THE DRAMATIC WORKS IN THE BEAUMONT AND FLETCHER CANON

THE
DRAMATIC WORKS IN
THE BEAUMONT AND
FLETCHER CANON

GENERAL EDITOR
FREDSON BOWERS
Linden Kent Professor Emeritus of English Literature
University of Virginia

VOLUME IV

THE WOMAN'S PRIZE   BONDUCA   VALENTINIAN

MONSIEUR THOMAS   THE CHANCES

CAMBRIDGE UNIVERSITY PRESS
CAMBRIDGE
LONDON · NEW YORK · MELBOURNE

Published by the Syndics of the Cambridge University Press
The Pitt Building, Trumpington Street, Cambridge CB2 1RP
Bentley House, 200 Euston Road, London NW1 2DB
32 East 57th Street, New York, NY 10022, USA
296 Beaconsfield Parade, Middle Park, Melbourne 3206, Australia

First published 1979

Printed in Great Britain
at the University Press, Cambridge

Library of Congress Cataloguing in Publication Data (*Revised*)
Beaumont, Francis, 1584–1616.
The dramatic works in the Beaumont and Fletcher canon.

  I. Fletcher, John, 1579–1625, joint author.
 II. Bowers, Fredson Thayer, ed.   III.   Title.
PR2420 1966   822'.3'09   66–74421

ISBN 0 521 20060 1 (vol. 4)

CONTENTS

FOREWORD

These volumes contain the text and apparatus for the plays conventionally assigned to the Beaumont and Fletcher canon, although in fact Fletcher collaborated with dramatists other than Beaumont in numerous plays of the canon and some of the preserved texts also represent revision at a later date by various hands. The plays have been grouped chiefly by authors; this arrangement makes for an order that conveniently approximates the probable date of composition for most of the works.

The texts of the several plays have been edited by a group of scholars according to editorial procedures set by the general editor, who closely supervised in matters of substance as well as of detail the initially contrived form of the texts. Thereafter the individual editors have been left free to develop their concepts of the plays according to their own views. We hope that the intimate connection of one individual, in this manner, with all the different editorial processes will lend to the results some uniformity not ordinarily found when diverse editors approach texts of such complexity. At the same time, the peculiar abilities of the several editors have had sufficient free play to ensure individuality of point of view in its proper role; and thus, we hope, the deadness of compromise that may fasten on collaborative effort has been avoided, even at the risk of occasional internal disagreement.

The principles on which each text has been edited have been set forth in detail in 'The Text of this Edition' prefixed to volume I, pp. ix–xxv, followed by an account on pp. xxvii–xxxv of the Folio of 1647. Necessary acknowledgements will be found in the present volume in each Textual Introduction.

F.B.

Charlottesville, Virginia
1978

THE WOMAN'S PRIZE
OR
THE TAMER TAMED

edited by

FREDSON BOWERS

TEXTUAL INTRODUCTION

The Woman's Prize, or The Tamer Tamed (Greg, no. 660) is generally regarded as the sole work of John Fletcher, composed early in his career and probably acted in 1611.[1] It was entered in the Stationers' Register on 4 September 1646 to H. Robinson and Humphrey Mosely, with numerous other plays for the 1647 Folio, and first appeared in this Folio, sigs. 5N1–5Q2, pp. 97–123 (sig. 5Q2v blank), in the section printed by Edward Griffin the Younger. After a transfer from Robinson to Martyn and Herringman on 13 May 1671, with other Folio plays, it was reprinted in the Folio of 1679, sigs. ²2F3–1I3v, pp. 229–54. In the Folger Shakespeare Library is preserved a manuscript (J.b.3) once originally bound in the Lambarde volume.

Only two pre-Restoration references to the play are known. It was acted before 18 October 1633 in a form that caused Sir Henry Herbert, Master of the Revels, to call it in for censorship; subsequently, it was presented at court on 28 November 1633.

Herbert's interference is well documented although some important questions remain unanswered in the account from his Office Book:

1633, October 18. On friday the nineteenth [an error for 'eighteenth'] of October, 1633, I sent a warrant by a messenger of the chamber to suppress

---

[1] For the authorship, see Cyrus Hoy, 'The Shares of Fletcher and his Collaborators in the Beaumont and Fletcher Canon', *Studies in Bibliography*, VIII (1956), 129–46. The evidence for the dating is considered by Baldwin Maxwell, 'The Woman's Prize, or the Tamer Tamed', *Modern Philology*, XXXII (1935), 353–63, utilized subsequently in his *Studies in Beaumont, Fletcher, and Massinger* (1939, repr. London, 1966), and Clifford Leech, *The John Fletcher Plays* (London, 1962). The earliest textual and historical study of the play is that by R. C. Bald, *Bibliographical Studies in the Beaumont and Fletcher Folio of 1647* (London, 1938). The text has been edited by George P. Ferguson (The Hague, 1966); the text of the Lambarde manuscript alone has been edited, with a careful examination of all pertinent evidence bearing on the textual transmission, by Graham C. Adams (unpublished doctoral dissertation, University of New Brunswick, Canada, 1974). Dr Adams generously made a copy of his dissertation available to me and I have laid it under heavy contribution. Any differences in our opinion about the textual situation are relatively minor.

The Tamer Tamd, to the Kings players, for that afternoone, and it was obeyd; upon complaints of foule and offensive matters conteyned therein.

They acted *The Scornful Lady* instead of it, I have entered the warrant here:

'These are to will and require you to forbeare the actinge of your play called *The Tamer Tamd, or the Taming of the Tamer*, this afternoone, or any more till you have leave from mee: and this at your perill. On friday morninge the 18 Octob. 1633.

To Mr. Taylor, Mr. Lowins, or any of the Kings players at the Blackfryers.'

On saterday morninge followinge the book was brought mee, and at my lord of Hollands request I returned it to the players yᵉ monday morninge after, purgd of oaths, prophaness, and ribaldrye, being yᵉ 21 of Octob. 1633.

Herbert then continues in a vein that indicates that the suppression of *The Woman's Prize* was not an isolated incident but the institution of a new policy:

Because the stoppinge of the acting of this play for that afternoone, it being an ould play, hath raysed some discourse in the players, thogh no disobedience, I have thought fitt to insert here their submission upon a former disobedience, and to declare that it concerns the Master of the Revells to bee carefull of their ould revived playes, as of their new, since they may conteyne offensive matter, which ought not to be allowed in any time.

The Master ought to have copies of their new playes left with him, that he may be able to shew what he hath allowed or disallowed.

All ould plays ought to bee brought to the Master of the Revells, and have his allowance to them, for which he should have his fee, since they may be full of offensive things against church and state; yᵉ rather that in former time the poetts tooke greater liberty than is allowed by mee.

The players ought not to study their parts till I have allowed of the booke.

When on the following Monday Herbert (evidently under some pressure to be expeditious) returned the censored manuscript to the company, he added the following letter to the book-keeper:

'Mr. Knight,

In many things you have saved mee labour; yet wher your judgement or penn fayld you, I have made boulde to use mine. Purge ther parts, as I have the booke. And I hope every hearer and player will thinke that I have done God good servise, and the quality no wronge; who hath no greater enemies than oaths, prophaness, and publique ribaldry, wᶜʰ for the future I doe absolutely forbid to bee presented unto mee in any playbooke, as you will answer it at your perill. 21 Octob. 1633.'

This was subscribed to their play of *The Tamer Tamd*, and directed to Knight, their book-keeper (*Dramatic Records*, ed. J. Q. Adams (repr. New York, 1963), pp. 20–1).

There is general agreement that the Folger manuscript was copied from a prompt-book,[1] cut for acting before Herbert's interference with the text. The manuscript is a folio of fifty-two leaves written on both sides and bound irregularly in 6's. A slip with writing only on the verso side is found as fol. 22, containing a passage of eighteen written lines from II.vi.144 (second half) to II.vi.156. Whether the slip repairs an inadvertent omission (as Bald suggests, p. 52) or whether (as Adams thinks it possible, pp. xxvii–xxviii) the leaf had been normally copied but damaged parts cut away, is uncertain. The catchword on fol. 21[v] agrees with the first words of the slip, and the slip's catchword agrees with the following word at the top of fol. 23. On the whole, the writing on only one side of the paper suggests the repair of some accident in transcription, the nature of which can be subject only to speculation. Eighteen lines might seem to be too few to justify a hypothesis that the scribe inadvertently turned over two pages of his copy at a time; it may be that there was also some form of slip in the copy that caused the difficulty.

In the inscription the scribe wrote the speech-prefixes and stage-directions in a larger hand. Speeches or stage-directions are not marked off by rules, but most of the directions are preceded by a long dash. The manuscript is divided into acts but only the second scene of Act I is numbered although there is a generally observed custom of indicating scenes by centrally placed opening stage-directions. No title-page, prologue, or epilogue is present. A corrector, different from the transcriber, made fifteen definite and four probable alterations, apparently by reference to copy.[2] The date

---

[1] Bald, p. 60; Ferguson, p. 31; Adams, pp. xxiiiff.

[2] These are recorded in the Historical Collation. Most correct such simple misreadings as at II.vi.92 where the 'o' of Ms 'bone' is altered to an 'a' to form the correct word 'bane'. Most substantive variants are fairly obvious alterations of the MS scribe's careless slips, yet they indicate some care in reading over the MS and ordinarily bring the variant into conformity with the F1 reading, as in the interlined 'yet' in II.vi.90 which for some reason had been deleted by the scribe in the course of his inscription, or in the wrong speech-prefix *Pedro* for *Rowland* at I.iv.6, or the addition of 'ly' to 'learned' at II.vi.64. The most puzzling variant is that at II.vi.104, in which 'recant' is deleted and 'recreant' interlined although the F1 reading is also

of the manuscript is uncertain: the watermark of a five-pointed Foolscap with countermark RP or PR is, as usual, not to be dated with any precision.[1] That the transcript was made before the appearance of the 1647 Folio is clear on practical grounds, but the rest is subject only to conjecture. Like the scribal manuscript of *Beggars' Bush*, which we owe to a court performance, the performance in November 1633 before the king may have occasioned sufficient interest for a private transcript to be requested which came into the hands of the private collector whose papers were utilized in the preparation of *Beggars' Bush* and *The Woman's Prize* for the 1679 Folio. This Folio supplies some authoritative matter missing from the 1647 Folio but present in the manuscripts of both plays; and indeed the Lambarde manuscript itself of *The Woman's Prize* may have been the document that was collated with some occasional care against the 1647 text used as printer's copy for 1679.[2] The *Beggars' Bush* manuscript may be dated as late as 1637/8 but could be earlier. Whether the 1633 or some unknown later revival of *The Woman's Prize* occasioned its private transcription is not to be determined.

Griffin used three compositors to set the 1647 Folio text of the play, two working simultaneously on the two pages of each forme in rough alternation. These three workmen had sufficiently different spelling characteristics so that the pages (and sometimes columns) that each set may be distinguished with relative certainty.[3]

'recant'. The reading 'recreant' is almost certainly correct but how it could have been recovered from copy is difficult to imagine without the strain of hypothesizing double error by MS scribe and F 1 compositor misreading a perhaps unclear inscription. It may be, then, that this word is instead an inspired guess by the corrector. For a description of the correcting hand see Bald, pp. 51–2, modified and elaborated by Adams, pp. xxxii–xxxiii.

[1] It may be the twin of Churchill's no. 341 of 1644; see W. A. Churchill, *Watermarks in Paper* (1935, repr. Meppel, Netherlands, 1967), pp. 42–3, 81. But the moulds may have been in use earlier or the paper identified in 1644 may have been old stock.

[2] For the relationship of the Lambarde manuscript of *Beggars' Bush* to F 2, and its general textual and theatrical history, see the Textual Introduction in the present *Works*, vol. III (Cambridge, 1976). That MS itself may have been the collating agent for *The Woman's Prize* is suggested by the omission in F 2 of any variants from F 1 (except for normal compositorial error or sophistication) that are not present in MS except for the song. On the contrary, F 2 of *Beggars' Bush* may have some authorial readings that derive from the prompt-book from which the preserved MS was copied.

[3] I am indebted to Professor Standish Henning's unpublished analysis of the fifth

Compositor *A*	Compositor *B*	Compositor *C*
I'le (Ile)	Ile	I'le (Ile)
i'le (ile)	ile	i'le (ile)
doe (do)	do (doe)	do
beleeve	believe	believe
Mistresse	Mistris	Mistris
Countrey	Countrey	Country
'tis	tis	tis
'twill *etc.*	twill *etc.*	'twill *etc.*

Compositor *A* is largely indifferent whether he set 'I'le' ('i'le') or 'Ile' ('ile'); Compositor *B* invariably set 'Ile' ('ile'); Compositor *C* has a preference for 'I'le' ('i'le') but will admit 'Ile' ('ile'). Compositor *A* has a strong preference for 'doe' but admits a few 'do' spellings, whereas Compositor *B*'s characteristic is precisely the opposite and Compositor *C* is invariable in setting 'do'. The other words are sufficiently indicated in the list as invariant spellings.

Compositor *A* set sigs. 5N3^v–5O1^r (I.iii.212–II.iv.20) and sigs. 5P1^v–5P3^r (IV.i.63–IV.v.97).

Compositor *B* set sigs. 5N1^r–5N3^r (I.i.0–I.iii.211), sigs. 5O1^v–5O2^{va} (II.iv.21–III.i.18), sig. 5O3^{rb} (III.ii.23–III.iii.24), sigs. 5O4^r–5P1^r (III.iii.128 (*2nd half*)–IV.i.62) and sigs. 5P4^v–5Q1^v (V.i.70–V.iv.90.1).

Compositor *C* set sigs. 5O2^{vb}–5O3^{ra} (III.i.15–III.ii.22), sig. 5O3^v (III.iii.25–128 (*1st half*)), sigs. 5P3^v–4^r (IV.v.98–V.i.69) and sig. 5Q2^r (Prologue and Epilogue).

In all, Compositor *A* set in round numbers (taking account of prose) about 812 lines or 30·4% of the text; Compositor *B* set about 1415 lines or 53%; and Compositor *C* set 410 lines or 16·6%. Proofreading was casual. The inner forme of the outer sheet 5O (5O1^v: 4) and the outer forme of the inner sheet (5O3^v) had certain literals corrected in press but with no indication of reference to copy.

The main textual problem concerns first the nature of the copy behind both the Lambarde manuscript and F1, and then the various

section of the 1647 Folio, which includes an identification of the three cases by types that provides valuable evidence for the compositorial identification in a few columns where the spelling is not wholly satisfactory as evidence. I have modified his account of the spellings in only minor detail.

7

authority of the two documents and their relationship. There is general agreement that MS is a favor copy made by permission of the players from a prompt-book that was at least comparatively uncensored since it contains various oaths and bawdry that have been modified in the F1 text.[1] Moreover, certain cuts for acting purposes had been made in comparison with the fuller text offered by F1. In brief, MS omits two scenes – II.i and IV.i – which do little or nothing to further the plot: other small omissions seem to be inadvertent mistakes in the copying or else minor improvements.[2] The staging of two scenes has been altered. In III.v lines 55–64 are omitted, a device that saves two characters, the Doctor and Apothecary; and instead of their report MS substitutes a general order by Petronius for a doctor to be summoned and if Petruchio remains uncured then for him to be transported to Bedlam. The ostensible reason is to reduce the number of actors (or of doubled parts), and this may well represent the central purpose. However, it should be remarked that as the fuller scene is found in F1 the circumstances of the Doctor's prior consultation with Petruchio are obscure, and thus the rewriting may have been as much for clarification as for reducing the requirements for actors.

The second alteration is more significant in that it reflects a change in the conditions of staging. In V.i in the stage-direction in F1 at line 68.1 the direction reads, '*Enter* Livia *discovered abed, and* Moroso *by her*', a clear-cut use of a discovery space, which at line 157 is confirmed by Byancha's 'draw all the Curtaines close',

[1] It has not been remarked that some censorship was also applied to MS, i.e. to the prompt-book underlying the present copy. For instance, in I.i.1, 21, I.iii.120 and V.ii.11 MS substitutes 'Heaven' for F1 'God' when an oath is not in question. (Many of the MS oaths invoking 'Heaven', which have milder F1 equivalents, may also be in the same category.) In I.ii.41 MS reads 'indeed' whereas 'Yfaith' slipped into F1; in I.iii.64 MS reads 'loves sake' for F1 'Heavens sake'; in I.iv.8 some oath (probably 'God') indicated by a dash in F1 is omitted in MS altogether. In II.vi.34 F1 'God' is MS 'long' (F2 'Heaven'). In IV.iv.7 both F1 'on my word' and MS 'I protest' are very likely softened paraphrases; but in V.iii.35 where MS reads 'I sweare' and F1 'By ——' there is clear evidence of the reduction in MS from a stronger original.

[2] The only omission in MS that could be another theatrical cut is Pedro's seven-line description at II.iv.78–85 of the revolted women's provisions, although the four missing lines at V.i.36–9 might also be argued for as a deliberate omission. The Historical Collation may be consulted for a record of the minor omissions that do not appear to have a theatrical origin, as for example in I.iii.132, I.iv.69, II.vi.134–5, III.v.102, IV.ii.101, V.i.72 and V.i.82.

which corresponds to Livia's exit from the scene. On the contrary, the performance guided by the prompt-book underlying the MS was unable to utilize a discovery space. Instead, the MS direction reads, 'Enter Livia sick carryed in a chaire by servants: Moroso by her', and Byancha's instructions to draw the curtains, later, is simply omitted.

That the manuscript derives from a prompt-book, therefore, is suggested not by indubitable internal evidence recognizable if it had been the only preserved text, but instead by comparison with the different form of the text as found in F1. The presence of oaths and of bawdry in this acting version represented by the manuscript copy indicates quite clearly that the text is in a state prior to Herbert's operations on it in October 1633, and indeed it may well represent the form of the play about which the complaints were made that led Herbert to suppress further performance until it had been reformed. Whether this was the original prompt-book of *ca* 1611 or a later copy for a revival is not to be determined.

The nature of the copy behind the F1 text is more conjectural, although some inferences may be drawn from the evidence that point towards a working hypothesis of some plausibility. It is generally agreed that the copy from which F1 was set was the actual document worked over first by Knight (in an attempt no doubt to forestall as many of Herbert's objections as possible) and later by Herbert. Critics then part company. Taking Herbert's use of the word 'book' in its technical sense as prompt-book, and assuming that it would be the official prompt-copy that the players would supply to Herbert's requirement, Bald (p. 60) assumed that 'when a private transcript was allowed [i.e. MS] the scribe was given the older acting version, now supplanted, as his copy, instead of the more recently made prompt-book which had had to submit to Herbert's censorings'. On the other hand, Adams (pp. xxxviff) suggests that Knight brought to Herbert not the current prompt-book (whether or not represented by the text in its MS form) but, instead, some basic non-theatrical manuscript which could have been either the author's own papers or a scribal fair copy made from them at a pre-prompt-book stage. Some evidence of irregularities in the F1 text would appear to support this position.

9

An immediate derivation of the MS text from the F1 manuscript text (in its pre-Herbert state) is impossible to demonstrate although some close connection of the two is indicated by the various examples of identical mislining of the verse or treatment of prose as verse. On the other hand, significant differences occur that are odd if one prompt-book copied another. The two cut scenes might impose no insuperable difficulty, but the rearrangement of the other two scenes would require a special hypothesis of a prompt-copy made up for performance under circumstances different from those governing the original. It is even odder to find that the stage-directions in the two documents differ ordinarily in their form and content: one prompt-book made up from another might be expected to retain more of the original directions, whereas they might be in part rewritten if a non-theatrical copy were being made into a prompt-book.[1] If oaths were satisfactory in one prompt-copy, they should be in another; yet some of the purged oaths represented by dashes in F1 when normally filled out are stronger than the bland form found in MS and sometimes quite clearly had been written at first in a different form. Some disruptions in the text of F1 appear that are not necessarily representative of copy in a prompt-book state. The most prominent of these is the brief duplicated scene of the three maids which appears first, improperly, in F1 as II.iii and is then hitched without scene number or other indication to the end of what is called II.v (properly II.iv), after which the next scene is misnumbered '*Scena tertia*'. The manuscript, with slightly different text and assignment of speeches (the final one being due, it would seem, to a misreading of a speech-prefix as text), places the scene

---

[1] For example, F1 adds '*with Rosemary*' in I.i.0.1, wanting in MS. The direction for I.iv.0.1 in MS reads '*Enter Rowland at one doore. Pedro hastly at the other*' but in F1 '*Enter Rowland, and Pedro, at severall doores*'. In this same scene at line 40 the MS direction reads '*Enter Livia and Moroso as unseene by her*' whereas F1 has '*Enter Livia at one doore, and Moroso at another harkning*'. In the entry at II.iv.0.1 Sophocles precedes Moroso but in F1 he follows Moroso. In the same scene at 57.1 MS reads '*Enter above Maria, Bianca, a Citty wife, a Country wife, and 3 Women*'; in F1 the only direction is '*All women above*'. At V.i.0.1 a trunk is specified in the MS direction, but a chest in F1 (the text calls for a trunk). The entry for V.iv.0.1 in MS reads '*Enter Petronius, Sophocles, Moroso, Petruchio in a Coffin, carried by Servants*', whereas F1 reads simply '*Petruchio born in a coffin*'. A line later F1 omits Pedro's necessary entrance with Maria and Jaques, and at 65.1 the phrase '*as from marriage*' in MS is wanting in the F1 entrance.

correctly. (Without authority F 2 reprints the first scene but omits
the second.) In F 1 the stage-directions differ in the two versions
and there is one easy substantive variant 'your' and 'the' in the
first line. Whatever the explanation for the duplication in the copy
behind F 1, it seems clear that the text of the same scene was indeed
repeated, whether or not deleted in its first appearance, a sign of
revision more probably to be found in the reworking of a pre-
prompt-copy than in the prompt-book itself. This hypothesis is the
more likely if the reason for the transfer was to provide an intervening scene between II.iv and II.vi which would otherwise have
violated the principle of the open stage by permitting the entrance
in scene vi of the same characters who had previously made their
last exeunt in the preceding scene, now numbered iv.

Finally, in F 1 appear certain disruptions of the text that may
perhaps be assignable to alteration, addition or revision of the
original that was incompletely carried out or was misunderstood
by the compositor. One example occurs in II.iii.3–4, where in F 1
(but not in MS) Rowland's speech begins with 'Thou has heard
I am sure of *Esculapius*.' before transferring abruptly to 'So were
they not well acquainted?', a line concerned with the relation of
women to the devil that begins the scene in MS, whereas the line
about Æsculapius is repeated in its proper context in F 1 (as in MS
for the first time) as lines 13–14. Another comes in II.iv.85–6 as in
MS where the speech '*Sophocles*. Lo ye fierce *Petruchio*, | This
comes of your impatience.' appears instead after line 67 in F 1,
where according to the present fuller text it is out of place. A third,
of some significance, comes at III.v.124. Here in F 1 'I could raile
twenty daies' completes the line begun by 'Can ever stop againe:'
and this line is then followed by a short line 'Out on 'em hedge-
hogs,' whereas in F 1 and MS line 141 reads 'I could raile twenty
daies together now.' This last is a perfect pentameter, but in the
F 1 original position at line 124 'I could raile twenty daies' produces
a hexameter and it is 'Out on 'em hedge-hogs' that should complete
the line after 'Can ever stop againe'. Once more, only the hypothesis of expanded text in the copy misunderstood by the F 1
compositor can explain these anomalies.

Another disruption in the text, but one that in an inexplicable

manner seems to have been transferred to MS, may appear in
II.iii.34. Here in F1, lines 33ff read:

> Tell her I doe beseech you, even for love sake.——
>   *Tra.* I will *Rowland.*
>   *Row.* She may sooner
> Count the good I have thought her,
> Our old love and our friend-ship,
> Shed one true teare, meane one houre constantly,

whereas in MS the passage reads:

> tell her I doe beseech you ever for love's sake
> our old love and our freindship,
>   [*six or seven lines space*]
> · *Tra.* I will Rowland.
>   *Row.* She may sooner
> count the good I have thought her,
> shed one true teare, meane one houre constantly, *etc.*

It will be noticed that the short lines in F1 do not link to form
pentameters involving Tranio's speech placed where it is, although
the metrics of MS are regular. Some speculation has been devoted to
the significance of the space left in MS, obviously for (a) material
of which the scribe was aware but which was not available to him,
or (b) material that could have been deleted and he was uncertain
whether to copy it, or (c) indecipherable material. If one must guess,
the second may seem to represent the most plausible answer, and
the hypothesis may be assisted by the signs of disruption in F1,
not only in the metrics but also in the line of thought. The MS
version is definitely the superior and appears to represent a better
interpretation of the deletion than that made by the F1 compositor.

If this is the correct interpretation, one important consequence
follows in that it would substantially assist the hypothesis that the
prompt-book behind MS was copied immediately from the manuscript behind F1 without an intermediary document intervening.
Despite the occasional textual differences that go beyond misreadings or memorial error in paraphrasing normal in any process of
copying involving the scribe of the prompt-book, the scribe of the
present favor manuscript and the F1 compositors, no serious bar is
present to this working hypothesis. The two pieces of information
that are wanting are, first, whether the manuscript from which F1

immediately derives was Fletcher's own working papers or a scribal fair copy. To this no certain answer can be given. The inference from the smaller than usual transmission of the typical Fletcherian *ye* through three different compositors could be made that the copy was an intermediate transcript in which the attrition of the *ye* forms had already begun, a proposition that gains support from the fact that MS supplies some of the *ye* forms for F1 *you* but very far from all that would have been expected in authorial papers. The evidence for some reworking of the text that seems to be preserved in F1 by no means disqualifies the hypothesis for a non-theatrical manuscript as copy, since precisely such authorial revision may be found in similar copy in back of Shakespeare's *Julius Cæsar* in the First Folio. The second piece of missing information is whether the copy from which MS immediately derives was the original prompt-book or a later book retranscribed (and perhaps slightly reworked in the two scenes of the Doctor visiting Petruchio and of Livia's deception) for the 1633 (or some earlier) revival. If some of the carelessnesses in copying are not attributable to the scribe of the present MS, it may be that the book was not the original one. However, the evidence of a direct connection between the copy for F1 and that for MS (especially the gap of six or seven lines in II.iii) may suggest at the least that whatever the status of the prompt-book in back of MS, it had been made up using the F1 manuscript as its source and not a preceding prompt-book, although in the nature of the case only conjecture is possible.

Since in textual work lost documents must be treated in general as if they had not existed, the editorial procedure based on the working hypothesis for this edition is relatively straightforward. The copy-text is necessarily F1 since it is the document closest to the author's original papers. Since MS derives in direct line from this F1 manuscript, it can have no independent authority apart from its correction of F1 compositorial errors of omission and commission and apart from its preservation in most but by no means in all places of words, phrases and lines censored in the manuscript behind F1 both by Knight and by Herbert. The authority of the two slight reworkings in III.v and V.i is moot. For certain plays it is evident that the publisher of the 1679 Folio consulted authoritative manuscripts which he had procured from a private collector and that some occasional variants in such cases may derive from authority superior to that of F 1. However, there is every evidence that the manuscript consulted in the preparation of the 1679 Folio was the preserved Lambarde MS. It follows that no agreement between F 2 and MS has any significance for authority and that the sole contribution of F 2 to the editing of the play consists in the addition of a song (which may possibly have been abstracted from a slip attached to MS) and to a few normal corrections of error or necessary improvements of minor details in the presentation of the edited text.

Prologue

Ladies to you, in whose defence and right,
  Fletchers *brave Muse prepar'd her self to fight*
A battaile without blood, 'twas well fought too,
  (The victory's yours, though got with much ado,)
We do present this Comedy, in which
  A rivulet of pure wit flowes, strong and rich
In Fancy, Language, and all parts that may
  Adde grace and ornament to a merry Play.
Which this may prove. Yet not to go too far
  In promises from this our female war,   10
We do intreat the angry men would not
  Expect the mazes of a subtle plot,
Set Speeches, high expressions; and what's worse,
  In a true Comedy, politique discourse.
The end we ayme at, is to make you sport;
  Yet neither gall the City, nor the Court.
Heare, and observe his Comique straine and when
  Y'are sick of melancholy, see't agen.
'Tis no deere Physick, since 'twill quit the cost:
  Or his intentions, with our pains, are lost.   20

The Persons represented in the Play

[Men.]

Moroso, *an old rich doating Citizen, suitor to* Livia.

Sophocles,⎱
Tranio, ⎰ *Two Gentlemen, friends to* Petruchio.

Petruchio, *An Italian Gentleman, Husband to* Maria.

Rowland, *A young Gentleman, in love with* Livia.

Petronius, *Father to* Maria *and* Livia.

Jaques,⎱
Pedro, ⎰ *Two witty servants to* Petruchio.

Doctor,

Apothecarie,   10

Watchmen,

Porters,

[Servants,]

Women.

Maria, *A chaste witty Lady,*⎱ *The two masculine daughters of*
Livia, *Mistriss to* Rowland.⎰ Petronius.

Biancha, *Their Cosin, and Commander in chief.*

City Wives,   ⎫
Countrey Wives, ⎬ *To the relief of the Ladies, of which, two*   20
Maids.   ⎭ *were drunk.*

The Scene London.

The Woman's Prize:

or,

The Tamer Tam'd

Enter Moroso, Sophocles, *and* Tranio, *with Rosemary*
as from a wedding

Moroso. God give 'em joy.
Tranio.   Amen.
Sophocles.   Amen, say I too:
  The Pudding's now i'th proof; alas poor wench,
  Through what a mine of patience must thou worke,
  Ere thou know'st good houre more?
Tranio.   Tis too true, certaine:
  Me thinks her father has dealt harshly with her,
  Exceeding harshly, and not like a Father,
  To match her to this Dragon; I protest
  I pity the poore Gentlewoman.
Moroso.   Me thinks now,
  He's not so terrible as people think him.
Sophocles [*aside*]. This old thiefe flatters, out of meere devotion, 10
  To please the father for his second daughter.
Tranio [*aside*]. But shall he have her?
Sophocles [*aside*].   Yes, when I have Rome.
  And yet the father's for him.
Moroso.   Ile assure ye,
  I hold him a good man.
Sophocles.   Yes sure a wealthy,
  But whether a good womans man, is doubtfull.
Tranio. Would 'twere no worse.
Moroso.   What though his other wife,

4 true, certaine:] Sympson; ~ : Certaine F1–2; ~, certaine, MS

17

Out of her most abundant stubbornesse,
Out of her daily huy and cries upon him,
(For sure she was a Rebell) turn'd his temper,
And forc'd him blow as high as she? do'st follow   20
He must retain that long since buried Tempest,
To this soft maid?
Sophocles.   I feare it.
Tranio.   So do I too:
And so far, that if God had made me woman,
And his wife that must be——
Moroso.   What would you doe sir?
Tranio. I would learn to eate Coales with an angry Cat,
And spit fire at him: I would (to prevent him)
Do all the ramping, roaring tricks, a whore
Being drunke, and tumbling ripe, would tremble at:
There is no safety else, nor morall wisdome,
To be a wife, and his.
Sophocles.   So I should think too.   30
Tranio. For yet the bare remembrance of his first wife
(I tell ye on my knowledge, and a truth too)
Will make him start in's sleep, and very often
Cry out for Cudgels, Colstaves, any thing;
Hiding his Breeches, out of feare her Ghost
Should walk, and weare 'em yet. Since his first marriage,
He is no more the still *Petruchio*,
Then I am *Babylon*.
Sophocles.   He's a good fellow,
And by my troth I love him: but to think
A fit match for this tender soule——   40
Tranio. His very frowne, if she but say her prayers
Louder then men talk treason, makes him tindar;
The motion of a Diall, when he's testy,
Is the same trouble to him as a water-worke;
She must do nothing of her selfe; not eate,
Drink, say sir how do ye, make her ready, pisse,

17 stubbornesse] MS (stubbornes); sobernesse F 1–2
39 by my troth] MS; on my word F 1–2   46 pisse] MS; unready F 1–2

18

Unlesse he bid her.
Sophocles. He will bury her,
Ten pound to twenty shillings, within these three weeks.
Tranio. Ile be your halfe.

Enter Jaques *with a pot of Wine.*

Moroso. He loves her most extreamly,
And so long 'twil be honey-moon. Now *Jaques* 50
You are a busie man I am sure.
Jaques. Yes certaine,
This old sport must have egges——
Sophocles. Not yet this ten daies.
Jaques. Sweet Gentlemen, with Muskadell.
Tranio. That's right sir.
Moroso. This fellow broods his Master: speed ye *Jaques.*
Sophocles. We shall be for you presently.
Jaques. Your worships
Shal have it rich and neat: and o' my conscience
As welcom as our Lady day: O my old sir,
When shall we see your worship run at Ring?
That houre a standing were worth money.
Moroso. So sir.
Jaques. Upon my little honesty, your Mistris,
If I have any speculation, 60
Must thinke this single thrumming of a Fiddle,
Without a Bow, but ev'n poore sport.
Moroso. Y'are merry
Jaques. Would I were wise too: oo God bless your worships.
Exit Jaques.
Tranio. The fellow tels you true.
Sophocles. When is the day man?
Come, come, you'ld steale a marriage.
Moroso. Nay believe me:
But when her father pleases I am ready,

64 worships] MS; worship F 1-2
66 you'ld] MS; you'l F 1-2

And all my friends shall know it.
Tranio.   Why not now?
  One charge had serv'd for both.
Moroso.   There's reason in't.
Sophocles [*aside*].   Call'd *Rowland*.
Moroso.   Will ye walke?   70
  They'l think we are lost: Come Gentlemen.
Tranio.   You have wip't him now.
Sophocles.   So will he never the wench I hope.
Tranio.   I wish it.
                                          Exeunt.

                Enter Rowland, *and* Livia   [I.] ii

Rowland.   Now *Livia*, if you'l goe away to night,
  If your affections be not made of words——
Livia.   I love you, and you know how dearly *Rowland*,
  Is there none neere us? my affections ever
  Have been your servants; with what superstition
  I have ever Sainted you——
Rowland.   Why then take this way?
Livia.   Twill be a childish and a lesse prosperous course,
  Then this that knows not care: why should we do
  Our honest and our hearty love such wrong,
  To over-run our fortunes?
Rowland.   Then you flatter.   10
Livia.   Alas you know I cannot.
Rowland.   What hope's left else
  But flying to enjoy ye?
Livia.   None so far,
  For let it be admitted we have time,
  And all things now in other expectation,
  My father's bent against us; what but ruine,
  Can such a by-way bring us? if your feares
  Would let you look with my eyes, I would shew you,

        *71 wip't him now] stet F1–2; impt him MS
        *8 this] MS; his F1–2

                        20

And certain, how our staying here would win us
A course, though somewhat longer, yet far surer.
Rowland.   And then *Moroso* h'as ye.
Livia.   No such matter: 20
  For hold this certaine, begging, stealing, whoring,
  Selling, (which is a sin unpardonable)
  Of counterfeit Cods, or musty English Crocus,
  Switches, or stones for th' toothache sooner finds me,
  Then that drawn Fox *Moroso.*
Rowland.   But his money,
  If wealth may win you——
Livia.   If a Hog may be
  High Priest among the Jewes: his money *Rowland?*
  Oh Love forgive me, what a faith hast thou?
  Why, can his money kisse me?
Rowland.   Yes.
Livia.   Behind,
  Laid out upon a Petticote: or graspe me   30
  While I cry, O good thank you? o' my troth
  Thou makst me merry with thy feare: or lie with me,
  As you may do? alas, what fooles you men are?
  His mouldy money? half a dozen Riders,
  That cannot sit but stampt fast to their Saddles?
  No *Rowland*, no man shall make use of me;
  My beauty was born free, and free Ile give it
  To him that loves, not buys me. You yet doubt me.
Rowland.   I cannot say I doubt ye.
Livia.   Goe thy waies,
  Thou art the prettiest puling piece of passion·   40
  Yfaith I will not faile thee.
Rowland.   I had rather——
Livia.   Prethee believe me, if I do not carry it,
  For both our goods——

           *23 Crocus] MS; Cracus F1, Coacus F2
           25 Fox] MS, F2; Fox and F1
           28 a] MS; *om.* F1–2
           30 Laid] MS, F2; Lasd F1

                        21

Rowland. But——
Livia. What but?
Rowland. I would tell you—
Livia. I know all you can tell me; all's but this,
You would have me, and lie with me; is't not so?
Rowland. Yes.
Livia. Why you shall; will that content you? Goe.
Rowland. I am very loth to goe.

Enter Byancha, *and* Maria.

Livia. Now o' my conscience
Thou art an honest fellow: here's my sister;
Go, prethee goe; this kisse, and credit me,
Ere I am three nights older, I am for thee: 50
You shall heare what I do.
Rowland. I had rather feele it.
Livia. Farewell.
Rowland. Farewell.

Exit Rowland.

Livia. Alas poore foole, how it looks?
It would ev'n hang it selfe, should I but crosse it.
For pure love to the matter I must hatch it.
Byancha. Nay never look for merry houre *Maria*,
If now ye make it not; let not your blushes,
Your modesty, and tendernesse of spirit,
Make you continuall Anvile to his anger:
Believe me, since his first wife set him going,
Nothing can bind his rage: Take your own Councell, 60
You shall not say that I perswaded you.
But if you suffer him——
Maria. Stay, shall I do it?
Byancha. Have you a stomack to't?
Maria. I never shew'd it.
Byancha. Twill shew the rarer, and the stranger in you.

51–52 *Rowland.* I...it.] MS; *om.* F 1–2
56 ye] MS; you F 1–2
64 stranger] MS; stronger F 1–2

22

But do not say I urg'd you.
Maria.   I am perfect,
Like *Curtius* to redeeme my Countrey, have I
Leap'd into this gulph of marriage, and Ile do it.
Farewell all poorer thoughts, but spight and anger,
Till I have wrought a miracle. Now cosen,
I am no more the gentle tame *Maria*;   70
Mistake me not; I have a new soule in me
Made of a North-wind, nothing but tempest;
And like a tempest shall it make all ruins,
Till I have run my will out.
Byancha.   This is brave now,
If you continue it; but your own will lead you.
Maria. Adieu all tendernesse, I dare continue;
Maides that are made of feares and modest blushes,
View me, and love example.
Byancha.   Here is your sister.
Maria. Here is the brave old mans love.
Byancha.   That loves the young man.
Maria. I and hold thee there wench: what a grief of heart is't,   80
When *Paphos* Revels should up rowse old night,
To sweat against a Cork; to lie and tell
The clock o'th lungs, to rise sport-starv'd?
Livia.   Deere sister,
Where have you been you talke thus?
Maria.   Why at Church, wench;
Where I am tide to talke thus: I am a wife now.
Livia. It seems so, and a modest.
Maria.   Y'are an asse;
When thou art married once, thy modesty
Will never buy thee Pins.
Livia.   'Blesse me.
Maria.   From what?
Byancha. From such a tame foole as our cozen *Livia.*
Livia. You are not mad?

81 Revels] MS (revels), F 2; Rebels F 1
83 lungs] MS, F 2; longs F 1   86 Y'are] MS; You are F 1–2

Maria.   Yes wench, and so must you be,   90
Or none of our acquaintance, marke me *Livia*,
Or indeed fit for our sex: Tis bed time.
Pardon me yellow *Hymen*, that I meane
Thine offrings to protract, or to keepe fasting
My valiant Bridegroome.
Livia.   Whether will this woman?
Byancha.   You may perceive her end.
Livia.   Or rather feare it.
Maria.   Dare you be partner in't?
Livia.   Leave it *Maria*,
I feare I have mark'd too much, for goodnesse leave it;
Devest you with obedient hands; to bed.
Maria.   To bed? No *Livia*, there are Comets hang   100
Prodigious over that yet; there's a fellow
Must yet before I know that heat (nere start wench)
Be made a man, for yet he is a monster;
Here must his head be *Livia*.
Livia.   Never hope it.
Tis as easie with a Sive to scoope the Ocean,
As to tame *Petruchio*.
Maria.   Stay: *Lucina* heare me,
Never unlock the treasure of my womb
For humane fruit, to make it capable;
Nor never with thy secret hand make briefe
A mothers labour to me; if I doe   110
Give way unto my married husbands will,
Or be a wife, in any thing but hopes:
Till I have made him easie as a child,
And tame as feare; he shall not win a smile,
Or a pleas'd look, from this austerity,
Though it would pull another Joynture from him,
And make him ev'ry day another man;
And when I kisse him, till I have my will,
May I be barren of delights, and know
Onely what pleasures are in dreams, and guesses.   120

94 or] *stet* F 1–2; and MS   112 hopes:] ~, F 1–2; ~ˌ MS

24

Livia.   A strange Exordium.

Byancha.   All the severall wrongs
Done by Emperious husbands to their wives
These thousand yeeres and upwards, strengthen thee:
Thou hast a brave cause.

Maria. ·   And Ile doe it bravely
Or may I knit my life out ever after.

Livia.   In what part of the world got she this spirit?
Yet pray *Maria*, looke before you truly,
Besides the disobedience of a wife,
(Which you will finde a heavy imputation)
Which yet I cannot thinke your own, it shews   130
So distant from your sweetnesse.

Maria.   Tis I sweare.

Livia.   Weigh but the person, and the hopes you have,
To worke this desperate cure.

Maria.   A weaker subject
Would shame the end I aime at: disobedience?
You talk too tamely: By the faith I have
In mine own Noble will, that childish woman
That lives a prisoner to her husbands pleasure,
Has lost her making, and becomes a beast,
Created for his use, not fellowship.

Livia.   His first wife said as much.

Maria.   She was a foole,   140
And took a scurvy course; let her be nam'd
'Mongst those that wish for things, but dare not do 'em:
I have a new daunce for him, and a mad one.

Livia.   Are you of this faith?

Byancha.   Yes truly, and wil die in't.

Livia.   Why then let's all weare breeches.

Byancha.   That's a good wench.

Maria.   Now thou comst neere the nature of a woman;
Hang these tame hearted Eyasses, that no sooner

128 disobedience] MS; obedience F1–2
143 him, and a mad one.] MS; him. F1–2
145 *Byancha.* That's...wench.] MS (wench,); *om.* F1–2

See the Lure out, and heare their husbands halla,
But cry like Kites upon 'em: The free Haggard
(Which is that woman, that has wing, and knowes it,   150
Spirit, and plume) will make an hundred checks,
To shew her freedome, saile in ev'ry ayre,
And look out ev'ry pleasure; not regarding
Lure, nor quarry, till her pitch command
What she desires, making her foundred keeper
Be glad to fling out traines, and golden ones,
To take her down again.
Livia.   You are learned sister;
Yet I say still, take heed.
Maria.   A witty saying;
Ile tell thee *Livia*, had this fellow tired
As many wives as horses under him,   170   160
With spurring of their patience; had he got
A Patent, with an Office to reclaime us
Confirm'd by Parliament; had he all the malice
And subtilty of Devils, or of us,
Or any thing that's worse then both——
Livia. Hey, hey boyes, this is excellent.
Maria.   Or could he
Cast his wives new again, like Bels to make 'em
Sound to his will; or had the fearfull name
Of the first breaker of wilde women: yet,
Yet would I undertake this man, thus single,   170
And spight of all the freedom he has reach'd to,
Turn him and bend him as I list, and mold him
Into a babe again; that aged women,
Wanting both teeth and spleen, may Master him.
Byancha. Thou wilt be chronicl'd.
Maria.   That's all I aime at.
Livia. I must confesse, I do with all my heart
Hate an Emperious husband, and in time
Might be so wrought upon——
Byancha.   To make him cuckold?

150 has] MS; hath F 1–2

Maria.   If he deserve it.
Livia.   Then Ile leave ye Ladies.
Byancha.   Thou has not so much Noble anger in thee.   180
Maria.   Goe sleep, goe sleep, what we intend to do,
Lies not for such starv'd soules as thou hast *Livia.*
Livia.   Good night: the Bridegroom will be with you presently.
Maria.   That's more then you know.
Livia.   If ye worke upon him,
As ye have promised, ye may give example,
Which no doubt will be followed.
Maria.   So.
Byancha.   Good night: we'l trouble you no further.
Maria.   If you intend no good, pray doe no harm.
Livia.   None, but pray for ye.   *Exit* Livia.
Byancha.   'Cheere wench?
Maria.   Now *Byancha,*
Those wits we have, let's wind 'em to the height,   190
My rest is up wench, and I pull for that
Will make me ever famous. They that lay
Foundations, are halfe builders all men say.

Enter Jaques.

Jaques.   My Master forsooth——
Maria.   Oh how do's thy Master? prethee commend me to him.
Jaques.   How's this? my Master staies forsooth——
Maria.   Why let him stay, who hinders him forsooth?
Jaques.   The Revel's ended now, to visit you.
Maria.   I am not sick.
Jaques.   I mean to see his chamber, forsooth.
Maria.   Am I his Groom? where lay he last night, forsooth?   200
Jaques.   In the low matted Parlour.
Maria.   There lies his way by the long Gallery.
Jaques.   I mean your chamber: y'ar very merry Mistris.
Maria.   Tis a good signe I am sound hearted *Jaques*:
But if you'l know where I lie, follow me;
And what thou seest, deliver to thy Master.

185, 189 'ye] MS; you F 1–2

Byancha.   Do gentle *Jaques.*   *Exeunt* Maria *and* Byancha.
Jaques.   Ha, is the wind in that dore?
  By'r Lady we shall have foule weather then:
  I doe not like the shuffling of these women,
  They are mad beasts when they knock their heads together: 210
  I have observ'd 'em all this day; their whispers,
  One in anothers eare, their signes, and pinches,
  And breaking often into violent laughters:
  As if the end they purpos'd were their own.
  Call you this weddings? Sure this is a knavery,
  A very trick, and dainty knavery,
  Marvellous finely carried, that's the comfort:
  What would these women doe in waies of honour,
  That are such Masters this way? Well, my Sir
  Has been as good at finding out these toyes,   220
  As any living; if he lose it now,
  At his own perill be it. I must follow.

                                            Exit.

        Enter Servants with lights, Petruchio, Petronius,   [I.] iii
                Moroso, Tranio, *and* Sophocles.

Petruchio.   You that are married, Gentlemen, have at ye
  For a round wager now.
Sophocles.   Of this nights Stage?
Petruchio.   Yes.
Sophocles.   I am your first man: a paire of Gloves of twenty shillings.
Petruchio.   Done: who takes me up next? I am for all bets.
Moroso.   Faith lusty *Laurence*, were but my night now,
  Old as I am, I would make you clap on Spurs,
  But I would reach you, and bring you to your trot too:
  I would Gallants.
Petruchio.   Well said good Will; but where's the stuffe boy, ha?
  Old father time, your houre-glasse is empty.   10
Tranio.   A good tough traine would break thee all to pieces;

Thou hast not breath enough to say thy prayers.

Petronius.   See how these boyes despise us. Will you to bed sonne?
This pride will have a fall.

Petruchio.   Upon your daughter;
But I shall rise again, if there be truth
In Egges, and butter'd Pasnips.

Petronius.   Wil you to bed son, and leave talking;
To morrow morning we shall have you looke,
For all your great words, like Saint *George* at *Kingston*,
Running a foot-back from the furious Dragon,   20
That with her angry tayle belabours him
For being lazie.

Sophocles.   His warlike launce
Bent like a crosse bow lath, alas the while.

Tranio.   His courage quench'd, and so far quench'd——

Petruchio.   Tis well sir.

Tranio.   That anie privie Saint even small Saint Davy
May lash him with a leeke.

Petruchio.   What then?

Sophocles.   Fly, fly, quoth then the fearfull dwarfe;
Here is no place for living man.

Petruchio.   Well my masters, if I doe sinke under my businesse,
as I finde tis very possible, I am not the first that has miscarried 30
so, that's my comfort; what may be done without impeach or
waste, I can and will doe.

Enter Jaques.

How now is my faire Bride a bed?

Jaques.   No truly sir.

Petronius.   Not a bed yet? body o' me: we'l up and rifle her:
here's a coyle with a mayden-head, tis not intayl'd, is it?

Petruchio.   If it be, ile try all the Law i'th Land, but Ile cut it
off: let's up, let's up, come.

Jaques.   That you cannot neither.

22–23 *Sophocles.* His...while.] MS (while,); *om.* F 1–2
25–26 *Tranio.* That...leeke.] MS; *om.* F 1–2
30–31 miscarried so,] MS; ~ ; So F 1–2

Petruchio. Why? 40

Jaques. Unlesse you'll drop through the Chimney like a Daw, or force a breach i'th windows: you may untile the house, tis possible.

Petruchio. What dost thou meane?

Jaques. A morall sir, the Ballat will expresse it:

> *The wind and the rain,*
> *Has turnd you back again,*
> *Ye cannot be lodged there.*

The truth is all the doores are baracadoed; not a Cathole, but holds a murd'rer in't. She's victual'd for this moneth.

Petruchio. Art not thou drunk? 50

Sophocles. He's drunk, he's drunk; come, come, let's up.

Jaques. Yes, yes, I am drunke: ye may goe up, ye may Gentlemen, but take heed to your heads: I say no more.

Sophocles. Ile try that. *Exit* Sophocles.

Petronius. How dost thou say? the door fast lock'd fellow?

Jaques. Yes truly sir, tis lock'd, and guarded too; and two as desperate tongues planted behind it, as ere yet batterd: they stand upon their honours, and will not give up without strange composition, Ile assure you; marching away with their Pieces cockt, and Bullets in their mouthes will not satisfie them. 60

Petruchio. How's this? how's this? they are? Is there another with her?

Jaques. Yes marry is there, and an Engineir.

Moroso. Who's that for Heavens sake?

Jaques. Colonell *Byancha*, she commands the workes: *Spinola*'s but a ditcher to her; there's a halfe-moon: I am but a poore man, but if you'ld give me leave, sir, Ile venture a yeeres wages, draw all your force before it, and mount your ablest piece of battery, you shall not enter in't these three nights yet.

Enter Sophocles.

Petruchio. I should laugh at that good *Jaques.* 70

Sophocles. Beat back again, she's fortified for ever.

Jaques. Am I drunk now sir?

47 *Ye*] MS (*rom.*); *And you* F 1–2   67 you'ld] MS; you'l F 1–2
69 in't] MS; it F 1–2

Sophocles.   He that dares most, goe up now, and be cool'd. I have scap'd a pretty scowring.

Petruchio.   What are they mad? have we another Bedlam? She doth not talke I hope?

Sophocles.   Oh terribly, extreamly fearfull, the noise at London-bridge is nothing neere her.

Petruchio.   How got she tongue?

Sophocles.   As you got taile, she was born to't.   80

Petruchio.   Lock'd out a doors, and on my wedding-night? Nay, and I suffer this, I may goe graze: come Gentlemen, Ile batter; are these vertues?

Sophocles.   Do, and be beaten off with shame, as I was: I went up, came to th' doore, knockd, no body answered; knock'd lowder, yet heard nothing: would have broke in by force; when suddenly a water-worke flew from the window with such violence, that had I not duck'd quickly like a Fryer, *cœtera quis nescit?* The chamber's nothing but a meere *Ostend*, in every window Pewter cannons mounted, you'l quickly finde with what they are charg'd sir.   90

Petruchio.   Why then *tantara* for us.

Sophocles.   And all the lower works lin'd sure with small shot, long tongues with Fire-locks, that at twelve score blanke hit to the heart: now and ye dare go up——

Enter Maria *and* Byanca *above.*

Moroso.   The window opens, beat a parley first; I am so much amaz'd my very haire stands.

Petronius   Why how now daughter: what intrench'd?

Maria.   A little guarded for my safety sir.

Petruchio.   For your safety Sweet-heart? why who offends you? I come not to use violence.   100

Maria.   I thinke you cannot sir, I am better fortified.

Petruchio.   I know your end, you would faine reprieve your Maiden-head a night, or two.

Maria.   Yes, or ten, or twenty, sir, or say an hundred; or indeed, till I list lie with you.

Sophocles.   That's a shrewd saying; from this present houre,

75 She doth] MS; They doe F 1–2

I never will believe a silent woman. When they break out they are
bonfires.

Petronius.   Till you list lie with him? why who are you Madam?

Byancha.   That trim Gentlemans wife, sir.   110

Petruchio.   Cry ye mercy, do ye command too?

Maria.   Yes marry do's she, and in chiefe.

Byancha.   I doe command, and you shall go without: (I mean your
wife, for this night.)

Maria.   And for the next too wench, and so as't follows.

Petronius.   Thou wilt not, wilt 'a?

Maria.   Yes indeed deere father, and till he seale to what I shall
set down, for any thing I know, for ever.

Sophocles.   By'r Lady these are Bugs-words.

Tranio.   You heare sir, she can talke, God be thanked.   120

Petruchio.   I would I heard it not sir.

Sophocles.   I finde that all the pity bestowd upon this woman,
makes but an Anagram of an ill wife, for she was never vertuous.

Petruchio.   Youl let me in I hope, for all this jesting.

Maria.   Hope still Sir.

Petronius.   You will come down I am sure.

Maria.   I am sure I will not.

Petronius.   Ile fetch you then.

Byancha.   The power of the whole County cannot sir, unlesse we
please to yeild, which yet I thinke we shal not; charge when you   130
please, you shall heare quickly from us.

Moroso.   'Blesse me from a Chicken of thy hatching, is this wiving?

Petruchio.   Prethee *Maria* tell me what's the reason,
And do it freely, you deale thus strangely with me?
You were not forc'd to marry, your consent
Went equally with mine, if not before it:
I hope you do not doubt I want that mettle
A man should have to keepe a woman waking;
I would be sorry to be such a Saint yet:
My person, as it is not excellent,   140

111 (*twice*), 165 (*twice*), 175, 214, 225, 266 ye] MS; you F 1–2
119 By'r Lady] MS (Birlady); Indeed F 1–2
*132 ' Blesse] *stet* F 1–2 ±; Heaven blesse MS

So tis not old, nor lame, nor weak with Physick,
But wel enough to please an honest woman,
That keeps her house, and loves her husband.
Maria.   Tis so.
Petruchio.   My means and my conditions are no shamers
Of him that owes 'em, all the world knows that,
And my friends no reliers on my fortunes.
Maria.   All this I believe, and none of all these parcels
I dare except against; nay more, so far
I am from making these the ends I aime at,
These idle outward things, these womens feares,   150
That were I yet unmarried, free to choose
Through all the Tribes of man, i'ld take *Petruchio*
In's shirt, with one ten Groats to pay the Priest,
Before the best man living, or the ablest
That ev'r leap'd out of Lancashire, and they are right ones.
Petronius.   Why do you play the foole then, and stand prating
Out of the window like a broken Miller!
Petruchio.   If you wil have me credit you *Maria*,
Come down, and let your love confirme it.
Maria.   Stay there sir, that bargain's yet to make.   160
Byancha.   Play sure wench, the pack's in thine own hand.
Sophocles.   Let me die lowsie, if these two wenches be not brewing
knavery to stock a Kingdome.
Petruchio.   Death, this is a Riddle:
I love ye, and I love ye not.
Maria.   It is so:
And till your own experience do untie it,
This distance I must keep.
Petruchio.   If you talk more,
I am angry, very angry.
Maria.   I am glad on't, and I wil talke.
Petruchio.   Prethee peace,
Let me not think thou art mad. I tell thee woman,   170
If thou goest forward, I am still *Petruchio*.
Maria.   And I am worse, a woman that can feare

164 Death,] MS (~ ‸); Why‸ F 1–2

33

Neither *Petruchio Furius*, nor his fame,
Nor any thing that tends to our allegeance;
There's a short method for ye, now you know me.
Petruchio.   If you can carry't so, tis very wel.
Byancha.   No you shall carry it, sir.
Petruchio.   Peace gentle Low-bel.
Petronius.   Use no more words, but come down instantly,
I charge thee by the duty of a child.
Petruchio.   Prethee come *Maria*, I forgive all.   180
Maria.   Stay there; That duty, that you charge me by
(If you consider truly what you say)
Is now another mans, you gave't away
I'th Church, if you remember, to my husband:
So all you can exact now, is no more
But onely a due reverence to your person,
Which thus I pay: Your blessing, and I am gone
To bed for this night.
Petronius.   This is monstrous:
That blessing that Saint *Dunstan* gave the Devil,
If I were neere thee, I would give thee——   190
Pull thee down by th' nose.
Byancha.   Saints should not rave, sir;
A little Rubarb now were excellent.
Petruchio.   Then by that duty you owe to me *Maria*,
Open the doore, and be obedient:
I am quiet yet.
Maria.   I do confesse that duty; make your best on't.
Petruchio.   Why give me leave, I will.
Byancha.   Sir, there's no learning
An old stiffe Jade to trot: you know the morall.
Maria.   Yet as I take it, sir, I owe no more
Then you owe back again.
Petruchio.   You wil not Article?   200
All I owe, presently, let me but up, ile pay.
Maria.   Y'are too hot, and such prove Jades at length;
You do confesse a duty or respect to me from you again,

*190 thee——] *stet* F1–2; ~, MS

34

That's very neere, or full the same with mine?
Petruchio.   Yes.
Maria.   Then by that duty, or respect, or what
You please to have it, goe to bed and leave me,
And trouble me no longer with your fooling;
For know, I am not for you.
Petruchio.   Well, what remedy?
Petronius.   A fine smart Cudgell. Oh that I were neer thee.   210
Byancha.   If you had teeth now, what a case were we in?
Moroso.   These are the most authentique Rebels, next *Tyrone*, I
ever read of.
Maria.   A weeke hence, or a fortnight, as you beare ye,
And as I finde my will observ'd, I may
With intercession of some friends be brought
May be to kisse you; and so quarterly
To pay a little rent by composition,
You understand me?
Sophocles.   Thou Boy, thou.   220
Petruchio.   Well there are more Maides then *Maudlin*, that's my
          comfort.
Maria.   Yes, and more men then *Michael*.
Petruchio.   I must not to bed with this stomach, and no meat Lady.
Maria.   Feed where you will, so it be sound, and wholsome,
Else live at livery, for i'le none with ye.
Byancha.   You had best back one of the dairy maids, they'l carry.
But take heed to your girthes, you'l get a bruise else.
Petruchio.   Now if thou would'st come down, and tender me
All the delights due to a marriage bed,
Studdy such kisses as would melt a man,   230
And turne thy selfe into a thousand figures,
To adde new flames unto me, I would stand
Thus heavy, thus regardlesse, thus despising
Thee, and thy best allurings: all the beauty
That's laid upon your bodies, mark me well,
For without doubt your minds are miserable,
You have no maskes for them: all this rare beauty,

234 the] MS, F2; thy F1

35

Lay but the Painter, and the silke worme by,
The Doctor with his dyets, and the Taylor,
And you appeare like flead Cats, not so handsome.   240
Maria.   And we appeare like her that sent us hither,
That onely excellent and beauteous nature;
Truly our selves, for men to wonder at,
But too divine to handle; we are Gold,
In our own natures pure; but when we suffer
The husbands stamp upon us, then alayes,
And base ones of you men are mingled with us,
And make us blush like Copper.
Petruchio.   Then, and never
Till then are women to be spoken of,
For till that time you have no soules I take it: 250
Good night: come Gentlemen; i'le fast for this night,
But by this hand——well: I shall come up yet?
Maria.   Noe.
Petruchio.   There will I watch thee like a wither'd Jewry,
Thou shalt neither have meat, fire, nor Candle,
Nor any thing that's easie: doe you rebell so soone?
Yet take mercy.
Byancha.   Put up your Pipes: to bed sir; i'le assure you
A moneths seige will not shake us.
Moroso.   Well said Colonell.   260
Maria.   To bed, to bed *Petruchio*: good night Gentlemen,
You'l make my Father sicke with sitting up:
Here you shall finde us any time these ten dayes,
Unlesse we may march off with our contentment.
Petruchio.   Ile hang first.
Maria.   And i'le quarter if I doe not,
Ile make ye know, and feare a wife *Petruchio*,
There my cause lies.
You have been famous for a woman tamer,
And beare the fear'd-name of a brave wife-breaker:
A woman now shall take those honours off,   270
And tame you;
Nay, never look so bigge, she shall, beleeve me,

36

And I am she: what thinke ye; good night to all,
Ye shall finde Centinels.
Byancha.   If ye dare sally.   *Exeunt above.*
Petronius. The devill's in 'em, ev'n the very devill, the downe
right devill.
Petruchio. Ile devill 'em: by these ten bones I will: i'le bring it to
the old Proverb, no sport no pie: death, taken down i'th top of all
my speed; this is fine dancing: Gentlemen, stick to me. You see
our Freehold's touch'd, and by this light, we will beleaguer 'em,   280
and either starve 'em out, or make 'em recreant.
Petronius. Ile see all passages stopt, but those about 'em: if the
good women of the Towne dare succour 'em, we shall have warres
indeed.
Sophocles. Ile stand perdue upon 'em.
Moroso.   My regiment shall lye before.
Jaques [aside].   I think so, 'tis grown too old to stand.
Petruchio.   Let's in, and each provide his tackle,
We'l fire 'em out, or make 'em take their pardons,
Heare what I say, on their bare knees I vow: 290
Am I *Petruchio*, fear'd, and spoken of,
And on my wedding night am I thus jaded?
                                               Exeunt Omnes.

          Enter Rowland, and Pedro, *at severall doores.*   [I.] iv

Rowland.   Now *Pedro?*
Pedro.   Very busie Master *Rowland.*
Rowland.   What haste man?
Pedro.   I beseech you pardon me,
I am not mine own man.
Rowland.   Thou art not mad?
Pedro.   No; but beleeve me, as hasty——
Rowland.   The cause good *Pedro?*
Pedro.   There be a thousand sir; you are not married?

          278 death,] MS (~ ∧); —— F1-2
          *290 I vow:] MS (~ ~∧); —— F1-2

Rowland.   Not yet.
Pedro.   Keepe your selfe quiet then.
Rowland.   Why?
Pedro.   You'l finde a Fiddle that never will be tun'd else:
From all such women God deliver me.   *Exit.*

Enter Jaques.

Rowland.   What ailes the fellow, tro? *Jaques?*
Jaques.   Your friend sir.
But very full of businesse.
Rowland.   Nothing but businesse?   10
Prethee the reason; is there any dying?
Jaques.   I would there were sir.
Rowland.   But thy businesse?
Jaques.   Ile tell you in a word, I am sent to lay
An imposition upon Sowse and Puddings,
Pasties, and Penny Custards, that the women
May not releeve yon Rebels: Fare ye well sir.
Rowland.   How does my Mistresse?
Jaques.   Like a resty jade.
She's spoil'd for riding.   *Exit* Jaques.

Enter Sophocles.

Rowland.   What a devill ayle they?
Custards, and penney Pasties, Fooles and Fiddles,
What's this to'th purpose? O well met.
Sophocles.   Now *Rowland.*   20
1 cannot stay to talk long.
Rowland.   What's the matter?
Here's stirring but to what end? whether goe you?
Sophocles.   To view the works.
Rowland.   What workes?
Sophocles.   The womens Trenches.
Rowland.   Trenches? are such to see?
Sophocles.   I doe not jest sir.
Rowland.   I cannot understand you.

8 all...me.] all women—— F 1–2; all such women deliver me. MS

38

Sophocles.   Doe not you heare
In what a state of quarrell the new Bride
Stands with her husband?
Rowland.   Let him stand with her,
And there's an end.
Sophocles.   It should be, but by'r Lady
She holds him out at Pikes end, and defies him,
And now is fortifide; such a Regiment of Rutters
Never defied men braver: I am sent
To view their preparation.   30
Rowland.   This is newes
Stranger then Armies in the ayre, you saw not
My gentle Mistresse?
Sophocles.   Yes, and meditating
Upon some secret businesse, when she had found it
She leapt for joy, and laugh'd, and straight retir'd
To shun *Moroso.*
Rowland.   This may be for me.
Sophocles. Will you along?
Rowland.   No.
Sophocles.   Farewell.   *Exit* Sophocles.
Rowland.   Farewell sir.
What should her musing meane, and what her joy in't,
If not for my advantage?

> *Enter* Livia *at one doore, and* Moroso *at another lurkning*

                                Stay ye; may not
That Bob-taile Jade *Moroso*, with his Gold,
His gew-gaudes, and the hope she has to send him   40
Quickly to dust, excite this? here she comes,
And yonder walkes the Stallion to discover:
Yet i'le salute her: save you beauteous mistresse.
Livia [aside].   The Fox is kennell'd for me:——save you sir.
Rowland. Why doe you look so strange?
Livia.   I use to looke sir
Without examination.

33 Armies] MS (armies); Armes F 1–2

Moroso.   Twenty Spur-Royals for that word.
Rowland.   Belike then
  The objects discontents you?
Livia.   Yes it does.   50
Rowland.   Is't come to this? you know me, doe you not?
Livia.   Yes as I may know many by repentance.
Rowland.   Why doe ye breake your faith?
Livia.   Ile tell you that too,
  You are under age, and no band holds upon you.
Moroso.   Excellent wench.
Livia.   Sue out your understanding,
  And get more haire, to cover your bare knuckle
  (For Boyes were made for nothing, but dry kisses,)
  And if you can, more manners.
Moroso.   Better still.
Livia.   And then if I want Spanish gloves, or stockings,
  A ten-pound waste-coate, or a Nag to hunt on,   60
  It may be I shall grace you to accept 'em.
Rowland.   Farewell, and when I credit women more,
  May I to Smith-field, and there buy a Jade,
  (And know him to be so) that breakes my neck.
Livia.   Because I have knowne you, Ile be thus kinde to you;
  Farewell, and be a man, and i'le provide you,
  Because I see y'are desperate, some staid Chamber-maid
  That may relieve your youth, with wholesome doctrin.
Moroso.   She's mine from all the world: ha wench?
Livia.   Ha Chicken?
                    Gives him a box o'th eare and Exit.
Moroso.   How's this? I do not love these favours: save you.   70
Rowland.   The devill take thee——   *Wrings him byth' nose.*
Moroso.   Oh!
Rowland.   There's a love token for you: thank me now.   *Exit.*
Moroso.   Ile thinke on some of ye, and if I live,
  My nose alone shall not be plaid withall.
                                    Exit.

                53 ye] MS; you F 1–2

                    40

Enter Petronius, *and* Moroso.   II. i

Petronius.   A Box o'th eare doe you say?
Moroso.   Yes sure a sound one,
  Beside my nose blown to my hand; if *Cupid*
  Shoot Arrows of that waight, i'le sweare devoutly,
  H'as sude his liverie, and is no more a Boy.
Petronius.   You gave her some ill language?
Moroso.   Not a word.
Petronius.   Or might be you weare fumbling?
Moroso.   Would I had sir.
  I had been a forehand then; but to be baffel'd,
  And have no feeling of the cause——
Petronius.   Be patient,
  I have a medicine clapt to her back will cure her.
Moroso.   No sure it must be afore sir.
Petronius.   O' my Conscience,   10
  When I got these two wenches (who till now
  Ne'r shew'd their riding) I was drunck with Bastard,
  Whose nature is to forme things like it selfe
  Heady, and monstrous: did she slight him too?
Moroso.   That's all my comfort: a meere Hobby-horse
  She made childe *Rowland*: s'foot she would not know him,
  Not give him a free look, not reckon him
  Among her thoughts, which I held more then wonder,
  I having seene her within's three dayes kisse him
  With such an appetite as though she would eat him.   20
Petronius.   There is some trick in this: how did he take it?
Moroso.   Ready to cry; he ran away.
Petronius.   I feare her.
  And yet I tell you, ever to my anger,
  She is as tame as Innocency; it may be
  This blow was but a favour.
Moroso.   Ile be sworne
  'Twas well tye'd on then.
Petronius.   Goe too, pray forget it,

II.i] *om. scene* MS   4 is] F2; *om.* F1

41

I have bespoke a Priest: and within's two houres
Ile have ye married; will that please you?
Moroso.   Yes.
Petronius.   Ile see it done my selfe, and give the Lady
Such a sound exhortation for this knavery   30
Ile warrant you, shall make her smell this Moneth on't.
Moroso.   Nay good sir, be not violent.
Petronius.   Neither——
Moroso.   It may be
Out of her earnest love, there grew a longing
(As you know women have such toyes) in kindnesse,
To give me a box o'th eare or so.
Petronius.   It may be.
Moroso.   I reckon for the best still: this night then
I shall enjoy her.
Petronius.   You shall hansell her.
Moroso.   Old as I am, i'le give her one blow for't
Shall make her groane this twelve-moneth.
Petronius.   Where's your joynture?
Moroso.   I have a joynture for her.
Petronius.   Have your Councell   40
Perus'd it yet?
Moroso.   No Councell, but the night, and your sweet daughter
Shall ere peruse that Joynture.
Petronius.   Very well sir.
Moroso.   Ile no demurrers on't nor no rejoynders.
The other's ready seal'd.
Petronius.   Come then let's comfort
My Son *Petruchio*, he's like little Children
That loose their Bables, crying ripe.
Moroso.   Pray tell me,
Is this stern woman still upon the flaunt
Of bold defiance?
Petronius.   Still, and still she shall be
Till she be starv'd out: you shall see such justice,   50
That women shall be glad after this tempest
To tye their husbands shooes, and walke their horses.

42

Moroso.   That were a merry world: doe you heare the rumour,
They say the women are in Insurrection,
And meane to make a ——
Petronius.   They'l sooner
Draw upon walls as we doe: Let 'em, let 'em,
We'l ship 'em out in Cuck-stooles, there they'l saile
As brave *Columbus* did, till they discover
The happy Islands of obedience.
We stay too long, Come.
Moroso.   Now Saint *George* be with us.   60
                                        Exeunt.

                        Enter Livia *alone.*   [II.] ii

Livia.   Now if I can but get in hansomely,
Father I shall deceive you, and this night
For all your private plotting, i'le no wedlock;
I have shifted saile, and finde my Sisters safety
A sure retirement; pray to heaven that *Rowland*
Do not beleeve too farre, what I said to him,
For y'on old Foxcase forc'd me, that's my feare.
Stay, let me see, this quarter fierce *Petruchio*
Keepes with his Myrmidons: I must be suddaine,
If he seize on me, I can looke for nothing   10
But Marshall Law; to this place have I scap'd him;
Above there.

                    Enter Maria, *and* Byancha *above.*

Maria.   *Qui va la?*
Livia.   A Friend.
Byancha.   Who are you?
Livia.   Looke out and know.
Maria.   Alas poore wench, who sent thee,
What weake foole made thy tongue his Orator?
I know ye come to parly.

53 *Moroso.*] F2; *om.* F1   *55 a ——] *stet* F1–2
12 *Qui va la?*] MS (là); *Cheval'a.* F1–2   15, 68, 84, 119 ye] MS; you F1–2

43

Livia.   Y'are deceiv'd,
Urg'd by the goodnes of your cause I come
To doe as you doe.
Maria.   Y'ar too weake, too foolish,
To cheat us with your smoothnesse: doe not we know
Thou hast been kept up tame?
Livia.   Beleeve me.
Maria.   No, prethee good *Livia*   20
Utter thy Eloquence somewhere else.
Byancha.   Good Cosen
Put up your Pipes; we are not for your palat,
Alas we know who sent you.
Livia.   O' my faith——
Byancha.   Stay there; you must not thinke your faith, or troth,
Or by your Maydenhead, or such Sonday oathes
Sworne after Even-Song, can inveigle us
To loose our hand-fast: did their wisdomes thinke
That sent you hither, we would be so foolish,
To entertaine our gentle Sister *Sinon*,
And give her credit, while the woodden Jade   30
Petruchio stole upon us: no good Sister,
Goe home, and tell the merry Greekes that sent you,
Ilium shall burn, and I, as did *Æneas*,
Will on my back, spite of the Myrmidons,
Carry this warlike Lady, and through Seas
Unknown, and unbeleev'd, seek out a Land,
Where like a race of noble *Amaʒons*,
We'le root our selves, and to our endlesse glory
Live, and despise base men.
Livia.   Ile second ye.
Byancha.   How long have you been thus?
Livia.   That's all one, Cosen.   40
I stand for freedome now.
Byancha.   Take heed of lying;
For by this light, if we doe credit you,

23 faith——] MS (~ .); word—— F 1–2
24 faith, or troth,] MS; word, F 1–2

And finde you tripping, his infliction
That kill'd the Prince of *Orenge*, will be sport
To what we purpose.
Livia.   Let me feele the heaviest.
Maria.   Swear by thy Sweet-heart *Rowland* (for by your mayden-
          head,
I feare 'twill be too late to swear) you meane
Nothing but faire and safe, and honourable
To us, and to your selfe.
Livia.   I sweare.
Byancha.   Stay yet,
Sweare as you hate *Moroso*, that's the surest,   50
And as you have a Christian feare to finde him
Worse then a poore dride Jack, full of more Aches
Then *Autumne* has; more knavery, and usury,
And foolery, and brokery, then doggs-ditch:
As you doe constantly beleeve he's nothing
But an old empty bagge with a grey beard,
And that beard such a Bob-taile, that it lookes
Worse then a Mares taile eaten off with Fillyes:
As you acknowledge, that young hansome wench
That lyes by such a Bilbo blade, that bends   60
With ev'ry passe he makes to'th hilts, most miserable,
A dry nurse to his Coughes, a fewterer
To such a nasty fellow, a rob'd thing
Of all delights youth lookes for: and to end,
One cast away on course beef, born to brush
That everlasting Cassock that has worne
As many Servants out, as the Northeast passage
Has consum'd Saylors: if ye sweare this, and truly
Without the reservation of a gowne
Or any meritorious Petticoate,   70
'Tis like we shall beleeve you.
Livia.   I doe sweare it.
Maria.   Stay yet a little; came this wholesome motion
(Deale truly Sister) from your own opinion,

51 Christian] MS; certaine F 1–2   63 rob'd] *i.e.* robb'd *as in* F 2

Or some suggestion of the Foe?
Livia.   Nev'r feare me,
For by that little faith I have in husbands,
And the great zeale I beare your cause, I come
Full of that liberty, you stand for, Sister.
Maria.   If we beleeve, and you prove recreant *Livia,*
Think what a maym you give the noble Cause
We now stand up for: Thinke what women shall   80
An hundred yeare hence speak thee, when examples
Are look'd for, and so great ones, whose relations
Spoke as we doe 'em wench, shall make new customs.
Byancha.   If ye be false, repent, goe home, and pray,
And to the serious women of the City
Confesse your selfe; bring not a sinne so heynous
To load thy soule, to this place: mark me *Livia,*
If thou bee'st double, and betray'st our honours,
And we fail in our purpose: get thee where
There is no women living, nor no hope   90
There ever shall be.
Maria.   If a Mothers daughter,
That ever heard the name of stubborn husband
Find thee, and know thy sinne——
Byancha.   Nay, if old age,
One that has worne away the name of woman,
And no more left to know her by, but railing,
No teeth, nor eyes, nor legges but woodden ones,
Come but i'th wind-ward of thee, for sure she'l smell thee
Thou'lt be so ranck, she'l ride thee like a night-mare,
And say her Prayers back-ward to undoe thee,
She'l curse thy meat and drink, and when thou marriest,   100
Clap a sound spell for ever on thy pleasures.
Maria.   Children of five yeare old, like little Fayries
Will pinch thee into motley; all that ever
Shall live, and heare of thee, I meane all women,
Will (like so many furies) shake their Keyes,
And tosse their flaming distaffes o're their heads,

83 'em] MS, F 2; th'em F 1   93 Find] MS, F 2; Found F 1

46

Crying Revenge: take heed, 'tis hideous,
Oh 'tis a fearefull office: if thou had'st
(Though thou bee'st perfect now) when thou cam'st hither,
A false Imagination, get thee gone,   110
And as my learned Cozen said repent,
This place is sought by soundnesse.
Livia.   So I seeke it,
Or let me be a most despis'd example.
Maria.   I doe beleeve thee, be thou worthy of it.
You come not empty?
Livia.   No, Here's Cakes, and cold meat,
And tripe of proofe: behold here's wine, and beere,
Be suddaine, l shall be surpriz'd else.
Maria.   Meet at the low Parlor doore, there lyes a close way:
What fond obedience ye have living in you,
Or duty to a man, before you enter,   120
Fling it away, 'twill but defile our Offrings.
Byancha.   Be wary as you come.
Livia.   I warrant ye.

                       Exeunt.

        Enter Rowland *and* Tranio *at severall doores.*   **[II.] iii**

Tranio.   Now *Rowland?*
Rowland.   How doe you?
Tranio.   How do'st thou man?
Thou look'st ill.
Rowland.   Yes, pray can you tell me *Tranio,*
Who knew the devill first?
Tranio.   A woman.
Rowland.   So,
Were they not well acquainted?
Tranio.   May be so,
For they had certaine Dialogues together.

II.iii] *om. scene* MS. *In* F1–2 *scene* v *in the present edition follows* II.ii, *headed*
'Scæna Tertia'.
   3–4 *Rowland. So...acquainted?*] MS, F2; *Row.* Thou hast heard I am sure of
Esculapius. | So were they not well acquainted? F1

Rowland. He sold her fruit, I take it?
Tranio. Yes, and Cheese
That choak'd all mankinde after.
Rowland. Canst thou tell me
Whether that woman ever had a faith
After she had eaten?
Tranio. That's a great Schoole question.
Rowland. No 'tis no question, for beleeve me *Tranio*,   10
That cold fruit after eating bred naught in her
But windy promises, and chollick vowes
That broke out both wayes; thou ha'st heard I am sure
Of *Esculapius*, a farre famed Surgeon,
One that could set together quarter'd Traytors,
And make 'em honest men.
Tranio. How do'st thou *Rowland*?
Rowland. Let him but take, (if he dare doe a cure
Shall get him fame indeed) a faithlesse woman,
There will be credit for him, that will speake him,
A broken woman *Tranio*, a base woman,   20
And if he can cure such a rack of honour
Let him come here, and practise.
Tranio. Now for Heavens sake
Why what ayl'st thou *Rowland*?
Rowland. I am ridden *Tranio*,
And Spur-gald to the life of patience
(Heaven keepe my wits together) by a thing
Our worst thoughts are too noble for, a woman.
Tranio. Your Mistresse has a little frown'd it may be?
Rowland. She was my Mistresse.
Tranio. Is she not?
Rowland. No *Tranio*.
She has done me such disgrace, so spitefully,
So like a woman bent to my undoing,   30
That henceforth a good horse shall be my Mistresse,
A good Sword, or a Booke: and if you see her,

---

*9 great] MS; *om.* F 1–2   13 thou] MS; *Row.* Thou F 1–2
22 Heavens] MS (heavens); honours F 1–2

48

Tell her I doe beseech you, even for loves sake,
Our old love and our friend-ship——
Tranio.   I will *Rowland.*
Rowland.   She may sooner count the good I have thought her,
Shed one true teare, meane one houre constantly,
Be old, and honest, married, and a maide,
Then make me see her more, or more beleeve her:
And now 1 have met a Messenger, farewell sir.   *Exit.*
Tranio.   Alas poore *Rowland,* I will doe it for thee:
This is that dogge *Moroso,* but I hope   40
To see him cold i'th mouth first er he enjoy her:
Ile watch this young man, desperate thoughts may seize him,
And if my purse, or councell can, i'le ease him.

                                             Exit.

          Enter Petruchio, Petronius, Moroso, *and* Sophocles.   [II.] iv

Petruchio.   For looke you Gentlemen, say that I grant her
Out of my free and liberall love, a pardon,
Which you and all men else know she deserves not,
(*Teneatis amici*) can all the world leave laughing?
Petronius.   I thinke not.
Petruchio.   No by —— they cannot;
For pray consider, have you ever read,
Or heard of, or can any man imagine,
So stiffe a Tom-boy, of so set a malice,
And such a brazen resolution,
As this young Crab-tree? and then answer me,   10
And marke but this too friends, without a cause,
Not a foule word come crosse her, not a feare,
She justly can take hold on, and doe you thinke
I must sleepe out my anger, and endure it,
Sew pillows to her ease, and lull her mischiefe?
Give me a Spindle first: no, no my Masters,

          33 loves] MS; love F1–2
          *34 Our...friend-ship——] MS (freindship); F1–2 *place after line* 35
          *5 by ——] *stet* F1–2; by this hand MS
          12 come] MS; comes F1–2   15 Sew] MS; Sow F1–2

Were she as faire as *Nell* a *Greece*, and house-wife
As good as the wise Saylors wife, and young still,
Never above fifteene; and these tricks to it,
She should ride the wild Mare once a week, she should,   20
(Believe me friends she should.) I would tabor her,
Till all the Legions that are crept into her,
Flew out with fire i'th tailes.
Sophocles.   Methinks you erre now,
For to me seems, a little sufferance
Were a far surer cure.
Petruchio.   Yes, I can suffer,
Where I see promises of peace and amendment.
Moroso.   Give her a few conditions.
Petruchio.   Ile be hangd first.
Petronius.   Give her a crab-tree-cudgell.
Petruchio.   So I will;
And after it a flock-bed for her bones,
And hard egges, till they brace her like a Drum.   30
She shall be pamperd with ——
    She shall not know a stoole in ten moneths Gentlemen.
Sophocles.   This must not be.

Enter Jaques.

Jaques.   Arme, arme, out with your weapons,
For all the women in the Kingdom's on ye;
They swarm like waspes, and nothing can destroy 'em,
But stopping of their hive, and smothering of 'em.

Enter Pedro.

Pedro.   Stand to your guard sir, all the devils extant
Are broke upon us, like a cloud of thunder;
There are more women, marching hitherward,
In rescue of my Mistris, then ere turn'd taile   40
At Sturbridge Faire; and I believe, as fiery.
Jaques.   The forlorn-hope's led by a Tanners wife,
I know her by her hide; a desperate woman:
She flead her husband in her youth, and made

50

Raynes of his hide to ride the Parish, her plackett
Lookes like the straights of Gibralter, still wider
Downe to the gulphe, all sun-burnt Barbary
Lyes in her breech; take 'em all together,
They are genealogy of Jennets, gotten
And born thus, by the boysterous breath of husbands;   50
They serve sure, and are swift to catch occasion,
(I meane their foes, or husbands) by the fore-locks,
And there they hang like favours; cry they can,
But more for Noble spight, then feare: and crying
Like the old Gyants that were foes to Heaven,
They heave ye stoole on stoole, and fling main Potlids
Like massie rocks, dart ladles, tosting Irons,
And tongs like Thunderbolts, till overlayd,
They fall beneath the waight; yet still aspiring
At those Emperious Codsheads, that would tame 'em.   60
There's nere a one of these, the worst and weakest,
(Choose where you will) but dare attempt the raysing
Against the soveraigne peace of Puritans,
A May-pole, and a Morris, maugre mainly
Their zeale, and Dudgeon-daggers: and yet more,
Dares plant a stand of battring Ale against 'em,
And drinke 'em out o'th Parish.
Pedro.   There's one brought in the Beares against the Canons
Of two church-wardens, made it good, and fought 'em,
And in the churchyard after even song.   70
Jaques.   Another, to her everlasting fame, erected
Two Ale-houses of ease: the quarter-sessions
Running against her roundly; in which businesse
Two of the disannullers lost their night-caps,
A third stood excommunicate by the cudgell:
The Cunstable, to her eternall glory,
Drunke hard, and was converted, and she victor.

45–48 her plackett...breech;] MS; *om.* F1–2 (Parish. Take)
*57 tosting] MS; tossing F1–2
67 Parish.] MS; F1–2 *add as next line*: Soph. Lo you fierce *Petruchio*, this comes
of your impatience. (*see lines* 85–86)
69 two church-wardens] MS; the Town F1–2   70 And...song.] MS; *om.* F1–2

Pedro.   Then are they victualed with pies and puddings,
  (The trappings of good stomacks) noble Ale
  The true defendor, Sawsages, and smoak'd ones,   80
  If need be, such as serve for Pikes; and Porke,
  (Better the Jewes never hated:) here and there
  A bottle of Metheglin, a stout Britaine
  That wil stand to 'em; what else they want, they war for.
Sophocles.   Lo ye fierce *Petruchio*,
  This comes of your impatience.
Petruchio.   Come to councell.
Sophocles.   Now ye must grant conditions or the Kingdom
  Will have no other talke but this.
Petronius.   Away then,
  And let's advise the best.
Sophocles.   Why doe you tremble?
Moroso.   Have I liv'd thus long to be knockt o'th head,   90
  With halfe a washing beetle? pray be wise sir.
Petruchio.   Come, something Ile doe; but what it is I know not.
Sophocles.   To councel then, and let's avoyd their follies.
  Guard all the doors, or we shal not have a cloke left.

                                             Exeunt.

                Enter three Maides, at severall doors.   [II. v]

1. How goes your businesse Girles?
2.   A foot, and faire――――
3. If fortune favour us: away to your strength,
  The Country Forces are ariv'd, be gone.
  We are discover'd else.
1.   Arme, and be valiant.
2. Think of our cause.
3.   Our Justice.
1.   'Tis sufficient.   *Exeunt.*

*85–86 *Sophocles.* Lo...impatience.] MS; F 1–2 *place after line 67*
85, 87 ye] MS; you F 1–2
II.v] *om. scene heading* F 1, MS; *om. scene* F 2. *Copy-text in the present edition is* F 1'*s
first text printed as* II.iii
  0.1 *at severall doors*] F 1 (*scene* iii), MS; *om.* F 1 (*scene* v), F 2

Enter Petronius, Petruchio, Moroso, Sophocles, *and* Tranio.   [II. vi]

Petronius.   I am indifferent, though I must confesse,
  I had rather see her carted.
Tranio.   No more of that sir.
Sophocles.   Are ye resolv'd to give her fair conditions?
  Twill be the safest way.
Petruchio.   I am distracted,
  Would I had run my head into a halter
  When I first woo'd her: if I offer peace,
  She'l urge her own conditions, that's the devil.
Sophocles.   Why say she do?
Petruchio.   Say, I am made an Asse, then;
  I know her aime: may I with reputation
  (Answer me this) with safety of mine honour,   10
  (After the mighty mannage of my first wife,
  Which was indeed a fury to this Filly,
  After my twelve strong labours to reclaime her,
  Which would have made *Don Hercules* horn mad,
  And hid him in his hide) suffer this *Sicely*,
  Ere she have warm'd my sheets, ere grappel'd with me,
  This Pinck, this painted Foyst, this Cockle-boat,
  To hang her Fights out, and defie me friends,
  A wel known man of war? if this be equal,
  And I may suffer, say, and I have done.   20
Petronius.   I do not think you may.
Tranio.   You'l make it worse sir.
Sophocles.   Pray heare me good *Petruchio*: but ev'n now,
  You were contented to give all conditions,
  To try how far she would carry: Tis a folly,
  (And you wil find it so) to clap the curb on,
  Er ye be sure it proves a naturall wildnesse,
  And not a forc'd. Give her conditions,
  For on my life this tricke is put into her.
Petronius.   I should believe so too.
Sophocles.   And not her own.

26, 153, 156, 167, 169 ye] MS; you F1–2

53

Tranio. You'l finde it so.

Sophocles. Then if she flownder with you, 30
Clap spurs on, and in this you'l deale with temperance,
Avoyd the hurry of the world.

Tranio. And loose—— *Musick above.*

Moroso. No honour on my life, sir.

Petruchio. I wil do it.

Petronius. It seems they are very merry.

Enter Jaques.

Petruchio. Why God hold it.

Moroso. Now *Jaques?*

Jaques. They are i'th flaunt sir.

Sophocles. Yes we heare 'em.

Jaques. They have got a stick of Fiddles, and they firke it
In wondrous waies, the two grand Capitanos,
(They brought the Auxiliary Regiments)
Daunce with their coats tuckt up to their bare breeches,
And bid the Kingdom kisse 'em, that's the burden; 40
They have got Metheglin, and audacious Ale,
And talke like Tyrants.

Petronius. How knowest thou?

Jaques. I peep't in
At a loose Lansket.

Tranio. Harke.

Petronius. A Song, pray silence.

SONG.

A Health for all this day
To the woman that bears the sway
And wears the breeches;
Let it come, let it come.
Let this health be a Seal,
For the good of the Common-weal
the woman shall wear the breeches. 50

40 the Kingdom] MS (Kingdome), F2; them F1
44–57 *A...pound.*] F2; *om.* F1, MS (*both have only marginal direction* 'Song')
(F1 'Song.')

54

Let's drink then and laugh it
And merrily merrily quaff it
And tipple, and tipple a round;
here's to thy fool,
and to my fool.
Come, to all fools
though it cost us wench, many a pound.

Enter above Maria, Bianca, *a City wife, a Country wife,*
and 3 mayds.

Moroso. They look out.
Petruchio. Good ev'n Ladies.
Maria.   Good you good ev'n sir.
Petruchio. How have you slept to night?
Maria.   Exceeding well sir.   60
Petruchio. Did you not wish me with you?
Maria.   No, believe me,
  I never thought upon you.
Country wife.   Is that he?
Byancha.   Yes.
Country wife. Sir?
Sophocles.   She has drunk hard, mark her hood.
Country wife.   You are——
Sophocles. Learnedly drunk, Ile hang else: let her utter.
Country wife. And I must tell you, *viva voce* friend,
  A very foolish fellow.
Tranio.   There's an Ale figure.
Petruchio. I thank you *Susan Brotes.*
Citty wife.   Forward sister.
Country wife. You have espoused here a hearty woman,
  A comely, and couragious.
Petruchio.   Wel I have so.
Country wife. And to the comfort of distressed damsels,   70
  Weomen out-worn in wedlock, and such vessels,
  This woman has defied you.

57.1–2 *Enter...mayds.*] MS; *All the women above.* F1; *All the Women above,*
citizens and Countrey women. F2

Petruchio.   It should seem so.

Country wife.   And why?

Petruchio.   Yes, can you tell?

Country wife.   For thirteen causes.

Petruchio.   Pray by your patience Mistris——

Citty wife.   Forward sister.

Petruchio.   Do you mean to treat of all these?

Citty wife.   Who shall let her?

Petronius.   Doe you heare, Velvet-hood, we come not now
To heare your doctrine.

Country wife.   For the first, I take it,
It doth divide it selfe into seven branches.

Petruchio.   Harke you good *Maria*,
Have you got a Catechiser here?

Tranio.   Good zeale.   80

Sophocles.   Good three pil'd predication, will you peace,
And heare the cause we come for?

Country wife.   Yes Bob-tailes
We know the cause you come for, here's the cause,
But never hope to carry her, never dream
Or flatter your opinions with a thought
Of base repentance in her.

Citty wife.   Give me sack,
By this, and next strong Ale——

Country wife.   Sweare forward sister.

Citty wife.   By all that's cordiall, in this place we'l bury
Our bones, fames, tongues, our triumphs; and ev'n all
That ever yet was chronicl'd of woman;   90
But this brave wench, this excellent despiser,
This bane of dull obedience, shall inherit
Her liberall wil, and march off with conditions
Noble, and worth her selfe.

Country wife.   She shall *Tom Tilers*,
And brave ones too; My hood shal make a hearse-cloth,
And I lie under it, like *Jone o Gaunt*,
Ere I goe lesse, my Distaffe stucke up by me,

89 ev'n] MS; then F1; *om.* F2   93 Her] MS; His F1–2

For the eternall Trophee of my conquests;
And loud fame at my head, with two main Bottles,
Shall fill to all the world the glorious fall   100
Of old *Don Gillian.*
Citty wife.   Yet a little further,
We have taken Armes in rescue of this Lady;
Most just and Noble: if ye beat us off
Without conditions, and we recreant,
Use us as we deserve; and first degrade us
Of all our ancient chambering: next that
The Symbols of our secrecy, silke Stockings,
Hew of our heeles; our petticotes of Armes
Teare of our bodies, and our Bodkins breake
Over our coward heads.   110
Country wife.   And ever after
To make the tainture most notorious,
At all our Crests, *videlicet* our Plackets,
Let Laces hang, and we returne againe
Into our former titles, Dayry maids.
Petruchio.   No more wars: puissant Ladies, shew conditions,
And freely I accept 'em.
Maria.   Call in *Livia;*
She's in the treaty too.

                Enter Livia *above.*

Moroso.   How, *Livia?*
Maria.   Heare you that sir?
There's the conditions for ye, pray peruse 'em.   120
Petronius.   Yes, there she is: t'had been no right rebellion,
Had she held off; what think you man?
Moroso.   Nay nothing.
I have enough o'th prospect: o'my conscience,
The worlds end, and the goodnesse of a woman
Will come together.
Petronius.   Are you there sweet Lady?
Livia.   Cry you mercy sir, I saw you not: your blessing.

        *104 recreant] MS ('recant' *del.*); recant F 1–2

Petronius. Yes when I blesse a jade, that stumbles with me.
How are the Articles?

Livia. This is for you sir; [*To* Petruchio.]
And I shal think upon't.

Moroso. You have us'd me finely.

Livia. There's no other use of thee now extant,
But to be hung up; cassock, cap, and all, 130
For some strange monster at Apothecaries.

Petronius. I heare you whore.

Livia. It must be his then sir,
For need wil then compell me.

Citty wife. Blessing on thee.

Livia. He wil undoe me in meere pans of Coles
To make him lustie.

Petronius. There's no talking to 'em;
How are they sir?

Petruchio. As I expected: Liberty and clothes, *Reads.*
When, and in what way she wil: continuall moneys,
Company, and all the house at her dispose;
No tongue to say, why is this? or whether wil it;
New Coaches, and some buildings, she appoints here; 140
Hangings, and hunting-horses: and for Plate
And Jewels for her private use, I take it,
Two thousand pound in present: then for Musick,
And women to read French ——

Petronius. This must not be.

Petruchio. And at the latter end a clause put in,
That *Livia* shal by no man be importun'd,
This whole moneth yet, to marry.

Petronius. This is monstrous.

Petruchio. This shall be done, Ile humor her awhile:
If nothing but repentance, and undoing
Can win her love, Ile make a shift for one. 150

Sophocles. When ye are once a bed, all these conditions
Lie under your own seale.

Maria. Do ye like 'em?

152 ye] MS; yo F1; you F2

58

Petruchio.   Yes.
And by that faith I gave ye fore the Priest
Ile ratifie 'em.
Country wife.   Stay, what pledges?
Maria.   No, Ile take that oath;
But have a care ye keep it.
Citty wife.   Tis not now
As when *Andrea* liv'd.
Country wife.   If ye do juggle,
Or alter but a Letter of this creed
We have set down, the self-same persecution——
Maria.   Mistrust him not.
Petruchio.   By all my honesty——   160
Maria.   Enough. I yield.
Petronius.   What's this inserted here?
Sophocles.   That the two valiant women that command here
Shall have a Supper made 'em, and a large one,
And liberall entertainment without grudging,
And pay for all their Souldiers.
Petruchio.   That shall be too;
And if a tun of Wine wil serve to pay 'em,
They shall have justice: I ordaine ye all
Pay-masters, Gentlemen.
Tranio.   Then we shall have sport boyes.
Maria.   We'l meet ye in the Parlour.   [*Exeunt above.*]
Petruchio.   Ne'r looke sad, sir,   [*To* Petronius.]
For I will doe it.
Sophocles.   There's no danger in't.   170
Petruchio.   For *Livia's* Article, you shall observe it,
I have tyde my selfe.
Petronius.   I wil.
Petruchio.   Along then: now
Either I break, or this stiffe plant must bow.

                                                Exeunt.

*155–156 No...it.] stet lining F1–2; No, | Ile...it. MS
*158 this creed] MS; these Articles F1–2

Enter Tranio, *and* Rowland.   III. i

Tranio.   Come, ye shall take my counsell.
Rowland.   I shall hang first.
  Ile no more love, that's certaine, tis a bane,
  (Next that they poyson Rats with) the most mortall:
  No, I thank Heaven, I have got my sleep again,
  And now begin to write sence; I can walk ye
  A long howre in my chamber like a man,
  And think of something that may better me;
  Some serious point of Learning, or my state;
  No more ay-mees, and *misereris, Tranio,*
  Come neer my brain. Ile tell thee, had the devil   10
  But any essence in him of a man,
  And could be brought to love, and love a woman,
  Twould make his head ake worser than his hornes doe;
  And firke him with a fire he never felt yet,
  Would make him dance. I tell thee there is nothing
  (It may be thy case *Tranio,* therefore heare me:)
  Under the Sun (reckon the masse of follies
  Crept into th' world with man) so desperate,
  So madde, so sencelesse, poor and base, so wretched,
  Roguy, and scurvy——
Tranio.   Whether wilt thou *Rowland?*   20
Rowland.   As tis to be in love.
Tranio.   And why for Heavens sake?
Rowland.   And why for Heavens sake? do'st thou not conceive me?
Tranio.   No by my troth.
Rowland.   Pray then, and hartely
  For fear thou fall into't: l'le tell thee why too,
  (For I have hope to save thee) when thou lovest,
  And first beginst to worship the calfe with the white face,
  Imprimis, thou hast lost thy gentry,

1, 77 (*twice*), 80, 81, 85, 87 ye] MS; you F 1–2
9 *misereris,*] Colman (miscreri's); miseries‸ F 1; mistrisses MS, F 2
*21 Heavens] Ms (heavens); vertue F 1–2
22 Heavens] MS (heavens); vertues F 1–2
26 calfe with the white face] MS; gilt calfe F 1–2

And like a prentice flung away thy freedom.
Forthwith thou art a slave.
Tranio.   That's a new Doctrine.
Rowland.   Next thou art no more man.
Tranio.   What then?
Rowland.   A Fryppery; 30
  Nothing but brayded haire, and penny riband,
  Glove, garter, ring, rose, or at best a swabber:
  If thou canst love so neer to keep thy making,
  Yet thou wilt loose thy language.
Tranio.   Why?
Rowland.   O *Tranio*,
  Those things in love, ne'r talke as we do.
Tranio.   No?
Rowland.   No without doubt, they sigh and shake the head,
  And sometimes whistle dolefully.
Tranio.   No tongue?
Rowland. Yes *Tranio*, but no truth in't, nor no reason,
  And when they cant (for tis a kind of canting)
  Ye shall hear (if you reach to understand 'em   40
  Which you must be a foole first, or you cannot)
  Such gibbrish; such believe me, I protest Sweet,
  And oh deer Heavens, in which such constellations
  Raigne at the births of lovers, this is too well,
  And daigne me Lady, daigne me I beseech ye
  Your poor unworthy lump, and then she licks him.
Tranio.   O, pox on't, this is nothing.
Rowland.   Thou ha'st hit it:
  Then talks she ten times worse, and wryes and wriggles,
  As though she had the itch (and so it may be.)
Tranio.   Of what religion are they?
Rowland.   Good old Catholikes,   50
  They deale by intercession all, they keepe

40–41 hear (if...'em) | Which] MS; ~, ~ ...~ | (Which F 1–2
46 Your] MS; You F 1–2
*47 O, pox] MS; (O ‸ pox); A —— F 1–2
50–57 *Tranio.* Of...ended——] MS; *om.* F 1–2

61

A kind of household Gods, call'd chamber-maides,
Which being pray'd to, and their offerings brought,
(Which are in gold, yet some observe the old law
And give 'em flesh) probatum est, you shall have
As good love for your monie, and as tydie
As ere you turn'd your legge ore, and that ended——
Tranio. Why thou art grown a strange discoverer.
Rowland. Of mine own follies *Tranio.*
Tranio.   Wilt thou *Rowland*,
  Certaine ne'r love again?
Rowland.   I think so, certain,   60
  And if I be not dead drunk, I shall keep it.
Tranio. Tell me but this; what do'st thou think of women?
Rowland. Why as I think of fiddles, they delight me,
  Till their strings break.
Tranio.   What strings?
Rowland.   Their modesties,
  Faithes, vowes and maidenheads, for they are like Kits,
  They have but foure strings to 'em.
Tranio.   What wilt thou
  Give me for ten pound now, when thou next lovest,
  And the same woman still?
Rowland.   Give me the money;
  A hundred, and my Bond for't.
Tranio.   But pray hear me,
  I'le work all meanes I can to reconcile ye.   70
Rowland. Do, do, give me the money.
Tranio.   There.
Rowland.   Work *Tranio.*
Tranio. You shall go sometimes where she is.
Rowland.   Yes straight.
  This is the first good I ere got by woman.
Tranio. You would think it strange now, if an other beauty
  As good as hers, say better——
Rowland.   Well?
Tranio.   Conceive me,
  This is no point o'th wager.

Rowland.   That's all one.

Tranio.   Love ye as much, or more, then she now hates ye.

Rowland.   Tis a good hearing, let 'em love: ten pound more,
I never love that woman.

Tranio.   There it is;
And so an hundred, if ye lose.

Rowland.   Tis done;   80
Have ye an other to put in?

Tranio.   No, no sir.

Rowland.   I am very sorry: now will I erect
A new Game and go hate for th' bell; I am sure
I am in excellent case to win.

Tranio.   I must have leave
To tell ye, and tell truth too, what she is,
And how shee suffers for you.

Rowland.   Ten pound more,
I never believe ye.

Tranio.   No sir, I am stinted.

Rowland.   Well, take your best way then.

Tranio.   Let's walk, I am glad
Your sullen feavor's off.

Rowland.   Shal't see me *Tranio*
A monstrous merry man now: let's to the Wedding,   90
And as we go, tell me the generall hurry
Of these madde wenches, and their workes.

Tranio.   I will.

Rowland.   And do thy worst.

Tranio.   Something i'le do.

Rowland.   Do *Tranio.*
                                        Exeunt.

                    Enter Pedro, *and* Jaques.   [III.] ii

Pedro.   A paire of stocks bestride 'em, are they gone?

Jaques.   Yes they are gon; and all the pans i'th Town
Beating before 'em: what strange admonitions
They gave my Master, and how fearfully

They threaten'd, if he brok 'em?
Pedro. O' my conscience
H'as found his full match now.
Jaques. That I believe too.
Pedro. How did she entertaine him?
Jaques. She lookt on him——
Pedro. But scurvely.
Jaques. Faith with no great affection
That I saw: and I heard some say he kiss'd her,
But 'twas upon a treaty, and some coppies 10
Say but her cheek.
Pedro. Faith *Jaques*, what wouldst thou give
For such a wife now?
Jaques. Full as many prayers
As the most zealous Puritane conceives
Out of the meditation of fat veale,
Or birds of prey, cram'd capons, against Players,
And to as good a tune too, but against her,
That heaven would blesse me from her: mark it *Pedro*,
If this house be not turn'd within this fortnight
With the foundation upward, i'le be carted.
My comfort is yet that those Amorites, 20
That came to back her cause, those heathen whores
Had their hoods hallowed with sack.
Pedro. How div'lish drunk they were?
Jaques. And how they tumbled, *Pedro*, didst thou marke
The Countrey Cavaliero?
Pedro. Out upon her,
How she turn'd down the Bragget?
Jaques. I that sunke her.
Pedro. That drink was wel put to her; what a somer salt
When the chaire fel, she fetch'd, with her heels upward?
Jaques. And what a piece of Landskip she discoverd?

8, 11 Faith] MS; *om.* F1–2
20 Amorites] MS; Amorities F1–2
26 Bragget] MS (Bragett), F2; Bagget F1
27 somer salt] F2 (Somer); sober salt F1; Sumersett MS

Pedro.   Didst mark her, when her hood fel in the Posset?   30
Jaques.   Yes, and there rid, like a Dutch hoy; the Tumbrel,
 When she had got her ballasse.
Pedro.   That I saw too.
Jaques.   How faine she would have drawn on *Sophocles*
 To come aboord, and how she simperd it——
Pedro.   I warrant her, she has been a worthy striker.
Jaques.   I'th heat of Summer there had been some hope on't,
 For then old women are coole cellars.
Pedro.   Hang her.
Jaques.   She offerd him a Harry-groat, and belcht out,
 Her stomack being blown with Ale, such Courtship,
 Upon my life has givn him twenty stooles since: 40
 Believe my calculation, these old women
 When they are tippled, and a little heated
 Are like new wheels, theyl roare you all the Town ore
 Till they be greasd.
Pedro.   The City Cinque-pace
 Dame Tost and Butter, had her Bob too?
Jaques.   Yes,
 But she was sullen drunk, and given to filching,
 I see her offer at a Spoon; my master,
 I do not like his looke, I feare h'as fasted
 For all this preparation; lets steale by him.

                                                        Exeunt.

                 Enter Petruchio, *and* Sophocles.   [III.] iii

Sophocles.   Not let you touch her all this night?
Petruchio.   Not touch her.
Sophocles.   Where was your courage?
Petruchio.   Where was her obedience?
 Never poore man was sham'd so; never Rascall
 That keeps a stud of whores was us'd so basely.
Sophocles.   Pray tell me one thing truly; do you love her?

---

37 For...cellars.] MS (woemen); *om.* F1–2   45 Tost] MS (tost), F2; tosse F1
45 her] MS; he F1; the F2   48 h'as] MS, F2; has F1
*5 pray] MS; pray you F1–2

Petruchio.　　I would I did not, upon that condition
　I past thee halfe my Land.
Sophocles.　　　　　　　　It may be then,
　Her modesty requir'd a little violence?
　Some women love to struggle.
Petruchio.　　　　　　　　She had it,
　And so much that I sweat for't, so I did,　　　　　　　　10
　But to no end: I washt an Ethiope;
　She swore my force might weary her, but win her
　I never could, nor should, till she consented;
　And I might take her body prisoner,
　But for her mind or appetite——
Sophocles.　　　　　　　Tis strange;
　This woman is the first I ever read of,
　Refus'd a warranted occasion,
　And standing on so faire termes.
Petruchio.　　　　　　　　I shall quight her.
Sophocles.　Us'd you no more art?
Petruchio.　　　　　　　　Yes, I swore unto her,
　And by no little ones, if presently　　　　　　　　20
　Without more disputation on the matter,
　She grew not neerer to me, and dispatcht me
　Out of the pain I was, (for I was nettl'd)
　And willingly, and eagerly, and sweetly,
　I would to her Chamber-maid, and in her hearing
　Begin her such a huntes-up.
Sophocles.　　　　　　　Then she started?
Petruchio.　No more then I do now; marry she answered
　If I were so dispos'd, she could not help it;
　But there was one cal'd *Jaques*, a poor Butler,
　One that might well content a single woman.　　　　　　　　30
Sophocles.　And he should tilt her?
Petruchio.　　　　　　　To that sence, and last
　She bad me yet these six nights look for nothing,
　Nor strive to purchase it, but faire good night,

　　　　*18 quight] MS; quit F1–2　　　*19 unto] MS; to F1–2
　　　　*32 nights] *stet* F1–2; monthes MS

66

And so good morrow, and a kisse or two
To close my stomach, for her vow had seald it,
And she would keep it constant.
Sophocles.　　　　　　　　Stay ye, stay ye,
Was she thus when you woo'd her?
Petruchio.　　　　　　　　Nothing *Sophocles*,
More keenely eager, I was oft afraid
She had bin light, and easy, she would showre
Her kisses so upon me.
Sophocles.　　　　　Then I fear　　　　　　40
An other spoke's i'th wheele.
Petruchio.　　　　　Now thou hast found me,
There gnawes my devill, *Sophocles*, O patience
Preserve me; that I make her not example
By some unworthy way; as fleaing her,
Boyling, or making verjuce, drying her.
Sophocles. I hear her.
Petruchio.　　　　Mark her then, and see the heire
Of spight and prodigality, she has studied
A way to begger's both, and by this hand
She shall be if I live a Doxy.

　　　　　Maria *at the dore, and Servant and woman.*

Sophocles.　　　　　Fy Sir.
Maria. I do not like that dressing, tis too poor,　　50
Let me have six gold laces, broad and massy,
And betwixt ev'ry lace a rich embroydry,
Line the gown through with plush, perfum'd, and purffle
All the sleeves down with pearle.
Petruchio.　　　　　What think you *Sophocles*.
In what point stands my state now?
Maria.　　　　　For those hangings
Let 'em be carried where I gave appointment,
They are too base for my use, and bespeak
New pieces of the civill wars of *France*,
Let 'em be large and lively, and all silke work,

　　　　*38 keenely] *stet* F 1–2; kindly MS

The borders gold.

Sophocles.   I marry sir, this cuts it.   60

Maria.   That fourteen yardes of satten give my woman,
I do not like the colour, tis too civill:
Ther's too much silk i'th lace too; tell the Dutchman
That brought the mares, he must with all speed send me
An other suit of horses, and by all meanes
Ten cast of Hawkes for th' River, I much care not
What price they beare, so they be sound, and flying,
For the next winter, I am for the Country;
And mean to take my pleasure; wher's the horse man?

Petruchio.   She meanes to ride a great horse.

Sophocles.   With a side sadle?   70

Petruchio.   Yes, and shee'l run a tilt within this twelvemonth.

Maria.   To morrow Ile begin to learne, but pray sir
Have a great care he be an easy doer,
Twill spoyle a Scholler els.

Sophocles.   An easy doer,
Did you hear that?

Petruchio.   Yes, I shall meet her morals
Er it be long I fear not.

Maria.   O good morrow.

Sophocles.   Good morrow Lady, how is't now?

Maria.   Faith sickly,
This house stands in an ill ayre——

Petruchio.   Yet more charges?

Maria.   Subject to rots, and rhewms; out on't, tis nothing
But a tild fog.

Petruchio.   What think you of the Lodge then?   80

Maria.   I like the seate, but tis too little, *Sophocles*
Let me have thy opinion, thou hast judgement.

Petruchio.   Tis very well.

Maria.   What if I pluck it down,
And built a square upon it, with two courts
Still rising from the entrance?

79 rhewms] F 2 (rheums); hewms F 1; rhumes MS
80 you] MS, F 2; *om.* F 1

Petruchio.   And i'th midst
  A Colledge for yong Scolds.
Maria.   And to the Southward
  Take in a garden of some twenty acres,
  And cast it of the Italian fashion, hanging.
Petruchio [*aside*].   And you could cast your self so too;——pray
        Lady
  Will not this cost much money?
Maria.   Some five thousand,   90
  Say six: Ile have it battel'd too.
Petruchio.   And gilt; *Maria,*
  This is a fearfull course you take, pray think on't,
  You are a woman now, a wife, and his
  That must in honesty, and justice look for
  Some due obedience from you.
Maria.   That bare word
  Shall cost you many a pound more, build upon't;
  Tell me of due obedience? what's a husband?
  What are we married for, to carry sumpters?
  Are we not one peece with you, and as worthy
  Our own intentions, as you yours?
Petruchio.   Pray hear me.   100
Maria.   Take two small drops of water, equall weigh'd,
  Tell me which is the heaviest, and which ought
  First to discend in duty?
Petruchio.   You mistake me;
  I urge not service from you, nor obedience
  In way of duty, but of love, and credit;
  All I expect is but a noble care
  Of what I have brought you, and of what I am,
  And what our name may be.
Maria.   That's in my making.
Petruchio.   Tis true it is so.
Maria.   Yes it is *Petruchio,*
  For there was never man without our molding,   110
  Without our stampe upon him, and our justice,

*88 of] MS, F2; off F1

Left any thing three ages after him
Good, and his own.
Sophocles.   Good Lady understand him.
Maria.   I do too much, sweet *Sophocles*, he's one
Of a most spightfull self condition,
Never at peace with any thing but age,
That has no teeth left to return his anger:
A Bravery dwels in his blood yet, of abusing
His first good wife; he's sooner fire then powder,
And sooner mischief.
Petruchio.   If I be so sodain   120
Do not you fear me?
Maria.   No nor yet care for you,
And if it may be lawfull, I defie you.
Petruchio.   Do's this become you now?
Maria.   It shall become me.
Petruchio.   Thou disobedient, weak, vain-glorious woman,
Were I but half so wilfull, as thou spightfull,
I should now drag thee to thy duty.
Maria.   Drag me?
Petruchio.   But I am friends again: take all your pleasure.
Maria.   Now you perceive him *Sophocles*.
Petruchio.   I love thee
Above thy vanity, thou faithlesse creature.
Maria.   Would I had been so happy when I married,   130
But to have met an honest man like thee,
For I am sure thou art good, I know thou art honest,
A hansome hurtlesse man, a loving man,
Though never a penny with him; and these eyes,
That face, and that true heart; weare this for my sake,
And when thou thinkst upon me pity me:
I am cast away,   *Exit* Maria.
Sophocles.   Why how now man?
Petruchio.   Pray leave me,
And follow your advices.
Sophocles.   The man's jealous.
Petruchio.   I shall find a time ere it be long, to aske you

70

One or two foolish questions.

Sophocles.   I shall answer   140
As wel as I am able, when you call me:——
If she mean true, tis but a little killing,
And if I do not venture it, rots take me.——
Farewel sir.   *Exit* Sophocles.

Petruchio.   Pray farewell. Is there no keeping
A wife to one mans use? no wintering
These cattell without straying? tis hard dealing,
Very hard dealing, Gentlemen, strange dealing:
Now in the name of madnesse, what star raign'd,
What dog-star, bull, or bear-star, when I married
This second wife, this whirlwind, that takes all   150
Within her compasse? was I not wel warnd,
(I thought I had, and I believe I know it,)
And beaten to repentance in the daies
Of my first doting? had I not wife enough
To turn my tooles to? did I want vexation,
Or any speciall care to kill my heart?
Had I not ev'ry morning a rare breakfast,
Mixt with a learned Lecture of ill language,
Louder then *Tom* o' Lincoln; and at dinner,
A dyet of the same dish? was there evening   160
That ere past over us, without thou knave,
Or thou whore, for digestion? had I ever
A pull at this same poor sport men run mad for,
But like a cur I was faine to shew my teeth first,
And almost worry her? and did Heaven forgive me,
And take this Serpent from me? and am I
Keeping tame devils now again? my heart akes;
Something I must do speedily: Ile die,
If I can hansomely, for that's the way
To make a Rascall of her; I am sick,   170
And Ile go very neer it, but Ile perish.

                                      Exit.

143 it, rots take me.——] MS (me.ₐ); its—— F1; it's—— F2
155 tooles] MS; love F1–2   155 to] F2; too F1, MS

Enter Livia, Byancha, Tranio, *and* Rowland. [III.] iv

Livia. Then I must be content sir, with my fortune.

Rowland. And I with mine.

Livia. I did not think, a look,
Or a poore word or two, could have displanted
Such a fix'd constancy, and for your end too.

Rowland. Come, come, I know your courses: there's your
gew-gaws,
Your Rings, and Bracelets, and the Purse you gave me,
The money's spent in entertaining you
At Plays, and Cherry-gardens.

Livia. There's your Chain too.
But if you'l give me leave, Ile weare the haire still;
I would yet remember you.

Byancha. Give him his love wench; 10
The yong man has imployment for't.

Tranio. Fie *Rowland.*

Rowland. You cannot fie me out a hundred pound
With this poore plot: yet, let me nere see day more,
If something do not struggle strangely in me.

Byancha. Young man, let me talk with you.

Rowland. Wel young woman.

Byancha. This was your Mistris once.

Rowland. Yes.

Byancha. Are ye honest?
I see you are young, and hansome.

Rowland. I am honest.

Byancha. Why that's wel said: and there's no doubt your judgement
Is good enough, and strong enough to tell you
Who are your foes, and friends: why did you leave her? 20

Rowland. She made a puppy of me.

Byancha. Be that granted:
She must doe so sometimes, and oftentimes;
Love were too serious else.

Rowland. A witty woman.

5 ²your] MS, F2; no F1

72

Byancha. Had ye lov'd me——
Rowland.   I would I had.
Byancha.   And deerly;
And I had lov'd you so: you may love worse sir,
But that is not materiall.
Rowland.   1 shal loose.
Byancha. Some time or other for variety
I should have cal'd ye foole, or boy, or bid ye
Play with the Pages: but have lov'd you stil,
Out of all question, and extreamly too;   30
You are a man made to be loved.
Rowland [aside].   This woman
Either abuses me, or loves me dearely.
Byancha. Ile tell you one thing, if I were to choose
A husband to mine own mind, I should think
One of your mothers making would content me,
For o' my conscience she makes good ones.
Rowland.   Lady,
Ile leave you to your commendations:——
I am in again, The divel take their tongues.
Byancha. You shall not goe.
Rowland.   I wil: yet thus far *Livia*,
Your sorrow may induce me to forgive ye,   40
But never love again;——if I stay longer,
I have lost two hundred pound.
Livia.   Good sir, but thus much——
Tranio. Turn if thou beest a man.
Livia.   But one kisse of ye;
One parting kisse, and I am gone too.
Rowland.   Come,
I shall kisse fifty pound away at this clap:
We'l have one more, and then farewel.
Livia.   Farewel, sir.
Byancha. Wel, go thy waies, thou bearst a kind heart with thee.
Tranio. H'as made a stand.

24, 28 (*twice*), 40, 43 ye] MS; you F 1–2   32 dearely] MS; deadly F 1–2
*45 clap:] *stet* F 1–2; ~ .—— MS   46 , sir] MS; *om.* F 1–2

Byancha.   A noble, brave young fellow,
  Worthy a wench indeed.
Rowland.   I wil: I wil not.   *Exit* Rowland.
Tranio.   'Is gone: but shot agen; play you but your part,   50
  And I will keep my promise: forty Angels
  In fair gold Lady: wipe your eyes: he's yours
  If I have any wit.   [*To* Livia.]
Livia.   Ile pay the forfeit.
Byancha.   Come then, lets see your sister, how she fares now,
  After her skirmish: and be sure, *Moroso*,
  Be kept in good hand; then all's perfect, *Livia*.

                                              Exeunt.

                    Enter Jaques *and* Pedro.   [III.] v

Pedro.   O *Jaques*, *Jaques*, what becomes of us?
  Oh my sweet Master.
Jaques.   Run for a Physitian,
  And a whole peck of Pothecaries, *Pedro*.
  He wil die, didle, didle die, if they come not quickly:
  And bring all Empyricks straight and Mountebankes
  Skilfull in Lungs and Livers: raise the neighbours,
  And all the Aquavite-bottles extant;
  And, O the Parson, *Pedro*; O the Parson!
  A little of his comfort, never so little;
  Twenty to one you finde him at the Bush,   10
  There's the best Ale.
Pedro.   I fly.   *Exit* Pedro.

   Enter Maria. *Servants carrying out houshold stuff and truncks.*

Maria.   Out with the Trunks, ho:
  Why are you idle? Sirha, up to th' Chamber,
  And take the hangings down, and see the Linnen
  Packt up, and sent away within this halfe houre.
  What are the Carts come yet? some honest body

---

*50 'Is] MS; He's F1–2   5 Empyricks...Mountebankes] MS; people that are F1–2
11 s.d. Maria...truncks.] MS; Maria, *and servants.* F 1–2±

                              74

Help down the chests of Plate, and some the wardrobe,
Alas we are undone else.
Jaques.   Pray forsooth,
And I beseech ye, tell me, is he dead yet?
Maria.   No, but 'is drawing on: out with the Armour.
Jaques.   Then Ile goe see him.
Maria.   Thou art undone then fellow: 20
No man that has been neere him come neere me.

Enter Sophocles, *and* Petronius.

Sophocles.   Why how now Lady, what means this?
Petronius.   Now daughter,
How do's my sonne?
Maria.   Save all ye can for Heavens sake.

Enter Livia, Byancha, *and* Tranio.

Livia.   Be of good comfort sister.
Maria.   O my Casket.
Petronius.   How do's thy husband woman?
Maria.   Get ye gon,
If you mean to save your lives: the sicknesse——
Petronius.   Stand further off, I prethee.
Maria.   Is i'th house sir, my husband has it now;
Alas he is infected, and raves extreamly:
Give me some counsell friends.
Byancha.   Why lock the doores up,   30
And send him in a woman to attend him.
Maria.   I have bespoke two women; and the City
Has sent a watch by this time: meat nor money
He shall not want, nor prayers.
Petronius.   How long is't
Since it first tooke him?
Maria.   But within this three houres.
                                   Enter Watch.

19 'is] ₐis F 1–2, MS
23, 25, 73, 81, 82, 83, 95 (*twice*), 97 ye] MS; you F 1–2
23 Heavens] MS (heavens), F 2; Heaven F 1
*29 Alas he is infected] *stet* F 1–2; *om.* MS   33 Has] MS; Hath F 1–2

75

I am frighted from my wits:——O here's the watch;
Pray doe your Office, lock the doores up friends,
And patience be his Angel.   *They lock the door.*
Tranio.   This comes unlook'd for.
Maria.   Ile to the lodge; some that are kind and love me,
  I know wil visit me.
Petruchio.   Doe you heare my Masters: 40
                                    Petruchio *within.*

Ho, you that locke the doores up.
Petronius.   Tis his voyce.
Tranio.   Hold, and let's heare him.
Petruchio.   Wil ye starve me here:
  Am I a Traytor, or an Heretick.
  Or am I grown infectious?
Petronius.   Pray sir, pray.
Petruchio.   I am as wel as you are, goodman puppy.
Maria.   Pray have patience, you shall want nothing sir.
Petruchio.   I want a cudgell, and thee, thou wickednesse.
Petronius.   He speakes wel enough.
Maria.   'Had ever a strong heart sir.
Petruchio.   Wil ye heare me? first be pleas'd
  To think I know ye all, and can distinguish   50
  Ev'ry mans severall voyce: you that spoke first,
  I know my father in law; the other *Tranio,*
  And I heard *Sophocles;* the last, pray marke me,
  Is my dam'd wife *Maria:* Gentlemen,
  If any man misdoubt me for infected,
  There is mine arme, let any mon looke on't.

                Enter Doctor and Pothecary.

Doctor.   Save ye Gentlemen.
Petronius.   O welcome Doctor,
  Ye come in happy time; pray your opinion,
  What think you of his pulse?
Doctor.   It beats with busiest,

38 *s.d. They...door.*] MS (doore); *om.* F 1–2
54 Gentlemen,] MS (gentlemen); *om.* F 1–2

And shews a general inflammation,   60
Which is the symptome of a pestilent feaver,
Take twenty ounces from him.
Petruchio.   Take a foole;
Take an ounce from mine arme, and Doctor Deuz-ace,
Ile make a close-stoole of your Velvet costard.
Death, Gentlemen, doe ye make a may-game on me?
I tell ye once againe, I am as sound,
As wel, as wholsome, and as sensible,
As any of ye all: Let me out quickly,
Or as I am a man, Ile beat the wals down,
And the first thing I light upon shall pay for't.   70
                                   Exit Doctor and Pothecary
Petronius.   Nay we'l go with you Doctor.
Maria.   Tis the safest;
I saw the tokens sir.
Petronius.   Then there is but one way.
Petruchio.   Wil it please ye open?
Tranio.   His fit grows stronger still.
Maria.   Let's save our selves sir,
He's past all worldly cure.
Petronius.   Friends do your office.
And what he wants, if money, love, or labour,
Or any way may win it, let him have it.
Farewell, and pray my honest friends——
                                   Exeunt: manent Watchmen.
Petruchio.   Why Rascals,
Friends, Gentlemen, thou beastly wife, *Jaques*;
None heare me? who's at the doore there?
1. Watchman.   Thinke I pray sir,   80
Whether ye are going, and prepare your selfe.
2. Watchman.   These idle thoughts disturbe ye, the good
        Gentlewoman
Your wife has taken care ye shall want nothing.

65 Death,] MS; —— F 1–2
78 *s.d. Exeunt: manent Watchmen.*] MS (Exeunt.); *Exeunt.* F 1–2
80 who's] MS; who F 1–2

Petruchio.   The blessing of her grandam Eve light on her,
Nothing but thin fig leaves to hide her knavery.
Shall I come out in quiet, answer me,
Or shall I charge a fowling-piece, and make
Mine own way? two of ye I cannot misse,
If I misse three; ye come here to assault me.
1. Watchman.   There's onions rosting for your sore, Sir.
Petruchio.   People, 90
I am as excellent wel, I thank Heav'n for't,
And have as good a stomacke at this instant——
2. Watchman.   That's an ill signe.
1. Watchman.   I he draws on; he's a dead man.
Petruchio.   And sleep as soundly; wil ye looke upon me?
1. Watchman.   Do ye want Pen and Inke? while ye have sence sir,
Settle your state.
Petruchio.   Sirs, I am as wel, as you are;
Or any Rascall living.
2. Watchman.   Would ye were sir.
Petruchio   Look to your selves, and if ye love your lives,
Open the doore, and fly me, for I shoot else;
1 sweare Ile shoot, and presently, chain-bullets;   100
And under foure I will not kill.
1. Watchman.   Let's quit him,
It may be it is a trick: he's dangerous.
2. Watchman.   The devill take the hinmost, I cry.

                                         Exit watch running.

        Enter Petruchio *with a piece, and forces the doore open.*

Petruchio.   Have among ye;
The doore shall open too, Ile have a faire shoot;
Are ye all gone? tricks in my old daies, crackers
Put now upon me? and by Lady *Green-sleeves?*

84–85 The. . .knavery.] MS; *om.* F 1–2
90 *1. Watchman*. . .People,] MS; *om.* F 1–2   93 I] MS; *om.* F 1–2
96 ¹as] MS; *om.* F 1–2   100 I sweare] MS; —— F 1–2
102 is a] F 2; is F 1; tis a MS   103 *s.d., and*. . .*open*] MS; *om.* F 1–2

Am I grown so tame after all my triumphs?
But that I should be thought mad, if I rail'd
As much as they deserve against these women,
I would now rip up from the primitive cuckold,   110
All their arch-villanies, and all their dobles,
Which are more then a hunted Hare ere thought on:
When a man has the fairest, and the sweetest
Of all their sex, and as he thinks the noblest,
What has he then? and Ile speake modestly,
He has a Quartern-ague, that shall shake
All his estate to nothing; never cur'd,
Nor never dying; H'as a ship to venture
His fame, and credit in, which if he man not
With more continuall labour then a Gally   120
To make her tith, either she grows a Tumbrell
Not worth the cloth she weares, or springs more leakes
Then all the fame of his posterity
Can ever stop againe: out on 'em hedge-hogs,
He that shal touch 'em, has a thousand thorns
Runs through his fingers: If I were unmarried,
I would do any thing below repentance,
Any base dunhill slavery; be a hang-man,
Ere I would be a husband: O the thousand,
Thousand, ten thousand waies they have to kil us!   130
Some fall with too much stringing of the Fiddles,
And those are fooles; some, that they are not suffer'd,
And those are Maudlin-lovers: some, like Scorpions,
They poyson with their tailes, and those are Martyrs;
Some die with doing good, those Benefactors,
And leave 'em land to leap away: some few,
For those are rarest, they are said to kill
With kindnesse, and faire usage; but what they are
My Catologue discovers not: onely tis thought
They are buried in old wals with their heeles upward.   140
I could raile twenty daies together now.

*124 Can...-hogs,] MS; Can...againe: I could raile twenty daies; | Out on 'em
hedge-hogs, F 1–2

Ile seek 'em out, and if I have not reason,
And very sensible, why this was done,
Ile go a birding yet, and some shall smart for't.

Exit.

Enter Moroso *and* Petronius.   IV. i

Moroso.   That I do love her, is without all question,
And most extreamly, deerly, most exactly;
And that I would ev'n now, this present Monday,
Before all others, maids, wives, women, widdows,
Of what degree or calling, marry her,
As certaine too; but to be made a whim-wham,
A Jib-crack, and a Gentleman o'th first house
For all my kindnesse to her——
Petronius.   How you take it?
Thou get a wench, thou get a dozen night-caps;
Wouldst have her come, and lick thee like a calfe,   10
And blow thy nose, and busse thee?
Moroso.   Not so neither.
Petronius.   What wouldst thou have her do?
Moroso.   Do as she should do;
Put on a clean smock, and to Church, and marry,
And then to bed a Gods name, this is faire play,
And keeps the Kings peace; let her leave her bobs,
I have had too many of them, and her quillets,
She is as nimble that way as an Eele;
But in the way she ought to me especially,
A sow of Lead is swifter.
Petronius.   Quoat your griefes down.
Moroso.   Give faire quarter, I am old and crasie,   20
And subject to much fumbling, I confesse it;
Yet something I would have that's warme, to hatch me:
But understand me I would have it so,
I buy not more repentance in the bargaine
Then the ware's worth I have; if you allow me

IV.i] *om. scene* MS   9 a dozen] F2; dozen F1

Worthy your Son-in-law, and your allowance,
Do it a way of credit; let me show so,
And not be troubled in my visitations,
With blows, and bitternesse, and down right railings,
As if we were to couple like two cats,   30
With clawing, and loud clamour.
Petronius.   Thou fond man
Hast thou forgot the Ballad, crabbed age,
Can *May* and *January* match together,
And nev'r a storm between 'em? say she abuse thee,
Put case she doe.
Moroso.   Wel.
Petronius.   Nay, believe she do's.
Moroso.   I doe believe she do's.
Petronius.   And div'lishly:
Art thou a whit the worse?
Moroso.   That's not the matter,
I know, being old, tis fit I am abus'd;
I know tis hansome, and I know moreover
I am to love her for't.
Petronius.   Now you come to me.   40
Moroso.   Nay more then this; I find too, and finde certain,
What Gold I have, Pearle, Bracelets, Rings, or Owches,
Or what she can desire, Gowns, Petticotes,
Wastcotes, Embroydered-stockings, Scarffs, Cals, Feathers,
Hats, five pound Garters, Muffs, Masks, Ruffs, and Ribands,
I am to give her for't.
Petronius.   Tis right, you are so.
Moroso.   But when I have done all this, and think it duty,
Is't requisit an other bore my nostrils?
Riddle me that.
Petronius.   Go get you gone, and dreame
She's thine within these two daies, for she is so;   50
The boy's beside the saddle: get warm broths,
And feed apace; think not of worldly businesse,
It cools the blood; leave off your tricks, they are hateful,

31 and] F2; add F1

81

And meere forerunners of the ancient measures;
Contrive your beard o'th top cut like Verdugoes;
It shows you would be wise, and burn your night-cap,
It looks like halfe a winding-sheet, and urges
From a young wench nothing but cold repentance:
You may eate Onyons, so you'l not be lavish.

Moroso. I am glad of that.

Petronius.   They purge the blood, and quicken,   60
But after 'em, conceive me, sweep your mouth,
And where there wants a tooth, stick in a clove.

Moroso. Shall I hope once againe, say't.

Petronius.   You shall sir:
And you shall have your hope.

            Enter Byancha *and* Tranio.

Moroso.   Why there's a match then.

Byancha. You shall not finde me wanting, get you gon.
Here's the old man, he'l think you are plotting else
Something against his new Sonne.   *Exit* Tranio.

Moroso.   Fare ye well sir.

                   Exit Moroso.

Byancha. *And ev'ry Buck had his Doe,*
  And ev'ry Cuckold a Bell at his Toe:
Oh what sport should we have then, then Boyes then,   70
   O what sport should we have then?

Petronius. This is the spirit, that inspires 'em all.

Byancha. Give you good ev'n.

Petronius.   A word with you Sweet Lady.

Byancha. I am very hasty sir.

Petronius.   So you were ever.

Byancha. Well what's your will?

Petronius.   Was not your skilfull hand
In this last stratagem? were not your mischiefes
Eeking the matter on?

Byancha.   In's shutting up?
Is that it?

          74 you] F2; your F1

Petronius.   Yes.
Byancha.   Ile tell you.
Petronius.   Doe.
Byancha.   And truly.
  Good old man, I doe grieve exceeding much,
  I feare too much.
Petronius.   I am sorry for your heavinesse.   80
  Belike you can repent then?
Byancha.   There you are wide too.
  Not that the thing was done (conceive me rightly)
  Do's any way molest me.
Petronius.   What then Lady?
Byancha.   But that I was not in't, there's my sorrow, there;
  Now you understand me, for Ile tell you,
  It was so sound a peece, and so well carried,
  And if you marke the way, so hansomely,
  Of such a heigth, and excellence, and art
  I have not known a braver, for conceive me,
  When the grosse foole her husband would be sick——   90
Petronius.   Pray stay.
Byancha.   Nay, good, your patience: and no sence for't,
  Then stept your daughter in.
Petronius.   By your appointment.
Byancha.   I would it had, on that condition
  I had but one halfe smock, I like it so well;
  And like an excellent cunning woman, cur'd me
  One madnesse with an other, which was rare,
  And to our weake beleifes, a wonder.
Petronius.   Hang ye,
  For surely, if your husband looke not to ye,
  I know what will.
Byancha.   I humbly thank your worship.
  And so I take my leave.   100
Petronius.   You have a hand I heare too——
Byancha.   I have two sir.
Petronius.   In my yong daughters businesse.
Byancha.   You will finde there

83

A fitter hand then mine, to reach her frets,
And play down diddle to her.
Petronius.   I shall watch ye.
Byancha.   Doe.
Petronius.   And I shall have justice.
Byancha.   Where?
Petronius.   That's all one;
I shall be with you at a turne hence forward.
Byancha.   Get you a posset too; and so good ev'n sir.

Exeunt.

Enter Petruchio, Jaques, *and* Pedro.   [IV. ii]

Jaques.   And as I told your worship, all the hangings,
Brasse, Pewter, Plate, ev'n to the very pispots——
Pedro.   And that that hung for our defence, the Armor,
And the march Beere was going too: Oh *Jaques*
What a sad sight was that?
Jaques.   Even the two Rundlets,
The two that was our hope, of Muskadell,
(Better nev'r tongue tript over) those two Cannons,
To batter brawne withall at Christmas sir,
Ev'n those two lovely twyns, the enemy
Had almost cut off cleane.
Petruchio.   Goe trim the house up,   10
And put the things in order as they were.

Exit Pedro *and* Jaques.

I shall finde time for all this: could I finde her
But constant any way, I had done my businesse;
Were she a whore directly, or a scold,
An unthrift, or a woman made to hate me,
I had my wish, and knew which way to rayne her:
But while she shewes all these, and all their losses,
A kinde of linsey woolsey mingled mischiefe
Not to be ghest at, and whether true, or borrowed,

2 pispots——] MS (~ .); looking glasses. F1–2
7 those] MS, F2; these F1

84

Not certaine neither, what a hap had I,   20

Enter Maria [*apart*].

And what a tydie fortune, when my fate
Flung me upon this Beare-whelp? here she comes,
Now if she have a colour, for the fault is
A cleanly one, upon my conscience
I shall forgive her yet, and finde a something
Certaine, I married for: her wit: Ile marke her.
Maria.   Not let his wife come neere him in his sicknes,
Not come to comfort him? she that all lawes
Of heaven, and Nations have ordain'd his second,
Is she refus'd? and two old Paradoxes,   30
Peeces of five and fifty, without faith
Clapt in upon him? h'as a little pet,
That all young wives must follow necessary,
Having their Mayden-heads——
Petruchio.   This is an Axiome
I never heard before.
Maria.   Or say rebellion
If we durst be so foule, which two faire words
Alas win us from, in an houre, an instant,
We are so easie, make him so forgetfull
Both of his reason, honesty, and credit,
As to deny his wife a visitation?   40
His wife, that (though she was a little foolish,)
Lov'd him, Oh heaven forgive her for't! nay doted,
Nay had run mad, had she not married him.
Petruchio.   Though I doe know this falser then the devill,
I cannot choose but love it.
Maria.   What doe I know
But those that came to keepe him, might have kill'd him,
In what a case had I been then? I dare not
Beleeve him such a base, debosh'd companion,
That one refusall of a tender maide
Would make him faigne this sicknesse out of need,   50
And take a Keeper to him of fourescore

85

To play at Billiards; one that mew'd content
And all her teeth together; not come neere him?
Petruchio.   This woman would have made a most rare Jesuite,
She can prevaricate on any thing:
There was not to be thought a way to save her
In all imagination, beside this.
Maria.   His unkinde dealing, which was worst of all,
In sending, heaven knowes whether, all the plate,
And all the houshold-stuffe, had I not crost it,   60
By a great providence, and my friends assistance
Which he will thanke me one day for: alas,
I could have watch'd as well as they, have serv'd him
In any use, better, and willinger.
The Law commands me to doe it, love commands me;
And my own duty charges me.
Petruchio.   Heav'n blesse me.
And now I have said my Prayers, Ile goe to her:
Are you a wife for any man?
Maria.   For you Sir.
If I were worse, I were better; That ye are well,
(At least, that ye appeare so) I thanke heaven,   70
Long may it hold, and that you are here, I am glad too,
But that you have abus'd me wretchedly,
And such a way that shames the name of husband,
Such a malicious mangy way, so mingled,
(Never looke strangely on me, I dare tell you)
With breach of honesty, care, kindnesse, manners——
Petruchio.   Holla, ye kick too fast.
Maria.   Was I a stranger?
Or had I vow'd perdition to your person?
Am I not married to you, tell me that?
Petruchio.   I would I could not tell you.
Maria.   Is my presence,   80
The stock I come of, which is worshipfull,
If I should say right worshipfull, I ly'd not,
My Grandsire was a Knight——

Petruchio.　　　　　　　　　O' the Shire?

Maria.　　　　　　　　　　　　　　　A Souldier,
Which none of all thy Family e're heard off,
But one conductor of thy name, a Grasier
That ran away with pay: or am I grown
(Because I have been a little peevish to you,
Onely to try your temper) such a dogge-leech
I could not be admitted to your presence?

Petruchio.　If I endure this, hang me.

Maria.　　　　　　　　　　And two deaths heads,　　90
Two *Harry* Groats, that had their faces worne,
Almost their names away too——

Petruchio.　　　　　　　　Now heare me.
For I will stay no longer.

Maria.　　　　　　　　This you shall:
However you shall think to flatter me,
For this offence, which no submission
Can ever mediate for, you'l finde it so,
What ever ye shall doe by intercession,
What ye can offer, what your Land can purchase,
What all your friends, or families can win,
Shall be but this, not to forsweare your knowledge,　　100
But ever to forbeare it: now your will sir.

Petruchio.　Thou art the subtlest woman I think living,
I am sure the lewdest; now be still, and marke me;
Were I but any way addicted to the devill,
I should now think I had met a play-fellow
To profit by, and that way the most learned
That ever taught to murmur. Tell me thou,
Thou most poor, paltry spitefull whore: doe you cry?
Ile make you roare, before I leave.

Maria.　　　　　　　　　Your pleasure.

Petruchio.　Was it not sinne enough, thou Fruiterer　　110
Full of the fall thou eat'st: thou devils broker,
Thou Seminary of all sedition,
Thou sword of veng'ance, with a thred hung o're us,

88 -leech] MS, F2; -latch F1

87

Was it not sinne enough, and wickednes
In full abundance? was it not vexation
At all points, cap a pe? nay, I shall pinch ye,
Thus like a rotten rascall to abuse
The name of heaven, the tye of marriage,
The honour of thy friends; the expectation
Of all that thought thee vertuous, with rebellion,   120
Childish and base rebellion, but continuing
After forgivenesse too, and worse, your mischiefe,
And against him, setting the hope of heaven by,
And the deere reservation of his honour,
Nothing above ground could have won to hate thee:
Well goe thy wayes.
Maria.   Yes.
Petruchio.   You shall heare me out first:
What punishment mai'st thou deserve, thou thing,
Thou Idle thing of nothing, thou pull'd Primrose,
That two houres after, art a weed, and wither'd,
For this last flourish on me? am I one   130
Selected out of all the husbands living,
To be so ridden by a Tit of ten pence,
Am I so blind and Bed-rid? I was mad,
And had the Plague, and no man must come neere me,
I must be shut up, and my substance bezel'd,
And an old woman watch me.
Maria.   Well sir, well,
You may well glory in't.
Petruchio.   And when it comes to opening, 'tis my plot,
I must undoe my selfe forsooth: do'st heare me?
If I should beat thee now, as much may be,   140
Do'st thou not well deserve it, o' thy conscience,
Do'st thou not cry, come beat me?
Maria.   I defie you.
And my last loving teares farwell: the first stroke,
The very first you give me, if you dare strike,
Try me, and you shall finde it so, for ever
Never to be recall'd: I know you love me,

88

Mad till you have enjoy'd me; I doe turne
Utterly from you, and what man I meet first
That has but spirit to deserve a favour,
Let him beare any shape, the worse the better,   150
Shall kill you, and enjoy me; what I have said
About your foolish sicknesse, e're you have me
As you would have me, you shall sweare, is certaine,
And challenge any man, that dares deny it;
And in all companies approve my actions,
And so farwell for this time.   *Exit* Maria.
Petruchio.   Grief goe with thee,
If there be any witchcrafts, herbes, or potions,
Saying my Prayers back-ward, Fiends, or Fayries
That can againe unlove me, I am made.

                                                        Exit.

                    Enter Byancha, *and* Tranio.   [IV.] iii

Tranio.   Faith Mistresse, you must doe it.
Byancha.   Are the writings
Ready I told ye of?
Tranio.   Yes they are ready,
But to what use I know not.
Byancha.   Y'are an Asse,
You must have all things constru'd.
Tranio.   Yes, and peirc'd too,
Or I finde little pleasure.
Byancha.   Now you are knavish,
Goe too, fetch *Rowland* hither presently,
Your twenty pound lies bleeding else: she is married
Within these twelve houres, if we crosse it not,
And see the Papers of one size.
Tranio.   I have ye.
Byancha.   And for disposing of 'em——
Tranio.   If I faile ye   10
Now I have found the way, use Marshall Law
And cut my head off with a hand Saw.

        1 Faith] MS; *om.* F1–2   2, 10, 42, 47 ye] MS; you F1–2

Byancha.   Wel sir.
Petronius and *Moroso* I'le see sent for:
About your businesse; goe.
Tranio.   I am gone.   *Exit* Tranio.
Byancha.   Ho *Livia.*

Enter Livia.

Livia.   Who's that?
Byancha.   A friend of yours, Lord how you looke now,
As if you had lost a Carrick.
Livia.   O *Byancha*!
I am the most undone, unhappy woman.
Byancha.   Be quiet wench, thou shalt be done, and done,
And done, and double done, or all shall split for't,
No more of these minc'd passions, they are mangy,   20
And ease thee of nothing, but a little wind,
An apple will doe more: thou fear'st *Moroso.*
Livia.   Even as I feare the Gallowes.
Byancha.   Keepe thee there still.
And you love *Rowland?* say.
Livia.   If I say not
I am sure I lye.
Byancha.   What would'st thou give that woman,
In spight of all his anger, and thy feare,
And all thy Fathers policy, that could
Clap ye within these two nights quietly
Into a Bed together?
Livia.   How?
Byancha.   Why fairely,
At half sword man and wife: now the red blood comes,   30
I marry now the matter's chang'd.
Livia.   *Byancha,*
Me thinks you should not mock me.
Byancha.   Mock a pudding.
I speake good honest English, and good meaning.
Livia.   I should not be ungratefull to that woman.
Byancha.   I know thou would'st not, follow but my Councell

And if thou hast him not, despight of fortune,
Let me nev'r know a good night more; you must
By very sick o'th instant.
Livia.   Well, what follows?
Byancha. And in that sicknesse send for all your friends,
Your Father, and your feavor old *Moroso*,   40
And *Rowland* shall be there too.
Livia.   What of these?
Byancha. Doe ye not twitter yet? of this shall follow
That that shall make thy heart leape, and thy lips
Venture as many kisses, as the Merchants
Doe dollars to the East-Indies: you shall know all,
But first walke in, and practise, pray be sick.
Livia. I doe beleeve ye: and I am sick.
Byancha.   So.
To bed then, come, Ile send away your Servants,
Post for your Foole, and Father; and good fortune,
As we meane honestly, now strike an up-shot.   50

                                        Exeunt.

                  Enter Tranio, *and* Rowland.   [IV.] iv

Tranio.   Nay, on my conscience, I have lost my money,
But that's all one: Ile never more perswade ye,
I see you are resolute, and I commend ye.
Rowland. But did she send for me?
Tranio.   Ye dare beleeve me.
Rowland I cannot tell, you have your waies for profit
Allow'd ye *Tranio*, as well as I
Have to avoid 'em feare.
Tranio.   No, on my word sir
I deale directly with ye.

                  Enter Servant.

43 That that] MS; that which F 1–2   47 So.] MS; Doe‸] F 1–2
50 honestly] MS; honesty F 1–2
2, 3, 4, 6, 8, 16, 27, 37, 43, 44 ye] MS; you F 1–2
*7 feare.] *stet* F 1 (~ :); *om.* MS, F 2

Rowland. How now fellow,
Whither Post you so fast?
Servant. O sir my Master,
Pray did you see my Master?
Rowland. Why your Master? 10
Servant. Sir his Jewell——
Rowland. With the gilded Button?
Servant. My pretty Mistresse *Livia.*
Rowland. What of her?
Servant. Is falne sick o'th suddaine.
Rowland. How, o'th sullens?
Servant. O'th suddaine sir, I say, and very sick.
Rowland. It seemes she hath got the toothach with raw apples.
Servant. It seemes you have got the headach, fare ye well sir.
You did not see my Master?
Rowland. Who told you so?
Tranio. No, no, he did not see him.
Rowland. Farewell blew bottle.
Exit Servant.
What should her sicknesse be?
Tranio. For you it may be.
Rowland. Yes when my braines are out, I may beleeve it, 20
Never before I am sure: yet I may see her,
'Twill be a point of honesty.
Tranio. It will so.
Rowland. It may be not too: you would faine be fingring
This old sinne-offring of two hundred, *Tranio.*
How daintily, and cunningly you drive me
Up like a Deere to'th toyle, yet I may leape it,
And what's the woodman then?
Tranio. A looser by ye.
Speake will you go or not? to me 'tis equall.
Rowland. Come, what goes lesse?
Tranio. Nay not a penny *Rowland.*
Rowland. Shall I have liberty of conscience 30
Which by interpretation, is ten kisses?

14 and] MS; *om.* F 1–2

Hang me if I affect her: yet it may be,
This whorson manners will require a strugling,
Of two and twenty, or by'r-Lady thirty.
Tranio.   By'r-lady Ile require my wager then,
For if you kisse so often, and no kindnesse,
I have lost my speculation, i'le allow ye——
Rowland.   Speake like a Gamster now.
Tranio.   It may be two.
Rowland.   Under a dozen *Tranio*, ther's no setting,
You shall have forty shillings, winck at small faults.   40
Say I take twenty, come, by all that's honest
I doe it but to vex her.
Tranio.   Ile no by-blowes.
If you can love her doe, if ye can hate her,
Or any else that loves ye——
Rowland.   Prethee *Tranio.*
Tranio.   Why farewell twenty pound, twill not undoe me;
You have my resolution.
Rowland.   And your money,
Which since you are so stubborne, if I forfeit,
Make me a Jack o' Lent, and breake my shins
For untag'd points and Compters: Ile goe with you,
But if thou gett'st a penny by the bargaine——   50
A parting kisse is lawfull?——
Tranio.   I allow it.
Rowland.   Knock out my braines with Apples; yet a bargaine.
Tranio.   I tell you, i'le no bargaines; win, and weare it.
Rowland.   Thou art the strangest fellow.
Tranio.   That's all one.
Rowland.   Along then,——twenty pound more if thou dar'st,
I give her not a good word.
Tranio.   Not a Penny.

Exeunt.

42 by-blowes] MS ($\sim_\wedge\sim$), F2; by-lowes F1   48 my] MS, F2; *om.* F1

Enter Petruchio, Jaques, *and* Pedro. [IV.] v

Petruchio.   Prethee, entreat her come, I will not trouble her
Above a word or two; ere I endure   *Exit* Pedro.
This life, and with a woman, and a vow'd one
To all the mischiefes she can lay upon me,
Ile goe to Plough again, and eat leeke Porridge;
Begging's a pleasure to't not to be numberd:
No there be other Countries *Jaques* for me,
And other people, yea, and other women.
If I have need, here's money, there's your ware,
Which is faire dealing, and the Sunne, they say   10
Shines as warme there, as here, and till I have lost
Either my selfe, or her, I care not whether
Nor which first——
Jaques.   Will your worship heare me?
Petruchio.   And utterly outworne the memory
Of such a curse as this, none of my Nation
Shall ever know me more.
Jaques.   Out alas sir
What a strange way doe you runne?
Petruchio.   Any way,
So I out-runne this rascall.
Jaques.   Me thinkes now,
If your good worship could but have the patience——
Petruchio.   The patience, why the patience?
Jaques.   Why i'le tell you,   20
Could you but have the patience——
Petruchio.   Well the patience.
Jaques.   To laugh at all she do's, or when she railes,
To have a drum beaten o'th top o'th house,
To give the neighbours warning of her Larme,
As I doe when my wife rebels.
Petruchio.   Thy wife?
Thy wife's a Pigeon to her, a meere slumber,
The dead of night's not stiller.
Jaques.   Nor an Iron Mill.

94

Petruchio.   But thy wife is certaine.
Jaques.   That's false Doctrine,
You never read yet of a certaine woman.
Petruchio.   Thou know'st her way.
Jaques.   I should doe, I am sure.   30
I have ridden it night, and day, this twenty yeare.
Petruchio.   But mine is such a drench of Balderdash,
Such a strange carded cunningnesse, the Rayne-bow
When she hangs bent in heaven, sheds not her colours
Quicker and more then this deceitfull woman

Enter Pedro.

Weaves in her dyes of wickednesse:——what sayes she?
Pedro.   Nay not a word sir, but she pointed to me,
As though she meant to follow; pray sir bear it
Ev'n as you may, I need not teach your worship,
The best men have their crosses, we are all mortall.   40
Petruchio.   What ailes the fellow?
Pedro.   And no doubt she may sir——
Petruchio.   What may she, or what do's she, or what is she?
Speake and be hang'd.
Pedro.   She's mad Sir.
Petruchio.   Heaven continue it.
Pedro.   Amen if't be his pleasure.
Petruchio.   How mad is she?
Pedro.   As mad as heart can wish sir: she has drest her self
(Saving your worships reverence) just i'th cut
Of one of those that multiply i'th Suburbs
For single money, and as durtlly :
If any speake to her, first she whistles,
And then begins her compasse with her fingers,   50
And points to what she would have.
Petruchio.   What new waye's this?
Pedro.   There came in Master *Sophocles*——
Petruchio   And what
Did Master *Sophocles* when he came in?

29 yet] MS; *om.* F1–2

95

Get my Truncks ready sirha, i'le be gone straight.
Pedro.   He's here to tell you.

Enter Sophocles.

She's horne mad *Jaques.*
Sophocles.   Call ye this a woman?
Petruchio.   Yes sir, shee's a woman.
Sophocles.   Sir, I doubt it.
Petruchio.   I had thought you had made experience.
Sophocles.   Yes I did so.
And almost with my life.
Petruchio.   You rid too fast sir.
Sophocles.   Pray be not you mistaken: by this light   60
Your wife's as chaste, and honest as a virgin,
For any thing I know: 'tis true she gave me
A Ring.
Petruchio.   For rutting.
Sophocles.   You are much deceiv'd still,
I sweare I never kist her since, and now
Coming in visitation, like a friend,
I thinke she is mad sir, suddainly she started,
And snatch'd the Ring away, and drew her knife out,
To what intent I know not.
Petruchio.   Is this certaine?
Sophocles.   As I am here sir.
Petruchio.   I beleeve ye honest.

Enter Maria.

And pray continue so.
Sophocles.   She comes.
Petruchio.   Now Damsell,   70
What will your beauty doe, if I forsake you?
Doe you deale by signes, and tokens? as I ghesse then,

57 shee's] MS; she is F 1–2   58 made] MS, F 2; make F 1
60 you] MS; *om.* F 1–2   60 light] MS; hand F 1–2
64 I sweare̞] MS; Beleeve me, F 1–2
    69, 82, 127, 129, 130, 131 (*twice*), 141, 143, 145 (*twice*), 164, 182, 197, 208, 213,
222 ye] MS; you F 1–2

You'l walke abroad, this Sommer, and catch Captaines,
Or hire a peece of holy ground i'th Suburbs,
And keepe a neast of Nuns?
Sophocles.   O doe not stir her!
You see in what a case she is?
Petruchio.   She is dogged,
And in a beastly case I am sure: Ile make her
If she have any tongue, yet tatle. *Sophocles*
Prethee observe this woman seriously,
And eye her well, and when thou hast done, but tell me   80
(For thou hast understanding) in what case
My sence was, when I chose this thing.
Sophocles.   Ile tell ye,
I have seene a sweeter——
Petruchio.   An hundred times cry oysters.
Ther's a poore Begger wench about Black-Fryers
Runs on her breech may be an Empresse to her.
Sophocles.   Nay, now you are too bitter.
Petruchio.   Nev'r a whit sir:
Ile tell thee woman; for now I have day to see thee,
And all my wits about me, and I speake
Not out of passion neither (leave your mumping,
I know y'ar' well enough:)——Now would I give   90
A million but to vex her:——when I chose thee
To make a Bedfellow, I tooke more trouble,
Then twenty Termes can come too, such a cause,
Of such a title, and so everlasting
That *Adams* Genealogie may be ended
Ere any law find thee: I tooke a Leprosie,
Nay worse, the plague, nay worse yet, a possession
And had the devill with thee, if not more:
And yet worse, was a beast, and like a beast
Had my reward, a Jade to fling my fortunes;   100
For who that had but reason to distinguish
The light from darknesse, wine from water, hunger
From full satiety, and Fox from ferne bush
That would have married thee?

97

Sophocles.   She is not so ill.
Petruchio.   She's worse then I dare think of: she's so lewd,
  No Court is strong enough to bear her cause,
  She hath neither manners, honesty, behaviour,
  Wife-hood, nor woman-hood, nor any morall
  Can force me think she had a mother, no
  I do believe her stedfastly, and know her   110
  To be a woman-Woolfe by transmigration,
  Her first forme was a Ferrets undergrounde,
  She kils the memories of men: not yet?
Sophocles.   Do you think she's sensible of this?
Petruchio.   I care not,
  Be what she will: the pleasure I take in her,
  Thus I blow off; the care I took to love her,
  Like this point I unty, and thus I loose it,
  The husband I am to her, thus I sever:
  My vanity farwell: yet, for you have bin
  So neer me as to bear the name of wife,   120
  My unquench'd charity shall tell you thus much
  (Though you deserve it well) you shall not beg,
  What I ordan'd your Jointure, honestly
  You shall have setled on you: and half my house,
  The other half shall be imploy'd in prayers,
  (That meritorious charge Ile be at also
  Yet to confirm ye christian) your apparrell,
  And what belongs to build up such a folly,
  Keep I beseech ye, it infects our uses,
  And now I am for travell.
Maria.   Now I love ye,   130
  And now I see ye are a man ile talk to ye,
  And I forget your bitternesse.
Sophocles.   How now man?
Petruchio.   O *Pliny*, if thou wilt be ever famous
  Make but this woman all thy wonders.
Maria.   Sure sir
  You have hit upon a happy course, a blessed,
  And what will make you vertuous.

Petruchio.　　　　　　　　　　She'l ship me.
Maria.　A way of understanding I long wishd for,
And now tis come, take heed you fly not back sir,
Me thinks you look a new man to me now,
A man of excellence, and now I see　　　　　　　　140
Some great design set in ye: you may think now
(And so may most that know me) 'twere my part
Weakly to weep your losse, and to resist ye,
Nay hang about your neck, and like a dotard
Urge my strong tie upon ye: but I love ye,
And all the world shall know it, beyond woman,
And more prefer the honour of your Country,
Which chiefly you are born for, and may perfect,
The uses you may make of other Nations,
The ripening of your knowledge, conversation,　　150
The full ability, and strength of judgement,
Then any private love, or wanton kisses.
Go worthy man, and bring home understanding.
Sophocles.　This were an excellent woman to breed Schoolmen.
Maria.　For if the Merchant through unknown Seas plough
To get his wealth, then deer sir, what must you
To gather wisdom? go, and go alone,
Only your noble mind for your companion,
And if a woman may win credit with you,
Go far: too far you cannot: still the farther　　160
The more experience finds you: and go sparing,
One meale a week will serve you, and one sute,
Through all your travels: for you'l find it certaine,
The poorer and the baser ye appear,
The more you look through still.
Petruchio.　　　　　　　　Do'st hear her?
Sophocles.　　　　　　　　　　　　　Yes.
Petruchio.　What would this woman do if she were suffer'd,
Upon a new religion?
Sophocles.　　　　　　Make us pagans,
I wonder that she writes not.

167 religion] MS, F 2; adventure F 1　　167 pagans] MS; F 2 (Pagans); nothing F 1

Maria.   Then when time,
And fulnesse of occasion have new made you,
And squard you from a sot into a Signior,   170
Or neerer from a Jade into a courser;
Come home an aged man, as did *Ulysses*,
And I your glad *Penelope.*
Petruchio.   That must have
As many lovers as I languages,
And what she do's with one i'th day, i'th night
Undoe it with an other.
Maria.   Much that way sir;
For in your absence, it must be my honour,
That, that must make me spoken of hereafter,
To have temptations, and not little ones
Daily and hourely offer'd me, and strongly,   180
Almost believed against me, to set off
The faith, and loyalty of her that loves ye.
Petruchio.   What should I do?
Sophocles.   Why by my troth, I would travell,
Did not you mean so?
Petruchio.   Alas no, nothing lesse man!
I did it but to try her, shee's the devill,
And now I find it, for she drives me, I must go:
Are my trunks down there, and my horses ready?
Maria.   Sir, for your house, and if you please to trust me
With that you leave behinde——
Petruchio.   Bring down the money.
Maria.   As I am able, and to my poor fortunes,   190
I'le govern as a widow: I shall long
To hear of your wel-doing, and your profit:
And when I hear not from you once a quarter,
I'le wish you in the *Indies*, or *Cataya*,
Those are the climes must make you.
Petruchio.   How's the wind?
She'l wish me out o'th world anon.
Maria.   For *France?*

183 troth] MS; —— F1–2   185 her,] MS; sir, F1; Sir, F2

Tis very faire; get ye aboard to night sir,
And loose no time, you know the tide staies no man,
I have cold meats ready for you.

Petruchio   Far thee well,
Thou ha'st foold me out o'th Kingdom with a vengeance,   200
And thou canst foole me in againe.

Maria   Not I sir,
I love you better, take your time, and pleasure,
Ile see you hors'd.

Petruchio.   I think thou wouldst see me hangd too,
Were I but halfe as willing.

Maria.   Any thing
That you think well of, I dare look upon.

Petruchio.   You'l bear me to the lands end *Sophocles*,
And other of my friends I hope.

Maria.   Nev'r doubt sir,
Ye cannot want companions for your good:
I am sure you'l kisse me ere I go; I have businesse,
And stay long here I must not.

Petruchio.   Get thee going,   210
For if thou tarriest but an other Dialogue
Ile kick thee to thy Chamber.

Maria.   Far you well Sir,
And bear your selfe, I do beseech ye once more,
Since you have undertaken doing wisely,
Manly, and worthily, tis for my credit;
And for those flying fames here of your follies,
Your gambols, and ill breeding of your youth,
(For which I understand you take this travell,
Nothing should make me leave you els) ile deale
So like a wife, that loves your reputation,   220
And the most large addition of your credit,
That those shall die: if ye want Limon-water,
Or any thing to take the edge o'th Sea off,
Pray speak, and be provided.

Petruchio.   Now the Devill,

200 out] MS, F 2; *om.* F 1   222 -water] MS (ᴧ -); -waters F 1–2

That was your first good master, shoure his blessing
Upon ye all: into whose custody——
Maria.   I do commit your Reformation,
And so I leave you to your *Stilo novo.*   *Exit* Maria.
Petruchio.   I will go: yet I will not: once more *Sophocles*
Ile put her to the test.
Sophocles.   You had better go.   230
Petruchio.   I will go then: let's seek my father out,
And all my friends to see me faire aboard:
Then women, if there be a storme at Sea,
Worse then your tongues can make, and waves more broken
Then your dissembling fayths are, let me feele
Nothing but tempests, till they cracke my Keele.

Exeunt.

Enter Petronius, *and* Byancha *with foure papers.*   V. i

Byancha.   Now whether I deserve that blame you gave me,
Let all the world discern sir.
Petronius.   If this motion,
(I mean this fair repentance of my Daughter)
Spring from your good perswasion, as it seems so,
I must confesse I have spoke too boldly of you,
And I repent.
Byancha.   The first touch was her own,
Taken no doubt from disobeying you,
The second I put to her, when I told her
How good, and gentle yet, with free contrition
Again you might be purchas'd: loving woman,   10
She heard me, and I thank her, thought me worthy
Observing in this point: yet all my councell,
And comfort in this case, could not so heal her
But that grief got his share too, and she sickend.
Petronius.   I am sorry she's so ill, yet glad her sicknesse
Has got so good a ground.

Enter Moroso.

102

Byancha.   Here comes *Moroso.*
Petronius.   O you are very welcome,
  Now you shall know your happinesse.
Moroso.   I am glad on't.
  What makes this Lady here?
Byancha.   A dish for you sir
  You'l thank me for hereafter.
Petronius.   True *Moroso,*   20
  Go get you in, and see your Mistris.
Byancha.   She is sick sir,
  But you may kisse her whole.
Moroso.   How?
Byancha.   Comfort her.
Moroso.   Why am I sent for sir?
Petronius.   Will you in, and see?
Byancha.   May be she needs confession.
Moroso.   By Saint *Mary,*
  She shall have absolution then and pennance,
  But not above her carriage.
Petronius.   Get you in foole.   *Exit* Moroso.
Byancha.   Here comes the other too.

                Enter Rowland *and* Tranio.

Petronius.   Now *Tranio.*
  Goodde'n to you too, and y'are welcome.
Rowland.   Thank you.
Petronius.   I have a certaine Daughter——
Rowland.   Would you had sir.
Petronius.   No doubt you know her well.
Rowland.   Nor never shall sir.   30
  She is a woman, and the waies into her
  Are like the finding of a certaine path
  After a deep falne Snow.
Petronius.   Well thats by'th by still.
  This Daughter that I tell you of is falne

---

*28 Goodde'n] MS; Good ev'n F1–2   28 y'are] MS you are F1–2
*31 into] MS; unto F1–2

103

A little crop sick, with the dangerous surfeit
She took of your affection.
Rowland. Mine sir?
Petronius. Yes sir.
Or rather, as it seemes, repenting. And there
She lies within, debating on't.
Rowland. Well sir.
Petronius. I think 'twere well you would see her.
Rowland. If you please sir;
I am not squeamish of my visitation. 40
Petronius. But, this ile tell you, she is alter'd much,
You'l finde her now an other *Livia.*
Rowland. I had enough o'th old sir.
Petronius. No more foole,
To look gay babies in your eyes yong *Rowland,*
And hang about your prety neck.
Rowland. I am glad on't,
And thank my Fates I have scapd such execution.
Petronius. And busse you till you blush againe.
Rowland. Thats hard sir,
She must kisse shamefully ere I blush at it,
I never was so boyish; well, what followes?
Petronius. She's mine now, as I please to settle her, 50
At my command, and where I please to plant her:
Only she would take a kind of farwell of ye,
And give you back a wandring vow or two,
You left in pawn; and two or three slight oaths
She lent you too, she looks for.
Rowland. She shall have 'em
With all my heart sir, and if you like it better,
A free release in writing.
Petronius. That's the matter,
And you from her, you shall have an other *Rowland,*
And then turne taile to taile, and peace be with you.
Rowland. Why so be it: your twenty pound sweats *Tranio.* 60

*43 had] MS; have F1–2   52, 103, 115 ye] MS; you F1–2
59 be] MS, F2; by F1   *60 Why] MS; *om.* F1–2

104

Tranio.   'Twill not undoe me *Rowland*, do your worst.
Rowland.   Come, shall we see her Sir?
Byancha.   What ere she saies
  You must beare manly *Rowland*, for her sicknesse
  Has made her somewhat teatish.
Rowland.   Let her talke
  Till her tongue ake I care not: by this hand
  Thou hast a handsome face wench, and a body
  Daintely mounted; now do I feele an hundred
  Running directly from me, as I pist it.

Enter Livia *discovered abed, and* Moroso *by her.*

Byancha.   Pray draw 'em softly, the least hurry sir
                                          [*Draw curtains.*]
  Puts her to much impatience.
Petronius.   How is't daughter?   70
Livia.   O very sick, very sick, yet somewhat
  Better I hope; a little lightsommer,
  Because this goodman has forgiven me;
  Pray set me higher; Oh my head.
Byancha [*aside*].   Wel done wench.
Livia.   Father, and all good people that shal heare me,
  I have abus'd this man perniciously;
  Was never old man humbled so; I have scornd him,
  And cal'd him nasty names, I have spit at him,
  Flung Candles ends in's beard, and cald him harrow,
  That must be drawn to all he do's: contemn'd him,   80
  For me thought then he was a beastly fellow.
  (Oh God my side) a very beastly fellow:
  And gave it out, his cassock was a Barge-cloth,
  Pawnd to his predecessor by a Sculler,
  The man yet extant: I gave him purging-comfits
  At a great christning once,
  That spoyl'd his Chamblet breeches; and one night
  I strewd the staires with pease, as he past down;
  And the good Gentleman (woe worth me for't)

85 extant] MS; living F 1–2

Ev'n with his reverent head, this head of wisdome,   90
Told two and twenty staires, good and true;
Mist not a step, and as we say verbatim
Fell to the bottome, broke his casting Bottle,
Lost a fair toad-stone of some eighteen shillings,
Jumbled his joynts together, had two stooles,
And was translated. All this villany
Did I: I *Livia*, I alone, untaught.
Moroso.   And I unask'd, forgive it.
Livia.   Where's *Byancha*?
Byancha.   Here Cozen.
Livia.   Give me drinke.
Byancha.   There.
Livia.   Who's that?
Moroso.   *Rowland.*
Livia.   O my dissembler, you and I must part.   100
Come neerer sir.
Rowland.   I am sorry for your sicknesse.
Livia.   Be sorry for your selfe sir, you have wrong'd me,
But I forgive ye; are the papers ready?
Byancha.   I have 'em here; wilt please you view 'em?
Petronius.   Yes.
Livia.   Shew 'em the young man too, I know he's willing
To shift his sailes too: tis for his more advancement;
Alas, we might have beggerd one another;
We are young both, and a world of children
Might have been left behind to curse our follies:
We had been undone *Byancha*, had we married,   110
Undone for ever: I confesse I lov'd him,
I care not who shall know it, most intirely;
And once, upon my conscience, he lov'd me;
But farewell that, we must be wiser cosen.
Love must not leave us to the world: have ye done?
Rowland.   Yes, and am ready to subscribe.
Livia.   Pray stay then:
Give me the papers, and let me peruse 'em,
And so much time, as may afford a teare

At our last parting.
Byancha.　　　　Pray retire, and leave her,
　Ile call ye presently.
Petronius.　　　　Come Gentlemen,　　　　　120
　The showre must fall.
Rowland.　　　　Would I had never seen her.
　　　　　　Exeunt all, but Biancha *and* Livia.
Byancha.　Thou hast done bravely wench.
Livia.　　　　　　Pray Heaven it prove so.
Byancha.　There are the other papers: when they come
　Begin you first, and let the rest subscribe
　Hard by your side; give 'em as little light
　As Drapers doe their wares.
Livia.　　　　　　Didst mark *Moroso*,
　In what an agony he was, and how he cry'd most
　When I abus'd him most?
Byancha.　　　　That was but reason.
Livia.　Oh what a stinking thief is this?
　Though I was but to counterfeit, he made me　　　130
　Directly sick indeed. Tames-street to him
　Is a meere Pomander.
Byancha.　Let him be hang'd.
Livia.　　　　　Amen.
Byancha.　　　　And lie you still.
　And once more to your businesse.
Livia.　　　　　Call 'em in.
　Now if there be a power that pities lovers,
　Helpe now, and heare my prayers.

　　　Enter Petronius, Rowland, Tranio, Moroso.

Petronius.　　　　　Is she ready?
Byancha.　She has done her lamentations: pray go to her.
Livia.　*Rowland*, come neer me, and before you seale,
　Give me your hand: take it again; now kisse me,
　This is the last acquaintance we must have;　　　140
　I wish you ever happy: there's the paper.

　　121.1 *Exeunt...Livia.*] MS; *om.* F 1; *Exeunt.* F 2

Rowland.   Pray stay a little.
Petronius.   Let me never live more
But I do begin to pity this young fellow;
How heartily he weeps!
Byancha.   There's Pen and Inke sir.
Livia.   Ev'n here I pray you. Tis a little Emblem
How neere you have been to me.
Rowland.   There.
Byancha.   Your hands too,
As witnesses.
Petronius.   By any means: to th' booke sonne.
Moroso.   With all my heart.
Byancha.   You must deliver it.
Rowland.   There *Livia*, and a better love light on thee,
I can no more.   150
Byancha.   To this you must be witnesse too.
Petronius.   We wil.
Byancha.   Doe you deliver it now.
Livia.   Pray set me up;——
There *Rowland*, all thy old love back: and may
A new to come exceed mine, and be happy.
I must no more.
Rowland.   Farewell.
Livia.   A long farewell.   *Exit* Rowland.
Byancha.   Leave her by any means, till this wild passion
Be off her head; draw all the Curtaines close,
A day hence you may see her, twil be better,
She is now for little company.
Petronius.   Pray tend her.
I must to horse straight: you must needs along too,   160
To see my sonne aboard; were but his wife
As fit for pity, as this wench, I were happy.
Byancha.   Time must do that too: fare ye wel; tomorrow
You shall receive a wife to quit your sorrow.
                                        Exeunt.

Enter Jaques, Pedro, *and Porters, with a trunke and Hampers.*　　V. [ii]

Jaques.　　Bring 'em away sirs.
Pedro.　　　　　　　　　　Must the great Trunke go too?
Jaques.　　Yes, and the Hampers; nay be speedy Masters;
　He'l be at Sea before us else.
Pedro.　　　　　　　　　　O *Jaques,*
　What a most blessed turn hast thou?
Jaques.　　　　　　　　　　I hope so.
Pedro.　　To have the Sea between thee and this woman,
　Nothing can drown her tongue, but a storm.
Jaques.　　　　　　　　　　By your leave,
　We'l get us up to *Paris* with all speed;
　For on my soule, as far as *Amyens*
　She'l carry blanke; away to *Lyon* key
　And ship 'em presently, we'l follow ye.　　　　　　　10
Pedro.　　Now could I wish her in that Trunk.
Jaques.　　　　　　　　　　God shield man,
　I had rather have a Beare in't.
Pearo.　　　　　　　　　　Yes, Ile tell ye:
　For in the passage if a Tempest take ye,
　As many doe, and you lie beating for it,
　Then, if it pleas'd the fates, I would have the Master
　Out of a powerfull providence, to cry,
　Lighten the ship of all hands, or we perish;
　Then this for one, as best spar'd, should by all means
　Over-board presently.
Jaques.　　　　　　　　O' that condition,
　So we were certaine to be rid of her,　　　　　　　20
　I would wish her with us: But believe me *Pedro,*
　She would spoyle the fishing on this coast for ever,
　For none would keepe her company, but Dog-fish,
　As currish as her selfe; or Porpisces,
　Made to all fatall uses: The two Fish-streets
　Were she but once ariv'd amongst the Whitings,
　Would sing a wofull *misereri Pedro,*

0.1. *a trunke*] MS; *Chest* F 1–2　　　*1 Trunke*] MS; Trunks F 1–2

And mourn in poor John, till her memory
Were cast o'shore agen, with a strong Sea-breach:
She would make god *Neptune*, and his fire-forke,   30
And all his demi-gods, and goddesses,
As weary of the Flemmish channell *Pedro*,
As ever boy was of the schoole: tis certain,
If she but meet him faire, and were wel angred,
She would break his god-head.

Pedro.   Oh her tongue, her tongue.
Jaques.   Rather her many tongues.
Pedro.   Or rather strange tongues.
Jaques.   Her lying tongue.
Pedro.   Her lisping tongue.
Jaques.   Her long tongue.
Pedro.   Her lawlesse tongue.
Jaques.   Her loud tongue.
Pedro.   And her lickrish——
Jaques.   Many other tongues, and many stranger tongues
Then ever Babel had to tell his ruines,   40
Were women rais'd withall; but never a true one.

Enter Sophocles.

Sophocles.   Home with your stuffe agen; the journey's ended.
Jaques.   What do's your worship meane?
Sophocles.   Your Master, O *Petruchio*, O poore fellows.
Pedro.   O *Jaques, Jaques.*
Sophocles.   O your Master's dead,
His body comming back; his wife, his devil;
The griefe of her——
Jaques.   Has kild him?
Sophocles.   Kild him, kild him.
Pedro.   Is there no law to hang her.
Sophocles.   Get ye in,
And let her know her misery, I dare not
For feare impatience seize me, see her more,   50
I must away agen: Bid her for wife-hood,

For honesty, if she have any in her,
Even to avoyd the shame that follows her,
Cry if she can: your weeping cannot mend it.
The body will be here within this houre, so tell her;
And all his friends to curse her. Farewell fellowes.

                                        Exit Sophocles.

Pedro.   O *Jaques, Jaques.*
Jaques.   O my worthy Master.
Pedro.   O my most beastly Mistris, hang her.
Jaques.   Split her.
Pedro.   Drown her directly.
Jaques.   Starve her.
Pedro.   Stinke upon her.
Jaques.   Stone her to death: may all she eate be Eggs,   60
   Till she run kicking mad for men.
Pedro.   And he,
   That man, that gives her remedy, pray Heav'n
   He may ev'n *ipso facto*, lose his fadings.
Jaques.   Let's goe discharge our selves, and he that serves her,
   Or speaks a good word of her from this houre,
   A seagly curse light on him; which is, *Pedro,*
   The feind ride through him booted, and spurd, with a Sythe at's
      back.

                                        Exeunt.

         Enter Rowland, *and* Tranio *stealing behind him.*   [V.] iii

Rowland.   What a dull asse was I to let her go thus?
   Upon my life she loves me still: wel Paper,
   Thou onely monument of what I have had,
   Thou all the love now left me, and now lost,
   Let me yet kisse her hand, yet take my leave
   Of what I must leave ever: Farewell *Livia.*——
   Oh bitter words, Ile read ye once again,
   And then for ever study to forget ye.——
   How's this? let me look better on't:——A Contract!

   63 fadings] MS; longings F1; Fadding F2   *66 seagly] *stet* F1, MS; Sedgly F2

                              111

By Heaven a Contract, seal'd, and ratified,   10
Her fathers hand set to it, and *Moroso's*:
I do not dream sure, let me read again——
The same still: tis a contract.
Tranio [*comes forward*].   Tis so *Rowland*;
And by the vertue of the same, you pay me
Two hundred pound to morrow.
Rowland.   Art sure *Tranio*,
We are both alive now?
Tranio.   Wonder not, ye have lost.
Rowland.   If this be true, I grant it.
Tranio.   Tis most certaine,
There's a Ring for you to, you know it.
Rowland.   Yes.
Tranio.   When shall 1 have my money?
Rowland.   Stay ye, stay ye,
When shall I marry her?
Tranio.   To night.
Rowland.   Take heed now   20
You do not trifle with me; if you doe,
You'l finde more payment, then your money comes to:
Come sweare; I know I am a man, and finde
I may deceive my selfe: Sweare faithfully,
Sweare me directly, am I *Rowland*?
Tranio.   Yes.
Rowland.   Am I awake?
Tranio.   Ye are.
Rowland.   Am I in health?
Tranio.   As far as I conceive.
Rowland.   Was I with *Livia*?
Tranio.   You were, and had this contract.
Rowland.   And shall I enjoy her?
Tranio.   Yes, if ye dare.
Rowland.   Sweare to all these.

10 By Heaven a] Sympson; —— a F 1; —— A F 2; I sweare a MS
15 Two] An F 1–2; a MS   21 with] MS; *om.* F 1–2
28 this] MS, F 2; his F 1

Tranio.   I will.

Rowland.   As thou art honest, as thou hast a conscience,   30
  As that may wring thee if thou lyest; all these
  To be no vision, but a truth, and serious.

Tranio.   Then by my honesty, and faith, and conscience;
  All this is certaine.

Rowland.   Let's remove our places.
  Sweare it again.

Tranio.   I sweare by Heaven tis true.

Rowland.   I have lost then, and Heaven knows I am glad ont.
  Let's goe, and tell me all, and tell me how,
  For yet I am a Pagan in it.

Tranio.   I have a Priest too,
And all shall come as even as two Testers.

                                        Exeunt.

                Enter Petronius, Sophocles, Moroso,   [V.] iv
                    and Petruchio *born in a Coffin.*

Petronius.   Set down the body, and one call her out.

              Enter Maria *in blacke,* Jaques, *and* Pedro.

You are welcome to the last cast of your fortunes;
There lies your husband, there your loving husband,
There he that was *Petruchio,* too good for ye;
Your stubborn, and unworthy way has kild him
Ere he could reach the Sea; if ye can weep,
Now ye have cause begin, and after death
Do something yet to th'world, to thinke ye honest.
So many teares had sav'd him, shed in time;
And as they are (so a good mind goe with 'em)   10
Yet they may move compassion.

Maria.   Pray ye all heare me,
And judge me as I am, not as you covet,
For that would make me yet more miserable:

        35 I sweare by Heaven] By ——— F 1–2; I sweare MS
        1.1 Jaques, *and* Pedro] MS (Jaques, Pedro); Pedro *and* Jaques F 1–2
        13 yet] MS, F 2; ye F 1

                                113

Tis true, I have cause to grieve, and mighty cause;
And truely and unfainedly I weep it.
Sophocles. I see there's some good nature yet left in her.
Maria. But what's the cause? mistake me not, not this man,
 As he is dead, I weep for; Heaven defend it,
 I never was so childish: but his life,
 His poore unmanly wretched foolish life, 20
 Is that my full eyes pity, there's my mourning.
Petronius. Dost thou not shame?
Maria. I do, and even to water,
 To think what this man was, to think how simple,
 How far below a man, how far from reason,
 From common understanding, and all Gentry,
 While he was living here he walkt amongst us.
 He had a happy turn he dyed; ile tell ye,
 These are the wants I weep for, not his person:
 The memory of this man, had he liv'd
 But two yeers longer, had begot more follies, 30
 Then wealthy Autumne flyes: But let him rest,
 He was a foole, and farewell he; not pitied,
 I meane in way of life, or action
 By any understanding man that's honest;
 But onely in's posterity, which I
 Out of the feare his ruines might out live him
 In some bad issue, like a carefull woman,
 Like one indeed born onely to preserve him,
 Denyd him meanes to raise.

Petruchio *rises out of the coffin.*

Petruchio. Unbutton me,
 By Heaven I die indeed else.——O *Maria*, 40
 Oh my unhappinesse, my misery.
Petronius. Go to him whore; by Heaven if he perish,
 Ile see thee hang'd my selfe.

39 *s.d.* Petruchio...*coffin.*] MS; *om.* F1–2
*40 By Heaven] MS; —— F1–2
42 by Heaven] Colman; —— F1–2; I sweare MS

114

Petruchio.   Why, why, *Maria.*
Maria.   I have done my worst, and have my end, forgive me;
  From this houre make me what you please: I have tam'd ye,
  And now am vowd your servant: Look not strangely,
  Nor feare what I say to you. Dare you kisse me?
  Thus I begin my new love.
Petruchio.   Once againe?
Maria.   With all my heart, sir.
Petruchio.   Once again *Maria*!——
  O Gentlemen, I know not where I am.   50
Sophocles.   Get ye to bed then: there you'l quickly know sir.
Petruchio.   Never no more your old tricks?
Maria.   Never sir.
Petruchio.   You shall not need, for as I have a faith
  No cause shall give occasion.
Maria.   As I am honest,
  And as I am a maid yet, all my life
  From this houre, since ye make so free profession,
  I dedicate in service to your pleasure.
Sophocles.   I marry, this goes roundly off.
Petruchio.   Go *Jaques,*
  Get all the best meat may be bought for money,
  And let the hogsheds blood, I am born again: 60
  Well little *England*, when I see a husband
  Of any other Nation stern or jealous,
  Ile wish him but a woman of thy breeding,
  And if he have not butter to his bread,
  Till his teeth bleed, ile never trust my travell.

  Enter Rowland, Livia, Byancha, *and* Tranio, *as from marriage.*

Petruchio.   What have we here?
Rowland.   Another morris, sir.
  That you must pipe too.
Tranio.   A poore married couple
  Desire an offering sir.

49 sir] MS; *om.* F 1–2   56 houre, since] MS, F 2; houre‿ since, since F 1
64, 65 his] MS, F 2; they F 1   65.1 *as from marriage*] MS (mariage); *om.* F 1–2

115

Byancha.   Never frown at it,
You cannot mend it now: there's your own hand;
And yours *Moroso*, to confirme the bargaine.   70
Petronius. My hand?
Moroso.   Or mine?
Byancha.   You'l finde it so.
Petronius.   A trick,
By Heaven, a trick.
Byancha.   Yes sir, we trickt ye.
Livia.   Father.
Petronius. Hast thou lyen with him? speake?
Livia.   Yes truly sir.
Petronius. And hast thou done the deed boy?
Rowland.   I have done sir,
That, that will serve the turne, I think.
Petruchio.   A match then,
Ile be the maker up of this: *Moroso*,
There's now no remedy you see, be willing;
For be, or be not, he must have the wench.
Moroso.   Since I am over-reach'd, let's in to dinner,
And if I can Ile drink't away.
Tranio.   That's wel said.   80
Petronius.   Well sirha, ye have playd a tricke, look to't,
And let me be a grandsire within's twelvemoneth,
Or by this hand, Ile curtaile halfe your fortunes.
Rowland.   There shall not want my labour sir: your money;
Here's one has undertaken.
Tranio.   Well, Ile trust her,
And glad I have so good a pawn.
Rowland.   Ile watch ye.
Petruchio.   Lets in, and drink of all hands, and be joviall:
I have my colt again, and now she carries;
And Gentlemen, whoever marries next,
Let him be sure he keep him to his Text.   90

                                        Exeunt.

72 By Heaven,] Colman; By —— F1–2; I sweare, MS
81 ye] MS; you F1–2

EPILOGUE

The Tamer's tam'd, but so, as nor the men
  Can finde one just cause to complaine of, when
They fitly do consider in their lives,
  They should not raign as Tyrants o'r their wives.
Nor can the women from this president
  Insult, or triumph: it being aptly meant,
To teach both Sexes due equality;
  And as they stand bound, to love mutually.
If this effect, arising from a cause
  Well layd, and grounded, may deserve applause,   10
We something more then hope, our honest ends
  Will keep the men, and women too, our friends.

TEXTUAL NOTES

I.i

71 wip't him now] For F1 'wip't him now' MS reads 'impt him'. One or other is clearly a minim misreading of the source: the question is, which. Metrically, 'impt' (in the MS version without the F1 'now') completes a fairly regular pentameter with the part-line 'They'l think...Gentlemen.' However, the F1 reading is perhaps sufficiently metrical if 'gentlemen' is slurred as a dissyllable and 'you have' is pronounced 'y'ave'; however, the question of the authority of the 'now' and its complication of the metrics, while paradoxically in favor of the 'wip't' reading, has, in fact, nothing to do with whether F1 or MS misread its copy. If 'impt' is the reading, Tranio could be suggesting that by his encouragement Sophocles has *imped*, i.e. (as in falconry) increased Moroso's powers, or strengthened him. Sophocles could then glance at the other sense, which refers to *planting* or *grafting shoots*, or *enlarging* something by addition, and respond that it is not likely that Moroso will get the young woman with child. The chief difficulty with accepting 'impt' is that Tranio (as in lines 68–69) has encouraged Moroso as much as Sophocles in lines 65–66 so that there is no reason for him to make a point of Sophocles' original jocularity. Since F1, in general, seems more accurate in its substantive transmission than MS, its 'wip't' must be taken seriously. In fact, the *OED* (without knowledge of the MS variant) quotes this line under 'wipe' as one of its illustrations for *vb* 7, 'To attack or strike with blows or with mockery, sarcasm'. This sense is perhaps more applicable than 'impt', for it could refer specifically to Sophocles' palpable hit (whether or not an aside from Moroso) naming Rowland as one of Moroso's reasons for delay in the marriage. The sense of 'wiped' in Sophocles' reply is less clear but could be related to *vb* 5, 'to deprive, cheat, do out of some advantage', a sense *OED* illustrates from *The Spanish Curate*, IV.iv.

I.ii

8 this] F1 'his' has a doubtful reference since if 'his' refers to Rowland (who, Livia says, knows no 'care' in his proposal), the natural reference would be 'your'. Hence it would seem that MS 'this' is right, and one could paraphrase: The course you propose is one that will cost me my inheritance, whereas if we pursue our present temporizing course we are not placed in poverty and want ('care'). The same variant in the work of Compositor *B* may also be resolved in favour of MS in V.iii.28.

23 Crocus]   This line is used in *OED* in the F 1 form 'Cracus' as an illustration of the name *Craccus* for a kind of tobacco as found, uniquely, in a
clearly defined context in Middleton and Rowley's *A Fair Quarrel* (1617),
the only illustration cited. However, F 1 'Cracus' seems to be a misreading
of an unfamiliar term and MS 'Crocus' to be correct. All of the items in the
list are false remedies for toothache. For instance, a 'cod' is a civet or musk
bag (*OED* quotes this line as *sb*¹ 1b). This would be followed most naturally
by some other scent-remedy. The smoking of tobacco was so firmly
believed to be a remedy to ease toothache as scarcely to qualify with the
rest as a quack nostrum. Moreover, the specification 'English' and the
adjective 'musty' for the *cracus* is not applicable to tobacco. Crocus is
used in a bag (like the 'cod' of musk') to scent clothing as noted in *OED*
under *sb* 5 in 1699; but the ancient Roman use of crocus as a scent is
mentioned only from a source in 1885. It is this latter origin, no doubt, that
was in Fletcher's mind as a nostrum.

94 or]   MS 'and' is very likely a natural sophistication that lumps the two
parts. In F 1 Maria seems to be asking pardon of Hymen for what she is
doing first to herself ('protract') and then to Petruchio ('keep fasting').

I.iii

9 stuffe]   The MS reading 'stuffe' is so natural (see line 10) that the sexual
meaning of 'staff' as cited by *OED* 7c from *Much Ado about Nothing*,
V.iv.125–126 ('there is no staff more reverend than one tipped with horn')
is insufficient to justify retention of the copy-text.

132 'Blesse]   Since MS reads 'Heaven blesse' it might be a natural assumption
that F 1 ''Blesse' exhibits censorship or else that the source had some such
phrase as 'God blesse', altered by MS, characteristically, to 'Heaven'.
Indeed, Seward followed by Colman and Weger inserted 'Heaven'; and
Ferguson adopted the word from MS. However, Dyce pointed out that
''Blesse' appears in F 1 at I.ii.88, and his parallel appears to be the stronger
when, as we now know, MS agrees at this point with F 1. It seems possible,
therefore, that in I.iii.132 MS has expanded the phrase and that F 1 correctly
represents the source.

190 thee——]   The comma in MS for the F 1 dash would seem to indicate
broken-off speech instead of a censored word, as Colman took it when he
supplied 'whore'. But even if some word has been dropped, 'whore' does
not seem to have been censored in this play. Instead of applying an epithet,
Petruchio very likely stops short of some violent threat and weakly substitutes 'Pull thee down by th' nose' for fear of further offending Maria.
'I am quiet yet' he remarks in line 195; but what he had in mind by the dash
is perhaps some threat near to 'A fine smart Cudgell' in line 210.

290 I vow]   Whatever the oath was that is represented by the F 1 long dash,

it was almost certainly not the mild asseveration 'I vow' of MS. Censorship of oaths is less frequent in MS than in F 1, but it appears to have operated here.

II.i

55 a ——] Whatever (three-syllable?) indecency probably involving urination, and perhaps piss-pot, is represented by the F 1 dash is unknowable since MS is not a witness to this scene. It is clear that the dash is not to indicate a suspension of speech.

II.iii

9 great] The addition of 'great' from MS (missing in F 1) smooths the meter. On the other hand, MS joins F 1 in lining Rowland's response 'No | 'Tis no question, for beleeve me *Tranio*,' which can be scanned, though roughly, without the 'great'. It is possible, then, that 'great' is a metrical sophistication, but with it or without it the meter would be extremely rough if 'No' were to complete line 9 instead of begin line 10. Concurrence of MS and F 1 in faulty lining is common enough not to be significant evidence in the present case.

34 Our...friend-ship——] MS seems to be correct in the placement of this part-line since Tranio can then complete it with 'I will *Rowland*.' On the contrary, the F 1 positioning after line 35 interrupts the sequence of lines 35 and 36 and produces a series of non-linked short lines:

> *Tranio.* I will *Rowland*.
> *Rowland.* She may sooner
> Count the good I have thought her,

Curiously, in MS a space sufficient for about seven lines of text occurs between 'Our old love and our friend-ship' and Tranio's response. It may be that this space represents some lost deleted text, in which case MS 'ever' in line 33 may just possibly be correct instead of F 1 'even'. In this event, however, the linking into a pentameter of Rowland's last line and Tranio's response would be accidental, a possibility not to be overlooked since both MS and F 1 agree in lining 35 as 'She may sooner | Count...her,' which would require a three-syllable ending of a speech by Rowland before Tranio's 'I will *Rowland*.' On the other hand, agreement in mislining is not unusual between MS and F 1, and the gap in the MS is difficult to explain except by the possibility that deleted text was present there which the scribe allowed for in case it was wanted or could be deciphered.

II.iv

5 by ——] MS 'by this hand' would seem to be a censored form of some three-syllable oath, perhaps 'by my faith' or 'by my troth'. That these have been admitted in MS, as at II.ii.23–24, though softened in F1, means little since the reduction of oaths in MS is irregular in comparison to F1.

57 tosting] The same mistake in F1, correct in MS, is found in III.ii.45.

85–86 Lo . . . impatience.] The metrics seem to indicate that this position of the line, as in MS, is better than that in F1, in which it follows line 67 and is a hexameter that cannot readily be divided to complete part-line 67 as a pentameter. On the other hand, the division of the line in MS links readily. In its F1 position Sophocles' interjection works well enough between the speeches of Jaques and Pedro, but in the MS position each servant has his antiphonal report without interruption followed by the comments of the gentlemen beginning with Sophocles' line reproving Petruchio, continued by his lines 87–88 and 93–94.

II.vi

104 recreant] F1 reads 'recant' but in MS original 'recant' is deleted and 'recreant' written in in the same hand that had altered 'yet ever' to correct 'ever yet' at line 91. The meter is slightly improved by the choice of 'recreant', for 'recant' requires 'conditions' to be scanned as four syllables, a good enough seventeenth-century device but not one highly typical of Fletcher. 'Recreant', for what it is worth, is the more difficult reading since it requires the elision of an expected verb. Mainly, however, it is preferable because it continues the military imagery characteristic of the women; moreover, see its use in I.iii.281 and II.ii.78.

155–156 No . . . it.] In contrast to the F1 lining adopted here, MS lines: 'No, | Ile . . . it.' This is attractive since the final 'No' balances the final 'Yes' in line 152 (a favorite device as in III.ii.45), and it would complete a pentameter begun with 'Ile ratifie 'em.', followed by the pentameter 'Ile take . . . keep it.' The difficulty in accepting such lining comes in what follows, however. The next part-line by the City Wife 'Tis not now' would need to form a pentameter with its continuation 'as when *Andrea* liv'd.', but in both texts the line is divided. Moreover, in MS this part-line 'Tis not now' ends the inserted slip (see Textual Introduction) and the next sheet begins 'as when Andrea liv'd.' If the explanation is correct that the lines on the slip were omitted from MS in error as it was copied, owing to a page being turned over, then in the document being copied by MS the City Wife's two part-lines were not a single pentameter but intended to link with others, in which case the F1 lining appears to be vindicated. In either case an independent part-line occurs in the passage. It is preferable, by the usual custom in dramatic blank verse, to have a part-line like 'Ile ratifie 'em' end a speech rather than to begin a speech with an unstopped short line as would be necessary for 'If ye do juggle' were it not linked with the part-line 'As when *Andrea* liv'd.'

158 this creed]   The difference between this MS reading and the 'these articles' of F 1 may have been produced by just such objection to a religious reference as Adams (p. lvi) finds in the omission of the concluding part of the line at I.iv.8. Here in F 1 Pedro exclaims 'from all women———', which in MS reads 'from all such women deliver me' (with the omission of the subject 'God' or 'Heaven') necessary to complete the meter. The difficulty is that (given the partial censorship in MS) one cannot be quite positive that it was not the oath instead of the reference to the litany that caused the removal of the conclusion in F 1. However, the censor of F 1 was sensitive to religious references, as witness the substitution of 'certaine' at II.ii.51 for MS 'Christian', the omission of the reference to 'two church-wardens' and the substitution of 'the Town' at II.iv.69, or the substitution of 'adventure' for 'religion' at IV.v.167 accompanied by the change from 'pagans' to 'nothing'.

III.i

21 Heavens]   Very possibly the reading in the source for both texts was 'Gods', toned down differently in MS and in F 1.

47 O, pox]   Since F 1 censors this phrase by substituting a dash for 'pox', the odds might seem to favor MS 'O' instead of F 1 'A'. 'A pox' might be a natural sophistication if the scribe, or compositor, did not understand that a comma (wanting in MS) should ideally follow 'O', as emended for clarity in this edition.

III.iii

5 pray]   MS 'pray', not F 1 'pray you' is the customary phrase: see III.iii.89, 92, 100, 137, 144; III.v.17, 46, 53, 80, etc.

18 quight]   The MS spelling gives the sense of 'requite' better than F 1 'quit' which could (and may in error) mean 'leave' her.

19 unto]   F 1 'to' forces the stress of the tenth syllable on 'her', whereas the characteristic meter of this play places 'her' (or 'him') as the feminine ending produced by MS 'unto': see III.ii.9, 16, 25, 26, 37, 49; III.iii.1, 5, 12, 18, etc. But for the terminal stress see III.ii.7; III.iii.44, 45.

32 nights]   MS 'monthes' would give a more comic effect by its gross exaggeration; but F 1 'six nights' may seem to be more authentic: added to the night that has just passed, a full week of seven nights would be produced, better prefaced by 'yet' in the sence of *still* than six months.

38 keenely]   MS 'kindly' with its wordplay on 'by nature' and 'doing a favor' poses a temptation to an editor, especially since F 1 'keenely' is tautological in connection with 'eager' and could have been a compositorial sophistication or misreading. However, the case is not certain enough to forsake the general authority of F 1; moreover, in the play there is a

general emphasis on Maria's sexual love for Petruchio, and 'keenely' might
well give him the concern that he expresses whether she was 'light, and easy'.
88 of] Fı 'off' (an occasional spelling of 'of') is liable to misconstruction
if retained instead of MS 'of'. *OED* lists no sense of 'cast off' except to di-
vest oneself, whereas under *cast* (*vb* VIII.45) it is completely appropriate:
'to lay out in order, to plan, devise...a piece of ground, piece of work,
or other thing material', quoting, among others, Shute's *Architecture* (1563),
'Ye must first have knowledge how to cast your ground plotte.'

III.iv

45 clap:] After this word, and also at the end of the next line, MS places
a long dash. Since such a dash in MS is customary between the last word
of a line and a stage-direction to the right, it is possible here that either
(a) stage-directions for the two lines have been omitted but have left their
trace in the dashes, or (b) the dashes signify a pause in the dialogue to allow
for some action. However, dashes in the second sense do not occur in MS:
a mark like a dash after line 55 in this scene is different in length and
placement and does not appear to represent an intentional mark of
punctuation.
50 'Is] For another use of this contraction for 'He's' in both Fı and MS
(although without the apostrophe), see III.v.19, 'No, but is drawing on'.

III.v

29 Alas...infected] MS varies in reading 'have a care' in line 26 for Fı
'mean' and omitting in line 29 the phrase 'Alas he is infected' so that the
line reads 'My husband has it now, and raves extreamly'. This version may
be said to provide the more 'normal' form in that it is metrically regular:
'Is i'th house sir' completes Petronius' short line 27, 'Stand further off,
I prethee'; in line 26 'care to' produces a regular pentameter, whereas
with 'mean' the line is a foot short if the first foot is an anapest but could
be considered regular if, less naturally, the first foot were an iamb with
a truncated first weak syllable. Given the working hypothesis that both the
copy behind Fı and the present MS were transcribed at different removes
from the same source document, it would seem possible to speculate (a) one
or other misinterpreted revisions in this transmitted source so that one
reads with the original and the other with the alterations, or (b) a revision
was introduced into the source in the interval between the copying out of
the two documents, or (c) MS is sophisticating a slightly irregular passage.
The evidence is insufficient to guide an editor. In the present edition Fı
has been followed on the hypothesis that the more irregular form has
a better chance of being authoritative, even though it is possible that
a revision is being ignored. In fact, the revision could be in reverse since
it would be more irregular to break the linked pentameter with Petronius'
speech than to write it originally as a linked line. Moreover, it could be

argued that the F1 early introduction of 'infection' clarifies the situation in a desirable manner.

124 Can...hogs;] The addition in F1 of 'I could raile twenty daies' appears to be the setting of a trial, presumably deleted in the original copy when the passage was expanded(?), this on the evidence of line 141 'I could raile twenty daies together now.'

IV.iv

7 feare] The reason for MS's omission of this word (followed by F2, probably from consultation) is not clear except that it seems to have been based on some puzzlement about the syntax and meaning. The syntax is, indeed, misleading since one expects 'waies' to be elided before 'to avoid'. But it would seem that 'feare' is the object of the second 'have' as 'waies' had been the object of the first. The sense is roughly: you have allowable ways to make a profit and I have allowable fears of your plots.

V.i

28 Goodde'n] The inherent probability is great that MS is correct in this colloquial contraction for F1 'Good ev'n', to be followed by MS 'y'are' for F1 'you are'. This emendation of the F1 copy-text allows an editor to complete Petronius' line with Rowland's 'Thank you' instead of beginning a roughly linked pentameter line 29 with 'Thank you' as has been customary.

31 into] F1 'unto' could be a minim error or else a censorship of MS's patent indecency. The passage has sexual overtones beginning with Rowland's playing on 'certain' as an implication that Livia is not perhaps so *certain* or *sure* (i.e. in virtue). The play is carried on by the usual double meaning of 'know', which practically enforces the MS 'into' and the sexual innuendo that follows.

43 had] MS 'had' for F1 'have' continues the sexual innuendo noted in the Note above to line 31.

60 Why] MS 'Why', omitted by F1, is necessary to preserve the meter so that '*Tranio*' becomes a slurred dissyllable with a feminine ending, as in all earlier occurrences, at II.iii.2, 10, 23; III.i.9, 34, 59; and IV.iv.24. The accent on the final syllable is found at V.i.27, however.

V.ii

1 Trunke] MS 'Trunke' agrees with the '*Chest*' of the F1 stage-direction (emended in the present edition to 'a trunke' from MS). Possibly the final 's' was picked up from the plural 'Hampers' or else is a misreading of final 'e'.

66 seagly] The spelling of the common source seems to be established by the agreement of MS and F1. Weber identifies Sedgley (see F2 Sedgly) as near Dudley in Staffordshire, quoting Francis Grose's *Proverbs*.

PRESS-VARIANTS IN F1 (1647)

[Copies collated: BL (British Library, C.39.k.5), Ger (private copy, Johann Gerritsen, Groningen), Hoy (private copy, Cyrus Hoy, University of Rochester), ICN (Newberry Library), IU¹ (University of Illinois, 822/B38/ 1647), IU² (q822/B38/1647 cop. 2), MB (Boston Public Library), MnU (University of Minnesota), NcD (Duke University 429544), (Z823B38/fOCa), NIC (Cornell University A951587), NjP (Princeton University Ex 3623.1/ 1647q cop. 2), PSt (Pennsylvania State University PR2420/1647/Q), ViU¹ (University of Virginia 570973), ViU² (217972), WaU (University of Washington 29424), WMU¹ (University of Wisconsin–Milwaukee copy 1), WMU² (copy 2), WMU³ (copy 3), WU (University of Wisconsin–Madison 1543420).]

GATHERING O, outer sheet (*inner forme*)

Uncorrected: BL, NIC, WMU¹, WU

Sig. 5O1ᵛ
II.iv.30 Drum,] Drum.
    72 feſſions] feſſiions
II.vi.4 *Petru*:] *Petru*.
    16 me,] me.
    17 -boat,] -boat;
    23 contented] cotented
    25 (And] And
    32 lOOfe] loofe.
    34 *s.d. Jaques*] *Jaquer*

Sig. 5O4
III.iii.131 thee,] thee;
    133 loving man,] loving man;
    170 make] meke

GATHERING O, inner sheet (*outer forme*)

Uncorrected: Ger

Sig. 5O3ᵛ
III.iii.49 *s.d. the*] *the*.
    52 rich] rieh
    61 fatten] fatten,
    77 Faith fickly] Faithfickly
    79 out on't] out 'ont
    91 gilt] git
    102 ought] aught

EMENDATIONS OF ACCIDENTALS

Prologue

4 *ado*,] ~ . F 1–2

14 *In*] F 2: *in* F 1

Persons

4, 5 Gentleman,] Gent. F 2

21 Maids.] *not braced* F 2

I.i

I.i] *Actus Primus——Scæna Prima.* F 1–2; Actus Primus | Scæna j.^ma MS
1 too] MS, F 2; to F 1
2 Pudding's] F 2 (pudding's); Puddings F 1, MS

47 her,] MS, F 2; ~ ˄ F 1
48 pound] F 2; ponnd F 1
52 egges——] ~ , F 1–2; ~ . MS
53 Gentlemen,] MS; ~ ˄ F 1–2
61–62 If...Fiddle] If...thinke | This...Fiddle F 1–2, MS

I.ii

I.ii] *Scæna secunda.* F 1–2; Actus j.^mus Scæna ij^da. Ms
2 words——] ~ . F 1–2; ~ , MS
6 way?] MS; ~ . F 1–2
11 hope's] MS, F 2; hopes F 1
30 Laid] MS (layd), F 2; Lasd F 1 (Lafd)
43 you——] ~ . F 1–2; ~ , MS
89 *Livia.*] MS; ~ ? F 1–2
90 mad?] MS; ~ . F 1–2
91 *Livia*,] MS, F 2; ~ . F 1
99 hands;] ~ ˄ F 1–2; ~ , MS
105–106 Ocean, | As to] Ocean, as | To F 1–2, MS
114 feare;] MS (*slightly uncertain*); ~ , F 1–2

129 (Which...imputation)] MS; ˄ ~ ... ~ , F 1–2
133 desperate] MS, F 2; disperate F 1
134 at: disobedience?] ~ , ~ . F 1–2; ~ ˄ ~ . MS
158 still,] MS; ~ ˄ F 1–2
165 both——] ~ . F 1–2, MS
178 upon——] ~ . F 1–2; ~ ˄ MS
190 have,] MS, F 2; ~ ˄ F 1
194, 196 forsooth——] ~ . F 1–2; ~ , MS
198 The...you.] MS; now, | To F 1–2
207 Maria *and* Byancha] MS (Bian:); *om.* F 1–2
219 way?] MS, F 2; ~ . F 1

I.iii

I.iii] *Scena tertia.* F 1–2; *om.* MS
19 Saint] St. F 1–2, MS
19 *Kingston*] F 2; *rom.* F 1, MS
31 comfort;] ~ , F 1–2; ~ ₐ MS
45–46 *The . . . again,*] MS; *one line*
F 1–2
52–53 Yes . . . more.] may | Gentle-
men MS, F 1–2
61–62 How's . . . her?] are? | Is
F 1–2, MS
61 ²this?] MS, F 2; ~ ₐ F 1
65 *Spinola*'s] MS, F 2; *Spinala*'s F 1
66 her;] MS; ~ , F 1–2
81–83 Lock'd . . . vertues?] Lock'd
. . .-night? | Nay . . . graze: |
Come . . . vertues? F 1–2, MS
89 *Ostend*] F 2; *rom.* F 1, MS
94 up——] ~ ₐ F 1; ~ . MS, F 2
95–96 The . . . stands.] first; | I
F 1–2, MS
97 intrench'd] MS, F 2; intrenc'd F 1
99–100 For . . . violence.] you? | I
F 1–2, MS
102–103 I . . . two.] MS; I . . . and, |
You . . .-head | A . . . two. F 1–2
104–105 Yes . . . you.] Yes . . . hun-
dred; | Or . . . you. F 1–2; Yes, |
Or . . . hundred | Or . . . you. MS
106–108 That's . . . bonfires.] That's
. . . houre, | I . . . woman. |
When . . . bonfires. F 1–2, MS
113–114 I . . . night.)] without: | (I
F 1–2, MS

114 night.)] ~ ₐ) F 1–2; ~ . ₐ MS
117–118 Yes . . . ever.] Yes . . . father,
| And . . . down, | For . . . ever.
F 1–2, MS
122–123 I . . . vertuous.] I . . . wo-
man, | Makes . . . wife, | For . . .
vertuous. F 1–2, MS
129–131 The . . . us.] The . . . sir, |
Unlesse . . . thinke | We . . . shall
| Heare . . . us. F 1–2, MS
132 'Blesse . . . wiving?] hatching, |
Is F 1–2
161 pack's] MS (packe's); Pack's
F 2; packs F 1
162–163 Let . . . Kingdome.] wen-
ches | Be F 1–2; Lett . . lowsie |
If . . . knavery. | To . . . king-
dome. MS
194–195 Open . . . yet.] *one line* F 1–
2, MS
203 again,] MS; ~ : F 1–2
221 Well . . . comfort.] MS; *prose*
F 1–2
228 me,] MS; ~ : F 1–2
236 minds] MS; mind's F 1–2
247 you,] MS, F 2; ~ , F 1
271–272 And . . . me,] *one line* F 1–2;
MS *lines:* And tame . . . bigg, |
She . . . yee?
272 shall,] ~ ₐ F 1–2, MS
278 Proverb,] F 2; ~ ₐ (*space*) F 1;
~ ; MS

I.iv

I.iv] *Scæna quarta.* F 1–2 ± ; *om.* MS
7–8 You'l . . . me.] MS; You'l . . .
Fiddle | That . . . women——
F 1–2
9 fellow,] ~ ₐ F 1–2, MS
11 reason;] MS; ~ ₐ F 1; ~ , F 2
13 Ile . . . lay] MS; word, | I F 1–2

27–28 Let . . . end.] *one line* F 1–2, MS
40 Stay] stay F 1–2, MS
46 me:— —] ~ : ₐ F 1–2; ~ , ₐ
MS
47–48 I . . . examination.] MS; sir |
Without F 1–2
73 *Exit.*] MS; *om.* F 1–2

II.i

II.i] *Actus secundus. Scæna prima.*
  F 1–2 ±
 4 H'as] F 2; Has F 1
 5 word.] ~ , F 1–2

31 on't.] F 2; ~ , F 1
45 let's] F 2; lets' F 1
52 horses.] F 2; ~ ; F 1

II.ii

II.ii] Scæna Secunda.] F 1–2; Actus
  II.ᵘˢ Scæna j.ᵐᵃ MS
 13 wench,] MS, F 2; ~ ₐ F 1
 34 Will] F 2; will F 1, MS
 38 selves,] MS, F 2; F 1 *uncertain*
 40 one,] F 2; ~ ₐ F 1, MS
 46 mayden-|head] ~ - ~ F 1–2,
  MS
 93 sinne——] ~ . F 1–2, MS
 96 eyes,...legges ₐ...ones,] ~ ₐ

... ~ ,... ~ ₐ F 1; ~ ,...
~ ,... ~ ₐ F 2; ~ ,... ~ ₐ
... ~ ₐ MS
103–104 motley;...women,] ~ ,
 ... ~ ; F 1; ~ :... ~ , F 2;
 ~ ,... ~ ₐ MS
107–108 hideous,...office:] ~ :
 ... ~ , F 1–2; ~ ₐ ... ~ , MS
122 come.] MS; ~ , F 1–2

II.iii

II.iii] *Scæna quarta.* F 1–2 ± ; *om.* MS
 1 doe] MS, F 2; yoe F 1
 1 man?] F 2; ~ , F 1; ~ ₐ MS
 2 ill.] ~ : F 1–2; ~ ? MS
 3–4 So...acquainted] *one line* F 1–
  2, MS
 9 question.] ~ ₐ F 1–2, MS
 10 No...*Tranio*,] No | 'Tis F 1–2,
  MS

11 bred] MS; bread F 1–2
21 such] MS, F 2; snch F 1
23 *Tranio*,] MS; ~ . F 1–2
33 sake,] ~ .—— F 1–2; ~ ₐ MS
35 She...her,] sooner | Count
 F 1–2, MS
42 er] 'er F 1; ere MS; e'r F 2

II.iv

II.iv] *Scæna quinta,* F 1–2 ± ; *om.* MS
 7 imagine,] ~ . F 1–2; ~ ₐ MS
 8 Tom-] MS, F 2 (*Tom*-); Tomb-
  F 1
 8 malice] MS, F 2; ma ice F 1
 17 -wife ₐ] MS; ~ , F 1–2
 20 should,] MS, F 2; ~ . F 1
 21 Believe] beleeve F 1 *cw*
 21 should.)] ~ ₐ) F 1–2; ~ ; ₐ MS
 29 bones,] ~ . F 1–2, MS
 30 Drum.] MS; ~ , F 1–2

36.1 *Enter* Pedro.] MS; F 1 *in line*
 34; F 2 *as line* 34 +
45 Parish,] MS (parish,); ~ . F 1–2
69 'em,] ~ . F 1–2; ~ ₐ MS
74–75 -caps,...cudgell:] ~ :...
 ~ . F 1; ~ : ... ~ ; F 2;
 ~ ,... ~ , MS
80 The] F 2; the F 1, MS
86 councell.] MS, F 2; ~ , F 1
88–89 Away...best.] MS; *one line*
  F 1–2

128

II.v

II.v] *Scæna Tertia.* F1–2; *om.* MS
  1 faire——] ~ . F1–2, MS

2 strength,] F1², F2; ~ ₐ F1¹, MS

II.vi

II.vi] *Scena tertia.* F1; *Scæna Quarta.*
  F2; *om.* MS
  0.1 Petruchio,] F2; ~ . F1, MS
  20 done.] MS (~ -); ~ ? F1–2
  32 loose——] ~ ₐ F1, MS; ~ . F2
  53 *round;*] ~ ₐ F2
  62 *et seq. Country wife.*] *Cun.* F1–2;
  Country MS
  64 Learnedly] MS, F2; Learuedly
  F1
  67 *et seq. Citty wife.*] *Cit.* F1–2;
  Citty MS
  74 Mistris——] ~ . F1–2, MS
  87 Ale——] ~ . F1–2; ~ ₐ MS

106 chambering] MS; chambring
  F1–2
112 Plackets,] MS; ~ . F1–2
143 thousand] MS, F2; twousand F1
144 French——] ~ ; F1–2; ~ . MS
146 importun'd,] ~ . F1–2; ~ ₐ MS
159 persecution——] ~ . F1–2; ~ₐ
  MS
161 What's...here?] F2; this | In-
  serted F1, MS
163 'cm] MS, F2; ₐ ~ F1
169–170 Ne'er...it.] *one line* F1–2,
  MS

III.i

III.i] *Actus tertius, Scæna prima.* F1;
  Actus Tertius. | *Scæna Prima.*
  F2; Actus III. Scæna j.ᵐᵃ· MS
  9 *Tranio,*] MS, F2; ~ ₐ F1
  20 scurvy——] ~ . F1; ~ , MS,
  F2
  32 swabber:] ~ , F1–2, MS
  34 Why?] MS, F2; ~ . F1
  35 do.] MS (*uncertain*); ~ , F1–2

46 him.] MS, F2; ~ ₐ F1
50 they?] ~ , MS
57 ended——] ~ , MS
65 Kits,] ~ ₐ F1–2, MS
70 ye.] MS; ~ : F1–2
75 better——] ~ . F1–2, MS
75 Well?] ~ . F1–2, MS
84 leave,] MS; ~ . F1–2

III.ii

III.ii] *Scæna Secunda.* F1–2; *om.* MS
  6 H'as] F2; Has F1; 'has MS
  7 him——] ~ . F1–2; ~ , MS
  16 her,] MS; ~ : F1–2
  21–22 That...sack.] MS, F2;
  prose F1

36 on't,] MS; ~ . F1–2
47 master,] ~ ₐ F1, MS; ~ ——
  F2

III.iii

III.iii] *Scena tertia.* F 1; *Scæna Tertia.*
F 2; *om.* MS
5 Pray...her?] MS; truly; | Do
F 1–2
23 (for...nettl'd)] MS; , ~ ...
~ , F 1–2
29 Butler,] ~ ∧ F 1–2, MS
31 her?] MS; ~ . F 1–2, MS
44 fleaing] F 2. fieaing F 1; flaying
MS
49.1 Maria...*woman.*] *s.d. in* F 1–2
in three lines at right opposite

lines 48–49; in MS *in two lines
opposite line* 50
58 *France*] F 2; *rom.* F 1, MS
66 for th'] MS, F 2; for 'th F 1
71 twelvemonth] ~ - | ~ F 1–2;
~ ∧ ~ MS
77 now?] MS; ~ ∧ F 1–2
78 ayre——] ~ . F 1–2, MS
89 too;——] ~ ; ∧ F 1–2, MS
122 you.] MS; ~ : F 1–2
138 jealous.] MS; ~ : F 1–2
141 me:——] ~ : F 1–2; ~ . MS

III.iv

III.iv] *Scæna Quarta.* F 1–2; *om.* MS
5 gew-gaws] MS; ~ — | ~ F 1–2
11 yong] youg F 1; young MS, F 2
37 commendations:——] ~ : ∧

F 1–2; ~ , ∧ MS
41 again;——] ~ ; ∧ F 1–2; ~ . ∧
MS

III.v

III.v] *Scena quinta.* F 1; *Scæna
Quinta.* F 2; *om.* MS
4 ²die,...quickly:] ~ : ...~ ,
F 1–2; ~ ∧ ...~ , MS
5–6 F 1–2 *line*: people that are
skilfull | In
8 Parson!] MS (parson); ~ ,
F 1–2
20–21 Thou...me.] MS; Thou...
has | Been...me. F 1–2
22–23 Now...sonne?] MS; *one
line* F 1–2
23 do's] dos F 1; does MS, F 2
25–26 Get...sicknesse——] MS;
one line F 1–2
26 sicknesse——] ~ . F 1–2, MS
28 Is...now;] sir, | My F 1–2, MS

38 for.] MS; ~ : F 1–2
40–41 Doe...up.] *one line* F 1–2,
MS (ho)
42–43 Wil...Heretick.] MS; *one
line* F 1–2
46–47 Pray...wickednesse.] Pray
...patience, | You...sir. | I...
cudgell, | And...wickednesse.
F 1–2, MS
49 Wil...pleas'd] MS; me? | First
F 1–2
62 from] MS, F 2; frow F 1
86 quiet,] MS; ~ ? F 1–2
88 way?] MS; ~ ; F 1–2
93 man.] MS, F 2; ~ , F 1
97 Would] MS, F 2; would F 1

IV.i

IV.i] *Actus Quartus. Scæna prima.*
  F 1–2 ± ; *om. scene* MS
8 her——] ~ . F 1–2
31 clamour.] ~ : F 1–2
32 Ballad] F 2; Ballard F 1
44 Feathers,] F 2; ~ ∧ F 1

63 *Moroso.*] F 2; *Mar.* F 1
78 Doe.] F 2; ~ , F 1
84 there;] ~ ∧ F 1–2
100 too——] ~ . F 1–2
101 yong] F 2 (young); youg F 1

IV.ii

IV.ii] *om.* F 1–2; Actus III. Scæna
  j.ᵐᵃ MS
8 Christmas∧] ~ , F 1–2, MS
8 sir,] F 2; ~ ∧ F 1; ~ . MS
10 up,] MS; ~ . F 1–2
18 woolsey∧] MS; ~, , F 1–2
22 comes,] MS, F 2; ~ ∧ F 1
43 him.] MS, F 2; ~ , F 1

45 Jesuite,] MS, F 2; ~ ∧ | F 1
70 (At...so)] MS; ~ ∧... ~ , ∧
  F 1–2
71 hold,] MS, F 2; ~ ∧ F 1
76 manners——] ~ . F 1–2, MS
83 Knight——] ~ . F 1–2, MS
92 too——] ~, . F 1–2, MS
124 honour,] MS (Honor,) ~ ∧ F 1–2

IV.iii

IV.iii] *Scæna Secunda.* F 1–2; *om.* MS
1–2 Are...of?] *one line* F 1–2;
  readie. | I MS
2–4 Yes...constru'd.] MS; *each
  one line* F 1–2
4 constru'd.] MS; ~ , F 1–2
10 'em——] ~ . F 1–2, MS

12 Saw.] MS; ~ : F 1–2
13 for:] ~ ∧ F 1, MS; ~ , F 2
16 *Byancha*!] MS (Bianca!); ~ .
  F 1–2
31 matter's] MS; matters F 1–2
36 fortune,] MS; ~ ∧ F 1–2
48 Servants,] ~ ∧ F 1–2, MS

IV.iv

IV.v] *Scæna Tertia.* F 1–2, *om.* MS
9 Master,] MS, F 2; ~ ∧ F 1
11 Jewell——] ~ . F 1–2; ~ ∧ MS
13 How,] ~ ∧ F 1–2, MS
14 sick.] MS; ~ : F 1–2
21 her,] ~ ∧ F 1, MS; ~ ; F 2
22 honesty.] MS; ~ : F 1–2
29 Come,] MS, F 2; ~ ∧ F 1

44 ye——] ~ . F 1–2, MS
50 bargaine——] ~ ; F 1–2; ~ ∧
  MS
51 lawfull?——] ~ ? ∧ F 1–2; ~, ∧
  MS
52 bargaine.] MS; ~ : F 1–2
55 then,——] MS; ~ ∧ F 1–2

IV.v

IV.v] *Scæna quarta.* F 1–2 ± ; *om.* MS
7–8 No...women.] MS; *prose*
  F 1–2

13 first——] ~ . F 1–2; ~ ∧ MS
19 patience——] ~ . F 1–2; ~ ∧
  MS

21 patience——] ~ . F 1–2, MS
26 her,] MS, F 2; ~ ∧ F 1
36 wickednesse:——] MS (wicked-
    nes.——); ~ : ∧ F 1–2
41 sir——] ~ ∧ F 1; ~ . MS, F 2
44 pleasure.] MS, F 2; ~ ∧ F 1
52 *Sophocles*——] ~ , F 1–2; ~ .
    MS
55 you.] MS; ~ ∧ F 1–2
57 woman.] MS; ~ , F 1–2
58 experience.] MS; ~ , F 1–2
78 tatle.] MS, F 2; ~ ∧ F 1
82 ye,] MS; ~ ∧ F 1–2
89–90 mumping,. . . enough:)] ~)
    . . . ~ : F 1–2; ~). . . ~ , MS
90 y'ar'] MS; you're F 1–2
90–91 enough: ——. . . her: ——]
    ~ : ∧. . . ~ : ∧ F 1–2; ~ , ∧. . .
    ~ , ∧ MS

103 satiety] MS, F 2; saciety F 1
107 behaviour] MS, F 2; behavour
    F 1
144 neck,] MS, F 2; ~ ∧ F 1 (*un-
    certain*)
154 Schoolmen] MS; ~ - | ~ F 1;
    ~ - ~ F 2
170 Signior] F 2; senior MS; Signour
    F 1
184 man !] MS; ~ : F 1–2
189 behinde——] ~ . F 1–2, MS
194, 196 *Indies*. . .*Cataya*. . .*France*]
    F 2; rom. F 1, MS
196 *France?*] ~ . F 1–2; ~ ∧ MS
201 thou] MS, F 2; thouc F 1
210 going,] MS; ~ . F 1–2
215 credit;] MS; ~ , F 1–2
218–219 (For. . .els)] MS (else);
    ∧ ~ . . . ~ , F 1–2

V.i

V.i] *Actus Quintus, Scæna Prima.*
    F 1–2; Actus V. Scæna j.ᵐᵃ MS
4 seems] MS, F 2; sems F 1
16 Has] MS, F 2; H'as F 1
22 How?] MS; ~ . F 1–2
24 Saint] St. F 1–2, MS
29 Daughter——] ~ . F 1–2, MS
37–38 Or. . .on't.] MS; repenting. |
    And F 1–2
38 on't.] ~ , F 1–2
57 That's] MS, F 2; Thats F 1
69 Pray] MS, F 2; pray F 1
74 head.] MS; ~ : F 1–2
76–78 I. . .him,] I. . .so; | I. . .

names, | I. . .him, F 1–2; I. . .
    perintiously; | Was. . .so, | I
    . . .names, | I. . .him, MS
80 do's] dos F 1; does MS, F 2
99 drinke.] MS; ~ , F 1–2
100 O] MS, F 2; O' F 1
120–1 Come. . .fall.] *one line* F 1–2,
    MS
147 By. . .sonne.] means: | To F 1–
    2, MS
147 means:] MS; ~ ∧ F 1–2
152 up;——] MS; ~ ; ∧ F 1–2
155 Farewell.] MS; ~ : F 1–2

V.ii

V.ii] *Scæna secunda.* F . 1–2±; om. MS
9 *Lyon*] F 2; rom. F 1
11 Trunk.] MS; ~ : F 1–2
28 John] MS; *John* F 1–2
42 journey's] MS, F 2; journeys F 1

47 of her——] of——her∧ F 1–2;
    of her. MS
53 her,] ~ . F 1–2; ~ ∧ MS
66 him;. . .*Pedro*,] ~ ,. . .~ ;
    F 1–2; ~ ,. . .~ , MS

V.iii

V.iii] *Scæna tertia.* F 1–2 ±; *om.* MS
  6 *Livia.*——] MS (~ ˄ ——);
    ~ . ˄ F 1–2
  8 ye.——] MS (~ , ——); ~ . ˄
    F 1–2

9 on't:——] MS (~ ˄ —); ~ : ˄
  F 1–2
9 Contract!] MS; ~ ? F 1 (Con-
  rract), F 2
12 again——] MS; ~ , ˄ F 1–2

V.iv

V.iv] *Scæna Quarta.* F 1–2; *om.* MS
40 else.——] MS; ~ ? ˄ F 1–2
46 strangely] MS, F 2; strangly | F 1

49 *Maria!*——] ~ ! ˄ F 1–2;
  ~ ˄ —— MS

HISTORICAL COLLATION

[NOTE: The following editions are herein collated: MS (Lambarde Manuscript), F1 (Folio 1647), F2 (Folio 1679), L (*Works*, 1711, ed. Gerard Langbaine the Younger and others), S (*Works*, 1750, ed. Theobald, Seward and Sympson), C (*Works*, 1778, ed. George Colman the Younger), W (*Works*, 1812, ed. Henry Weber), D (*Works*, rev. ed. 1877, ed. Alexander Dyce), Fg (*Womans Prize*, ed. G. B. Ferguson, 1966).]

Prologue] *om.* MS   Persons] *om.* F1, MS

I.i

0.1 *with Rosemary*] *om.* MS
1 God] Heaven MS
4 true, certaine:] ~ : ~ , F1–2, Fg; ~ , ~ , MS
17 stubbornesse] sobernesse F1–2, L, S, C, W; sourness D (*after* Mason)
18 huy] hue MS, F2+
23 God] heaven MS
23 woman] a woman MS
24 be——] ~ , MS
35 Breeches,...feareₐ] ~ ₐ ... ~ , F2
39 by my troth] on my word F1+ (−Fg)

40 this] his MS
40 soule——] ~ , MS
46 pisse] unready F1+ (−Fg)
48 pound] pounds MS, W
48 these] this MS
49 *s.d. with a pot of Wine*] *om.* MS
53 Gentlemen] Gentleman S
57 O] a' MS
59 a] at MS
64 God] heaven MS
64 worships] worship F1+ (−Fg)
64.1 *s.d.* Jaques] *om.* MS
66 you'ld] you'l F1+
71 wip't him now] impt him MS

I.ii

1 Now] Nay MS
6 you——] ~ , MS
7, 64 Twill] 'Till C
7 ²a] *om.* MS, S
8 this] his F1+
9 love] loves MS
20 h'as] has MS
23 Cods] Gods Fg
23 Crocus] Cracus F1, Fg; Croacus F2, L
25 Fox] Fox and F1

26 you——] ~ . MS
28 a] *om.* F1–2, L, C, W
30 Laid] Lasd F1; Lac'd S, C, W
30 graspe] gasp D
41 Yfaith] Indeed MS
41 rather——] ~ , MS
43 But——] ~ , MS
51–52 *Rowland.* I...it. | *Livia.*] *om.* F1+ (−Fg)
62 But...him——] *om.* MS
63 to't] to it MS

64 stranger] stronger F1+ (−S, Fg)
65 I am perfect] Ile doe it MS
66–67 Like...it.] leap'd | Into C+ (−Fg)
66 have I] I have F2, L; I've S
67 into] in MS
67 and...it] om. MS
68 poorer] poore MS
69–74 Now...out.] upon him. MS
72 tempest] [a] tempest D
77 feares] 's' added MS
78 example.] MS adds lines 70–74 'I...out.'
78, 79 Here is] Here's C+ (−Fg)
80–83 MS lines: I...Wench, | What...revels | Should... corke; | To...-starv'd.
80 of] o'the MS
80 is't,] ∼ ? F2, S
81 Revels] Rebels F1
81 up rowse] rowze up F2
83 lungs] longs F1
83 -starv'd] start'd MS
83–84 Deere...thus?] one line in MS
84–85 Why...now.] MS lines: Why...thus | I...now.
86–88 Y'are...Pins.] MS lines: Y'are...once | Thy...pins.
90–92 Yes...time.] Yes wench, and so must you be, marke me Livia, | Or none of our acquaintance, or indeed fit for our sex: MS
94–95 Thine...Bridegroome.] MS lines: Thy...keepe ['f' del.] | Fasting...Bridegroome.
94 Thine] Thy MS

94 or] and MS
99 hands;] ∼ ∧ Fg
100 are] be MS
101 there's] there is MS
105 as easie] om. MS
110 mothers] womans MS
112 hopes,] ∼ ∧ MS
114 feare;] ∼ , F1–2, Fg
120 pleasures are] pleasure is MS
128 disobedience] obedience F1–2 L, S
134 end∧...at,] ∼ , ... ∼ ∧ MS
143 and...one] om. F1+ (−Fg)
145 Byancha. That's...wench.] om. F1+ (−Fg)
146 Maria.] om. MS
147 these] those MS
148 halla] hallow MS, F2; hollow S+ (−D, Fg)
150 has] hath F1+
151 an] a MS
163 all] om. MS
174 Wanting] Wonting F2
179 Then] There (C qy. (after Mason), D)
179 ye] you MS
189 Now Byancha] MS assigns sp. pref. Maria and places as separate line above 'Byancha. 'Cheere wench?'
200 Maria.] Jaq. L
203 y'ar] you are MS
205 you'l] you will MS
210 together] om. MS
215 this] these MS
215 weddings] wedding Mason
215 a] om. MS
216 trick] ranck MS

I.iii

0.1 *s.d. with lights,*] (~ ~ ,) MS
0.1 *s.d. and*] *om.* MS
1 have] home F 1, Fg
2 nights] night MS
4 next] els MS
5 Faith] Well F 1 + (−Fg)
7–9 MS *lines*: But...to | You...
gallant.
7 ¹you] *om.* S
7 your trot] you troth MS
8 Gallants] gallant MS
9 stuffe] staffe F 1 + (−S[*conj.*],
Fg)
11–12 *Tranio.* A...prayers.] *om.*
MS
11 all to] to all S
13 Will...sonne?] well son, well_∧
MS
22–23 *Sophocles.* His...while.] *om.*
F 1 + (−Fg)
24 Tis] Tis very S
25–26 *Tranio.* That...leeke.] *om.*
F 1 + (−Fg)
28 man] men D
32–33 *One line in* MS
32 and] or MS
32.1 *Enter* Jaques.] MS *places on
line* 31
35–36 MS *lines:* Not...her, | Here's
...intayl'd, | Is yet?
35 o' me] a me MS
36 it] yet MS
37–38 *Lined:* of | Let's MS, Fg
41–42 *Lined:* Unlesse...daw, | Or
...the | House, 'tis possible. MS,
Fg
47–49 *Lined:* Ye...is | All...
-hole | But...victuall'd | For
...month. MS, Fg; F 1–2 *as
prose but And*...doores | Are
...in't | She's...moneth. MS,
Fg; F 1–2 *as prose but And*...

doores | Are...in't. | She's...
moneth.
47 *Ye*] *And you* F 1 +
49 murd'rer] murder MS
50 not thou] thou not MS
57 ere] are MS
58 will not] wont S
58–59 composition,...you;] ~ ;
... ~ , MS
61 ²this?] ~ _∧ F 1
61 are?] ~ —— F 2
64 Heavens] loves MS
67 but] *om.* MS
67 you'ld] you'l F 1 +
67, 104 sir,] *om.* F 1 +
69 in't] it F 1 +
73 cool'd] cold MS
75 She doth] They doe F 1 + (−Fg)
77–78 MS *lines*: noyse | At
77 fearfull] fearfully MS
79 tongue] this tongue S
84–90 MS *lines*: Doe...was. | I...
answer'd, | Knock'd...have |
Broke...worke | Flew...vio-
lence | That...nescit? | The...
Ostend, | In...mounted, |
You'le...Sir.
87, 89, 95 window] windore MS
87 such] such a MS
94 ye dare] you deare MS
97 what] what are you S
99 who] pray who S
106 present] *om.* MS
107 never will] will never MS
112 do's] doth MS
113–114 (I...night).]_∧ ~ ... ~ ·_∧
MS
117 seale] sealer MS
119 By'r Lady] Indeed F 1 + (−Fg)
119 Bugs-words] Bug-words F 2, L,
S, C
120 heare] heare her MS

120 God] heaven MS
121 sir] *om.* MS
122 that] *om.* S
130 charge] charge us S
132 'Blesse] ˌBless F2; Heaven
blesse MS, S, C, W, Fg
132 is this wiving?] *om.* MS
134 do it freely] freely do it S
141 nor...nor] or...or MS
145 'em] them MS
148 except] *alt. fr.* 'accept' MS;
accept F2, L
152 i'ld] I would MS; I'll F2, S, C,
W; I'd D
160 MS *lines:* Sir, | That
164 Death] Why F1+ (−Fg)
165–166 It...it,] *one line in* MS
172–173 MS *lines:* And...feare |
Neither...fame.
173 *Furius*] furious MS
190 come] come down S
190 thee——] ~ , MS; thee, whore
C, W
196 on't] out MS
212–213 F2 *lines:* next | *Tyrone*
219 me?] me now? S
221 MS *lines:* Maudlin. | That's

223 MS *lines:* stomach | And
226–227 MS *lines:* You...maydes. |
They'l...girths, | You'l...els.
234 allurings] alluring S
234 the] thy F1
237 maskes] markes MS
240 And] *om.* MS
244 too] for MS
246 alayes] ['like' *del.*] alayes MS
252 hand——] ~ , MS, F2
252 I shall] shall I S
254 Jewry] Jury F2, S, C, W, D
262 sitting] setting MS
267–268 MS *lines:* There...famous
| For...Tamer
267 my cause lies] lyes my cause MS
273 to] *om.* S
274 Ye] You MS
278 death] —— F1–2, S; Pox C,
D, W
282 those] these MS
285 upon] on S
288 MS *lines:* each | Provide
290 I vow] —— F1–2, L, S; *om.*
C, W, D
292.1 *Omnes*] *om.* MS, S

I.iv

0.1 *Enter...doores.*] Enter Rowland at one doore. Pedro hastily
at the other. MS
2–3 I...man.] *one line in* MS
3 mine] my MS
4 hasty——] ~ . MS
6 *Rowland. Why*] 'Rowland' *over*
'Pedro' MS
8 such] *om.* F1+ (−Fg)
8 women God] women—— F1+
(−Fg); women, MS, Fg
8 deliver me] *om.* S, C
9–10 Your...businesse.] *one line*
in MS

10 very] *om.* S
16 yon] you MS, F2
16, 74 ye] you MS
17 my] thy MS
18 *s.d.* Jaques] *om.* MS
18 *s.d. Enter Sophocles.*] MS *marks*
to follow line 19
20–21 MS *lines:* Now...stay | To
...long.
33 Armies] Armes F1–2, L, S
38 (*twice*) Farewell] Fare you well
MS
40 ye] *om.* MS
40 *s.d. Enter...harkning.*] Enter

Livia and Moroso as unseene by her MS (*against lines* 42–43)
42 -gaudes] 'u' *intrl.* MS
47–48 I . . . examination.] *one line in* MS
48 Twenty Spur-Royals] I thanke thee MS
55 Excellent] Gramercy for that MS
56 knuckle] knockle MS; noddle Mason
62 women] woman MS

64 breakes] breake MS
66 you] for you MS
69 She's . . . world:] *om.* MS
69.1 *Gives*] She gives MS
69.1 *o'th*] a'th MS
70 How's . . . you.] Is't come to this. | Save you. MS
71 thee——] you. MS
71 *s.d. Wrings . . . nose.*] *om.* MS
73 thank] thuck MS

II.i

0.1–60.1 *om. scene* MS
4 is] *om.* F1
7 I] *om.* S, C

17 Not] Nor S
53 *Moroso.*] *om.* F1

II.ii

0.1 *alone*] *om.* MS
1 but get in] gett in but MS
4 finde] finds MS
6 Do not beleeve] Beleeve not MS
7 y'on] yo'nd MS; yon F2+ (−Fg)
12 *Qui va la*] *Cheval'a* F1–2; *Che va la?* S
23 O'] A MS
23 faith——] word—— F1+ (−Fg)
24 your] upon your S
24 faith, or troth] word F1+ (−Fg)
26 can] can e'er S
29 *Sinon*] Simon L
34 of] *alt. fr.* 'off' MS
49 your selfe] our cause MS
51 Christian] certaine F1+ (−Fg)
58 off] *om.* MS
58 Fillyes] Flies S–D

60 Bilbo] *Bilboa* F2, L–W
61 most] *om.* F2, L
68 Has] Hath MS
68 and] *om.* MS
81 An] A MS
81 yeare] years F2 L–D
87 soule, . . . place:] ~ ; . . . ~ MS
89 fail] fall MS
93 Find] Found F1
96 nor legges] no legs MS
97 i'th] a'th MS
97 for] *om.* S
98 Thou'lt] The root MS
105 (like . . . furies)]ᴧ ~ . . . ~ , MS
106 distaffes] distaves MS
108 office] offence D (*after* Heath)
109 hither] first MS
118 Meet] Meet | Me MS
121 our] your D

II.iii

II.iii] F 1–2, L–W *reprint first version of* Scene v *as* Scene iii
  0.1 *Enter...doores.*] Enter Rowland at one doore, Tranio at yᵉ other. MS
  2 can] *om.* MS
  3 knew] kew MS
  3–4 *Rowland. So...acquainted?*] *Row.* Thou hast heard I am sure of *Esculapius*, | So were... acquainted? F 1
  9 great] *om.* F 1+
  13 thou] *Row.* Thou F 1–2
  15 could] coo'd MS

17 he] be F 2
21 rack] wreck, C, W, D
22 Heavens] honours F 1+ (−Fg)
23 Why] *om.* MS
32 or] *om.* MS
33 doe] *om.* F 2
33 even] ever MS
33 loves] love F 1–2, L, D
34 Our...friend-ship——] *follows line* 35 F 1+
35 She] That she S
38 ᵗher] here MS
42 first] *om.* MS
42 enjoy] joy MS

II.iv

  0.1 Moroso, *and* Sophocles] Sophocles. Moroso MS
  5 ——] this hand MS; Heaven C, W, D
  8 of] or Fg
  12 come] comes F 1–2, L, S
  15 Sew] Sow F 1–2, L–W
  17 a] of MS
  19 these] those MS
  21 (Believe...should.)] (~ ... ~ ₐ) F 1–2; ₐ ~ ... ~ ,ₐ MS; ₐ ~ ... ; ₐ S; ₐ ~ ... ~ ! ₐ C, W
  21 me] my S
  24 For] And MS
  25 surer] sooner MS
  26 amendment] mendment MS
  31 with ——] ~ , MS
  37 devils] evils MS
  44–48 her plackett...breech;] *om.* F 1+ (−Fg)
  56 main] manie MS

57 tosting] tossing F 1+ (−C)
60 Codsheads] Godheads F 2, L, S
64 and] or MS
65 zeale] zcales MS
67, 90 o'th] a'th MS
67 F 1+ *add next line:* *Soph.* Lo you fierce *Petruchio*, this comes of your impatience. (*see lines* 86–87)
68–70 MS *lines*: There's...against | The...good | And...song.
68 brought] first brought MS
69 two church-wardens] The Town F 1+ (−Fg)
70 And song] *om.* F 1+ (−Fg)
70 And] *intrl.* MS
77 she] the Fg
78–84 Then...for.] *om.* MS
83 Britaine] Briton W, D
92 MS *lines*: doe, | But
93 their] these MS

II.v

0.1–5.1 *om.* F2; F2 *prints this*
scene only as II.iii; MS *only as*
II.v; F1 *duplicates* II.iii *at* II.v
with slightly variant text

0.1 *Maides*] Country wenches MS

0.1 *at severall doors*] *om.* F1 (*scene*
iii), F2+ (−Fg)

1 your] the F1 (*scene* v), D

1 Girles] girles F1 (*scene* v)–F2

2 strength] strengths | We are
discover'd els. MS

3–4 The...else.] *one line in* F1
(*scene* v)

3 The] 1. The MS

3 Forces] forces F1 (*scene* v), MS

3 ariv'd,] ~ ; F1 (*scene* v)

3 gone.] ~ ₍ F1 (*scene* v); ~ , F2

4 We...else] MS *places as line* 2

4 discover'd] discovered F1
(*scene* v)

4 *1.* Arme...valiant.] II. Arme
and be valliant, thinke of our
cause. MS

5 *2.* Think...cause.] MS *assigns*
to 'II.' *in line above*

5 *3.* Our...sufficient.] III. Our
Justice I: I: I: 'tis sufficient. MS

5 Justice] justice F1 (*scene* v)

5 'Tis] ₍ ~ F1 (*scene* v)

II.vi

7 that's] there's MS

8 Why] They MS

11 wife,] ~) MS

14 *Don*] Dom MS

16 have] ['v' *over* 'd'] MS

30 flownder] founder MS

32 *s.d. Musick above.*] MS *places*
after 'world' *line* 32

33 on] a MS

34 God] long MS; Heaven F2, L,
S, D

38 They] That MS

40 the Kingdom] them F1

42 Tyrants.] Tyrants. *Song.* MS

42–43 I...Lansket.] *one line in* MS

42 in] in   *Song*! F1

43 pray] pray you MS

44–57 *A...pound.*] *om.* F1, MS

46 *wears*] wear C, W

48 this] his S

57 S *adds:* Tra. Hark. | Pedro. A
Song, pray silence. *after line* 57

61–62 No...you.] *one line in* MS

63 drunk] drank F2, L–W

63 are——] ~ . MS

64 Learnedly] 'ly' *added* MS

68–69 You...couragious.] *one line*
in MS

69 A] *om.* MS

75 these] this MS

75 shall] sall MS

78 into] in MS

79 you] ['good' *del.*] you MS

82 come] came MS

89 ev'n] then F1 C, W, D, Fg;
om. F2, L, S

90 ever yet] ['yet' *del.*] ever *yet
[*intrl.*] MS

92 bane] 'a' *over* 'o' MS (MS *cw*
this bone)

93 Her] His F1–2

95 hood] *intrl.* MS

96 I] I'll F2, L, S, C, W

96 o] of MS; o' F2+ (−Fg)

97 goe lesse] ~ ; ~ ₍ MS

99 two main] too manie MS

104 recreant] recant F1–2, S–W
('recant' *del.* MS)

114 Into] Unto, S, C, W

117 She's] shee is MS
118 Heare] Heard MS
119 ye] you MS
129 There's] There is MS
131 Apothecaries] the' apothecary S, C
132 It] I Mason, W
132 sir] *om.* MS
134–135 *Livia.* He...lustie.] *om.* MS, F 2, L, S
136 *Reads.*] *om.* MS
143 pound] pounds MS

144–156 *Petronius.* This...now] MS *originally omitted but supplied on slip*
147 monstrous] monstruous MS
148 awhile] a while MS
158 this creed] these Articles F 1–2 +
160 honesty——] ~ ₐ MS
162 command] commanded F 2, L, S, C
169 Ne'r] Never MS
171 *Petruchio.*] *Petro.* F 2

III.i

0.1 *Enter...Rowland.*] Enter Rowland & Tranio. MS
9 *misereris*] miscries F 1, W; mistrisses MS, F 2, L, S
15 I] I'le MS
15 there is] *alt. fr.* 'there's' MS
21 Heavens] vertue F 1 + (−Fg)
22 Heavens] vertues F 1 + (−Fg)
22 do'st thou not] Don't you S
23 hartely] hartly MS
26 calfe with the white face] gilt calfe F 1–2 +
30 man] a man MS
32 best] the best MS
40 Ye] you MS
44 Raigne] raignes MS
46 Your] You F 1–2, I.

46 licks] *alt. fr.* 'like' MS
47 O, pox] A —— F 1–2, L, S; A pox C, W, D, Fg
50–57 *Tranio.* Of...ended——] *om.* F 1 + (−Fg)
55 give] guie Fg
62 women?] woman. MS
67, 86 pound] pounds MS
69 and] an MS
71 do,] ~ ₐ MS
77 she now] now she F 2, L, S
80 an] a MS
81 no] more MS
83 for th' bell] forthbell MS (?)
85 too,] to ₐ MS
86 how] what MS
89 Shal't] 'Shalt MS

III.ii

5 O'] A MS
8, 11 Faith] *om.* F 1 + (−Fg)
9 he kiss'd her] she kist him MS
12 prayers] Payers F 2
20 those] these MS
24 thou] *om.* MS
25 Cavaliero] Cavelero MS
27 somer salt] sober salt F 1; Summersett MS

34 it——] ~ . MS
37 For..cellars.] *om.* F 1 + (−Fg)
44 Cinque-pace] cinque-a-pace MS, C; Cinque-a-pace F 2, L, S
45 Tost] tosse F 1
45 her] he F 1; the F 2 + (−Fg)
47 see] saw D

III.iii

0.1 *and*] *om.* MS
5 Pray] pray you F 1+
7 past] had past MS
9 *Petruchio.*] *Petro.* MS
11 washt] wash MS
15 appetite——] ~ ? MS
19 unto] to F 1+
21 on] of MS
23 pain] pains F 2
23 was] was in S
26 started] startled MS
32 nights] monthes MS
36 Stay...ye] Stay, stay MS
38 keenely] kindly MS
41 spoke's] spoke is MS
49 *s.d. and...woman*] *and servants* MS
54 pearle] pearles MS
55 those] these MS
60 cuts] cutte MS
65 suit] set S

74–75 An...that?] *one line in* MS
80 you] *om.* F 1
82 thy] your MS
84 And] ['What if I pluck it downe' *del.*] And MS
84 built] build S
86 yong] your young MS
88 of] off F 1
94 and justice] *om.* MS
101 weigh'd] way'd MS
114 sweet] good MS
127 friends] friend MS
143 it,...me.——] its—— F 1; it's—— F 2, L, S, C, W, D; it. Mason; it,...me. Fg
145 wintering] wyntring MS
146 These] this MS
155 tooles] love F 1+ (−Fg)
155 to] too MS, F 1
157 rare] reare MS
165 did͜] ~ ; MS

III.iv

0.1 Tranio, *and* Rowland] Rowland Tranio MS
4 end] Ends S
5 ²your] no F 1
7–8 MS *lines*: you at playes | &
10 him] *om.* MS
11 yong man] youngman MS
12 out] out of S
13 poore] pure MS

15 woman] man MS
32 dearely] deadly F 1+ (−Fg)
34 mine] my MS
36 o'] a' MS
36 makes] gets MS
42 much——] ~ . MS
46 sir] *om.* F 1+
50 'Is] He's F 1+
52 Lady:] lady to MS

III.v

0. Scene IV. W, D
0.1 Jaques *and* Pedro] Pedro & Jaques MS
5 Empyricks . . . Mountebankes] people that are F 1+ (−Fg)

11 *s.d. Maria...truncks.*] Maria, *and servants.* F 1+ (−Fg)
12 th'] yᵉ MS
18 ye] you MS
18 he] 'a MS

142

19 'is] he's S, C, W; is F 1–2, MS,
    L, D, Fg
20–21 *Lined*: Thou...has | Been
    ...me. F 1–2
21.1 Sophocles, *and* Petronius]
    Sophocles, Petronius, Livia,
    Bianca & Tranio MS
22 Now] How MS
23 Heavens] Heaven F 1, C, W, D
23.1 *s.d.*] *om.* MS
26 mean] have a care MS
29 Alas he is infected] *om.* MS
    (My...extremely *one line*)
30 me] *om.* MS
33 Has] Hath F 1+
33 by this time] I thanke 'em MS
34–35 How...him?] *one line in* MS
35 this] these D
35.1 *Watch*] ye Watchmen MS
36 wits:—— O here's] wits, my
    freinds, MS
37 friends] fast MS
38 *s.d. They...door.*] *om.* F 1+
    (−Fg)
40 *Petruchio.*] Petruch. w^thin. MS
41 Ho] *om.* MS
48 'Had] H'had C, D; He had W
49 Wil...pleas'd] *one line in* MS,
    Fg
54 Gentlemen,] *om.* F 1+ (−Fg)
55–72 MS *follows line* 54 *with lines*
    65–70 *and then interpolates*
    '*Petro.* Fetch a Doctor presently
    | And if he can doe no good on
    him, he must to Bedlam.' *After*
    these lines MS *continues with*
    lines 73ff. 'Wil it please ye
    open?'
55–64 If...costard.] *om.* MS
59 beats] bears Fg
65 Death,] —— F 1–2, L, S; Pox
    C, W, D

65 ye] you MS
74–75 Let's...cure.] MS *lines*:
    Let's...all | Worldly cure.
74 sir] *om.* MS
78 *s.d. Exeunt*: ... *Watchmen.*]
    Exeunt. F 1–2, S
80 who's] who F 1–2
82–83 MS *lines*: These...ye, | The
    ...care | Ye...nothing.
84–85 The...knavery.] *om.* F 1+
    (−Fg)
90
1 Watchman. ...People,] *om.*
    F 1+ (−Fg)
92 instant——] ~ , MS
93 I] *om.* F 1+
96 as wel] wel F 1+
98 lives] lifes MS
100 I sweare] —— F 1–2, L, S; By
    heav'n, C, W, D
101 *1*] 2 MS
102 is a] is F 1; tis a MS
102 he's dangerous] *om.* MS
103 *2*] *1* MS
103 The devill] de de'il C
103 *s.d. Exit watch running.*] Exeunt
    running. MS
103 *s.d. , and...open*] *om.* F 1+
    (−Fg)
104 shoot] shot MS
105 ye] *om.* MS
106 mad, if] ~ : If MS
118 H'as] has MS; He'as F 2
119 he] a [*intrl.*] MS
121 Tumbrell] thumbrell MS
124 Can...hogs;] Can,,.againe:
    I could raile twenty daies; | Out
    on 'em hedgehogs, F 1–2, L, S
131 too] two F 2
137 those] these MS

IV.i

1–106 *om. scene* MS
9 a dozen] dozen F 1
12 she] you D
12 should] would F 2
14 a] i' C
20 Give] Give me S

31 and] add F 1
61 sweep] sweet S, C
70 *then, then*] then, S, C, W
74 you] your F 1
107 too] do S, C

IV.ii

2 pispots] looking-glasses F 1 +
(−Fg)
7 (Better...over)] ∧ ~ ... ~ ∧
MS
7 those] these F 1
9 those] these MS
11.1 Pedro *and* Jaques] Jaques and
Pedro MS
13 done] none D
23 the fault is] this fault MS
26 for:] ~ ∧ MS
30 two] the two MS
34 -heads——] ~ . MS
36 two] too MS
37 win] would (*intrl.*) win MS
38 make] made MS
41 (though...foolish,)] ∧ ~ ...
~ ∧ ∧ MS
42 Oh] on, D
42 Oh...for't!] (~ ... ~ ∧) MS
44 doe] *om.* S
44 this] this is S
46 came] come MS
47 a] *om.* MS
50 this] his S
53 come] to come MS
56 to be] *om.* MS
58 dealing] meaning MS

59 heaven] who F 1 + (−Fg)
59 whether] *ab. del.* 'away' MS
62 thanke me one day] one day
thank me W
62 alas,] *om.* MS
63 watch'd] watch MS
65 to] *om.* MS
76 breach] breach MS ('c' *intrl.*)
86 ran] runne MS
87–88 (Because...temper)] ∧ ~
... ~ , ∧ MS
88 -leech] -latch F 1
92 away] *om.* MS
99 families] family S, D
101 But...sir.] *om.* MS
116 cap a pe] *italic* F 2
121 continuing] continue MS
127 ²thou] thoug MS
137 well] *om.* MS
140 much] much as MS
142–143 I...stroke,] *one line in* MS
147 till] tell MS
147 I doe] doe I MS
149 but] a MS
156 *s.d.* Maria] *om.* MS
158 Fayries] furies MS
159 made] a man MS

IV.iii

1 Faith] *om.* F1+ (−Fg)
2 of] *om.* MS
4 constru'd] conster'd MS
5 little] a little MS
7 pound] pounds MS, F2
10 'em] them MS
14 *s.d.* Tranio] *om.* MS

20 minc'd] mixed MS
38 o'th] a'th MS
41 these] this MS
43 that] which F1+
46 pray] pray ye MS
47 So] Doe F1+
50 honestly] honesty F1+

IV.iv

1 on] a MS
5 your] *intrl.* MS (yor)
7 'em feare] them MS; 'em F2
7 on my word] I protest MS
8 *s.d.* Servant] *final* 's' *del.* MS, *which places after completed line* 7
11 Servant...Button?] MS *places after line* 12; 'button' *added later*
13 (*twice*), 14 o'th] a'th MS
14 and] *om.* F1+

15 MS *lines:* toothache | With
18.1 *Exit Servant.*] MS *places after first half of line*
24 old] od MS
25 daintily] daintly MS
26 to'th] to the MS
37, 44 ye——] ~ ˄ MS
48 o'] a MS
48 my] *om.* F1

IV.v

0.1 *and*] *om.* MS
5 again] *om.* F2, L
16–17 Out...runne?] *one line in* MS
24 the] *om.* MS
29 read yet] yet read S
29 yet] *om.* F1+ (−S)
31 ridden] rid S
35.1 *Enter*] *Enter's* MS
36 Weaves] waves MS
39 Ev'n] easie MS
39 teach] to teach MS
40 men have their] man hath his MS
43 She's] Shee is MS
44 if't] if it MS
46 (Saving...reverence)] ˄ ~ ...
   ~ ˄ MS
49 any] any one S
52–53 And...in?] *one line in* MS

54 sirha] *om.* MS
55.1 *Enter* Sophocles.] MS *places after the first half of line* 52
57 Sir,] *om.* MS
58 made] make F1
59 rid] ride MS
60 Pray] Pray, Sir, S
60 you] *om.* F1+
60 light] hand F1+
61 wife's] wife is MS
64 I sweare] Beleeve me F1+
69.1 *Enter* Maria.] F2 *places after first half of line* 70
76 a] *om.* MS
81 understanding)] ~ ˄ MS
83 sweeter——] ~ . MS
83 An] A MS
87 day] a day MS
88 I] Ile MS

105 She's] She is MS
108 woman-hood] man-hood MS
108 morall] mortal F2+ (−Fg)
110 know] I know MS
126–127 (That...christian)] ∧ ∼
   ... ∼ , MS
127 christian] a Christian MS
132 forget] forgive MS
135 happy] double S
142 (And...me)] ∧ ∼ ... ∼ ,
   MS
155 through...plough] plough...
   Seas S
155 Seas] sea MS
167 religion] adventure F1+ (−Fg)
167 pagans] nothing F1+ (−Fg:
   Pagans)
171 neerer] neere Fg
171 Jade] lade Fg
171 courser] courier C
175 i'th] in the MS

178 That...hereafter,] MS places
   after line 180
183 troth] —— F1–2, L, S; soul
   C, W, D
184 not you] you not MS
184 no] om. MS
185 her] Sir F1+ (−D, Fg)
186 for] om. MS
189 that] those MS
194 Cataya] Catayna MS
195 climes] climats MS
196 o'th] of the MS
197 aboard] abroad MS
200 out] om. F1
200 o'th] a'th MS
203 wouldst] would MS
207 of] a' MS
222 -water] -waters F1+
223 o'th] ['of' del.] o'th MS
226 custody——] ∼ ∧ MS
228 s.d. Maria] om. MS

V.i

0.1 with...papers] om. MS
2 discern] discern it MS
5 spoke] spake ['a' over 'o'] MS
14 that] om. MS
26 Petronius.] om. MS
26 Get] Will MS
27 too] two MS
27 s.d. Enter...Tranio.] MS places
   in line 26 after 'carriage'
28 Goodde'n] Good ev'n F1+
28 too,] intrl. MS
31 into] unto F1+
36–39 Petronius. Yes...sir.] om.
   MS
39 'twere] it MS
43 had] have F1+
45 your] you MS
46 execution] executions MS
47 till] tell MS
47 never was] was never MS

52 kind of] kind MS
58 you shall] shall MS, C
60 Why so] So F1+
60 pound sweats] pounds sweat MS
62–64 What...teatish.] MS lines:
   What...manly. | For...
   peevish.
63 Rowland,] om. MS
64 teatish] peevish MS; pettish F2
67 an] a MS
68.1 Enter....] Enter Livia sick
   carryed in a chaire by servants:
   Moroso by her. MS (marginal,
   starting on line 68)
69 draw 'em] beare her MS; draw
   her S, C, W
71–73 MS lines: O...better | Be-
   cause...me:
71 very sick, very] sick, very MS
72 I...lightsommer] om. MS

73 goodman] good man MS
76 perniciously] perintiously MS
79 in's] in his MS
82 (Oh...fellow:] *om.* MS
82 God] *om.* F2
85 extant] living F1+
85 purging-] *om.* MS
88 as] and as D
90 his] this MS, F2, L, S, Fg
95 Jumbled] I-['t' *del.*]umbled MS
105 young man] youngman MS
106 ʰhis] *om.* S.
116–117 MS *lines:* Pray...papers, |
    And...them,
117 'em] them MS
120 ye] you MS

120–121 Come...fall.] *one line in*
    MS
124 Begin] Being D
124 you] your MS
129 is this] it is MS
133 lie] sitt MS
134 your] our MS
135 Now] and MS
136 heare] have MS
136 *s.d.* Rowland...Moroso] Mor-
    oso. Rowland. Tranio MS
137 MS *lines:* lamentations, | Pray
144 Pen] the Pen MS
157 draw...close,] *om.* MS
163 fare ye wel] farewell MS
164 quit] quight ['g' *over* 'h'] MS

V.ii

0.1 ʰand] *om.* MS
0.1 *a trunke*] *Chest* F1+
1 Trunke] Trunks F1+
8 soule] word MS
10 'em] them MS
11 God] Heaven MS
12 ye] thee MS
13, 48 ye] you MS
16 powerfull] carefull MS
19 presently] instantly MS
19 O'] A MS
21 me] *intrl.* MS
26 amongst] among MS
27 *misereri*] Miscrere MS

29 o'] a MS
34 meet] met D
35 her tongue, her tongue.] her
    tongue! MS
38 lickrish——] ~ , MS
39 other] more MS
46 body] Body's S
56.1 Sophocles] *om.* MS
61–62 And...Heav'n] *one line in*
    MS
63 lose] lost Fg
63 fadings] longings F1, C, W, D;
    Fadding F2, L, S
67 MS *lines:* spurd. | With

V.iii

0.1 *and*] *om.* MS
10 By Heaven] —— F1; —— A
    F2, L; I sweare a MS, Fg
15 Two] An F1–2+; a MS
16, 26, 29 ye] you MS
19 Stay ye, stay ye] Stay, stay MS

21 with] *om.* F1–2, L
28 this] his F1
29 these] this MS
35 I sweare by Heaven] By ——
    F1–2, L, S; By Heaven C, W,
    D; I sweare MS, Fg

V.iv

0.1 *and...Coffin*] in a Coffin, carried by Servants MS
2.1 Jaques, *and* Pedro] *and* Jaques F1+ (−D); Jaques, Pedro MS
6, 7, 11, 51, 56 ye] you MS
7 after] after's S
14 and] a MS
39 *s.d.* Petruchio...*coffin.*] *om.* F1–2
40 By Heaven] ⸻ F1–2, L, S; I vow MS, Fg; Oh, God C
42 by Heaven] ⸻ F1–2, L, S; I sweare MS, Fg
49 sir] *om.* F1+
49 Once] Nay, once S

56 houre, since] houre‸ since, sicen F1
64, 65 his] thy F1
65.1 *and*] *om.* MS
65.1 *as from marriage*] *om.* F1+ (−Fg)
71–72 A...trick.] *one line in* MS
72 By Heaven] By ⸻ F1–2, L, S; I sweare, MS, Fg
74 ²done] *om.* F2
75 *Petruchio.*] *Petro.* MS
76 this:] ~ ‸ MS
90 he] to S
90.1 *Exeunt.*] *Exeunt.* | *Finis.* MS

Epilogue

1–12] *om.* MS

BONDUCA

edited by

CYRUS HOY

TEXTUAL INTRODUCTION

Fletcher's *Bonduca* was first printed in the 1647 Folio, but a manuscript of the play, written some ten to twenty years before, is preserved as Add. MS 36758 in the British Library. It was evidently prepared for a private patron, and is the work of the scribe Edward Knight, book-keeper of the King's Company in the later 1620s and the early 1630s. The prompt-book of *The Honest Man's Fortune* (licensed by Sir Henry Herbert, Master of the Revels, on 8 February 1625) was transcribed by Knight. His work as a theatrical adapter can be traced in the additions made in his hand to the manuscript prompt-books of Clavell's *The Soddered Citizen* (*ca* 1630) and Massinger's *Believe as You List* (licensed on 6 May 1631).

The manuscript of *Bonduca* has been described in detail by W. W. Greg[1] and by R. C. Bald.[2] It is a transcript, as the scribe tells us in a famous note, of Fletcher's 'fowle papers', these being all that were available in the absence of the prompt-book ('the booke where by it was first Acted from') which is reported lost. But the author's foul papers were themselves defective, and the scribe is reduced to summarizing (somewhat incorrectly) the action of the scenes (all of V.i–ii and the first thirty-six and one half lines of V.iii) missing from his copy. The foul papers clearly gave him trouble; the Historical Collation to the present edition sets forth in full the numerous occasions when Knight has misread his copy, or has omitted single words or phrases because he was not able to decipher it. We can judge of this because the prompt-book, missing when the manuscript was prepared sometime during the decade 1625–35,[3] had reappeared by 1647, when it served as the basis for the text of *Bonduca* in the first Beaumont and Fletcher

[1] In his 'Prompt Copies, Private Transcripts, and the Playhouse Scrivner', *The Library*, 4th ser. VI (1925), 151–3; in his *Dramatic Documents from the Elizabethan Playhouses* (Oxford, 1931), pp. 321–4; and in his edition of the manuscript for the Malone Society (Oxford, 1951).
[2] In his *Bibliographical Studies in the Beaumont and Fletcher Folio of 1647*, Supplement to the Bibliographical Society's Transactions, no. 13 (Oxford, 1938).
[3] Greg, Introduction to his Malone Society edition of the manuscript, p. x.

Folio. A comparison of the two texts shows signs of revision in F1, notably in the scene between Penyus and Petillius in IV.iii. The end of the play has been reworked in F1, with the introduction of six lines (not present in the manuscript) at V.iii.196–201. But not all the departures on exhibit between the manuscript and the First Folio texts necessarily imply revision; some of them, as Greg noted in the Introduction to his Malone Society edition of the manuscript (p. xii), 'can be explained by uncertainty regarding the intended position of marginal additions or the nature of alterations made in the foul papers'. The rough-draft status of the foul papers that lie behind the manuscript is suggested by its opening stage-direction, wherein Bonduca is found to have but a single daughter; Fletcher provided her with another as work on the play progressed. In transcribing Fletcher's foul papers, Knight frequently changed the author's characteristic second-person pronoun *ye* to *you*.[1] On the other hand, the contraction *'um* (for *them*), possibly a Fletcherian form, is found throughout the manuscript; in F1 it always occurs as *'em*. The F1 text is divided into acts and scenes; the text of the manuscript into acts only. The stage-directions differ widely in the two texts, as Greg (in *Dramatic Documents*, p. 322) noted, and he thus described the difference: 'While each has directions not found in the other, those of the manuscript are perhaps in general more numerous, and in particular tend to be fuller and more graphic. They suggest amplifications by the scribe writing for readers and with recollections of actual performance in mind.' Occasionally, as at II.iii.66, 116, 130; II.iv.41.1; IV.iv.133, 153, the manuscript supplies directions missing from F1, and these have been received into the text of the present edition.

For all its priority of date, there is no question of the British Library manuscript of *Bonduca* serving as copy-text for an edition of the play. With its large lacuna at the beginning of Act V, to say nothing of its numerous omissions of words, phrases and single lines elsewhere, its many misreadings and its unrevised state, it provides a distinctly inferior text to that of F1, on which the present

---

[1] *Ye* is found 352 times in the First Folio text of *Bonduca*; in Knight's manuscript it is found but 147 times. I have discussed the matter in 'The Shares of Fletcher and his Collaborators in the Beaumont and Fletcher Canon (1)', *Studies in Bibliography*, VIII (1956), 139.

edition is based. Nonetheless, the manuscript is far from useless to the editor of the play, for it preserves some eight important substantive readings that have been either altered or mistaken in the F1 text. In the Introduction to his edition of the manuscript (p. xii), Greg plausibly suggested that the censor was responsible for the F1 readings at I.i.37 ('tainted pleasures') and 87 ('hated ravisher'); the manuscript readings, surely the authoritative ones, are respectively '*Cæsars* pleasures' and 'high sett ravisher'. The manuscript corrects the text of the First Folio in the following additional places: I.i.144 ('barre their mentions' for F1 'burn their mentions'), I.ii.89 ('cheese and chibballs' for F1 'these, and Chibbals'), II.ii.56 ('*has liberty*' for F1 'his libertie'), III.v.79 ('sett vp stales for victories' for F1 'set up scales for Victories'), IV.iii.166 ('Eating Envy' for F1 'melting envie'), and IV.iv.76 ('bloody Sears' for F1 'bloody fears').[1] In addition to these substantive readings, the manuscript solves a problem, recognized by editors since Colman, concerning the division of speeches at the end of II.i. The present edition of *Bonduca* is the first to avail itself of the authority of the British Library manuscript. A complete record of the variants between it and the text of the play in the First Folio is published for the first time in the Historical Collation to this edition.

The Tragedy of Bonduca was printed in Section 5 of the 1647 Folio, the section assigned to R. Raworth. It occupies sigs. 4F4 through 4I4 (4I4^v is blank). The evidence of running titles suggests two-skeleton work for the three quires, with two verso and two recto titles appearing in an orderly sequence:

Verso: I   F4^v, G1^v, G3^v, H3^v, I1^v, I2^v
      III G2^v, G4^v, H1^v, H2^v, H4^v, I3^v
Recto: II G1, G3, H1, H3, H4, I1, I2
      IV G2, G4, H2, I3, I4

The Folio text seems to have been set by at least two compositors. Their work is distinguishable chiefly by certain differences in the

---

[1] Emendations by previous editors arrived independently at the manuscript reading in three of the cases that have just been cited: Sympson for II.ii.56 and III.v.79, and Dyce for IV.iv.76. To this list of manuscript corrections of F1 errors, Greg, in the Introduction to his edition of the manuscript (p. xii), added another, at II.iv.61 ('rouncing banquet' for F1 'running banquet'), but in this he was wrong. See the Textual Note on the passage following the text of the present edition.

abbreviation of speech-prefixes for Bonduca, Macer and Hengo. From the beginning of the play through sig. 4H3 these appear normally (though not invariantly) as *Bon.*, *Ma.* and *Hen.* From 4H3^v to the end, the forms are *Bond.*, *Mac.* (or *Macer*) and *Heng.* (though there is much variation of abbreviated forms for this character's speech headings on sig. 4I3^v). The compositor who set the opening of the play (sigs. 4F4–4F4^v) consistently italicized the words *Romanes* and *Britains*, a practice that ceases abruptly with the first line on sig. 4G1, and does not recur in the F1 text thereafter. In italicizing these words, the compositor may have been following copy; they are italicized throughout the manuscript.

The F1 text has been purged of oaths. In it, a dash regularly stands in such phrases as 'By——' or 'a —— consume ye'. Greg, in the Introduction to his edition of the manuscript (p. xii), noted that 'In some cases the manuscript supplies what is presumably the original reading, but in others the mildness of the manuscript expression or a difference of construction suggests that the scribe undertook some purging of his own.' This seems altogether likely when one considers that the scribe was the same Knight to whom Sir Henry Herbert, Master of the Revels, addressed his stern injunction of 21 October 1633 forbidding any 'oaths, prophaness, and publique ribaldry' to be presented to him 'in any playbooke, as you will answer it at your perill'.[1] In the text of the present edition, it has seemed best not to attempt to differentiate among what in the manuscript are Fletcher's original oaths and what are Knight's softened substitutions, but instead to adhere strictly to the copy-text and to reproduce the F1 dashes wherever they occur. The manuscript replacements for the dashes, together with the sundry oaths suggested by past editors, are recorded in the Historical Collation.

The present edition is based on a collation of six copies of F1: Cambridge University Library copy 1 (Aston a.Sel.19) and copy 2 (SSS.10.8), the Bodleian Library copy (B.1.8.Art.), the Folger Shakespeare Library copy, a copy in the Rush Rhees Library in the University of Rochester and a copy in my possession. No press-variants have been discovered.

[1] *The Dramatic Records of Sir Henry Herbert*, ed. J. Q. Adams (New Haven, 1917), p. 21.

The Persons Represented in the Play.

Caratach, *General of the* Britains, *Cosin to* Bonduca.
Nenius, *A great Soldier, a* Britain *Commander.*
Hengo, *A brave boy, Nephew to* Caratach.
Suetonius, *General to the* Roman *Army in* Britain.
Penius, *A brave* Roman *Commander, but stubborn to the General.*
Junius, *A* Roman *Captain, in love with* Bonduca's *Daughter.*
Petilus, *A merry Captain, but somewhat wanton.*
Demetrius, ⎫
⎬ *Two* Roman *Commanders.*
Decius, ⎭
Regulus,⎫   10
Drusus, ⎪
⎬*Four* Roman *Officers.*
Macer, ⎪
Curius, ⎭
Judas, *A Corporal, a merry hungry knave.*
Herald.
Druides.
Soldiers.
[Guides, Servants, A Messenger.]

WOMEN

Bonduca, *Queen of the* Iceni, *a brave* Virago.
Her two Daughters, by Prosutagus.   20

The Scene Britain.

The Principal Actors were

Richard Burbadge,	*Nich. Toolie,*	*John Underwood,*
Henry Condel,	*William Ostler,*	*Richard Robinson.*
William Eglestone,	*John Lowin,*	

The Persons...in the Play] *from* F 2; *om.* F 1
20 *by* Prosutagus] S; *after* Virago (*line* 19) *in* F 2, L

156

THE TRAGEDIE OF BONDUCA

Bonduca.   The hardy *Romanes?* O ye gods of *Britain,*
The rust of Arms, the blushing shame of souldiers;
Are these the men that conquer by inheritance?
The Fortune-makers? these the *Julians,*

Enter Caratach.

That with the Sun measure the end of Nature,
Making the world but one *Rome* and one *Cæsar?*
Shame, how they flee! *Cæsars* soft soul dwells in 'em;
Their mothers got 'em sleeping, pleasure nurst 'em,
Their bodies sweat with sweet oils, loves allurements,
Not lustie Arms. Dare they send these to seek us,   10
These *Romane* Girls? Is *Britain* grown so wanton?
Twice we have beat 'em, *Nennius,* scatter'd 'em,
And through their big-bon'd *Germans,* on whose Pikes
The honour of their actions sit in triumph,
Made Themes for songs to shame 'em, and a woman,
A woman beat 'em, *Nennius*; a weak woman,
A woman beat these *Romanes.*
Caratach.   So it seems.
A man would shame to talk so.
Bonduca.   Who's that?
Caratach.   I,
Bonduca.   Cousin, do ye grieve my fortunes?
Caratach.   No, *Bonduca,*
If I grieve, 'tis the bearing of your fortunes;   20
You put too much winde to your sail: Discretion
And hardie Valour are the twins of Honour,
And nurs'd together, make a Conquerour:
Divided, but a talker. 'Tis a truth,

19 ye] MS; you F1

157

That *Rome* has fled before us twice, and routed;
A truth we ought to crown the gods for, Lady,
And not our tongues. A truth is none of ours,
Nor in our ends, more then the noble bearing:
For then it leaves to be a vertue, Lady;
And we that have been Victors, beat our selves,   30
When we insult upon our honours subject.
Bonduca.   My valiant Cousin, is it foul to say
What liberty and honour bid us do,
And what the gods allow us?
Caratach.   No, *Bonduca,*
So what we say, exceed not what we do.
Ye call the *Romanes* fearful, fleeing *Romanes,*
And *Romane* Girls, the lees of *Cæsars* pleasures:
Does this become a doer? are they such?
Bonduca.   They are no more.
Caratach.   Where is your Conquest then?
Why are your Altars crown'd with wreathes of flowers,   40
The beasts with gilt horns waiting for the fire?
The holy *Druides* composing songs
Of everlasting life to Victory?
Why are these triumphs, Lady? for a *May*-game?
For hunting a poor herd of wretched *Romanes?*
Is it no more? shut up your Temples, *Britains,*
And let the Husband-man redeem his heifers;
Put out your holy fires; no Timbrel ring;
Let's home, and sleep; for such great overthrows,
A Candle burns too bright a sacrifice,   50
A Glow-worms tail too full a flame. O *Nennius,*
Thou hadst a noble Uncle knew a *Romane,*
And how to speak him, how to give him weight
In both his fortunes.
Bonduca.   By——I think
Ye doat upon these *Romanes, Caratach.*
Caratach.   Witnesse these wounds, I do; they were fairly given.
I love an enemy: I was born a souldier;

37 *Cæsars*] MS; tainted F 1   48 your] MS; our F 1

And he that in the head on's Troop defies me,
Bending my manly body with his sword,
I make a Mistris. Yellow-tressed *Hymen*   60
Ne'er ty'd a longing Virgin with more joy,
Then I am married to that man that wounds me:
And are not all these *Romane*? Ten struck Battels
I suckt these honour'd scars from, and all *Romane*:
Ten yeers of bitter nights and heavie marches,
When many a frozen storm sung thorow my Curasse,
And made it doubtful whether that or I
Were the more stubborn metal, have I wrought thorow,
And all to try these *Romanes*. Ten times a night
I have swom the Rivers, when the stars of *Rome*   70
Shot at me as I floated, and the billows
Tumbled their watry ruines on my shoulders,
Charging my batter'd sides with troops of Agues;
And still to try these *Romanes*, whom I found
(And if I lye, my wounds be henceforth backward,
And be you witnesse, gods, and all my dangers)
As ready, and as full of that I brought
(Which was not fear nor flight) as valiant,
As vigilant, as wise, to do and suffer,
Ever advanced as forward as the *Britains*,   80
Their sleeps as short, their hopes as high as ours,
I, and as subtil, Lady. 'Tis dishonour,
And, follow'd, will be impudence, *Bonduca*,
And grow to no belief, to taint these *Romanes*.
Have not I seen the *Britains*——
Bonduca.   What?
Caratach.   Dishearted,
Run, run, *Bonduca*, not the quick rack swifter;
The virgin from the high sett ravisher
Not half so fearful? not a flight drawn home,
A round stone from a Sling, a lovers wish
Ere made that haste that they have. By——   90

87 high sett] MS; hated F1

159

I have seen these *Britains*, that you magnifie,
Run as they would have out-run time, and roaring
Basely for mercy, roaring: the light shadows,
That in a thought scur ore the fields of Corn,
Halted on crutches to 'em.
Bonduca.   O ye Powers,
What scandals do I suffer?
Caratach.   Yes, *Bonduca*,
I have seen thee run too, and thee, *Nennius*;
Yea, run apace, both; then when *Penyus*
The *Romane* Girl cut thorow your armed Carts,   100
And drove 'em headlong on ye down the hill;
Then when he hunted ye, like *Britain*-Foxes,
More by the sent then sight: then did I see
These valiant and approved men of *Britain*,
Like boading Owls, creep into tods of Ivie,
And hoot their fears to one another nightly.
Nennius.   And what did you then, *Caratach*?
Caratach.   I fled too,
But not so fast; your Jewel had been lost then,
Young *Hengo* there; he trasht me, *Nennius*:
For when your fears out-run him, then stept I,
And in the head of all the *Romane* fury   110
Took him, and with my tough Belt to my back
I buckled him; behinde him, my sure Shield;
And then I follow'd. If I say I fought
Five times in bringing off this bud of *Britain*,
I lye not, *Nennius*. Neither had ye heard
Me speak this, or ever seen the childe more,
But that the son of vertue, *Penyus*,
Seeing me steer thorow all these storms of danger,
My helm still in my hand (my sword), my prow
Turn'd to my fo (my face), he cri'd out nobly,
Go, *Britain*, bear thy Lions whelp off safely;   120
Thy manly sword has ransom'd thee: grow strong,
And let me meet thee once again in arms;

100 drove] L; drive MS, F 1–2

160

Then if thou stand'st, thou art mine. I took his offer,
And here I am to honour him.
Bonduca.   O Cousin,
From what a flight of honour hast thou checkt me?
What wouldst thou make me, *Caratach?*
Caratach.   See, Lady,
The noble use of others in our losses;
Does this afflict ye? Had the *Romanes* cri'd this,
And as we have done theirs, sung out these fortunes,   130
Rail'd on our base condition, hooted at us,
Made marks as far as the earth was ours, to shew us
Nothing but sea could stop our flights; despis'd us,
And held it equal whether banquetting
Or beating of the *Britains* were more businesse,
It would have gall'd ye.
Bonduca.   Let me think we conquer'd.
Caratach. Do; but so think, as we may be conquer'd:
And where we have found vertue, though in those
That came to make us slaves, let's cherish it.
There's not a blowe we gave since *Julius* landed,   140
That was of strength and worth, but like Records
They file to after-ages. Our Registers,
The *Romanes*, are for noble deeds of honour;
And shall we barre their mentions with upbraidings?
Bonduca.   No more, I see my self: thou hast made me, Cousin,
More then my fortunes durst; for they abus'd me,
And wound me up so high, I swell'd with glory:
Thy temperance has cur'd that Tympany,
And given me health again, nay, more discretion.
Shall we have peace? for now I love these *Romanes*.   150
Caratach.   Thy love and hate are both unwise ones, Lady.
Bonduca.   Your reason?
Nennius.   Is not Peace the end of Arms?
Caratach.   Not where the cause implies a general Conquest:
Had we a difference with some pettie Isle,
Or with our neighbours (Lady) for our Land-marks,

144 barre] MS; burn F 1

The taking in of some rebellious Lord,
Or making a head against Commotions,
After a day of Blood, Peace might be argued:
But where we grapple for the ground we live on,
The Libertie we hold as dear as life,   160
The gods we worship, and next those, our Honours,
And with those swords that know no end of Battel:
Those men beside themselves allow no neighbour;
Those mindes that where the day is claim inheritance,
And where the sun makes ripe the fruits, their harvest,
And where they march, but measure out more ground
To adde to *Rome*, and here i' th' bowels on us;
It must not be; no, as they are our foes,
And those that must be so until we tire 'em,
Let's use the peace of Honour, that's fair dealing,   170
But in our ends, our swords. That hardy *Romane*
That hopes to graft himself into my stock,
Must first begin his kindred under ground,
And be alli'd in ashes.
Bonduca   *Caratach*,
As thou hast nobly spoken, shall be done;
And *Hengo* to thy charge I here deliver:
The *Romanes* shall have worthy Wars.
Caratach.   They shall.
And, little Sir, when your young bones grow stiffer,
And when I see ye able in a morning
To beat a dozen boys, and then to breakfast,
I'll tye ye to a sword.   180
Hengo.   And what then, Uncle?
Caratach.   Then ye must kill, Sir, the next valiant Romane
That calls ye knave.
Hengo.   And must I kill but one?
Caratach.   An hundred, boy, I hope.
Hengo.   I hope five hundred.
Caratach. That's a noble boy. Come, worthy Lady,
Let's to our several charges, and henceforth
Allow an enemy both weight and worth.   *Exeunt*.

Enter Junius *and* Petillius, *two Romane Captains.*

Petillius.   What ailst thou, man? dost thou want meat?
Junius.   No.
Petillius.   Clothes?
Junius.   Neither. For heavens love, leave me.
Petillius.   Drink?
Junius.   Ye tire me.
Petillius.   Come, 'tis drink; I know 'tis drink.
Junius.   'Tis no drink.
Petillius.   I say 'tis drink: for what affliction
  Can light so heavie on a Souldier,
  To dry him up as thou art, but no drink?
  Thou shalt have drink.
Junius.   Prethee, *Petillius*——
Petillius.   And by mine honour, much drink, valiant drink:
  Never tell me, thou shalt have drink. I see,
  Like a true friend, into thy wants: 'tis drink;   10
  And when I leave thee to a desolation,
  Especially of that dry nature, hang me.
Junius.   Why do you do this to me?
Petillius.   For I see,
  Although your modestie would fain conceal it,
  Which sits as sweetly on a Souldier,
  As an old side-saddle——
Junius.   What do you see?
Petillius.   I see as fair as day, that thou want'st drink.
  Did I not finde thee gaping like an Oyster
  For a new tide? thy very thoughts lie bare
  Like a lowe ebbe? thy soul that rid in Sack,   20
  Lies moor'd for want of liquor? Do but see
  Into thy self; for by——I do:
  For all thy body's chapt, and crackt like timber
  For want of moisture; what thou wantst there, *Junius*,
  And if it be not drink?
Junius.   You have too much on't.

17 fair] S; far MS, F 1–2

Petillius.   It may be a whore too; say it be: come, meecher,
  Thou shalt have both: a pretty valiant fellow,
  Die for a little lap and lechery?
  No, it shall ne'er be said in our Countrey,
  Thou dy'dst o' th' Chin-cough. Heare, thou noble Romane,   30
  The son of her that loves a Souldier,
  Hear what I promised for thee; thus I said,
  Lady, I take thy son to my companion,
  Lady, I love thy son, thy son loves war,
  The war loves danger, danger drink, drink discipline,
  Which is society and lechery;
  These two beget Commanders: fear not, Lady,
  Thy son shall lead.
Junius.   'Tis a strange thing, *Petillius,*
  That so ridiculous and loose a mirth
  Can master your affections.
Petillius.   Any mirth,   40
  And any way, of any subject, *Junius,*
  Is better then unmanly mustinesse:
  What harm's in drink, in a good wholesom wench?
  I do beseech ye, Sir, what errour? yet
  It cannot out of my head handsomly,
  But thou wouldst fain be drunk: come, no more fooling,
  The General has new wine, new come over.
Junius.   He must have new acquaintance for it too,
  For I will none, I thank ye.
Petillius.   None, I thank ye?
  A short and touchie answer. None I thank ye: 50
  Ye do not scorn it, do ye?
Junius.   Gods defend Sir;
  I owe him still more honour.
Petillius.   None, I thank ye:
  No company, no drink, no wench, I thank ye.
  Ye shall be worse intreated, Sir.
Junius.   *Petillius,*
  As thou art honest, leave me.
Petillius.   None, I thank ye;

A modest and a decent resolution,
And well put on. Yes, I will leave ye, *Junius*,
And leave ye to the boys, that very shortly
Shall all salute ye, by your new sirname
Of *Junius* none I thank ye. I would starve now,   60
Hang, drown, despair, deserve the forks, lie open
To all the dangerous passes of a wench,
Bound to believe her tears, and wed her aches,
Ere I would own thy follies. I have found ye,
Your lays, and out-leaps *Junius*, haunts, and lodges:
I have view'd ye, and I have found ye by my skill
To be a fool o' th' first head, *Junius*,
And I will hunt ye: ye are in love, I know it:
Ye are an asse, and all the Camp shall know it:
A peevish idle boy; your dame shall know it;   70
A wronger of my care; your self shall know it.

Enter Corporal Judas, *and four souldiers.*

Judas.   A Bean? a princely diet, a full banquet,
To what we compasse.
1. Souldier.   Fight like hogs for Acorns?
2. Souldier.   Venture our lives for pig-nuts?
Petillius.   What ail these Rascals?
3. Souldier.   If this hold, we are starv'd.
Judas.   For my part, friends,
Which is but twenty Beans a day, a hard world
For Officers, and men of action;
And those so clipt by master mouse, and rotten:
For understand 'em French Beans, where the fruits
Are ripen'd like the people, in old tubs.   80
For mine own part, I say, I am starv'd already,
Not worth another Bean, consum'd to nothing,
Nothing but flesh and bones left, miserable:
Now if this mustie provender can prick me
To honourable matters of atchievement, Gentlemen,
Why there's the point.

4. Souldier.   I'll fight no more.
Petillius.   You'll hang then,
A soveraign help for hunger. Ye eating Rascals,
Whose gods are Beef and Brewis, whose brave angers
Do execution upon cheese, and Chibbals:
Ye dogs heads i' th' porridge pot; you fight no more?   90
Does *Rome* depend upon your resolution
For eating mouldy pie-crust?
3. Souldier.   Would we had it.
Judas.   I may do service, Captain.
Petillius.   In a Fish-market.
You, Corporal Curry-comb, what will your fighting
Profit the Common-wealth? do you hope to triumph,
Or dare your vamping valour, good man Cobler,
Clap a new soal to th' Kingdom? s'death, ye dog-whelps
You, fight, or not fight.
Judas.   Captain.
Petillius.   Out, ye flesh-flyes,
Nothing but noyce and nastinesse.
Judas.   Give us meat,
Whereby we may do.
Petillius.   Whereby hangs your valor?   100
Judas.   Good bits afford good blows.
Petillius.   A good position:
How long is't since thou eat'st last? wipe thy mouth,
And then tell truth.
Judas.   I have not eat to th' purpose——
Petillius.   To th' purpose? what's that? half a Cow, and Garlick?
Ye Rogues, my Company eat Turf, and talk not;
Timber they can digest, and fight upon't;
Old matts, and mud with spoons, rare meats. Your shoes, slaves,
Dare ye cry out of hunger, and those extant?
Suck your Sword-hilts, ye slaves, if ye be valiant;
Honour will make 'em march-pain: to the purpose?   110
A grievous penance. Dost thou see that Gentleman,
That melancholy Monsieur?

89 cheese] MS; these F1–2

166

Junius.   Pray ye, *Petillius.*
Petillius.   He has not eat these three weeks.
2. Souldier.   'Has drunk the more then,
3. Souldier.   And that's all one.
Petillius.   Nor drunk nor slept these two months.
Judas.   Captain, we do beseech ye as poor Souldiers,
  Men that have seen good days, whose mortal stomacks
  May somtime feel afflictions.
Junius.   This, *Petillius,*
  Is not so nobly done.
Petillius.   'Tis common profit;
  Urge him to th' point, he'll finde ye out a food
  That needs no teeth nor stomack; a strange formity   120
  Will feed ye up as fat as hens i' th' foreheads,
  And make ye fight like Fichocks, to him.
Judas.   Captain.
Junius.   Do you long to have your throats cut?
Petillius.   See what metal
  It makes in him: two meals more of this melancholy,
  And there lies *Caratach.*
Judas.   We do beseech ye.
2. Souldier.   Humbly beseech your valour.
Junius.   Am I onely
  Become your sport, *Petillius?*
Judas.   But to render
  In way of general good, in preservation.
Junius.   Out of my thoughts, ye slaves.
4. Souldier.   Or rather pitie.
3. Souldier.   Your warlike remedy against the maw-worms.   130
Judas.   Or notable receipt to live by nothing.
Petillius.   Out with your Table-books.
Junius.   Is this true friendship?
  And must my killing griefs make others *May*-games?
  Stand from my swords point, slaves; your poor starv'd spirits
  Can make me no oblations; else, O love,
  Thou proudly blind destruction, I would send thee

115, 119 ye] MS; you F1–2

Whole Hecatombs of hearts, to bleed my sorrows.
Judas.   Alas, he lives by love, Sir.   *Exit* Junius.
Petillius.   So he does, Sir,
  And cannot you do so too? All my Company
  Are now in love, ne'er think of meat, nor talk   140
  Of what Provant is: aymees, and hearty hey-hoes,
  Are Sallets fit for Souldiers. Live by meat,
  By larding up your bodies? 'tis lewd, and lazie,
  And shews ye meerly mortal, dull, and drives ye
  To fight like Camels, with baskets at your noses.
  Get ye in love; ye can whore well enough,
  That all the world knows: fast ye into Famine,
  Yet ye can crawl like Crabs to wenches, handsomly.
  Fall but in love now, as ye see example,
  And follow it but with all your thoughts, *probatum*,   150
  There's so much charge sav'd, and your hungers ended.
  Away, I hear the General: get ye in love all,   *Drum afar off.*
  Up to the ears in love, that I may hear
  No more of these rude murmurings; and discreetly
  Carry your stomacks, or I prophesie
  A pickel'd rope will choke ye. Jog, and talk not.
                      Exeunt [Judas *and four Soldiers*].

        Enter Swetonius, Demetrius, Decius, *Drum, Colours.*

Swetonius.   *Demetrius*, is the messenger dispatch'd
  To *Penyus*, to command him to bring up
  The Volans Regiment?
Demetrius.   He's there by this time.
Swetonius.   And are the horse well view'd we brought from
        Mona?   160
Decius.   The Troops are full, and lusty.
Swetonius.   Good *Petillius*,
  Look to those eating Rogues, that bawl for victuals,
  And stop their throats a day or two: provision
  Waits but the winde to reach us.
Petillius.   Sir, already
  I have been tampring with their stomacks, which I finde

As deaf as Adders to delays: your clemency
Hath made their murmurs, mutinies, nay, rebellions:
Now, and they want but Mustard, they're in uproars:
No oil but Candy, Lucitanian figs,
And wine from Lesbos, now can satisfie 'em: 170
The British waters are grown dull and muddy,
The fruit disgustful: Orontes must be sought for,
And Apples from the happie Isles: the truth is,
They are more curious now in having nothing,
Then if the sea and land turn'd up their treasures:
This lost the Colonies, and gave *Bonduca*
(With shame we must record it) time and strength
To look into our Fortunes; great discretion
To follow offered Victory; and last, full pride
To brave us to our teeth, and scorn our ruines.   180
Swetonius.   Nay, chide not, good *Petillius*, I confesse
My will to conquer Mona, and long stay
To execute that will, let in these losses:
All shall be right again, and as a pine
Rent from Oeta by a sweeping tempest,
Joynted again, and made a Mast, defies
Those angry windes that split him: so will I,
Piec'd to my never-failing strength and fortune,
Steer thorow these swelling dangers, plow their prides up,
And bear like thunder through their loudest tempests: 190
They keep the field still.
Demetrius.   Confident and full.
Petillius.   In such a number, one would swear they grew,
The hills are wooded with their partizans,
And all the valleys over-grown with darts,
As moors are with rank rushes: no ground left us
To charge upon, no room to strike: say fortune
And our endeavours bring us in to 'em,
They are so infinite, so ever-springing,
We shall be kill'd with killing; of desperate women,
That neither fear, or shame ere found, the devill   200

170 Lesbos] MS; Lestos F1

Has rankt amongst 'em multitudes: say the men fail,
They'll poison us with their petticoats: say they fail,
They have priests enough to pray us into nothing.
Swetonius.   These are imaginations, dreams of nothings,
The man that doubts or fears.
Decius.   I am free of both.
Demetrius.   The self-same I.
Petillius.   And I as free as any;
As carelesse of my flesh, of that we call life,
So I may lose it nobly; as indifferent
As if it were my diet. Yet, noble General,
It was a wisedom learn'd from you; I learn'd it,   210
And worthy of a Souldiers care, most worthy,
To weigh with most deliberate circumstance
The ends of accidents, above their offers;
How to go on and get, to save a Romane,
Whose one life is more worth in way of doing,
Then millions of these painted wasps; how viewing
To finde advantage out; how, found, to follow it
With counsel and discretion, lest meer fortune
Should claim the victory.
Swetonius.   'Tis true, *Petillius,*
And worthily remembred: the rule's certain,   220
Their uses no lesse excellent: but where time
Cuts off occasions, danger, time and all
Tend to a present peril, 'tis required
Our Swords and Manhoods be best counsellors,
Our expeditions, presidents. To win, is nothing,
Where reason, time and counsel are our Camp-masters:
But there to bear the field, then to be conquerours,
Where pale destruction takes us, takes us beaten,
In wants, and mutinies, our selves but handfuls,
And to our selves our own fears, needs a new way,   230
A sudden and a desperate execution:
Here, how to save, is losse; to be wise, dangerous;
Onely a present well-united strength,
And mindes made up for all attempts, dispatch it:

Disputing and delay here, cools the courage;
Necessity gives no time for doubts; things infinite,
According to the spirit they are preach'd to,
Rewards like them; and names for after-ages,
Must steel the Souldier; his own shame help to arm him;
And having forc'd his spirit, ere he cools,   240
Fling him upon his enemies; sudden and swift,
Like Tygers amongst Foxes, we must fight for't:
Fury must be our Fortune; shame we have lost,
Spurs ever in our sides to prick us forward:
There is no other wisedom nor discretion
Due to this day of ruine, but destruction;
The Souldiers order first, and then his anger.
Demetrius.   No doubt they dare redeem all.
Swetonius.   Then no doubt
The day must needs be ours. That the proud woman
Is infinite in number, better likes me,   250
Then if we dealt with squadrons: half her Army
Shall choke themselves, their own swords dig their graves.
I'll tell ye all my fears, one single valour,
The vertues of the valiant *Caratach*
More doubts me then all *Britain*: he's a Souldier
So forg'd out, and so temper'd for great fortunes,
So much man thrust into him, so old in dangers,
So fortunate in all attempts, that his meer name
Fights in a thousand men, himself in millions,
To make him Romane. But no more. *Petillius,*   260
How stands your charge?
Petillius.   Ready for all employments,
To be commanded too, Sir.
Swetonius.   'Tis well govern'd;
To morrow we'll draw out, and view the Cohorts:
I'th' mean time, all apply their Offices.
Where's *Junius?*
Petillius.   In's Cabbin, sick o'th' mumps, Sir.
Swetonius.   How?

236 no] W (*conj.* C); *om.* MS, F 1–2

Petillius.   In love, indeed in love, most lamentably loving,
To the tune of Queen *Dido.*
Decius.   Alas poor Gentleman.
Swetonius.   'Twill make him fight the nobler. With what Lady?
I'll be a spokesman for him.
Petillius.   You'll scant speed, Sir.
Swetonius.   Who is't?
Petillius.   The devils dam, *Bonduca*'s daughter,   270
Her youngest, crackt i'th' ring.
Swetonius.   I am sorry for him:
But sure his own discretion will reclaim him,
He must deserve our anger else. Good Captains,
Apply your selves in all the pleasing forms
Ye can, unto the Souldiers; fire their spirits,
And set 'em fit to run this action;
Mine own provision shall be shar'd amongst 'em,
Till more come in: tell 'em, if now they conquer,
The fat of all the kingdom lies before 'em,
Their shames forgot, their honours infinite,   280
And want for ever banisht. Two days hence,
Our fortunes, and our swords, and gods be for us.   *Exeunt.*

                   Enter Penyus, Regulus, Macer, Drusus.   II. i

Penyus.   I must come?
Macer.   So the General commands, Sir.
Penyus.   I must bring up my Regiment?
Macer.   Believe, Sir,
I bring no lye.
Penyus.   But did he say, I must come?
Macer.   So delivered.
Penyus.   How long is't, *Regulus*, since I commanded
In *Britain* here?
Regulus.   About five yeers, great *Penyus.*
Penyus.   The General some five months. Are all my actions
So poor, and lost, my services so barren,
That I'm remembred in no nobler language

But Must come up?
Macer.　　　　　　I do beseech ye, Sir,　　　　　10
　Weigh but the times estate.
Penyus.　　　　　　Yes, good Lieutenant,
　I do, and his that sways it. Must come up?
　Am I turn'd bare Centurion? Must, and shall,
　Fit embasses to court my honour?
Macer.　　　　　　　Sir——
Penyus. Set me to lead a handful of my men
　Against an hundred thousand barbarous slaves
　That have marcht name by name with *Romes* best doers?
　Serve 'em up some other meat; I'll bring no food
　To stop the jaws of all those hungry wolfs.
　My Regiment's mine own. I must, my language.　　　　20

　　　　　Enter Curius.

Curius. *Penyus,* where lies the host?
Penyus.　　　　　　Where Fate may finde 'em.
Curius. Are they ingirt?
Penyus.　　　　The Battel's lost.
Curius.　　　　　　So soon?
Penyus. No; but 'tis lost, because it must be won:
　The Britains must be Victors. Who ere saw
　A troop of bloody Vultures hovering
　About a few corrupted carcases,
　Let him behold the silly Romane host,
　Girded with millions of fierce Britain Swains,
　With deaths as many as they have had hopes;
　And then go thither, he that loves his shame;　　　　30
　I scorn my life, yet dare not lose my name.
Curius. Do not you hold it a most famous end,
　When both our names and lives are sacrific'd
　For *Romes* encrease?
Penyus.　　　　　Yes, *Curius;* but mark this too;
　What glory is there, or what lasting fame
　Can be to *Rome,* or us? what full example,
　When one is smother'd with a multitude,

And crowded in amongst a namelesse presse?
Honour got out of flint, and on their heads
Whose vertues, like the Sun, exhal'd all valours, 40
Must not be lost in mists and fogs of people,
Notelesse, and out of name, but rude and naked:
Nor can *Rome* task us with impossibilities,
Or bid us fight against a flood: we serve her,
That she may proudly say she has good souldiers,
Not slaves to choke all hazards. Who but fools,
That make no difference betwixt certain dying,
And dying well, would fling their fames and fortunes
Into this Britain-gulf, this quicksand-ruine,
That sinking, swallows us? What noble hand 50
Can finde a subject fit for blood there? or what sword
Room for his execution? What air to cool us,
But poison'd with their blasting breaths and curses,
Where we lie buried quick above the ground,
And are with labouring sweat, and breathlesse pain,
Kill'd like to slaves, and cannot kill again?
Drusus. *Penyus*, mark ancient Wars, and know that then
A Captain weigh'd an hundred thousand men.
Penyus. *Drusus*, mark ancient wisdom, and you'll finde then
He gave the overthrow that sav'd his men. 60
I must not go.
Regulus. The souldiers are desirous,
Their Eagles all drawn out, Sir.
Penyus. Who drew up, *Regulus*?
Ha? speak: did you? whose bold will durst attempt this?
Drawn out? why, who commands, Sir? on whose warrant
Durst they advance?
Regulus. I keep mine own obedience.
Drusus. 'Tis like the general cause, their love of honour,
Relieving of their wants.
Penyus. Without my knowledge?
Am I no more? my place but at their pleasures?
Come, who did this?

46 Not] MS; nor F1   58 A Captain] C; the Captaines MS; Captains F1–2

174

Drusus.   By—— Sir, I am ignorant.

Drum softly within: then enter Souldiers with Drum and Colours.

Penyus.   What, am I grown a shadow? Heark, they march.
I will know, and will be my self. Stand, disobedience;   70
He that advances one foot higher, dies for't.
Run thorow the Regiment upon your duties,
And charge 'em on command: beat back again,
By——I'll tith 'em all else.
Regulus.   We'll do our best.

Exeunt Drusus *and* Regulus.

Penyus.   Back; cease your bawling Drums there,
I'll beat the Tubs about your brains else. Back:
Do I speak with lesse fear then Thunder to ye?
Must I stand to beseech ye? home, home: ha?
Do ye stare upon me? Are those mindes I moulded,
Those honest valiant tempers I was proud   80
To be a fellow to, those great discretions
Made your names fear'd and honour'd, turn'd to wildfires?
O gods, to disobedience? Command, farewel;
And be ye witnesse with me, all things sacred,
I have no share in these mens shames. March, Souldiers,
And seek your own sad ruines; your old *Penyus*
Dares not behold your murders.
1. Souldier.   Captain.
2. Souldier.   Captain.
3. Souldier.   Dear honour'd Captain.
Penyus.   Too too dear lov'd Souldiers,
Which made ye weary of me: and heaven yet knows,
Though in your mutinies, I dare not hate you;   90
Take your own wills; 'tis fit your long experience
Should now know how to rule your selves: I wrong ye,
In wishing ye to save your lives and credits,
To keep your necks whole from the Ax hangs ore ye:
Alas, I much dishonour'd ye: go, seek the Britains,
And say ye come to glut their Sacrifices;

88 1. Souldier.] MS; Sould. F1–2

But do not say I sent ye. What ye have been,
How excellent in all parts, good, and govern'd,
Is onely left of my Command, for story; 100
What now ye are, for pitie. Fare ye well.

Enter Drusus *and* Regulus.

Drusus. Oh turn again, great *Penyus*; see the Souldier
In all points apt for duty.
Regulus.   See his sorrow
For his disobedience, which he says was haste,
And haste (he thought) to please you with. See, Captain,
The toughnesse of his courage turn'd to water;
See how his manly heart melts.
Penyus.   Go, beat homeward,
There learn to eat your little with obedience,
And henceforth strive to do as I direct ye.

Exeunt Souldiers.

Macer. My answer, Sir.
Penyus.   Tell the great General, 110
My Companies are no fagots to fill breaches;
My self no man that must, or shall, can carry:
Bid him be wise; and where he is, he's safe then;
And when he findes out possibilities,
He may command me. Commend me to the Captains.
Macer. All this I shall deliver.
Penyus.   Farewel, *Macer.*

Exit Penyus.

Curius. Pray gods this breed no mischief.
Regulus.   It must needs,
If stout *Swetonius* win; for then his anger,
Besides the Souldiers losse of due, and honour,
Will break together on him.
Drusus.   He's a brave fellow; 120
And but a little hide his haughtinesse,
(Which is but sometimes neither, on some causes)
He shews the worthiest *Romane* this day living.
You may, good *Curius*, to the General

176

Make all things seem the best.
Curius.   I shall endeavour:
Pray for our fortunes, Gentlemen. If we fall,
This one farewel serves for a Funeral.
Regulus. The gods make sharp your swords, and steel your hearts;
We dare, alas, but cannot fight our parts.

Exeunt.

Enter Junius, Petillius *and a* Herald.   II. ii

Petillius. Let him go on: stay, now he talks.
Junius.   Why?
Why should I love mine enemie? what is beauty?
Of what strange violence, that like the plague,
It works upon our spirits? blind they faign him,
I am sure, I find it so.
Petillius.   A dog shall lead ye.
Junius. His fond affections blinder.
Petillius.   Hold ye there still.
Junius. It takes away my sleep——
Petillius.   Alas, poor chicken.
Junius. My company, content; almost my fashion.
Petillius. Yes, and your weight too, if you follow it.
Junius. 'Tis sure the plague, for no man dare come neer me   10
Without an Antidote: 'tis far worse; Hell.
Petillius. Thou art damn'd without redemption then.
Junius.   The way to't
Strow'd with fair Western smiles, and April blushes,
Led by the brightest constellations; eyes,
And sweet proportions, envying heaven: but from thence
No way to guide, no path, no wisdome brings us.
Petillius. Yes, a smart water, *Junius.*
Junius.   Do I fool?
Know all this, and fool still? Do I know further,
That when we have enjoy'd our ends, we lose 'em,
And all our appetites are but as dreams   20

*128 *Regulus.*] MS; *om.* F1–2   128 your...your] MS; our...our F1–2

Wee laugh at in our ages.
Petillius. Sweet Philosopher!
Junius. Do I know on still, and yet know nothing? Mercie gods,
Why am I thus ridiculous?
Petillius. Motley on thee,
Thou art an arrant Asse.
Junius. Can red and white,
An eye, a nose, a cheek——
Petillius. But one cheek, *Junius?*
An half-fac'd Mistris?
Junius. With a little trim,
That wanton fools call Fashion, thus abuse mee?
Take me beyond my reason? Why should not I
Doat on my horse well trapt, my sword well hatch'd?
They are as handsom things, to mee more usefull, 30
And possible to rule too. Did I but love,
Yet 'twere excusable, my youth would bear it;
But to love there, and that no time can give me,
Mine honour dare not ask: shee has been ravish'd
My nature, must not know; she hates our Nation.
Thus to dispose my spirit!
Petillius. Stay a little,
He will declame again.
Junius. I will not love; I am a man, have reason,
And I will use it: I'll no more tormenting,
Nor whining for a wench, there are a thousand—— 40
Petillius. Hold thee there boy.
Junius. A thousand will intreat me.
Petillius. Ten thousand, *Junius.*
Junius. I am young and lustie,
And to my fashion valiant; can please nightly.
Petillius. I'll swear thy back's *probatum,* for I have known thee
Leap at sixteen like a strong Stallion.
Junius. I will be man again.
Petillius. Now mark the working,
The divell and the spirit tug for't: twenty pound
Upon the divels head.

Junius.   I must be wretched.
Petillius.   I knew I had won.
Junius.   Nor have I so much power
To shun my fortune.
Petillius.   I will haunt thy fortune   50
With all the shapes imagination breeds,   *Musick.*
But I will fright thy divell: Stay, he sings now.
            Song, by Junius, *and* Petillius *after him in mockage.*
Junius.   Must I be thus abus'd?
Petillius.   Yes mary must ye.
Let's follow him close: oh, there he is, now read it.
*Herald (reads). It is the Generals command, that all sick, persons old
and unable, retire within the Trenches; hee that fears has libertie, to
leave the Field: Fools, boyes, and lovers must not come neer the
Regiments, for fear of their infections; especially those Cowards they
call Lovers.*
Junius.   Hah?   60
Petillius.   Read on.
*Herald. If any common Souldier love an Enemie, hee's whip'd and
made a slave: If any Captain; cast, with losse of honours, flung out
o'th' Army, and made unable ever after to bear the name of a Souldier.*
Junius.   The——consume ye all, Rogues.
                                                    Exit Junius.
Petillius.   Let this work:
H'as something now to chew upon: he's gone,
Come, shake no more.
Herald.   Well, Sir, you may command me,
But not to doe the like again for Europe:
I would have given my life for a bent two-pence,
If I ere read to lovers whilst I live again,   70
Or come within their confines——
Petillius.   There's your payment,
And keep this private.
Herald.   I am school'd for talking.
                                                    Exit Herald.

50 haunt] MS; hunt F 1–2   56 *has*] MS; *his* F 1–2

Enter Demetrius.

Petillius.   How now, *Demetrius*, are we drawn?
Demetrius.   'Tis doing:
  Your Company stands fair; but pray ye, where's *Junius*?
  Half his command are wanting, with some forty
  That *Decius* leads.
Petillius.   Hunting for victuals:
  Upon my life free-booting Rogues, their stomacks
  Are like a widows lust, nere satisfied.
Demetrius.   I wonder how they dare stir, knowing the enemy
  Master of all the Countrey.
Petillius.   Resolute hungers   80
  Know neither fears, nor faiths, they tread on ladders,
  Ropes, gallowes, and overdoe all dangers.
Demetrius.   They may be hang'd though.
Petillius.   There's their joyfull supper,
  And no doubt they are at it.
Demetrius.   But for heavens sake,
  How does young *Junius*?
Petillius.   Drawing on, poor Gentleman.
Demetrius.   What, to his end?
Petillius.   To th' end of all flesh: woman.
Demetrius.   This Love has made him a stout Souldier.
Petillius.   O, a great one,
  Fit to command young goslings: but what news?
Demetrius.   I think the messenger's come back from *Penyus*
  By this time, let's go know.
Petillius.   What will you say now   90
  If he deny to come, and take exceptions
  At some half syllable, or sound deliverd
  With an ill accent, or some stile left out?
Demetrius.   I cannot think he dare.
Petillius.   He dare speak treason,
  Dare say, what no man dares beleeve, dares doe——
  But that's all one: I'd lay ye my black armour

96 ye] MS; you F 1–2

To twenty crowns, he comes not.
Demetrius.   Done.
Petillius.   You'll pay.
Demetrius. I will.
Petillius.   Then keep thine old use *Penyus,*
Be stubborn and vain glorious, and I thank thee.
Come let's go pray for six hours: most of us   100
I fear, will trouble heaven no more: two good blowes
Struck home at two Commanders of the Britains,
And my part's done.
Demetrius.   I do not think of dying.
Petillius. 'Tis possible we may live. But *Demetrius,*
With what strange legs, and arms, and eyes, and noses,
Let Carpenters and Copper-smiths consider.
If I can keep my heart whole, and my wind-pipe,
That I may drink yet like a Souldier——
Demetrius. Come, let's have better thoughts; mine's on your
Armour.
Petillius. Mine's in your purse, Sir: Let's go try the wager.   110
                                        Exeunt.

Enter Judas *and his four Companions* (*halters about their necks*) II. iii
        Bonduca, *her* Daughters, Nennius *following.*

Bonduca. Come, hang 'm presently.
Nennius.   What made your Rogueships
Harrying for victuals here? Are we your friends?
Or doe you come for Spies? tell me directly,
Would you not willingly be hang'd now? do not ye long for't?
Judas. What say ye? shall wee hang in this vain? Hang we must,
And 'tis as good to dispatch it merrily,
As pull an arse like dogs to't.
1. Souldier.   Any way,
So it be handsome.
3. Souldier. I had as lief 'twere toothsom too: but all agree,
And I'll not out Boyes.
4. Souldier.   Let's hang plesantly.   10

Judas. Then plesantly be it: Captain, the truth is,
We had as lief hang with meat in our mouthes,
As ask your pardon empty.

Bonduca. These are brave hungers.
What say you to a leg of Beef now, sirha?

Judas. Bring me acquainted with it, and I'll tell ye.

Bonduca. Torment 'em wenches: I must back; then hang 'em.

[*Exit* Bonduca.]

Judas. We humbly thank your Grace.

1. Daughter. The Rogues laugh at us.

2. Daughter. Sirha, What think you of a wench now?

Judas. A wench, Lady?
I do beseech your Ladiship, retire,
I'll tell ye presently, ye see the time's short; 20
One crash; even to the setling of my conscience.

Nennius. Why, is't no more but up, boyes?

Judas. Yes, ride too Captain.
Will you but see my seat?

1. Daughter. Ye shall be set, Sir,
Upon a Jade shall shake ye.

Judas. Sheets, good Madam,
Will do it ten times better.

1. Daughter. Whips, good Souldier,
Which ye shall taste before ye hang, to mortifie ye;
'Tis pitie ye should die thus desperate.

2. Daughter. These are the merry Romans, the brave madcaps.
'Tis ten to one wee'll cool your resolutions.
Bring out the whips.

Judas. Would your good Ladyships 30
Would exercise 'em too.

4. Souldier. Surely Ladies,
We'ld shew you a strange patience.

Nennius. Hang 'em, Rascals,
They'l talk thus on the wheel.

Enter Caratach.

182

Caratach.   Now what's the matter?
What are these fellows? whats the crime committed,
That they wear necklaces?
Nennius.   They are Roman Rogues,
Taken a forraging.
Caratach.   Is that all, *Nennius?*
Judas.   Would I were fairly hang'd; this is the divell,
The kill-cow *Caratach.*
Caratach.   And you would hang 'em.
Nennius.   Are they not enemies?
1. Souldier.   My breech makes buttons.
1. Daughter.   Are they not our tormentors?
Caratach.   Tormentors? Flea-traps. 40
Pluck off your halters, fellows.
Nennius.   Take heed, *Caratach,*
Taint not your wisdome.
Caratach.   Wisdome, *Nennius?*
Why, who shall fight against us, make our honours,
And give a glorious day into our hands,
If we dispatch our foes thus? what's their offence?
Stealing a loafe or two to keep out hunger,
A piece of greazie bacon, or a pudding?
Do these deserve the gallows? They are hungry,
Poor hungry knaves, no meat at home left, starv'd:
Art thou not hungry?
Judas.   Monstrous hungry.   50
Caratach.   He looks like hungers self: get 'em some victuals,
And wine to cheer their hearts, quick: Hang up poor pilchers?
2. Souldier.   This is the bravest Captain——
Nennius.   *Caratach,*
I'll leave you to your will.
Caratach.   I'll answer all, Sir.   [*Exit* Nennius.]
2. Daughter.   Let's up, and view his entertainment of 'em.
I am glad they are shifted any way, their tongues else
Would still have murdred us.
1. Daughter.   Let's up, and see it.
                                   Exeunt [Daughters].

Enter Hengo.

Caratach.   Sit down poor knaves: why, where's this wine and
   victuals?
   Who waites there?
Servant (within).   Sir, 'tis coming.
Hengo.   Who are these Uncle?
Caratach.   They are Romans, Boy.
Hengo.   Are these they   60
   That vex mine Aunt so? can these fight? they look
   Like emptie scabbards, all, no mettle in 'em,
   Like men of clouts, set to keep crows from orchards;
   Why, I dare fight with these.
Caratach.   That's my good chicken. And how do ye?
   How do you feel your stomacks?

Enter [*Servant*] *with wine and meate.*

Judas.   Wondrous apt, Sir,
   As shall appear when time calls.
Caratach.   That's wel, down with't,
   A little grace will serve your turns: eat softly,
   You'll choak ye knaves else: give 'em wine.
Judas.   Not yet, Sir,
   We're even a little busie.
Hengo.   Can that fellow   70
   Do any thing but eat? thou fellow.
Judas.   Away Boy,
   Away, this is no boyes play.
Hengo.   By——, Uncle,
   If his valour lie in's teeth, he's the most valiant.
Caratach.   I am glad to hear ye talk, Sir.
Hengo.   Good Uncle tell me,
   What's the price of a couple of cramm'd Romans?
Caratach.   Some twenty Britains boy; these are good soldiers.
Hengo.   Do not the cowards eat hard too?

59 *Servant*] S; *om.* MS; *Suit.* F 1; *Swet.* F 2
66 *Enter...meate.*] MS; *om.* F 1–2

184

By——thou didst, I over-heard thee, there,
There where thou standst now, deliver me for rascal,
Poor, dead, cold coward, miserable, wretched,
If I out-liv'd this ruine?
Petillius.   I?
Penyus.   And thou didst it nobly,
Like a true man, a souldier: and I thank thee,
I thank thee, good *Petillius*; thus I thank thee.   110
Petillius.   Since ye are so justly made up, let me tell ye
'Tis fit ye die indeed.
Penyus.   O how thou lovest me!
Petillius.   For say he had forgiven ye; say the peoples whispers
Were tame again, the time run out for wonder,
What must your own Command think, from whose Swords
Ye have taken off the edges, from whose valours
The due and recompence of Arms; nay, made it doubtful
Whether they knew obedience? must not these kill ye?
Say they are won to pardon ye, by meer miracle
Brought to forgive ye; what old valiant Souldier,   120
What man that loves to fight, and fight for *Rome*,
Will ever follow you more? dare ye know these ventures?
If so, I bring ye comfort; dare ye take it?
Penyus.   No, no, *Petillius*, no.
Petillius.   If your minde serve ye,
Ye may live still; but how? yet pardon me,
You may outwear all too; but when? and certain
There is a mercy for each fault, if tamely
A man will take't upon conditions.
Penyus.   No, by no means: I am onely thinking now, Sir,
(For I am resolved to go) of a most base death,   130
Fitting the basenesse of my fault. I'll hang.
Petillius.   Ye shall not; y'are a Gentleman I honour,
I would else flatter ye, and force ye live,
Which is far baser. Hanging? 'tis a dogs death,
An end for slaves.
Penyus.   The fitter for my basenesse.
Petillius.   Besides, the man that's hang'd, preaches his end,

And sits a signe for all the world to gape at.
Penyus.   That's true: I'll take a fitter; poison.
Petillius.   No,
  'Tis equal ill; the death of rats, and women,
  Lovers, and lazie boys, that fear correction.   140
  Die like a man.
Penyus.   Why my sword then.
Petillius.   I, if your sword be sharp, Sir,
  There's nothing under heaven that's like your sword;
  Your sword's a death indeed.
Penyus.   It shall be sharp, Sir.
Petillius.   Why *Mithridates* was an arrant asse
  To die by poison, if all *Bosphorus*
  Could lend him swords: your sword must do the deed:
  'Tis shame to die choak'd, fame to die and bleed.
Penyus.   Thou hast confirmed me: and, my good *Petillius*,
  Tell me no more I may live.
Petillius.   'Twas my Commission;
  But now I see ye in a nobler way,   150
  A way to make all even.
Penyus.   Fare-well, Captain:
  Be a good man, and fight well: be obedient:
  Command thy self, and then thy men. Why shakest thou?
Petillius.   I do not, Sir.
Penyus.   I would thou hadst, *Petillius*:
  I would finde something to forsake the world with
  Worthy the man that dies: a kinde of earth-quake
  Thorow all stern valours but mine own.
Petillius.   I feel now
  A kinde of trembling in me.
Penyus.   Keep it still,
  As thou lov'st vertue, keep it.
Petillius.   And brave Captain,
  The great and honoured *Penyus*——
Penyus.   That again: 160
  O how it heightens me! again, *Petillius*.
Petillius.   Most excellent Commander.

Penyus.   Those were mine,
Mine, onely mine.
Petillius.   They are still.
Penyus.   Then to keep 'em
For ever falling more, have at ye, heavens,   [*Stabs himself.*]
Ye everlasting powers, I am yours: The work's done,
That neither fire, nor age, nor Eating envie
Shall ever conquer. Carry my last words
To the great General: kisse his hands, and say,
My soul I give to heaven, my fault to justice
Which I have done upon my self: my vertue,   170
If ever there was any in poor *Penyus*,
Made more, and happier, light on him. I faint.
And where there is a foe, I wish him fortune.
I die: lie lightly on my ashes, gentle earth.
Petillius.   And on my sin. Fare-well, great *Penyus*,   *Noise within.*
The souldier is in fury. Now I am glad
'Tis done before he comes. This way, for me,
The way of toil; for thee, the way of honour.   *Exit.*

          Enter Drusus *and* Regulus, *with* Souldiers.

Souldiers.   Kill him, kill him, kill him.
Drusus.   What will ye do?
Regulus.   Good souldiers, honest souldiers.
Souldiers.   Kill him, kill him, kill him.   180
Drusus.   Kill us first; we command too.
Regulus.   Valiant Souldiers,
Consider but whose life ye seek. O *Drusus*,
Bid him be gone, he dies else. Shall *Rome* say
(Ye most approved souldiers) her dear children
Devoured the fathers of the fights? shall rage
And stubborn fury guide those swords to slaughter,
To slaughter of their own, to Civil ruine?
Drusus.   O let 'em in: all's done, all's ended, *Regulus*,
Penyus has found his last eclipse. Come, Souldiers,
Come, and behold your miseries: come bravely,   190

          166 Eating] MS; melting F 1-2

Full of your mutinous and bloody angers,
And here bestow your darts. O onely Romane,
O father of the Wars.
Regulus.   Why stand ye stupid?
Where be your killing furies? whose sword now
Shall first be sheath'd in *Penyus*? do ye weep?
Howl out, ye wretches, ye have cause: howl ever.
Who shall now lead ye fortunate? whose valour
Preserve ye to the glory of your Countrey?
Who shall march out before ye, coy'd and courted
By all the mistrisses of War, care, counsel,   200
Quick-ey'd experience, and victory twin'd to him?
Who shall beget ye deeds beyond inheritance
To speak your names, and keep your honours living,
When children fail, and time that takes all with him,
Builds houses for ye to oblivion?
Drusus.   O ye poor desperate fools: no more now, souldiers;
Go home, and hang your arms up; let rust rot 'em;
And humble your stern valours to soft prayers;
For ye have sunk the frame of all your vertues;
The sun that warm'd your bloods is set for ever: 210
I'll kisse thy honour'd cheek. Fare well, great *Penyus*,
Thou thunder-bolt, fare-well. Take up the body:
To morrow morning to the Camp convey it,
There to receive due Ceremonies.   That eye
That blindes himself with weeping, gets most glory.
                    Exeunt with a dead march.
                                        IV. iv

Enter Swetonius, Junius, Decius, Demetrius, Curius, *and*
Souldiers: Bonduca, *two* Daughters, *and* Nennius, *above.*
                    Drum and Colours.

Swetonius.   Bring up the Catapults and shake the wall,
We will not be out-brav'd thus.
Nennius.   Shake the earth,
Ye cannot shake our souls. Bring up your Rams,

205 Builds] MS; build F 1–2

And with their armed heads, make the Fort totter,
Ye do but rock us into death.   *Exit* Nennius.
Junius.   See Sir,
See the Icenian Queen in all her glory
From the strong battlements proudly appearing,
As if she meant to give us lashes.
Decius.   Yeeld, Queen.
Bonduca.   I am unacquainted with that language, Roman.
Swetonius.   Yeeld, honour'd Lady, and expect our mercie,   10
                                   Exit Decius.
We love thy noblenesse.
Bonduca.   I thank ye, ye say well;
But mercie and love are sins in *Rome* and hell.
Swetonius.   Ye cannot scape our strength; ye must yeeld, Ladie,
Ye must adore and fear the power of *Rome.*
Bonduca.   If *Rome* be earthly, why should any knee
With bending adoration worship her?
She's vitious; and your partiall selves confesse,
Aspires the height of all impietie:
Therefore 'tis fitter I should reverence
The thatched houses where the Britains dwell   20
In carelesse mirth, where the blest houshold gods
See nought but chaste and simple puritie.
'Tis not high power that makes a place divine,
Nor that the men from gods derive their line.
But sacred thoughts in holy bosoms stor'd,
Make people noble, and the place ador'd.
Swetonius.   Beat the wall deeper.
Bonduca.   Beat it to the center,
We will not sink one thought.
Swetonius.   I'll make ye.
Bonduca.   No.
2. Daughter.   O mother, these are fearfull hours: speak gently

Enter Petillius.

To these fierce men, they will afford ye pitie.   30
Bonduca.   Pitie? thou fearful girl; 'tis for those wretches

That miserie makes tame. Wouldst thou live lesse?
Wast not thou born a Princesse? Can my blood,
And thy brave fathers spirit, suffer in thee
So base a separation from thy self,
As mercie from these Tyrants? Thou lov'st lust sure,
And long'st to prostitute thy youth and beautie
To common slaves for bread. Say they had mercie;
The divel a relenting conscience:
The lives of Kings rest in their Diadems,   40
Which to their bodies lively souls do give,
And ceasing to be Kings, they cease to live.
Show such another fear, and——
I'll fling thee to their furie.
Swetonius.   He is dead then?
Petillius.   I think so certainly; yet all my means, Sir,
Even to the hazzard of my life——
Swetonius.   No more:
Wee must not seem to mourn here.

                    Enter Decius.

Decius.   There's a breach made,
Is it your will we charge, Sir?
Swetonius.   Once more mercie,
Mercie to all that yeeld.
Bonduca.   I scorn to answer:
Speak to him girle; and hear thy sister.
1. Daughter   Generall,   50
Hear me, and mark me well, and look upon me
Directly in my face, my womans face,
Whose onely beautie is the hate it bears ye;
See with thy narrowest eyes, thy sharpest wishes,
Into my soul, and see what there inhabits;
See if one fear, one shadow of a terrour,
One palenesse dare appear but from my anger,
To lay hold on your mercies. No, ye fools,
Poor Fortunes fools, we were not born for triumphs,
To follow your gay sports, and fill your slaves   60

                    222

With hoots and acclamations.
Petillius.   Brave behaviour.
1. Daughter.   The children of as great as *Rome,* as noble,
Our names before her, and our deeds her envie;
Must we gild ore your Conquest, make your State,
That is not fairly strong, but fortunate?
No, no, ye Romanes, we have ways to scape ye,
To make yee poor again, indeed our prisoners,
And stick our triumphs full.
Petillius.   'S death, I shall love her.
1. Daughter.   To torture ye with suffering, like our slaves;
To make ye curse our patience, wish the world   70
Were lost again, to win us onely, and esteem it
The end of all ambitions.
Bonduca.   Do ye wonder?
We'll make our monuments in spite of fortune,
In spight of all your Eagles wings: we'll work
A pitch above ye; and from our height we'll stoop
As fearlesse of your bloody Sears; and fortunate,
As if we prey'd on heartlesse doves.
Swetonius.   Strange stiffnesse.
Decius, go charge the breach.   *Exit* Decius.
Bonduca.   Charge it home, Romane,
We shall deceive thee else. Where's *Nennius?*

Enter Nennius.

Nennius.   They have made a mighty breach.
Bonduca.   Stick in thy body,   80
And make it good but half an hour.
Nennius.   I'll do it.
1. Daughter.   And then be sure to die.
Nennius.   It shall go hard else.
Bonduca.   Fare well with all my heart; we shall meet yonder,
Where few of these must come.
Nennius.   Gods take thee, Lady.
                                        Exit Nennius.

71 it] MS; *om.* F1–2   *76 Sears] MS; fears F1; soars F2

Bonduca.   Bring up the swords, and poison.

Enter one with swords, and a great cup.

2. Daughter.   O my fortune!
Bonduca.   How, how, ye whore?
2. Daughter.   Good mother, nothing to offend ye.
Bonduca.   Here, wench:
  Behold us, Romanes.
Swetonius.   Mercy yet.
Bonduca.   No talking:
  Puff; there goes all your pitie. Come, short prayers,
  And let's dispatch the businesse: you begin,   90
  Shrink not; I'll see ye do't.
2. Daughter.   O gentle mother,
  O Romanes, O my heart; I dare not.
Swetonius.   Woman, woman,
  Unnaturall woman.
2. Daughter.   O perswade her, Romanes:
  Alas, I am young, and would live. Noble mother,
  Can ye kill that ye gave life? are my yeers
  Fit for destruction?
Swetonius.   Yeeld, and be a Queen still,
  A mother, and a friend.
Bonduca.   Ye talk: come, hold it,
  And put it home.
1. Daughter.   Fie, sister, fie,
  What would ye live to be?
Bonduca.   A whore still.
2. Daughter.   Mercie.
Swetonius.   Hear her, thou wretched woman.
2. Daughter.   Mercie, mother: 100
  O whither will you send me? I was once
  Your darling, your delight.
Bonduca.   O gods,
  Fear in my family? do it, and nobly.
2. Daughter.   O do not frown then.

99 ye] MS; you F1-2

1. Daughter.　　　　　　　　　　　Do it, worthy sister:
'Tis nothing, 'tis a pleasure; we'll go with ye.
2. Daughter.　O if I knew but whither.
1. Daughter　　　　　　　　To the blessed,
Where we shall meet our father.
Swetonius.　　　　　　　Woman.
Bonduca.　　　　　　　　　　Talk not.
1. Daughter.　Where nothing but true joy is.
Bonduca.　　　　　　　　　That's a good wench,
Mine own sweet girl; put it close to thee.
2. Daughter.　O comfort me still, for heavens sake.
1. Daughter.　　　　　　　　　Where eternal　110
Our youths are, and our beauties; where no Wars come,
Nor lustful slaves to ravish us.
2. Daughter.　　　　　　That steels me:
A long farewel to this world. [*2. Daughter stabs herself and dies.*]
Bonduca.　　　　　　Good: I'll help thee.
1. Daughter.　The next is mine.
Shew me a Romane Lady in all your stories,
Dare do this for her honour: they are cowards,
Eat coals like compell'd Cats: your great Saint *Lucrece*
Di'd not for honour; *Tarquin* topt her well,
And mad she could not hold him, bled.
Petillius.　　　　　　　　By——
I am in love: I would give an hundred pound now　120
But to lie with this womans behaviour. O the devil.
1. Daughter.　Ye shall see me example. All your *Rome*,
If I were proud, and lov'd ambition;
If I were lustful, all your ways of pleasure;
If I were greedie, all the wealth ye conquer——
Bonduca.　Make haste.
1. Daughter.　　　　　I will. Could not intice to live
But two short hours this frailty: would ye learn
How to die bravely, Romanes, to fling off
This case of flesh, lose all your cares for ever?
Live as we have done, well, and fear the gods,　130
Hunt Honour, and not Nations with your swords,

Keep your mindes humble, your devotions high;
So shall ye learn the noblest part, to die. *Dyes.*
Bonduca. I come, wench; to ye all Fates hang-men; you
  That ease the aged destinies, and cut
  The threds of Kingdoms, as they draw 'em: here,
  Here's a draught would ask no lesse then *Cæsar*
  To pledge it for the glories sake.
Curius. Great Lady.
Swetonius. Make up your own conditions.
Bonduca. So we will.
Swetonius. Stay.
Demetrius. Stay.
Swetonius. Be any thing.
Bonduca. A Saint, *Swetonius,* 140
  When thou shalt fear, and die like a slave. Ye fools,
  Ye should have ti'd up death first, when ye conquer'd,
  Ye sweat for us in vain else: see him here,
  He's ours still, and our friend; laughs at your pities;
  And we command him with as easie reins
  As do our enemies. I feel the poison.
  Poor vanquish'd Romanes, with what matchlesse tortures
  Could I now rack ye? But I pitie ye,
  Desiring to die quiet: nay, so much
  I hate to prosecute my victory, 150
  That I will give ye counsel ere I die.
  If you will keep your Laws and Empire whole,
  Place in your Romane flesh a Britain soul. *Dyes.*

Enter Decius.

Swetonius. Desperate and strange.
Decius. 'Tis won, Sir, and the Britains
  All put to th' sword.
Swetonius. Give her fair Funeral;
  She was truely noble, and a Queen.
Petillius. ——take it,
  A love-mange grown upon me? what, a spirit?

133, 153 *Dyes*] MS; *om.* F 1–2

226

Junius.   I am glad of this, I have found ye.
Petillius.   In my belly,
  O how it tumbles?
Junius.   Ye good gods, I thank ye.

                                              Exeunt.

        Enter Caratach *upon a rock, and* Hengo *by him, sleeping.*   V. i

Caratach.   Thus we afflicted Britains climb for safeties,
  And to avoid our dangers, seek destructions;
  Thus we awake to sorrows. O thou woman,
  Thou agent for adversities, what curses
  This day belong to thy improvidence?
  To *Britanie* by thy means, what sad millions
  Of widows weeping eyes? The strong mans valour
  Thou hast betraid to fury; the childes fortune
  To fear, and want of friends: whose pieties
  Might wipe his mournings off, and build his sorrows   10
  A house of rest by his blest ancestors:
  The virgins thou hast rob'd of all their wishes,
  Blasted their blowing hopes, turn'd their songs,
  Their mirthful Marriage songs to Funerals,
  The Land thou hast left a wildernesse of wretches.
  The boy begins to stir: thy safety made,
  Would my soul were in heaven.
Hengo.   O noble Uncle,
  Look out; I dream'd we were betraid.
                              A soft dead march within.
Caratach.   No harm, boy,
  'Tis but thy emptinesse that breeds these fancies;
  Thou shalt have meat anon.
Hengo.   A little, Uncle,   20
  And I shall hold out bravely. What are those?
  Look, Uncle, look, those multitudes that march there?
  They come upon us stealing by.
Caratach.   I see 'em;
  And prethee be not fearful.

                        227

Hengo.   Now ye hate me,
  Would I were dead.
Caratach.   Thou know'st I love thee dearly.
Hengo.   Did I ere shrink yet, Uncle? were I a man now,
  I should be angry with ye.

Enter Drusus, Regulus, *and* Souldiers, *with Penyus Herse,
Drums and Colours.*

Caratach.   My sweet chicken,
  See, they have reach'd us, and as it seems they bear
  Some Souldiers body, by their solemn gestures,
  And sad solemnities; it well appears too   30
  To be of eminence. Most worthy Souldiers,
  Let me intreat your knowledge to inform me
  What noble body that is which you bear
  With such a sad and ceremonious grief,
  As if ye meant to woo the world and nature
  To be in love with death? Most honourable
  Excellent Romanes, by your ancient valours,
  As ye love fame, resolve me.
Souldier.   'Tis the body
  Of the great Captain *Penyus,* by himself
  Made cold and spiritlesse.
Caratach.   O stay, ye Romanes,   40
  By the religion which you owe those gods
  That lead ye on to Victories, by those glories
  Which made even pride a vertue in ye.
Drusus.   Stay:
  What's thy will, *Caratach?*
Caratach.   Set down the body,
  The body of the noblest of all Romanes,
  As ye expect an offering at your graves
  From your friends sorrows, set it down a while,
  That with your griefs an enemy may mingle;
  A noble enemy that loves a Souldier;
  And lend a tear to vertue: even your foes,   50

Your wild foes, as you call'd us, are yet stor'd
With fair affections, our hearts fresh, our spirits,
Though sometimes stubborn, yet when vertue dies,
Soft and relenting as a virgins prayers.
O set it down.
Drusus.   Set down the body, souldiers.
Caratach.   Thou hallowed relique, thou rich diamond
Cut with thine own dust; thou for whose wide fame
The world appears too narrow, mans all thoughts,
Had they all tongues, too silent; thus I bow
To thy most honour'd ashes; though an enemy,   60
Yet friend to all thy worths: sleep peaceably;
Happinesse crown thy soul, and in thy earth
Some Lawrel fix his seat, there grow, and flourish,
And make thy grave an everlasting triumph.
Fare well all glorious Wars, now thou art gone,
And honest Arms adieu: all noble Battels
Maintain'd in thirst of honour, not of blood,
Fare well for ever.
Hengo.   Was this Romane, Uncle,
So good a man?
Caratach.   Thou never knew'st thy father.
Hengo.   He di'd before I was born.
Caratach.   This worthy Romane   70
Was such another piece of endlesse honour,
Such a brave soul dwelt in him: their proportions
And faces were not much unlike, boy: excellent natures,
See how it works into his eyes, mine own boy.
Hengo.   The multitudes of these men, and their fortunes,
Could never make me fear yet: one mans goodnesse——
Caratach.   O now thou pleasest me: weep still, my childe,
As if thou saw'st me dead; with such a flux
Or flood of sorrow: still thou pleasest me.
And worthy souldiers, pray receive these pledges,   80
These hatchments of our griefs, and grace us so much
To place 'em on his Hearse. Now if ye please,
Bear off the noble burden; raise his pile

High as *Olympus*, making heaven to wonder
To see a star upon earth outshining theirs.
And ever loved, ever living be
Thy honoured and most sacred memory.
Drusus.   Thou hast done honestly, good *Caratach*,
And when thou diest, a thousand vertuous Romanes
Shall sing thy soul to heaven. Now march on, souldiers.   90
> *Exeunt [Romans]. A dead march.*
Caratach.   Now dry thine eyes, my boy.
Hengo.   Are they all gone?
I could have wept this hour yet.
Caratach.   Come, take cheer,
And raise thy spirit, childe: if but this day
Thou canst bear out thy faintnesse, the night coming
I'll fashion our escape.
Hengo.   Pray fear not me;
Indeed I am very heartie.
Caratach.   Be so still;
His mischiefs lessen, that controls his ill.

> *Exeunt.*

Enter Petillius.   V. ii

Petillius.   What do I ail, i'th' name of heaven? I did but see her,
And see her die: she stinks by this time strongly,
Abominably stinks: she was a woman,
A thing I never car'd for: but to die so,
So confidently, bravely, strongly; O the devil,
I have the bots, by——; she scorn'd us, strangely,
All we could do, or durst do; threatned us
With such a noble anger, and so governed
With such a fiery spirit——; the plain bots;
A——upon the bots, the love-bots: hang me,   10
Hang me even out o'th' way, directly hang me.
O pennie pipers, and most painful penners
Of bountiful new ballads, what a subject,
What a sweet subject for your silver sounds,
Is crept upon ye?

Enter Junius.

Junius.   Here he is; have at him.   *Sings.*
  She set the sword unto her brest,
  Great pitie it was to see,
  That three drops of her life-warm blood,
  Run trickling down her knee.
Art thou there, bonny boy? and ifaith how dost thou?
Petillius. Well, gramercie, how dost thou? h'as found me,
Sented me out: the shame the devil ow'd me,   20
H'as kept his day with. And what news, *Junius?*
Junius.   *It was an old tale ten thousand times told,*
  Of a young Lady was turn'd into mold,
  Her life it was lovely, her death it was bold.
Petillius. A cruel rogue; now h'as drawn pursue on me,
He hunts me like a devil. No more singing;
Thou hast got a cold: come, let's go drink some Sack, boy.
Junius. Ha, ha, ha, ha, ha, ha.
Petillius.   Why dost thou laugh?
What Mares nest hast thou found?
Junius.   Ha, ha, ha.   30
I cannot laugh alone: *Decius, Demetrius,*
Curius: O my sides. Ha, ha, ha, ha,
The strangest jest.
Petillius.   Prethee no more.
Junius.   The admirablest fooling.
Petillius. Thou art the prettiest fellow.
Junius.   Sirs.
Petillius.   Why *Junius,*
Prethee away, sweet *Junius.*
Junius.   Let me sing then.
Petillius. Whoa, here's a stir now: sing a song o' six pence,
By—— (if) prethee; —— on't: *Junius.*
Junius. I must either sing, or laugh.
Petillius.   And what's your reason?
Junius. What's that to you?

26 *life it was*] F2; life was F1; *om.* MS

Petillius.   And I must whistle.

Junius.   Do so.   40

O, I hear 'em coming.

Petillius.   I have a little businesse.

Junius.   Thou shalt not go, believe it: what a Gentleman

Of thy sweet conversation?

Petillius.   Captain *Junius*,

Sweet Captain, let me go with all celerity;

Things are not always one: and do not question,

Nor jeer, nor gybe: none of your doleful ditties,

Nor your sweet conversation: you will finde then

I may be anger'd.

Junius.   By no means, *Petillius*;

Anger a man that never knew passion?

'Tis most impossible: a noble Captain,   50

A wise and generous Gentleman?

Petillius.   Tom puppie,

Leave this way to abuse me: I have found ye,

But for your mothers sake I will forgive ye.

Your subtil understanding may discover

(As you think) some trim toy to make you merry;

Some straw to tickle ye; but do not trust to't;

Y'are a young man, and may do well; be sober;

Carry your self discreetly.

Enter Decius, Demetrius, Curius.

Junius.   Yes forsooth.

Demetrius.   How does the brave *Petillius*?

Junius.   Monstrous merry:

We two were talking what a kinde of thing   60

I was when I was in love; what a strange monster

For little boys and girls to wonder at;

How like a fool I lookt.

Decius.   So they do all,

Like great dull slavering fools.

232

Junius.   *Petillius* saw too.
Petillius.   No more of this; 'tis scurvie: peace.
Junius.   How nastily,
  Indeed how beastly all I did became me?
  How I forgot to blow my nose? there he stands,
  An honest and a wise man; if himself
  (I dare avouch it boldly, for I know it)
  Should finde himself in love——
Petillius.   I am angry.   70
Junius.   Surely his wise self would hang his beastly self,
  His understanding self so mawl his asse-self——
Decius.   He's bound to do it; for he knows the follies,
  The poverties, and basenesse that belongs to't,
  H'as read upon the reformations long.
Petillius.   He has so.
Junius.   'Tis true, and he must do't:
  Nor is it fit indeed any such coward——
Petillius.   You'll leave prating.
Junius.   Should dare come neer the Regiments, specially
  Those curious puppies (for believe there are such)
  That onely love behaviours: those are dog-whelps,   80
  Dwindle away, because a woman dies well;
  Commit with passions onely: fornicate
  With the free spirit meerly: you, *Petillius,*
  For you have long observ'd the world——
Petillius.   Dost thou hear?
  I'll beat thee damnably within these three hours:
  Go pray; may be I'll kill thee. Farewel, Jack-daws.   *Exit.*
Decius.   What a strange thing he's grown?
Junius.   I am glad he is so:
  And stranger he shall be, before I leave him.
Curius.   Is't possible her meer death——
Junius.   I observ'd him,
  And found him taken, infinitely taken   90
  With her bravery: I have follow'd him,
  And seen him kisse his sword since, court his scabbard,
  Call dying, dainty deer; her brave minde, mistris;

Casting a thousand ways, to give those forms,
That he might lie with 'em, and get old Armors:
He had got me o'th' hip once: it shall go hard, friends,
But he shall find his own coin.

Enter Macer.

Decius.   How now *Macer?*
Is *Judas* yet come in?

Enter Judas.

Macer.   Yes, and has lost
Most of his men too. Here he is.
Curius.   What news?
Judas.   I have lodg'd him; rouze him he that dares.
Demetrius.   Where, *Judas?*   100
Judas.   On a steep rock, i'th' woods, the boy too with him,
And there he swears he will keep his Christmas, Gentlemen,
But he will come away with full conditions,
Bravely, and like a Britain: he paid part of us,
Yet I think we fought bravely: for mine own part,
I was four several times at half sword with him,
Twice stood his partizan: but the plain truth is,
He's a meer devil, and no man: i'th' end he swing'd us,
And swing'd us soundly too: he fights by Witch-craft:
Yet for all that I see him lodg'd.
Junius.   Take more men,   110
And scout him round. *Macer*, march you along.
What victuals has he?
Judas.   Not a piece of Bisket,
Not so much as will stop a tooth; nor water,
More then they make themselves: they lie
Just like a brace of bear-whelps, close, and crafty,
Sucking their fingers for their food.
Decius.   Cut off then
All hope of that way: take sufficient forces.
Junius.   But use no foul play, on your lives: that man

109 Witch-craft] F2; With-craft F1; *om.* MS

That does him mischief by deceit, I'll kill him.
Macer.   He shall have fair play, he deserves it.
Judas.   Heark ye,   120
  What should I do there then? you are brave Captains,
  Most valiant men; go up your selves; use vertue,
  See what will come on't: pray the Gentleman
  To come down, and be taken. Ye all know him,
  I think ye have felt him too: there ye shall finde him,
  His sword by his side, plums of a pound weight by him
  Will make your chops ake: you'll finde it a more labour
  To win him living, then climbing of a Crowes nest.
Decius.   Away, and compasse him; we shall come up
  I am sure within these two hours. Watch him close.   130
Macer.   He shall flee thorow the air, if he escape us.
                              A sad noise within.

Junius.   What's this loud lamentation?
Macer.   The dead body
  Of the great *Penyus* is new come to th' Camp Sir.
Demetrius.   Dead!
Macer.   By himself, they say.
Junius.   I fear'd that fortune.
Curius.   Peace guide him up to heaven.
Junius.   Away good *Macer.*
                              Exeunt Macer *and* Judas.

          Enter Swetonius, Drusus, Regulus, Petillius.

Swetonius.   If thou be'st guilty,
  Some sullen plague thou hat'st most light upon thee:
  The Regiment return on *Junius,*
  Hee well deserves it.
Petillius.   So.
Swetonius.   Draw out three Companies,
  Yours *Decius, Junius,* and thou *Petillius,*
  And make up instantly to *Caratach,*   140
  He's in the wood before ye; we shall follow
  After due ceremony done to the dead,
  The noble dead: Come, let's go burn the body.
                              Exeunt all but Petillius.

Petillius.   The Regiment given from me; disgrac'd openly;
In love too with a trifle to abuse me?
A merry world, a fine world: serv'd seven yeers
To be an asse o' both sides, sweet *Petillius,*
You have brought your hogs to a fine market: you are wise, Sir,
Your honourable brain-pan full of crotchets,   150
An understanding Gentleman; your projects
Cast with assurance ever: wouldst not thou now
Be bang'd about the pate, *Petillius?*
Answer to that sweet souldier; surely, surely,
I think ye would; pull'd by the nose, kick'd; hang thee,
Thou art the arrant'st rascall: trust thy wisdome
With any thing of weight; the winde with feathers.
Out ye blind puppie; you command? you govern?
Dig for a groat a day, or serve a swine-herd;
Too noble for thy nature too. I must up;   160
But what I shall do there, let time discover.   *Exit.*

Enter Macer and Judas, with meat and a bottle.   V.iii

Macer.   Hang it o'th' side o'th' rock, as though the Britains
Stole hither to relieve him; who first ventures
To fetch it off, is ours. I cannot see him.
Judas.   He lies close in a hole above, I know it,
Gnawing upon his anger: ha? no, 'tis not he.
Macer.   'Tis but the shaking of the boughs.
Judas.   —— shake 'em,
I am sure they shake me soundly. There.
Macer.   'Tis nothing.
Judas.   Make no noise: if he stir, a deadly tempest
Of huge stones fall upon us: 'tis done: away close.
                                              Exeunt.
Enter Caratach [on the Rock, above].

Caratach.   Sleep stil, sleep sweetly child, 'tis all thou feedst on.   10
No gentle Britain neer; no valiant charitie
To bring thee food? poor knave, thou art sick, extreme sick,
Almost grown wild for meat; and yet thy goodnesse

236

Will not confesse, nor show it. All the woods
Are double lin'd with souldiers; no way left us
To make a noble scape: I'll sit down by thee,
And when thou wak'st, either get meat to save thee,
Or lose my life i'th' purchase. Good gods comfort thee.

[*Exit above.*]

Enter Junius, Decius, Petillius, Guide.

Guide.   Ye are not far off now, Sir.
Junius.   Draw the Companies
The closest way thorow the woods; we'll keep on this way.   20
Guide.   I will Sir: half a furlong more you'll come
Within the sight o'th' Rock; keep on the left side,
You'll be discoverd else: I'll lodge your Companies
In the wilde vines beyond ye.
Decius.   Do ye mark him?
Junius.   Yes, and am sorry for him.
Petillius.   *Junius,*
Pray let me speak two words with you.
Junius.   Walk afore,
I'll overtake ye straight.
Decius.   I will.   *Exit* [Decius *and* Guide].
Junius.   Now, Captain.
Petillius.   You have oft told me, you have lov'd me, *Junius.*
Junius.   Most sure I told you truth then.
Petillius.   And that love
Should not deny me any honest thing.   30
Junius.   It shall not.
Petillius.   Dare ye swear it?
I have forgot all passages between us
That have been ill, forgiven too, forgot you.
Junius.   What would this man have? By—— I do, Sir,
So it be fit to grant ye.
Petillius.   'Tis most honest.
Junius.   Why, then I'll do it.
Petillius   Kill mee.
Junius.   How?

Petillius.   Pray kill me.
Junius.   Kill ye?
Petillius.   I, kill me quickly, suddenly,
Now kill me.
Junius.   On what reason? ye amaze me.
Petillius.   If ye do love me, kill me, ask me not why:
I would be kill'd, and by you.
Junius.   Mercy on me,   40
What ails this man? *Petillius.*
Petillius.   Pray ye dispatch me,
Ye are not safe whilest I live: I am dangerous,
Troubled extremely, even to mischief, *Junius,*
An enemie to all good men: fear not, 'tis justice;
I shall kill you else.
Junius.   Tell me but the cause,
And I will do it.
Petillius.   I am disgrac'd, my service
Slighted, and unrewarded by the Generall,
My hopes left wilde and naked; besides these,
I am grown ridiculous, an asse, a folly
I dare not trust my self with: Prethee kill me.   50
Junius.   All these may be redeem'd as easily
As you would heal your finger.
Petillius.   Nay——
Junius.   Stay, I'll do it,
You shall not need your anger: But first, *Petillius,*
You shall unarm your self; I dare not trust
A man so bent to mischief.
Petillius.   There's my sword;
And do it handsomely.
Junius.   Yes, I will kill ye,
Beleeve that certaine: but first i'll lay before ye
The most extreme fool ye have plaid in this,
The honour purpos'd for ye, the great honour
The Generall intended ye.
Petillius.   How?
Junius.   And then I'll kill ye,   60

Because ye shall die miserable. Know Sir,
The Regiment was given me, but till time
Call'd ye to do some worthie deed might stop
The peoples ill thoughts of ye for Lord *Penyus*,
I mean his death. How soon this time's come to ye,
And hasted by *Swetonius?* Go, sayes he,
Junius and *Decius*, and go thou *Petillius*;
Distinctly, thou *Petillius*, and draw up,
To take stout *Caratach*: there's the deed purpos'd,
A deed to take off all faults, of all natures: 70
And thou *Petillius*; Mark it, there's the honour,
And that done, all made even.
Petillius.   Stay.
Junius.   No, I'll kill ye.
He knew thee absolute, and full in souldier,
Daring beyond all dangers, found thee out
According to the boldnesse of thy spirit,
A subject, such a subject.
Petillius.   Heark ye *Junius*,
I will live now.
Junius.   By no means. Wooed thy worth,
Held thee by the chin up, as thou sankst, and shew'd thee
How honour held her arms out: Come, make ready,
Since ye will die an asse.
Petillius.   Thou wilt not kill me.   80
Junius.   By—— but I will Sir: I'll have no man dangerous
Live to destroy me afterward. Besides, you have gotten
Honour enough, let young men rise now. Nay,
I do perceive too by the Generall, (which is
One main cause ye shall die) how ere he carry it,
Such a strong doting on ye, that I fear,
You shall command in chief: how are we paid then?
Come, if you will pray, dispatch it.
Petillius.   Is there no way?
Junius.   Not any way to live.
Petillius.   I will do any thing,
Redeem my self at any price: good *Junius*,   90

239

Let me but die upon the Rock, but offer
My life up like a Souldier.
Junius.   You will seek then
To out-doe every man.
Petillius.   Beleeve it *Junius*,
You shall goe stroak by stroak with me.
Junius.   You'll leave off too,
As ye are noble, and a souldier,
For ever these mad fancies.
Petillius.   Dare ye trust me?
By all that's good and honest.
Junius.   There's your sword then,
And now come on a new man: Vertue guide thee.   *Exeunt.*

        Enter Caratach *and* Hengo *on the Rock.*

Caratach.   Courage my Boy, I have found meat: look *Hengo*,
Look where some blessed Britain, to preserve thee,   100
Has hung a little food and drink: cheer up Boy,
Do not forsake me now.
Hengo.   O Uncle, Uncle,
I feel I cannot stay long: yet I'll fetch it,
To keep your noble life: Uncle, I am heart whole,
And would live.
Caratach.   Thou shalt, long I hope.
Hengo.   But my head, Uncle:
Me thinks the Rock goes round.

            Enter Macer *and* Judas.

Macer.   Mark 'em well, *Judas.*
Judas.   Peace, as you love your life.
Hengo.   Do not you hear
The noise of bels?
Caratach.   Of bels Boy? 'tis thy fancie,
Alas, thy bodie's full of wind.
Hengo.   Me thinks Sir,
They ring a strange sad knell, a preparation   110
To some neer funerall of State: nay, weep not,

        95 ye] MS; you F 1–2

                    240

Mine owne sweet Uncle, you will kill me sooner.
Caratach.　　O my poor chicken.
Hengo.　　　　　　　　　　　Fie, faint-hearted Uncle:
Come, tie me in your belt, and let me down.
Caratach.　　I'll go my self, Boy.
Hengo.　　　　　　　　　　　No, as ye love mee, Uncle;
I will not eat it, if I doe not fetch it;
The danger onely I desire: pray tie me.
Caratach.　　I will, and all my care hang ore thee: come child,
My valiant child.
Hengo.　　　　　Let me down apace, Uncle,
And ye shall see how like a Daw I'll whip it　　　　　　　120
From all their policies: for 'tis most certain
A Roman train: and ye must hold me sure too,
You'll spoil all else. When I have brought it Uncle,
Wee'll be as merry——
Caratach.　　　　　　　Go i'th' name of heaven Boy.
Hengo.　　Quick, quick, Uncle, I have it. Oh.

　　　　　　　　　　　　　　　Judas shoots Hengo.
Caratach.　　　　　　　　　What ailest thou?
Hengo.　　O my best Uncle, I am slain.
Caratach.　　I see yee, and heaven direct my hand: destruction
　　　　　　Caratach kils Judas with a stone from the Rock.
Go with thy coward soul. How dost thou Boy?
Oh villain, pocky villain.
Hengo.　　　　　　　O Uncle, Uncle,
Oh how it pricks mee: am I preserv'd for this?　　　　　130
Extremely pricks me.
Caratach.　　　　　　　Coward, rascall Coward,
Dogs eat thy flesh.
Hengo.　　Oh I bleed hard: I faint too, out upon't,
How sick I am? the lean Rogue, Uncle.
Caratach.　　　　　　　　Look Boy,
I have laid him sure enough.
Hengo.　　　　　　　　Have ye knockt his brains out?
Caratach.　　I warrant thee for stirring more: cheer up, child.
Hengo.　　Hold my sides hard, stop, stop, oh wretched fortune,

Must we part thus? Still I grow sicker, Uncle.

Caratach.   Heaven look upon this noble child.

Hengo.   I once hop'd
I should have liv'd to have met these bloody Romans   140
At my swords point, to have reveng'd my father,
To have beaten 'em: oh hold me hard. But Uncle——

Caratach.   Thou shalt live still I hope Boy. Shall I draw it?

Hengo.   Ye draw away my soul then. I would live
A little longer; spare me heavens, but onely
To thank you for your tender love. Good Uncle,
Good noble Uncle weep not.

Caratach.   Oh my chicken,
My deer Boy, what shall I lose?

Hengo.   Why, a child,
That must have died how-ever: had this scap'd me,
Feaver or famine: I was born to die, Sir.   150

Caratach.   But thus unblown, my Boy?

Hengo.   I goe the straighter
My journey to the gods: Sure I shall know ye
When ye come, Uncle.

Caratach.   Yes, Boy.

Hengo.   And I hope
Wee shall enjoy together that great blessednesse
You told me of.

Caratach.   Most certain, child.

Hengo.   I grow cold,
Mine eyes are going.

Caratach.   Lift 'em up.

Hengo.   Pray for me;
And noble Uncle, when my bones are ashes,
Think of your little Nephew. Mercie.

Caratach.   Mercie.
You blessed angels take him.

Hengo.   Kisse me: so.
Farewell, farewell.   *Dies.*

Caratach.   Farewell the hopes of *Britain*,   160
Thou Royall graft, Farewell for ever. Time and Death

Ye have done your worst. Fortune now see, now proudly
Pluck off thy vail, and view thy triumph: Look,
Look what thou hast brought this Land to. Oh fair flower,
How lovely yet thy ruines show, how sweetly
Even death embraces thee! The peace of heaven,
The fellowship of all great souls be with thee.

Enter Petillius *and* Junius *on the rock.*

Hah? dare ye Romans? ye shall win me bravely.
Thou art mine.   *Fight.*
Junius.   Not yet, Sir.
Caratach.   Breathe ye, ye poor Romans,
And come up all, with all your ancient valours,   170
Like a rough winde I'll shake your souls, and send 'em——

Enter Swetonius, *and all the Roman Captains.*

Swetonius.   Yeeld thee bold *Caratach*; by all——
As I am souldier, as I envie thee,
I'll use thee like thy self, the valiant Britain.
Petillius.   Brave soldier yeeld; thou stock of Arms and Honor,
Thou filler of the world with fame and glory.
Junius.   Most worthy man, we'l woo thee, be thy prisoners.
Swetonius.   Excellent Britain, do me but that honour,
That more to me then Conquests, that true happinesse,
To be my friend.
Caratach.   O Romans, see what here is: 180
Had this Boy liv'd——
Swetonius.   For Fames sake, for thy Swords sake,
As thou desirest to build thy vertues greater:
By all that's excellent in man, and honest——
Caratach.   I do beleeve: Ye have had me a brave foe;
Make me a noble friend, and from your goodnesse,
Give this Boy honourable earth to lie in.
Swetonius.   He shall have fitting Funerall.
Caratach.   I yeeld then,
Not to your blowes, but your brave courtesies.
Petillius.   Thus we conduct then to the arms of Peace

The wonder of the world.

Swetonius.   Thus I embrace thee,   *Flourish.* 190
And let it be no flattery that I tell thee,
Thou art the onely Souldier.

Caratach.   How to thank ye
I must hereafter finde upon your usage.
I am for *Rome?*

Swetonius   Ye must.

Caratach.   Then *Rome* shall know
The man that makes her spring of glory grow.

Swetonius.   *Petillius,* you have shown much worth this day,
Redeem'd much errour,
Ye have my love again, preserve it. *Junius,*
With you I make him equall in the Regiment.

Junius.   The elder and the nobler: I'll give place, Sir.   200

Swetonius.   Ye shew a friends soul.
March on, and through the Camp in every tongue,
The Vertues of great *Caratach* be sung.

                                               Exeunt.

Finis

TEXTUAL NOTES

II.i

128 *Regulus.*] The speech-prefix is omitted from both Folios, where the last two lines of the scene are printed as part of Curius' preceding speech. Colman (followed by Weber and Dyce) noted that the final line of the scene 'must be spoke by either *Drusus* or *Regulus*', it being 'expressive of their discontent at being kept from the field', whereas '*Curius* is going to the engagement'. Colman, Weber and Dyce accordingly assign line 129 ('We dare, alas, but cannot fight our parts') to Regulus. The MS assigns the last two lines of the scene to Regulus; in MS, the pronouns of line 128 'our' in both Folios) read appropriately 'your'. This division, whereby Regulus is given a couplet that closes the scene, seems the preferable arrangement.

II.iv

61 running banquet] This, the F1 reading, Greg (in the introduction to his Malone Society edition of the *Bonduca* MS, pp. xi–xii) considered to be one of the Folio errors which the MS (reading 'rouncing banquet') corrected. But the phrase 'running banquet' occurs elsewhere in Fletcher. Cf. *The Loyal Subject*, V.iv.14 and *Henry VIII*, I.iv.12, V.iii.65.

IV.iv

76 Sears] The word (which means 'talons') is preserved in the MS, and confirms Dyce's independent emendation 'seres'. The word appears in F1 as 'fears', and in F2 (followed by Langbaine, Sympson, Colman and Weber) as 'soars'.

EMENDATIONS OF ACCIDENTALS

[NOTE: The periods in the MS entries represent a typographical convention adopted by Greg in his edition of the manuscript of *Bonduca* for the Malone Society. In the Introduction to his edition (p. vii), he wrote of the manuscript punctuation: 'Commas and full stops are often clearly formed, but at other times they pass insensibly into one another, and no real distinction is made in their use. If anything the tailed form appears to be treated as the more emphatic and is generally used at the end of a speech, whereas the mere dot tends to mark lighter pauses within the sentence. An attempt to differentiate them according to the sense having proved unsatisfactory, it was decided to render all alike by periods.']

I.i

I.i] *Actus primus. Scæna prima.* F 1,
MS
119 hand$_\wedge$ (my sword), my prow$_\wedge$]
C; ~ ,$_\wedge$ ~ ~ $_{\wedge\wedge}$ ~ ~ , F 1–2;
~ .$_\wedge$ ~ ~ $_\wedge$. ~ ~ $_\wedge$ MS

120 fo (my face)] C; ~ $_\wedge$ ~ ~ $_\wedge$
F 1–2; ~ .$_\wedge$ ~ *fate* $_\wedge$ MS
173 kindred] MS; kinred F 1

I.ii

I.ii] *Scæna Secunda.* F 1
16 saddle——] ~ . F 1–2, MS
25 drink?] F 2; ~ . F 1, MS

115 we] MS, F 2; We F 1
265 In's. . .Sir] F 1 *lines:* Cabbin, |
sick

II.i

II.i] *Actus secundus. Scæna Prima.*
F 1; *Act: 2: Scæna: i:* MS
0.1, 59, 101.1 Drusus] MS; *Drusius*
F 1–2

76 Drusus] *Drus:* MS; *Drusius*
F 1–2

II.ii

II.ii] *Scæna Secunda.* F 1
7 sleep——] ~ , F 1–2; ~ . MS
25 cheek——] ~ , F 1–2; ~ $_\wedge$ MS

40 thousand——] ~ , F 1–2; ~ $_\wedge$
MS
55 (*reads*)] $_\wedge$ ~ $_\wedge$ F 1–2; *om.* MS

II.iii

II.iii] *Scæna Tertia* F 1   59 (*within*)] $_\wedge$ ~ $_\wedge$ F 1–2, MS

II.iv

II.iv] *Scæna quarta.* F 1   63 dog's] F 2; dogs F 1, MS
48 Forks,] ~ . F 1–2; ~ $_\wedge$ MS

III.i

III.i] *Actus Tertius. Scæna Prima.* F 1, MS

III.ii

III.ii] *Scæna Secunda.* F 1   73 bones$_\wedge$ with your vertues.] MS;
9 (*reads*)] $_\wedge$ ~ $_\wedge$ F 1–2, MS   ~ . With ~ ~ , F 1 2
35 *Bonvica.*——] MS; ~ . $_\wedge$ F 1–2

III.iii

III.iii] *Scæna tertia.* F 1

III.iv

III.iv] *Scæna quarta.* F 1

III.v

III.v] *Scæna quinta.* F 1   38 has,] ~ $_\wedge$ F 1–2; ~ . MS
8 charge,] ~ . F 1–2; ~ $_\wedge$ MS

IV.i

IV.i] *Actus Quartus. Scæna Prima.*   9 *sleek,*] ~ . F 1–2, MS
   F 1, MS   59 *Petillius*——] ~ , F 1–2; ~ $_\wedge$
5 *viewing.*] MS; ~ , F 1–2   MS
6 *thigh,*] F 2; ~ . F 1, MS   61 honour——] ~ , F 1–2; ~ . MS

IV.ii

IV.ii] *Scæna Secunda,* F 1   84 endure$_\wedge$] MS, F 2; ~ . F 1
27 What$_\wedge$] MS; ~ , F 1–2

IV.iii

IV.iii] *Scæna Tertia,* F1
9 breaches,] ~ ∧ F1–2, MS
35.1 Drusus] MS; *Drusius* F1–2
36 ye.——] ~ . ∧ F1–2; *om.* MS

138 fitter;] ~ ∧ F1–2; *om.* MS
160 *Penyus*——] ~ . F1–2, MS
213 it,] ~ . F1–2, MS

IV.iv

IV.iv] *Scæna Quarta.* F1

108–109 That's...thee] MS; *one line in* F1–2

V.i

V.i] *Actus Quintus. Scæna Prima* F1; *Actus: Quinti: Scæna: pri^a: MS*

V.ii

V.ii] *Scæna secunda.* F1
24–26 *It was...bold*] F2; *roman in* F1; *om.* MS

84 world——] ~ . F1–2; *om.* MS

V.iii

V.iii] *Scæna tertia.* F1

202 tongue,] ~ . F1–2; ~ ∧ MS

HISTORICAL COLLATION

[NOTE: The F1 copy-text has been collated with the British Library manuscript (MS) as this is presented in the edition prepared by W. W. Greg for the Malone Society and published in 1951. Other editions collated herein are as follows: F2 (1679), L (*Works*, 1711, ed. Gerard Langbaine the Younger), S (*Works*, 1750, ed. Theobald, Seward and Sympson), C (*Works*, 1778, ed. George Colman the Younger), W (*Works*, 1812, ed. Henry Weber), D (*Works*, 1843–6, ed. Alexander Dyce).

The pronominal form 'ye', so favored by Fletcher, was often changed to 'you' by Knight, who transcribed the manuscript, and has been freely altered by subsequent editors. The collation that follows records all first folio and manuscript variants concerning 'ye', but not such variants as arise between F1 and subsequent editions. F2, L and S tend to follow quite closely the practice of F1 concerning the use of 'ye'. Beginning with C, Fletcher's 'ye' is freely altered (to 'y'' or 'you'), and W and D continue the tendency.

No attempt has been made to record all the minor differences of phrasing that sometimes exist between F1 and manuscript stage-directions.

I.i

0.1 Bonduca, Daughters,] Bonduca: (*hir Daughter*) MS
4.1 *Enter* Caratach] *in margin to right of lines 6–7 in* MS
7 flee] fly MS
7 dwells] is MS
8 pleasure] pleasures MS
14 sit] sits, S, C, W
15 to shame 'em] *om.* MS
19 ye] you F1+
19 grieve my] grieve at my F2, L, S
20 'tis the] 'tis at the F2, S; 'tis as the L
33 bid] bids MS
36 fleeing] fflying MS
37 *Cæsars*] tainted F1–2, L–D
40 Why] where MS
48 your] our F1–2, L, S, C

51 a flame] of flame F2, L, S, C, W
54 By——] by the gods MS, C, W, D
55 these] the MS
75–76 And if...dangers] *order of lines reversed in* MS
82 I, and] found MS
85 Dishearted] Disheartned, F2, L, S, C, W
87 high sett] hated F1–2, L D
90 haste] wish MS
90 By——] by the gods MS, C, W, D
94 scur] sturr MS
98 Yea] ye MS
99 Carts] troopes MS
100 drove] drive F1–2, MS
103 These] the MS
107 so fast] for fast F2

108 trasht] trac't MS (*replacing* trasht *which is marked for deletion*)
109 stept] stopt MS
116 speak] speaking MS
116 the childe more] this child MS
117 son] *Sunne* MS
120 to my fo] to ffoe MS
120 face] *fate* MS
121 Lions] lyon MS
131 condition] conditions MS
132 the] *om.* MS
134 held] made MS
137 think, as] thinke it as MS, S
144 barre] burn F 1–2, L, S, W, D; brand C (*conj.* S)

144 upbraidings] abraydings MS
150 these] the MS
151 ones] on MS
152 *Nennius.*] *om.* MS
153 *Caratach.*] *pen*: MS (*which places Caratach's speech-prefix on line* 154)
157 a] *om.* MS
163 neighbour] neighbors MS
171 ends] Hands S
178 stiffer] stiffe MS
179 ye] you MS
184 An] a MS
185 That's] why thats MS; That is S, C, W

I.ii

2 heavens love] heaven sake MS
13 do you do this] do you this F 2; do ye this L; do ye do this S
17 fair] far MS, F 1–2, L
18 Did I not] did not I MS
22 by——] by this hand MS; by the gods, C, W, D
23 chapt] chopt MS
24 what thou] what is't thou F 2, L–D
26 It may] may MS
50 touchie] *om.* MS
51 Ye do] you do MS
54, 69, 90, 275 Ye] you MS
55, 57, 58, 60, 98, 125, 149 ye] you MS
59 ye] *om.* MS
62 wench] whore MS
63 aches] ashes MS
65 out-leaps] out leys MS
69 it] *om.* MS, F 1
71 A wronger...it.] *om.* F 2, L
72 Bean? a] beane is a MS
89 cheese] these F 1–2, L–D
91 resolution] resolutions MS

97 s'death, ye] death you MS
99 Give] Good, Give, L, S
101 A] *om.* MS
105 Ye Rogues] you rogue MS
106 Timber they] *om.* MS
107 mud with] *om.* MS
107 spoons...slaves] spoons. yor shooes slaues rare MS
108 of] for F 2, L–D
109 Suck] Eate MS
109 ye be] you be MS
111 A...penance] *Iud:* a...pennance MS
112 ye] *om.* MS
115 ye] you F 1+
117 somtime] sometimes MS
119 ye] you F 1+
129 *4. Souldier.*] *om.* MS
130 *3. Souldier.*] · 4 · MS
131 *Judas.*] · 3 · MS
132 true] yor MS
134 your] you MS
136 destruction] *om.* MS
144 shews ye] showes you MS
145 at your] on the MS

146 ye can] you can MS
148 ye can] you will MS
152 *Drum afar off.*] *om.* MS
154 these] this MS
156 choke ye. Jog] make you. away MS
156.2 *Drum, Colours*] *om.* MS
165 their] the MS
166 As deaf] Is deaffe MS
167 Hath] have MS
168 they're] they are MS
170 Lesbos] Lestos F1
179 full] our MS
182 Mona] more MS (*the word* mona *has been added to the* MS *text in a hand other than Knight's at line* 160 *above*)
196 strike] sticke MS
199 of] *om.* MS
200 devill] devills MS
204 nothings] nothing F2, L, S, C

205 The] that MS
206 selfe-same] selfe am MS
210 was] is MS
214 get] yet W (*conj.* S), D
217 how,] how; how, F2
217 found] fond MS
227 there] then MS
236 no] *om.* MS, F1–2, L, S, C (*where conj. but not received in text*)
236 infinite] in MS
237 spirit] spiritts MS
237 preach'd] *om.* MS
239 help] helpes MS
240 forc'd] *om.* MS
254 vertues] vertue MS
255 he's] he is MS
257 thrust] trust MS
266 In love,] *om.* MS
277 provision] Provisions, S, C, W

II.i

3 he say] his word MS
9 I'm] I am MS
10, 80, 90, 94, 97, 109 ye] you MS
14 my] myne MS
14 Sir] nay sir MS
16 an] a MS
18 up] *om.* MS
19 wolfs] wolves L–D
28 Swaino] Swanns MS
42 out] not W
42 but] both S, C, D
46 Not] not F1
48 fling] fly MS
50 swallows] swallow MS
51 there] here MS
54 lie] *om.* MS
58 A Captain] the Captaines MS; Captains F1–2; L; Ten Captains S
58 an] a MS

69 By——Sir] I sweare sir MS; By Heaven, sir C, W, D
69.1 *Drum . . . Colours.*] *Drums beate | A March w^{th}in:* MS
70 What] death MS
72 higher] further MS
75 By ——] by this blest light MS; By Heaven C, W, D
85 be ye] be you MS; ye be L, S, C
88 Dares] dare MS
93 know] finde MS
98, 101 ye...ye] you...you MS
101 for] meere MS
104 his] *om.* MS
106 toughnesse] roughnes MS
106 courage] carriage MS
112 shall] *om.* MS
113 he's] is MS
114 when] where MS

120 He's] Is MS
121 his] this MS
127 This] then MS

128 *Regulus.*] *om.* F 1–2, L, S; *on line* 129 *in* C, W, D
128 your...your] our...our F 1–2, L–D

II.ii

0.1 Junius, Petillius] Iunius: (*after him:*) petillius MS
4 our] the MS
5, 6, 53 ye] you MS
6 still] sir MS
8 *Junius.*] *om.* MS
12 to't] *om.* MS
16 brings] bring F 2, L, S
26 An] a MS
32 Yet 'twere] It were MS
39 tormenting] tormentings MS
40 whining] whynings MS
50 shun my fortune.] MS *adds marginal s.d.:* '*he sitts downe:*'
50 haunt] hunt F 1–2, L–D
51 *Musick.*] *Songe:* MS
52.1 *Song...in mockage.*] *om.* MS (*but cf. line* 54 *below*)

54 oh,] *om.* MS
54 read it.] read it in mockage. MS
56 *has*] *his* F 1–2, L
57 *lovers*] cowards S, C, W
64 *a*] *om.* MS
65 The——consume ye] The rott consume you MS; The pox consume ye C, W, D
66 chew] chaw MS
70 I ere] ere I MS
82 gallowes] gallosses MS
82 overdoe] overlook S
87 Souldier] leader MS
94 dare...dare] dares...dares MS
96 ye] you F 1 +
109 lets have] lets have have F 2

II.iii

2 your] not MS
5, 15, 27, 65, 69, 74, 84, 89, 116, 132, 136 ye] you MS
9 *3. Souldier.*] · 2 · sold: MS
9, 12 lief] live MS; lieve L–W
10 not out] not stick out S, C, W
10 *4. Souldier.*] *All sold:* MS
17, 18 *1. Daughter, 2. Daughter*] *referred to respectively as* Eldest Daughter *and* Youngest Daughter *throughout* MS
20 ye...ye] you...you MS
21 even] ene MS
21 conscience] consciences MS
23 Ye] you MS
26 ye...ye...ye] you...you... you MS

30 *Judas.*] · 1 · sold: MS
31 *4. Souldier.*] *Iud:* MS
31 Surely] Securely S
32 We'ld] wee wolld MS
34 What] who MS
39 *1. Souldier.*] · 2 · Sold: MS
50 Art...hungry] art not thow hungry fellow MS
52 quick] *om.* MS
53 *2. Souldier* · 1 · sold: MS
58–59 Sit downe...'tis coming] *after* chicken (*line* 65) *in* MS
70 We're even] wee are Ene MS
72, 81 By——] by my life MS; By Heaven C, W, D
78 by me] my MS
80 hearing] heareing still MS

87 thee] you MS
90 this] the MS
90.1 Daughters *above.*] *the · 2 ·*
    Daughters (Aboue:) MS (*on lines*
    87–88)
100 whelp] whelpes MS
100 my Uncle] my noble vncle MS;
    me Uncle F2
106–109 *Judas. By* this...do it.]
    after Do it. (*line* 97) *in* MS
110 Uncle...pin.] *after* were a man.
    (*line* 106) *in* MS

123 your] our MS
125 *Enter...Servant] Enter: younger*
    Daughter: & an Attendant:
    *she shewes her selfe but at y*ᵉ
    Doore MS
128.1 *a* Guide] *Guides* MS
131, 136 *Servant.*] *Attend:* MS
135 boyes] boy MS
136 Keep...there] knowe yoʳ file
    then MS
138 'Blesse] god blesse MS

II.iv

13 Falanx] *om.* MS
24 too] *om.* MS
31 *at the end of this line* MS *contains*
    s.d. Exit Demetrius
38 could] should MS
38 ye] you MS
41.2 *company*]   *Company · 4 ·*
    Soldiers MS
43 ——confound] a pox confound
    MS; Pox confound C, W, D
44, 49, 62, 67, 75, 80, 86, 90, 93 ye]
    you MS
46 devises] deuills MS
48 even] ene MS
48 Forks] fforke MS

54 the] *om.* L, S
55 *1. Souldier] Soldiers* MS
57 By this——] by this hand MS;
    by this Heaven C; by this light
    W, D
59, 82, 85 Ye] you MS
61 running] rouncing MS
69 yern] erne MS
83 one call'd] an old MS
86 drag] dril MS
91–92 Arm, arm...more] *after*
    boyes (*line* 94) *in* MS; *after* more
    (*line* 92) MS *has the words* 'Iust
    Decius'

III.i

4 doubt] *om.* MS
4 valours] valor MS
6 due to] vnto MS
11 these] this MS
14, 49, 51 ye] you MS
18 place] plac'd F2, L
24 strik'st] struck'st MS
26 thou god] *om.* MS
29 their] the S
29 the] thy MS
44 hourly] *om.* MS
46 *Prosutagus*] Prasutagus D
47 Ye] see MS
50 O] *om.* MS

50.1 *A smoak...Altar.*] *om.* MS
53 fretfull] fearefull MS, F2, L, S;
    fetrfull F1
59, 74 *Andate*] *Audate* F1; *An-*
    drasta S
61 roll'st] row'st S
75 *A flame arises.*] *om.* MS
76 *Musick.*] *om.* MS
79 in] on MS
80 him] her F2, L, S
81 His] Her F2, L, S
83 *Messenger.*] Seruᵗ: MS
83 He's] Is MS
86.1 *Recorders.*] *om.* MS

III.ii

3, 39, 49, 51, 53, 55, 58, 59, 63 ye]
　you MS
7 likelihood] *om.* MS
12 new] no MS
22 beheld] behold MS
23 Thy] yor MS
26 I am] I'm F2, L, S, C
28 parents] parent C, W, D
36 This] *Cur.* This F1–2
47 Ye] you MS
48, 67 ye...ye] you...you MS
48.1 Macer] *om.* MS

62 honour] honors MS
68 Perinine] *perimine* MS; Apenine
　F2–D
70 deserts] desert MS
70 where the snow dwels] *between
　the words* Apennine, and (*line* 68)
　in C
72 death and sleep] sleepe and
　death MS
77 myst] mixt MS
78 burning] *om.* MS
86 *March.*] *om.* MS

III.iii

2–2.1 *A March.* | *Drums within...
　off*] *Drums Beate* w^th*in* MS (*on
　line* 0.1)
4 by——a] I sweare a MS: By
　Heaven a C, W, D

13 square] great MS
20 place] part MS
22.1 *Drums...off.*] *om.* MS
25 hound] *om.* MS
26 I'll] I MS

III.iv

1 yee] you MS
4, 13 ye] you MS
7 nor] not, L, S

8 end's] end' F2
14.2–3 *Alarms,...Battell.*] *om.* MS

III.v

1, 40, 45, 47, 51, 54, 55, 60, 86,
　112, 119, 120, 123, 135, 148,
　151, 159, 162, 173 ye] you MS
5 halloa] holoe MS; hollo F2;
　Hollow L; halo S–D
5 *Loud Shouts.*] *om.* MS
8 charge] change MS
18 *Loud.*] *om.* MS
27 with...Souldiers] *Soldiers* (*bring-
　ing in*)...*others* MS
29 death] deaths S, D
31 *Servant.*] *Guide:* MS; *First Sold.*
　D

36 prate] prattle MS
43 Ye...improvident...ye] you
　...vnprouident...you MS
44, 67 ye...ye] you...you MS
46 to your wanton livers] to waite
　on your louers MS
48 itcht] itch F2–C
48 master] masters MS
49 topt] tupt MS, C, W
52 fell] self F2, L
58 us'd] vse MS
61 th' battell] the battell MS
69 ye] *om.* MS

69 By——] I vowe MS; By
   Heaven C, W, D
70 By——] good cozen MS; By
   Heaven, C W, D
74 one] our MS
76 must we] we must F 2, L, S
76 whence] whome MS
79 stales] scales F 1–2, L
83 The——] the devill MS, C, W,
   D
88.1 *Drums...again.*] *om.* MS
92 By——] I sweare MS; By
   Heaven, C W, D
95 mountains] mountaine MS
96 Dragons] Dragon L
106 ground] playnes MS
109 face] plume MS; fate F 2, L
110 Y'have] you haue MS
115 despight the] despight o'th' S
116 line] live MS
123 to't] to you MS
124 now] *om.* F 2, L, S
124 'Tis I] "Tis now I S
125 'em...ye] on...you MS
131 ——on't] pox on't MS, C, W;
   a pox on't D
134 mens] mans MS
136 ruind] ruine F 1–2, L
136 How,] *om.* MS
136 *Showts within.*] *om.* MS
137 by——] I sweare MS; by
   Heaven C, W, D

137 *Victoria within.*] *om.* MS
138.1 *Exeunt*] *Exit Caratack* MS
141.1 *Enter . . . Captains*] *Enter:
   Swetonius: Iunius: & Soldiers:
   vpon the chase:* MS
147 ye, ye] you. you MS
150 your Queen] yor great *Queene*
   MS
150.1 Caratach] *Caratacke: (at their
   backs:)* MS
151 rape] rapes MS
152 Ye...ye] you...you MS
152.1 *Loud...within.*] *om.* MS
153 tread] treads MS
153 all's lost, all's lost] alls lost. lost
   MS
154 *Exeunt* Bonduca] *Bonduca flyes
   & hir Daughters* MS
155 thy] the F 2, L
157 breech ye...ye] brich you...
   you MS
159.1 *Fight. Drums*] *fights* MS
160 sledges] *om.* MS
161 *Decius.*] *om.* MS
161 *Petillius.*] *Drus:* MS
163 I] ô. I MS
164 these] they MS
170 rul'd ye] ruled you MS
172 *Retreat.*] *om.* MS
172.1 *Demetrius...Colours*] *om.* MS
179 at no] at not L; not at S
181 Let's] let's us F 1

IV.i

19 nesh] *om.* MS; Mesh F 2
21 ballads] madness F 2, L, S
28 I am counsell'd,] *om.* MS
30 Ye] you MS
32 whistling] whiskling MS
32 snatcht] *om.* MS
33 They're] they are MS
34 and] a MS

41 crush] crash MS
45 Wench] a wench MS
50 trim] *om.* MS
51 I have] ye have F 2
57 H'as] h'has MS
65 ye] you MS
71.2 *Short Flourish.*] *om.* MS

IV.ii

4 saw] see MS
9–28] MS *om. all speech-prefixes*
22 fully...you] full...ye MS
23 those] these MS
31 *people to the door*] *Company (peeping at the Doore:)* MS
32 dare] dares MS
36 A——on ye] a curse on you MS; A pox on you C, W, D
37, 39, 44, 61, 62 ye] you MS
38 in's] in his MS
39 *They retire.*] *om.* MS
45 the] this MS
46 at bay] at a bay MS
47 Stand] w*th*in*:* stand MS
47 ye...ye] you...you
47 *Exit*] *om.* MS
53 Thou...charge] thow man made of matt. come charge MS
54 Hang thee] away thow MS
56 scabb'd] scald MS
57 I] Ile MS

60 By——] I sweare MS; By Heaven C, W, D
62 Sir?] *om.* MS
63–64] *lines reversed in* MS
63 kill] eate MS
66 A dwarf, devil] the damnd devill MS
67–68 I have kill'd...him thus.] *after* bloody staff (*line* 65) *in* MS
68 Look here,] *the words occur in the* MS *but are marked for deletion*
69 charge] shake MS
70 Flee, flee] fly. fly MS
72 ye Rogues] you rogues MS
73 A...a...a...a] he...he...he ...he MS
74 , *with a head*] *om.* MS
77 And a strange] and by a stronge MS
85 The] thy MS
87 nay,] *om.* F 2, L
88 these] the MS

IV.iii

1 grieve ye] greeve you MS
2, 31, 57, 119, 120, 122, 124, 150, 179, 182, 195, 197, 198, 205 ye] you MS
6 ye...ye] you...you MS
10–11] *lines reversed in* MS
12 ever, ever, ever] ever. ever MS
14 pointing] poyntings MS
16 disputing] dispatching MS
19 by——] I sweare MS; by Heaven C, W, D
21 I have robb'd...seek me,] *om.* MS
22 lost] last C
26 not] *om.* MS
29 I'll] I MS
33–35 *Drusus.* Good...winter.

Exeunt] *Drus:* I feare thy nature | and will not be far of. good *Regulus* | step to the soldier. and allay his anger. | for he is wild as winter. | *Regu:* Ile doe my best. | and when occasion offers. call. | *Drus:* I will: ——*Exeunt:* MS
36–49 O, are ye...he rises.] *om.* MS
50 How...ye see.] *petill:* how does lord *penius.* | *peni:* sure he mocks me. | *petill:* sir. how doe ye. | *peni:* as you see sir MS
50–51 I am glad...still.] *om.* MS
58, 59, 125 Ye] you MS
60 The gods defend, Sir.] *om.* MS
72 It] that MS

73 and] o MS

73–74 Yet...again] It may be cur'd though MS

74 Never] never with credit MS

74–80 Petillius. Your leave... None, Petillius] petill: now ye are ith right on't. | peni: I am ith right: I knowe petillius MS

76 along] om. F2, L

87 the General——] the Generall. the noble Generall. | you doe not knowe sir MS

87 He's] Is MS

95 a General] a Iust Generall MS

97–110 Petillius. What would... thank thee.] om. MS

105 By——] Dy Heaven C, W, D

112–113 'Tis fit...ye; say] nor is it fit you should. ye foole yor waight in't. | breake yor owne grounds of rule. that have cōmande. | nay say he had sir. say MS

112 how] now D

118 knew] knowe MS

118–119 kill ye? | Say] kill you. | dare you stay so long penius. | peni: honest captaine | petill: say MS

123 dare ye] dare you MS

131–141 fault. I'll hang...sword then] faulte. | petill: by no meanes: that were abhominable. | and wolld still showe you poorer and poorer. | peni: why then my sword petillius MS

157 stern...own] om. MS

157 now] none MS

164 Stabs himself] the words are marked for deletion in MS, which replaces them with 'strikes him-selfe'

166 nor age] nor age. nor age MS

166 Eating] melting F1–2, L–D

174 earth.] MS adds s.d.: 'dyes:'

178.1 with Souldiers] (stopping the Soldiers. at the Doore.) MS

179 Souldiers.] Soldiers· wthin. MS

180 Regulus.] om. MS

180 Kill him, kill him, kill him] kill him. kill him MS

185 Devoured] devoure MS

195–197] Marginal s.d. in MS: 'the Soldiers kneele about &. weeps:'

196 ye wretches] you wretches MS

199 coy'd] loued MS

205 Builds] build F1–2, L–W

213 morning] mourning C (conj. S)

214 Ceremonies] cerimonye MS

IV.iv

0.3 Drum and Colours.] om. MS

2 out-brav'd] out out-brav'd F2

5 Exit Nennius.] om. MS

6 Icenian] Ilenian. MS

8 lashes] lawes MS

8 Decius.] Curi: MS

10.1 Exit Decius.] om. MS

17 She's] she is

18 Aspires] aperes MS

29.1 Petillius.] petillius: (talkes wth ye Generall: MS

33 not thou] thow not MS

40 their] the MS

43 and——] and by the gods MS, C, W, D

44 their] the MS

47 Enter Decius.] om. MS

47 Decius.] Demet: MS

52 my womans] no womans MS

56 if one fear, one] it on feare on MS

57 One...but] on...out MS

58 To] om. MS

63 envie] Envyes MS

66, 86 ye...ye] you...you MS

67 yee] you MS
68 'S death] death MS
71 it] *om.* F1–2, L–W
72, 75, 91, 133, 134 ye] you MS
76 Sears] fears F1; soars F2, L–W
77 Strange] stronge MS
78 *Exit* Decius.] *om.* MS
82 *1. Daughter.*] *Bondu:* MS
89 Come] some MS
90 begin] *om.* MS
95 ye kill] you kill MS
99 ye] you F1+
102 O gods] o ye gods MS
113 help thee] MS *adds s.d.:* 'she dyes'
115 in all your stories] *om.* MS (*but cf. line* 117 *below*)
115 your] our F2
117 Eat] and all yor storyes. Eate MS
118 topt] tupt C, W

119 By——] I sweare MS; By Heaven C, W, D
120 an] a MS
132 mindes] hearts MS
135 aged] *om.* MS
137 a] the F2, L, S
138 glories] glorye MS
139 up] *om.* MS
141 like] *om.* MS
142 ye conquer'd] yo^u conquerd MS
153.1 *Enter* Decius.] *om.* MS
155 th' sword] the sword MS
156 ——take] pox take MS, C, W, D
157 grown] growes MS
157 what, a spirit?] *om.* MS (*but cf. line* 159 *below*)
159 tumbles?] tumbles. | what a spirit MS

V.i

V.i–V.iii.37 (*Junius.* Kill ye?)] *Missing from* MS *which explains thus:* 'Here should A Scæne. be betwene Iunius. & petillius: (Iunius mocking petillius for being in loue wth Bonducas Daughter that Killd her selfe: to them: Enterd Suetonius: (blameing petillius for the Death of pænius: The next scæne. the solemnitye of pænius his ffunerall mournd by Caracticus: The begining of this following Scæne betweene petillius & Iunius is wanting. – the occa-

sion. why these are wanting here. the booke where by it was first Acted from is lost: and this hath beene transcrib'd from the fowle papers of the Authors wch were found:'
6 *Britanie*] Britain L, C
14 songs] sons F2
53 sometimes] sometime F2, L–W
61 worths] Worth L, S
70 before] 'fore S, C
73 natures] nature F2, L–D
84 making] make F2, L
85 upon] on S

V.ii

6 by——] by Heaven C, W, D
10 A——] A pox C, W, D
15 he is] is he L, S, C

26 *life it was*] life was F1, W
27 pursue on] pursue it on F2, L; pursuit on S, C, W

38 By——] By Heaven C, W, D
38 ——on't] pox on't C, W, D
51 wise and] wise and and F2
77 it] *om.* L, S

78 specially] especially F2, L–D
110 see] saw L–D
133 th' Camp] the Camp F2, L, D

V.iii

6 ——shake] Pox shake C, W, D
9 fall] falls S, C, W
25 am sorry] am very sorry L, S
33 forgot you] forget you S, C; forgot W
34 By——] By the gods, C, W, D
38, 39, 80, 153 ye] you MS
39 ask me not] aske not MS
50 I dare not trust] I am asham'd to truot MS
52 do it,] MS *adds s.d.:* 'drawes'
65 time's come] *Iunius* comes MS
78 the chin] th chin MS
78 sankst] sunkst MS, F2, L–W
81 By——] by my faith MS; By Heaven C, W, D
86 ye] *om.* MS
91 Rock] racke MS
95 ye] you F1+
98.1 *on the Rock*] *om.* MS
99 my] *om.* MS
105 *Hengo.* But my head, Uncle:] *om.* MS
124 Boy] *om.* MS
125 Quick, quick...have it.] *after* What ailest thou? *in* MS
125 *Iudas shoots Hengo*] *Iudas steales nere him and shoots him: & startes back:* MS
127.1 *Caratach...Rock.*] *flings and tumbles him ouer: pulls him vp againe:* MS
129–131 pocky villain...pricks me] pockye villaine. am I preseru'd

for this. | *Hen:* ô it pricks me | extreamely prickes me MS
137 wretched] sciruy MS
138 grow] am MS
139 I once hop'd] I bleede MS
141 father] vncle MS
142 Uncle] *om.* MS
143 Shall I draw it?] *om.* MS
144 I would live] *om.* MS
145 heavens] heaven MS
150 Feaver] ſfeavers MS
158–159 Mercie. | *Caratach.* Mercie. | You blessed] mercy | mercy | *Cara:* you blessed MS
163–164 Look, | Look what] looke what MS
167.1 *on the rock*] *climing the rock:* MS
172 by all——] by all thats honorable MS; By all the gods C, W, D
173 As I...envie thee,] *om.* MS
176 Thou filler...glory.] *om.* MS
179 true] new MS
182 vertues] vertue MS
188–189 MS *contains marginal s.d.:* 'they come of|the rocke'
189 then] theé MS
190 The] thow MS
190 *Flourish.*] *om.* MS
196–201 *Swetonius*...friends soul.] *om.* MS
202 in] on MS

THE TRAGEDY OF VALENTINIAN

edited by

ROBERT K. TURNER, JNR

TEXTUAL INTRODUCTION

Entitled *The Emperor Valentinian, The Tragedy of Valentinian* (Greg, *Bibliography*, no. 667) was included in the list of Beaumont and Fletcher plays entered in the Stationers' Register in September, 1646. It occupies sigs. 7A1–7D2ᵛ in the Folio of 1647. Using materials from the 'Histoire d'Eudoxe, Valentinian, et Ursace' in the Second Part of *L'Astrée de Messire Honoré d'Urfé* (Paris, 1610) and from Procopius' discourses about the Vandal War, which was available in several Latin translations as well as in the Greek, Fletcher composed the play without the aid of a collaborator. He wrote it after the publication of *L'Astrée* but, if I am right about the adaptation of 'Care charming sleep' (V.ii.13ff) to the occasion of Prince Henry's death, before that event, 6 November 1612.[1] Like others in the Folio of 1647, the text was thus over thirty years old when it was first published.

There are still a good many unanswered questions about the printing of Section 7, which, comprising only *Valentinian* and *The Fair Maid of the Inn*, is the briefest in the Folio.[2] Although no certain link has been established, Section 7 was probably a product, as Johan Gerritsen observes, of the shop of Susan Islip, who was responsible as well for Section 3.[3] It is set in a different fount, however, and could have been printed concurrently with the latter part of the earlier section, which ends with Beaumont's Letter on sig. 3X4. Section 7 may have been created, in fact, because Islip, having been asked to handle *Valentinian* in addition to the pieces in

---

[1] See the Textual Note on the passage. The posterior date was previously set at 1614, when William Ostler died; he was, according to the Folio of 1672, one of the tragedy's principal actors. For the date and sources, see R. G. Martin (ed.), *Valentinian*, in *The Works of Francis Beaumont and John Fletcher* (1912), IV, 209–11. For the authorship, see Cyrus Hoy, 'The Shares of Fletcher and his Collaborators in the Beaumont and Fletcher Canon (I)', *Studies in Bibliography*, VIII (1956), 129–46.

[2] The subject has most recently been studied by James P. Hammersmith, *The Printers and the Beaumont and Fletcher Folio of 1647, Section 7* (Ann Arbor, 1974), summarized in *Papers of the Bibliographical Society of America*, LXIX (1975), 206–25. Most of the following details are drawn from this monograph.

[3] 'The Printing of the Beaumont and Fletcher Folio of 1647', *The Library*, 5th ser., III (1949), 233–64.

263

Section 3, needed a new signature alphabet, there being an inadequate number of leaves remaining in 3 to accommodate the play; and the fact that *Valentinian* ends with an internal two-leaf quire (7D) suggests that *The Fair Maid* was a further late addition which came to the printer's hand when *Valentinian* was nearly completed. These matters would be of small consequence to the text of *Valentinian* were it not that there seem to have been peculiarities in the printing which are perhaps the product of unusual expedients for publication.

Two compositors set the type. Their takes and the order in which they proceeded may be represented as follows:

Compositor:	*A*	*A*	*B*	*B*	*B*	*B*	*A*	*B*	*A?*
Signature:	A2^v	A3a^1	A3a^2	A3b	A2a	A2b^1	A2b^2	A3^{v}a	A3^{v}b

Compositor:	?	*A*	*B*	*B*	*B*	*B*	*B?*	*A*	*B*
Signature:	A1	A4^{v}a^1	A4^{v}a^2	A4^{v}b	A4	A1^{v}a	A1^{v}b	B3	B2^v

Compositor:	*B*	*B*	*A*	*B*	*B*	*A*	*B*	*B*	*B*
Signature:	B2	B3^v	B4	B1^v	B1	B4^v	C2^v	C3	C2

Compositor:	*B*	*B*	*B*	*B*	*A*	*B*	*B*	*B*	*B*
Signature:	C3^v	C1^v	C4	C1	C4^v	D2	D1^v	D1	D2^v

Divided columns: A3a^1 to F lines 23–40; A2b^1 to F line 49; A4^{v}a^1 to F line 39

Leaving A1 aside, Compositor *A* thus was more or less certainly responsible for A2b^2–A3a^1 (I.iii.25–I.iii.177–98, the limit being unclear), A3^{v}b (II.ii.6–51), A4^{v}a^1 (II.iii.85–116), B3 (III.i.272–382), B4–B4^v (III.iii.23–IV.i.79), and C4^v (V.ii.120–V.iv.29), between six and seven folio pages. Compositor *B* was responsible for the rest, between twenty-one and twenty-two pages. Evidence from reappearing types indicates fairly clearly that only one typecase was employed and the division of labour in Quire A that at first the services of the compositors were but occasionally available for work on *Valentinian*. In the later quires the typesetting became essentially a one-man affair, with the second compositor lending a hand now and then. This no doubt explains why three, instead of two or four, sets of rules and running titles were assembled for the skeleton formes, causing the sheets to be printed, in effect, in one and one half skeletons. Since, as Hammersmith has shown, there was no shortage of the rules or types used for this purpose, it appears that construction of a second skeleton was half done when the first forme, with two sets of rules and running titles, was returned from the press, making it more convenient to combine one of its sets with the third than to assemble a fourth. Subsequently, the three sets were employed, two for each forme, in what must have been combinations of convenience, it never having become advantageous to construct the fourth set. Between each forme, therefore, there was a suspension in the printing of a duration at least sufficient for the stripping of one side of the old forme; and, since some wrought-off formes were distributed out of the order in which they were machined, the work probably proceeded slowly. Even if Compositor *B* remained fairly steadily on the job (perhaps rinsing formes or doing similar chores while Compositor *A* was typesetting), the press may have performed other work between the formes of *Valentinian* or have been operated at half-press.

Some strangely haphazard proofreading seems to have been done, although too few variants have been discovered to permit much generalization. A collation of twenty-one copies turned up only four certain variants on three pages – the repositioning of a scene head (I.iii.0.1) a rather puzzling alteration in a line of a song (II.v.44), a correction to punctuation (IV.i.156), and a trivial change to a speech-prefix abbreviation (IV.i.182). What makes these remarkable is that they occur amidst untouched errors, both substantive and accidental, that cry out for attention; it seems nearly impossible that the corrections are second-round. On the evidence available it appears instead that some, if not all, sheets were merely glanced at and an error or two almost arbitrarily selected for repair. Nothing indicates that the proofreader ever looked at the copy, even that of the song, for there several mistakes survive, including one in the line above the corrected line.

As the text is divided into acts and scenes, is in general properly lined, and is supplied with stage-directions and speech-prefixes in a reasonably uniform style, it strikes one immediately as having been derived from a transcript of some sort, the tangles usually characterizing foul papers being largely absent. R. C. Bald undoubtedly was impressed by these features when he noted that

Valentinian has the look of a private transcript, 'private' perhaps because there are few conspicuous signs of theatrical connection.[1] Even if we accept the initial assumption of a transcript, however, it is important to know what was being transcribed and by whom. We must, therefore, separate out those features of the text which can be attributed to the compositors and analyse those remaining for what they can tell about the nature of the printer's copy, a rather delicate task, for transcripts have a way of hiding as much as they reveal.

Act and Scene Division

Valentinian is correctly divided into acts and scenes, except that II.v, II.vi and III.ii are unmarked and II.iii, IV.iv and V.viii are all headed 'Scæn. 2.'. With respect to the undesignated scenes, II.iv, v and vi (which concludes Act II) are closely related; all follow Lucina through the palace just before her ravishing, and it is apparent only on fairly close inspection that the stage is clear between them. Someone not intimately familiar with the play could easily have understood the three to be one long scene.[2] III.ii, however, is another matter, for it employs characters different from those in III.i and it is followed by III.iii, properly headed 'Scæn. 3.'. The implication here is that 'Scæn. 2.' at one time was in the text and was omitted through carelessness somewhere along the line of transmission. With respect to the second anomaly, the fact that all the scenes are mismarked 'Scæn. 2.' suggests that Compositor *B*, in whose takes they all fall, may have reused a standing scene head without altering its number. If this is so, however, it is a bit curious that only 'Scæn. 2.' and no other such head was incorrectly repeated. The play, incidentally, was designed for production with intervals between the acts: twice characters who exit at the end of scenes concluding acts reappear at the beginning of the acts following (II.i and V.i).

---

[1] *Bibliographical Studies in the Beaumont and Fletcher Folio of 1647* (Oxford, 1938), p. 110.
[2] The stage is momentarily clear at V.ii.12, but here the following entrance seems to be into the locale just vacated.

Lineation

The F1 lineation is correct except in about twenty places, a low number by comparison with some other plays in the canon. At IV.iv.81, 92 and 94, all near the foot of 7C2b, Compositor B almost certainly divided single lines into two in order to fill the column, 7C2ᵛ having been previously set. I suspect that II.ii.5 (Compositor B) and V.iv.29 (Compositor A), both the last lines in their columns, were also divided for mechanical reasons, perhaps to maintain conformity between the type lines and the casting off. Here and there, however, there are five other instances of single lines being printed as two; IV.i.106, IV.ii.20 and V.ii.95 could have been divided by the author to indicate pauses in delivery, but the reason for dividing II.iv.30 and IV.iv.245 is not immediately apparent. Mislineation most frequently occurs (seven times) when a pentameter is shared by two or more speakers. In one instance a short line is run in with a pentameter (V.viii.100) and in another the final word of one pentameter is carried down to the next (III.i.123–4); neither of these is a particularly revealing error. One other, however, may be. III.i.331 is a perfectly good pentameter if 'Aecius' is given four syllables, as it must be at I.iii.244, III.i.298 and IV.ii.11. In F1 line 331 is run in with the last half of line 330, the result being hopelessly hypermetrical – 'Why then I care not, I can live wel enough Aecius'. The creator of this mishmash seems to have thought that 'Aecius' takes three syllables, as it usually does, or possibly two, as it never does. Fletcher would not have made this mistake, and a compositor setting cast-off copy is not likely to alter lineation except to fit copy, a consideration that does not pertain here. The culprit, then, would seem to have been an intermediary.

Speech Assignments

As is true of the lineation, the speech assignments are generally right, although not absolutely so. At IV.i.15 a speech evidently intended for Lycinius is given to the Emperour, who also has the speeches immediately preceding and following; this kind of error, probably memorial, is without special significance. At IV.i.193 a speech-prefix is omitted, an eyeskip error which also reveals nothing. At IV.iii.23 a prefix is dropped one line, a more interesting accident. F1 prints

> *Pon.* Out of a mischiefe meerly: did you mark it?
> Yes well enough.
> *Pro.* Now ye have meanes to quit it. . . .

Pontius' speech is a complete pentameter; 'Yes well enough', which answers the question, obviously belongs to Proculus, and these words, joined to those F1 gives him, also make up a pentameter and should with them occupy one line. The error, however, could not have arisen had 'Yes well enough' not occupied a line to itself in the printer's copy, perhaps as an interlineation which was mis-interpreted. If it was an interlineation, however, we are no closer to the nature of the F1 copy, for Fletcher or a transcriber may have made it.

Several other speech-prefixes are similarly tantalizing. At V.iv.0.1 three Senators, new characters at this point, are brought on. Their speeches are tagged 1., 2. and 3., although the dialogue makes it clear that 1. is Fulvius and 3. is Sempronius, 2. for the moment remaining unnamed. They reappear as members of the procession which opens V.viii ('*the* Senators', line 0.2), after which Sempronius orates. His prefix is '*Sen. Semp.* 3.' (line 1). This oddity evidently came about because some such prefix as '*Sen.* 3.' was cancelled and '*Semp.*' substituted, but in such a way that the compositor conflated the two. Subsequently the Senator is '*Semp.*' and may have been so in the copy, the first prefix having been altered to bring it into conformity with the later occurrences. And the same thing happens again. At line 56, 2. *Senator* is finally identified as Lucius, and at line 57, his only speech in the scene, his prefix is '2. *Sen. Luc.*', the compositor having again conflated a cancellation and a substitution. What we have, then, is evidence that in the printer's copy numbered prefixes were replaced by names, but once more nothing to show whether the reviser was the author or another agent.

Stage-Directions

The text is pretty adequately supplied with stage-directions. For ease of reading I have added thirty or so describing business, but all of these are inferential from the text and would not be strictly necessary to regulate performance. Occasionally F1 itself supplies similar aids ('*Jewells shewd*' (II.v.84), '*Letter red*' (IV.i.107)). A half-dozen exits are lacking, but these omissions occur in conjunction with lines of dialogue which send the character off (e.g. 'be gone then' (I.iii.103)). Supernumeraries may be specified (e.g. the Attendants at V.ii.12.2; they will be needed to take Aretus' and Valentinian's bodies away) or they may not be (e.g. the Ladies at II.v.92.1), a not uncommon omission. Somewhat more serious are several places where necessary characters are not brought on or where the action is left unclear. The entrance of Proculus at IV.i.79.1 is omitted (see the Textual Note on IV.i.80) as are the entrances of Lucina and the Emperour at II.vi.4.1 and the Messenger at V.vi.0.1 (that this character is a messenger, incidentally, is Weber's guess and that he is the same messenger who enters at V.vi.53 is mine). The first of these omissions is almost certainly compositorial and the second may be, but the third, like the Ladies just mentioned, was probably not in the manuscript. The only place where the action is egregiously muddled, however, is at the beginning of V.viii where, as the Textual Note explains more fully, several separate directions appear to have been run together. I suspect that the difficulty over the '*Musicke, Song, wreath*', if the words are not the crude preliminary notations of a prompter, may have arisen from the provision of the lyric in a separate manuscript, a matter we shall reach in a moment, and that the direction was given its F1 form by someone, not the author, who simply pulled together several directions pertaining to the song which were unclear because the lyric was absent or on another leaf. The language of several stage-directions is authorial rather than theatrical, in the technical sense of that word. Several of the subordinate characters are provided, usually upon their first appearance, with generic descriptions in addition to their names: 'Pontius *the Captaine*' (II.iii.0.1), 'Lycias *the Eunuch*' (II.i.51 and II.ii.39.1; he is the character whom d'Urfé, with splendid inaptness, called Heracles the Eunuch), 'Eudoxa *the Empresse*' (V.ii.12.1), 'Paulus (*a Poet*) *and* Lycippus (*a Gentleman*)' (V.v.0.1). The author's hand may also be detected in '*as at Dice*' (II.i.0.1), '*Enter* Maximus *alone*' (IV.ii.0.1), '*runs away*' (IV.iv.125), and 'Phidias *with his dagger in him, and* Aretus *poysond*' (V.i.0.1–0.2). On the other hand, several directions involving aspects of production such as sounds and stage movements could have had theatrical origin, although none seems to me decisively prompt-booklike. They include '*Tumult and noise within*' (II.iii.0.1), '*at one dore...at another*' (II.iv.0.1), '*running over the Stage*' (IV.iv.244.1), '*Exeunt severally*' (V.i.34.1) and '*sicke in a Chaire*' (V.ii.12.1), as well as flourishes, a sennet with trumpets, and music upon oboes. There are no directions of a strictly theatrical sort, such as those that name actors or anticipate entrances, business or properties.

The most striking feature of the stage-directions, however, is that, following the initial direction of each scene, those within the scene, whether centered or marginal, are frequently preceded by dashes or hyphens linking them with the text or attempting to do so. Those that run to two lines or more are often preceded by a brace or sometimes a brace and a dash.[1] The compositors thus took some trouble to bring over into the print the device used in the manuscript to show at what point in the text marginal directions were to be effective.[2] Even so, in this edition it has been thought desirable to

---

[1] The braces and dashes are eliminated from the present edition, but I have thought a record of the removed dashes worth preserving in the Emendations of Accidentals because F1 sometimes seems to regard them as punctuation. In the Emendations of Accidentals the dash is considered to follow the last word of the sentence if there is no other punctuation after that word. If there is, the dash is considered to precede the stage-direction.

[2] Dashes, braces, or a combination of the two used to connect stage-directions and the text are fairly common in dramatic manuscripts – e.g. *Richard II* (BM MS Egerton 1994), *Sir Thomas More* (BM MS Harl. 7368), the Lambarde MS of *The Woman's Prize*, the Malone MS of *A Game at Chess*, Crane's transcripts of *Demetrius, Barnavelt* and *The Witch*, and Knight's of *Bonduca, The Honest Man's Fortune* and *Believe as You List*. The compositors of *Valentinian* also employ both dashes and braces in *The Fair Maid of the Inn*, although less frequently than in *Valentinian*. In Section 3 of the Folio, which may have been typeset in the same shop as Section 7, braces are fairly common but dashes occur only and very occasionally in *The Humourous Lieutenant* (3S2 and 3S4ᵛ; according to Hoy, 'Fletcher and his Collaborators', VIII, 139, the copy is supposed to derive from prompt) and *The Nice Valour* (3T4ᵛ; copy un-

move some ten directions by a line or two, although in not all of these instances is it certain that F1 is wrong: in a few the characters may be intended to enter shortly before they speak (e.g. the Servant at III.iii.55 and Proculus and the two others at IV.iv.270). Of another order are two radically misplaced directions, both of which furnish important clues to the nature of the copy. The entrance of Lucina and the others at II.v.4.1 in F1 is placed after line 44, following the song which Lucina is obviously intended to hear (cf. lines 49–50). The most likely reason for the error is that the lyric was written on a leaf of manuscript not integral with the text, and this combined with the mix-up at the beginning of V.viii, which also in part involves a song, and the fact that for none of the songs are the singers indicated leads me to believe that all the songs were provided in separate copy. The second badly misplaced direction is at V.ii.54; in F1 it occurs after line 30, where it has no business at all. Between line 31 and line 54 the plot does not advance, the dialogue being devoted primarily to Valentinian's descriptions of the agonizing effects of the poison and appropriate comments and replies from others present. This idea is introduced and somewhat developed in lines 23–31; from line 31 through line 54 it is merely developed further. Valentinian's speech at line 32 is prefixed 'Em.', the only use in the entire play of this abbreviation ('Emp.' or 'Empe.' being the ordinary forms). Lines 31–54 thus seem to be an authorial interpolation – a writing up of Valentinian's sufferings for increased dramatic effect – which was inserted into the manuscript, perhaps on an additional leaf, in such a way as to obscure the correct position of the stage-direction. In this connection it might also be observed that another stage-direction (II.v.0.1) which is misplaced by one line may show, because of its unusual phrasing ('Enter Lycinius, and Proculus, Balbus'), signs of touching up.

ascertained). The one or the other device may be found elsewhere in the Folio, e.g. in *The Spanish Curate* (Section 1; dashes), *The Captain* (Section 2; dashes), *The Woman's Prize* (dashes on 5N4), *Love's Pilgrimage* (Section 8; braces).

Other Special Features

Two more details of the text should be noticed. First, in two places (IV.iv.109 and V.ii.63) dashes have replaced oaths. Since the same is found in *The Fair Maid of the Inn* ('A —— upon them', 7G1ᵛa), the purgation was probably compositorial. Paulus' 'By'th masse' (V.v.20), incidentally, was allowed to stand. Secondly, at IV.i.157–8 the numerals 1. and 2. are set at the beginning of each line, their original intention evidently having been to show the correct order of the two. What is remarkable is that insofar as meaning is concerned the order is quite indifferent and insofar as rhetorical effect is concerned there is also little to choose. I myself find the reverse order preferable. There can be no doubt, however, that the numerals came from the manuscript, but whether they show the author revising his own work, a scribe correcting his transcript or the author correcting a scribe is an open question.

The Quality of the Text

Although it has a superficial orderliness, the text actually contains a considerable number of errors, many of which seem to arise from the compositors' difficulties with the handwriting. I count about twenty-five involving the terminations of words; some of these may be foul case, but they cannot all be. All but one or two are in Compositor *B*'s stints. Examples are 'aske' for 'askd' (I.i.88), 'marke' for 'markt' (II.ii.31), 'Empires' for 'Empire' (III.i.36), 'laught' for 'laugh' (IV.i.147) and 'hope' for 'hop'd' (V.iv.45). Four errors, equally divided between *A* and *B*, drop letters – e.g. 'filing' for 'fidling' (I.iii.148). Some twenty-seven mistakes, their incidence being roughly proportional to the workmen's contributions to the whole, appear to arise from other misreadings or possibly, in a few instances, from foul case. Examples are 'think' for 'thank' (I.ii.28), 'forgive' for 'forget' (II.iii.41), 'misery' for 'mistery' and 'againe' for 'a game' (III.i.12–13), 'breed' for 'bread' (IV.i.40) and 'masses' for 'masts' (V.iii.35). The number of these errors is greater in the last half of the play. Latin names caused particular trouble; *Aretus* is *Aretius* thrice, *Proculus* is *Proclus* twice,

Bruti appears as *Brutij*, *Meroe* as *Nero*, *Bellona* as *Bellonia*, and *Titius* as *Tituis*. Since the work of both compositors is affected, the manuscript must have been at fault, yet the compositors may also have contributed a share of corruption, either because they were not very proficient or because they were working under unfavorable circumstances.

The syntax of some of the speeches is extravagant, and F 1's punctuation is often wrong or misleading. Occasionally it is evident that whoever supplied the punctuation had entirely lost his grasp of the meaning, as at III.i.45–7, which is rendered as

> good men raze thee
> For ever being read again,—but vicious
> Women, and fearefull Maids, make vows against thee...

Frequently, and especially after short speeches, the terminal punctuation is lighter than a full stop, a style that is not prominent in Section 3 but which reappears in the work of both compositors in *The Fair Maid of the Inn*.[1] One cannot be certain to what extent the compositors were influenced by faulty punctuation in the copy, but the impression given is that the copy was lightly pointed and that the compositors were left to do their best with the more florid passages. Their best was not always very good.

Discounting the features of the text which seem most obviously compositorial and ignoring for the present those that are most ambiguous, we are left with the following details which seem to bear on the nature of the copy.

1. The division into scenes was not made in the printing house, for *The Fair Maid of the Inn* is divided into acts only, as are *The Lovers' Progress*, *The Island Princess* and *The Nice Valour* in Section 3. Because so many of his plays descend from prompt-books or from other transcripts, it is difficult to know what Fletcher's attitude toward scene division was, but *A Wife for a Month*, thought to derive from foul papers or an unsophisticated transcript of them, and *The Sea Voyage*, perhaps given its final form by Fletcher, are divided into acts only.[2] So is the Lambarde manuscript of *The*

---

[1] According to the conventions of this edition, commas, semicolons and colons at the ends of complete speeches are silently emended.

[2] See Hoy, 'Fletcher and his Collaborators', VIII, 141 and IX, 153.

Woman's Prize. So too is the transcript of the *Bonduca* foul papers, yet *Demetrius and Enanthe,* which Greg believes also to have come from foul papers (*Shakespeare First Folio* (1955), p. 154), has scenes marked, as does F1 *The Humourous Lieutenant.* Perhaps all one can say is that the scene division in *Valentinian* at least raises the possibility of scribal intervention.

2. The mislineation of III.i.331 also hints at scribal copy, as explained above. So, I think, do other instances of mislining, for they are found in the work of both compositors, and thus are likely to have been in the copy, where someone other than the author appears to have misconstrued the arrangement of material he was copying.

3. The misplaced stage-direction at V.ii.54 suggests that the copy contained authorial revisions, of which the 1. and 2. at IV.i.157–8, the possible interlineation at IV.i.193, and the alterations of the Senators' speech-prefixes in V.viii could be other examples.

The evidence is fragile, but I think what there is points towards the printer's copy as being a scribal transcript of Fletcher's working papers made before the lyrics of the songs were available. This manuscript was subsequently worked over by the author, although it is impossible to say how extensive his revisions were. The rather high incidence of misreadings suggests a number of ill-written changes which could not be entirely deciphered by the compositors or difficulties on the part of the scribe in making out Fletcher's draft, errors having thus been introduced into the transcript and missed by Fletcher in his review. It is also possible that the manuscript contained some preliminary notes by the prompter, but there are no positive traces of his hand. The printer's copy was, of course, provided with the song lyrics, these perhaps having been added to the manuscript on separate leaves during the course of revision. If this hypothesis is correct, the F1 text of *Valentinian* is essentially at two removes from Fletcher's papers, and, because it is uncertain how thorough or careful his revision was, the F1 readings need careful evaluation.

After its publication in F1, *Valentinian* next appeared in the Folio of 1679, which provides a dramatis personae, an indication of the scene, and a list of the principal actors, viz. 'Richard Burbadge, Henry Condel, John Lowin, William Ostler, John Underwood'. The F2 editor reviewed the text pretty carefully, supplying a number of substantive corrections and mending some punctuation, yet his alterations are not always to be trusted. The apparatus he added and some of his readings suggest that he may have had access to a prompt-book or other theatrical documents; if so, however, he did not make use of them to disentangle the action of V.viii. On the whole, the changes he made seem not beyond an intelligent man working on his own or making only occasional reference to another text. Subsequently, except for a separate edition in 1717, the play was published only in the standard editions of the canon. Upon all these the Historical Collation of this edition is based. I have ignored Rochester's adaptation of 1685 as adding nothing of importance to the textual tradition.

Readings advocated by J. Monck Mason, *Comments on the Plays of Beaumont and Fletcher* ... (London, 1798) are included in the Historical Collation when they differ from those of the present edition. Also consulted have been John Mitford, *Cursory Notes on* ...*Beaumont and Fletcher*... (London, 1856) and K. Deighton, *The Old Dramatists: Conjectural Readings*... (Westminster, 1896). The one reading proposed by Mitford is in the Textual Note on III.iii.138; the one proposed by Deighton in that on IV.iv.151. Benjamin Heath's *MS Notes* are quoted from Dyce's edition. In the Historical Collation changes of 'ye' to 'you' are not noted unless the variant arises in F2. In later editions this alteration is frequent; regardless of the reading of the early editions, Dyce, for example, ordinarily prints 'you' in addresses to an equal or superior but 'ye' in addresses to an inferior.

Four of the play's songs have been discovered in manuscript ('Care charming Sleep' in nine manuscripts), four are included in *Poems*: by Francis Beaumont, Gent. (1653), and two are in John Wilson's *Cheerful Ayres* (1660). Substantive variants from these sources are in the Historical Collation. I obtained photostats of the lyrics as well as advice about their readings from L. A. Beaurline, to whom I am very grateful.

For other help I am indebted to Prudence Byers, James Hammersmith, James O'Donnell, Jeanne Roberts and John Velz, as well as to the Graduate Research Committee of the University of Wisconsin–Milwaukee.

Valentinian, *Emperour of* Rome.

Aecius, *the Emperours Loyal General.*

Balbus,
Proculus,
Chilax, } *four Noble Panders, and flatterers to the Emperour.*
Lycinius,

Maximus, *a great Souldier, Husband to* Lucina

Lycias, *an Eunuch.*

Pontius, *an honest Cashier'd Captaine.*   10

Phidias, } *two bold and faithful Eunuchs, Servants to* Aecius.
Aretus,

Affranius, *an eminent Captaine.*

Paulus, *a Poet.*

Lycippus, *a Courtier.*

(Fulvius, Lucius, Sempronius,) *three Senators.*

(A Boy.)

(A Messenger.)

Physicians, Gentlemen, Souldiers.

WOMEN.

Eudoxa, *Empress, Wife to* Valentinian.   20

Lucina, *the chast abused Wife of* Maximus.

Claudia,
Marcellina, } Lucinas *waiting Women.*

Ardelia,
Phorba, } *two of the Emperours Bawds.*

(*Ladies.*)

The Scene Rome.]

Persons Represented] *Based on the list in* F2; *om.* F1

276

THE TRAGEDIE

OF

VALENTINIAN.

Balbus. I never saw the like, shee's no more stirr'd,
No more another woman, no more alter'd
With any hopes or promises layd to her
(Let 'em be nev'r so waighty, nev'r so winning)
Then I am with the motion of my owne legs.
Proculus. *Chilax,*
You are a stranger yet in these designes,
At least in *Rome*; tell me, and tell me truth,
Did you ere know in all your course of practise,
In all the wayes of woman you have runne through   10
(For I presume you have been brought up *Chilax,*
As we to fetch and carry)——
Chilax.   True I have so.
Proculus. Did you I say againe in all this progresse,
Ever discover such a peece of beauty,
Ever so rare a Creature (and no doubt
One that must know her worth too, and affect it,
I and be flatter'd, else tis none) and honest?
Honest against the tide of all temptations,
Honest to one man, to her husband only,
And yet not eighteene, not of age to know   20
Why she is honest?
Chilax.   I confesse it freely,
I never saw her fellow, nor er'e shall,
For all our Græcian Dames, all I have tri'd,
(And sure I have tri'd a hunderd, if I say two

0.1 I.i] *Actus primus. Scæna prima.* F 1

I speake within my compasse) all these beauties,
And all the constancy of all these faces,
Mayds, Widdows, Wives, of what degree or calling,
(So they be Greekes, and fat, for there's my cunning)
I would undertake and not sweat for't, *Proculus*,
Were they to try againe, say twice as many,   30
Under a thousand pound, to lay 'em em bedrid;
But this Wench staggers me.
Lycinius.   Doe you see these Jewells?
You would thinke these pretty baytes; now Ile assure ye
Here's halfe the wealth of *Asia*.
Balbus.   These are nothing
To the full honours I propounded to her;
I bid her think, and be, and presently,
What ever her ambition, what the Councell
Of others would adde to her, what her dreames
Could more enlarge, what any President
Of any woman rising up to glory,   40
And standing certaine there, and in the highest,
Could give her more; nay to be Empresse.
Proculus.   And cold at all these offers?
Balbus.   Cold as Christall,
Never to be thaw'd again.
Chilax.   I trid her further,
And so farre, that I think she is no woman,
At least as women goe now.
Lycinius.   Why what did you?
Chilax.   I offerd that, that had she been but Mistris,
Of as much spleene as Doves have, I had reach'd her,
A safe revenge of all that ever hates her,
The crying down for ever of all beauties   50
That may be thought come neare her.
Proculus.   That was pretty.
Chilax.   I never knew that way faile, yet Ile tell ye
I offerd her a gift beyond all yours,
That, that had made a Sainct start, well considerd:

50 of] F2; *om.* F1

278

The Law to be her creature, she to make it,
Her mouth to give it, every creature living
From her aspect to draw their good or evill,
Fixd in'em spight of Fortune; a new Nature
She should be called, and mother of all ages;
Time should be hers, and what she did lame vertue   60
Should blesse to all posterities: her aire
Should give us life, her earth and water feed us.
And last, to none but to the Emperour,
(And then but when she pleas'd to have it so,)
She should be held for mortall.
Lycinius.   And she heard you?
Chilax.   Yes, as a Sick man heares a noise, or he
  That stands condemn'd his Judgment: let me perish,
  But if there can be vertue, if that name
  Be any thing but name and emptie title,
  It if be so as fooles have been pleas'd to faigne it,   70
  A power that can preserve us after ashes,
  And make the names of men out-reckon ages,
  This Woman has a God of vertue in her.
Balbus.   I would the Emperor were that God.
Chilax.   She has in her
  All the contempt of glory and vaine seeming
  Of all the *Stoicks,* all the truth of *Christians,*
  And all their Constancy: Modesty was made
  When she was first intended: When she blushes
  It is the holyest thing to looke upon,
  The purest temple of her sect, that ever   80
  Made nature a blest Founder.
Proculus.   Is there no way
  To take this *Phenix?*
Lycinius.   None but in her ashes.
Chilax.   If she were fat, or any way inclining
  To ease or pleasure, or affected glory,
  Proud to be seene and worship'd, t'were a venture;
  But on my soule she is chaster then cold Camphire.

---

*60 lame] *stet* F 1–2   *63 Emperour] *Emperour* F 1–2

Balbus.   I thinke so too; for all the wayes of woman,
Like a full saile she bears against: I askd her
After my many offers, walking with her,
And her as many down-denyals, how   90
If the Emperor grown mad with love should force her?
She pointed to a *Lucrece*, that hung by,
And with an angry looke, that from her eyes
Shot Vestall fire against me, she departed.
Proculus.   This is the first wench I was ever pos'd in,
Yet I have brought young loving things together
This two and thirty yeare.
Chilax.   I find by this wench
The calling of a Bawd to be a strange,
A wise, and subtile calling; and for none
But staid, discreet, and understanding people: 100
And as the Tutor to great *Alexander*
Would say, a young man should not dare to read
His morall books, till after five and twenty;
So must that he or she, that will be bawdy,
(I meane discreetly bawdy, and be trusted)
If they will rise, and gaine experience,
Wel steept in yeares, and discipline, begin it;
I take it tis no boys play.
Balbus.   Well, what's thought off?
Proculus.   The Emperour must know it.
Lycinius.   If the women
Should chance to faile too?
Chilax.   As tis ten to one.   110
Proculus.   Why what remaines, but new nets for the purchase?
Chilax.   Let's goe consider then: and if all faile,
This is the first quick Eele, that sav'd her taile.

                                                Exeunt.

                88 askd] F2 (askt); aske F1

                            280

Enter Lucina, Ardelia, *and* Phorba.   [I.] ii

Ardelia.   You still insist upon that Idoll, Honour:
Can it renue your youth: can it adde wealth,
That takes off wrinkles: can it draw mens eyes,
To gaze upon you in your age? can honour,
That truly is a Saint to none but Souldiers,
And lookd into, bears no reward but danger,
Leave you the most respected person living?
Or can the common kisses of a husband,
(Which to a sprightly Lady is a labour)
Make ye almost Immortall? ye are cozend,   10
The honour of a woman is her praises;
The way to get these, to be seene, and sought too,
And not to bury such a happy sweetnesse
Under a smoaky roofe.
Lucina.   Ile heare no more.
Phorba.   That white, and red, and all that blessed beauty,
Kept from the eyes, that make it so, is nothing;
Then you are rarely faire, when men proclaime it:
The *Phenix,* were she never seene, were doubted;
That most unvalued Horne the Unicorne
Beares to oppose the Huntsman, were it nothing   20
But talc, and meere tradition, would help no man;
But when the vertue's knowne, the honor's dobled:
Vertue, is either lame, or not at all,
And Love a sacriledge, and not a Saint,
When it bars up the way to mens Petitions.
Ardelia.   Nay ye shal love your husband too; we come not
To make a Monster of yee.
Lucina.   Are ye women?
Ardelia.   You'l find us so, and women you shall thank too,
If you have grace to make your use.
Lucina.   Fye on yee.
Phorba.   Alas poore bashfull Lady: by my soule,   30

o.1 I.ii] Scæne 2. F1   6 bears] F2; beare F1
*12 too] *i.e.* to   28 thank] F2; think F1

10   281   B B F

Had ye no other vertue, but your blushes,
And I a man, I should run mad for those:
How daintily they set her off, how sweetly?
Ardelia.   Come Goddesse, come, you move too neer the earth,
It must not be, a better orbe staies for you:
Here: be a mayd, and take 'em.   [*Offers Jewells.*]
Lucina.   Pray leave me.
Phorba.   That were a sin sweet Lady, and a way
To make us guilty of your melancholly;
You must not be alone; In conversation
Doubts are resolvd, and what sticks neer the conscience   40
Made easie, and allowable.
Lucina.   Ye are Devills.
Ardelia.   That you may one day blesse for your damnation.
Lucina.   I charge ye in the name of Chastity,
Tempt me no more; how ugly ye seem to me?
There is no wonder men defame our Sex,
And lay the vices of all ages on us,
When such as you shall beare the names of women;
If ye had eyes to see yourselves, or sence
Above the base rewards ye play the bawds for:
If ever in your lives ye heard of goodnesse,   50
(Though many Regions off, as men heare thunder)
If ever ye had Mothers, and they soules:
If ever Fathers, and not such as you are;
If ever any thing were constant in you,
Beside your sins, or comming but your curses;
If ever any of your Ancestors
Dyde worth a noble deed, that would be cherishd:
Soule-frighted with this black infection,
You would run from one another, to repentance,
And from your guilty eyes drop out those sins,   60
That made ye blind, and beasts.
Phorba.   Ye speak well Lady;
A signe of fruitfull education,

If your religious Zeale had wisdome with it.
Ardelia.   This Lady was ordain'd to blesse the Empire,
And we may all give thanks for't.
Phorba.   I beleive ye.
Ardelia.   If any thing redeem the Emperour,
From his wild flying courses, this is she;
She can instruct him if ye mark; she is wise too.
Phorba.   Exceeding wise, which is a wonder in her,
And so religious, that I well believe,   70
Though she would sinne she cannot.
Ardelia.   And besides,
She has the Empires cause in hand, not loves;
There lies the maine consideration,
For which she is chiefly borne.
Phorba.   She finds that point
Stronger then we can tell her, and belicve it,
I look by her meanes for a reformation,
And such a one, and such a rare way carried
That all the world shall wonder at.
Ardelia.   Tis true;
I never thought the Emperor had wisdom,
Pittie, or faire affection to his Country,   80
Till he profest this love: gods give 'em Children,
Such as her vertues merit, and his zeale.
I looke to see a *Numa* from this Lady,
Or greater then *Octavius.*
Phorba.   Do you mark too,
Which is a Noble vertue, how she blushes,
And what a flowing modesty runs through her,
When we but name the Emperour?
Ardelia.   But mark it,
Yes, and admire it too, for she considers,
Though she be faire as heaven, and vertuous
As holy truth, yet to the Emperour   90
She is a kind of nothing but her service,
Which she is bound to offer, and shee'l do it;
And when her Countries cause commands affection,

She knows obedience is the key of vertues:
Then flye the blushes out like Cupids arrowes,
And though the tye of marriage to her Lord
Would faine cry stay *Lucina*, yet the cause
And generall wisdom of the Princes love,
Makes her find surer ends and happier,
And if the first were chaste, this is twice dobled.   100
Phorba. Her tartnes unto us too——
Ardelia.   That's a wise one.
Phorba. I rarely like, it shewes a rising wisdom,
  That chides all common fooles as dare enquire
  What Princes would have private.
Ardelia.   What a Lady
  Shall we be blest to serve?
Lucina.   Goe get ye from me.
  Ye are your purses Agents, not the Princes:
  Is this the vertuous Lure yee traind me out too?
  Am I a woman fit to imp your vices?
  But that I had a Mother, and a woman
  Whose ever living fame turnes all it touches   110
  Into the good it selfe is, I should now
  Even doubt my selfe, I have been search't so neere
  The very soule of honour: why should you two,
  That happily have been as chast as I am,
  (Fairer, I think, by much, for yet your faces,
  Like ancient well built piles, shew worthy ruines)
  After that Angell age, turne mortall Devills?
  For shame, for woman-hood, for what ye have been,
  (For rotten Cedars have borne goodly branches)
  If ye have hope of any Heaven, but Court,   120
  Which like a Dreame, you'l find hereafter vanish,
  Or at the best but subject to repentance,
  Study no more to be ill spoken of;
  Let women live themselves, if they must fall,
  Their owne destruction find 'em, not your fevours.
Ardelia. Madam, yee are so excellent in all,

*107 Lure] Weber (Mason); Lore F 1–2

And I must tell it you with admiration,
So true a joy ye have, so sweet a feare,
And when ye come to anger, tis so noble,
That for mine own part, I could still offend, 130
To heare you angry; women that want that,
And your way guided (else I count it nothing)
Are either Fooles, or Cowards.

Phorba. She were a Mistris for no private greatnesse,
Could she not frowne: a ravishd kisse from anger,
And such an anger as this Lady learnes us,
Stuck with such pleasing dangers (Gods, I aske ye)
Which of ye all could hold from?

Lucina.   I perceive ye,
Your owne dark sins dwell with yee, and that price
You sell the chastitie of modest wives at 140
Runs to diseases with your bones: I scorne ye,
And all the nets ye have pitcht to catch my vertues,
Like Spiders Webs, I sweep a way before me.
Goe tell the Emperour, yee have met a woman,
That neither his owne person, which is God-like,
The world he rules, nor what that world can purchase,
Nor all the glories subject to a *Cesar,*
The honours that he offers for my body,
The hopes, gifts, everlasting flatteries,
Nor any thing that's his, and apt to tempt me, 150
No not to be the Mother of the Empire,
And Queene of all the holy fires he worships,
Can make a Whore of.

Ardelia.   You mistake us Lady.

Lucina. Yet tell him this: h'as thus much weakend me,
That I have heard his knaves, and you his Matrons,
Fit Nurses for his sins, which gods forgive me;
But ever to be leaning to his folly,
Or to be brought to love his lust, assure him,
And from her mouth, whose life shal make it certain,
I never can: I have a Noble husband, 160

154 this: h'as] this, ha's F 1–2   155 heard] F 2; here F 1

(Pray tell him that too) yet a noble name,
A Noble Family, and last a Conscience:
Thus much for your answer: For your selves,
Ye have liv'd the shame of women, dye the better.   *Exit* Lucina.
Phorba.   What's now to doe?
Ardelia.   Ev'n as she said, to dye,
For ther's no living here, and women thus,
I am sure, for us two.
Phorba.   Nothing stick upon her?
Ardelia.   We have lost a masse of mony; wel Dame Vertue,
Yet ye may halt if good luck serve.
Phorba.   Wormes take her,
She has almost spoil'd our trade.
Ardelia.   So godly;   170
This is ill breeding *Phorba.*
Phorba.   If the women
Should have a longing now to see this Monster,
And she convert 'em all?
Ardelia.   That may be *Phorba*,
But if it be, Ile have the young men gelded:
Come, let's goe think, she must not scape us thus;
There is a certain season, if we hit,
That women may be rid without a bit.

                                        Exeunt.

                    Enter Maximus *and* Aecius.   [I.] iii

Maximus.   I cannot blame the Nations, noble friend,
That they fall off so fast from this wild man,
When (under our Allegeance be it spoken,
And the most happy tye of our affections)
The worlds weight groanes beneath him; where lives vertue,
Honour, discretion, wisdom? who are cald
And chosen to the steering of the Empire
But Baudes, and singing Girles? ô my *Aecius*,
The glory of a Souldier, and the truth

        0.1 I.iii] Scæn. 3. F1   *0.1 Aecius] *Æcius* F1

Of men made up for goodnesse sake, like shells
Grow to the ragged walls for want of action:
Only your happy selfe, and I that love ye,
Which is a larger meanes to me then favour——
Aecius.   No more my worthy friend, though these be truths,
And though these truthes would aske a Reformation,
At least a little squaring; yet remember,
We are but subjects *Maximus*; obedience
To what is done, and griefe for what is ill done,
Is all we can call ours: the hearts of Princes
Are like the Temples of the gods; pure incense,   20
Untill unhallowed hands defile those offrings,
Burnes ever there; we must not put 'em out,
Because the Priests that touch those sweetes are wicked,
We dare not deerest friend, nay more we cannot,
(While we consider why we are, and how,
To what lawes bound, much more to what Law-giver;
Whilest majestie is made to be obeyed
And not inquired into, whilest Gods and Angels
Make but a rule as we do, though a stricter)
Like desperate and unseason'd fooles let fly   30
Our killing angers, and forsake our honors.
Maximus.   My noble Freind, from whose Instructions
I never yet tooke surfet, weigh but thus much,
Nor thinke I speake it with ambition,
For by the Gods I do not: why *Aecius*,
Why are we thus, or how become thus wretched?
Aecius.   You'l fall againe into your fit.
Maximus.   I will not.
Or are we now no more the sons of *Romanes*,
No more the followers of their happy fortunes,
But conquer'd *Gaules*, or Quivers for the *Parthians*?   40
Why is this Emperor, this man we honor,
This God that ought to be——
Aecius.   You are too curious.
Maximus.   Good, give me leave, why is this Author of us——

*25 why] stet F 1

Aecius.   I dare not heare ye speake thus.

Maximus.   Ile be modest,——
Thus led away, thus vainly led away,
And we beholders? misconceive me not,
I sow no danger in my words; but wherefore
And to what end, are we the sonnes of Fathers
Famous, and fast to *Rome*? Why are their vertues
Stampt in the dangers of a thousand Battailes,   50
For goodnesse sake? their honors, time out daring?
I thinke for our example.

Aecius.   Ye speake nobly.

Maximus.   Why are we seeds of these then, to shake hands
With Bawdes and base Informers, kisse discredit,
And court her like a Mistris? pray, your leave yet;
You'l say the Emperor is young, and apt
To take impression rather from his pleasures
Then any constant worthynesse, it may be.
But why do these, the people call his pleasures,
Exceed the moderation of a man?   60
Nay to say justly freind, why are they vices
And such as shake our worthes with forraigne Nations?

Aecius.   You search the soare too deep, and I must tel ye,
In any other man this had been boldnesse,
And so rewarded; pray depresse your spirit,
For though I constantly beleeve ye honest,
(Ye were no freind for me else) and what now
Ye freely spake, but good ye owe toth Empire,
Yet take heed worthy *Maximus*; all eares
Heare not with that distinction mine doe, few   70
You'l find admonishers, but urgers of your actions,
And to the heaviest (freind;) and pray consider
We are but shadowes, motions others give us,
And though our pitties may become the times,
Justly our powers cannot; make me worthy
To be your ever freind in faire allegiance,

*50–51 Battailes,...sake?] Langbaine ($\sim_{\wedge}...\sim$;); $\sim$,...$\sim$, F1; $\sim$?...$\sim$, F2
*51 out daring] *stet* F1   65 your] F2; you F1

288

But not in force: For durst mine own soule urge me
(And by that soule, I speake my just affections)
To turn my hand from truth, which is obedience,
And give the helme my vertue holds, to Anger,   80
Though I had both the blessings of the *Bruti*,
And both their Instigations, though my cause
Carried a face of Justice beyond theirs,
And (as I am) a servant to my fortunes,
That daring soule, that first taught disobedience,
Should feele the first example: Say the Prince,
As I may well beleeve, seemes vitious,
Who justly knowes tis not to try our honors?
Or say he be an ill Prince, are we therefore
Fit fires to purge him? No, my dearest freind,   90
The Elephant is never won with anger,
Nor must that man that would reclaime a Lyon,
Take him by'th teeth.
Maximus.   I pray mistake me not.
Aecius.   Our honest actions, and the light that breakes
Like morning from our service, chaste and blushing,
Is that, that pulls a Prince backe; then he sees,
And not till then truly repents his errors,
When subjects Chrystall soules are glasses to him.
Maximus.   My ever honored freind, Ile take your councel:
The Emperor appeares, Ile leave ye to him,   100
And as we both affect him, may he flourish.   *Exit* Maximus.

            Enter the Emperor *and* Chilax.

Emperor.   Is that the best newes?
Chilax.   Yet the best we know Sir.
Emperor.   Bid *Maximus* come to me, and be gone then:
                                            [*Exit* Chilax.]
Mine own head be my helper, these are fooles;——
How now *Aecius*, are the Souldiers quiet?
Aecius.   Better I hope Sir, then they were.

            81 *Bruti*] F2; *Brutij* F1
            84 (as I am)] Colman (And,...am,); ‸~ ~ ~‸ F1–2

Emperor. They are pleas'd I heare,
To censure me extremely for my pleasures,
Shortly they'l fight against me.
Aecius. Gods defend Sir.
And for their censures they are such shrew'd Judgers, 110
A donative of ten Sesterties
Ile undertake shall make 'em ring your praises,
More then they sang your pleasures.
Emperor. I beleeve thee.
Art thou in love *Aecius* yet?
Aecius. O no Sir.
I am too course for Ladies; my embraces,
That only am acquainted with Alarums,
Would break their tender bodies.
Emperor. Never feare it,
They are stronger then ye think, they'le hold the hammer.
My Empresse sweares thou art a lusty Souldier,
A good one I beleeve thee.
Aecius. All that goodnesse 120
Is but your Graces creature.
Emperor. Tell me truly,
For thou darst tell me——
Aecius. Any thing concernes ye,
That's fit for me to speake and you to pardon.
Emperor. What say the soldiers of me? and the same words,
Mince 'em not good *Aecius*, but deliver
The very forms and tongues they talke withall.
Aecius. Ile tell your Grace, but with this caution,
You be not stirr'd, for should the Gods live with us,
Even those we certainly beleeve are righteous,
Give 'em but drinke, they would censure them too. 130
Emperor. Forward.
Aecius. Then to begin, they say you sleep too much
By which they judge your Majesty too sensuall,
Apt to decline your strength to ease and pleasures;
And when you do not sleepe, you drink too much,
From which they feare suspitions first, then ruines;

And when ye neither drinke nor sleepe, ye wench much,
Which they affirm first breakes your understanding,
Then takes the edge of honor, makes us seeme,
That are the ribbes, and rampires of the Empire,   140
Fencers, and beaten Fooles, and so regarded;
But I beleive 'em not; for were these truths,
Your vertue can correct them.
Emperor.   They speake plainly.
Aecius.   They say moreover (since your grace wil have it,
For they will talke their freedoms, though the sword
Were in their throat) that of late time, like *Nero*,
And with the same forgetfullnes of glory,
You have got a vaine of fidling, so they terme it.
Emperor.   Some drunken dreames *Aecius.*
Aecius.   So I hope Sir.
And that you rather study cruelty,   150
And to be feared for blood, then lov'd for bounty,
Which makes the Nations, as they say, despise ye,
Telling your yeares and actions by their deathes,
Whose truth, and strength of duty made you *Cæsar.*
They say besides you nourish strange devourers,
Fed with the fat o'th Empire, they call Bawdes,
Lazie and lustfull creatures that abuse ye,
And people, as they terme 'em made of paper,
In which the secret sins of each mans monyes
Are sealed and sent a working.
Emperor.   What sin's next?   160
For I perceive they have no mind to spare me.
Aecius.   Nor hurt ye o' my soule Sir; but such people
(Nor can the power of man restraine it)
When they are full of meat and ease, must prattle.
Emperor.   Forward.
Aecius.   I have spoken too much Sir.
Emperor.   Ile have all.
Aecius.   It fits not

139 of] *i.e.* off   148 fidling]F2; filing F1
158 And] Dyce (Mason); A F1-2   *162 o'] F2; ô F1

Your eares should heare their vanities; no profit
Can justly rise to you from their behaviour,
Unless ye were guilty of those crimes.
Emperor.   It may be
I am so, therefore forward.
Aecius.   I have ever   170
Learn'd to obey, nor shall my life resist it.
Emperor.   No more Apologies.
Aecius.   They greive besides Sir,
To see the nations, whom our ancient vertue
With many a weary march and hunger conquer'd,
With losse of many a daring life subdude,
Fall from their faire obedience, and even murmure
To see the warlike Eagles mew their honors
In obscure Townes, that wont to prey on Princes;
They cry for enemies, and tel the Captaines
The fruits of *Italy* are luscious, give us *Ægypt,*   180
Or sandy *Affrick* to display our valours,
There where our Swords may make us meat, and danger
Digest our well got Vyands: here our weapons
And bodyes that were made for shining brasse,
Are both unedg'd and old with ease, and women;
And then they cry agen, where are the *Germaines,*
Linde with hot *Spain,* or *Gallia?* bring 'em on,
And let the son of war, steel'd *Mithridates,*
Lead up his winged *Parthians* like a storme,
Hiding the face of Heaven with showres of arrowes;   190
Yet we dare fight like *Romanes;* then as Souldiers
Tyr'd with a weary march, they tell their wounds,
Even weeping ripe they were no more nor deeper,
And glory in those scarrs that make 'em lovely,
And sitting where a Campe was, like sad Pilgrims
They reckon up the times, and living labours
Of *Julius* or *Germanicus,* and wonder
That *Rome,* whose turrets once were topt with honours,
Can now forget the Custome of her conquests:
And then they blame your Grace, and say, who leads us,   200

Shall we stand here like Statues? were our Fathers
The Sonnes of lazie Moores, our Princes *Persians*,
Nothing but silkes, and softnesse? curses on 'em
That first taught *Nero* wantonnesse, and bloud,
Tiberius doubts, *Caligula* all vices;
For from the spring of these, succeeding Princes——
Thus they talke Sir.

Emperor. Well,
Why doe you heare these things?

Aecius.   Why do you do 'em?
I take the gods to witnesse, with more sorrow   210
And more vexation, doe I heare these taintures,
Then were my life dropt from me through an hour-glasse.

Emperor. Belike then you beleeve 'em, or at least
Are glad they should be so; take heed, you were better
Build your own Tomb, and runne into it living,
Then dare a Princes anger.

Aecius.   I am old Sir,   [*Kneels.*]
And ten yeares more addition, is but nothing:
Now if my life be pleasing to ye, take it;
Upon my knees, if ever any service,
(As let me brag, some have bin worthy notice)   220
If ever any worth, or trust ye gave me,
Descrv'd a faire respect, if all my actions,
The hazards of my youth, colds, burnings, wants,
For you and for the Empire, be not vices;
By that stile ye have stampt upon me, Souldier,
Let me not fall into the hands of wretches.

Emperor. I understand ye not.

Aecius.   Let not this body,
That has lookd bravely in his bloud for *Cesar*,
And covetous of wounds, and for your safety,
After the scape of Swords, Speares, Slings, and Arrows,   230
(Gainst which my beaten body was mine Armour)
The Seas, and thirstie deserts, now be purchase
For Slaves, and base Informers: I see anger,
And death look through your eyes: I am markt for slaughter

And know the telling of this truth has made me
A man cleane lost to this world; I embrace it;
Only my last Petition sacred *Cesar*,
Is, I may dye a *Roman*.
Emperor.   Rise my friend still,   [*Raising him.*]
And worthy of my love; Reclaime the Souldier,
Ile study to doe so upon my selfe too,   240
Goe keep your command, and prosper.
Aecius.   Life to *Cesar*.   *Exit* Aecius.

Enter Chilax.

Chilax.   Lord *Maximus* attends your Grace.
Emperor.   Goe tell him,
Ile meete him in the gallery.   [*Exit* Chilax.]
The honesty of this *Aecius*,
Who is indeed the Bull-wark of the Empire,
Has div'd so deep into me, that of all
The sins I covet, but this womans beautie,
With much repentance, now I could be quit of:
But she is such a pleasure, being good,
That though I were a god, she would fire my bloud.   250
                                                        Exit.

Enter the Emperour, Maximus, Lycinius, Proculus, Chilax,   II. i
                        as at Dice.

Emperour.   Nay ye shall set my hand out, tis not just
I should neglect my fortune, now tis prosperous.
Lycinius.   If I have any thing to set your Grace,
But Clothes or good conditions, let me perish;
You have all my mony Sir.
Proculus.   And mine.
Chilax.   And mine too.
Maximus.   Unless your Grace will credit us——
Emperour.   No bare boord.
Lycinius.   Then at my Garden-House.

0.1 II.i] *Actus Secundus. Scæna prima.* F1

294

Emperour.   The Orchard too?
Lycinius.   And't please your Grace.
Emperour.   Have at 'em.   [*Throws.*]
Proculus.   They are lost.
Lycinius.   Why farewell Fig-trees.
Emperour.   Who sets more?
Chilax.   At my Horse Sir.
Emperour.   The dapl'd *Spaniard*?
Chilax.   He.   [*Emperour throws.*]
Emperour.   He's mine.
Chilax.   He is so.   10
Maximus.   Your short horse is soone curried!
Chilax.   So it seemes Sir,——
So may your Mare be too, if luck serve.
Maximus.   Ha?
Chilax.   Nothing my Lord but grieving at my fortune.
Emperour.   Come *Maximus*, you were not wont to flinch thus.
Maximus.   By Heaven Sir, I have lost all.
Emperour.   Ther's a ring yet.
Maximus.   This was not made to loose Sir.
Emperour.   Some love token;
Set it I say.
Maximus.   I doe beseech your Grace,
Rather name any house I have.
Emperour.   How strange,
And curious you are growne of toyes? redeem't
If so I win it, when you please, to morrow,   20
Or next day as ye will, I care not;
But only for my luck sake: Tis not Kings
Can make me richer.
Maximus.   Will you throw Sir? there 'tis.
Emperour.   Why then have at it fairely:——myne.   [*Throws.*]
Maximus.   Your Grace
Is only ever fortunate: to morrow,
An't be your pleasure Sir, Ile pay the price on't.
Emperour.   To morrow you shall have it without price Sir,
But this day 'tis my victory: good *Maximus*,

Now I bethink my selfe, goe to *Aecius*,
And bid him muster all the Cohorts presently,   30
(They mutiny for pay I heare) and be you
Assistant to him; when you know their numbers,
Ye shall have monyes for 'em, and above
Something to stop their tongues withall.
Maximus.   I will Sir,
And gods preserve you in this mind still.
Emperour.   Shortly
Ile see 'em march my selfe.
Maximus.   Gods ever keep ye.   *Exit* Maximus.
Emperour.   To what end doe you think this ring shall serve now?
For you are fellowes only know by roate,
As birds record their lessons.
Chilax.   For the Lady.
Emperour.   But how for her?
Chilax.   That I confesse I know not.   40
Emperour.   Then pray for him that do's: fetch me an Eunuch
That never saw her yet: and you two see   *Exit* Chilax.
The Court made like a Paradise.
Lycinius.   We will Sir.
Emperour.   Full of faire shewes and Musiques; all your arts
(As I shall give instructions) screw to'th highest,
For my maine peece is now a doing: and for feare
You should not take, Ile have an other engine,
Such as if vertue be not only in her,
She shall not choose but leane to: let the women
Put on a graver shew of welcome.
Proculus.   Well Sir.   50
Emperour.   They are a thought too eager.

Enter Chilax *and* Lycias *the Eunuch.*

Chilax.   Here's the Eunuch.
Eunuch.   Long life to *Cesar.*
Emperour.   I must use you *Lycias*:
Come let's walk in, and then Ile shew ye all:

If women may be fraile, this wench shall fall.

Exeunt.

Enter Claudia, *and* Marcellina.   [II.] ii

Claudia.   Sirrha, what ayles my Lady, that of late
She never cares for company?
Marcellina.   I know not,
Unless it be that company causes Cuckolds.
Claudia.   That were a childish feare.
Marcellina.   What were those Ladyes,
Came to her lately? from the Court?
Claudia.   The same, wench.
Some grave Instructors on my life, they look
For all the world like old hatcht hilts.
Marcellina.   Tis true wench.
For here and there (and yet they painted well too)
One might discover where the gold was worne
Their Iron ages.
Claudia.   If my judgment faile not,   10
They have been sheathed like rotten ships——
Marcellina.   It may be.
Claudia.   For if ye mark their rudders, they hang weakly.
Marcellina.   They have past the line belike: wouldst live *Claudia*
Till thou wert such as they are?
Claudia.   Chimney pieces.
Now heaven have mercy on me, and young men;
I had rather make a drallery till thirty:
While I were able to endure a tempest,
And beare my fights out bravely, till my tackle
Whistled i'th wind, and held against all weathers,
While I were able to beare with my tyres   20
And so discharg 'em, I would willingly
Live *Marcellina*, not till barnacles
Bred in my sides.
Marcellina.   Thou art i'th right wench.

0.1 II.ii] Scæne 2. F 1   *16 drallery] stet F 1

For who would live, whom pleasures had forsaken,
To stand at marke, and cry a bow short signeur?
Were there not men came hither too?
Claudia.   Brave fellowes.
I feare me Bawdes of five i'th' pound.
Marcellina.   How know you?
Claudia.   They gave me great lights to it.
Marcellina.   Take heed *Claudia.*
Claudia.   Let them take heed, the spring comes on.
Marcellina.   To me now,
They seem'd as noble visitants.
Claudia.   To me now   30
Nothing lesse *Marcellina,* for I markt 'em,
And by this honest light (for yet tis morning)
Saving the reverence of their guilded doublets
And Millan skins——
Marcellina.   Thou art a strange wench *Claudia.*
Claudia.   Ye are deceived,——they shew'd to me directly
Court crabbs that creepe a side way for their living:
I know 'em by the breeches that they beg'd last.
Marcellina.   Peace,
My Lady comes.

Enter Lucina, *and* Lycias *the Eunuch.*

What may that be?

Claudia.   A Sumner
That cites her to appeare.
Marcellina.   No more of that wench.   40
Eunuch.   Madam, what answer to your Lord?
Lucina.   Pray tell him,
I am subject to his will.
Eunuch.   Why weepe you Madam?
Excellent Lady, there are none will hurt you.
Lucina.   I do beseech you tell me Sir——
Eunuch.   What Lady?

31 markt] F2; marke F1

298

Lucina.   Serve ye the Emperor?
Eunuch.   I do.
Lucina.   In what place?
Eunuch.   In's chamber Madam.
Lucina.   Do ye serve his will too?
Eunuch.   In faire and just commands.
Lucina.   Are ye a *Romane*?
Eunuch.   Yes noble Lady, and a *Mantuan*.
Lucina.   What office bore your parents?
Eunuch.   One was Pretor.
Lucina.   Take heed then how you staine his reputation.   50
Eunuch.   Why worthy Lady?
Lucina.   If ye know, I charge ye,
Ought in this Message, but what honesty,
The trust and faire obedience of a servant,
May well deliver, yet take heed, and help me.
Eunuch.   Madam, I am no Broker——
Claudia [*aside*].   Ile be hangd then.
Eunuch.   Nor base procurer of mens lusts; Your husband,
Praid me to doe this office, I have done it,
It rests in you to come, or no.
Lucina.   I will Sir.
Eunuch.   If ye mistrust me, doe not.
Lucina.   Ye appeare
So worthy, and to all my sence so honest,   60
And this is such a certaine signe ye have brought me,
That I believe.
Eunuch.   Why should I couzen you?
Or were I brib'd to doe this villany,
Can mony prosper, or the foole that takes it,
When such a vertue falls?
Lucina.   Ye speake well Sir;
Would all the rest that serve the Emperour,
Had but your way.
Claudia [*aside*].   And so they have *ad unguem*.
Lucina.   Pray tell my Lord, I have receivd his Token,
And will not faile to meet him.   [Eunuch *offers to go.*]

                              Yet good Sir, thus much
Before you goe, I doe beseech ye too,   70
As little notice as ye can, deliver
Of my appearance there.
Eunuch.   It shall be Madam,
And so I wish you happinesse.
Lucina.   I thank you.

                                                        Exeunt.

        Tumult and noise within. Enter Aecius *pursuing* Pontius   [II.] iii
            the Captaine, and Maximus *following.*

Maximus.   Temper your selfe *Aecius.*
Pontius.   Hold my Lord,
    I am a *Roman*, and a Souldier.
Maximus.   Pray Sir——
Aecius.   Thou art a lying Villaine, and a Traytor;——
                                        [*Maximus holds him.*]
    Give me my selfe, or by the Gods my friend
    You'l make me dangerous;——how dar'st thou pluck
    The Souldiers to sedition, and I living,
    And sow Rebellion in 'em, and even then
    When I am drawing out to action?
Pontius.   Heare me.
Maximus.   Are yee a man?
Aecius.   I am a true hearted, *Maximus*,
    And if the Villaine live, we are dishonourd.   10
Maximus.   But heare him what he can say.
Aecius.   That's the way,
    To pardon him; I am so easie naturd,
    That if he speak but humbly I forgive him.
Pontius.   I doe beseech yee Noble Generall——
Aecius.   Has found the way already, give me rome,
    One stroake, and if he scape me then ha's mercy.
Pontius.   I doe not call yee Noble, that I feare ye,
    I never care'd for death; if ye will kill me,

Consider first for what, not what you can doe;
Tis true, I know ye for my Generall,   20
And by that great Prerogative may kill:
But doe it justly then.
Aecius.   He argues with me.
By Heaven a made up Rebell.
Maximus.   Pray consider,
What certaine grounds ye have for this.
Aecius.   What grounds?
Did I not take him preaching to the Souldiers
How lazily they liv'd, and what dishonours
It was to serve a Prince so full of woman?
Those were his very words, friend.
Maximus.   These, *Aecius*,
Though they were rashly spoke, which was an errour
(A great one *Pontius*) yet from him that hungers   30
For warres, and brave imployment, might be pardond.
The heart, and harbourd thoughts of ill, make Traytors,
Not spleeny speeches.
Aecius.   Why should you protect him?
Goe too, it shewes not honest.
Maximus.   Taynt me not,
For that shewes worse *Aecius*: All your friendship
And that pretended love ye lay upon me,
(Hold back my honesty) is like a favour
You doe your slave to day, to morrow hang him,
Was I your bosome peece for this?
Aecius.   Forgive me.
The nature of my zeale, and for my Country,   40
Makes me sometimes forget my selfe; for know,
Though I most strive to be without my passions,
I am no God:——For you Sir, whose infection
Ha's spread it selfe like poyson through the Army,
And cast a killing fogge on faire Allegiance,
First thank this Noble Gentleman, y'had dy'de else.
Next from your place, and honour of a Souldier,

I here seclude you——
Pontius.   May I speak yet?
Maximus.   Heare him.
Aecius. And while *Aecius* holds a reputation,
  At least command, ye beare no Armes for *Rome* Sir.   50
Pontius. Against her I shall never: The condemnd man,
  Ha's yet that priviledge to speak my Lord;
  Law were not equall else.
Maximus.   Pray heare *Aecius*,
  For happily the fault he has committed,
  Though I believe it mighty, yet considered,
  (If mercy may be thought upon) will prove
  Rather a hastie sin, then heynous.
Aecius.   Speake.
Pontius. Tis true my Lord, ye took me tir'de with peace,
  My words, almost as ragged as my fortunes.
  Tis true I told the Souldier, whom we serv'd,   60
  And then bewaild, we had an Emperour
  Led from us by the flourishes of Fencers;
  I blam'd him too for women.
Aecius.   To the rest Sir.
Pontius. And like enough I blest him then as Souldiers
  Will doe sometimes: Tis true I told 'em too,
  We lay at home, to show our Country
  We durst goe naked, durst want meate, and mony,
  And when the Slave drinkes Wine, we durst be thirstie:
  I told 'em this too, that the Trees and Roots
  Were our best pay-masters; the Charity   70
  Of longing women, that had bought our bodies,
  Our beds, fires, Taylers, Nurses: Nay I told 'em,
  (For you shall heare the greatest sin, I said Sir)
  By that time there be wars agen, our bodies
  Laden with scarres, and aches, and ill lodgings,
  Heates, and perpetuall wants, were fitter praires,
  And certaine graves, then cope the foe on crutches:
  Tis likely too, I counselld 'em to turne
  Their Warlike pikes to plough-shares, their sure Targets

And Swords hatcht with the bloud of many Nations,   80
To Spades, and pruning Knives, for those get mony,
Their warlike Eagles, into Dawes, or Starlings,
To give an *Ave Cesar* as he passes,
And be rewarded with a thousand dragma's,
For thus we get but yeares and beets.
Aecius.   What think you,
Were these words to be spoken by a Captain,
One that should give example?
Maximus.   'Twas too much.
Pontius. My Lord, I did not wooe 'em from the Empire,
Nor bid 'em turne their daring steel gainst *Cæsar*,
The Gods for ever hate me, if that motion   90
Were part of me: Give me but imployment, Sir,
And way to live, and where you hold me vicious,
Bred up in mutiny, my Sword shall tell ye,
(And if you please, that place I held, maintaine it,
Gainst the most daring foes of *Rome*) I am honest,
A lover of my Country, one that holds
His life no longer his, then kept for *Cæsar*.
Weigh not (I thus low on my knee beseech you)   [*Kneels.*]
What my rude tongue discovered, t'was my want,
No other part of *Pontius*: you have seen me,   100
And you my Lord, doe something for my Country,
And both beheld the wounds I gave and took,
Not like a backward Traytor.
Aecius.   All this language,
Makes but against you *Pontius*, you are cast,
And by mine honor, and my love to *Cæsar*,
By me shall never be restord; In my Campe
I will not have a tongue, though to himselfe,
Dare talke but neere sedition; as I governe,
All shall obey, and when they want, their duty
And ready service shall redresse their needs,   110
Not prating what they would be.
Pontius.   Thus I leave ye,   [*Rises.*]

*85 yeares and beets] *stet* F 1

303

Yet shall my praires still, although my fortunes
Must follow you no more, be still about ye;
Gods give ye where ye fight the Victory,
Ye cannot cast my wishes.   [*Exit.*]
Aecius.   Come my Lord,
  Now to the Field agen.
Maximus.   Alas poore *Pontius.*

                                                    Exeunt.

        Enter Chilax *at one dore,* Lycinius, *and* Balbus *at another.*   [II.] iv

Lycinius.   How now?
Chilax.   Shee's come.
Balbus.   Then Ile to'th Emperor.
Chilax.   Doe: *Exit* Balbus.
              Is the Musick placed well?
Lycinius.   Excellent.
Chilax.   *Lycinius,* you and *Proculus* receive her,
  In the great Chamber, at her entrance
  Let me alone; and (doe you heare *Lycinius?*)
  Pray let the Ladies ply her further off,
  And with much more discretion: one word more——
Lycinius.   Well?
Chilax.   Are the Jewells, and those ropes of Pearle,
  Layd in the way she passes?
Lycinius.   Take no care man.   *Exit* Lycinius.

        Enter Emperor, Balbus *and* Proculus.

Emperor.   What is she come?
Chilax.   She is Sir; but t'wer best,   10
  Your Grace were seen last to her.
Emperor.   So I mean;
  Keep the Court emptie *Proculus.*
Proculus.   Tis done Sir.

          0.1 II.iv] Scæn. 4. F 1
          3 *Proculus*] *Tragedy of Valentinian* (1717); *Proclus* F 1–2
          6 Pray] F 2; Bray F 1
          9.1 Proculus] Langbaine; *Proclus* F 1–2
                          304

Emperor.   Be not too sudaine to hir.
Chilax.   Good your Grace,
  Retire, and man your selfe; let us alone,
  We are no children this way: doe you heare Sir?
  Tis necessary that her waiting women
  Be cut off in the Lobby, by some Ladies,
  They'd break the businesse else.
Emperor.   Tis true, they shall.
Chilax.   Remember your place *Proculus.*
Proculus.   I warrant ye.
                    Exeunt Emperor, Balbus *and* Proculus.
Chilax.   She enters:

                Enter Lucina, Claudia, *and* Marcellina.

                Who are waytors there? the Emperor   20
  Calls for his Horse to ayre himselfe.
Lucina [*aside*].   I am glad,
  I come so happily to take him absent,
  This takes away a little feare; I know him,
  Now I begin to feare agen: Oh honour,
  If ever thou hadst temple in weak woman,
  And sacrifice of modesty burnt to thee,
  Hold me fast now, and help me.
Chilax.   Noble Madam,
  Ye are welcome to the Court, most nobly welcome,
  Ye are a stranger Lady.
Lucina.   I desire so.
Chilax.   A wondrous stranger here, nothing so strange: 30
  And therefore need a guide I think.
Lucina.   I doe Sir,
  And that a good one too.
Chilax.   My service Lady,
  Shall be your guide in this place; But pray ye tell me,
  Are ye resolv'd a Courtier?
Lucina.   No I hope Sir.
Claudia.   You are Sir?

                *33 guide] F2; guard F1
                        305

Chilax. Yes my faire one.

Claudia. So it seemes,
You are so ready to bestow your selfe;
Pray what might cost those Breeches?

Chilax. Would you weare 'em?
Madam ye have a witty woman.

Marcellina. Two Sir,
Or else yee underbuy us.

Lucina. Leave your talking:
But is my Lord here, I beseech ye Sir? 40

Chilax. He is sweet Lady, and must take this kindly,
Exceeding kindly of ye, wondrous kindly,
Ye come so farre to visit him: Ile guide ye.

Lucina. Whether?

Chilax. Why to your Lord.

Lucina. Is it so hard Sir,
To find him in this place without a Guide?
For I would willingly not trouble you.

Chilax. It will be so for you that are a stranger;
Nor can it be a trouble to doe service
To such a worthy beauty, and besides——

Marcellina. I see he will goe with us.

Claudia. Let him amble. 50

Chilax. It fits not that a Lady of your reckoning,
Should passe without attendants.

Lucina. I have two Sir.

Chilax. I mean without a man; You'l see the Emperor?

Lucina. Alas I am not fit Sir.

Chilax. You are well enough.
Hee'l take it wondrous kindly: Harke. [*Whispers.*]

Lucina. Ye flatter,
Good Sir, no more of that.

Chilax. Well, I but tell ye——

Lucina. Will ye goe forward? since I must be mand,
Pray take your place.

Claudia. Cannot ye man us too Sir?

Chilax. Give me but time.

306

Marcellina.   And you'l try all things.
Chilax.   No,
  Ile make ye no such promise.   60
Claudia.   If ye doe Sir,
  Take heed ye stand to't.
Chilax.   Wondrous merry Ladies.
Lucina.   The wenches are disposd, pray keep your way Sir.
                                             Exeunt.

             Enter Lycinius, Proculus *and* Balbus.   [II. v]

Lycinius.   She is comming up the staires; Now the Musick;
  And as that stirs her, let's set on: perfumes there.
Proculus.   Discover all the Jewells.
Lycinius.   Peace.   *Musicke.*

       Enter Chilax, Lucina, Claudia, *and* Marcellina.

                SONGS.

                [FIRST.]

        Now the lusty Spring is scene,
          Golden yellow, gaudy Blew,
          Daintily invite the view,
        Every where, on every Greene.
        Roses blushing as they blow,
          And inticing men to pull,   10
        Lillies whiter then the snow,
          Woodbines of sweet hony full:
            All loves Emblems and all cry,
            Ladyes, if not pluck't we dye.

        Yet the lusty Spring hath stayd,
          Blushing red and purest white,
          Daintily to love invite,

60 Ile make] F 2 (I'le); Hmake F 1
  0.1 ‸*Enter*. . .Balbus.] Langbaine; ——*Enter Lycinius, and Proculus, Balbus.*
(*following* II.iv.61) F 1–2
  4.1 *Enter*. . .Marcellina.] Weber; *following line* 44 F 1–2
  *4.2–24 SONGS. . .dye.] *stet* F 1

Every Woman, every Mayd;
Cherries kissing as they grow,
  And inviting men to taste,   20
Apples even ripe below,
  Winding gently to the waste:
    All loves emblems and all cry,
    Ladies, if not pluckt we dye.

SECOND.

Heare ye Ladies that despise,
  What the mighty love has done,
Feare examples, and be wise:
  Faire Calisto *was a Nun;*
Læda *sayling on the streame,*
  To deceive the hopes of man,   30
Love accounting but a dream,
  Doted on a silver Swan;
    Danae *in a Braʒen Tower,*
    Where no love was, lov'd a Showre.

Heare yee Ladyes that are coy,
  What the mighty love can doe,
Feare the fiercenesse of the Boy:
  The chaste Moon he makes to woe,
Vesta *kindling holy fires,*
  Circled round about with spies,   40
Never dreaming loose desires,
  Doting at the Altar dies.
    Ilion *in a short hower higher*
    He can build, and once more fire.

Lucina [*aside*].   Pray Heaven my Lord be here, for now I feare it.
Well Ring, if thou bee'st counterfeit, or stolne,
As by this preparation I suspect it,

*24.1–44 SECOND...fire.] stet F1
34 *Showre*] MS² (shower); *Flowre* F1
43 *hower higher*ᴀ] F2 (hour); *Tower higher,* F1
44 *can build*] F1(c)–F2; *can once more build* F1(u)

Thou hast betraid thy Mistris:——pray Sir forward,
I would faine see my Lord.
Chilax.   But tell me Madam,
How doe ye like the Song?
Lucina.   I like the ayre well,   50
But for the words, they are lascivious,
And over-light for Ladies.
Chilax.   All ours love 'em.
Lucina.   Tis like enough, for yours are loving Ladies.
Lycinius.   Madam, ye are welcome to the Court. Who waits?
Attendants for this Lady.
Lucina.   Ye mistake Sir;
I bring no triumph with me.
Lycinius.   But much honour.
Proculus.   Why this was nobly done; and like a neighbour,
So freely of your selfe to be a visitant,
The Emperour shall give ye thanks for this.
Lucina.   O no Sir;
Ther's nothing to deserve 'em.
Proculus.   Yes, your presence.   60
Lucina.   Good Gentlemen be patient, and believe
I come to see my husband, on command too,
I were no Courtier else.
Lycinius.   That's all one Lady,
Now ye are here, y'are welcome, and the Emperor
Who loves ye, but too well——
Lucina.   No more of that Sir,
I came not to be Catechizd.
Proculus.   Ah Sirah,
And have we got you here? faith Noble Lady,
Wee'l keep you one month Courtier.
Lucina.   Gods defend Sir,
I never likd a trade worse.
Proculus.   Harke ye.   [*Whispers.*]
Lucina.   No Sir.
Proculus. Ye are grown the strangest Lady.   [*Whispers.*]
Lucina.   How?

Proculus.   By Heaven,   70
  Tis true I tell ye, and you'l find it.
Lucina.   I?
  Ile rather find my grave, and so informe him.
Proculus.   Is it not pity Gentlemen, this Lady,
  (Nay Ile deale roughly with ye, yet not hurt ye)
  Should live alone, and give such heavenly beauty,
  Only to walls, and hangings?
Lucina.   Good Sir, patience:
  I am no wonder, neither come to that end;
  Ye doe my Lord an injury to stay me,
  Who though ye are the Princes, yet dare tell ye
  He keeps no wife for your wayes.
Balbus.   Well, well Lady;   80
  How ever you are pleasd to think of us,
  Ye are welcome, and ye shall be welcome.
Lucina.   Shew it
  In that I come for then, in leading me
  Where my lov'd Lord is, not in flattery: *Jewells shewd.*
  Nay ye may draw the Curtain, I have seen 'em
  But none worth halfe my honesty.
Claudia.   Are these Sir,
  Layd here to take?
Proculus.   Yes, for your Lady Gentlewoman.
Marcellina.   We had been doing else.
Balbus.   Meaner Jewels
  Would fit your worths.
Claudia.   And meaner clothes your bodies.
Lucina.   The Gods shall kill me first.
Lycinius.   Ther's better dying   90
  I'th Emperors arms; goe too, but be not angry,
  These are but talkes sweet Lady.

         Enter Phorba, *and* Ardelia [*with Ladyes*].

Phorba.   Where is this stranger? rushes, Ladyes, rushes,
  Rushes as greene as Summer for this stranger.

         79 Princes] *i.e.* Prince's   87 Lady] F 2; Ladys F 1

                              310

Proculus.   Heer's Ladies come to see you.
Lucina.   You are gone then?
 I take it tis your *Que.*
Proculus.   Or rather manners:
 You are better fitted Madam, we but tire ye,
 Therefore wee'l leave you for an houre, and bring
 Your much lov'd Lord unto you.
Lucina.   Then Ile thank ye,——

           Exeunt [Chilax, Lycinius, Proculus *and* Balbus].

 [*Aside*] I am betraid for certaine; well *Lucina*,   100
 If thou do'st fall from vertue, may the earth
 That after death should shout up gardens of thee,
 Spreading thy living goodnesse into branches,
 Fly from thee, and the hot Sun find thy vices.
Phorba.   You are a welcom woman.
Ardelia.   Blesse me heaven,
 How did you find the way to Court?
Lucina.   I know not.
 Would I had never trod it.
Phorba.   Pre-thee tell me,
 Good Noble Lady (and good sweet heart love us,
 For we love thee extreamly) is not this place
 A Paradice to live in?
Lucina.   To those people   110
 That know no other Paradice but pleasure;
 That little I enjoy contents me better.
Ardelia.   What, heard ye any Musick yet?
Lucina.   Too much.
Phorba.   You must not be thus froward; what, this gown
 Is one o'th prettiest by my troth *Ardelia*,
 I ever saw yet; t'was not to frowne in Lady,
 Ye put this gowne on when ye came.
Ardelia.   How doe ye?
 Alas poore wretch how cold it is!
Lucina.   Content ye;

           102 shout] *i.e.* shoot

I am as well as may be, and as temperate,
If ye will let me be so: wher's my Lord?   120
For ther's the businesse that I came for Ladies.
Phorba.   Wee'l lead ye to him, hee's i'th Gallery.
Ardelia.   Wee'l shew ye all the Court too.
Lucina.   Shew me him,
And ye have shewd me all I come to look on.
Phorba.   Come on, wee'l be your guides, and as ye goe,
We have some pretty tales to tell ye Lady,
Shall make ye merry too; ye come not here,
To be a sad *Lucina.*
Lucina.   Would I might not.

                                                        Exeunt.

                    Enter Chilax *and* Balbus.   [II.vi]

Chilax.   Now the soft Musick; *Balbus* run.
Balbus.   I flye Boy.
                                                    Exit Balbus.
Chilax.   The women by this time are worming of her:
If she can hold out them, the Emperour
Takes her to taske: he h'as her; hark the Musick.   *Musicke.*
                                                        [*Exit.*]

                    Enter Emperour *and* Lucina.

Lucina.   Good your Grace,
Where are my women Sir?
Emperour.   They are wise, beholding
What you thinke scorne to looke on, the Courts bravery:
Would you have run away so slily Lady,
And not have seen me?
Lucina.   I beseech your Majestie,
Consider what I am, and whose.
Emperour.   I doe so.   10
Lucina.   Believe me, I shall never make a Whore Sir.
Emperour.   A friend ye may, and to that man that loves ye,

                4.1 *Enter*...Lucina.] F2 (Emperour,); *om.* F1

                              312

More then you love your vertue.
Lucina.   Sacred *Cesar*——   [*Kneels.*]
Emperour.   You shall not kneel to me Sweet.
Lucina.   Look upon me,
And if ye be so cruell to abuse me,
Think how the Gods will take it; do's this beauty
Aflict your soule? Ile hide it from you ever,
Nay more, I will become so leprous,
That ye shall curse me from ye: My deer Lord,
H'as serv'd ye ever truly, fought your Battailes,   20
As if he daily longd to dye for *Cesar*,
Was never Traytor Sir, nor never tainted
In all the actions of his life.
Emperour.   I know it.
Lucina. His fame and family have growne together,
And spred together like two sayling Cedars,
Over the *Roman* Diadem; ô let not,
(As ye have any flesh that's humane in you)
The having of a modest wife decline him,
Let not my vertue be the wedge to break him:
I doe not think ye are lascivious,   30
These wanton men belye ye; you are *Cesar*,
Which is the Father of the Empires honour,
Ye are too neere the nature of the Gods,
To wrong the weakest of all creatures: Women.
Emperour [*aside*].   I dare not do it here, ——rise faire *Lucina*,
I did but try your temper; ye are honest,
And with the commendations waite on that
Ile lead ye to your Lord, and give ye to him:
Wipe your faire eyes: ——[*aside*] he that endeavours ill,
May well delay, but never quench his hell.   40
                                              Exeunt.

25 two] Seward (Sympson); to F1–2
38 give] F2; *om.* F1

Enter Chilax, Lycinius, Proculus, *and* Balbus.   III. i

Chilax. Tis done *Lycinius.*
Lycinius.   Ha?
Chilax.   I shame to tell it:
  If there be any justice, we are Villaines,
  And must be so rewarded.
Balbus.   If it be done,
  I take it tis no time now to repent it;
  Let's make the best o'th trade.
Proculus.   Now veng'ance take it.
  Why should not he have setled on a beauty,
  Whose honesty stuck in a peece of tissue,
  Or one a Ring might rule, or such a one
  That had an itching husband to be honourable,
  And ground to get it: if he must have women,   10
  And no allay without 'em, why not those
  That know the mistery, and are best able
  To play a game with judgment? such as she is,
  Grant they be won with long seidge, endlesse travell,
  And brought to opportunity with millions,
  Yet when they come to motion, their cold vertue
  Keeps 'em like cakes of yce; Ile melt a Christall,
  And make a dead flint fire himselfe, ere they
  Give greater heate, then now departing embers
  Gives to old men that watch 'em.
Lycinius.   A good Whore   20
  Had sav'd all this, and happily as wholsome,
  I, and the thing once done too, as well thought of,
  But this same chastity forsooth——
Proculus.   A Pox on't,
  Why should not women be as free as we are?
  They are, but not in open, and far freer,
  And the more bold ye beare your selfe, more welcome,

0.1 III.i] *Actus Tertius. Scæna prima.* F1   1 Ha] Ho F1; How F2
12 mistery] Seward; misery F1–2   13 a game] F2; againe F1
*19 now] *stet* F1

314

And there is nothing you dare say, but truth,
But they dare heare.

Enter Emperor *and* Lucina.

Chilax.   The Emperour! away,
And if we can repent, let's home and pray.   *Exeunt* [Courtiers].
Emperour.   Your only vertue now is patience,   30
Take heede, and save your honour; if you talke——
Lucina.   As long as there is motion in my body,
And life to give me words, Ile cry for justice.
Emperour.   Justice shall never heare ye, I am justice.
Lucina.   Wilt thou not kill me, Monster, Ravisher?
Thou bitter bane o'th Empire, look upon me,
And if thy guilty eyes dare see these ruines,
Thy wild lust hath layd levell with dishonour,
The sacrilegious razing of this Temple,
The mother of thy black sins would have blushed at,   40
Behold and curse thy selfe; the Gods will find thee,
(That's all my refuge now) for they are righteous,
Vengeance and horror circle thee; the Empire,
In which thou liv'st a strong continued surfeit,
Like poyson will disgorge thee, good men raze thee
For ever being read again but vicious,
Women, and fearefull Maids, make vows against thee:
Thy own Slaves, if they heare of this, shall hate thee;
And those thou hast corrupted, first fall from thee;
And if thou let'st me live, the Souldier,   50
Tyrde with thy Tyrannies, break through obedience,
And shake his strong Steele at thee.
Emperour.   This prevailes not;
Nor any Agony ye utter Lady:
If I have done a sin, curse her that drew me,
Curse the first cause, the witchcraft that abusd me,
Curse those faire eyes, and curse that heavenly beauty,
And curse your being good too.

36 Empire,] F 2; Empires‸ F 1
*46 again‸‸ but vicious,] Colman; ~ , —— ~ ~ ‸ F 1–2

Lucina.   Glorious theife,
What restitution canst thou make to save me?
Emperour.   Ile ever love, and honour you.
Lucina.   Thou canst not,
For that which was mine honour, thou hast murdred,   60
And can there be a love in violence?
Emperour.   You shall be only mine.
Lucina.   Yet I like better
Thy villany, then flattery, that's thine owne,
The other basely counterfeit; flye from me,
Or for thy safety sake and wisdome kill me,
For I am worse then thou art; thou mayst pray,
And so recover grace; I am lost for ever,
And if thou lets't me live, th'art lost thy selfe too.
Emperour.   I feare no losse but love, I stand above it.
Lucina.   Call in your Lady Bawdes, and guilded Pander's   70
And let them triumph too, and sing to *Cesar*,
Lucina's falne, the chast *Lucina*'s conquerd;
Gods, what a wretched thing has this man made me?
For I am now no wife for *Maximus*,
No company for women that are vertuous,
No familie I now can claime, nor Country,
Nor name, but *Cesars* Whore; O sacred *Cesar*,
(For that should be your title) was your Empire,
Your Rods, and Axes, that are types of Justice,
Those fires that ever burne, to beg you blessings,   80
The peoples adoration, feare of Nations,
What victory can bring ye home, what else
The usefull Elements can make your servants,
Even light it selfe, and sons of light (truth, justice,
Mercy, and starlike pietie) sent to you,
And from the gods themselves, to ravish women?
The curses that I owe to Enemies,
Even those the *Sabines* sent, when *Romulus*,
(As thou hast me) ravishd their noble Maydes,
Made more, and heavier, light on thee.

*84 sons] Seward; suns F1-2

Emperour.   This helps not. 90
Lucina.   The sins of *Tarquin* be rememberd in thee,
And where there has a chast wife been abusde,
Let it be thine, the shame thine, thine the slaughter,
And last, for ever thine, the feard example.
Where shall poore vertue live, now I am falne?
What can your honours now, and Empire make me,
But a more glorious Whore?
Emperour.   A better woman,
But if ye will be blind, and scorne it, who can help it?
Come leave these lamentations, they doe nothing,
But make a noyse; I am the same man still, 100
Were it to doe again (therefore be wiser)
By all this holy light, I should attempt it:
Ye are so excellent, and made to ravish,
(There were no pleasure in ye else)——
Lucina.   Oh villaine.
Emperour.   So bred for mans amazement, that my reason
And every help to hold me right has lost me;
The God of love himselfe had been before me,
Had he but power to see ye; tell me justly,
How can I choose but erre then? if ye dare
Be mine, and only mine (for ye are so pretious, 110
I envie any other should enjoy ye,
Almost look on ye; and your daring husband
Shall know h'as kept an Offring from the Empire,
Too holy for his Altars) be the mightiest,
More then my selfe Ile make it: if ye will not,
Sit down with this, and silence, for which wisdom,
Ye shall have use of me, and much honour ever,
And be the same you were; if ye divulge it,
Know I am far above the faults I doe,
And those I doe I am able to forgive too; 120
And where your credit in the knowledge of it,
May be with glosse enough suspected, mine
Is as mine owne command shall make it: princes
Though they be somtime subject to loose whispers,

Yet weare they two edged swords for open censures:
Your husband cannot help ye, nor the Souldier,
Your husband is my creature, they my weapons,
And only where I bid 'em, strike; I feed 'em:
Nor can the Gods be angry at this action,
For as they make me most, they meane me happiest, 130
Which I had never bin without this pleasure:
Consider, and farewell: you'l find your women
At home before ye, they have had some sport too,
But are more thankfull for it. *Exit* Emperor.
Lucina.   Destruction finde thee.
Now which way must I goe? my honest house
Will shake to shelter me, my husband flye me,
My Family, because they are honest, and desire to be so,
Must not endure me, not a neighbour know me:
What woman now dare see me without blushes,
And pointing as I passe: there, there, behold her, 140
Look on her little Children, that is she,
That hansome Lady, mark; O my sad fortunes,
Is this the end of goodnesse, this the price
Of all my early praiers to protect me?
Why then I see there is no God but power,
Nor vertue now alive that cares for us,
But what is either lame or sensuall;
How had I bin thus wretched else? [*Sits.*]

   Enter Maximus *and* Aecius.

Aecius.   Let *Titius*
Command the company that *Pontius* lost,
And see the Fosses deeper.
Maximus.   How now sweet heart, 150
What make you here, and thus?
Aecius.   *Lucina* weeping?
This must be much offence.
Maximus.   Look up and tell me,
Why are you thus? My Ring? ô friend, I have found it,

   *148–150 Aecius. Let...deeper.] stet F1

318

Ye were at Court, Sweet?
Lucina.   Yes, this brought me thither.
Maximus.   Rise, and goe home: I have my feares *Aecius*:
Oh my best friend, I am ruind; goe *Lucina*,
Already in thy teares, I have read thy wrongs,
Already found a *Cesar*; go thou Lilly,
Thou sweetly drooping floure: go silver Swan,
And sing thine owne sad requiem: goe *Lucina*,   160
And if thou dar'st, out live this wrong.
Lucina.   I dare not.
Aecius.   Is that the Ring ye lost?
Maximus.   That, that, *Aecius*,
That cursed Ring, my selfe, and all my fortunes:
T'has pleasd the Emperor, my Noble master,
For all my services, and dangers for him,
To make me mine owne Pandar: was this justice?
Oh my *Aecius*, have I liv'd to beare this?
Lucina.   Farewell for ever Sir.
Maximus.   That's a sad saying,
But such a one becomes ye well *Lucina*:
And yet me thinkes we should not part so lightly,   170
Our loves have been of longer growth, more rooted
Then the sharp word of one farewell can scatter.
Kisse me: I find no *Cesar* here; these lips
Taste not of Ravisher in my opinion.
Was it not so?
Lucina.   O Yes.
Maximus.   I dare believe thee,
For thou wert ever truth it selfe, and sweetnesse:——
Indeed she was *Aecius*.
Aecius.   So she is still.
Maximus.   Once more: [*Kisses her again.*]
                O my *Lucina*; ô my comfort,
The blessing of my youth, the life of my life.
Aecius.   I have seene enough to stagger my obedience: 180
Hold me ye equall Gods, this is too sinfull.

*154 were...thither] stet F1

319

Maximus.   Why wert thou chosen out to make a whore of?
 To me thou wert too chast: fall Christall fountaines,
 And ever feed your streames you rising sorrowes,
 Till you have dropt your mistris into marble.
 Now goe for ever from me.
Lucina.   Long farewell Sir.
 And as I have been loyall, Gods think on me.
Maximus.   Stay, let me once more bid farewell *Lucina*,
 Farewell thou excellent example of us,
 Thou starry vertue, farethee-well; seeke heaven,   190
 And there by *Cassiopeia* shine in glory,
 We are too base and dirty to preserve thee.
Aecius.   Nay, I must kisse too: such a kisse againe,
 And from a woman of so ripe a vertue,
 Aecius must not take: Farewell thou *Phenix*:
 If thou wilt dye *Lucina*; which well weighd,
 If you can cease a while from these strange thoughts,
 I wish were rather alterd.
Lucina.   No.
Aecius.   Mistake not.
 I would not staine your honour for the Empire,
 Nor any way decline you to discredit,   200
 Tis not my faire profession, but a Villaines:
 I find and feele your losse as deep as you doe,
 And am the same *Aecius*, still as honest,
 The same life I have still for *Maximus*,
 The same sword weare for you, where justice wills mee,
 And tis no dull one: therefore misconceave not:
 Only I would have you live a little longer,
 But a short yeare.
Maximus.   She must not.
Lucina.   Why so long Sir,
 Am I not grey enough with griefe already?
Aecius.   To draw from that wild man a sweet repentance,   210
 And goodnesse in his daies to come.
Maximus.   They are so,
 And will be ever comming my *Aecius*.

Aecius.   For who knowes but the sight of you, presenting
 His swolne sins at the full, and your faire vertues,
 May like a fearefull vision fright his follies,
 And once more bend him right again? which blessing
 (If your dark wrongs would give you leave to read)
 Is more then death, and the reward more glorious:
 Death only eases you; this, the whole Empire:
 Besides, compeld and forcd with violence   220
 To what ye have done, the deed is none of yours,
 No nor the justice neither; ye may live,
 And still a worthier woman, still more honoured:
 For are those trees the worse we teare the fruits from?
 Or should the eternall Gods desire to perish,
 Because we daily violate their truths,
 Which is the chastitie of heaven? No Lady,
 If ye dare live, ye may: and as our sins
 Makes them more full of equitie and justice,
 So this compulsive wrong, makes you more perfect: 230
 The Empire too will blesse ye.
Maximus.   Noble Sir;
 If she were any thing to me but honour,
 And that that's wedded to me too, layd in,
 Not to be worne away without my being:
 Or could the wrong be hers alone, or mine,
 Or both our wrongs, not tide to after issues,
 Not borne a new in all our names and kindreds,
 I would desire her live, nay more, compell her:
 But since it was not youth, but malice did it,
 And not her own, nor mine, but both our losses,   240
 Nor staies it there, but that our names must find it,
 Even those to come; and when they read, she livd,
 Must they not aske how often she was ravishd,
 And make a doubt she lov'd that more then Wedlock?
 Therefore she must not live.
Aecius.   Therefore she must live,
 To teach the world such deaths are superstitious.
Lucina.   The tongues of Angels cannot alter me;

321

For could the world again restore my credit,
As faire and absolute as first I bred it,
That world I should not trust agen: The Empire   250
By my life can get nothing but my story,
Which whilst I breath must be but his abuses:
And where ye councell me to live, that *Cesar*
May see his errors, and repent, Ile tell ye,
His penitence is but encrease of pleasures,
His prayers never said but to deceave us,
And when he weeps (as you think for his vices)
Tis but as killing drops from balefull Ewgh trees
That rot their honest neighbour: If he can grieve,
As one that yet desires his free conversion,   260
And almost glories in his penitence,
Ile leave him robes to mourn in, my sad ashes.
Aecius.   The farewells then of happy soules be with thee,
And to thy memory be ever sung
The praises of a just and constant Lady;
This sad day whilst I live, a Souldiers teares
Ile offer on thy Monument, and bring
Full of thy noble selfe with teares untold yet,
Many a worthy wife, to weep thy ruine.
Maximus.   All that is chast, upon thy Tomb shal flourish,   270
All living Epitaphs be thine; Time, Story,
And what is left behind to peice our lives,
Shall be no more abus'd with tales and trifles,
But full of thee, stand to eternitie.
Aecius.   Once more farewell, go find *Elysium,*
There where the happy soules are crownd with blessings,
There where tis ever spring, and ever summer.
Maximus.   There where no bedrid justice comes; truth, honor,
Are keepers of that blessed place; go thither,
For here thou livest chaste fire in rotten timber.   280
Aecius.   And so our last farewells.
Maximus.   Gods give the justice.
                                                        Exit Lucina.

281 the] *i.e.* thee

322

Aecius [*aside*]. His thoughts begin to worke; I feare him, yet
  He ever was a noble *Romane*, but
  I know not what to thinke on't: he hath suffered
  Beyond a man, if he stand this.
Maximus.   *Aecius*,
  Am I a live, or has a dead sleepe seized me?
  It was my wife the Emperor abus'd thus;
  And I must say, I am glad I had her for him;
  Must I not my *Aecius*?
Aecius.   I am stricken
  With such a stiffe amazement, that no answer   290
  Can readily come from me, nor no comfort:
  Will ye go home, or go to my house?
Maximus.   Neither:
  I have no home, and you are mad *Aecius*
  To keepe me company, I am a fellow
  My own Sword would forsake, not tyed unto me:
  A Pandar is a Prince, to what I am falne;
  By heaven I dare do nothing.
Aecius.   Ye do better.
Maximus. I am made a branded slave *Aecius*,
  And yet I blesse the maker;
  Death o' my soule, must I endure this tamely?   300
  Must *Maximus* be mention'd for his tales?
  I am a child too; what should I do rayling?
  I cannot mend my selfe, tis *Cæsar* did it,
  And what am I to him?
Aecius.   Tis well consider'd;
  How ever you are tainted, be no Traitor.
  Time may out-weare the first, the last lives ever.
Maximus. O that thou wert not living, and my freind.
Aecius [*aside*].   Ile beare a wary eye upon your actions,
  I feare ye *Maximus*, nor can I blame thee
  If thou breakest out, for by the Gods thy wrong   310
  Deserves a generall ruine:——do ye love me?
Maximus. That's all I have to live on.

  *300, 316 o'] F2; ô F1   *301 tales] *stet* F1

Aecius.   Then go with me,
Ye shall not to your own house.
Maximus.   Nor to any,
My greifs are greater far, then walls can compasse,
And yet I wonder how it happens with me,
I am not dangerous; and o' my conscience
Should I now see the Emperor i'th heat on't,
I should not chide him for't: an awe runs through me,
I feele it sensibly, that bindes me to it,
Tis at my heart now, there it sits and rules,   320
And me thinkes tis a pleasure to obey it.
Aecius [*aside*].   This is a maske to cozen me; I know ye,
And how far ye dare do; no *Romane* farther,
Nor with more fearlesse valour; and ile watch ye:——
Keepe that obedience still.
Maximus.   Is a wives losse
(For her abuse much good may do his grace,
Ile make as bold with his wife, if I can)
More then the fading of a few fresh colours,
More then a lusty spring lost?
Aecius.   No more *Maximus*,
To one that truly lives.
Maximus.   Why then I care not,   330
I can live wel enough *Aecius*.
For looke you freind, for vertue, and those triffles,
They may be bought they say.
Aecius [*aside*].   He's craz'd a little.
His greife has made him talke things from his nature.
Maximus.   But chastitie is not a thing I take it
To get in *Rome*, unlesse it be bespoken
A hundred yeare before; is it *Aecius?*
By'r lady, and well handled too i'th breeding.
Aecius.   Will ye go any way?
Maximus.   Ile tell thee freind,
If my wife for all this should be a whore now,   340
A kind of kicker out of sheetes, t'would vex me,
For I am not angry yet; the Emperor

Is young and hansome, and the woman flesh,
And may not these two couple without scratching?
Aecius.   Alasse my noble freind.
Maximus.   Alasse not me,
I am not wretched, for ther's no man miserable
But he that makes himselfe so.
Aecius.   Will ye walke yet?
Maximus.   Come, come, she dare not dye freind, that's the
      truth on't;
She knowes the inticing sweets and delicacies
Of a young Princes pleasures, and I thanke her   350
She has made a way for *Maximus* to rise by.
Wilt not become me bravely? why do you think
She wept, and said she was ravish'd? keep it here
And Ile discover to you.
Aecius.   Well.
Maximus.   She knowes
I love no bitten flesh, and out of that hope
She might be from me, she contriv'd this knavery;
Was it not monstrous freind?
Aecius [*aside*].   Do's he but seeme so,
Or is he made indeed?
Maximus.   Oh Gods, my heart!
Aecius.   Would it would fairly breake.
Maximus.   Me thinks I am somewhat wilder then I was,   360
And yet I thanke the gods I know my duty.

Enter Claudia.

Claudia.   Nay ye may spare your tears; she's dead. She is so.
Maximus.   Why so it should be: how?
Claudia.   When first she enter'd
Into her house, after a world of weeping,
And blushing like the Sun-set, as we saw her;
Dare I, said she, defile this house with whore,
In which his noble family has flourish'd?
At which she fel, and stird no more; we rubd her——

355 made] *i.e.* mad (*cf.* IV.i.115)   365 saw] Seward; see F 1–2

Maximus. No more of that: be gon: *Exit* Claudia.
                     now my *Aecius*,
  If thou wilt do me pleasure, weepe a little,   370
  I am so parch'd I cannot: Your example
  Has brought the raine down now: now lead me freind,
  And as we walke together let's pray together truly
  I may not fall from faith.
Aecius.   That's nobly spoken.
Maximus. Was I not wilde, *Aecius*?
Aecius.   Somewhat troubled.
Maximus. I felt no sorrow then: Now ile goe with ye,
  But do not name the woman: fye what foole
  Am I to weepe thus? God's, *Lucina*, take thee,
  For thou wert even the best, and worthiest Lady.
Aecius. Good Sir no more, I shall be melted with it.   380
Maximus. I have done, and good Sir comfort me;
  Would there were wars now.
Aecius.   Settle your thoughts, come.
Maximus. So I have now friend,
  Of my deep lamentations here's an end.

                          Exeunt.

         Enter Pontius, Phidias, *and* Aretus.   [III. ii]

Phidias. By my faith Captain *Pontius*, besides pitie
  Of your falne fortunes, what to say I know not,
  For tis too true the Emperor desires not,
  But my best Master, any Souldier neere him.
Aretus. And when he understands, he cast your fortunes
  For disobedience, how can we incline him,
  (That are but under persons to his favours)
  To any faire opinion? Can ye sing?
Pontius. Not to please him *Aretus*, for my Songs
  Goe not to'th Lute, or Violl, but to'th Trumpet,   10
  My tune kept on a Target, and my subject
  The well struck wounds of men, not love, or women.
Phidias. And those he understands not.

Pontius.   He should *Phidias.*
Aretus.   Could you not leave this killing way a little,
  (You must if here you would plant your selfe) and rather
  Learne as we doe, to like what those affect
  That are above us: weare their actions,
  And think they keep us warme too: what they say,
  Though oftentimes they speake a little foolishly,
  Not stay to construe, but prepare to execute,   20
  And think how ever the end falls, the businesse
  Cannot run empty handed?
Phidias.   Can yee flatter,
  And if it were put to you, lye a little?
Pontius.   Yes, if it be a living.
Aretus.   That's well said then.
Pontius.   But must these lyes and flatteries be beleev'd then?
Phidias.   Oh yes by any meanes.
Pontius.   By any meanes then,
  I cannot lye, nor flatter.
Aretus.   Ye must sweare too,
  If ye be there.
Pontius.   I can sweare, if they move me.
Phidias.   Cannot ye forsweare too?
Pontius.   The Court for ever,
  If it be growne so wicked.   30
Aretus.   You should procure a little too.
Pontius.   What's that?
  Mens honest sayings for my truth?
Aretus.   Oh no Sir:
  But womens honest actions for your triall.
Pontius.   Doe you doe all these things?
Phidias.   Doe you not like 'em?
Pontius.   Do ye aske me seriously, or trifle with me?
  I am not so low yet, to be your mirth.
Aretus.   You do mistake us Captain, for sincerely,
  We aske you how you like 'em.
Pontius.   Then sincerely

18 think] F2; thinks F1

I tell ye I abhor 'em: they are ill wayes,
And I will starve before I fall into 'em.   40
The doers of 'em wretches, their base hungers
Cares not whose bread they eate, nor how they get it.
Aretus.   What then Sir?
Pontius.   If you professe this wickednesse,
Because ye have bin Souldiers, and borne Armes,
The servants of the brave *Aecius*,
And by him put to'th Emperor, give me leave,
Or I must take it else, to say ye are villaines,
For all your Golden Coates, deboshd, base villaines,
Yet I doe weare a sword to tell ye so:
Is this the way you mark out for a Souldier,   50
A man that has commanded for the Empire,
And borne the reputation of a man?
Are there not lazie things enough cald fooles, and cowards,
And poore enough to be preferr'd for Panders,
But wanting Souldiers must be knaves too? ha:
This the trim course of life? were not ye born Bawdes,
And so inherit but your rights? I am poore
And may expect a worse; yet digging, pruning,
Mending of broken wayes, carrying of water,
Planting of Worts, and Onyons, any thing   60
That's honest, and a mans, Ile rather choose,
I and live better on it, which is juster;
Drink my well gotten water, with more pleasure,
When my endeavours done, and wages payd me,
Then you doe wine; eate my course bread not curst,
And mend upon't (your diets are diseases)
And sleep as soundly, when my labour bids me,
As any forward Pander of ye all,
And rise a great deale honester; my Garments,
Though not as yours, the soft sins of the Empire,   70
Yet may be warme, and keep the biting wind out,
When every single breath of poore opinion
Finds you through all your Velvets.

55 knaves] F2 (Knaves); knave F1   62 I] *i.e.* ay

328

Aretus.   You have hit it,
  Nor are we those we seeme: the Lord *Aecius*
  Put us good men to'th Emperor, so we have serv'd him,
  Though much neglected for it: So dare be still:
  Your curses are not ours: we have seen your fortune,
  But yet know no way to redeem it: Meanes,
  Such as we have, ye shall not want brave *Pontius*,
  But pray be temperate; if we can wipe out   80
  The way of your offences, we are yours Sir;
  And you shall live at Court an honest man too.
Phidias.   That little meat and means we have, wee'l share it,
  Feare not to be as we are; what we told ye,
  Were but meere tryalls of your truth: y'are worthie,
  And so wee'l ever hold ye; suffer better,
  And then ye are a right man *Pontius*,
  If my good Master be not ever angry,
  Ye shall command againe.
Pontius.   I have found two good men: use my life,   90
  For it is yours, and all I have to thank ye.

                                                   Exeunt.

                    Enter Maximus.   [III.] iii

Maximus.   Ther's no way else to doe it, he must die,
  This friend must die, this soule of *Maximus*,
  Without whom I am nothing but my shame,
  This perfectnesse that keeps me from opinion,
  Must dye, or I must live thus branded ever:
  A hard choice, and a fatall; God's ye have given me
  A way to credit, but the ground to goe on,
  Ye have levelld with that pretious life I love most,
  Yet I must on, and through; for if I offer
  To take my way without him, like a Sea   10
  He bares his high command, twixt me and vengeance,
  And in my owne road sinkes me: he is honest,
  Of a most constant loyaltie to *Cesar*,
  And when he shall but doubt, I dare attempt him,

            0.1 III.iii] Scæn. 3. F1   11 bares] *i.e.* bears

But make a question of his ill, but say,
What is a *Cesar*, that he dare doe this,
Dead sure he cuts me off: *Aecius* dies,
Or I have lost my selfe: why should I kill him?
Why should I kill my selfe? for tis my killing,
Aecius is my roote, and whither him,   20
Like a decaying branch, I fall to nothing.
Is he not more to me, then wife? then *Cesar*,
Though I had now my safe revenge upon him?
Is he not more then honour, and his freindship
Sweeter then the love of women? What is honor
We all so strangly are bewitch'd withall?
Can it relieve me if I want? he has;
Can honor, twixt the incensed Prince, and Envy,
Beare up the lives of worthy men? he has;
Can honor pull the wings of fearefull cowards   30
And make 'em turne againe like Tigers? he has,
And I have liv'd to see this, and preserv'd so;
Why should this empty word incite me then
To what is ill, and cruell? let her perish.
A freind is more then all the world, then honor;
She is a woman and her losse the lesse,
And with her go my greifs:——but hark ye *Maximus*,
Was she not yours? Did she not dye to tell ye
She was a ravish'd woman? did not justice
Nobly begin with her, that not deserv'd it,   40
And shall he live that did it? Stay a little,
Can this abuse dye here? Shall not mens tongues
Dispute it afterward, and say I gave
(Affecting dul obedience, and tame duty,
And led away with fondnes of a freindship)
The only vertue of the world to slander?
Is not this certaine, was not she a chaste one,
And such a one, that no compare dwelt with her?

20 whither] *i.e.* wither (*but cf.* IV.ii.40)
*24 honour] Colman (Theobald and Sympson); rumour F 1–2
*30 of] *stet* F 1   41 he] F 2; ye F 1

One of so sweete a vertue, that *Aecius*,
Even he himselfe, this freind that holds me from it,   50
Out of his worthy love to me, and justice,
Had it not been on *Cæsar*, h'ad reveng'd her?
By heaven he told me so; what shall I do then?
Can other men affect it, and I cold?
I feare he must not live.

Enter a Servant.

Servant.   My Lord, the Generall
Is come to seeke ye.
Maximus.   Go, intreate him to enter: [*Exit* Servant.]
O brave *Aecius*, I could wish thee now
As far from freindship to me, as from feares,
That I might cut thee off, like that I weigh'd not:
Is there no way without him, to come neare it?   60
For out of honesty he must destroy me
If I attempt it, he must dye as others,
And I must loose him; tis necessity,
Only the time, and meanes is all the difference;
But yet I would not make a murther of him,
Take him directly for my doubts; he shall dye,
I have found a way to do it, and a safe one,
It shall be honor to him too: I know not
What to determine certaine, I am so troubled,
And such a deale of conscience presses me;   70
Would I were dead my selfe.

Enter Aecius.

Aecius.   You run away well;
How got you from me freind?
Maximus.   That that leads mad men,
A strong Imagination, made me wander.
Aecius. I thought ye had been more setled.

55 *Enter a* Servant.] Weber; *following line* 53 F 1–2
71 *Enter* Aecius.] Langbaine; *following line* 70 F 1–2

Maximus.   I am well,
  But you must give me leave a little sometimes
  To have a buzzing in my brains.
Aecius [*aside*].   Ye are dangerous,
  But Ile prevent it if I can;—— ye told me
  You would go to'th Army.
Maximus.   Why, to have my throat cut?
  Must he not be the bravest man *Aecius*
  That strikes me first?
Aecius.   You promised me a freedom   80
  From all these thoughts, and why should any strike you?
Maximus.   I am an Enemy, a wicked one,
  Worse then the foes of *Rome*, I am a Coward,
  A Cuckold, and a Coward, that's two causes
  Why every one should beat me.
Aecius.   Ye are neither,
  And durst another tell me so, he dyde for't:
  For thus far on mine honor, Ile assure you
  No man more lov'd then you, and for your valour;
  And what ye may be, faire, no man more follow'd.
Maximus.   A doughty man indeed, but that's all one: 90
  The Emperor, nor all the Princes living
  Shall find a flaw in my coat; I have sufferd,
  And can yet; let them find inflictions,
  Ile find a body for 'em, or Ile break it.
  Tis not a wife can thrust me out; some lookt for't,
  But let 'em looke till they are blind with looking,
  They are but fooles, yet there is anger in me,
  That I would faine disperse, and now I think on't,
  You told me freind the Provinces are stirring,
  We shall have sport I hope then, and what's dangerous,   100
  A Battle shall beat from me.
Aecius.   Why do ye eye me
  With such a setled looke?
Maximus.   Pray tell me this,
  Do we not love extremely? I love you so.

*88–89 valour;...faire,] ~ ,... ~ ; F1–2

Aecius.   If I should say I lov'd not you as truly,
I should do that I never durst do, lye.
Maximus.   If I should dye, would it not greive you much?
Aecius.   Without all doubt.
Maximus.   And could you live without me?
Aecius.   It would much trouble me to live without ye.
Our loves, and loving soules have been so us'd
But to one houshold in us: But to dye   110
Because I could not make you live, were woman,
Far much too weake: were it to save your worth,
Or to redeeme your name from rooting out,
To quit you bravely fighting from the foe,
Or fetch ye off, where honor had ingag'd ye,
I ought, and would dye for ye.
Maximus.   Truly spoken.
[*Aside*].   What beast but I, that must, could hurt this man now?
Would he had ravish'd me, I would have payd him,
I would have taught him such a trick, his Eunuches
Nor all his black-eyd boyes dreamt of yet;   120
By all the Gods I am mad now; Now were *Cæsar*
Within my reach, and on his glorious top
The pile of all the world, he went to nothing;
The destinies, nor all the dames of hell,
Were I once grappl'd with him, should relieve him,
No not the hope of mankind more; all perished;
But this is words, and weaknesse.
Aecius.   Ye looke strangely.
Maximus.   I looke but as I am, I am a stranger.
Aecius.   To me?
Maximus.   To every one, I am no *Romane*;
Nor what I am do I know.
Aecius.   Then Ile leave ye.   130
Maximus.   I find I am best so, if ye meet with *Maximus*
Pray bid him to be an honest man for my sake,
You may do much upon him; for his shadow,
Let me alone.
Aecius.   Ye were not wont to talke thus,

333

And to your freind; ye have some danger in you,
That willingly would run to action.
Take heed, by all our love take heed.
Maximus.   I danger?
I, willing to do any thing? I die?
Has not my wife been dead two dayes already?
Are not my mournings by this time moath-eaten?   140
Are not her sins dispers'd to other women,
And many one ravish'd to relieve her?
Have I shed teares these twelve houres?
Aecius.   Now ye weepe.
Maximus.   Some lazie drops that staid behind.
Aecius.   Ile tell ye
And I must tell ye truth, were it not hazard,
And almost certaine losse of all the Empire,
I would joyne with ye: were it any mans
But his life, that is life of us, he lost it
For doing of this mischeife: I would take it,
And to your rest give ye a brave revenge: 150
But as the rule now stands, and as he rules,
And as the Nations hold, in disobedience
One pillar failing, all must fall; I dare not:
Nor is it just you should be suffer'd in it,
Therefore againe take heed: On forraigne foes
We are our own revengers, but at home
On Princes that are eminent and ours,
Tis fit the Gods should judge us: Be not rash,
Nor let your angry steele cut those ye know not,
For by this fatall blow, if ye dare strike it,   160
(As I see great aymes in ye) those unborne yet,
And those to come of them, and those succeding
Shall bleed the wrath of *Maximus*: For me
As ye now beare your selfe, I am your freind still,
If ye fall off (I will not flatter ye)
And in my hands, were ye my soule, you perish'd:

*138 die] Colman; dig F 1–2   *147 joyne] F 2 (join); wyne F 1
162 them, and those] Dyce; ~ ˄ ~ these F 1; ~ , ~ these F 2

334

Once more be carefull, stand, and still be worthy,
Ile leave ye for this howre.
Maximus.   Pray do:———tis done; *Exit* [Aecius].
And freindship, since thou canst not hold in dangers,
Give me a certaine ruin, I must through it.   170

                                        Exit.

                Enter Emperor, Lycinius, Chilax, *and* Balbus.   IV. i

Emperor.   Dead?
Chilax.   So tis thought Sir.
Emperor.   How?
Lycinius.   Greife, and disgrace,
As people say.
Emperor.   No more, I have too much on't,
Too much by you, you whetters of my follies,
Ye Angell formers of my sins, but devills;
Where is your cunning now? you would worke wonders,
There was no chastity above your practise,
You would undertake to make her love her wrongs,
And doate upon her rape: mark what I tell ye,
If she be dead———
Chilax.   Alas Sir.
Emperor.   Hang ye rascalls,
Ye blasters of my youth, if she be gon,   10
T'wer better ye had been your fathers Camells,
Ground under dayly waights of wood and water
(Am I not *Cæsar?*)———
Lycinius.   Mighty and our maker.
Emperor.   Then thus have given my pleasures to destruction.
Looke she be living slaves.
Lycinius.   We are no Gods Sir,
If she be dead, to make her new againe.
Emperor.   She cannot dye, she must not dye; are those

168 *Exit.*] Langbaine; *following* howre F 1–2
0.1 IV.i] *Actus Quartus. Scæna prima.* F 1
15 *Lycinius.*] F 2 (*Lici.*); *Empe.* F 1

I plant my love upon but common livers?
Their howres as others, told 'em? can they be ashes?
Why do ye flatter a beliefe into me   20
That I am all that is, the world's my creature,
The Trees bring forth their fruits when I say Summer,
The Wind, that knowes no limit but his wildnesse,
At my command moves not a leafe: The sea
With his proud mountaine waters envying heaven,
When I say still, run into christall mirrors?
Can I do this and she dye? Why ye bubbles
That with my least breath break, no more remembred;
Ye moaths that fly about my flame and perish,
Ye golden cancker-wormes, that eate my honors,   30
Living no longer then my spring of favour:
Why do ye make me God that can do nothing?
Is she not dead?
Chilax.   All women are not with her.
Emperor.   A common whore serves you, and far above ye,
The pleasures of a body lam'd with lewdnesse;
A meare perpetuall motion makes ye happy:
Am I a man to traffique with diseases?
Can any but a chastity serve *Cæsar*?
And such a one the Gods would kneele to purchase?
You think because you have bread me up to pleasures,   40
And almost run me over all the rare ones,
Your wives will serve the turne: I care not for 'em,
Your wives are Fencers whores, and shall be Footmens,
Though sometimes my nyce will, or rather anger,
Have made ye Cuckolds for variety,
I would not have ye hope, nor dreame ye poore ones,
Alwaies so great a blessing from me; go
Get your own infamy hereafter, rascalls,
I have done too nobly for ye; ye enjoy
Each one an heire, the royall seed of *Cæsar*,   50
And I may curse ye for't; your wanton Gennets
That are so proud, the wind get's 'em with fillies,

19 others] *i.e.* others'   40 bread] F 2 (bred); breed F 1

Taught me this foule intemperance: Thou *Lycinius*
Hast such a *Messalina*, such a *Lais*,
The backs of bulls cannot content, nor Stallions,
The sweate of fifty men a night do's nothing.
Lycinius.   Your Grace but jests I hope.
Emperor.   Tis Oracle.
The sins of other women put by hers
Shew off like sanctities:——Thine's a foole *Chilax*,   60
Yet she can tell to twenty, and all lovers,
And all lien with her too, and all as she is,
Rotten, and ready for an hospitall.——
Yours is a holy whore freind *Balbus.*
Balbus.   Well Sir.
Emperor.   One that can pray away the sins she suffers,
But not the punishments: She hus had ten bastards,
Five of 'em now are lictors, yet she praies;
She has been the song of *Rome*, and common *Pasquill*;
Since I durst see a wench, she was Campe mistris,
And musterd all the cohorts, paid 'em too,
(They have it yet to shew) and yet she prayes;   70
She is now to enter old men that are children,
And have forgot their rudiments: am I
Left for these withered vices? and but one,
But one of all the world that could content me,
And snatch'd away in shewing? If your wives
Be not yet witches, or your selves, now be so
And save your lives, raise me this noble beauty
As when I forc'd her, full of constancy,
Or by the Gods——
Lycinius.   Most sacred *Cæsar.*
Emperor.   Slaves.

Enter Proculus.

Lycinius.   Good *Proculus*——
Proculus.   By heaven you shall not see it,   80
It may concerne the Empire.

79.1 *Enter* Proculus.] F 2; *om.* F 1   *80 *Lycinius.*] F 2 (*Lici.*); *Lycias.* F 1

Emperor.   Ha: what said'st thou?
  Is she not dead?
Proculus.   Not any one I know Sir;
  I come to bring your Grace a letter here,
  Scatterd belike i'th Court: Tis sent to *Maximus*,
  And bearing danger in it.
Emperor.   Danger? where?
  Double our Guard.
Proculus.   Nay no where, but i'th letter.
Emperor [*aside*].   What an afflicted conscience doe I live with,
  And what a beast I am growne? I had forgotten
  To aske heaven mercy for my fault, and was now
  Even ravishing againe her memory.   90
  I find there must be danger in this deed:
  Why doe I stand disputing then, and whining
  For what is not the gods to give? they cannot
  Though they would linck their powers in one, do mischiefe.
  This Letter may betray me,——get ye gon
  And waite me in the Garden, guard the house well,
  And keep this from the Empresse;   *Exeunt* [Courtiers].
                                        The name *Maximus*
  Runnes through me like a feavour, this may be
  Some private Letter upon private businesse,
  Nothing concerning me: why should I open't?   100
  I have done him wrong enough already; yet
  It may concerne me too, the time so tells me;
  The wicked deed I have done, assures me tis so.
  Be what it will, ile see it, if that be not
  Part of my feares, among my other sins,
  Ile purge it out in prayers: How? what's this?

  Lord *Maximus*, you love *Aecius*,   *Letter red.*
  And are his noble friend too; bid him be lesse,
  I meane lesse with the people: times are dangerous,
  The Army's his, the Emperor in doubts,   110
  And as some will not stick to say, declining;

    97 *Exeunt.*] Weber; *following line* 95 F 1–2   112 fortune] F 2; fortunes F 1

You stand a constant man in either fortune;
Perswade him, he is lost else: Though ambition
Be the last sin he touches at, or never;
Yet what the people, made with loving him
And as they willingly desire another,
May tempt him too, or rather force his goodnesse,
Is to be doubted mainly: he is all,
(As he stands now) but the meer name of *Cesar*,
And should the Emperor inforce him lesser,   120
Not comming from himselfe, it were more dangerous:
He is honest, and will heare you: doubts are scatterd,
And almost come to growth in every houshold:
Yet in my foolish judgment, were this masterd,
The people that are now but rage, and his,
Might be againe obedience: you shall know me
When *Rome* is faire againe; till when I love you.

No name! this may be cunning, yet it seemes not;
For there is nothing in it but is certain:
Besides my safety——
               Had not good *Germanicus*,   130
That was as loyall, and as straight as he is,
If not prevented by *Tiberius*,
Bin by the Souldiers forcd their Emperor?
He had, and tis my wisdom to remember it.
And was not *Corbulo* (even that *Corbulo*,
That ever fortunate and living *Roman*,
That broake the heart strings of the *Parthians*,
And brought *Arsases* line upon their knees,
Chaind to the awe of *Rome*) because he was thought
(And but in wine once) fit to make a *Cesar*,   140
Cut off by *Nero*? I must seeke my safety:
For tis the same againe, if not beyond it:
I know the Souldier loves him more then heaven,
And will adventure all his gods to raise him;
Me he hates more then peace: what this may breed,

    115 made] *i.e.* mad (*cf.* III.i.358)
   *129–130 certain:...safety——] Seward; ~ ,... ~ . F1–2

If dull security and confidence
Let him grow up, a foole may find, and laugh at.
But why Lord *Maximus* I injurd so,
Should be the man to councell him, I know not,   150
More then he has been friend, and lov'd allegeance:
What now he is I feare, for his abuses,
Without the people, dare draw bloud; who waits there?

Enter a Servant.

Servant.   Your Grace.
Emperor.   Call *Phidias* and *Aretus* hither:

                               [*Exit* Servant.]

Ile find a day for him too; *times are dangerous,*   [*Reads.*]
The Army his, the Emperor in doubts:
I find it is too true; did he not tell me
As if he had intent to make me odious,
And to my face, and by a way of terror,
What vices I was grounded in, and almost   160
Proclaimd the Souldiers hate against me? is not
The sacred name and dignity of *Cesar*
(Were this *Aecius* more then man) sufficient
To shake off all his honesty? Hee's dangerous
Though he be good, and though a friend, a feard one,
And such I must not sleep by: are they come yet?
I doe beleeve this fellow, and I thank him;
T'was time to look about: if I must perish,
Yet shall my feares go foremost.

Enter Phidias, *and* Aretus.

Phidias.   Life to *Cesar.*
Emperor.   Is Lord *Aecius* waiting?
Phidias.   Not this morning,
I rather think hee's with the Army.   170
Emperor [*aside*].   Army?
I doe not like that Army:——goe unto him,

147 laugh] Langbaine; laught F 1–2
*157–158 As...And] *Tragedy of Valentinian* (1717); 1. As...2. And F 1–2
*168 go] F 2; goes F 1

And bid him straight attend me, and doe ye heare,
Come private without any; I have businesse
Only for him.
Phidias.   Your Graces pleasure.
Emperor.   Goe;   *Exit* Phidias.
What Souldier is the same (I have seene him often)
That keepes you company *Aretus*?
Aretus.   Me Sir?
Emperor.   I you Sir.
Aretus.   One they call *Pontius*,
And't please your Grace.
Emperor.   A Captaine?
Aretus.   Yes, he was so;
But speaking somthing roughly in his want,
Especially of warres, the noble Generall   180
Out of a strict allegiance cast his fortunes.
Emperor.   Ha's been a valiant fellow?
Aretus.   So hee's still.
Emperor.   Alas, the Generall might have pardond follies,
Souldiers will talke sometimes.
Aretus [*aside*].   I am glad of this.
Emperor.   He wants preferment as I take it.
Aretus.   Yes Sir;
And for that noble Grace his life shall serve.
Emperor.   I have a service for him;
I shame a Souldier should become a Begger:
I like the man *Aretus*.
Aretus.   Gods protect ye.
Emperor.   Bid him repaire to *Proculus*, and there   190
He shall receive the businesse, and reward for't:
Ile see him setled too, and as a Souldier,
We shall want such.
Aretus.   The sweets of Heaven still crowne yee.
Emperor [*aside*].   I have a fearefull darknesse in my soule,
And till I be deliverd, still am dying.

                              Exeunt.

174 *Exit* Phidias.] Dyce; *following* pleasure F 1–2
193 *Aretus.*] F 2; *om.* F 1   194 *Emperor.*] F 2; *om.* F 1

341

Enter Maximus *alone.*

Maximus.   My way has taken: all the Court's in guard,
And business every where, and every corner
Full of strange whispers: I am least in rumour,

Enter Aecius *and* Phidias.

And so Ile keep my selfe. Here comes *Aecius,*
I see the bait is swallow'd: If he be lost
He is my Martyr, and my way stands open,
And honour, on thy head his bloud is reckond.
Aecius.   Why how now friend, what make ye here unarmd:
Are ye turnd Merchant?
Maximus.   By your faire perswasions,
And such a Marchant trafficks without danger;   10
I have forgotten all *Aecius,*
And which is more, forgiven.
Aecius.   Now I love ye,
Truly I doe, ye are a worthy *Roman.*
Maximus.   The faire repentance of my Prince to me
Is more then sacrifice of bloud and vengeance,
No eyes shall weep her ruins, but mine owne.
Aecius.   Still ye take more love from me: vertuous friend,
The gods make poore *Aecius* worthy of thee.
Maximus.   Only in me y'are poore Sir, and I worthy
Only in being yours: But why your arme thus,   20
Have ye bin hurt *Aecius?*
Aecius.   Bruisd a little:
My horse fell with me friend, which till this morning
I never knew him doe.
Maximus.   Pray gods it boade well;
And now I think on't better, ye shall back,
Let my perswasions rule ye.
Aecius.   Back, why *Maximus?*
The Emperor commands me come.
Maximus.   I like not

0.1 IV.ii] Scæn. 2. F1

At this time his command.
Aecius.   I doe at all times,
And all times will obey it, why not now then?
Maximus.   Ile tell ye why, and as I have bin governd,
Be you so noble Friend: The Courts in Guard,   30
Armd strongly, for what purpose, let me feare;
I doe not like your going.
Aecius.   Were it fire,
And that fire certain to consume this body,
If *Cesar* sent, I would goe; never feare man,
If he take me, he takes his armes away.
I am too plaine and true to be suspected.
Maximus [*aside*].   Then I have dealt unwisely.
Aecius.   If the Emperor,
Because he meerely may, will have my life,
That's all he has to worke on, and all shall have:
Let him, 'a loves me better: here I wither,   40
And happily may live, till ignorantly
I run into a fault worth death, nay more, dishonour.
Now all my sinnes, I dare say those of duty,
Are printed here, and if I fall so happy,
I blesse the grave, I lye in, and the gods,
Equall as dying on the Enemy,
Must take me up a Sacrifice.
Maximus.   Goe on then,
And Ile go with ye.
Aecius.   No, ye may not friend.
Maximus.   He cannot be a friend, bars me *Aecius*,
Shall I forsake ye in my doubts?
Aecius.   Ye must.
Maximus.   I must not, nor I will not; have I liv'd   50
Only to be a Carpet friend for pleasure?
I can endure a death as well as *Cato*.
Aecius.   There is no death nor danger in my going,
Nor none must goe along.
Maximus.   I have a sword too,
And once I could have usd it for my friend.

Aecius.   I need no sword, nor friend in this, pray leave me;
And as ye love me, do not overlove me;
I am commanded none shall come: At supper
Ile meet ye, and weele drink a cup or two,   60
Ye need good Wine, ye have bin sad: Farwell.
Maximus.   Farwell my noble Friend, let me embrace ye
Ere ye depart; it may be one of us
Shall never doe the like agen.
Aecius.   Yes often.
Maximus. Farwell good deer *Aecius.*
Aecius.   Farwell *Maximus*
Till night: indeed you doubt too much.
Maximus.   I doe not:
                              Exit [Aecius, *with* Phidias].
Goe worthy innocent, and make the number
Of *Cesars* sinnes so great, heaven may want mercy:
Ile hover hereabout to know what passes:
And if he be so divelish to destroy thee,   70
In thy bloud shall begin his Tragedy.
                                                    Exit.

                    Enter Proculus, *and* Pontius.   [IV.] iii

Proculus.   Besides this, if you do it, you enjoy
The noble name Patrician: more than that too,
The Friend of *Cesar* ye are stild: ther's nothing
Within the hopes of *Rome*, or present being
But you may safely say is yours.
Pontius.   Pray stay Sir;
What has *Aecius* done to be destroyd?
At least I would have a colour.
Proculus.   Ye have more,
Nay all that may be given: he is a Traitor,
One, any man would strike that were a subject.
Pontius.   Is he so fowle?

66.1 *Exit.*] Dyce; *following* much F 1–2
0.1 IV.iii] Scæn. 3. F 1

344

Proculus.   Yes, a most fearefull Traytor.   10
Pontius [*aside*].   A fearefull plague upon thee, for thou lyest;——
I ever thought the Souldier would undoe him
With his too much affection.
Proculus.   Ye have hit it,
They have brought him to ambition.
Pontius.   Then he is gone.
Proculus.   The Emperor out of a foolish pittie,
Would save him yet.
Pontius.   Is he so mad?
Proculus.   He's madder!
Would goe to'th Army to him.
Pontius.   Would 'a so?
Proculus.   Yes *Pontius*; but we consider——
Pontius.   Wisely.
Proculus.   How else man?——that the state lies in it.
Pontius.   And your lives too.
Proculus.   And every mans.
Pontius.   He did me   20
All the disgrace he could.
Proculus.   And scurvily.
Pontius.   Out of a mischiefe meerly: did you mark it?
Proculus.   Yes well enough. Now ye have meanes to quit it,
The deed done, take his place.
Pontius.   Pray let me thinke on't,
Tis ten to one I doe it.
Proculus.   Doe and be happy.   *Exit* Proculus.
Pontius.   This Emperor is made of naught but mischiefe,
Sure, Murther was his Mother: none to lop,
But the maine linck he had? upon my conscience
The man is truly honest, and that kills him;
For to live here, and study to be true,   30
Is all one to be Traitors: why should he die?
Have they not Slaves and Rascalls for their Offrings

---

*17 Would...him.] *stet* F1
22–23 *Pontius.* Out...it? | *Proculus.* Yes...it,] F2 (Yes well enough. | Now...
it,); *Pon.* Out...it? | Yes well enough. | *Pro.* Now...it, F1

In full abundance; Bawds more then beasts for slaughter?
Have they not singing whores enough, and knaves too,
And millions of such Martyrs to sink *Charon*,
But the best sons of *Rome* must saile too? I will shew him
(Since he must dye) a way to doe it truly:
And though he beares me hard, yet shall he know,
I am born to make him blesse me for a blow.

Exit.

Enter Phidias, Aretus, and Aecius. [IV.] iv

Phidias. Yet ye may scape to'th Camp, wee'l hazard with ye.
Aretus. Loose not your life so basely Sir: ye are armd,
And many when they see your sword out, and know why,
Must follow your adventure.
Aecius. Get ye from me:
Is not the doom of *Cesar* on this body?
Doe not I beare my last houre here, now sent me?
Am I not old *Aecius*, ever dying?
You think this tendernesse and love you bring me:
Tis treason, and the strength of disobedience,
And if ye tempt me further, ye shall feele it: 10
I seek the Camp for safety, when my death
(Ten times more glorious then my life, and lasting)
Bids me be happie? Let the foole feare dying,
Or he that weds a woman for his humour,
Dreaming no other life to come but kisses;
Aecius is not now to learne to suffer:
If ye dare shew a just affection, kill me,
I stay but those that must: why do ye weep?
Am I so wretched to deserve mens pities?
Goe give your teares to those that lose their worths,   20
Bewaile their miseries: for me wear Garlands,
Drink wine, and much; sing Peans to my praise;
I am to triumph friends, and more then *Cesar*,
For *Cesar* feares to die, I love to die.

0.1 IV.iv] Scæn. 2. F1   14 humour] Dyce (Mason); honour F1–2

Phidias.   O my deare Lord!

Aecius.   No more, goe, goe I say;
   Shew me not signes of sorrow, I deserve none:
   Dare any man lament, I should die nobly?
   Am I grown old to have such enemies?
   When I am dead, speake honourably of me,
   That is, preserve my memory from dying;   30
   Then if you needs must weep your ruind Master,
   A teare or two will seem well: this I charge ye,
   (Because ye say you yet love old *Aecius*)
   See my poore body burnt, and some to sing
   About my Pile, and what I have done and sufferd,
   If *Cæsar* kill not that too: at your banquets
   When I am gone, if any chance to number
   The times that have been sad and dangerous,
   Say how I fell, and tis sufficient:
   No more I say, he that laments my end
   By all the gods dishonours me; be gone
   And sodainly, and wisely from my dangers,
   My death is catching else.

Phidias.   We feare not dying.

Aecius.   Yet feare a wilfull death, the just Gods hate it,
   I need no company to that that children
   Dare doe alone, and Slaves are proud to purchase;
   Live till your honesties, as mine has done,
   Make this corrupted age sicke of your vertues,
   Then dye a sacrifice, and then ye know
   The noble use of dying well, and *Roman*.   50

Aretus.   And must we leave ye Sir?

Aecius.   We must all die,
   All leave our selves; it matters not, where, when,
   Nor how, so we die well: and can that man that does so
   Need lamentation for him? Children weep
   Because they have offended, or for feare,
   Women for want of will, and anger; is there
   In noble man, that truly feeles both poyses

31 Then] Dyce (*conj.*); There F 1–2

Of life and death, so much of this wet weaknesse,
To drown a glorious death in child and woman?
I am a shamd to see ye; yet ye move me,   60
And were it not my manhood would accuse me
For covetous to live, I should weep with ye.
Phidias.   O we shall never see you more.
Aecius.   Tis true;
Nor I the miseries that *Rome* shall suffer,
Which is a benefit life cannot reckon:
But what I have been, which is just, and faithfull;
One that grew old for *Rome*, when *Rome* forgot him,
And for he was an honest man durst die,
Ye shall have daily with ye: could that dye too,
And I returne no trafficke of my travells,   70
No pay to have bin Souldier, but this silver,
No *Annalls* of *Aecius*, but he liv'd,
My friends ye had cause to weep, and bitterly;
The common overflowes of tender women,
And children new borne crying, were too little
To shew me then most wretched: if teares must be,
I should in justice weep 'em, and for you,
You are to live, and yet behold those slaughters
The drie, and witherd bones of death would bleed at:
But sooner then I have time to thinke what must bee,   80
I feare you'l find what shall be; if ye love me,
(Let that word serve for all) be gone and leave me;
I have some little practise with my soule,
And then the sharpest sword is welcom'st; goe,
Pray be gon, ye have obeyd me living,
Be not for shame now stubborn; so I thank ye,
And faryewell, a better fortune guide yee.
                         Exeunt Phidias *and* Aretus.
I am a little thirstie, not for feare,
And yet it is a kind of feare, I say so;
Is it to be a just man now againe,   90
And leave my flesh unthought of? tis departed:

70 travells] *i.e.* travails

348

I heare 'em come, who strikes first? I stay for ye:

Enter Balbus, Chilax, Lycinius.

Yet I will dye a Souldier, my sword drawne,
But against none: why doe ye feare? come forward.
Balbus.   You were a Souldier *Chilax.*
Chilax.   Yes, I musterd
But never saw the Enemy.
Lycinius.   Hee's drawne,
By heaven I dare not doe it.
Aecius.   Why doe ye tremble?
I am to die, come ye not now from *Cesar,*
To that end? speake.
Balbus.   We due, and we must kill ye,
Tis *Cesars* will.
Chilax.   I charge you put your sword up,   100
That we may doe it hansomly.
Aecius.   Ha, ha, ha,
My sword up! hansomly! where were ye bred?
Ye are the merriest murderers my masters
I ever met withall; Come forward fooles,
Why doe ye stare? upon mine honour Bawds,
I will not strike ye.
Lycinius.   Ile not be first.
Balbus.   Nor I.
Chilax.   You had best die quietly: the Emperour
Sees how you beare your selfe.
Aecius.   I would die Rascalls,
If you would kill me, quietly.
Balbus.   Pox of *Proculus,*
He promisd us to bring a Captaine hither,   110
That has been used to kill.
Aecius.   Ile call the Guard,
Unlesse you will kill me quickly, and proclaim
What beastly, base, and cowardly companions,
The Emperor has trusted with his safetie:

109 Pox] Colman; —— F1-2

Nay Ile give out, ye fell of my side, villaines.
Strike home ye bawdy slaves.
Chilax.   By heaven he will kill us,
I markd his hand, he waits but time to reach us:
Now doe you offer.
Aecius.   If ye doe mangle me,
And kill me not at two blowes, or at three,
Or not so stagger me, my sences faile me,   120
Look to your selves.
Chilax.   I told ye.
Aecius.   Strike me manly,
And take a thousand strokes.

                    Enter Pontius.

Balbus.   Heer's *Pontius.*
Pontius.   Not kild him yet?
Is this the love ye beare the Emperor?
Nay then I see yee are Traitors all, have at yee.
                    [*Wounds* Chilax *and* Balbus.] Lycinius *runs away.*
Chilax.   Oh I am hurt.
Balbus.   And I am killd.
                    Exeunt Chilax *and* Balbus.
Pontius.   Dye Bawdes;
As ye have liv'd and flourish'd.
Aecius.   Wretched fellow,
What hast thou done?
Pontius.   Killd them that durst not kill,
And you are next.
Aecius.   Art thou not *Pontius?*
Pontius.   I am the same you cast *Aecius,*   130
And in the face of all the Camp disgracd.
Aecius.   Then so much nobler, as thou wert a Souldier,
Shall my death be: is it revenge provoked thee,
Or art thou hir'd to kill me?
Pontius.   Both.
Aecius.   Then doe it.

                    116 slaves] F2; slave F1

Pontius.   Is that all?
Aecius.   Yes.
Pontius.   Would you not live?
Aecius.   Why should I,
   To thanke thee for my life?
Pontius.   Yes, if I spare it.
Aecius.   Be not deceiv'd, I was not made to thank
   For any curtesie, but killing me,
   A fellow of thy fortune; doe thy duty.
Pontius.   Doe not you feare me?
Aecius.   No.
Pontius.   Nor love me for it?   140
Aecius.   That's as thou dost thy businesse.
Pontius.   When you are dead,
   Your place is mine *Aecius.*
Aecius.   Now I feare thee,
   And not alone thee *Pontius*, but the Empire.
Pontius.   Why, I can governe Sir.
Aecius.   I would thou couldst,
   And first thy selfe: Thou canst fight well, and bravely,
   Thou canst endure all dangers, heates, colds, hungers;
   Heavens angry flashes are not sodainer
   Then I have seene thee execute, nor more mortall;
   The winged feete of flying enemies
   I have stood and viewd thee mow away like rushes,   150
   And still kill the killer: were thy minde,
   But halfe so sweet in peace, as rough in dangers,
   I died to leave a happy heire behind me;
   Come strike, and be a Generall.
Pontius.   Prepare then:
   And for I see your honour cannot lessen,
   And 'twere a shame for me to strike a dead man,
   Fight your short span out.
Aecius.   No thou knowst I must not,
   I dare not give thee so much vantage of me
   As disobedience.

*151 still...killer] stet F1

351

Pontius.   Dare ye not defend ye
Against your enemy?
Aecius.   Not sent from *Cesar*,   160
I have no power to make such enemies;
For as I am condemn'd, my naked sword
Stands but a hatchment by me, only held
To shew I was a Souldier; had not *Cesar*
Chaind all defence in this doom, *let him die*,
Old as I am, and quenchd with scarres, and sorrowes,
Yet would I make this witherd Arme do wonders,
And open in an enemy such wounds
Mercy would weep to look on.
Pontius.   Then have at ye,
And look upon me, and be sure ye feare not: 170
Remember who you are, and why you live,
And what I have been to you: cry not hold,
Nor think it base injustice I should kill ye.
Aecius.   I am prepard for all.
Pontius.   For now *Aecius*,
Thou shalt behold and find I was no traitor,
And as I doe it, blesse me; die as I doe.

                              Pontius *kills himselfe.*

Aecius.   Thou hast deceiv'd me *Pontius*, and I thank thee;
By all my hopes in heaven, thou art a *Roman*.
Pontius.   To shew you what you ought to doe, this is not;
For slanders selfe would shame to find you coward,   180
Or willing to out-live your honestie:
But noble Sir, ye have been jealous of me,
And held me in the rancks of dangerous persons,
And I must dying say it was but justice,
Ye cast me from my credit; yet believe me,
(For there is nothing now but truth to save me,
And your forgivenesse) though ye held me hainous,
And of a troubled spirit, that like fire
Turnes all to flames it meets with, ye mistook me;
If I were foe to any thing, t'was ease,   190
Want of the Souldiers due, the Enemy;

The nakednesse we found at home, and scorne,
Children of peace, and pleasures; no regard
Nor comfort for our scarres, but how we got 'em;
To rusty time, that eate our bodies up,
And even began to prey upon our honours;
To wants at home, and more then wants, abuses;
To them, that when the Enemy invaded,
Made us their Saints, but now the sores of *Rome*;
To silken flattery, and pride plumd over,   200
Forgetting with what wind their feathers saile,
And under whose protection their soft pleasures
Grow full and numberlesse: to this I am foe,
Not to the state, or any point of duty:
And let me speake but what a Souldier may,
(Truly I ought to be so); yet I errd,
Because a far more noble sufferer
Shewd me the way to patience, and I lost it:
This is the end I die Sir; to live basely,
And not the follower of him that bred me,   210
In full account and vertue *Pontius* dare not,
Much lesse to out-live what is good, and flatter.
Aecius.   I want a name to give thy vertue Souldier,
For only *good* is farre below thee *Pontius*,
The gods shall find thee one; thou hast fashiond death,
In such an excellent, and beauteous manner,
I wonder men can live: Canst thou speake once more?
For thy words are such harmony, a soule
Would choose to flye to heaven in.
Pontius.   A farewell:
Good noble Generall your hand, forgive me,   220
And think what ever was displeasing you,
Was none of mine: ye cannot live.
Aecius.   I will not:
Yet one word more.
Pontius.   Dye nobly:——*Rome* farewell:
And *Valentinian* fall, thou hast broke thy basis;

195 eate] *past tense*   200 plumd] Seward; plaind F 1–2   224 basis] F 2; bases F 1

In joy ye have given me a quiet death,
I would strike more wounds, if I had more breath.   *He dyes.*
Aecius.   Is there an houre of goodnesse beyond this?
   Or any man would out-live such a dying?
   Would *Cesar* double all my honours on me,
   And stick me ore with favours, like a Mistris;   230
   Yet would I grow to this man: I have loved,
   But never doated on a face till now:
   O death thou art more than beautie, and thy pleasure
   Beyond posterity: Come friends and kill me;
   Cesar be kind, and send a thousand swords,
   The more, the greater is my fall: why stay ye?
   Come, and Ile kisse your weapons: feare me not,
   By all the gods Ile honour ye for killing:
   Appeare, or through the Court, and world, Ile search ye:
   My sword is gone;   [*Throws it from him.*]
                    ye are Traitors if ye spare me,   240
   And *Cesar* must consume ye: all base cowards?
   Ile follow ye, and ere I dye proclaime ye,
   The weeds of *Italy*; the drosse of nature.
   Where are ye, villaines, traytors, slaves?   *Exit.*

           Enter Proculus, *and* 3. *others running over the Stage.*

Proculus.   I knew h'ad killd the Captain.
1.   Here's his sword.
Proculus.   Let it alone, 'twill fight it selfe else; friends,
   An hundred men are not enough to doe it:
   Ile to the Emperor, and get more ayd.
Aecius [*within*].   None strike a poore condemnd man?
Proculus.   He is mad:
   Shift for your selves my masters.   *Exeunt.*

                    Enter Aecius.

Aecius.   Then *Aecius*,   250
   See what thou darst thy selfe;   [*Takes up sword.*]
                    hold my good sword,

                    354

Thou hast been kept from bloud too long: Ile kisse thee,
For thou art more then friend now, my preserver:
Shew me the way to happinesse, I seeke it:
And all you great ones, that have falne as I do,
To keep your memories, and honours living,
Be present in your vertues, and assist me,
That like strong *Cato*, I may put away
All promises, but what shall crown my ashes;
Rome, fartheewell: stand long, and know to conquer   260
Whilst there is people, and ambition:
Now for a stroak shall turne me to a Star:
I come ye blessed spirits, make me room
To live for ever in *Eli*ʒ*ium*:   [*Wounds himselfe.*]
Doe men feare this? O that posterity
Could learne from him but this, that loves his wound,
There is no paine at all in dying well,
Nor none are lost, but those that make their hell.   *Kills himselfe.*
1 (within).   Hee's dead,
Draw in the Guard againe.

               Enter Proculus *and two others.*

Proculus.   Hee's dead indeed,   270
And I am glad hee's gone; he was a devill:
His body, if his Eunuches come, is theirs;
The Emperor out of his love to vertue,
Has given 'em that: Let no man stop their entrance.   *Exeunt.*

               Enter Phidias *and* Aretus.

Phidias.   O my most Noble Lord,——look here *Aretus*,
Heer's a sad sight.
Aretus.   O cruelty! O *Cesar*!
O times that bring forth nothing but destruction,
And overflowes of bloud: why wa'st thou kild?
Is it to be a just man now againe,
As when *Tiberius* and wild *Nero* raignd,   280
Only assurance of his over-throw?

          *270 Enter...others.] Dyce; following line 268 F 1–2

                         355

Phidias. It is *Aretus*: he that would live now,
Must like the Toad, feed only on corruptions,
And grow with those to greatnesse: honest vertue,
And the true *Roman* honour, faith and valour
That have been all the riches of the Empire,
Now like the fearefull tokens of the Plague,
Are meer fore-runners of their ends that owe 'em.
Aretus.   Never enough lamented Lord, deer master:

Enter Maximus [*unseen*].

Of whom now shal we learn to live like men?   290
From whom draw out our actions just, and worthy?
O thou art gone, and gone with thee all goodnesse,
The great example of all equitie,
(O thou alone a *Roman*, thou art perishd)
Faith, fortitude, and constant noblenesse,
Weep *Rome*, weep *Italy*, weep all that knew him,
And you that feard him as a noble Foe,
(If Enemies have honourable teares)
Weep this decayd *Aecius* falne, and scatterd   Maximus *advances.*
By foule, and base suggestion.
Phidias.   O Lord *Maximus*,   300
This was your worthy friend.
Maximus [*aside*].   The gods forgive me:——
Think not the worse my friends, I shed not teares,
Great griefes lament within; yet now I have found 'em:
Would I had never knowne the world, nor women,
Nor what that cursed name of honour was,
So this were once againe *Aecius*:
But I am destin'd to a mighty action,
And begge my pardon friend; my vengance taken,
I will not be long from thee:——ye have a great losse,
But beare it patiently, yet to say truth
In justice tis not sufferable: I am next,   310
And were it now, I would be glad on't: friends,

*293–294 The...equitie, | (O... perishd)] *stet* F1 (‸O...perishd,)
*299 Maximus *advances.*] *om.* F1–2

Who shall preserve you now?

Aretus.   Nay we are lost too.

Maximus.   I feare ye are, for likely such as love
 The man that's falne, and have been nourishd by him,
 Doe not stay long behind: Tis held no wisdom,
 I know what I must doe:———ô my *Aecius,*
 Canst thou thus perish, pluckt up by the rootes,
 And no man feele thy worthinesse?———From boyes
 He bred you both I think.

Phidias.   And from the poorest.   320

Maximus.   And lov'd ye as his owne.

Aretus.   We found it Sir.

Maximus.   Is not this a losse then?

Phidias.   O, a losse of losses;
 Our lives, and ruines of our families,
 The utter being nothing of our names,
 Were nothing neere it.

Maximus.   As I take it too,
 He put ye to the Emperor.

Aretus.   He did so.

Maximus.   And kept ye still in credit.

Phidias.   Tis most true Sir.

Maximus.   He fed your Fathers too, and made them meanes,
 Your Sisters he preferd to Noble Wedlocks,
 Did he not friends?

Aretus.   Oh yes Sir.

Maximus.   As I take it   330
 This worthy man would not be now forgotten:
 I tell ye to my griefe, he was basely murdred;
 And something would be done, by those that lov'd him:
 And something may be: pray stand off a little.
 Let me bewaile him private:———ô my dearest.

Phidias.   *Aretus,* if we be not sodaine, he out does us,
 I know he points at vengance; we are cold,
 And base ungratefull wretches, if we shun it:
 Are we to hope for more rewards, or greatnesse,
 Or any thing but death, now he is dead?   340

Dar'st thou resolve?
Aretus.   I am perfect.
Phidias.   Then like flowers
  That grew together all, wee'l fall together,
  And with us that that bore us: when tis done
  The world shall stile us two deserving servants:
  I feare he will be before us.
Aretus.   This night *Phidias*——
Phidias. No more.
Maximus.   Now worthy friends I have done my mournings,
  Let's burn this Noble body: Sweetes as many
  As sun-burnt *Meroe* breeds Ile make a flame of,
  Shall reach his soule in heaven: he that shall live   350
  Ten ages hence, but to reherse this story,
  Shall with the sad discourse on't, darken Heaven,
  And force the painefull burdens from the wombs
  Conceivd a new with sorrow: even the Grave
  Where mighty *Sylla* sleeps shall rend asunder
  And give her shadow up, to come and groane
  About our piles, which will be more, and greater
  Then greene *Olimpus*, *Ida*, or old *Latmus*
  Can feed with Cedar, or the East with Gums,
  Greece with her wines, or *Thessalie* with flowers,   360
  Or willing heaven can weep for in her showres.

                              Exeunt [*with body*].

          Enter Phidias *with his dagger in him, and* Aretus *poysond.*   V. i

Aretus.   He h'as his last.
Phidias.   Then come the worst of danger;
  Aecius to thy soule we give a *Cesar*:
  How long is't since ye gave it him?
Aretus.   An houre,
  Mine owne two houres before him: how it boyles mee!
Phidias.   It was not to be cur'd I hope.

    349 sun-burnt, *Meroe*] F 2; sun-burnt: *Neroe* F 1
    0.1 V.i] *Actus Quintus. Scæna prima.* F 1

Aretus.   No *Phidias*,
I delt above his Antidotes: Physicians
May finde the cause, but where the cure?
Phidias.   Done bravely,
We are got before his Tyrrany *Aretus.*
Aretus.   We had lost our worthiest end els *Phidias.*
Phidias.   Canst thou hold out a while?
Aretus.   To torture him   10
Anger would give me leave, to live an age yet;
That man is poorely spirited, whose life
Runs in his bloud alone, and not in's wishes.
And yet I swell, and burne like flaming *A'etna*,
A thousand new found fires are kindled in me,
But yet I must not die this foure houres *Phidias.*
Phidias.   Remember who dies with thee, and despise death.
Aretus.   I need no exhortation, the joy in me
Of what I have done, and why, makes poyson pleasure,
And my most killing torments mistresses.   20
For how can he have time to dye or pleasure,
That falls as fooles unsatisfied, and simple?
Phidias.   This that consumes my life, yet keeps it in me,
Nor doe I feele the danger of a dying,
And if I but endure to heare the curses
Of this fell Tyrant dead, I have halfe my heaven.
Aretus.   Hold thy soule fast but foure houres *Phidias*,
And thou shalt see to wishes beyond ours,
Nay more beyond our meanings.
Phidias.   Thou hast steeld me:
Farwell *Aretus*, and the soules of good men,   30
That as ours doe, have left their *Roman* bodies
In brave revenge for vertue, guide our shadowes.
I would not faint yet.
Aretus.   Farwell *Phidius*
And as we have done nobly, gods look on us.
                                        Exeunt severally.

Enter Lycias, *and* Proculus.

Lycias.   Sicker, and sicker *Proculus?*
Proculus.   Oh *Lycias,*
What shall become of us? would we had dide
With happy *Chilax*, or with *Balbus*, bedrid
And made too lame for justice.

Enter Lycinius.

Lycinius.   The soft Musick;
And let one sing to fasten sleep upon him:——
Oh friends, the Emperor.
Proculus.   What say the Doctors?
Lycinius.   For us a most sad saying, he is poysond,
Beyond all cure too.
Lycias.   Who?
Lycinius.   The wretch *Aretus,*
That most unhappy villaine.
Lycias.   How doe you know it?
Lycinius.   He gave him drink last: let's disperse and find him;   10
And since he has opend misery to all,
Let it begin with him first: Softly he slumbers.   [*Exeunt.*]

Enter Emperor *sicke in a Chaire, with* Eudoxa, *the Empresse,*
and Physitians, *and Attendants.*

Musick and Song.

Care charming sleep, thou easer of all woes,
Brother to death, sweetly thy selfe dispose
On this afflicted Prince; fall like a Cloud
In gentle showres, give nothing that is lowd,
Or painfull to his slumbers; easie, light,
And as a purling stream, thou son of night,
Passe by his troubled senses; sing his paine

0.1 V.ii] Scæn. 2. F1
*12.1 Eudoxa] *Eudoxia* F1–2   *12.3–22 Musick...*Bride.] stet F1
14 *selfe*] MS3 (self); *life* F1   17 *his*] MS3; *her* F1
17 *light*] MS11; *sweet* F1–2, MSS   19 *sing*] MS3; *sings* F1

Like hollow murmuring winds, or silver Rayne.   20
Into this Prince gently, Oh gently slide,
And kisse him into slumbers like a Bride.

Emperor.   Oh gods, gods: drink, drink, colder, colder
Then snow on *Scythian* Mountaines: ô my heart strings.
Eudoxa.   How do's your Grace?
Phisitian.   The Empresse speakes Sir.
Emperor.   Dying,
Dying *Eudoxa,* dying.
Physitian.   Good Sir patience.
Eudoxa.   What have ye given him?
Physitian.   Pretious things deere Lady
We hope shall comfort him.
Emperor.   O flatterd foole,
See what thy god-heads come to:——Oh *Eudoxa.*
Eudoxa.   Oh patience, patience Sir.
Emperor.   *Danubius,*   30
Ile have brought through my body——
Eudoxa.   Gods give comfort.
Emperor.   And *Volga,* on whose face the North wind freezes;
I am an hundred hells, an hundred Piles
Already to my Funeralls are flaming.
Shall I not drink?
Physitian.   You must not Sir.
Emperor.   By heaven
Ile let my breath out that shall burne ye all
If yo deny me longer: tempests blow me,
And inundations that have drunk up kingdomes
Flow over me, and quench me: wher's the Villaine?
Am I immortall now ye slaves? by *Numa*   40
If he doe scape: Oh, oh——
Eudoxa.   Deere Sir.
Emperor.   Like *Nero,*
But farre more terrible, and full of slaughter,
I'th midst of all my flames ile fire the Empire:

20 *winds*] MS3; *winde* F1–2   21 *Prince*] F2; *om.* F1
*32 *wind*] F2; *om* F1   33 *am*] Seward; *and* F1; *find* F2

A thousand fans, a thousand fans to coole me:
Invite the gentle windes *Eudoxa*.

Eudoxa.   Sir.

Emperor. Oh doe not flatter me, I am but flesh,
A man, a mortall man: drink, drink, ye dunces;
What can your doses now doe, and your scrapings,
Your oyles, and Mithridates? if I doe die,
You only words of health, and names of sicknesse   50
Finding no true disease in man but mony,
That talke your selves into Revenues,—oh——
And ere ye kill your patients, begger 'em,
Ile have ye flead, and dride.

Enter Proculus, Licinius *with* Aretus.

Proculus.   The Villaine Sir;
The most accursed wretch.

Emperor.   Be gon my Queene,
This is no sight for thee: goe to the Vestalls,
Cast holy incense in the fire, and offer
One powerfull sacrifice to free thy *Cæsar*.

Proculus. Goe Goe and be happy.

Aretus.   Goe, but give no ease,——   *Exit* Eudoxa.
The Gods have set thy last houre *Valentinian*,   60
Thou art but man, a bad man too, a beast,
And like a sensuall bloudy thing thou diest.

Proculus.   Oh damned Traitor.

Aretus.   Curse your selves ye flatterers,
And howle your miseries to come ye wretches;
You taught him to be poysond.

Emperor.   Yet no comfort?

Aretus.   Be not abusd with Priests, nor Pothecaries,
They cannot help thee: Thou hast now to live
A short halfe houre, no more, and I ten minutes:
I gave thee poyson for *Aecius* sake,
Such a destroying poyson would kill nature;   70

54 ‸*Enter*...Aretus.] Seward; ——*Enter*...*Aretus. following* Sir., *line* 30 F1–2
63 damned] Weber; —— F1; *om.* F2

And for thou shalt not die alone, I took it.
If mankind had bin in thee at this murder,
No more to people earth again, the wings
Of old time clipt for ever, reason lost,
In what I had attempted, yet ô *Cæsar*
To purchase faire revenge, I had poysond them too.
Emperor.   Oh villaine:——I grow hotter, hotter.
Aretus.   Yes;
But not neere my heate yet; what thou feel'st now,
(Marke me with horror *Cæsar*) arc but Embers
Of lust and leachery thou hast committed: 80
But there be flames of murder.
Emperor.   Fetch out tortures.
Aretus.   Doe, and ile flatter thee, nay more ile love thee:
Thy tortures to what now I suffer *Cæsar*,
At which thou must arrive too, ere thou dy'est,
Are lighter, and more full of mirth then laughter.
Emperor.   Let 'em alone: I must drink.
Aretus.   Now be mad,
But not neere me yet.
Emperor.   Hold me, hold me, hold me;
Hold me, or I shall burst else.
Aretus.   See me *Cesar*,
And see to what thou must come for thy murder;
Millions of womens labours, all diseases——   90
Emperor.   Oh my afflicted soule too.
Aretus.   Womens feares, horrors,
Despaires, and all the Plagues the hot Sunne breeds——
Emperor.   *Aecius*, ô *Aecius*: ô *Lucyna*.
Aretus.   Are but my torments shadowes.
Emperor.   Hide me mountaines;
The gods have found my sinnes: now breake.
Aretus.   Not yet Sir;
Thou hast a pull beyond all these.
Emperor.   Oh hell,
Oh villaine, cursed villaine.

85 more…laughter] *i.e.* more full of mirth than laughter is

Aretus.   O brave villaine,
My poyson dances in me at this deed:
Now *Cesar*, now behold me, this is torment,
And this is thine before thou diest, I am wildfire: 100
The brazen Bull of *Phalaris* was feignd,
The miseries of soules despising Heaven,
But Emblems of my torments——
Emperor.   Oh quench me, quench me, quench me.
Aretus.   Fire a flattery;
And all the Poets tales of sad *Avernus*,
To my paines lesse then fictions: Yet to shew thee
What constant love I bore my murdred master,
Like a Southwind, I have sung through all these tempests.——
My heart, my witherd heart,——feare, feare thou Monster,
Feare the just gods, I have my peace.   *He dies.*
Emperor.   More drinke,   110
A thousand Aprill showres fall in my bosom:
How dare ye let me be tormented thus?
Away with that prodigious body, [*Exeunt Attendants with body.*]
                                   gods,
Gods, let me aske ye what I am, ye lay
All your inflictions on me: heare me, heare me;
I doe confesse I am a ravisher,
A murderer, a hated *Cesar*; oh,
Are there not vowes enough, and flaming Altars,
The fat of all the world for sacrifice,
And where that failes, the blood of thousand captives   120
To purge those sins, but I must make the incense?
I do despise ye all, ye have no mercy,
And wanting that, ye are no Gods, your paroale
Is only preach'd abroad to make Fooles fearfull,
And women made of awe, beleeve your heaven:——
Oh torments, torments, torments, paines above paines,——
If ye be any thing but dreames, and ghests,
And truly hold the guidance of things mortall;
Have in your selves times past, to come, and present;

127 ghests] *i.e.* ghosts

Fashion the soules of men, and make flesh for 'em,   130
Waighing our fates, and fortunes beyond reason;
Be more then all, ye Gods, great in forgivenesse:
Breake not the goodly frame ye build in anger;
For you are things men teach us, without passions:
Give me an howre to know ye in: Oh save me
But so much perfect time ye make a soule in:
Take this destruction from me; no ye cannot,
The more I would beleeve, the more I suffer,
My braines are ashes, now my heart, my eyes freinds;
I go, I goe, more aire, more aire; I am mortall.   *He dyes.* 140
Proculus.   Take in the body:

        [*Exeunt Attendants and* Physitians, *with body.*]

                 oh *Lycinius,*
The misery that we are left to suffer;
No pitty shall find us.
Licinius.   Our lives deserve none:
Would I were chain'd againe to slavery,
With any hope of life.
Proculus.   A quiet grave,
Or a consumption now *Lycinius,*
That we might be too poore to kill, were something.
Lycinius.   Let's make our best use, we have mony *Proculus,*
And if that cannot save us, we have swords.
Proculus.   Yes, but we dare not dye.
Lycinius.   I had forgot that: 150
There's other countries then.
Proculus.   But the same hate still,
Of what we are.
Lycinius.   Think any thing, Ile follow.

           Enter a Messenger.

Proculus.   How now what newes?
Messenger.   Shift for your selves, ye are lost else:
The Souldier is in armes for great *Aecius,*

132 all, ye] Seward; all‸ the F 1–2   133 build] *i.e.* built
138 beleeve, the] Dyce (Mason); beleeve ye, F 1–2

And their Lieutenant generall that stopt 'em,
Cut in a thousand peeces: they march hither:
Beside, the women of the Towne have murderd
Phorba, and loose *Ardelia, Cæsars* she-Bawdes.
Lycinius.   Then here's no staying *Proculus?*
Proculus.   O *Cæsar,*
That we had never known thy lusts: Lets fly,   160
And where we find no womans man lets dye.

                                                   Exeunt.

                        Enter Maximus.   [V.] iii

Maximus.   Gods, what a sluce of blood have I let open!
My happy ends are come to birth, he's dead,
And I reveng'd; the Empires all a fire,
And desolation everywhere inhabits:
And shall I live that am the author of it,
To know *Rome* from the awe o'th world, the pitty?
My freinds are gone before too of my sending,
And shall I stay? is ought else to be liv'd for?
Is there an other freind, an other wife,
Or any third holds halfe their worthynesse,   10
To linger here alive for? Is not vertue
In their two everlasting soules departed,
And in their bodies first flame fled to heaven?
Can any man discover this, and love me?
For though my justice were as white as truth,
My way was crooked to it, that condemnes me:
And now *Aecius*, and my honored Lady,
That were preparers to my rest and quiet,
The lines to lead me to *Eliȝium*;
You that but stept before me, on assurance   20
I would not leave your freindship unrewarded;
First smile upon the sacrifice I have sent ye,
Then see me comming boldly: stay, I am foolish,
Somewhat too suddaine to mine own destruction,

                    0.1 V.iii] Scæn. 3. F1
                           366

This great end of my vengance may grow greater:
Why may not I be *Cæsar*, yet no dying?
Why should not I catch at it? fooles and children
Have had that strength before me, and obtaind it,
And as the danger stands, my reason bids me:
I will, I dare; my deare freinds pardon me,   30
I am not fit to dye yet if not *Cæsar*;
I am sure the Souldier loves me, and the people,
And I will forward, and as goodly Cedars
Rent from *Oeta* by a sweeping tempest
Jointed againe and made tall masts, defie
Those angry winds that split 'em, so will I
New peec'd againe, above the fate of women,
And made more perfect far then growing privat,
Stand and defie bad fortunes: If I rise,
My wife was ravish'd well; If then I fall,
My great attempt honors my Funerall.   40

                                 Exit.

Enter 3 Senators [Fulvius, Lucius *and* Sempronius] *and*   [V.] iv
Affranius.

1. Senator.   Guard all the posternes to the Camp *Affranius*,
And see 'em fast, we shall be rifled else;
Thou art an honest, and a worthy Captaine.
2. Senator.   Promise the Souldier any thing.
3. Senator.   Speake gently,
And tell 'em we are now in councell for 'em,
Labouring to choose a *Cæsar* fit for them,
A Souldier, and a giver.
1. Senator.   Tell 'em further,
Their free and liberall voices shall go with us.
2. Senator.   Nay more, a negative say we allow 'em.
3. Senator.   And if our choice displease 'em, they shall name him. 10

26 *Cæsar*, yet] Dyce; *Cæsar*? Yet F1–2
*35 Jointed...masts] F2; Winted...masses F1
37 peec'd] Weber (Mason); peece F1–2
0.1 V.iv] Scæn. 4. F1   *9 say] *stet* F1

1. Senator.   Promise three donatives, and large, *Affranius.*

2. Senator.   And *Cæsar* once elected, present fees,
With distribution of all necessaries,
Corne, Wine, and Oyle.

3. Senator.   New garments, and new Armes,
And equall portions of the Provinces
To them, and to their families for ever.

1. Senator.   And see the City strengthned.

Affranius.   I shall do it.

                                        Exit Affranius.

2. Senator.   *Sempronius*, these are wofull times.

3. Senator.   O *Brutus*,
We want thy honesty againe; these *Cæsars*,
What noble Consuls got with blood, in blood   20
Consume againe, and scatter.

1. Senator.   Which way shall we?

2. Senator.   Not any way of safety I can thinke on.

3. Senator.   Now go our Wives to ruin, and our daughters,
And wee beholders *Fulvius.*

1. Senator.   Every thing
Is every mans that will.

2. Senator.   The vestalls now
Must only feed the Souldiers fire of lust,
And sensuall Gods be glutted with those Offerings,
Age like the hidden bowels of the earth
Open'd with swords for Treasure. Gods defend us,
We are chaffe before their fury else.

3. Senator.   Away,   30
Let's to the Temples.

1. Senator.   To the Capitoll,
Tis not a time to pray now, let's be strengthend.

Enter Affranius.

3. Senator.   How now *Affranius*: what good news?

Affranius.   A *Cesar.*

1. Senator. Oh who?

Affranius.   Lord *Maximus* is with the Souldier,
  And all the Camp rings, *Cesar, Cesar, Cesar*:
  He forcd the Empresse with him for more honour.
2. Senator.   A happy choice: let's meet him.
3. Senator.   Blessed fortune.
1. Senator.   Away, away, make room there, room there, room.
                              Exeunt Senators. *Flourish.*
Within. Lord *Maximus* is *Cesar, Cesar, Cesar*;
  Haile *Cesar Maximus.*
Affranius.   Oh turning people!   40
  Oh people excellent in war, and governd;
  In peace more raging then the furious North,
  When he ploughes up the Sea, and makes him brine,
  Or the lowd falls of *Nile*; I must give way,
  Although I neither love nor hop'd this *Cesar,*   *Flourish.*
  Or like a rotten bridge that dares a current
  When he is sweld and high, crack and farwell.

        Enter Maximus, Eudoxa, Senators, *and* Souldiers.

Senators.   Roome for the Emperor.
Soldiers.   Long life to *Cesar.*
Affranius.   Haile *Cesar Maximus.*
Emperor Maximus.   Your hand *Affranius.*——
  Lead to the Pallace, there my thanks in generall,   50
  Ile showre among ye all: gods give me life,
  First to defend the Empire, then you Fathers:
  And valiant friends, the heires of strength and vertue,
  The rampires of old *Rome,* of us the refuge;
  To you I open this day all I have,
  Even all the hazard that my youth hath purchasd:
  Ye are my children, family, and friends
  And ever so respected shall be: forward.——
  Ther's a Prescription grave *Sempronius,*
  Gainst all the flatterers, and lazie Bawdes   60

*45 hop'd this *Cesar,*   *Flourish.*] hope this.   *Cesar*ˌ *flourish.* F1; hope this: F2
47 high, crackˌ] Seward; highˌ crackt, F1–2
59 Prescription] *i.e.* proscription

Led loose-liv'd *Valentinian* to his vices,
See it effected.   *Flourish.*
Senators.   Honour wait on *Cesar.*
Soldiers.   Make room for *Cesar* there.   *Exeunt all but* Affranius.
Affranius.   Thou hast my feares,
But *Valentinian* keeps my vowes: oh gods,
Why doe we like to feed the greedy Raven
Of these blowne men, that must before they stand,
And fixt in eminence, cast life on life,
And trench their safeties in with wounds, and bodies?
Wel froward *Rome*, thou wilt grow weak with changing
And die without an Heire, that lov'st to breed   70
Sonnes for the killing hate of sons: for me,
I only live to find an enemy.

                                                              Exit.

        Enter Paulus (*a Poet*) *and* Lycippus, (*a Gentleman*).   [V.] v

Paulus.   When is the Inauguration?
Lycippus.   Why to morrow.
Paulus.   T'will be short time.
Lycippus.   Any devise that's hansom,
A *Cupid*, or the God o'th place will doe it,
Where he must take the Fasces.
Paulus.   Or a Grace.
Lycippus.   A good Grace ha's no fellow.
Paulus.   Let me see,
Wil not his name yeeld somthing (*Maximus*)
By'th way of Anagram? I have found out *Axis*,
You know he beares the Empire.
Lycippus.   Get him wheeles too,
T'will be a cruell carriage else.
Paulus.   Some songs too.
Lycippus.   By any meanes some songs: but very short ones,   10
And honest language *Paulus*, without bursting,
The ayre will fall the sweeter.

        65 Raven] *i.e.* ravin, voracity   0.1 V.v] Scæn. 5. F 1

                            370

Paulus.   A Grace must doe it.
Lycippus.   Why let a Grace then.
Paulus.   Yes it must be so;
  And in a robe of blew too, as I take it.
Lycippus [*aside*].   This poet is a little kin to'th Painter
  That could paint nothing but a ramping Lion,
  So all his learned fancies are blew Graces.
Paulus.   What think ye of a Sea-nymph, and a heaven?
Lycippus.   Why what shold she do there man? ther's no water.
Paulus.   By'th masse that's true, it must be a grace; and yet   20
  Me thinkes a Rain-bow——
Lycippus.   And in blew?
Paulus.   Oh yes;
  Hanging in arch above him, and i'th midle——
Lycippus.   A showre of raine?
Paulus.   No, no, it must bee a Grace.
Lycippus.   Why prethee Grace him then.
Paulus.   Or *Orpheus*,
  Comming from hell.
Lycippus.   In blew too?
Paulus.   Tis the better;
  And as he rises, full of fires——
Lycippus.   Now blesse us,
  Will not that spoile his Lute strings *Paulus*?
Paulus.   Singing,
  And crossing of his armes.
Lycippus.   How can he play then?
Paulus.   It shall be a Grace, ile doe it.
Lycippus.   Prethee doe,
  And with as good a grace as thou canst possible,   30
  Good fury *Paulus*; be i'th morning with me,
  And pray take measure of his mouth that speaks it.
                                        Exeunt.

Enter Maximus *and* Eudoxa, *with a Messenger.*   [V.] vi

Maximus.   Come my best lov'd *Eudoxa*:——Let the Souldier
  Want neither Wine nor any thing he calls for,
  And when the Senat's ready, give us notice;
  In the meane time leave us.   *Exit Messenger.*
  Oh my deere sweet.
Eudoxa.   Is't possible your Grace
  Should undertake such dangers for my beauty,
  If it were excellent?
Maximus.   By heaven tis all
  The world has left to bragge of.
Eudoxa.   Can a face
  Long since bequeath'd to wrinkles with my sorrowes,
  Long since razd out o'th book of youth and pleasure,   10
  Have power to make the strongest man o'th Empire,
  Nay the most staid, and knowing what is woman,
  The greatest aym of perfectnesse men liv'd by,
  The most true constant lover of his wedlock,
  (Such a stillblowing beauty, earth was proud of)
  Loose such a noble wife, and wilfully;
  Himselfe prepare the way, nay make the rape?
  Did ye not tell me so?
Maximus.   Tis true *Eudoxa.*
Eudoxa.   Lay desolate his deerest peece of friendship,
  Break his strong helme he steerd by, sinke that vertue,   20
  That valour, that even all the gods can give us,
  Without whom he was nothing, with whom worthiest;
  Nay more, arive at *Cesar*, and kill him too,
  And for my sake? either ye love too deerly,
  Or deeply ye dissemble Sir.
Maximus [*aside*].   I doe so;
  And till I am more strengthend, so I must doe;
  Yet would my joy, and wine had fashiond out
  Some safer lye:——Can these things be *Eudoxa*,

  0.1 V.vi] Scæn. 6. F1   0.1 *with a Messenger*] Weber; *om.* F1–2
  4 *Exit Messenger.*] Weber; *om.* F1–2   *7 If] *stet* F1–2

And I dissemble? Can there be but goodnesse
And onely thine deer Lady, any end,   30
Any imagination but a lost one,
Why I should run this hazard? O thou vertue!
Were it to doe againe, and *Valentinian*
Once more to hold thee, sinfull *Valentinian*,
In whom thou wert set, as pearles are in salt Oysters,
As Roses are in ranck weeds, I would find,
Yet to thy sacred selfe a deerer danger:
The God's know how I honour thee.
Eudoxa.   What love Sir,
Can I returne for this, but my obedience?
My life, if so you please, and tis too little.   40
Maximus.   Tis too much to redeem the world.
Eudoxa.   From this houre,
Ye sorrowes for my dead Lord, faryewell,
My living Lord has dride ye; And in token,
As Emperor this day I honor ye,
And the great caster new of all my wishes,
The wreath of living Lawrell, that must compasse
That sacred head, *Eudoxa* makes for *Cesar*:
I am me thinkes too much in love with fortune;
But with you, ever Royall Sir my maker,
The once more Summer of me, meere in love,   50
Is poore expression of my doting.
Maximus.   Sweetest.
Eudoxa.   Now of my troth ye have bought me deere, Sir.
Maximus.   No,
Had I at losse of mankinde——

                    Enter the Messenger.

Eudoxa.   Now ye flatter.
Messenger.   The Senat waites your Grace.
Maximus.   Let 'em come on,
And in a full forme bring the ceremony:
This day I am your servant (deere) and proudly,

        *42 Ye] Dyce (*conj.*);* The F1–2   53 *the]* a F1–2

                          373

Ile weare your honoured favour.

Eudoxa.   May it prove so.

Exeunt.

Enter Paulus, *and* Lycippus.   [V.] vii

Lycippus.   Is your Grace done?
Paulus.   Tis done.
Lycippus.   Who speakes?
Paulus.   A Boy.
Lycippus.   A dainty blew Boy *Paulus?*
Paulus.   Yes.
Lycippus.   Have ye viewed
The worke above?
Paulus.   Yes, and all up, and ready.
Lycippus.   The Empresse does you simple honour *Paulus,*
The wreath your blew Grace must present, she made.
But harke ye, for the Souldiers?
Paulus.   That's done too:
Ile bring 'em in I warrant ye.
Lycippus.   A Grace too?
Paulus.   The same Grace serves for both.
Lycippus.   About it then:
I must to'th Cupbord; and bee sure good *Paulus*
Your Grace be fasting, that he may hang cleanly: 10
If there should need an other voice, what then?
Paulus.   Ile hang an other Grace in.
Lycippus.   Grace be with ye.

Exeunt.

0.1 V.vii] Scæn. 7. F1

374

A Synnet with Trumpets. Enter in state Maximus, Eudoxa,   [V.] viii
with Souldiers and Gentlemen of Rome, the Senators, *and Rods
and Axes borne before them.* [*Attendants follow*] *with a Banket
prepard. Hoboies* [*play*].

Sempronius.   Haile to thy imperiall honour sacred *Cesar*,
And from the old *Rome* take these wishes;
You holy gods, that hitherto have held
As justice holds her Ballance, equall poysd,
This glory of our Nation, this full *Roman*,
And made him fit for what he is, confirme him:
Looke on this Son, ô *Jupiter* our helper,
And *Romulus*, thou Father of our honour,
Preserve him like thy selfe, just, valiant, noble,
A lover, and increaser of his people: 10
Let him begin with *Numa*, stand with *Cato*,
The first five yeares of *Nero* be his wishes,
Give him the age and fortune of *Emilius*,
And his whole raigne, renew a great *Augustus*.   *Musicke.*

[*A* Boy *descends and sings.*]

SONG.

> *Honour that is ever living,*
> *Honour that is ever giving,*
> *Honour that sees all and knowes,*
> *Both the ebbs of man and flowes,*
> *Honour that rewards the best,*
> *Sends thee thy rich labours rest;*   20

0.1 V.viii] SCENE VIII. F2; Scæn. 2. F1
*0.1–0.4 F1 *and* F2 (*substantially*) *arrange the stage-direction as follows*:

> *Enter in state Maximus, Eudoxa, with Souldiers
> and Gentlemen of Rome, the Senators, and Rods and
> Axes borne before them.*

> { *A Synnet with* }   { *With a Banket prepard, with* }
> { *Trumpets.* }   { *Hoboies, Musicke, Song, wreath.* }

1 *Sempronius.*] Weber; Sen. Semp. 3. F1; 3 Sen. F2
14 *Musicke.*] *in line* 0.4 F1–2

375

Thou hast studied still to please her,
Therefore now she calls thee Cesar.

Chorus.
Hayle, hayle, Cæsar, *hayle and stand,*
And thy name out live the Land.
Noble fathers to his browes,
Bind this wreath with thousand vows.

[*The* Boy *gives a*] *wreath.*
[Senators *place it on the head of Maximus.*]

All.   Stand to eternity.
Maximus.   I thank ye fathers,
And as I rule, may it stil grow or wither:
Now to the bancket, ye are all my guests;
This day be liberall friends, to wine we give it,   30
And smiling pleasures: Sit my Queen of beauty;
Fathers your places: These are faire Wars Souldiers,
And thus I give the first charge to ye all;   [*Drinks.*]
You are my second (sweet): to every cup,
I adde unto the Senat, a new honour,
And to the sonnes of *Mars* a donative.

[*The* Boy *sings again.*]

SONG.

God Lyeus *ever young,*
Ever honourd, ever sung;
Staind with bloud of lusty Grapes,
In a thousand lusty shapes;
Dance upon the Mazers brim,   40
In the Crimson liquor Swim;
From thy plenteous hand divine,
Let a River runne with Wine:
     God of mirth, let this day here,
     Enter neither care nor feare.

26.1 *wreath*] *in line* 0.4 F 1–2   37 Lyeus] F 2; Lizus F 1
*45 *mirth*] MS¹²(CA); *youth* F 1–2

Boy. *Bellona's* seed, the glory of old *Rome,*
Envie of conquerd Nations, nobly come
And to the fulnesse of your warlike noyce,
Let your feete move, make up this houre of joyes;   50
Come, come I say, range your faire Troop, at large,
And your hy measure turne into a charge.

[*Souldiers dance.* Maximus *falls back.*]

Sempronius.   The Emperor's growne heavie with his wine.
Affranius.   The Senat staies Sir for your thanks.
Sempronius.   Great *Cesar.*
Eudoxa [*aside*]. I have my wish.
Affranius.   Wilt please your Grace speake to him?
Eudoxa.   Yes, but he will not heare Lords.
Sempronius.   Stir him *Lucius*;
The Senat must have thankes.
Lucius.   Your Grace, Sir, *Cesar.*
Eudoxa.   Did I not tell you he was well? he's dead.
Sempronius.   Dead? treason, guard the Court, let no man passe:
Souldiers, your *Cesars* murdred.
Eudoxa.   Make no tumult,   60
Nor arme the Court, ye have his killer with ye;
And the just cause, if ye can stay the hearing:
I was his death; That wreath that made him *Cesar,*
Has made him earth.
Soldiers.   Cut her in thousand peeces.
Eudoxa.   Wise men would know the reason first: to die,
Is that I wish for *Romans,* and your swords,
The readiest way of death: yet Souldiers grant me
(That was your Empresse once, and honourd by ye)
But so much time to tell ye why I killd him,
And waigh my reasons well, if man be in you;   70
Then if ye dare doe cruelly, condemne me.
Affranius.   Heare her ye noble *Romans*; 'Tis a woman,
A subject not for swords, but pitty: Heaven,

57 *Lucius.*] Weber; 2. *Sen. Luc.* F 1–2   *67 readiest] Seward; heaviest F 1–2
68 honourd] F 2 (honour'd); honour F 1

If she be guilty of malitious murder,
H'as given us lawes to make example of her:
If only of revenge, and bloud hid from us,
Let us consider first, then execute.
Sempronius.   Speake bloudy woman.
Eudoxa.   Yes; This *Maximus*,
That was your *Cesar*, Lords, and noble Souldiers,
(And if I wrong the dead, heaven perish me;   80
Or speake to wyn your favours but the truth)
Was to his Country, to his friends, and *Cesar*
A most malitious Traytor.
Sempronius.   Take heed woman.
Eudoxa.   I speake not for compassion. Brave *Aecius*
(Whose blessed soule if I lye shall afflict me,)
The man that all the world lov'd, you adoard,
That was the master peece of Armes, and bounty,
(Mine own griefe shal come last) this friend of his,
This Souldier, this your right Arme noble *Romans*,
By a base letter to the Emperor,   90
Stufft full of feares, and poore suggestions,
And by himselfe, unto himselfe directed,
Was cut off basely, basely, cruelly;
(Oh losse, ô innocent, can ye now kill me?)
And the poore stale my Noble Lord, that knew not
More of this villaine, then his forcd feares;
Like one foreseene to satisfie, dy'd for it:
There was a murder too, *Rome* would have blusht at;
Was this worth being *Cesar*? or my patience?
Nay his wife,   100
By heaven he told it me in wine, and joy,
And swore it deeply, he himselfe prepard
To be abusd: how? let me grieve, not tell ye,
And weep the sins that did it: and his end
Was only me, and *Cesar*: But me he ly'd in:
These are my reasons *Romans*, and my soule
Tells me sufficient; and my deed is justice:

98 blusht] F2; blush F1   104 it] F2; yet F1   105 ly'd] F2 (lyed); lyd F1

Now as I have done well, or ill, look on me.
Affranius.   What lesse could nature doe, what lesse had we done,
    Had we knowne this before? *Romans*, she is righteous;   110
    And such a peece of justice, heaven must smile on:
    Bend all your swords on me, if this displease ye,
    For I must kneele, and on this vertuous hand
    Seale my new joy and thankes,——thou hast done truly.
Sempronius.   Up with your arms, ye strike a Saint els *Romans*,
    May'st thou live ever spoken our protector:
    Rome yet has many noble heires: Let's in
    And pray before we choose, then plant a *Cesar*
    Above the reach of envie, blood, and murder.
Affranius.   Take up the body, nobly to his urne,   120
    And may our sinnes, and his together burne.
                                        Exeunt. A dead March.

EPILOGUE

We would faine please yee, and as faine be pleasd;
Tis but a little liking, both are easd:
Wee have your money, and you have our ware,
And to our understanding good and faire:
For your own wisdomes sake, be not so mad,
To acknowledge ye have bought things deere and bad:
Let not a brack i'th stuffe, or here and there
The fading glosse, a general losse appeare:
We know yee take up worse Commodities,   10
And deerer pay, yet thinke your bargains wise;
Wee know in Meate and Wine, yee fling away
More time and wealth, which is but deerer pay,
And with the Reckoning all the pleasure lost.
We bid yee not unto repenting cost:
The price is easie, and so light the Play,
That ye may new digest it every day.
Then noble friends, as yee would choose a Misse,
Only to please the eye a while and kisse,
Till a good wife be got: So let this Play   20
Hold yee a while, untill a better may.

7 *i'th*] F 2 (*i'th'*); *'th* F 1
*12 *wealth*] *stet* F 1
17 *Misse*] F 2 (*Miss*); *Mistris* F 1

TEXTUAL NOTES

I.i

60 lame]   For 'lame' Virtue (instead of, perhaps, 'dame', as at I.ii.168), cf. I.ii.23.

63 Emperour]   The compositors spell this word both -*our* and -*or*, the latter termination being the more common. In the text of the play it is printed in italics here (7A 1), at I.iii.41 (7A 2ᵛ) and at I.iii.56 (7A 2ᵛ), but at I.i.74 (7A 1), I.i.91 (7A 1), I.i.109 (7A 1ᵛ), I.ii.66 (7A 1ᵛ), I.ii.79 (7A 1ᵛ), I.ii.87 (7A 1ᵛ), I.ii.90 (7A 1ᵛ), I.ii.144 (7A 2) and subsequently in roman. Because responsibility for 7A 1 is uncertain, the matter is not entirely clear, but I suspect the variation is compositorial, *A* having set 7A 2ᵛ and *B* 7A 1ᵛ (probably) and 7A 2. The italics may have been adopted initially because the title serves as Valentinian's dramatic name, but since F 1 also occasionally italicizes such ordinary titles as *Madam*, the word has been made roman throughout.

I.ii

12 too]   That this word here means 'to' is clear from other instances of the double-o spelling (II.iii.34 and IV.i.117, for example), but the 'too' preserved by the early editions probably was understood as 'also'. See the Historical Collation.

52–53 If...are]   Seward transposed 'Mothers' and 'Fathers' and later editors have followed him. It may be argued, however, that F 1's arrangement is preferable; If the mothers had souls (in addition, presumably, to senses) they would have been chaste; proper fathers would guard the chastity of their daughters. Men like Chilax and the other courtiers are as much bawds as Ardelia and Phorba, since the word denoted either a man or a woman until *ca* 1700 (*OED*). Cf. I.i.97ff.

55 comming...curses]   As the Historical Collation shows, this reading has seemed unsatisfactory, but F 1 is probably right, although somewhat ambiguous. Since *come* may be used in respect of what one receives (*OED*, *s.v.* Come, *v.* 8), Lucina may say, 'If anything were coming to you but the curses you deserve...'. Or since it may be used in respect of an attitude manifest in one (*s.v.* Coming, *ppl. a.* 2), she may say, 'If anything were eager to show itself in you but your curses...'. Of the two possibilities the second is preferable because 'comming' appears to be rhetorically parallel with 'constant' and thus to be followed by an understood 'in you'.

107 Lure]   Dyce quotes Mason: 'We should certainly read "lure", instead of "lore": the allusion is to falconry, and the word "train'd" proves it.'

381

Rather than 'train'd', the expression is 'traind out', which can have the general significance of 'draw, lead, conduct, bring' (*OED, s.v.* Train, *v.*[1] 3, 1549 quotation); but the hawking term 'imp' in line 108 serves to confirm the emendation.

I.iii

0.1 Aecius] Fletcher's character is based ultimately on the historical Roman general who checked the Huns near Châlons in A.D. 451. This general's name in Procopius' Greek is 'Αέτιος; translations of Procopius which Fletcher may have consulted and which I have seen render this as Aetius (*De rebus Gothorum, Persarum ac Vandalorum* (Basillae: Ex officina Ioannis Heruagii, 1531)), Aetio (*De la guerra...contra i Vandali* (In Vinegia: Per Michele Tramesino, 1547), a translation into 'vulgar Latin'), or Ætius (*Iustiniani Augusti historia* (Lugduni: Apud Franciscum le Preux, 1594)). In the last it appears that Aé has been interpreted as Aï. Cooper's *Thesaurus* (1565) nowhere employs the ligature; in the *Dictionarium Historicum & Poeticum* Aëtius is found, the ë distinguishing this name from others beginning in Ae. In *L'Astrée* it is Aetius and in Lovelace's commendatory poem in F1 (πb2ᵛ) Aëtius.

Two points are involved here, the first of no great consequence. In the Renaissance medial -c and -t in Latin names were often confused: John Velz points out to me that Shakespeare's Portia should be Porcia (after her father, Marcus Porcius Cato) and his Coriolanus' middle name is properly Martius, as the First Folio has him, rather than Marcius. Whether Fletcher, working from memory, misspelled his character's name or whether the scribe misread his -t as a -c there is no way of knowing, but because the -c spelling is uniform in F1 it must be accepted.

The rendition of the first two letters is of more significance because of the effect it has on the number of syllables in the word and the effect of this, in turn, upon meter. Æcius represents 'Ē-shus' or 'Ē-ci-us'; Aecius represents 'Ā-ē-shus' or 'Ā-ē-si-us'. F1's practice is various. The first forme composed was 7A2ᵛ: 3, of which Compositor *A* set 7A2ᵛ (I.iii.41–160) and 7A3 at least through line 23 (I.iii.177) but not beyond line 44 (I.iii.198). Compositor *B* then completed 7A3 (to II.i.12). Compositor *A* spells Æ- and Compositor *B* Ae-. On 7A2, the next page composed, *B* set '*Æcius*' at I.iii.0.1, then '*Aecius*' at line 8, then '*Æcius*' again at line 14; Compositor *A*, who took over at I.iii.25, consistently set '*Æcius*' through the rest of 7A2, 7A2ᵛ, and his part of 7A3 (to I.iii.177 at least). When *B* resumed work again (at least by I.iii.198), he began to spell *Ae-* once more. Subsequently, the spellings sometimes separate by compositors but more frequently are mixed, probably because variation was in part encouraged by occasional shortages of the Æ ligature. From this hodge-podge nothing can be deduced.

However, at four places in the play – I.iii.244, III.i.298, III.i.331 (as emended) and IV.ii.11 – the name, which usually requires three syllables, must be read with four to make meter. It is never dissyllabic. I take it from these facts that Fletcher probably spelt 'Aecius', and I suspect that the Æ- variant is the result of an incorrect rendition by the compositors.

25 why] F2 changes to 'who' and editors since Colman have followed. The F1 reading, however, seems acceptable: 'why we are' means 'the reason for our being' (implying 'to serve the Prince'); 'and how' signifies 'by sufferance of the Prince'.

50–51 Battailes,...sake?] Because F1 punctuates 'Battailes,...sake,' it is an open question whether 'For goodnesse sake' modifies 'Stampt' or 'out daring'. F2 elects the latter by putting a query after 'Battailes'. At I.iii.9–10, however, Maximus seems to associate the same phrase with 'truth' rather than with 'glory', which makes an attachment to 'vertues' (line 49) rather than to 'honors' slightly better here.

51 out daring] The Variorum emends to 'out-during', Bullen noting that, although Seward had let the word pass here, he had corrected 'out-dare the Sun' to 'out-dure' in The False One, II.i (F1: 2Q3ᵛb). Since, according to Hoy (ix, 148–50), Fletcher wrote Act II of The False One, the occurrence of the word there is all the more reason for keeping it here. It means 'defying, out-braving' (OED, s.v. Outdare).

162 o'] Here, at III.i.300 and at III.i.316, all the work of Compositor A, ô, which ordinarily means 'oh', appears for 'o''. Since the expressions are 'o' my soule' (twice) and 'o' my conscience', the compositor, misinterpreting apostrophes for circumflexes, may have thought the 'o''s ejaculations.

II.ii

16 drallery] Although he left it in the text, 'drallery' puzzled Seward (and Sympson), who thought the 'Context requires the Name of some Ship'. Colman also retained it, corrupt though it seemed, but suggested 'drollery', a French word 'signifying...pleasant things, and gay ladies'. Weber and later editors adopted 'drollery' and glossed it 'puppet show'. Drallery, however, is simply an alternative form of drollery, 'something humorous or funny' (OED, s.v. Drollery 2).

II.iii

85 yeares and beets] Editors' suspicion of this line has focussed on the word 'beets'. Weber printed 'beats', blows, the meaning recognized by the OED, which cites this line in illustration even though the spelling 'beets' was archaic by the seventeenth century. In his text Dyce followed Weber, but in his Addenda and Corrigenda he declared for 'heats', citing as an analogy The Mad Lover, II.i.189–90: 'Next by the glorious battells we have fought in, | By all the dangers, wounds, heats, colds, distresses...'. To this Martin

in the Variorum adds reference to II.iii.76 and IV.iv.146 of *Valentinian*. In two of these instances, however, 'heats' is joined with 'colds' to signify extremities of physical distress; in the third, line 76 above, Pontius probably means fevers. This sense would fit the present context, but there seems little point in repeating the idea.

The word more likely is all right as it stands and means the vegetable, which in 'A Country Life: To His Brother' Herrick lists with nettles, cole-worts and sour herbs as coarse fare. With 'beets', 'yeares', signifying aging, can pass, but if this line picks up the idea of trees and roots from line 69, another unpalatable food may be wanted.

II.iv

33 guide]   It is not certain that F1 is wrong here, for Chilax's service, his attendance upon Lucina, would furnish her protection, if only against the inconvenience of getting lost in the palace. Moreover, had there been a mistake it is more reasonable to think that F2 corrupted 'guard' to 'guide' under the influence of 'guide' in line 31 than that F1 did the reverse. Yet it would not be to Chilax's interest to say anything even remotely to arouse Lucina's suspicion, as the suggestion that she might require defense would do, and he later (lines 43 and 52) pretends to be no more than a ceremonial attendant to show the way. F1's reading, then, seems likely to have come from a misreading or trick of memory on the part of the compositor or the scribe.

II.v

4.2–24 SONGS...*dye*.]   Although MS¹ and *Cheerful Ayres* preserve at least one reading in the first stanza of the song which may be thought superior ('on eu'ry bush' instead of the more indefinite '*Every where*', line 8), there is no indication that these versions are anterior to F1 and at least one error ('you' for '*we*', line 14) which suggests that they are not.
24.1–44 SECOND...*fire*.]   The question whether F1 or MS² preserves the earlier version of the song is answered by their different renditions of line 40. As far as I know, there was no story current either in antiquity or in the Renaissance about Vesta herself dying for love in either sense of the word 'die'; but there were several tales about unchaste vestals who might, as her representatives, be called by the goddess' name. Certainly the action described by lines 39–42 is more appropriate to the priestess than to the goddess, although Vesta herself is associated with the flames of her altar ('Next holy Vesta with her flames of zeal | Presents herself...', Daniel, *The Vision of the Twelve Goddesses*, ed. Rees, in *A Book of Masques* (1967), pp. 304–5). But probably F1's image is not supposed to recall a specific incident in myth or story; it is merely another hyperbolical assertion of love's power, as the virgin priestess, guarded though she is,

384

is done to death by the flames of love sympathetically generated by the holy flame she kindles. F1 makes good sense; the MS, however, does not, for I can find no reference elsewhere to Vesta or any of her devotees being circled in silver ties or anything else that might give rise to the MS reading in line 40. It must then be a corruption of the reading as represented in F1, and the other variants in the MS appear to be products of a faulty memory, the version deriving probably from F2 (because of 'moment' for 'short hower' (line 43)).

The press-variant in line 44 is troublesome, for, while it may be possible to distinguish the corrected from the uncorrected state, it is not entirely certain which preserves the true reading. Since there is no indication that copy was elsewhere consulted during proofreading, there is little reason to think that 'can build' erroneously set by the compositor would have been altered to 'can once more build' as a result of the corrector's referring to the manuscript, and 'can build' certainly would not have been changed gratuitously. The change is more likely to have gone the other way in order to reduce the line to the tetrameters of the rest of the song. The corrected state, therefore, probably is 'can build'. The manuscript, however, could have read 'can once more build', the last line being elongated to accord with a final musical embellishment. On the other hand, the 'once more' may be merely a duplication of the same words later in the line. There is little to choose, but I have elected to print the shorter version as being safer because metrically consistent.

III.i

19 now]   F2's change to 'new', if indeed it is not merely a typographical error, is unnecessary: *now-departing* (= just-departing) makes sense and is an acceptable idiom (*OED*, *s.v.* Now, 17.b).

46 again‸‸ but vicious,]   In support of his emendation to 'again; all virtuous Women...', Seward offers the following: 'It is not very unnatural for a Transcriber or Printer to put some word into the Context that is accidentally raised in his Mind by a Glimpse of the true one: And Words as often raise an Idea of their direct Opposites, as of those Words that have an Affinity to them. Thus Black and White, Virtue and Vice, Wisdom and Folly, Truth and Falschood, &c. by their very Opposition have a near Connexion in our Ideas.' He evidently did not understand that 'but' may mean 'except as'. 'For' probably means 'against' (*OED*, *prep.*, 23.d).

84 sons]   F1's punctuation is a bit deceptive, but it is clear that 'truth', 'justice', 'Mercy', and 'pietie' are in apposition to 'sons', and, as Seward recognized, that F1's 'suns of light', in addition to being tautological, will not work with 'starlike pietie'. Colman and Weber defend the old reading, the former saying that 'suns of light' is a natural amplification (though 'starlike pietie' 'must be confessed an anticlimax') and the latter adding that 'this is not the only instance of Fletcher's being chargeable with such

exuberances'. 'Suns', however, is more likely to be a misreading. With 'starlike pietie' compare 'starry vertue' (line 190).

148–150 *Aecius. Let...deeper.*] Editors unnecessarily direct this speech 'to those without'. Although they are friends, Aecius holds the senior command (II.iii.49–50 and III.iii.11) and Maximus a subordinate, though high-ranking, post (cf. II.i.31–32). Here Aecius is merely directing Maximus to carry out certain orders.

154 were...thither] III.i is located at court, as evidenced by the presence of Chilax and the others as well as of Valentinian himself, a consideration which must have inspired F2's changes to 'are...hither'. But Fletcher seems to have conceived of the action as occurring in a more or less un-localized place, probably outdoors, different from the scenes within the palace (II.iv and v). In *L'Astrée* Valentinian ravishes Isidore (Lucina) in an arbor in the palace garden, whence the Emperor and Lucina may be emerging at III.i.28.

300, 316 0'] See the Textual Note on I.iii.162.

301 tales] Editors since Dyce, who found F1's reading nonsense, have adopted an emendation first proposed in Heath's *MS Notes* – 'tameness'. Maximus means, however, that he has been reduced to the helplessness of an old man, a teller of tales rather than a performer of actions. From this 'I am a child too' follows naturally.

III.iii

24 honour] Seward notes Theobald's and Sympson's preference for 'honour' but himself chose not to emend because '*Honour*, in this Place, must signify exactly the same with *Rumour.*' He no doubt had in mind *rumour* as 'Talk or report of a person...noted or distinguished' (*OED*, *sb.*, 1.b). Maximus' question in lines 25–26 and the linking of friendship and honour in line 35 seem to confirm the emendation, however.

30 of] 'Of' is an acceptable spelling of *off*, between which and *of* there is nothing to choose in this context. Because 'off' is spelt with two f's at lines 17, 115, and 165, however, 'of' seems to be intended. Line 17 was set by Compositor *B*, the rest by *A*.

88–89 valour;...faire,] Some editors accept Seward's change in line 89 of 'ye' to 'else', reading 'what else may be fair'; but F1's comma after 'be', in addition to the lack of graphical similarity between 'else' and 'ye', does little to encourage the emendation. The F1 reading is probably nearly all right as it stands; with the present emendation of punctuation lines 88–89 say: 'No man is more loved than you because of your valour; no man is more followed than you because of what you may become if you behave fairly (honourably).' This is similar to Heath's explanation of the F1 reading: 'and for your valour, and your great expectations, even those consistent with your honour and loyalty, no man more followed'.

138 die] F1's 'dig' looks like nothing more than a misreading or possibly

a foul-case error, and Colman's 'die' fits well, as Maximus is continuing to ask the same sort of questions, rhetorical and otherwise, that previously have figured in his speeches to Aecius (e.g. lines 78–80, 102–103, and 117). The idea of Maximus' death through some suicidally desperate action has been present from the beginning of the conversation, and here it is related naturally to its motivation, Lucina's dishonour and death (lines 139–142). Critics, however, have been dissatisfied with the emendation. Mitford suggests 'I'm willing to do anything; ay, die!'; Martin (Variorum) prints 'dig', noting that the true reading is irrecoverable; Dyce queries 'I am willing to do anything! Ay, dig', citing III.ii.58ff. as an analogy. Pontius' conventional comparison of honest toil with the courtiers' sleazy life hardly suggests, however, that Maximus would be thinking along the same lines.

147 joyne] Cf. V.iii.35, where F1 has 'Winted' for 'Iointed' (Weber's note).

IV.i

80 *Lycinius.*] F1's assignment of this speech to Lycias was the result of a compositorial mix-up. After the setting of 7B4ᵛ (which contains the earlier part of IV.i) by Compositor *A*, Compositor *B* set the pages of Quire C in the following order: 7C2ᵛ, 7C3, 7C2 (Lycinius enters at IV.iv.92.1; speech-prefix *Lyc.*), 7C3ᵛ (Lycias enters at V.ii.0.1; speech-prefixes *Lycias.* and *Lyc.*; Lycinius enters at V.ii.4; speech-prefixes *Lycin.* and *Lyci.*), 7C1ᵛ, 7C4 and 7C1, upon which IV.i.80 is the first line. Whatever abbreviation for Lycinius stood in the MS – probably *Lyci.*, judging by the prefixes on 7B4ᵛ – *B* misunderstood for Lycias' tag. The fact that Compositor *A* set IV.i.79, the last line of 7B4ᵛ, and Compositor *B* set IV.i.80 may also account for the omission of Proculus' entrance in F1.

129–130 certain...safety——] Although Seward indicated a suspension after 'safety', Colman and later editors returned, substantially, to the pointing of F1, except that they printed line 130 as one line rather than as two. This arrangement causes Valentinian to say, 'The letter may be cunning, but it seems not, because there is nothing in it except certainties, other than (besides) the question of my safety'. Yet the letter has alluded to the certainty of his danger because of Aecius' popularity. It appears that Seward was right, his interpretation being reinforced by F1's division of the line.

157–158 As...And] With reference to the numerals preceding these lines in F1, Seward noted, 'Here a marginal Direction how to place the Lines has been taken into the Text...' He seems to have been right, see p. 272.

168 go] Although lack of concord is common, this is a particularly egregious instance and, in view of the many other terminal errors in the text, probably a misprint.

IV.iii

17 Would...him.] I.e. because of foolish pity, the Emperour will endanger himself by visiting Aecius in the camp, there to dissuade him from the pursuit of ambitious plans. Pontius does not yet know that Aecius has been ordered to the court.

IV.iv

151 still...killer] Deighton remarks, 'Though no commentator has noticed [these] words, their want of meaning, their cacophony, and the imperfection of the metre, show, I think, that the line is corrupt. I would read "And still toil kill the killer": *i.e.* though you mowed them down like rushes, so great was their number that you were almost dead with the mere labour of slaying. The word *toil* is sufficiently like *kill* to have been accidentally omitted' (p. 64). He then cites two analogies, the nearer of which is 'We shall be kill'd with killing' from *Bonduca*, I.ii (F1: 4G1ᵛ).

Although the line is a syllable short, it does not for this reason demand emendation. If the passage is corrupt, it is more likely that a line has been omitted between 150 and 151 because of the incompleteness of 'viewd thee mow away like rushes'.

270 *Enter...others.*] The wrong placement in F1 of this direction and the metrical deficiency of lines 269 and 270 suggest that the F1 compositor incorrectly resolved a difficulty in the MS, where the direction was probably written in the margin. In addition to inserting the direction after rather than before the speech from within, the compositor may have omitted a part of the speech of Proculus' first companion which linked metrically with line 270.

293–294 The...equitie, | (O...perishd)] Weber notes, 'Mason, with some plausibility, proposes to transpose these lines. But by placing the latter between parentheses, the same purpose is answered, and the speech of the faithful eunuch rendered more expressive of his agitation, which embarrasses and disjoins his words.' In fact, Mason, at least in his *Comments* of 1798, does not make this proposal, but Weber's point is acceptable in any case.

299 Maximus *advances.*] That some such direction as this stood in the MS is suggested by the dash following 'scatterd' in F1.

V.ii

12.1 Eudoxa] Here (7C3ᵛ) the Empress' name is *Eudoxia* (the comma following suggesting that the scribe or the compositor thought Eudoxia and the Empress to be separate characters); at V.ii.26 and 29 (7C4a) and subsequently (eight times spelled out, all typeset by Compositor *B*) her name is *Eudoxa*. It is not easy to decide which was Fletcher's form. In

Procopius the name is $Εὐδοξία$, in d'Urfé Eudoxe, from which *Eudoxa* might have derived. I have chosen *Eudoxa* because the name always takes three syllables and because on another occasion Compositor *B* set an *-a* ending as *-ia* (*Bellonia* for *Bellona*, V.viii.47).

12.3–22 Musick...*Bride*.] F1, which incorrectly reads 'life' (line 14), 'her' and 'sweet' (line 17) and 'sings' (line 19) and is defective in line 21, was set from a debased or illegible version of the song. F2 rectifies all these mistakes but 'sweet'. The manuscripts, however, preserve a different tradition, one that may antedate the printing of F1.

Unique readings mark MS^4 (14 'of', 14 'disclose', 17 'but'), MS^{10} (18 'Come like', 22 'slumber'), MS^{11} (16 'pleasant', 17 'easily', 19 'troubled' omitted) and probably MS^6 (15 'man') and MS^7 (14 'depose') as terminal, leaving MS^3, MS^8, and MS^9 as possible intermediaries, MS^{8-9} being identical in substantives. These manuscripts differ from F1 as corrected by F2:

15 *Prince*] wight MSS
20 *winde*] winds MSS
21 *this Prince*] his sence MS^3; thy selfe MS^{8-9}
21 *gently, Oh gently*] gently MS^{8-9}

and all read 'sweet' (line 17). Of these variants, we may observe that the manuscripts generalize the song (by changing 'Prince' to 'wight') and that all appear to be struggling to restore sense to line 21, MS^3 somewhat more successfully than MS^{8-9}. The obvious inference is that all three manuscripts derive from F1.

That this is probably not the case, however, is suggested by the fact that MS^{8-9} (and MS^{11}) bear titles connecting the song with Prince Henry's death, which occurred in 1612. Public expressions of grief, most numerous in 1612–13, continued through the century (see Elkin Calhoun Wilson, *Prince Henry and English Literature* (Ithaca, New York, 1946), p. 174; but John Philip Edmond, 'Elegies and Other Tracts Issued on the Death of Henry, Prince of Wales, 1612', *Publications of the Edinburgh Bibliographical Society* VI (1906), 141–58, which covers 1612, 1613 and 1614, lists forty-one titles published during the first two of these years but only three published in the third). It is unlikely, however, that the song would have been re-fashioned to that occasion as late as 1647, and indeed MS^5 may prove otherwise. The original text of this manuscript is a late rendition of the MS tradition (it is related to MS^{10}), but it contains alterations in a second hand obviously made after comparison with F1. MS^5 seems to have been inscribed before the publication of F1 and altered after that text became available.

Because of the close connection of the lyric with the dramatic circumstances of the play, Fletcher probably did not take over and adapt a song already in existence. Instead it appears that behind both F1 and the manuscripts there lay a defective version, perhaps illegibly written, which read 'selfe' (14), 'Prince' (15), 'his' and 'sweet' (17), 'sing' (19), 'winde' or 'winds' (20), 'gently, Oh gently' (21) and which omitted a word after 'this' in line 21. From this source F1 and MS³ independently descended and from MS³ the other manuscript versions. The lyric was generalized by MS³ (or an antecedent of it), which could preserve the original music. A different musical setting is found in MS⁴⁻⁶, MS⁵⁻⁶ attributing it to Robert Johnson (see Edmund Fellowes, *Songs and Lyrics from the Plays of Beaumont and Fletcher with Contemporary Settings* (London, 1928), p. 54; John P. Cutts, 'Robert Johnson: King's Musician in His Majesty's Public Entertainment', *Music and Letters* XXXVI (1955), 118–19; Cutts, *La Musique de Scène de la Troupe de Shakespeare* (Paris, 1959), pp. 35–8, 140–2; Cutts believes Johnson to have been the original composer). The song in its generalized form was subsequently associated with Prince Henry's death.

The F2 editor may have had access to the version preserved in the prompt-book, but if he did he failed to correct two errors in F1. 'Sweet' (17) and 'light' (18) make a very imperfect rhyme (see the representation of these words in Kökeritz' transcription of Sonnet 30, *Shakespeare's Pronunciation* (New Haven, 1953), p. 346). 'Light', found in MS¹¹ and independently proposed by Weber, has no authority, but it is a sensible emendation. Because of F1's terminal misreading in 'sings' (19), its 'winde' (20) is suspect, and I have followed the MSS in 'winds'. In order to achieve consistency in accidentals, F1 rather than MS³ has served as copy-text.

32 wind]   Because the Emperour, despite his agony, speaks regular verse, there evidently is an omission in this line. F2's 'wind', a reasonable guess, has been accepted by all editors. Cf. 'Southwind', V.ii.108, but 'North', V.iv.42.

V.iii

35 Jointed...masts]   Cf. F1's 'wyne' for 'joyne' at III.iii.147 (Weber's note). Mason was the first to point out (pp. 159–60) that nearly the same simile occurs in *Bonduca*, I.ii: '...and as a *pine* | rent from *oeta* by a sweeping *Tempest* | Ioynted againe and made a mast. defyes | those angry windes that splitt him...' (*MSR* of *Bonduca* MS, lines 445–448, with which F1 substantially agrees).

V.iv

9 say]   The question is whether 'say' is a noun or a verb, whether the Second Senator says, 'Say [to them] we allow them a negative' or '[Tell them] we allow them a negative say'. Between these options there is little to choose. As a verb 'say' would parallel 'Tell 'em' (line 7) and 'Promise' (line 11). As a noun it may carry on the idea of the soldiers' free and liberal voices (line 8). Although 'to have a say' appears as early as 1614 (*OED*, *s.v.* Say, *sb.*⁴ 3), the noun in this context strikes me as unidiomatic, and I suspect the verb is intended.

12 fees]   F1's 'foes' has always passed muster, the meaning of the senators

presumably being 'Promise them three large donatives now, and, once Caesar is elected, that we will hand over to them their present enemies, along with such necessaries as corn, wine and oil.' The idea of ridding the soldiers of their enemies, however, does not sit easily with the senators' other bribes, all of which are of money or kind. 'Present fees' would be back wages (*OED*, *s.v.* Fee, *sb.*² 9 and 10), those immediately due.

30 *3. Senator.*] The fact that Compositor *A* set 7C4ᵛ, which includes the Second Senator's prefix at V.iv.25, and Compositor *B* set 7D 1, upon which this prefix falls, probably contributed to F 1's error.

45 hop'd this *Cesar*, *Flourish.*] The F 1 version of this line seems to result from two mistakes: the misreading of 'hop'd' as 'hope' and, probably in consequence, the interpretation of '*Cesar*' as a part of the stage-direction and the placing of a full stop after 'this'. The compositor lacked the courage of his convictions, however, for '*Cesar flourish.*' is set well in from the right margin. F 2 attempted to remedy matters by simply omitting these two words. Seward corrected 'hope' to 'hoped' (two syllables), thereby establishing the proper temporal relationship between the two verbs: in the past Affranius, because of his loyalty to Valentinian (lines 63 64), did not hope that Maximus would be Caesar; now that he is Caesar, Affranius does not like it. In this emendation Seward was followed by subsequent editors. Dyce transforms '*Cesar flourish*' into '*Flourish within, and cries of Caesar*', preceding the entrance at line 47.1.

V.vi

7 If] The Variorum marks a suspension after 'excellent', but the sentence is probably complete, 'If' meaning 'even though' (*OED*, 4.a).

42 Ye] Dyce compares F 1's 'the' for 'ye' at V.ii.132.

V.viii

0.1 ∩ 1 *A . . . Hoboies.*] F 1 masses what must at one time have been several separate, perhaps sketchy, directions, and it is difficult to extract some details of the action intended. '*A Synnet with Trumpets*' is easiest to deal with: the braces enclosing it suggest that it was marginal originally; it obviously belongs before the state entrance rather than after it. The other bracketed direction, perhaps also a prompter's note, refers mainly to the activities of unnamed attendants, although it contains other elements as well. First, a banquet with a table and chairs (cf. 'Sit my Queen of beauty', line 31) must be set out at least by line 29. I do not think it certain that the attendants would enter in the wake of the procession, but it is less awkward to have them do so than to bring them on later. '*With Hoboies*' could signify that musicians also enter with the instruments upon which they will play during the ceremony which follows; oboes, on the other hand, are the accompaniment for a royal entrance in *The Maid's Tragedy* (II.ii.98), and it seems likely that here as well they play offstage during the procession. The next three words – '*Musicke, Song, wreath*' – seem to describe the device, the music being the accompaniment of the Grace's song and '*Song*' being an intrusive repetition of the same word at line 14.2. The wreath is rather a puzzle. The Boy will descend (cf. V.vii.3, 10) and present it to the senators, who in turn place it on the head of Maximus, creating him Caesar (cf. V.vii.5, V.viii.25–30). The wreath could have been carried behind Maximus during the entrance and later handed to the Boy, yet, because it symbolizes Honour, its divine origin is better implied if the Boy brings it with him from the heavens.

45 *mirth*]   The texts of 'God Lyeus' form two clusters: F1, F2, and O on the one hand and CA and MS¹² on the other. F2 and O descend independently from F1; the relationship between MS¹² (which preserves music similar to CA's) and CA is an indifferent matter since their readings are identical. F1 and CA, however, could branch from a common ancestor (the evidence is inadequate for proof), and if so 'mirth' and 'youth' could be of equal authority. The appellation 'God of youth' is appropriate enough for a deity who is 'ever young' (line 37), but Lyeus is Bacchus, mirthful as well as youthful, and it seems preferable to invoke a god of mirth against care and fear (line 47). The version in CA may be a redaction by Wilson of a musical composition by Robert Johnson (see John P. Cutts, *La Musique de Scène de la Troupe de Shakespeare* (Paris, 1959), pp. 142–3).

67 readiest]   The Folios' 'heaviest' will not do, and there is not much to choose between the emendations adopted by various editors ('easiest', 'heavenliest'). Seward's 'readiest' could have given rise to the error about as well as any of the others, and it has the advantage of leading to Eudoxa's request for time (line 69).

Epilogue

12 *wealth*]   Editors after Colman rejected Seward's emendation and returned to 'wealth' under the influence of Mason's explanation: 'You pay dearer for worse commodities, meat and wine: for you fling away more time and more money to procure them, which is paying at a dearer rate. Besides, in these articles, all the pleasure is over when the reckoning comes to be paid; but the fare with which we treat you, you may digest every day, and enjoy from it a lasting pleasure.'

PRESS-VARIANTS IN F1 (1647)

[Copies collated: Bodl (Bodleian Library B.1.8.Art.), Camb¹ (University Library, Cambridge, Aston a.Sel.19), Camb² (SSS.10.8), Hoy (personal copy of Cyrus Hoy, University of Rochester), ICN (Newberry Library), IU¹ (University of Illinois, copy 1), IU² (copy 2), MB (Boston Public Library), MnU (University of Minnesota), NcD (Duke University), NIC (Cornell University), NjP (Princeton University), PSt (Pennsylvania State University), ViU¹ (University of Virginia 570973), ViU² (217972), WaU (University of Washington), WMU¹ (University of Wisconsin–Milwaukee, copy 1), WMU² (copy 2), WMU³ (copy 3), WMU⁴ (copy 4), WU (University of Wisconsin–Madison).]

SHEET 7A ii (*outer forme*)

Uncorrected: Bodl, Camb¹⁻², ICN, IU¹⁻², MB, MnU, NcD, NIC, NjP, PSt, WaU, WMU¹, WMU³, WMU⁴

Corrected: *The rest*

Sig. 7A2

I.iii.0.1 Scæn. 3. . . . Aecius.] *one half line lower*

Note: *The better-centered direction is presumed to be in the corrected state.*

SHEET 7B i (*outer forme*)

Uncorrected(?): Camb¹⁻², NjP, WaU

Corrected (?): *The rest*

Sig. 7B1

II.v.44 can build] can once more build

Note: *See Textual Note on* II.v.24.1–44.

SHEET 7B i (*inner forme*)

Uncorrected(?): IU¹⁻², NcD, NIC, PSt, ViU²

Corrected(?): *The rest*

Sig. 7B1ᵛ

cw Take] Take

Note: *Probably not a true press-variant.*

SHEET 7C i (*outer forme*)

Uncorrected: WMU¹, WU

1st stage corrected: The rest, except WMU²(?)

Sig. 7C1

IV.i.156 true;. . .me] true. . .me;

IV.i.182 Emp.] Empr.

393

2nd stage corrected: WMU²(?)

Sig. 7 C 1

    IV.i.97 Empresse;] Empresse,

Note: *The semi-colon in* IV.i.97, *if it is one, prints imperfectly, the dot being unusually small.*

EMENDATIONS OF ACCIDENTALS

[NOTE: (|) indicates that the reading occurs in a line that fills the measure.]

I.i

2 alter'd$_\Lambda$] F2; ~ , F1
4 winning)] F2; ~ , F1
6 *Chilax,*] F2; ~ . F1
12 carry$_\Lambda$)——] ~ .)$_\Lambda$ F1–2
15–17 Creature (and...none)] ~ ,
    ~ ... ~ : F1–2
28 (So...cunning)] $_\Lambda$ ~ ... ~,
    F1–2
36 presently,] ~ $_\Lambda$ F1–2
42 more;] ~ , F1–2
54 considerd:] ~ , F1–2

57 aspect$_\Lambda$ ...evill,] ~ , ... ~ $_\Lambda$
    F1–2
59 ages;] ~ , F1–2
67 Judgment:] ~ , F1–2
79 upon,] ~ ; F1–2
91 her?] ~ ; F1–2
101 *Alexander*$_\Lambda$] ~ , F1–2
102 say,] F2; ~ $_\Lambda$ F1
107 it;] ~ , F1–2
109–110 If...too?] *one line in* F1–2
110 too?] ~ , F1; ~ . F2

I.ii

1 Honour:] ~ , F1–2
2 youth:] ~ , F1–2
17 it:] ~ ; F1–2
18 doubted;] F2; ~, F1
21 man;] F2; ~ , F1
30 Lady:] ~ , F1–2
33 daintily] F2; daintlily F1
55 curses;] F2; ~ , F1
57 cherishd:] ~ , F1; ~ ; F2
71 And$_\Lambda$ besides,] F2; ~ , ~ $_\Lambda$ F1
75 it,] ~ $_\Lambda$ F1–2
92–93 it;...affection,] ~ , ... ~ ;
    F1; ~ , ... ~ , F2
94 vertues:] ~ , F1–2
96 Lord$_\Lambda$] F2; ~ , F1
101 too——] ~ . F1–2

110 touches$_\Lambda$] ~ , F1–2
115–116 (Fairer...ruines)] $_\Lambda$ ~ ...
    ~ , F1–2
119 (For...branches)] $_\Lambda$ ~ ...~ ,
    F1–2
135 frowne:] ~ $_\Lambda$ F1–2
137 dangers (Gods, I aske ye)]
    ~ . ~ (~ ~ ~) F1–2
142 vertues,] ~ $_\Lambda$ F1–2
156 me;] F2; ~ , F1
159 certain,] F2; ~ $_\Lambda$ F1
161 (Pray...too)]$_\Lambda$ ~ ...~ , F1–2
167 sure,] ~ $_\Lambda$ F1–2
168 Vertue] F2; vertue F1
173 all?] ~ , F1; ~ . F2

I.iii

1 Nations,] F2; ~ ₐ F1
13 favour——] ~ . F1–2
25–29 (While...stricter)] ₐ ~ ...
    ~ ; F1–2
27 obeyed₍₎] ~ , F1–2
35 not:] ~ , F1; ~ ; F2
41, 56 Emperor] *Emperor* F1–2±
42 be——] ~ ? F1–2
43 us——] ~ ? F1–2
44 modest,——] ~ , ₐ F1–2
46 beholders?] F2; ~ , F1
51 daring?] F2; ~ , F1
58 worthynesse] F2 (worthiness);
    worthynsse F1
67 (Ye...else)] ₐ ~ ... ~ , F1–2
69 *Maximus*;] ~ , F1–2
84 (as I am)] ₐ ~ ~ ~ ₐ F1–2
90 freind,] F2; ~ ₐ F1
95 blushing,] F2; ~ ₐ F1
104 fooles;——] ~ ; ₐ F1; ~ : ₐ
    F2
110 Judgers,] ~ ; F1–2
115 embraces,] F2; ~ ₐ F1

118 hammer.] F2; ~ ₐ F1
122 me——] ~ . F1–2
124 me?] ~ , F1–2
127 caution,] ~ ₐ F1–2
134 pleasures;] ~ , F1–2
158 people,...'em₍₎] ~ ₐ ... ~ ,
    F1–2
178 Princes;] ~ , F1–2
187 *Gallia*?] ~ , F1–2
192 wounds,] ~ ₐ F1–2
200 say,] ~ ₐ F1–2
206 these,] F2; ~ ₐ F1
206 Princes——] F2; ~ ₐ F1
210 sorrow₍₎] ~ , F1–2
218 it;] ~ , F1–2
220 (As...notice)] F2; ₐ ~ ... ~ ,
    F1
231 (Gainst...Armour)] ₐ ~ ...
    ~ , F1–2
241 *Cesar*....Aecius.] ~ —— ...
    ~ —— F1; ~ —— ... ~ ₐ
    F2
244 *Aecius*,] F2; ~ ₐ F1

II.i

4 perish;] ~ , F1; ~ . F2
6 us——] ~ , F1; ~ . F2
7 too?] ~ . F1–2
11 curried!] *In some copies of* F1 *the*
    exclamation point is broken and
    looks like an italic colon.
11 Sir,——] ~ , ₐ F1–2
21 not;] ~ , F1–2
24 fairely:——] ~ : ₐ F1; ~ , ₐ
    F2

30 presently,] ~ ; F1–2
31 (They...heare)] ₐ ~ ... ~ ,
    F1–2
35–36 Shortly...selfe.] *one line in*
    F1–2
36 ye.₍₎] ~ .—— F1; ~ ₐ —— F2
42 *Exit*₍₎] F2; ~ . F1
49 to:] ~ , F1–2
51 eager.₍₎] F2; ~ . —— F1

396

II.ii

5 Came...Court?] F1–2 *line*
  lately, | From
5 lately?] ~ , F1; ~ ∧ F2
5 same,] ~ ∧ F1–2
7 hatcht] F2; hactht F1
8 there (and...too)] ~ , ~ ...
  ~ , F1–2
11 ships——] ~ , F1; ~ . F2
13 *Claudia*∧] F2; *Clau.* F1 (|)
15 men;] ~ , F1–2
16 thirty:] ~ , F1–2
32 (for...morning)] , ~ ... ~ ,
  F1–2
34 skins—— —] ~ . F1–2

35 deceived,——] ~ , ∧ F1–2
36 living:] ~ ∧ F1; ~ , F2
38–39 Peace...be?] *one line in* F1–2
39 comes. What] ~ ; what F1–2
41–42 Pray...will.] *one line in*
  F1–2
44 Sir——] ~ . F1–2
55, 72 Madam] *Madam* F1–2
55 Broker——] ~ ; F1; ~ . F2
59–60 Ye...honest,] F1–2 *line*
  worthy, | And
69 him. Yet] ~ ; yet F1–2
73 you.∧] ~ . —— F1; ~ ∧ ——
  F2

II.iii

1–2 Lord,...Souldier.] F2; ~ .
  ... ~ , F1
2 Sir——] ~ ; F1; ~ . F2
3 Traytor;——] ~ , F1; ~ ∧ F1–2
5 dangerous;——] ~ ; ∧ F1–2
9 hearted,] F2; ~ ∧ F1
14 Generall——] ~ , F1; ~ . F2
27 woman?] F2; ~ . F1
37 (Hold...honesty)] ∧ ~ ... ~ ,
  F1–2
38 him.] ~ , F1–2
43 God:——] ~ : ∧ F1–2

46 y'had] y'e had F1; ye had F2
48 you——] ~ . F1–2
56 (If...upon)] ∧ ~ ... ~ , F1–2
72 Nurses:] ~ , F1; ~ . F2
84 dragma's,] F2; ~ ∧ F1
91 Sir,] ~ ; F1–2
94–95 (And...*Rome*)] ∧ ~ ... ~ ,
  F1; ∧ ~ ... ~ . F2
107 himselfe,] ~ ∧ F1–2
113 ye;] ~ , F1–2
116 *Pontius.*∧] ~ . —— F1–2

II iv

1 Emperor.∧] ~ . —— F1–2
2 Doe:] ~ ; F1–2
4 Chamber, at her∧ entrance∧]
  ~ ∧ ~ ~ , ~ , F1; ~ ,
  ~ ~ ∧ ~ , F2
5 (doe...*Lycinius?*)] ∧ ~ ... ~ ,∧
  F1–2
7 more——] ~ , F1; ~ . F2
8 Well?] ~ ; F1; ~ . F2
9 passes?∧] F2; ~ ? —— F1

9 man.] ~ —— F1–2
9 *Exit*] F2; *Exeunt* F1
10 best,] F2; ~ ; F1
18 They'd] F2; The'd F1
19 ye.∧] ~ . —— F1–2
20 Who] who F1–2
25 woman,] F2; ~ . F1
27, 38 Madam] *Madam* F1–2
30 A...strange:] F1–2 *line* here, |
  Nothing

397

32 Lady,] F2; ~ . F1
35 Sir?] F2; ~ . F1
36 selfe;] ~ , F1–2
37 'em?] F2; ~ , F1
42 kindly,] ~ ∧ F1–2

56 ye——] ~ ; F1; ~ . F2
57 forward?] ~ , F1–2
59 No,] ~ ? F1; ~ : F2
60 Sir,] F2; ~ ; F1
62.1 *Exeunt.*] *Exit.* F1; *Ex.* F2

II.v

7–8 *view,...Greene.*] ~ .... ~ ,
   F1–2
11 *snow,*] F2; ~ ∧ F1
12 *full:*] ~ . F1–2
18–19 *Mayd;...grow,*] ~ ,...~ ;
   F1–2
22 *waste:*] F2; ~ , F1
27 *wise:*] ~ , F1–2
28 *Nun;*] ~ , F1–2
32 *Swan;*] ~ , F1–2
37–38 *Boy:...woe,*] ~ , ... ~ :
   F1–2
46 counterfeit] F2; counrerfeit F1
48 Mistris:——] ~ : ∧ F1–2
49, 54, 97 Madam] *Madam* F1–2
65 well——] ~ : F1; ~ . F2
65–66 Sir,...Catechizd.] ~ ....
   ~ , F1; ~ .... ~ . F2

66–67 Sirah,...here?] ~ ; ... ~ ,
   F1; ~ ; ... ~ ? F2
77 end;] ~ , F1–2
84 flattery:∧] ~ : —— F1–2
90–91 dying ∧ ...arms;] ~ ; ...
   ~ ∧ F1–2
91 angry,] ~ —— F1–2
96 manners:] ~ , F1–2 (*possibly a
   period in* F1)
99 you.] ~ —— F1–2
99 ye,——] ~ , ∧ F1–2
108–109 Lady (and...extreamly)]
   ~ , ~ ...~ ; F1–2
111 pleasure;] ~ , F1–2
113 What,] F2; ~ ∧ F1
128 not.∧] ~ . —— F1–2
128.1 *Exeunt.*∧] F2; ~ . -- F1

II.vi

1 run.] ~ – F1–2
1 Boy.] ~ —— F1–2
2 her:] ~ , —— F1–2
13 *Cesar*——] ~ , F1; ~ . F2
27 (As...you)] ∧ ~ ...~ , F1–2
29 him:] ~ , F1; ~ . F2

31 ye;] ~ , F1–2
35 here,——] ~ , ∧ F1–2
36 temper;] ~ , F1–2
39 eyes:——] ~ : ∧ F1–2
40 hell.∧] ~ . —— F1–2

III.i

0.1 Chilax] F2; *Cbilax* F1
1 it:] ~ , F1–2
4 it;] ~ , F1–2
23 forsooth——] ~ , F1; ~ . F2
28 heare.∧] ~ . —— F1–2
31 talke——] ~ , F1; ~ . F2
35 Ravisher?] ~ , F1–2
42 (That's...now)] ∧ ~ ...~ ,
   F1–2

49 corrupted,] ~ ∧ F1–2
53 Lady:] ~ , F1–2
72 chast *Lucina's*] F2; chast
   Lucnia's F1
84–85 light (truth...pietie)] ~ ,
   ~ ...~ ∧ F1–2
86 themselves,] F2; ~ ∧ F1
94 last, for ever,∧] ~ ∧ ~ ~ , F1;
   ~ ∧ ~ ~ ∧ F2

100 noyse;] ∼ , F 1–2
101 again (therefore be wiser)] ∼ ;
    ∼ ∼ ∼ , F 1–2
102 it:] ∼ , F 1–2
104 (There...else)——] ∧ ∼ ...
    ∼ . ∧ F 1–2
109 dare∧] F 2; ∼ , F 1
110–114 (for...Altars)], ∼ ... ∼ ;
    F 1–2
121 knowledge] F 2; knowldge F 1
123–124 Is...whispers] F 1–2 line
    it: | Princes
128 feed 'em:] ∼ ∼ , F 1–2
134 it.] ∼ —— F 1–2
140 passe:] ∼ , F 1–2
144 me?] ∼ , F 1–2
147 sensuall,] ∼ , F 1–2
148 Titius] F 2; Tituis F 1
154 Sweet?] ∼ , F 1; ∼ . F 2
166 Pandar:] ∼ , F 1–2
176 sweetnesse:——] ∼ : ∧ F 1–2 ±
190 farethee-well;] ∼ , F 1–2
195 Phenix:] ∼ , F 1–2
196 weighd,] F 2; ∼ ∧ F 1
216 again?] F 2; ∼ , F 1
219 Death∧] ∼ , F 1–2
220 Besides, compeld∧] F 2; ∼ ∧ ∼ ,
    F 1
229 violence∧] ∼ , F 1–2

233 in,] F 2; ∼ ∧ F 1
250 agen:] F 2; ∼ , F 1
257 (as you think...vices)] , ∼ ∼
    ∼ ... ∼ , F 1; (∼ ∼ ∼)... ∼,
    F 2
265 Lady;] ∼ , F 1–2
271 thine; Time, Story,] ∼ , ∼ , ∼ ;
    F 1–2
281 justice.∧] ∼ . —— F 1–2 ±
284 on't:] ∼ , F 1–2
311 ruine:——] ∼ : ∧ F 1–2
316 dangerous;] ∼ , F 1–2
318 for't:] ∼ , F 1–2
319 sensibly,] ∼ ∧ F 1–2
324 ye:——] ∼ : ∧ F 1–2 ±
330–331 Why...Aecius.] one line in
    F 1–2
333 craz'd] F 2; craz'd F 1
339 freind,] ∼ . F 1; ∼ ; F 2
348 on't;] ∼ , F 1–2
351 by.] F 2; ∼ ? F 1
361 duty.] F 2; ∼ – F 1
362 F 1–2 line dead. | She
366 I, said she,] F 2; ∼ ∧ ∼ ∼ ∧ F 1
368 her——] ∼ . F 1–2
378 God's, Lucina,] F 2; ∼ ∧ ∼ ∧ F 1
381 me;] F 2; foot of type after me
    prints in F 1
384 end.∧] F 2; ∼ . —— F 1

III.ii

3 not,] F 2; ∼ ∧ F 1
9 Aretus] F 2; Aretius F 1
14 little,] ∼ ? F 1–2
15 (You...selfe)] ∧ ∼ ... ∼ , F 1–
    2
22 handed?] ∼ . F 1–2
29 too?] F 2; ∼ . F 1
43 wickednesse,] F 2; ∼ : F 1
49 so:] ∼ , F 1–2

56 life?] ∼ : F 1; ∼ ; F 2
62 juster;] ∼ , F 1–2
65 wine;] ∼ , F 1–2
66 (your...diseases)] , ∼ ... ∼ ,
    F 1–2
74 seeme:] ∼ , F 1–2
74 Lord] F 2; Lord F 1
80 temperate;] ∼ , F 1–2
91 ye.] ∼ —— F 1–2

III.iii

11 twixt] F2 ('twixt); twix F1
12 me:] ~ , F1–2
12 honest,] F2; ~ ∧ F1
15 say,] ~ ∧ F1–2
18 selfe:] F2; ~ ? F1
19 selfe?] F2; ~ , F1
22 wife? then *Cesar*,] ~ , ~ ~ ?
   F1–2
23 him?] ~ , F1–2
37 greifs:——] ~ : ∧ F1–2±
48 her?] ~ , F1–2
53 then?∧] F2; ~ ?—— F1
59 not:] ~ , F1–2
70 me;∧] F2; ~ ;—— F1
73 Imagination,] ~ ∧ F1–2
77 can;——] ~ ; ∧ F1–2
78 cut?] F2; ~ , F1
85–86 neither,...for't:] ~ ; ...
   ~ , F1–2

90 indeed,...one:] ~ : ... ~ ,
   F1–2
95 out;...for't,] ~ , ... ~ ;
   F1–2
111 woman,] F2; ~ ∧ F1
112 weake:] ~ , F1–2
129 me?] F2; ~ . F1
138 thing?...die?] ~ , ... ~ .
   F1–2
152 hold, in disobedience∧] ~ ∧
   ~ ~ , F1–2
161 (As...ye)] ∧ ~ ... ~ , F1–2
165 (I...ye)] ∧ ~ ... ~ , F1–2
168 howre.∧] F2; ~ .—— F1
168 do:——tis done;] ~ , ∧ ~ ~ :
   F1–2

IV.i

12–13 water∧ | (Am...*Cæsar?*)
   ——] ~ : | ∧ ~ ... ~ ?∧∧ F1–2
21 that is] F2; *possibly* that'is F1
23 knowes] F2 (knows); kdowes
   F1
26 mirrors?] ~ , F1–2
44 anger,] ~ ∧ F1–2
45 variety,] ~ ; F1–2
46 ones,] ~ ∧ F1–2
48 hereafter,] ~ ∧ F1–2
49 ye;] ~ , F1–2
55 Stallions] F2; *Stallions* F1
59 sancties:——] ~ : ∧ F1–2
59 Thine's] F2; Thin's F1
62 hospitall.——] ~ . ∧ F1–2
70 (They...shew)] ∧ ~ ... ~ ,
   F1–2
78 full] F2; fnll F1
80 *Proculus*——] ~ : F1; ~ . F2
83 letter∧ here,] ~ , ~ ∧ F1–2
90 memory.] ~ , F1–2

92 disputing∧ then,] ~ , ~ ∧ F1;
   ~ ∧ ~ ∧ F2
92 whining∧] ~ ? F1–2
93 gods∧ to give?] ~ ? ~ ~ ∧ F1;
   ~ ∧ ~ ~ , F2
94 one,] F2; ~ ∧ F1
95 me,——] ~ , ∧ F1–2
97 Empresse;] F1 (c?); ~ , F1
   (u?); ~ : F2
97 ∧*Exeunt*.] F2; —— ~ . F1
106 Ile...this?] F1–2 *line* prayers: |
   How?
109 people:...dangerous,] ~ , ...
   ~ : F1–2
110–111 doubts,...declining;] ~ ;
   ... ~ , F1–2
115–116 people, . . . him∧ . . . another,] ~ ∧...~ , ...~ ∧ F1–2
124 masterd,] F2; ~ ; F1
135–139 *Corbulo* (even...*Rome*)]
   ~ , ~ ... ~ , F1–2

149 not,] ~ ; F 1–2
151–152 abuses,...people,] ~ ‸...
  ~ ‸ F 1–2
152.1 ‸Enter] F 2; —— ~ F 1
154–155 times...doubts:] roman in
  F 1–2
156 true;...me‸] F 1(c)–2; ~ ‸...
  ~ ; F 1(u)
158 face,] ~ ; F 1–2

167 about:] ~ , F 1–2
168 ‸Enter] F 2; —— ~ F 1
169 Aecius] F 2; Æciuss F 1
171 Army:——] ~ : ‸ F 1–2
174 ‸Exit] —— ~ F 1–2
175 (I...often)] , ~ ...~ , F 1–2
182 fellow?] ~ . F 1–2
187 him;] ~ : F 1–2
195.1 ‸Exeunt] F 2; —— ~ F 1

IV.ii

3.1 ‸Enter] F 2; —— ~ F 1
4 selfe.] F 2; ~ , F 1
4 Aecius,] F 2; ~ ‸ F 1
6 Martyr] Martyr F 1–2
7 honour,...head‸] ~ ‸...~ ,
  F 1–2
17 friend,] ~ ‸ F 1–2
19 Sir,] ~ : F 1–2
20 Only...thus] F 1–2 line yours: |
  But

22 friend,] ~ : F 1–2
32 fire,] ~ ; F 1–2
42 death,] ~ : F 1–2
43 duty,] ~ ‸ F 1–2
45–46 gods, | Equall‸] ~ ‸ | ~ ,
  F 1–2
66.1 ‸Exit] F 2; -- ~ F 1
71.1 ‸Exit] F 2; —— ~ F 1

IV.iii

2 Patrician] Patrician F 1–2
8 given:] ~ , F 1–2
11 lyest;——] ~ ; ‸ F 1–2

19 man?——] ~ , ‸ F 1–2
25 ‸Exit] F 2; —— ~ F 1
39.1 ‸Exit] —— ~ F 1–2

IV.iv

3 why,] F 2; ~ ‸ F 1(|)
5 body?] ~ , F 1–2
8 me:] ~ , F 1–2
12 (Ten...lasting)] ‸ ~ ...~ ‸
  F 1–2
13 happie?] F 2; ~ : F 1
21 miseries:] ~ , F 1–2
22 praise;] ~ , F 1–2
27 nobly?] F 2; ~ ; F 1
51 die,] F 2; ~ ‸ F 1
52 selves;] ~ , F 1–2
61 me‸] ~ , F 1–2
80 sooner‸] ~ , F 1–2
81 I...me] F 1–2 line be; | If

82 (Let...all)] ‸ ~ ...~ , F 1–2
87 yee.] ~ —— F 1–2
87 Aretus] F 2; Aretius F 1
91 of?] F 2; ~ , F 1
92 I...ye] F 1–2 line first? | I
92.1 ‸Enter] —— ~ F 1–2
94 But...forward] F 1–2 line none:
  | Why
99 end? speake.] ~ , ~ ? F 1–2
102 up! hansomly!] ~ , ~ ‸ F 1;
  ~ , ~ ? F 2
109 me,] ~ ‸ F 1–2
117 us:] ~ , F 1–2
122 ‸Enter] F 2; —— ~ F 1

125 yee.] ~ —— F 1–2
126 killd.] ~ —— F 1–2
147 sodainer‸] ~ , F 1–2
148 execute,] ~ ; F 1–2
158 me‸] ~ , F 1–2
159 ye‸] F 2; ~ , F 1
163 me,] ~ ; F 1–2
176.1 ‸Pontius] —— ~ F 1–2
186–187 (For…forgivenesse)] ‸ ~
    …~ , F 1–2
191 Enemy;] ~ , F 1; ~ ‸ F 2
193 pleasures;] ~ , F 1–2
194 'em;] ~ , F 1–2
196 honours;] ~ , F 1–2
197 abuses;] ~ ‸ F 1; ~ , F 2
198 invaded,] ~ ‸ F 1–2
206 (Truly…so);] ‸ ~…~ ‸;
    F 1–2
217 more?] ~ , F 1–2
223 nobly:——] ~ : ‸ F 1–2
224 basis;] ~ , F 1; ~ . F 2
226 breath.] ~ —— F 1–2
228 dying?] F 2; ~ ‸ F 1
241 ye:] F 2; ~ , F 1
243–244 nature. | …slaves? ‸Exit.]
    ~ ——Exit. | … ~ . ——
    F 1; ~ —— | … ~ . ——
    [Exit. F 2
245 I…Captain] F 1–2 line knew |
    H'ad
247 it:] ~ , F 1–2
249 man?] F 2; ~ . F 1
250 ‸Exeunt] —— ~ F 1–2
250 ‸Enter] —— ~ F 1–2

252 long:] ~ , F 1–2
253 preserver:] ~ , F 1–2
268 hell.] ~ —— F 1–2
269–270 Hee's…againe.] one line
    in F 1–2
269 againe.] F 2; ~ , F 1
269 ‸Enter] —— ~ F 1–2
274 ‸‸Exeunt.] (——Exit. F 1;
    [——Exeunt. F 2 both following
    line 273
274.1 ‸Enter] —— ~ F 1–2
275 Lord,——] ~ , ‸ F 1–2
276 Cesar!] F 2; ~ , F 1
282 Phidias.] Phil. F 1–2
289 Lord, deer master:] ~ : ~ ~ --
    F 1–2
291 worthy?] F 2; ~ : F 1
294 (O…perishd)] ‸ ~ … ~ ,
    F 1–2
299 scatterd‸] ~ —— F 1–2
300 Phidias.] Pho. F 1–2
301 me:——] ~ : ‸ F 1–2
308 friend;] ~ , F 1–2
309 thee:——] ~ : ‸ F 1–2
317 doe:——] ~ ‸‸ F 1; ~ ·‸ F 2
319 worthinesse?——] ~ ? ‸ F 1–2
331 forgotten:] ~ , F 1–2
335 private:——] ~ : ‸ F 1–2
342 all,] ~ ‸ F 1–2
345 Phidias——] ~ : F 1–2±
347 mournings,] F 2; ~ ‸ F 1(|)
349 breeds‸…of,] ~ ,…~ ‸
    F 1; ~ ,…~ , F 2

V.i

0.1 Aretus] F 2; Aretius F 1
1 danger;] ~ , F 1–2
2 Cesar:] ~ , F 1; ~ . F 2

21 dye‸ or pleasure,] ~ , ~ ~ ‸
    F 1–2
34.1 ‸Exeunt] —— ~ F 1–2

V.ii

4 ₐ*Enter* Lycinius.] ⸻ ～ ～ .
 following line 3 F 1–2
5 him:⸻] ～ : ₐ F 1–2
12.1 ₐ*Enter* F 2; ⸻ ～ F 1
15 *Prince;*] ～ , F 1–2
20 *Rayne.*] ～ ? F 1; ～ , F 2
25 Grace?] F 2; ～ . F 1
29 to:⸻] ～ : ₐ F 1–2
31 body⸻] ～ . F 1–2
32 freezes;] ～ , F 1–2
34 flaming.] ～ , F 1–2
41 oh⸻] ～ , F 1; ～ . F 2
52 Revenues,—oh⸻] ～ , ₐ ～ ₐ
 F 1 2
59 ease,⸻] ～ , ₐ F 1–2
64 wretches;] ～ , F 1–2
77 villaine:⸻] ～ : ₐ F 1–2
79 (Marke...*Cæsar*)] ₐ ～...～ ,
 F 1–2
86 mad,] F 2; ～ . F 1
87–88 me; | Hold me,] ～ , | ～ ～ ;
 F 1–2
90 diseases⸻] ～ . F 1–2

92 breeds ₐ⸻] ～ . ⸻ F 1–2
95 The...breake] F 1–2 *line* sinnes:
 | Now
103 torments⸻] ～ . F 1–2
107 master,] ～ ; F 1–2
108 tempests.⸻] ～ ₘₘ F 1|–2
109 heart,⸻] ～ , ₐ F 1–2
110 ₐ*He*] ⸻ ～ F 1–2
115 on me:] ～ ～ , F 1–2
116 ravisher,] F 2; ～ , , F 1
121 sins,...incense?] ～ ?...～ :
 F 1; ～ ?...～ ? F 2
125 heaven:⸻] ～ : ₐ F 1–2
126 paines,⸻] ～ , ₐ F 1–2
129 present;] ～ , F 1–2
131 reason;] ～ , F 1–2
132 forgivenesse:] ～ , F 1–2
134 passions:] ～ , F 1–2
136 in:] ～ , F 1–2
140 ₐ*He*] ⸻ ～ F 1–2
152 follow.] ～ ⸻ F 1–2
161.1 ₐ*Exeunt*] ⸻ ～ F 1; *om.*
 s.d. F 2

V.iii

19 *Elizium;*] ～ : F 1–2
21 unrewarded;] ～ , F 1–2
26 *Cæsar*, yet no dying?] ～ ?
 Yet ～ ～ ; F 1–2

29 me:] ～ , F 1–2
38 far ₐ] ～ , F 1–2
41.1 ₐ*Exit*] ⸻ ～ F 1–2

V.iv

1 *1. Senator.*] 1. F 1–2 *which use
 numerals alone for the Senators'
 speech-prefixes throughout the
 scene*
2 else;] ～ , F 1–2
5 'em,] F 2; ～ . F 1
17.1 ₐ*Exit*] ⸻ ⸻ ～ F 1–2
23 to] F 2; ro F 1

26 the Souldiers] F 2; theSouldiers
 F 1
29 Open'd...us] F 1–2 *line* Trea-
 sure. | Gods
29 with] F 2; wirh F 1
30 before] F 2; besore F 1
32 strengthend.] ～ ⸻ F 1–2
33 news?] F 2; ～ , F 1

38.1 ˄*Exeunt*] ——— ~ F1–2
38.1 *Senators.*] ~ , F1–2
41 governd;] ~ , F1–2
43 brine,] F2; ~ : F1
46 current˄] ~ , F1–2
47.1 Senators] *Senat.* F1–2
49 *Affranius.*——] ~ . ˄ F1–2

52 Fathers:] ~ , F1–2
56 purchasd:] ~ , F1–2
58 be: forward.——] ~ , ~ . ˄
    F1–2
62 ˄*Flourish*] F2; ——— ~ F1
63 there.] F2; ~ ——— F1
72.1 ˄*Exit*] F2; ——— ~ F1

V.v

6 somthing (*Maximus*)] ~ ? ~ ˄
    F1–2
20 grace;] ~ , F1–2
21 Rain-bow——] ~ . F1–2
21 *Lycippus.*] F2 (*Lic.*); *Luy.* F1
21 blew?] ~ , F1; ~ . F2

22 midle——] F2; ~ ˄ F1
23 raine?] ~ . F1–2
25 too?] ~ . F1–2
26 fires——] ~ . F1–2
30–31 possible,...*Paulus*;] ~ ;
    ...~ , F1–2

V.vi

1 *Eudoxa:*——] ~ : ˄ F1–2
4 us.] F2; ~ , F1
12 woman,] ~ : F1; ~ ; F2
15 (Such...of)] ˄ ~ ... ~ , F1–2
17 rape?] ~ . F1–2
22 worthiest;] ~ , F1–2
23 more,] F2; ~ ˄ F1
25 Sir.] ~ ? F1–2
28 lye:——] ~ : ˄ F1–2
34 thee,] F2; ~ ˄ F1

37 danger:] ~ , F1–2
38 Sir,] F2; ~ ? F1
39 obedience?] F2; ~ ; F1
49 you,] ~ ˄ F1–2
51 Sweetest.] F2; ~ , F1
52 deere,] ~ ˄ F1–2
52 Sir.] F2; ~ ; F1
53 mankinde——] ~ ˄ F1; ~ . F2
53 ˄*Enter*] F2; ——— ~ F1
57.1 ˄*Exeunt*] F2; ——— ~ F1

V.vii

12.1 ˄*Exeunt*] F2; ——— ~ F1

V.viii

4 Ballance,] ~ ˄ F1–2
7 Son,] ~ ˄ F1–2
10 people:] ~ , F1–2
13 *Emilius*] F2 (*Emylius*); *Emelius*
    F1
24 *Land.*] F2; ~ , F1
29–30 guests;...it,] ~ ,...~ ;
    F1–2

34 second (sweet):] ~ (~) ˄ F1;
    ~ , ~ , ˄ F2
42 *Swim;*] ~ ˄ F1; ~ : F2
44 *Wine:*] F2; ~ ; F1
47 *Bellona's*] F2; *Bellonia's* F1
55 him?] F2; ~ . F1
56–57 Stir...thankes] *one line in*
    F1–2

404

57 Sir,] ~ ‸ F 1–2
58 well?] F 2; ~ : F 1
59 passe:] ~ , F 1–2
68 (That...ye)] ‸ ~ ... ~ ; F 1;
   ‸ ~ ... ~ , F 2
71 cruelly,] F 2; ~ ‸ F 1
72 *Romans*;] ~ , F 1–2
73 Heaven,] ~ ‸ F 1–2
75 her:] ~ , F 1–2
79 Souldiers,] F 2; ~ ; F 1
87 bounty,] ~ ; F 1–2
88 (Mine...last)] ‸ ~ ... ~ :
   F 1–2
89 *Romans*,] F 2; ~ : F 1
90 Emperor,] ~ ; F 1–2

92 directed,] ~ ; F 1–2
94 (Oh...me?)] ‸ ~ ... ~ ? ‸
   F 1–2
99–100 Was...wife] *one line in*
   F 1–2
100 wife,] ~ ‸ F 1–2
101 joy,] ~ ; F 1–2
103 abusd:] ~ , F 1–2
103 grieve,...ye,] ~ ‸ ... ~ ;
   F 1–2
105 in:] F 2; ~ ; F 1
113 hand‸] ~ ; F 1–2
114 thankes,——] ~ , ‸ F 1–2
121.1 ‸*Exeunt*] F 2; —— ~ F 1

Epilogue

7 *there*‸] F 2; ~ , F 1

[The seventeenth-century editions and a selection of modern editions are collated with the present text, substantive and important semi-substantive variants being recorded. Included as well are readings suggested by J. Monck Mason in his *Comments on the Plays of Beaumont and Fletcher* (1798). The lemmata are those of the present text; variants with their sigla appear after the bracket. The sigla are as follows:

C   *Works*, 1778, ed. Colman
D   *Works*, 1843–6, ed. Dyce
F1   *Comedies and Tragedies*, 1647
F2   *Fifty Comedies and Tragedies*, 1679
L   *Works*, 1711, with introduction by Langbaine
M   *Beaumont and Fletcher*, 1887, ed. Strachey (Mermaid series)
Ma Mason, *Comments*, 1798
S   *Works*, 1750, ed. Theobald, Seward and Sympson (*Valentinian* ed. Seward)
T   *The Tragedy of Valentinian*, 1717
V   *Works*, 1904–12, ed. Bullen *et al.* (Variorum edition; *Valentinian* ed. Martin)
W   *Works*, 1812, ed. Weber

Variants in the songs found in manuscripts and two printed anthologies are also included, the sigla being:

'Now the lusty Spring is seene' (II.v.4.2–24)
   MS1 Edinburgh University Library MS Dc 1, 60 (with music)
   O   *Poems:* by Francis Beaumont, Gent., 1653
   CA   *Cheerful Ayres*, 1660, edited by John Wilson
'Heare ye Ladies that despise' (II.v.24.1–44)
   MS2 Bodleian MS Eng. Poet. c. 50
   O   *Poems*, 1653

Note: This song is listed in the index of Drexel MS 4175 but is not in the manuscript itself. See John P. Cutts, '"Songs Vnto the Violl and Lute" – Drexel MS. 4175', *Musica Disciplina*, XVI (1962), 78, 84.

'Care charming Sleep' (V.ii.12.3–22)
   MS3 Bodleian MS MUS. Christ Church 87 (with music)
   MS4 Bodleian MS Don. c. 57 (with music)
   MS5 British Museum Add. 11608 (with music)
   MS6 Fitzwilliam Museum, Cambridge, MS 52.D.25 (with music)
   MS7 Folger MS V.a.170
   MS8 Folger MS V.a.319

MS⁹   Folger MS V.a.322
MS¹⁰   Rosenbach MS 243/4
MS¹¹   Rosenbach MS 1083/17

'Honour that is ever living' (V.viii.15–26)
    O   *Poems*, 1653

'God Lyeus ever young' (V.viii.36.1–46)
    MS¹² Edinburgh University Library MS Dc 1, 69 (with music)
    O   *Poems*, 1653
    CA   *Cheerful Ayres*, 1660, edited by John Wilson

Omission of a siglum indicates that the edition or manuscript concerned agrees with the text. The symbol + is used to show all editions subsequent to the one noted, less any exceptions signified by − : thus, 'C+ (−D)' may be read 'Colman and all later editions but Dyce'. Alterations of 'ye' to 'you' and vice versa are not recorded unless they begin in F2.]

I.i

10 woman] Women F2, W
44 thaw'd] thraw'd T
49 hates] hate L+ (−V)
50 of] *om.* F1
52 *Chilax.*] *om.* S

66 *Chilax.*] *Pro.* S
88 askd] aske F1
97 yeare] years F2, C, W
109 women] woman F2

I.ii

6 bears] beare F1
12 too] to Ma, W+
15 blessed] blissed T
28 thank] think F1
36 take 'em] take'en F1; take him C
52–53 Mothers...Fathers] fathers ...mothers S+
55 Beside] Besides W
55 comming] common S+

55 curses] courses F2, L, T; curtsies Ma
107 Lure] Lore F1–2, L, T, S, C
141 Runs] Run T+
142 ye have] ye've F2, C
154 this: h'as] this ha's F1+
155 heard] here F1, L, T
161 him] *om.* M

I.iii

6 cald] clad L, T, S
10 shells] shields S
12 ye] you F2+ (−L, T, S)
25 While] Whilst W, D, M
25 why] who F2+ (−L, T, S)
29 but] that Ma

41 Why‿] ∼ , F2
50–51 Battailes,...saker] ∼ ,... ∼ , F1; ∼ ?...∼ , F2
51 out daring] out-during V
58 worthynesse] Worthlessness S
65 your] you F1

66 ye] you F2+ (−L, T, S)
68 ye] you F2+ (−L, T, S)
76 ever freind] friend ever F2
81 *Bruti*] *Brutij* F1, L, T
84 (as I am)]_∧ ~ ~ ~ _∧ F1–2, L, T; _∧ ~ ~ ~ , S
86 feele_∧] fall, Ma
104 be] by T
111 Sesterties] Sestertias F2
148 fidling] filing F1, L, T, C

158 And] A F1+ (−D, M, V)
159 monyes] Body S
162 ye] you F2, D, M, V
162 o'] ô F1, L, T, S
166 spoken] spoke C
175 daring] darling T
194 'em] them F2
227 ye] you F2, W, D, M, V
250 she would] she'd F2, S+
250.1 *Exit*] *Exeunt* F2

II.i

4 Clothes] Cloaths F2, L, T, S, C
15 By Heaven Sir,] *om.* F2
21 ye] you F2, W, D, M, V
22 luck] lucks F2, V

38 you] ye F2
38 know] known D
41 an] a M
51 a] *om.* W

II.ii

12 ye] you F2, D, M, V
13 wouldst live] wouldst thou live S
17 were] am F2
26 came] come T

31 markt] marke F1, L, T, S
40 her to] to her T
45 the] *om.* T, S, C
49 was Pretor] was a prætor W
50 heed then] then heed T

II.iii

7 sow] so F1
9 am a true] am true C
15 Has] He has W
15 way] was F1
23 By Heaven] *om.* F2
25 Souldiers] Souldier F2

41 forget] forgive F1
42 most] must T
81 those] these L, T, S
85 beets] beats W, D; heats D (*Addenda and Corrigenda*), M, V

II.iv

1 now] how F2
3 *Proculus*] *Proclus* F1–2, L
6 Pray] Bray F1
9.1 Proculus] *Proclus* F1–2

33 guide] guard F1, L, T, S
33 ye] *om.* S, C, W
49 besides] beside T
60 Ile make] Hmake F1

II.v

0.1 ₄Enter...Balbus.] ——Enter
Lycinius, and Proculus, Balbus.
(following II.iv.61) F 1–2

1, 4 Lycinius.] Lucin. V

4.1 Enter...Marcellina.] following
line 44 F 1–2, L, T, S, C

4.2 FIRST.] untitled MS¹; First Song
to the Tragedy of Valentinian.
O; Cantus Primus. J. Wilson. CA

6 Golden₄] greene, MS¹, CA;
Golden, O

7 invite] invites MS¹, CA

8 Every where] on eu'ry bush MS¹,
CA

10 inticing] inuiteinge MS¹, CA

12 of'] with MS¹, CA

14 we] you MS¹, CA

15–24 Yet...dye.] om. MS¹, CA

24.1 SECOND.] untitled MS²; The
second Song. O

25 Heare] Harke MS²

25 ye] you MS²

26 has] hath MS²

27 Feare examples] heare example
MS²

30 deceive] delude MS²

34 Showre] Flowre F 1

35 Heare yee Ladyes] Harke you
meadens MS²

37 Feare] heare MS²

38 The] That MS²

38 Moon he makes] phoeboe made
MS²

40 round...spies] in her siluer ties
(?) MS²

41 Never] Little MS²

41 loose] loues MS²

42 at] afore MS²

43 short hower] short Tower F 1, O;
moment MS²

44 can build] can once more build F 1
(u), O

44 build...more] raise, and set on
MS²

87 Lady] Ladys F 1

87 Gentlewoman] Gentlewomen
F 2, L, T, S

II.vi

4.1 Enter...Lucina.] om. F 1

25 two] to F 1–2, L, T, C

38 give] om. F 1, L, T, S

38 ye] you F 2, C+

III.i

1 Ha] Ho F 1; How F 2+

10 ground] groan'd C, W

12 mistery] misery F 1–2, L, T

13 a game] againe F 1, L+ (−D,
M, V)

19 now] new F 2

20 Gives] Give F 2, T+

36 Empire,] Empires₄ F 1

46 again₄₄ but vicious,] ~ , ——
~ ~ ₄ F 1–2, L, T; ~ ; all
virtuous S

84 sons] suns F 1–2, L, T, C, W

124 somtime] sometimes C, W

136 flye] flee F 2

154 were....thither] are...hither
F 2+ (−L, T, S)

179 the] om. S

206 misconceave not] misconceive me not F2
229 Makes] Make F2+ (−L, T, S)
231 ye] you F2, C+
235 wrong] wrongs F2, C, W, D, M
271 Time, Story] Time's story C
297 By heaven] *om.* F2
300, 316 o'] ô F1

301 tales] tameness Ma, D, M, V
321 me thinkes tis] 'tis methinks S
337 yeare] years F2+ (−L, T, S)
362 ye] you F2+ (−L, T, S)
365 as] that S
365 saw] see F1–2, L, T
373 pray together truly] pray truly C, W, V

III.ii

18 think] thinks F1
35 ye] you F2, C+
42 Cares] Care F2+ (−L, T, S)
49 ye] you F2, V
55 knaves] knave F1

57 but] by W
75 us] *om.* M
81 way] stain C
87 ye] you F2+ (−L, T, S)

III.iii

12 my] mine F2, W, V
24 honour] rumour F1+ (−C)
41 he] ye F1
53 By heaven] *om.* F2
55 *Enter a* Servant.] *following line* 53 F1–2, L, T, S, C
56 him to enter] him enter S
60 Is…it?] There is no way without to come near it; Ma
64 all] *om.* F2
71 *Enter* Aecius.] *following line* 70 F1–2, C
74 ye] you F2+ (−L, T, S)
76 brains] brain S
88–89 valour;…ye may be, faire,] ~ ,… ~ ~ ~ , ~ ; F1–2, L, T; ~ ,…else may be∧ fair; S,

C, W, V±; ~ ,…you may be∧ fair, D, M
120 boyes dreamt] Boys e'er dreamt S, C, W
131 with] *om.* S
138 die] dig F1–2, L, T, S, V
142 many one ravish'd] many a one e'en ravish'd S, C
147 joyne] wyne F1, L, T; whine S, C
158 us] 'em S
162 them, and those] ~ ∧ ~ these F1, L+ (−D, M, V); ~ , ~ these F2
168 ye] you F2, C+
168 *Exit.*] *following* howre F1–2, T, S, C, W

IV.i

12 Ground] Groan'd F2, C+
15 *Lycinius.*] *Empe.* F1
26 run] runs S, C, W
39 the] that F2, C, W
40 bread] breed F1
79.1 *Enter* Proculus.] *om.* F1, L, T; *Enter Proculus and Lycias.* C, W

80 *Lycinius.*] *Lycias.* F1, C, W
80 By heaven] *om.* F2
88 I am] am I T
97 *Exeunt.*] *following line* 95 F1–2, L, S, C; *line* 96 T
112 fortune] fortunes F1, L, T, S, W

129–130 certain:...safety——] ~ ,
  ...~ . F1+ (−S)
147 laugh] laught F1–2
157–158 As...And] 1. As...2. And
  F1–2, L
168 go] goes F1

174 *Exit* Phidias.] *following* pleasure
  F1+ (−D, M, V)
175 the] that S
193 *Aretus.*] *om.* F1, L, T
194 *Emperor.*] *om.* F1, L, T

IV.ii

3.1 *Enter...*Phidias.] *following
  line 7* D, M, V
8 make] makes F2, C, W
40 'a] he F2+

54 *Aecius.* There...going,] *om.* T
66.1 *Exit.*] *following* much. F1+
  (−D)

IV.iii

17 Would 'a] Would he F2, C+
21–23 *Proculus.* And scurvily. |
  Pontius. Out...it? | *Proculus.*
  Yes...it,] *Pro.* And scurvily, |

Pon. Out...it? | Yes well
  enough. | *Pro.* Now...it, F1, L;
  Pro. And scurvily. | Out...it? |
  Pon. Yes, well enough. S

IV.iv

1 to] for M
14 humour] honour F1+ (−D, M,
  V)
31 Then] There F1+
73 ye] he W
87 faryewell] farewell L, T
109 Pox] —— F1–2, L, T, S
109 of] o' C, W
116 slaves] slave F1
116 By heaven] *om.* F2
122 *Enter* Pontius.] *following line* 122
  D, M
165 *let him die] not distinguished* F2,
  L, T
183 rancks] rank F2, T+ (−S, C)
200 plumd] plaind F1–2, L, T
209 Sir] for Ma
214 *good] not distinguished* F2, L, T,
  S

219 A] *om.* S
224 basis] bases F1, L, T
262 me to] to me L
268 Nor] For W
270 *Enter...others.*] *following line*
  268 F1+ (− D, M)
278 overflowes] oversows F2
289.1 *Enter* Maximus.] *following* suggestion. *line* 300 D, M
293–294 The...equitie, | (O...
  perishd)] Oh...perish'd! | The
  ...equity, Ma
299 Maximus *advances.*] *om.* F1+
308 my pardon] thy pardon S
342–343 all...with us] still...fall
  with S
349 sun-burnt, *Meroe*] sun-burnt:
  Neroe F1

V.i

16 this] these S, C, W

27 but foure] but for four T

V.ii

12.3 Musick and Song.] *untitled* MS³⁻⁴; Song. in The Tragedy of *Valentinian.* | by Beamont & Fletcher. 1647 [7 *written over 6, or vice versa*]. | Set to music by Robᵗ Johnson. MS⁵; Mʳ Robᵗ Johnson. MS⁶; A Sonnet. W. S. MS⁷; songe. | sung to Prince Henry at his departinge. MS⁸; A Song sung to Prince Henery | at his departinge‸ MS⁹; A wish to his discontented freinde. MS¹⁰; Vpon prince Henry being in a slumber | a little befor his death. MS¹¹

13 *thou*] the MS⁴,⁷,¹¹

14 *to*] of MS⁴

14 *selfe*] life MS⁵ (selfe *cancelled*), F 1, L, T, S

14 *dispose*] disclose MS⁴; depose MS⁷

15 *Prince*] wight MSS (−MS⁶; *in* MS⁵ wight *cancelled*, prince *substituted*, prince *struck out*); man MS⁶

15 *fall*] fale MS¹⁰(?)

16 *gentle*] pleasant MS¹¹

17 *his*] her F 1

17 *slumbers; easie*] slumbers but easy MS⁴

17 *easie*] easily MS¹¹

17 *light*] sweete MSS (−MS¹¹), F 1+ (−M)

18 *And as*] Come like MS¹⁰

18 *son*] sunne MS¹⁰⁻¹¹ (*in* MS⁵ sunne *cancelled*, son *substituted*)

19 *troubled*] om. MS¹¹

19 *sing*] sings F 1

20 *hollow*] hallow T

20 *winds*] wind MS⁵,¹⁰, F 1+

21 *Into*] Rule MS¹¹

21 *this Prince*] thy selfe MSS (−MS³,¹⁰; *in* MS⁵ his sense (?) *is altered first to* thy self *and then to* this); his sence MS³,¹⁰; *this* F 1

21 *gently, Oh gently*] gently, ôh gently, ô gently MS⁵; gently, o, o gently, o gently MS⁶; O gently, gently MS⁷; gently MS⁸⁻⁹

21 *slide*] glide MS¹¹

22 *slumbers*] slumber MS¹⁰

23 *gods, gods: drink, drink*] Gods, Gods, Gods: Drink, Drink, Drink S

32 *wind*] om. F 1

33 *am*] and F 1; find F 2, L, T

33 *an hundred Piles*] a hundred Piles F 2

34 *Funeralls*] funeral C, W, M

37 *tempests*] Tempest S

38 *drunk*] drank T

54 *Enter...Aretus.*] *following Sir. line* 30 F 1–2, L; *following Eudoxa. line* 29 T

63 *damned*] —— F 1; *om.* F 2; cursed C

85 *then*] and F 2

103 *torments*] torment C, W

132 *all, ye*] all‸ the F 1–2, L, T

138 *beleeve, the*] beleeve ye, F 1+ (−D, M, V)

V.iii

26 not I] I not L, T
26 *Cæsar,* yet] *Cæsar?* Yet F1+
   (−D, M, V)

35 Jointed...masts] Winted...
   masses F1
37 peec'd] peece F1–2, L, T, S, C

V.iv

9 negative$_\Lambda$ say$_\Lambda$] ∼ (∼) C, W,
   D, M
12 *2. Senator.*] *om.* M
12 fees] foes F1+
30 *3. Senator.*] *2.* F1–2, L, T;
   1 Sen. S+ (−D)
31 *1. Senator.*] *2 Sen.* S, C, W, M
45 hop'd this$_\Lambda$ *Cesar, Flourish.*]
   hope this. *Cesur$_\Lambda$ flourish. [the
   last word apparently part of dia-*

logue] F1; hope this: F2, L,
T±; hoped this. S, C±; hoped
this, [*Within,* Cæsar! W; hopèd
this,...*Flourish within, and cries
of* Cæsar. [*s.d. following line 47*]
D, M; hoped this, [Cæsar!
Flourish. V
47 high, crack$_\Lambda$] ∼ $_\Lambda$ crackt, F1–2,
   L, T
67 fixt] fix S, C, W

V.v

9 T'will] 'Till T

20 By'th masse] *om.* F2

V.vi

0.1 *with a Messenger*] *om.* F1–2,
    L, T, S, C
4 *Exit Messenger.*] *om.* F1–2, L,
   T, S, C
6–7 beauty,...excellent?] ∼ ?...
    ∼ —— V

7 By heaven] *om.* F2
13 liv'd] live M
20 his] the S
38 know] knows T
42 Ye] The F1+
53 the] a F1+ (−D); *om.* D

V.viii

0.1–0.4 *A...Hoboies*] *For* F1–2
reading, see footnote; L, T, S substantially agree. *A synnet, with
trumpets: A banquet prepared,
with musick. Enter, in state,
Maximus, Eudoxia, Senators,
Gentlemen, and Soldiers, rods and
axes borne before them.* C;...
Eudoxia, *Gentlemen and Soldiers;
then the three Senators,* Fulvius,
Lucius, Sempronius; *Lictors*

bearing rods and axes before them,
W; *A banquet laid out. A synnet
with trumpets. Enter, in state,*
Maximus, Eudoxia, Gentlemen,
and Soldiers; *then* Fulvius,
Lucius, Sempronius, *and other*
Senators, Lictors [*etc., as* W] D,
M; *A banquet laid out. Sennet.
Enter* [*etc., as* D] Sempronius,
Lictors [*etc., as* W] V

413

1 *Sempronius.*] *Sen. Semp.* 3. F1;
  3 *Sen.* F2, L, T, S, C
8 thou] the M
14 *Musicke.*] *See fn. on lines* 0.1–0.3.
14.2 SONG] The third Song O
26.1 *wreath*] *See fn. on lines* 0.1–0.3.
30 liberall‸] ~ , S+
36.2 SONG] *untitled* MS¹²; The
  fourth Song. O; *Cantus Primus
  J. Wilson* CA
37 Lyeus] Lizus F1, O; Lycus T,
  S
38 *honourd*] renown'd O

45 *mirth*] *youth* F1+
46 *Enter…feare*] *repeated* MS¹²,
  CA
57 *Lucius.*] 2. *Sen. Luc.* F1–2, L,
  T, S; 2. *Sen.* C
67 readiest] heaviest F1–2, L, T;
  easiest D, M; heavenliest Ma, W,
  V
68 honourd] honour F1
98 blusht] blush F1
104 it] yet F1
105 ly'd] lyd F1; lied C+

Epilogue

7 *i'th*] *'th* F1
12 *wealth*] *health* S, C

17 *Misse*] *Mistris* F1, L, T, S

MONSIEUR THOMAS

edited by

HANS WALTER GABLER

TEXTUAL INTRODUCTION

Monsieur Thomas, A Comedy (Greg, no. 558) was published in a Quarto of 1639 by John Waterson. On 22 January of that year, it was entered for Waterson in the Stationers' Register. Entry and title-page assign it to John Fletcher, whose sole authorship has never been held in doubt. The dedication to Charles Cotton and the commendatory verses prefixed to Q are signed by Richard Brome who in 1639 was principal playwright to the King and Queen's Young Company at the Cockpit. In a list of plays of 1639 drawn up by William Beeston, their manager, it is claimed as company property under the alternative title of *Father's Own Son*. Whether or not there was at the time a dispute over the ownership in which the property list and the publication were strategical moves has remained a matter of speculation. Its resolution depends in part on an assessment of the title-page statement 'Acted at the Private House in *Blacke Fryers*'. It does not clearly imply an acting company, since the theatre in question may have been the Blackfriars, or else a 'Private House' such as Porter's Hall in Blackfriars, where, for example, the Queen's Revels Children, corporate ancestors of Beeston's company of 1639, are known to have played in 1615/16; nor does it specify a date of the original or revival performance, whichever the title-page is assumed to refer to. Early or late the King's Men may have owned or laid claim to *Monsieur Thomas*. But it would seem likelier on the whole that it was an undisputed Children's play throughout. E. K. Chambers suggests (*Elizabethan Stage* (Oxford, 1923), vol. II, p. 60) that *Monsieur Thomas* and *The Nightwalker* were indeed Queen's Revels plays of 1610–13. Significantly or not, they happen to be linked verbally by one rather conspicuous tag of mock Welsh ('Du gat awhee', *MT* I.ii.8, recurring only once more in *The Custom of the Country*, I.ii). More importantly, Fletcher may within the period in question be expected to have written for the Children's theatre before he assumed the full duties of principal playwright to the King's Men. These considerations taken together would seem to allow more confidently than hitherto a dating of the play to the first years of the limit given by Chambers (vol. III, p. 228) as 1610–16.

There is general agreement that the *terminus a quo* is defined by the evident dependence on *L'Astrée de Messire Honoré d'Urfé*, Part II, as a source, which, containing the 'Histoire de Cellidée, Thamyre et Calidon', was published in February, 1610. The punchline in the final scene, 'Take her *Francisco*: now no more yong *Callidon*' (V.xii.89) has sometimes been thought to constitute a vestige of a lost original version of the play. But an hypothesis of revision cannot be substantiated, and an adequate and sufficient function of the line would seem to be that of a passing source acknowledgement to the readers of popular romances among the play's audience.

The Quarto of 1639 was machined in two skeleton formes in alternation. That the text was set up by at least two compositors is suggested by certain divergent features of orthography and typography which have, however, not proved sufficiently distinctive safely to differentiate and to tabulate compositorial stints. The absence of directions and notations of an exclusively theatrical nature and the presence in high proportion of Fletcherian linguistic forms according to Cyrus Hoy's classification suggests authorial papers as printer's copy, further defined as a fair copy in Fletcher's hand by the virtually error-free verse lining. Yet it cannot be conclusively determined whether the regular Latin act/scene divisions of Q are authorial, or in some manner editorial, or a mixture of both, nor whether the apparent breakdown in their transmission which occurs in sheet K is due to a passing obscurity of the printer's copy or to errors committed in the printing shop. Concealing as it does the point of division of Acts IV and V, it affects the structural proportions of the play as a whole and requires editorial emendation against all previous editions.

Sheet L opens with the head title *Actus Quintus, Scena Quarta*. This is unique, since it is each first scene only which in Acts I–IV is given an act and scene number. No first scene for Act V is marked in Q. On the pattern of the earlier act divisions, editors following F2 have taken the head title on L1 to indicate the beginning of Act V and have considered the scene number to be erroneous. Yet in doing so they have not taken into account that the preceding scene but one – V.ii if the scene opening on L1 is correctly V.iv – is actually headed *Scena secunda*. Beginning in the lower half of K3ᵛ and ending at the bottom of K4, it is sandwiched between a *Scena septima* of only twelve lines at the top of K3ᵛ and a *Scena Octava* of twenty-eight lines typographically padded to fill K4ᵛ. In the numbering of these scenes, the sequence of fourth-act scenes in K (*Scena Quinta* K1ᵛ, *Scena Sexta* K2) is carried on, though oddly by disregarding the scene division *Scena septima*/*Scena secunda* in K3ᵛ.

The true beginning of Act V, then, would appear to lie concealed in sheet K. Critically it is determinable with ease. There can be no doubt about the play's conscious five-act structure. The act divisions which Q preserves all show structural awareness and control of the phases of the dramatic movement. Act I ends on the first climax of the comic action, the reading of Thomas' offensive letter to Mary. Act II opens as the change in Francis' health has become manifest; in closing, it establishes Valentine's and Cellide's conflict. III.i brings on stage the Physicians in full activity, quickly relieved of their duties by Cellide. To end the third act, III.iii unleashes the comic action for the evening scene of Thomas' boisterous ballading and serenading, with all his efforts foiled by Mary. Act IV sets in the following morning. Francis has clandestinely departed, and Sebastian receives Launcelot's report of the night's misdeeds. By midday, Sebastian has renounced and reaccepted his son. On going out to dinner, Thomas is on the point of once more persuading Dorothy to help him in a design to win Mary. Meanwhile, Michael has tempered Valentine's despair and promised to bring Francis back if he can. Hylas and Sam in their turn have gone out in search of Thomas. In IV.v, Michael finds Francis as he is boarding a ship and has him arrested. This scene brings about a partial resolution of the action while kindling new suspense through the introduction of Francis' ring and jewel, the instruments of recognition in V.xii. On the seashore, the arrest takes place away from the action's main locality, to which it will require time (a sequence of three scenes in the play) for Michael and Francis to return. Yet the comedy reverts there immediately in the following evening scene (headed *Scena Sexta* in Q). Thomas is being disguised in his sister's clothes to carry out the designs hinted at at the end of IV.ii. This scene opening, set off as it is from IV.v by a shift in both plot and place of action, marks the beginning of the play's final comic night-and-morning sequence which in the present edition constitutes Act V.

But if *Scena secunda* (K3^v) and *Actus Quintus, Scena Quarta* (L1) are correctly the second and fourth scenes of V, the act ought to begin not with *Scena Sexta* (K2) but with *Scena septima* (K3^v). However, not only is the twelve-line *Scena septima* a brief and transitory scene without any of the dramatic focusing power of the opening scenes of Acts I–IV. An act division separating *Scena Sexta* and *Scena secunda* would also constitute an unwarranted break in the line of action from Thomas' first encounter in diguise with Sebastian to the second one with Valentine. On closer inspection, moreover, the *Scena septima/Scena secunda* division on K3^v appears unwarranted. Since the Maid is expressly ordered by Mary to remain and await Thomas, there is no moment of clear-stage. '*Scena septima*' and '*Scena secunda*' are one scene.

Bibliographically, sheet K proves to be the only sheet – except for initial sheet B – not regularly machined with two skeleton formes. Skeleton I prints both formes of B, naturally omitting the B2 running title in B1. Transferred to C(i), it shows a new running title for C2. The order of the first formes through the press was therefore B(i)–B(o)–C(i). Two-skeleton printing starts in sheet C with the construction of skeleton II for C(o). On the assumption of regularity according to generally favored printing habits, and following from the sequence pattern established in the initial formes, the press-work proceeded in a $(i)-$(o) alternation through sheet I. Skeleton I then printed both formes of K, L(o), M(i) and (with its running title from M1^v) N(i). The use of skeleton II was suspended for sheet K and resumed for L(i), M(o) and (with the running title from M1) N(o).

In accordance with the apparent compositorial practice through-out the book, sheet K was divided between two typesetters doing unequal stints. It was composed *seriatim*, though in a manner adaptable to the effect of a setting by formes. By spelling characteristics such as they can be made out, it is K2^v in K(o) which clearly differs from the remaining pages in the sheet as the work of a second compositor. This implies a speeding up of the composition of K(o). While the second compositor set K2^v, the first would have completed *Scena Sexta* (begun in the lower half of K2) on K3 and been free to proceed to *Scena Octava* on K4^v in order to make K(o) ready for the press. An hypothesis that he did so only after setting the scene heading *Scena septima* and a few lines of text for K3^v would best fit the bibliographical evidence. It is at the end of *Scena Octava*, and at the bibliographical point of transition from sheet K to sheet L, that the error in numbering appears to have been realized. The catchword *Actus* on K4^v may imply a glance at the textual continuation in the manuscript revealing that what followed was not the first, but the fourth, scene of Act V. Yet neither the '*Scena Octava*' in K(o) nor the '*Scena Sexta*' and '*Scena septima*' headings in K(i) were altered. A proper act heading in place of '*Scena Sexta*' in the lower half of K2 in particular would have violated the Quarto's apparent typographical rule of opening an act on a new page. If the inference is valid that K3^v and K4 were completed only after K4^v, and thus that the composition and printing of K(o) preceded that of K(i), the scene heading '*Scena secunda*' may have been compositorially introduced as a clue to the correctness of the anticipated *Actus Quintus, Scena Quarta* head-title of L1.

Contrary to the pattern established for sheets C–I, then, K(o) apparently preceded K(i) through the press. With skeleton I printing both formes of K, skeleton II from I(o) was available for imposition of L(i). But when K(i) came off the press L(i) seems to have been only half ready to succeed it, with just pages L1^v and L2, both the work of the second compositor, in position. The assembly of two brief scenes, and half of a third one not much longer, was combined with a beautiful touch of printing economy by which the faulty scene numbers from K(i) were quickly reused, now correctly, to complete L3^v and L4 for L(i). The identical settings of *Scena Sexta* and *Scena septima*, even accompanied by the same rules on the respective pages, appear in K2/L3^v and K3^v/L4. In the case of *Scena Sexta*, the letter-type and the rule which precedes it are transferred as a block, with identical spacing. In the case of *Scena septima*, the space between letter-type and rule below is adjusted to admit scenes of different length (twelve and seven lines respectively). It would thus seem a further pragmatic assumption that L(i) in skeleton II from I(o) preceded L(o) in skeleton I from K(i) through the press.

The second reversal in the use of the skeleton formes observable in sheets M–N appears to be related to a casting off of the text for the Quarto's completion. Throughout, the way in which the text is divided into page units by varying, though not always bibliographically systematic, density of typesetting, suggests that a casting off of copy took place predominantly for typographical reasons. A new act always begins a new page; and a new scene does so frequently, with space to spare on the preceding page. Signs of serious miscalculation appear in L. L4^v is only half filled; indeed, with less liberal spacing in L3^v and L4, its lines could conceivably have been accommodated within L(i). Perhaps the rapid reuse in L(i) of the scene headings from K(i) is to be explained as a padding out of type to conceal that casting off between sheets L and M was faulty by a whole page. But even with a full sheet L the remaining text of the play would have overshot sheet M by one page, as it now does by two. Evidence from M(i), which in all its pages is less crowded than M(o) – and is especially open in M4 which, with white space of seven lines, yet breaks off after the first line of a three-line speech – suggests that M(o) was composed before M(i), and M4^v in particular before M4. To know where to end M4^v would have determined the exactest possible allocation of text for N1–N1^v, the two pages of text to be printed with the title-page as a separate half-sheet. The completion of M(o) before M(i) explains the second reversal in the use of the skeleton formes. M(o) was printed in skeleton II from L(i), and M(i) in skeleton I from L(o).

To judge from Richard Brome's dedication and commendatory verses, *Monsieur Thomas* did not enjoy either an initial or a lasting theatrical success. Nor, apparently, was John Waterson's Quarto of 1639 a bestseller. In 1646, the rights to the title passed to Humphrey Moseley, who between 1653 and 1660 repeatedly advertised the play and appears to have continued to sell Waterson copies, of which forty-one exemplars are known to survive today. The undated Quarto entitled *Fathers own Son*, extant in two known copies, is a reissue from a new publisher, John Crofts, of the remainder sheets of the 1639 edition printing. Its title-page indicates that it was published to coincide with the play's revival by the King's Men during the 1661/2 theatrical season at the Theatre in Vere Street. Kirkman's *The WITS, or Sport upon Sport. In Select Pieces of Drollery, Digested into SCENES by way of DIALOGUE* contains as Droll 27 in the latter part of its 1662 edition 'The Doctors of Dulhead Colledge, out of Fathers own son', which is a verbatim rendition of II.iv and passages from III.i. Thomas Durfey's *Trick for Trick: or, The Debauched Hypocrite* of 1678 is a debased adaptation, while John Fletcher's *Monsieur Thomas* in its original garb was included in the second Beaumont and Fletcher Folio of 1679. It was there clearly printed from the 1639 edition, so that Q constitutes the only authoritative text and provides the copy-text for the present edition.

It is a pleasure to thank the libraries in the United Kingdom who allowed me to assemble their exemplars of *Monsieur Thomas* for Hinman collation kindly made possible at the Bodleian Library in Oxford and the Cambridge University Library, and my colleague Günter Kotzor in Munich for his expertise in hagiology and matters of historical English usage.

TO THE NOBLE

HONOURER OF

The dead Authors works and memory, Master

CHARLES COTTON

SIR,

My directing of this piece unto you, renders me obvious to many censures, which I would willingly prevent by declaring mine owne and your right thereto. Mine was the fortune to be made the unworthy preserver of it; yours is the worthy opinion you have of the Author and his Poems: neither can it easily be determined, 10 whether your affection to them hath made you (by observing) more able to judge of them, then your ability to judge of them hath made you to affect them, deservedly, not partially. In this presumptuous act of mine, I express my two-fold zeale; to him and your noble selfe, who have built him a more honourable monument in that faire opinion you have of him, then any inscription subject to the wearing of time can be. You will finde him in this Poem as active as in others, to many of which, the dull apprehensions of former times gave but slender allowance, from malitious custome more than reason: yet they have since by your candid selfe and 20 others beene cleerely vindicated. You shall oblige by your acceptance of this acknowledgement (which is the best I can render you, mine own weake labours being too unworthy your judicious perusall) him that is ambitious to be known

Your most humble servant;

RICHARD BROME.

424

In prayse of the Authour, and his following Poeme.

'*Tis both the life of Action and of wit,*
When Actors so the fanci'd humours hit,
As if'twixt them and th'Authour there were strife
How each to other should give mutuall life.
The last this wanted not. Invention strayes
Here in full many pleasant turning wayes,
That like Meanders their curld circles bend,
Yet in a smooth streame runne to crowne the end.
Then 'tis authoriz'd by the Authors name;
Who never writ but with such sprightly flame,   10
As if the Muses jointly did inspire,
His raptures only with their sacred fire.
And yet perhaps it did participate
At first presenting but of common fate;
When ignorance was judge, and but a few
What was legitimate, what bastard, knew.
The world's growne wiser now: each man can say
If Fletcher *made it 'tis an exc'lent play.*
   Thus Poemes like their Authors may be sed,
   Never to live 'till they have first beene dead.   20

Rich: Brome.

Valentine.
Francis, son to Valentine.
Sebastian.
Thomas, son to Sebastian.
Hylas.
Sam.
Launcelot, servant to Thomas.
Michael, neighbour to Valentine.
Three Physitians.
Apothecary.
Barber.
Fidler.

Alice, sister to Valentine.
Cellide, ward to Valentine.
Dorothy, daughter to Sebastian.
Abbesse, aunt to Thomas and Dorothy.
Mary, niece to Valentine.
Maid.
Madge.
Kate, disguised as a Moore.

Servants, Maids, Saylors, Officers, Nuns.]

MONSIEUR *THOMAS*

A COMEDY

Enter Alice *and* Valentine.

Alice.   How dearely welcome you are!
Valentine.   I know it,
  And my best sister, you as deer to my sight,
  And pray let this confirm it. How you have govern'd
  My poore state in my absence, how my servants,
  I dare and must beleeve, else I should wrong ye,
  The best and worthiest.
Alice.   As my womans wit Sir,
  Which is but weake and crazie.
Valentine.   But good *Alice*
  Tell me how fares the gentle *Cellide*,
  The life of my affection, since my travell,
  My long, and lazie travell? is her love still   10
  Upon the growing hand? do's it not stop
  And wither at my yeares? has she not view'd
  And entertain'd some yonger smooth behaviour,
  Some youth but in his blossome, as her selfe is?
  There lyes my feares.
Alice.   They need not, for beleeve me
  So well you have manag'd her, and won her minde,
  Even from her houres of childehood, to this ripenesse,
  And in your absence (that by me inforced stil)
  So well distill'd your gentlenesse into her,
  Observ'd her, fed her fancy, liv'd still in her,   20
  And though Love be a boy, and ever youthfull,
  And young and beauteous objects ever aym'd at,
  Yet here yee have gone beyond love, better'd nature,
  Made him appeare in yeares, in gray yeares fiery,

I.i] *Actus Primus, Scena Prima.* Q   *22 young‸] F2; ~, Q

427

His bow at full bent ever: feare not brother,
For though your body has been farre off from her,
Yet evcry houre your heart, which is your goodnesse,
I have forc'd into her, won a place prepar'd too,
And willingly to give it ever harbour:
Beleeve she is so much yours, and won by miracle,   30
(Which is by age) so deep a stamp set on her
By your observances, she cannot alter.
Were the childe living now ye lost at sea
Among the *Genoway* Gallies, what a happinesse,
What a maine blessing?
Valentine.   O no more good sister,
Touch no more that string, 'tis too harsh and jarring.
With that childe all my hopes went, and you know
The root of all those hopes, the mother too
Within few dayes.
Alice.   'Tis too true, and too fatall,
But peace be with their soules.
Valentine.   For her losse   40
I hope, the beauteous *Cellide*——
Alice.   You may Sir,
For all she is, is yours.
Valentine.   For the poore boyes losse,
I have brought a noble friend, I found in travell:
A worthier minde, and a more temperate spirit
If I have so much judgement to discerne 'em,
Man yet was never master of.
Alice.   What is he?
Valentine.   A Gentleman, I doe assure my selfe,
And of a worthy breeding, though he hide it:
I found him at *Valentia*, poore and needy,
Onely his minde the master of a treasure.   50
I sought his friendship, wonne him by much violence,
His honesty and modesty still fearing
To thrust a charge upon me; how I love him,
He shall now know, where want and he hereafter
Shall be no more companions: use him nobly,

It is my will, good sister, all I have
I make him free companion in, and partner,
But onely——
Alice.   I observe ye, hold your right there,
 Love and high rule allowes no rivals, brother:
 He shall have faire regard, and all observance.   60

Enter Hylas.

Hylas.   Ye are welcome noble Sir.
Valentine.   What, Monsieur *Hylas*,
 I'me glad to see your merry body well yet.
 Hylas.   Y'faith y'are welcome home; what news beyond seas?
Valentine.   None, but new men expected, such as you are
 To breed new admirations: 'tis my sister,
 Pray ye know her sir.
Hylas.   With all my heart, your leave Lady.
Alice.   Ye have it sir.
Hylas [*aside*].   A shrewd smart touch, which do's prognosticate
 A body keene and active, somewhat old,
 But that's all one: age brings experience   70
 And knowledge to dispatch. [*To* Valentine] I must be better
 And neerer in my service, with your leave sir,
 To this faire Lady.
Valentine.   What, the old squire of dames still?
Hylas.   Still the admirer of their goodnesse:
                        [*Aside*] With all my heart now
 I love a woman of her yeares, a pacer
 That, lay the bridle in her neck, will travell:
 Forty, and somewhat fulsome is a fine dish,
 These yong colts are too sketish.

Enter Mary.

Alice.   My cosin *Mary*
 In all her joy Sir to congratulate
 Your faire returne.
Valentine.   My loving, and kind cosin,   80
 A thousand welcomes.

Mary. A thousand thanks to heaven Sir
For your safe, voyage, and returne.
Valentine. I thanke ye:
But wher's my blessed *Cellide?* her slacknesse
In visitation——
Mary. Thinke not so deere Uncle,
I left her on her knees, thanking the gods
With teares and prayers.
Valentine. Ye have given me too much comfort.
Mary. She will not be long from ye.
Hylas. Your faire cosin?
Valentine. It is so, and a bait you cannot balke sir,
If your old rule raigne in you, ye may know her.
Hylas. A happy stocke ye have, [*to* Mary] right worthy Lady,   90
The poorest of your servants, vowes his duty
And obliged faith.
Mary. O 'tis a kisse you would sir,
Take it, and tye your tongue up.
Hylas. I am an asse
I doe perceive now: a blinde asse, a blockhead:
For this is handsomnesse, this that that drawes us,
Body and bones: oh what a mounted forehead,
What eyes and lips, what every thing about her?
How like a Swan she swims her pace, and beares
Her silver breasts? this is the woman, she,
And onely she, that I will so much honour   100
As to thinke worthy of my love; all older Idols
I heartily abhorre, and give to gunpowder,
And all complexions besides hers, to Gypsies.

Enter Francis *at one door, and* Cellide *at another.*

Valentine. O my deere life, my better heart, all dangers,
Distresses in my travell, all misfortunes,
Had they been endlesse like the houres upon me,
In this kisse, had been buried in oblivion:
How happy have ye made me, truely happy?

90 *Hylas.*] S; *om.* Q, F2, L

430

Cellide.   My joy has so much overmastered me,
That in my teares for your returne——
Valentine.   O deerest: 110
My noble friend too: what a blessednesse
Have I about me now? how full my wishes
Are come agen, a thousand hearty welcomes
I once more lay upon ye: all I have,
The faire and liberall use of all my servants
To be at your command, and all the uses
Of al within my power——
Francis.   Ye are too munificent,
Nor am I able to conceive those thanks sir.
Valentine.   Ye wrong my tender love now,——even my service,
Nothing excepted, nothing stuck between us   120
And our intire affections, but this woman,
This I beseech ye friend.
Francis.   It is a jewell
I doe confesse would make a thiefe, but never
Of him that's so much yours, and bound your servant,
That were a base ingratitude.
Valentine.   Ye are noble,
Pray be acquainted with her: keep your way sir,
My cosin and my sister.
Alice.   Ye are most welcome:
Mary.   If any thing in our poore powers faire sir
To render ye content, and liberall welcome
May but appeare, command it.
Alice.   Ye shall find us   130
Happy in our performance.
Francis.   The poore servant
Of both your goodnesses presents his service.
Valentine.   Come no more complement: custome has made it
Dull, old, and tedious: ye are once more welcome,
As your owne thoughts can make ye, and the same ever.
And so wee'l in to ratifie it.

*117–119 power‸——...now, ——] W; ~ · ‸ ··· ~ , ‸ Q
120 excepted] S; accepted Q, F2, L

431

Hylas.   Harke ye *Valentine,*
  Is wild oates yet come over?
Valentine.   Yes: with me Sir.
Mary.   How do's he beare himself?
Valentine.   A great deale better:
  Why doe you blush? the Gentleman will doe well.
Mary.   I should be glad on't Sir.
Valentine.   How do's his Father?   140
Hylas.   As mad a worme as ere he was.
Valentine.   I lookt for't:
  Shall we enjoy your companie?
Hylas.   Ile wayt on ye:
  Only a thought, or two.
Valentine.   We bar all prayers.

                           Exeunt all but Hylas.

Hylas.   This last wench, I this last wench was a faire one:
  A dainty wench, a right one: a devill take it,
  What doe I ayle; to have fifteene now in liking,
  Enough a man would thinke to stay my stomack,
  But what's fifteene, or fifteene score to my thoughts?
  And wherefore are mine eyes made, and have lights,
  But to encrease my objects? this last wench   150
  Sticks plaguy close unto me: a hundred pound
  I were as close to her: if I lov'd now
  As many foolish men doe, I should run mad.

                               [*Exit.*]

            Enter old Sebastian, *and* Launcelot.   [I.] ii

Sebastian.   Sirha, no more of your French shrugs I advise you,
  If you be lowzie, shift your selfe.
Launcelot.   May it please your worship——
Sebastian.   Onely to see my sonne, my sonne good *Launcelot:*
  Your Master, and my sonne: body o' me sir,
  No money, no more money Monsieur *Launcelot,*
  Not a deneere, sweet Signior: bring the person,

      141 ere] *stet* Q; e'er F2   I.ii] *Scæna Secunda.* Q

The person of my boy, my boy *Tom*, Monsieur *Thomas*:
Or get you gone agen, *du gat awhee* sir,
Bassa mi cu, good *Launcelot*, *valetote*.
My boy, or nothing.

Launcelot.   Then to answer punctually——   10
Sebastian.   I say to th' purpose.
Launcelot.   Then I say to th' purpose,
Because your Worships vulgar understanding
May meet me at the neerest: your sonne, my master,
Or Monsieur *Thomas*, (for so his travell stiles him)
Through many forraigne plots that vertue meets with,
And dangers (I beseech ye give attention)
Is at the last ariv'd
To aske your (as the French man cals it sweetly)
Benediction, *de jour en jour*.
Sebastian.   Sirha, do not conjure me with your French furies.   20
Launcelot.   *Che ditt'a vou*, Monsieur.
Sebastian.   *Che doga vou*, Rascall:
Leave me your rotten language, and tell me plainely
And quickly sirha, lest I crack your French crowne,
What your good Master meanes: I have maintain'd
You and your Monsieur, as I take it, *Launcelot*,
These two yeeres at your *ditty vous*, your *jours*:
Jour me no more, for not another penny
Shall passe my purse.
Launcelot.   Your Worship is erroneous,
For as I told you, your Sonne *Tom*, or *Thomas*,
My Master, and your sonne is now arriv'd   30
To aske ye, as our language beares it neerest,
Your quotidian blessing, and here he is in person.

Enter Thomas.

Sebastian.   What *Tom*, boy, welcome with all my heart boy,
Welcome 'faith, thou hast gladded me at soule boy,
Infinite glad I am, I have praied too, *Thomas*,
For you wilde *Thomas: Tom*, I thank thee hartily

* 8 *du gat awhee*] *du gata whee* Q

For comming home.
Thomas.   Sir, I doe finde your prayers
  Have much prevail'd above my sins.
Sebastian.   How's this?
Thomas.   Else certaine I had perish'd with my rudenesse,
  Ere I had won my selfe to that discretion   40
  I hope you shall hereafter finde.
  Sebastian.   Humh, humh,
  Discretion? is it come to that? the boy's spoild.
Thomas.   Sirah, you rogue, look for't, for I will make thee
  Ten times more miserable then thou thoughtst thy selfe
  Before thou travelledst: thou hast told my father
  I know it, and I finde it, all my rogueries
  By meere way of prevention to undoe me.
Launcelot.   Sir, as I speake eight languages, I onely
  Told him you came to aske his benediction,
  De jour en jour.
Thomas.   But that I must be civill,   50
  I would beat thee like a dog:——sir, howsoever
  The time I have mispent may make you doubtfull,
  Nay, harden your beliefe 'gainst my conversion——
Sebastian.   A pox o' travell, I say.
Thomas.   Yet deere father
  Your owne experience in my after courses——

                  Enter Dorothy.

Sebastian.   Prethee no more; 'tis scurvy; ther's thy sister:——
  Undon without redemption: he eates with picks,
  Utterly spoyld, his spirit baffell'd in him.
  How have I sind that this affliction
  Should light so heavie on me. I have no more sonnes;   60
  And this no more mine owne, no spark of nature
  Allows him mine now, he's growne tame: my grand curse
  Hang ore his head that thus transform'd thee: travell?
  Ile send my horse to travell next: *we* monsieur,
  Now will my most canonicall deere neighbours

        38 much] F2; much much Q   55.1 Dorothy] *Dorothea* Q
        64 *we*] [*i.e. oui*] F2 we; Q

Say I have found my sonne, and rejoyce with me
Because he has mew'd his mad tricks off. I know not,
But I am sure, this Monsieur, this fine gentleman
Will never be in my books like mad *Thomas*.
I must goe seeke an heire, for my inheritance   70
Must not turne secretary: my name and quality
Has kept my land three hundred yeers in madnesse,
And it slip now, may it sinke.   *Exit.*
Thomas.   Excellent sister,
  I am glad to see thee well: but wher's my father?
Dorothy.   Gone discontent, it seemes.
Thomas.   He did ill in it
  As he dos all: for I was uttering
  A handsome speech or two, I have been studying
  Ere since I came from *Paris:* how glad to see thee?
Dorothy.   I am gladder to see you, with more love too
  I dare maintaine it, then my father's sorry   80
  To see (as he supposes) your conversion:
  And I am sure he is vext, nay more I know it,
  He has prai'd against it mainely: but it appeares sir
  Ye had rather blinde him with that poore opinion,
  Then in your selfe correct it. Deerest brother,
  Since there is in our uniforme resemblance,
  No more to make us two, but our bare sexes:
  And since one happy birth produced us hither,
  Let one more happy minde——
Thomas.   It shallbe sister,
  For I can doe it when I list. and yet wench   90
  Be mad too when I please: I have the trick on't.
  Beware a traveller.
Dorothy.   Leave that trick too.
Thomas.   Not for the world: but wher's my Mistresse
  And prethee say how do's she? I melt to see her,
  And presently: I must a way.
Dorothy.   Then doe so.
  For o' my faith she will not see you brother.

96 you] F2; your Q

Thomas.   Not see me? I'le——
Dorothy.   Now you play your true self;
  How would my father love this! I'le assure ye
  She will not see you: she has heard, (and lowdly)
  The gambolls that you plaid since your departure,   100
  In every Towne ye came, your severall mischeifes,
  Your rowses, and your wenches: all your quarrells,
  And the no causes of 'em: these I take it
  Although she love ye well, to modest eares,
  To one that waited for your reformation,
  To which end travell was propounded by her Uncle,
  Must needs, and reason for it, be examined,
  And by her modesty, and fear'd too light too
  To fyle with her affections: ye have lost her
  For any thing I see, exil'd your selfe.   110
Thomas.   No more of that sweet *Doll*, I will be civill.
Dorothy.   But how long?
Thomas.   Wouldst thou have me lose my birth-
      right?
  For yond old thing will disinherit me
  If I grow too demure: good sweet *Doll*, prethee:
  Prethee deere sister, let me see her.
Dorothy.   No.
Thomas.   Nay, I beseech thee: by this light——
Dorothy.   I: swagger.
Thomas.   Kiss me, and be my friend, we two were twins.
  And shall we now grow strangers?
Dorothy.   'Tis not my fault.
Thomas.   Well, there be other women, and remember
  You, you were the cause of this: there be more lands too,   120
  And better people in 'em: fare ye well,
  And other loves: what shall become of me
  And of my vanities, because they grieve ye?
Dorothy.   Come hither, come, do you see that clowd that flyes
      there?
  So light are you, and blown with every fancy:
  Will ye but make me hope ye may be civill?

I know your nature's sweet enough, and tender,
Not grated on, nor curb'd: doe you love your Mistresse?
Thomas.   He lyes, that sayes I doe not.
Dorothy.   Would ye see her?
Thomas.   If you please: for it must be so.
Dorothy.   And appeare to her   130
A thing to be belov'd?
Thomas.   Yes.
Dorothy.   Change then
A little of your wildenesse into wisedome,
And put on a more smoothnesse:
I'le doe the best I can to helpe ye, yet
I doe protest she swore, and swore it deeply,
She would never see you more: where's your mans heart now?
What doe you faint at this?
Thomas.   She is a woman:
But he she entertaines next for a servant,
I shall be bold to quarter.
Dorothy.   No thought of fighting:
Goe in, and there wee'l talke more: be but rul'd,   140
And what lyes in my power, ye shall be sure of.

                                        Exeunt.

                   Enter Alice *and* Mary.   [I.] iii

Alice.   Hee cannot be so wilde still.
Mary.   'Tis most certaine,
I have now heard all, and all the truth.
Alice.   Grant all that:
Is he the first, that h'as bin giv'n a lost man,
And yet come fairely home? he is yong, and tender
And fit for that impression your affections
Shall stamp upon him; age brings on discretion,
A yeere hence, these mad toyes that now possesse him
Will shew like bugbeares to him, shapes to fright him;
Marriage dissolves all these like mists.

                   I.iii] *Scæna Tertia.* Q
                        437

Mary.   They are grounded
  Hereditary in him, from his father,   10
  And to his grave they will haunt him.
Alice.   'Tis your feare
  Which is a wise part in you; yet your love
  However you may seeme to lessen it
  With these dislikes, and choake it with these errors,
  Do what you can will break out to excuse him;
  Ye have him in your hart, and planted, Cosin,
  From whence the power of reason, nor discretion
  Can ever roote him.
Mary.   Planted in my heart Aunt?
  Beleeve it no, I never was so liberall:
  What though he shew a so so comely fellow   20
  Which we call pretty? or say it may be hansom?
  What though his promises may stumble at
  The power of goodnesse in him, sometimes use too?
Alice.   How willingly thy heart betrayes thee cosin?
  Cozen thy selfe no more: thou hast no more power
  To leave off loving him, then he that's thirsty
  Has to abstaine from drinke standing before him.
  His mind is not so monstrous; for his shape,
  If I have eyes, I have not seene his better.
  A hansom browne complexion——
Mary.   Reasonable   30
  Inclining to a tawney.
Alice.   Had I said so
  You would have wish'd my tongue out: then his making——
Mary.   Which may be mended: I have seene leggs straiter,
  And cleaner made.
Alice.   A body too,
Mary.   Far neater,
  And better set together.
Alice.   God forgive thee,
  For against thy conscience thou lyest stubbornely.
Mary.   I grant 'tis neat enough.
Alice.   'Tis excellent,

And where the outward parts are faire and lovely,
(Which are but molds o'th minde) what must the soule be?
Put case youth has his swinge, and fyery nature   40
Flames to mad uses many times.

Mary.   All this
You onely use, to make me say I love him:
I doe confesse I doe, but that my fondnesse
Should fling it selfe upon his desperate follies——

Alice.   I doe not counsell that, see him reclaim'd first,
Which will not prove a miracle, yet *Mary*
I am afraid 'twill vexe thee horribly
To stay so long.

Mary.   No, no Aunt, no beleeve me.

Alice.   What was your dreame to night? for I observ'd ye
Hugging of me; with good, deere, sweet *Tom.*

Mary.   Fye Aunt,   50
Upon my conscience.

Alice.   On my word 'tis true wench:
And then ye kiss'd me *Mary*, more then once too,
And sigh'd, and O sweet *Tom* againe: nay, doe not blush,
Ye have it at the heart wench.

Mary.   I'le be hang'd first,
But you must have your way.

                    Enter Dorothy.

Alice.   And so will you too,
Or breake down hedges for it:——*Dorothea,*
The welcom'st woman living: how do's thy brother?
I heare he's turn'd a wondrous civill gentleman
Since his short travell.

Dorothy.   Pray heaven he make it good *Alice.*

Mary.   How doe ye friend, I have a quarrell to ye,   60
Ye stole away, and left my company.

Dorothy.   O pardon me, deere friend, it was to welcome
A brother, that I have some cause to love well.

Mary.   Prethee how is he? thou speakst truth.

Dorothy.   Not perfect

I hope he will be.
Mary.   Never: ha's forgot me,
  I heare wench, and his hot love too.
Alice.   Thou wouldst howle then.
Mary.   And I am glad it should be so; his travels
  Have yeelded him variety of Mistresses,
  Fairer in his eye farre.
Alice.   O cogging rascall.
Mary.   I was a foole, but better thoughts I thank heaven——   70
Dorothy.   Pray do not think so, for he loves you deerely,
  Upon my troth most firmely: would faine see you.
Mary.   See me friend? doe you thinke it fit?
Dorothy.   It may be,
  Without the losse of credit too: he's not
  Such a prodigious thing, so monstrous,
  To fling from all society.
Mary.   He's so much contrary
  To my desires, such an antipathy
  That I must sooner see my grave.
Dorothy.   Deere friend,
  He was not so before he went.
Mary.   I grant it,
  For then I daily hop'd his faire conversion.   80
Alice.   Come, do not maske your selfe, but see him freely,
  Ye have a minde.
Mary.   That minde I'le master then.
Dorothy.   And is your hate so mortall?
Mary.   Not to his person,
  But to his qualities, his mad-cap follies,
  Which still like *Hydras* heads grow thicker on him.
  I have a credit friend, and maids of my sort,
  Love where their modesties may live untainted.
Dorothy.   I give up that hope then: pray, for your friends sake,
  If I have any interest within ye,
  Doe but this courtesie, accept this Letter.   90
Mary.   From him?

76 He's] F2; His Q

Dorothy.   The same: 'tis but a minutes reading,
And as we looke on shapes of painted divels,
Which for the present may disturb our fancy,
But with the next new object loose 'em, so
If this be foule, ye may forget it, 'pray.
Mary.   Have ye seene it friend?
Dorothy.   I will not lye: I have not,
But I presume, so much he honours you,
The worst part of himselfe was cast away
When to his best part he writ this.
Mary.   For your sake,
Not that I any way shall like his scribling.   100
Alice.   A shrewd dissembling queane.
Dorothy.   I thanke ye deere friend,——
I know she loves him.
Alice.   Yes, and will not loose him,
Unlesse he leap into the Moone, beleeve that,
And then shee'l scramble too: yong wenches loves
Are like the course of quartans, they may shift
And seeme to cease sometimes, and yet we see
The least distemper puls 'em backe againe,
And seats 'em in their old course: feare her not,
Unlesse he be a devill.
Mary.   Now heaven blesse me.
Dorothy.   What has he writ?
Mary.   Out, out upon him.   110
Dorothy.   Ha, what has the mad man done?
Mary.   Worse, worse, and worse still.
Alice.   Some northerne toy, a little broad.
Mary.   Still fowler?
Hay, hay boyes: goodnesse keep me: oh!
Dorothy.   What ayle ye?
Mary.   Here, take your spell againe, it burnes my fingers.
Was ever Lover writ so sweet a Letter,
So elegant a stile? pray looke upon't:
The rarest inventory of ranke oathes
That ever cut-purse cast.

Alice.   What a mad boy is this?

Mary.   Onely i'th bottome
A little julip gently sprinckled over   120
To coole his mouth, lest it breake out in blisters,
Indeed law. Yours for ever.

Dorothy.   I am sorry.

Mary.   You shall be welcome to me, come when you please,
And ever may command me vertuously,
But for your brother, you must pardon me,
Till I am of his nature, no accesse friend,
No word of visitation, as ye love me,
And so for now Ile leave ye.   *Exit.*

Alice.   What a letter
Has this thing written, how it roares like thunder?
With what a state he enters into stile: 130
Deere Mistresse.

Dorothy.   Out upon him bedlam.

Alice.   Well, there be waies to reach her yet: such likenesse
As you two carry me thinkes——

Dorothy.   I am mad too,
And yet can apprehend ye: fare ye well,
The foole shall now fish for himselfe.

Alice.   Be sure then
His tewgh be tith and strong: and next no swearing,
He'l catch no fish else. Farewell *Doll.*

Dorothy.   Farewell *Alice.*

                                                        Exeunt.

            Enter Valentine, Alice, *and* Cellide.   II. i

Cellide.   Indeed he's much chang'd, extreamely alter'd,
His colour faded strangely too.

Valentine.   The ayre,
The sharpe and nipping ayre of our new clymat
I hope is all, which will as well restore
To health againe th'affected body by it,

            II.i] *Actus Secundus, Scena Prima.* Q

                              442

And make it stronger far, as leave it dangerous;
How do's my sweet, our blessed houre comes on now
Apace my *Cellide*, (it knocks at dore)
In which our loves, and long desires like rivers
Rising asunder far, shall fall together: 10
Within these two daies deere——
Cellide.   When heaven, and you sir
Shall think it fit: for by your wils I am govern'd.
Alice. 'Twere good some preparation——

Enter Francis.

Valentine.   All that may be:
It shall be no blinde wedding: and all the joy
Of all our friends I hope: he lookes worse hourely:
How do's my friend, my selfe? he sweats too coldly,
His pulse, like the slow dropping of a spowt,
Scarce gives his function: how is't man, alas sir,
You looke extreme ill: is it any old griefe,
The weight of which?
Francis.   None, gentle sir, that I feele: 20
Your love is too too tender.
Nay beleeve sir——
Cellide. You cannot be the master of your health,
Either some feaver lyes in wait to catch ye,
Whose harbingers already in your face
We see preparing: or some discontent,
Which if it lye in this house, I dare say
Doth for this noble Gentleman, and all
That live within it, shall as readily
Be purg'd away, and with as much care soften'd,   30
And where the cause is.
Francis.   'Tis a joy to be ill,
Where such a vertuous faire Physitian
Is ready to releeve: your noble cares

*10–11 together, | ...deere——] ~, | ...~ . Q, F2
11 two] L; too Q, F2
25 harbingers] S; harbinger's Q, F2, L

I must, and ever shall be thankfull for,
And would my service (I dare not looke upon her)
But be not fearefull, I feele nothing dangerous,
A grudging caus'd by th'alteration
Of ayre, may hang upon me: my heart's whole,
(I would it were).
Valentine.   I knew the cause to be so.
Francis [aside].   No, you shall never know it.
Alice.   Some warme broths 40
  To purge the bloud, and keep your bed a day Sir,
  And sweat it out.
Cellide.   I have such cordials,
  That if you will but promise me to take 'em,
  Indeed you shall be well, and very quickly,
  I'le be your Doctor, you shall see how finely
  I'le fetch ye up againe.
Valentine.   He sweats extreamely:
  Hot, very hot: his pulse beats like a drum now,
  Feele sister, feele: feele sweet.
Francis [aside].   How that touch stung me?
Valentine.   My gowne there.
Cellide.   And those julips in the window.
Alice.   Some see his bed made.
Valentine.   This is most unhappy,   50
  Take courage man, 'tis nothing but an ague.
Cellide.   And this shall be the last fit.
Francis [aside].   Not by thousands:
  Now what 'tis to be truely miserable,
  I feele at full experience.
Alice.   He growes fainter.
Valentine.   Come, leade him in, he shall to bed: a vomit,
  I'le have a vomit for him.
Alice.   A purge first,
  And if he breath'd a veyne——
Valentine.   No, no, no bleeding,
  A Clyster will coole all.
Cellide.   Be of good cheere Sir.

Alice.   He's loth to speake.
Cellide.   How hard he holds my hand Aunt?
Alice.   I doe not like that signe.
Valentine.   Away to's chamber,   60
Softly, he's full of paine, be diligent
With all the care ye have: would I had scus'd him.

                                                        Exeunt.

                    Enter Dorothy *and* Thomas.   [II.] ii

Dorothy.   Why do you raile at me? do I dwell in her
To force her to do this or that? your Letter,
A wilde-fire on your Letter; your sweet Letter;
You are so learned in your writs: ye stand now
As if ye had worried sheepe: you must turne tippet,
And suddenly, and truely, and discreetly
Put on the shape of order and humanity,
Or you must marry *Malkyn* the May Lady:
You must, deere brother: doe you make me carrier
Of your confound-mee's, and your culverings?   10
Am I a seemely agent for your othes?
Who would have writ such a debosh'd——
Thomas.   Your patience,
May not a man professe his Love?
Dorothy.   In blasphemies?
Rack a maids tender eares, with dam's and divels?
Out, out upon thee.
Thomas.   How would you have me write?
Begin with my love premised? surely,
And by my truly Mistresse?
Dorothy.   Take your owne course
For I see all perswasions lost upon ye:
Humanitie, all drownd: from this howre fayrely

        II.ii] *Scena Secunda.* Q   *3 your sweet] F2; our sweet Q
        15 Out...thee.] S; *Thom.* Out...thee. Q, F2, L
        15 *Thomas.* How] S; how Q, F2, L
        18 perswasions] Q(u); perswasion's Q(c)

Ile wash may hands of all ye do: farewell Sir.　　　　　　20
Thomas.　　Thou art not mad?
Dorothy.　　　　　　　　　　No, if I were, deere brother
I would keep you company: get a new Mistresse
Som suburb Sant, that six pence, and som othes
Will draw to parley: carowse her health in Cans
And candles ends, and quarrell for her beauty,
Such a sweet hart must serve your turne: your old love
Releases ye of all your tyes; disclaimes ye
And utterly abjures your memory
Till time has better mannag'd ye.
Will ye comand me———　　　　　　　　　　　30
Thomas.　　What, bobd of all sides?
Dorothy.　　　　　　　　　　———any worthy service
Unto my father sir, that I may tell him
Even to his peace of heart, and much rejoycing
Ye are his true son *Thom* still? will it please ye
To beat some halfe a dozen of his servants presently
That I may testifie you have brought the same faith
Unblemishd home, ye carried out? or if it like you
There be two chambermaids within, yong wenches,
Handsom and apt for exercise: you have bin good, sir,　　40
And charitable though I say it Signiour
To such poore orphans: and now, by th' way I think on't
Your yong reare Admirall, I meane your last bastard
Don John, ye had by Lady *Blanch* the Dairy Maid,
Is by an Academy of learned Gypsies,
Foreseeing some strange wonder in the infant
Stolne from the Nurse, and wanders with those Prophets.
There is plate in the parlour, and good store sir,
When your wants shall supply it. So most humbly
(First rendring my due service) I take leave sir.　　*Exit.* 50
Thomas.　　Why *Doll*, why *Doll* I say: my letter fubd too,
And no accesse without I mend my manners?

20 Ile...Sir.] F2; *Tho.* Ile...Sir. Q　　21 *Thomas.* Thou] F2; Thou Q
23 othes] S; others Q, F2, L
*29–30 Till...ye. | Will...me———] *this ed.; one line* Q, F2, L+
*49 your wants] *stet* Q

All my designes in Limbo? I will have her,
Yes, I will have her, though the divell rore,
I am resolv'd that, if she live above ground,
I'le not be bobd i'th nose with every bobtaile:
I will be civill too: now I thinke better,
Exceeding civill, wondrous finely carried:
And yet be mad upon occasion,
And starke mad too, and save my land: my father: 60
I'le have my will of him, how ere my wench goes.

                                        Exit.

               Enter Sebastian *and* Launcelot.   [II. iii]

Sebastian.   Sirha, I say:
  Still you have spoild your Master: leave your stiches:
  I say thou hast spoild thy master.
Launcelot.   I say how sir?
Sebastian.   Marry thou hast taught him like an arrant rascall,
  First to reade perfectly: which on my blessing
  I warn'd him from: for I knew if he read once,
  He was a lost man. Secondly, sir *Launcelot,*
  Sir lowsie *Launcelot,* ye have suffer'd him
  Against my power first, then against my precept,
  To keepe that simpring sort of people company,   10
  That sober men call civill: marke ye that Sir?
Launcelot.   And't please your worship——
Sebastian.   It does not please my worship,
  Nor shall not please my worship: third and lastly,
  Which if the law were here, I would hang thee for,
  (However I will lame thee) like a villaine,
  Thou hast wrought him
  Cleane to forget what 'tis to doe a mischiefe,
  A handsome mischiefe, such as thou knew'st I lov'd well.
  My servants all are sound now, my drink sowrd,
  Not a horse pawnd, nor plaid away: no warrants   20
  Come for the breach of peace.

                II.iii] W; *om.* Q, F2, L–C

Men travell with their money, and nothing meets 'em:
I was accurs'd to send thee, thou wert ever
Leaning to lazinesse, and losse of spirit,
Thou slept'st still like a corke upon the water.
Launcelot.   Your worship knowes, I ever was accounted
The most debosh'd, and please you to remember,
Every day drunke too, for your worships credit,
I broke the Butlers head too.
Sebastian.   No base Palliard
I doe remember yet that anslaight, thou wast beaten,   30
And fledst before the Butler: a blacke jacke
Playing upon thee furiously, I saw it:
I saw thee scatter'd rogue; behold thy Master.

Enter Thomas *with a Booke.*

Thomas.   What sweet content dwels here?
Launcelot.   Put up your booke sir,
We are all undone else.
Sebastian.   *Tom*, when is the horse-race?
Thomas.   I know not sir.
Sebastian.   You will be there?
Thomas.   Not I sir,
I have forgot those journeyes.
Sebastian.   Spoild for ever,——
The cocking holds at *Derby*, and there will be
Jacke Wild-oats, and *Will* Purser.
Thomas.   I am sorry sir,
They should employ their time so slenderly,   40
Their understandings will beare better courses.
Sebastian [*aside*].   Yes, I will marry agen:——
                                        but Monsieur *Thomas*,
What say ye to the gentleman that challenged ye
Before ye went, and the fellow ye fell out with?
Thomas.   O good Sir,

26 *Launcelot.*] F2; *om.* Q
30 anslaight] *stet* Q, F2, D; *i.e.* onslaught L–W, V
44 ¹ye] C; he Q, F2, L, S

448

Remember not those follies: where I have wronged sir,
(So much I have now learn'd to discern my selfe)
My meanes, and my repentance shall make even,
Nor do I thinke it any imputation
To let the law perswade me.
Sebastian [aside].　　　　　　Any woman:　　　　　50
　I care not of what colour, or complexion,
　Any that can beare children:——rest ye merry.　　　Exit.
Launcelot.　Ye have utterly undone, cleane discharg'd me:
　I am for the ragged regiment.
Thomas.　　　　　　　　Eight languages,
　And wither at an old mans words?
Launcelot.　　　　　　　　O pardon me.
I know him but too well: eight score I take it
Will not keepe me from beating, if not killing:
I'le give him leave to breake a leg, and thank him:
You might have sav'd all this, and sworn a little.
What had an oath or two bin? or a head broke,　　　60
Though t'had been mine, to have satisfied the old man?
Thomas.　I'le breake it yet.
Launcelot.　　　　　　　Now 'tis too late, I take it:
　Will ye be drunk to night, (a lesse intreaty
　Has serv'd your turne) and save all yet? not mad drunk,
　For then ye are the divell, yet the drunker,
　The better for your father still: your state is desperate,
　And with a desperate cure ye must recover it:
　Doe something, doe sir: doe some drunken thing,
　Some mad thing, or some any thing to help us.
Thomas.　Goe for a Fidler then: the poore old Fidler　70
　That sayes his songs: but first where lyes my Mistresse,
　Did ye enquire out that?
Launcelot.　　　　　I'th Lodge, alone sir,
　None but her owne attendantes.
Thomas.　　　　　　　'Tis the happier:
　Away then, finde this Fidler, and doe not misse me
　By nine a clocke.
Launcelot.　　Via.　　　　　　　　　Exit.

Thomas.   My father's mad now,
And ten to one will disinherite me:
I'le put him to his plunge, and yet be merry.
What *Rybabalde?*

Enter Hylas *and* Sam.

Hylas.   *Don Thomasio.*
De bene venew.
Thomas.   I doe embrace your body:
How do'st thou *Sam.*
Sam.   The same *Sam* still: your friend sir.   80
Thomas.   And how is't bouncing boyes?
Hylas.   Thou art not alter'd,
They said thou wert all Monsieur.
Thomas.   O beleeve it,
I am much alter'd, much another way:
The civil'st Gentleman in all your Country:
Doe not ye see me alter'd? yea, and nay Gentlemen,
A much converted man: wher's the best wine boyes?
Hylas.   A sound Convertite.
Thomas.   What hast thou made up twenty yet?
Hylas.   By'r Lady,
I have giv'n a shrewd push at it, for as I take it,
The last I fell in love with, scor'd sixteene.   90
Thomas.   Look to your skin, *Rambaldo* the sleeping Gyant
Will rowze, and rent thee piece-meale.
Sam.   He nev'r perceives 'em
Longer then looking on.
Thomas.   Thou never meanest then
To marry any that thou lov'st?
Hylas.   No surely,
Nor any wise man I thinke; marriage?
Would you have me now begin to be prentize,
And learne to cobble other mens old boots?
Sam.   Why you may take a Maid.
Hylas.   Where? can you tell me?

85 yea] F 2; ye Q

450

Or if 'twere possible I might get a Maid,
To what use should I put her? looke upon her,   100
Dandle her upon my knee, and give her suger sops?
All the new gowns i'th parish will not please her,
If she be high bred, for ther's the sport she aymes at,
Nor all the feathers in the Fryars.
Thomas.   Then take a widow,
A good stanch wench, that's tith.
Hylas.   And begin a new order,
Live in a dead mans monument, not I sir,
I'le keep mine old road, a true mendicant:
What pleasure this day yeelds me, I never covet
To lay up for the morrow: and me thinks ever
Another mans cooke dresses my dyet neatest.   110
Thomas.   Thou wast wont to love old women, fat, and flat
    nosed,
And thou wouldst say they kist like Flounders, flat
All the face over.
Hylas.   I have had such damsels
I must confesse.
Thomas.   Thou hast been a pretious rogue.
Sam.   Onely his eyes: and o' my conscience
They lye with half the kingdome.

                Enter over the stage, Physitians *and others.*

Thomas.   What's the matter?
Whither goe all these men-menders, these Physitians?
Whooo dog lyes sicke o'th mulligrubs?
Sam.   O the Gentleman,
The yong smug Signiour, Master *Valentine*
Brought out of travell with him, as I heare   120
Is falne sick o'th sudden, desperate sicke,
And likely they goe thither.
Thomas.   Who? yong *Frank*?
The onely temper'd spirit, Scholler, Souldier,
Courtier: and all in one piece? 'tis not possible.

                105 that's] F2; that Q

                451

Enter Alice.

Sam.   Ther's one can better satisfie you.
Thomas.   Mistresse *Alice*,
  I joy to see you Lady.
Alice.   Good Monsieur *Thomas*,
  You'r welcome from your travell: I am hasty,
  A Gentleman lies sicke sir.
Thomas.   And how do'st thou?
  I must know, and I will know.
Alice.   Excellent well,
  As well as may be, thank ye.
Thomas.   I am glad on't,   130
  And prethee harke——
Alice.   I cannot stay.
Thomas.   ——a while *Alice*.
Sam.   Never looke so narrowly, the mark's in her mouth still.
Hylas.   I am looking at her legs, prethee be quiet.
Alice.   I cannot stay.
Thomas.   O sweet *Alice*——
Hylas.   A cleane instep,
  And that I love a life: I did not marke
  This woman half so well before, how quicke
  And nimble like a shadow, there her leg shew'd:
  By th' mas a neat one, the colour of her stocking,
  A much inviting colour.
Alice.   My good Monsieur,
  I have no time to talke now.
Hylas.   Pretty breeches,   140
  Finely becomming too.
Thomas.   By heaven——
Alice.   She will not,
  I can assure you that, and so——
Thomas.   But this word——
Alice.   I cannot, nor I will not: good Lord.   *Exit.*
Hylas.   Well you shall heare more from me.

*135 a]'stet Q

452

Thomas.   Wee'll goe visite,
'Tis charity: besides I know she is there:
And under visitation I shall see hir.
Will ye along?
Hylas.   By any meanes.
Thomas.   Be sure then
I be a civill man: I have a sport in hand boyes
Shall make mirth for a marriage day.
Hylas.   Away then.

                                        Exeunt.

          Enter three Physitians *with an Urinall.*   [II.] iv

1. Phisitian. A Plurisie. I see it.
2. Phisitian.   I rather hold it
For *tremor cordis.*
3. Phisitian.   Doe you marke the Pheses?
'Tis a most pestilent contagious feaver,
A surfet, a plaguy surfet: he must bleed.
1. Phisitian. By no meanes.
3. Phisitian.   I say bleed.
1. Phisitian.   I say 'tis dangerous:
The person being spent so much before hand,
And nature drawne so low: clysters, coole clysters.
2. Phisitian. Now with your favours, I should think a vomit:
For take away the cause, the effect must follow,
The stomack's foule and fur'd, the pot's unflam'd yet.   10
3. Phisitian. No, no, wee'l rectifie that part by milde meanes.
Nature so sunke, must finde no violence.

                    Enter a Servant.

Servant. Wilt please ye draw neere? the weake gentleman
Growes worse and worse still.
1. Phisitian.   Come, we will attend him.
2. Phisitian. He shall doe well my friend.

          II.iv] W; *Scæna Tertia* Q, F2, L–C
          *2 Pheses] *stet* Q   *10 unflam'd] *stet* Q

Servant.   My masters love sir.
1. Phisitian.   Excellent well I warrant thee, right and straight
friend.
3. Phisitian.   Ther's no doubt in him, none at all, nev'r feare
him.

                                             Exeunt.

                   Enter Valentine *and* Michael.   [II.] v

Michael.   That he is desperate sick, I do beleeve well,
   And that without a speedy cure, it kils him;
   But that it lyes within the helpe of physicke,
   Now to restore his health, or art to cure him:
   Beleeve it you are cosened: cleane beside it.
   I would tell ye the true cause too, but 'twould vexe ye,
   Nay, run ye mad.
Valentine.   May all I have restore him?
   So deerly and so tenderly I love him,
   I doe not know the cause why, yea my life too.
Michael.   Now I perceive ye so well set, I'le tell you,   10
   Hei mihi quod nullis amor, est medicabilis herbis.
Valentine.   'Twas that I onely fear'd: good friend go from me,
   I finde my heart too full for further conference:
   You are assur'd of this?
Michael.   'Twill prove too certaine,
   But beare it nobly sir, youth hath his errors.
Valentine.   I shall do, and I thank ye: pray ye no words on't.
Michael.   I doe not use to talke sir.   *Exit.*
Valentine.   Ye are welcome:
   Is there no constancy in earthly things:
   No happinesse in us, but what must alter,
   No life without the heavy load of fortune?   20
   What miseries we are, and to our selves,
   Even then when full content seemes to sit by us,
   What daily sores, and sorrowes?

                   II.v] W; *Scena Quarta.* Q, F2, L–C
                   17 *Michael.*] F2; *om.* Q

Enter Alice.

Alice.   O deere brother,
The Gentleman if ever you will see him
Alive as I think——

Enter Cellide.

Cellide.   O he faints, for heaven sake,
For heaven sake sir——
Valentine.   Goe comfort him deere sister.
                                              Exit Alice.
And one word sweet, with you: then we'l go to him.
What think you of this Gentleman?
Cellide.   My pity thinks sir,
'Tis great misfortune, that he should thus perish.
Valentine. It is indeed: but *Cellide*, he must dye.   30
Cellide. That were a cruelty, when care may cure him,
Why doe you weep so sir, he may recover?
Valentine. He may, but with much danger: my sweet *Cellide*
You have a powerfull tongue.
Cellide.   To doe you service.
Valentine. I will betray his griefe: he loves a gentlewoman,
A friend of yours, whose heart another holds,
He knowes it too: yet such a sway blinde fancy,
And his not daring to deliver it,
Have won upon him, that they must undoe him:
Never so hopefull and so sweet a spirit,   40
Misfortune fell so foule on.
Cellide.   Sure she's hard hearted,
That can looke on, and not relent, and deeply
At such a misery: she is not married?
Valentine. Not yet.
Cellide.   Nor neere it?
Valentine.   When she please.
Cellide.   And pray sir,
Do's he deserve her truely, that she loves so?
Valentine. His love may merit much: his person little,

For there the match lyes mangled.

Cellide. Is he your friend?

Valentine. He should be, for he is neere me.

Cellide. Will not he dye then?
When th'other shall recover?

Valentine. Ye have pos'd me.

Cellide. Me thinks he should go neere it, if he love her; 50
If she love him——

Valentine. She do's, and would doe equall.

Cellide. 'Tis a hard taske you put me: yet for your sake
I will speake to her: all the art I have:
My best endevors: all his youth, and person,
His mind more full of beauties: all his hopes,
The memory of such a sad example,
Ill spoken of, and never old: the curses
Of loving maids, and what may be aleagd
Ile lay before her: what's her name? I am ready.

Valentine. But will you deale effectually?

Cellide. Most truly: 60
Nay were it my selfe, at your entreaty.

Valentine. And could ye be so pittifull?

Cellide. So dutifull;
Because you urge it sir.

Valentine. It may be then
It is your selfe.

Cellide. It is in deed, I know it:
And now know how ye love me.

Valentine. O my dearest,
Let but your goodnesse judge: your owne part: pitty:
Set but your eyes on his afflictions:
He is mine, and so becomes your charge: but thinke
What ruine nature suffers in this yong man,
What losse humanity, and noble manhood: 70
Take to your better judgement my declining,
My age, hung full of impotence, and ils,
My body budding now no more: seere winter

58 aleagd] Q(u); alleag'd Q(c)

Hath seal'd that sap up, at the best and happiest
I can but be your infant: you my nurse,
And how unequall deerest: where his yeeres,
His sweetnesse, and his ever spring of goodnesse,
My fortunes growing in him, and my selfe too,
Which makes him all your old love: misconceive not,
I say not this, as weary of my bondage,   80
Or ready to infringe my faith: beare witnesse,
Those eyes that I adore still, those lamps that light me
To all the joy I have.
Cellide.   You have said enough sir,
And more then ere I thought that tongue could utter,
But ye are a man, a false man too.
Valentine.   Deere *Cellide.*
Cellide.   And now, to shew you that I am a woman
Rob'd of her rest, and fool'd out of her fondnesse,
The Gentleman shall live: and if he love me,
Ye shall be both my triumphs: I will to him,
And as you carelesly fling off your fortune,   90
And now grow weary of my casie winning,
So will I lose the name of *Valentine,*
From henceforth all his flatteries, and beleeve it,
Since ye have so slightly parted with affection,
And that affection you have pawn'd your faith for:
From this houre, no repentance, vowes, nor prayers
Shall plucke me backe agen: what I shall doe,
(Yet I will undertake his cure, expect it,)
Shall minister no comfort, no content
To either of ye, but hourely more vexations   100
Valentine.   Why let him dye then.
Cellide.   No, so much I have loved
To be commanded by you, that even now,
Even in my hate I will obey your wishes.
Valentine.   What shall I doe? Dye like a foole unsorrow'd?
A bankrupt foole, that flings away his treasure?

94 so] F2; so so Q
*104 Dye] *this ed.*; *Cellide.* Dye Q, F2, L+

Cellide. I must begin my cure.
Valentine. And I my crosses. *Exeunt.*

Enter Francis *sick*, Physitians, *and* a Pothecary. III. i

1. Phisitian. Clap on the Cataplasme.
Francis. Good Gentlemen,
Good learned Gentlemen——
2. Phisitian. And see those brothes there,
Ready within this houre: pray keep your armes in,
The ayre is raw, and ministers much evill.
Francis. Pray leave me: I beseech ye leave me gentlemen,
I have no other sicknesse but your presence,
Convey your Cataplasmes to those that need 'em,
Your Vomits, and your Clysters.
3. Phisitian. Pray be rul'd sir.
1. Phisitian. Bring in the Lettice cap: you must be shaved sir,
And then how suddenly wee'l make you sleep. 10
Francis. Till doomes-day: what unnecessary nothings
Are these about a wounded minde?
2. Phisitian. How doe ye?
Francis. What questions they propound too: how do you sir?
I am glad to see you well.
3. Phisitian. A great distemper, it growes hotter still.
1. Phisitian. Open your mouth I pray sir.
Francis. And can you tell me
How old I am then? there's my hand, pray shew me
How many broken shins within this two yeare.
Who would be thus in fetters, good master Doctor,
And you deere Doctor, and the third sweet Doctor, 20
And pretious master Apothecary, I doe pray ye
To give me leave to live a little longer,
Ye stand before me like my blacks.
2. Phisitian. 'Tis dangerous,
For now his fancy turnes too.

106 *Cellide.*] *this ed.; om.* Q, F2, L+
III.i] *Actus Tertius, Scena Prima.* Q   0.1 Francis] L; *Franck* Q, F2

Enter Cellide.

Cellide.   By your leave Gentlemen:
And pray ye your leave a while too, I have something
Of secret to impart unto the patient.
1. Phisitian.   With all our hearts.
3. Phisitian.   I mary such a Physicke
May chance to find the humour: be not long Lady,
For we must minister within this halfe houre.
                                Exeunt Physitians [*and* Apothecary].
Cellide.   You shall not stay for me.
Francis.   Would you were all rotten   30
That ye might only intend one anothers itches:
Or would the Gentlemen with one consent
Would drinke small Beere but seven yeare, and abolish
That wild fire of the bloud, unsatiate wenching,
That your two Indies, springs and fals might faile ye;
What torments these intruders into bodies.
Cellide.   How do you worthy Sir?
Francis.   Blesse me, what beames
Flew from these angell eyes: O what a misery,
What a most studdied torment tis to me now
To be an honest man: dare ye sit by me?   40
Cellide.   Yes; and do more then that too: comfort ye,
I see ye have need.
Francis.   You are a faire Physitian:
You bring no bitternesse gilt ore, to gull us,
No danger in your lookes, yet there my death lyes.
Cellide.   I would be sorry sir, my charity
And my good wishes for your health should merit
So stubborne a construction: will it please ye
To taste a little of this Cordiall——

                    Enter Valentine [*apart*].

For this I thinke must cure ye.
Francis.   Of which Lady?
——Sure she has found my griefe?——why do you blush so?   50

Cellide. Do you not understand? of this, this Cordiall.

[*Kisses him.*]

Valentine. O my afflicted heart: she is gon for ever.

Francis. What heaven ye have brought me Lady?

Cellide. Do not wonder:
For tis not impudence, nor want of honour
Makes me do this: but love to save your life sir,
Your life, too excellent to loose in wishes,
Love, virtuous love.

Francis. A vertuous blessing crowne ye:
O goodly sweet, can there be so much charity,
So noble a compassion in that heart
That's filled up with anothers faire affections? 60
Can mercy drop from those eyes?
Can miracles be wrought upon a dead man,
When all the power ye have, and perfect object
Lyes in anothers light: and his deserves it?

Cellide. Do not dispaire: nor do not thinke to boldly
I dare abuse my promise: 'twas your friends
And so fast tyde, I thought no time could ruine:
But so much has your danger, and that spell
The powerfull name of friend, prevail'd above him
To whom I ever owe obedience, 70
That here I am, by his command to cure ye,
Nay more for ever, by his full resignement,
And willingly I ratefie it.

Francis. Hold for heaven sake,
Must my friends misery make me a triumph?
Beare I that noble name, to be a Traitor?
O vertuous goodnes, keepe thy selfe untainted:
You have no power to yeeld, nor he to render,
Nor I to take: I am resolv'd to die first.

Valentine. Ha; saist thou so? nay then thou shalt not perish.

Francis. And though I love ye above the light shines on me, 80
Beyond the wealth of Kingdomes, free content
Sooner would snatch at such a blessing offer'd

52 O] F2; Of Q

Then at my pardon'd life by the law forfeited:
Yet, yet O noble beauty, yet O paradise,
For you are all the wonder reveal'd of it,
Yet is a gratitude to be preserv'd,
A worthy gratitude to one most worthy
The name, and noblenes of friend.
Cellide.   Pray tell me
If I had never knowne that gentleman
Would you not willingly embrace my offer?   90
Francis.   Do you make a doubt?
Cellide.   And can ye be unwilling
He being old and impotent: his aime too
Levell'd at you, for your good? not constrain'd,
But out of cure, and councell? alas consider,
Play but the woman with me, and consider
As he himselfe do's, and I now dare see it,
Truly consider sir, what misery——
Francis.   For vertues sake take heed.
Cellide.   What losse of youth,
What everlasting banishment from that
Our yeares doe only covet to arive at,   100
Equall affections aim'd and shot together:
What living name can dead age leave behind him,
What art of memory but fruitlesse doating?
Francis.   This cannot be.
Cellide.   To you unlesse ye apply it
With more and firmer faith, and so digest it:
I speake but of things possible, not done
Nor like to be: a posset cures your sicknesse
And yet I know ye grieve this; and howsoever
The worthines of Friend may make ye stagger,
Which is a faire thing in ye, yet my Patient,   110
My gentle Patient, I would faine say more
If you would understand.
Valentine.   O cruell Woman.

88 friend] D; friends Q–W   *101 aim'd] V; *om.* Q
*103 art of memory] *stet* Q

Cellide. Yet sure your sicknesse is not so forgetfull
Nor you so willing to be lost.
Francis.   Pray stay there:
Me thinks you are not faire now; me thinks more
That modest vertue men delivered of you
Shewes but like shadow to me, thin, and fading.
Valentine. Excellent Friend.
Francis.   Ye have no share in goodnesse:
Ye are belyde; you are not *Cellide,*
The modest, imaculate: who are ye?   120
For I will know: what devill to do mischiefe
Unto my vertuous Friend, hath shifted shapes
With that unblemished beauty.
Cellide.   Do not rave Sir,
Nor let the violence of thoughts distract ye,
You shall enjoy me: I am yours: I pitty,
By those faire eyes I do.
Francis.   O double hearted,
O woman, perfect woman: what distraction
Was meant to mankind when thou was't made a devill,
What an invyting hell invented? tell me,
And if you yet remember what is goodnesse,   130
Tell me by that, and truth, can one so cherish'd
So sainted in the soule of him, whose service
Is almost turn'd to supperstition,
Whose every day endeavours, and desires
Offer themselves like incense on your altar,
Whose heart holds no intelligence, but holy
And most religious with his love; whose life
(And let it ever be remembred Lady)
Is drawne out only for your ends——
Valentine.   O miracle.
Francis. Whose all, and every part of man: pray marke me: 140
Like ready Pages wait upon your pleasures;
Whose breath is but your bubble: Can ye, dare ye,

120 imaculate] F2; unaculate Q   140 marke] S; make Q, F2, L
143 of] *i.e.* off F2

462

Must ye cast of this man—though he were willing,
Though in a noblenes, to crosse my danger
His friendship durst confirme it—without basenesse,
Without the staine of honour? shall not people
Say liberally hereafter, ther's the Lady
That lost her Father, Friend, herselfe, her faith too,
To fawne upon a stranger, for ought you know
As faithlesse as your selfe, in love as fruitlesse?   150
Valentine.   Take her with all my heart, thou art so honest
That tis most necessary I be undone:
With all my soule possesse her.   *Exit* Valentine.
Cellide.   Till this minut
I scorn'd, and hated ye, and came to cosen ye:
Utter'd those things might draw a wonder on me,
To make ye mad.
Francis.   Good heaven, what is this woman?
Cellide.   Nor did your danger, but in charity,
Move me a whit: nor you appeare unto me
More then a common object, yet, now truely,
Truely, and nobly I doe love ye deerely,   160
And from this houre, ye are the man I honour,
You are the man, the excellence, the honesty,
The onely friend, and I am glad your sicknesse
Fell so most happily at this time on ye,
To make this truth the worlds.
Francis.   Whether doe you drive me?
Cellide.   Backe to your honesty, make that good ever,
'Tis like a strong built Castle, seated high,
That drawes on all ambitions, still repaire it,
Still fortifie it: there are thousand foes
Besides the tyrant beauty, will assaile it: 170
Looke to your Centinels that watch it hourely,
Your eyes, let them not wander.
Francis.   Is this serious?
Or do's she play still with me?

144 to] L; so Q, F2   153 With] S; *Cellide.* With Q, F2, L
153 *Cellide.*] S; *om.* Q, F2, L   173 Or] F2; *Cellide.* Or Q

Cellide.   Keep your eares,
The two maine ports that may betray ye, strongly
From light beliefe first, then from flattery,
Especially where woman beats the parley:
The body of your strength, your noble heart
From ever yeelding to dishonest ends,
Rigd round about with vertue, that no breaches,
No subtle mynes may meet ye.
Francis.   How like the Sun   180
Labouring in his eclipse, darke, and prodigious,
She shew'd till now? when having won his way,
How full of wonder he breakes out again,
And sheds his vertuous beames: excellent Angell,
For no lesse can that heavenly minde proclaime thee,
Honour of all thy sexe, let it be lawfull,
And like a pilgrim thus I kneele to beg it,
Not with prophane lips now, nor burnt affections,
But, reconcil'd to faith, with holy wishes,
To kisse that virgin hand.
Cellide.   Take your desire sir,   190
And in a nobler way, for I dare trust ye,
No other fruit my love must ever yeeld yee,
I feare no more: yet your most constant memory
(So much I am wedded to that worthinesse)
Shall ever be my friend, companion, husband;
Farewell, and fairely governe your affections,
Stand, and deceive me not: [*aside*] O noble yong man,
I love thee with my soule, but dare not say it:——
Once more farewell, and prosper.   *Exit.*
Francis.   Goodnesse guide thee:
My wonder like to fearefull shapes in dreames,   200
Has wakened me out of my fit of folly,
But not to shake it off: a spell dwels in me,
A hidden charme shot from this beauteous woman,
That fate can ne'r avoid, nor physicke finde,
And by her counsell strengthen'd: onely this

173 *Cellide.*] F2; *om.* Q   179 Rigd] *i.e.* Ridg'd L   182 his] L; her Q, F2

Is all the helpe I have, I love faire vertue.
Well, something I must doe, to be a friend,
Yet I am poore, and tardy: something for her too,
Though I can never reach her excellence,
Yet but to give an offer at a greatnesse.   210

  Enter Valentine, Thomas, Hylas, *and* Sam.

Valentine. Be not uncivill *Tom*, and take your pleasure.
Thomas. Doe you think I am mad? you'l give me leave
To try her fairely?
Valentine.   Doe your best.
Thomas.   Why there boy,——
But wher's the sicke man?
Hylas.   Where are the gentlewomen
That should attend him, ther's the patient.
Me thinks these women——
Thomas.   Thou thinkst nothing else.
Valentine. Goe to him friend, and comfort him: Ile leade ye:
O my best joy, my worthiest friend, pray pardon me,
I am so over-joy'd I want expression:
I may live to be thankfull: bid your friends welcome.   220
           Exit Valentine.
Thomas. How do'st thou *Frank?* how do'st thou boy, beare up
 man:
What, shrink i'th sinewes for a little sicknesse?
Deavolo morte.
Francis. I am o'th mending hand.
Thomas. How like a Flute thou speak'st: o'th mending hand
 man:
Gogs bores, I am well, speake like a man of worship.
Francis. Thou art a mad companion: never staid *Tom?*
Thomas. Let rogues be staid that have no habitation,
A gentleman may wander: sit thee down *Frank*,
And see what I have brought thee: come discover,
Open the sceane, and let the work appeare,   230
A friend at need you rogue is worth a million.

   215 patient] F2; patent Q

      465

Francis.   What hast thou there, a julip?
Hylas.   He must not touch it,
'Tis present death.
Thomas.   Ye are an Asse, a twirepipe,
A *Jeffrey John bo peepe*: thou minister?
Thou mend a left-handed pack-saddle? out puppey:
My friend *Frank*, but a very foolish fellow:
Do'st thou see that bottle? view it well.
Francis.   I doe *Tom*.
Thomas.   There be as many lives in't, as a Cat carries,
'Tis everlasting liquor.
Francis.   What?
Thomas.   Old Sack boy,
Old reverend Sack, which for ought that I can reade yet,   240
Was that Philosophers Stone the wise King *Ptolomeus*
Did all his wonders by.
Francis.   I see no harme *Tom*,
Drinke with a moderation.
Thomas.   Drinke with suger,
Which I have ready here, and here a glasse boy:
Take me without my tooles.
Sam.   Pray sir be temperate,
You know your owne state best.
Francis.   Sir, I much thanke ye,
And shall be carefull: yet a glasse or two
So fit I finde my body, and that so needfull.
Thomas.   Fill it, and leave your fooling: thou say'st true *Frank*.
Hylas.   Where are these women I say?
Thomas.   Tis most necessary,   250
Hang up your julips, and your portugall possets,
Your barly brothes, and sorrell sops, they are mangy,
And breed the scratches onely: give me Sack:
I wonder where this wench is though: have at thee.
Hylas.   So long, and yet no bolting?
Francis.   Doe, I'le pledge thee.
Thomas.   Take it off thrice, and then cry heigh like a Huntsman

234 minister] C; mimister Q, F2, L–S

466

With a cleere heart, and no more fits I warrant thee.
The onely Cordiall *Frank*.

Phisitians *within, and* Servant.

1. Phisitian.   Are the things ready?
And is the Barber come?
Servant.   An houre agoe sir.
1. Phisitian.   Bring out the oyles then.
Francis.   Now or never, gentlemen,   260
Doe me a kindnesse and deliver me.
Thomas.   From whom boy?
Francis.   From these things, that talke within there,
Physitians, *Tom*, Physitians, scowring-sticks,
They meane to reade upon me.
Enter three Phisitians, Apothecary, *and* Barber.
Hylas.   Let 'em enter.
Thomas.   And be thou confident, we will deliver thee:
For looke ye Doctor, say the divell were sicke now,
His hornes saw'd off and his head bound with a Biggin,
Sicke of a calenture, taken by a surfet
Of stinking soules at his nephews, and Saint *Dunstans*,
What would you minister upon the sudden?   270
Your judgement short and sound.
1. Phisitian.   A fooles head.
Thomas.   No sir,
It must be a Physitians for three causes,
The first because it is a bald head likely,
Which will down easily without apple-pap.
3. Phisitian.   A main cause.
Thomas.   So it is, and well consider'd;
The second, for 'tis fil'd with broken Greek sir,
Which will so tumble in his stomacke, Doctor,
And worke upon the crudities, conceive me,
The feares, and the fidle strings within it,
That those damn'd soules must disembogue againe.   280
Hylas.   Or meeting with the stygian humour——
Thomas.   Right sir.

467

Hylas.   Forc'd with a cataplasme of crackers——
Thomas.   Ever.
Hylas.   Scowre all before him, like a Scavenger.
Thomas.   *Satis fecisti domine:* my last cause,
  My last is, and not least, most learned Doctors,
  Because in most Physitians heads (I meane those
  That are most excellent, and old withall,
  And angry, though a patient say his prayers,
  And *Paracelsians* that doe trade with poysons)
  We have it by tradition of great writers,   290
  There is a kinde of toad-stone bread, whose vertue
  The Doctor being dri'd——
1. Phisitian.   We are abus'd sirs.
Hylas [*aside*].   I take it so, or shall be:——for, say, the
  belly-ake
Caus'd by an inundation of Pease-porridge,
Are we therefore to open the port veyne,
Or the port Esquiline?
Sam.   A learned question.
Hylas.   Or grant the diaphragma by a rupture,
  The signe being then in the head of *Capricorne*——
Thomas.   Meet with the passion Hupercondriaca,
  And so cause a carnositie in the kidneyes——   300
Hylas.   Must not the brains, being butter'd with this humour?
  Answer me that.
Sam.   Most excellently argued.
2. Phisitian.   The next fit you will have, my most fine scholler,
  Bedlam shall finde a salve for:——fare ye well sir,
  We came to doe you good, but these yong Doctors
  It seemes have boar'd our noses.
3. Phisitian.   Drinke hard Gentlemen,
  And get unwholesome drabs: 'tis ten to one then
  We shall heare further from ye, your note alter'd.
                      Exeunt [Phisitians, Apothecary, *and* Barber].

291 bread] *i.e.* bred *as in* F2   *293 belly-ake] *stet* Q
*297 *Hylas.*] *om.* Q   299 Hupercondriaca] *recte* Hupocondriaca
*301 *Hylas.*] *Tom.* Q   *301 humour?] *stet* Q

Thomas.   *And wilt thou be gone saies one?*
Hylas.   *And wilt thou be gone saies t'other?*   310
Thomas.   *Then take the odde crowne*
              To mend thy old gowne,
Sam.   *And we'l be gone all together.*
Francis. My learned *Tom.*

Enter Servant.

Servant.   Sir, the yong Gentlewomen
Sent me to see what company ye had with ye,
They much desire to visite ye.
Francis.   Pray ye thanke 'em,
And tell 'em my most sicknesse is their absence:
Ye see my company.
Thomas.   Come hither Crab,
What gentlewomen are these? my Mistresse?
Servant.   Yes sir.
Hylas. And who else?
Servant.   Mistresse *Alice.*
Hylas.   Oh.
Thomas.   Harke ye sirha,   320
No word of my being here, unlesse she know it.
Servant. I doe not thinke she do's.
Thomas.   Take that, and mum, then.
Servant. You have ty'd my tongue up.   *Exit.*
Thomas.   Sit you downe good *Francis,*
And not a word of me till ye heare from me,
And as you finde my humour, follow it:
You two come hither, and stand close, unseen boyes,
And doe as I shall tutor ye.
Francis.   What, new worke?
Thomas. Prethee no more, but helpe me now.
Hylas.   I would faine
Talke with the gentlewomen.
Thomas.   Talke with the gentlewomen?
Of what forsooth? whose maiden-head the last maske   330
Suffer'd impression, or whose clyster wrought best:

469

Take me as I shall tell thee.

Hylas.   To what end?
What other end came we along?

Sam.   Be rul'd though.

Thomas.   Your weezell face must needs be ferretting
About the farthingale: doe as I bid ye,
Or by this light——

Hylas.   Come then.

Thomas.   Stand close and marke me.

[*Hide* Thomas, Hylas, *and* Sam.]

Francis.   All this forc'd foolery will never doe it.

Enter Alice *and* Mary.

Alice.   I hope we bring ye health sir: how is't with ye?

Mary.   You look far better trust me: the fresh colour
Creeps now againe into his cheeks.

Alice.   Your enemy   340
I see has done his worst. Come, we must have ye
Lusty againe, and frolicke man; leave thinking.

Mary.   Indeed it do's ye harme sir.

Francis.   My best visitants,
I shall be govern'd by ye.

Alice.   You shall be well then,
And suddenly, and soundly well.

Mary.   This ayre sir
Having now season'd ye: will keep ye ever.

Thomas.   No, no, I have no hope, nor is it fit friends,
My life has bin so lewd, my loose condition,
Which I repent too late, so lamentable,
That any thing but curses light upon me,   350
Exorbitant in all my waies.

Alice.   Who's that sir,
Another sicke man?

Mary.   Sure, I know that voyce well.

Thomas.   In all my courses, curelesse disobedience.

Francis [*aside*].   What a strange fellow's this?

Thomas.   No counsell friends,
No looke before I leapt.

470

Alice.   Doe yo' know the voyce sir?
Francis.   Yes, 'tis a gentlemans that's much afflicted
  In's minde: great pitty Ladies.
Alice.   Now heaven help him.
Francis.   He came to me, to aske free pardon of me,
  For some things done long since, which his distemper
  Made to appeare like wrong, but 'twas not so.   360
Mary.   O that this could be truth.
Hylas.   Perswade your selfe.
Thomas.   To what end gentlemen, when all is perish'd
  Upon a wrack, is there a hope remaining?
  The sea, that nev'r knew sorrow, may be pittifull,
  My credit's split, and sunke, nor is it possible,
  Were my life lengthened out as long as——
Mary.   I like this well.
Sam.   Your minde is too mistrustfull.
Thomas.   I have a vertuous sister, but I scorn'd her,
  A Mistresse too, a noble gentlewoman,
  For goodnesse all out-going——
Alice.   Now I know him.   370
Thomas.   Which these eyes friends, my eyes must nev'r see more.
Alice.   This is for your sake *Mary:* take heed cosen,
  A man is not so soone made.
Thomas.   O my fortune,
  But it is just, I be despis'd and hated.
Hylas.   Despaire not, 'tis not manly: one houres goodnesse
  Strikes off an infinite of ils.
Alice.   Weepe truly
  And with compassion Cosin.
Francis [*aside*].   How exactly
  This cunning yong theefe plaies his part.
Mary.   Well *Tom,*
  My *Tom* againe, if this be truth.
Hylas.   She weepes boy.
Thomas.   O I shall die.
Mary.   Now heaven defend.

*365 split] F2; spilt Q   371 Which] S; With Q, F2, L

Sam.   Thou hast her.   380
Thomas.   Come lead me to my Friend to take his farewell,
And then what fortune shall befall me, welcome.
——How do's it show?
Hylas.   O rarely well.
Mary.   Say you so Sir.
Francis [*aside*].   O ye grand Asse.
Mary.   And are ye there my Juggler:
Away we are abus'd *Alice*.
Alice.   Foole be with thee.
                                        Exeunt Mary *and* Alice.
Thomas.   Where is she?
Francis.   Gon; she found you out, and finely,
In your own nooze she halter'd ye: you must be whispering
To know how things showd: not content to fare well
But you must roare out rost meate; till that suspition
You carried it most neately, she beleeved too   390
And wept most tenderly; had you continew'd,
Without doubt you had brought her off.
Thomas.   This was thy Rouging,
For thou wert ever whispering: fye upon thee
Now I could breeks thy head.
Hylas.   You spoke to me first.
Thomas.   Do not anger me,
For by this hand ile beate thee buzard-blind then.
She shall not scape me thus: farewell for this time.
Francis.   Good night, tis almost bed time: yet no sleepe
Must enter these eyes, till I worke a wonder.   *Exit.*
Thomas.   Thou shalt along too, for I meane to plague thee   400
For this nights sins, I will nev'r leave walking of thee
Till I have worne thee out.
Hylas.   Your will be done Sir.
Thomas.   You will not leave me *Sam*.
Sam.   Not I.

*394 breeks] *i.e.* break *as in* F2
396 thee buzard-blind] C; the buzard blind Q, F2, L–S
404 guid. Now, if] C; ~∧ now, ~ Q, F2; ~ ∧ now. If L–S

Thomas.   Away then:
Ile be your guid. Now, if my man be trusty,
My spightfull Dame, ile pipe ye such a huntsup
Shall make ye daunce a tipvaes: keepe close to me.

                                                              Exeunt.

               Enter Sebastian, *and* Dorothy.   [III.] ii

Sebastian.   Never perswade me, I will marry againe.
What should I leave my state to pins and poaking sticks,
To Farthingals, and frownces? two fore-horses
And a old leather bawdy house behind'en
To thee?
Dorothy.   You have a sonne Sir.
Sebastian.   Where, what is he?
Who is he like?
Dorothy.   Your selfe.
Sebastian.   Thou lyest, thou hast mard him,
Thou, and thy praier bookes: I do disclaime him:
Did not I take him singing yesternight
A godly Ballad, to a godly tune too,
And had a catechizme in's pocket, Damsell,   10
One of your deare disciples, I perceive it.
When did he ride abroad since he came over?
What Taverne has he us'd to? what things done
That shewes a man, and mettle? when was my house
At such a shame before, to creep to bed
At ten a clocke, and twelve, for want of company?
No singing, nor no daunring, nor no drinking?
Thou think'st not of these scandals; when, and where
Has he but shewd his sword of late?
Dorothy.   Dispaire not
I do beseech you Sir, nor tempt your weaknesse,   20
For if you like it so, I can assure you
He is the same man still.
Sebastian.   Would thou wert ashes

          406 tipvaes] stet Q   III.ii] *Scena Secunda.* Q
          3 two] this ed.; to Q, F 2, L +   *4 behind'en] stet* Q

On that condition; but beleeve it gossip
You shall know you have wrong.
Dorothy.   You never Sir.
So will I know my duty: and for heaven sake,
Take but this councell with ye ere you marry,
You were wont to heare me: take him, and confesse him,
Search him toth' quicke, and if you find him false
Do as please you; a Mothers name I honour.
Sebastian. He is lost, and spoil'd, I am resolv'd my rooffe   30
Shall never harbour him: and for you Minion
Ile keepe you close enough, least you breake loose
And do more mischiefe; get ye in: who waits?   *Exit* Dorothy.

                   Enter Servant.

Servant.   Do you call Sir?
Sebastian.   Seeke the Boy: and bid him wait
My pleasure in the morning: marke what house
He is in, and what he do's: and truly tell me.
Servant.   I will not faile Sir.
Sebastian.   If ye do, ile hang ye.

                                         Exeunt.

                   Enter Thomas, Hylas, *and* Sam.   [III.] iii

Thomas.   Keepe you the backe doore there, and be sure
None of her servants enter, or goe out,
If any woman passe, she is lawfull prize, boyes,
Cut off all convoyes.
Hylas.   Who shall answere this?
Thomas.   Why, I shall answere it, you fearefull widgen,
I shall appeare to th' action.
Hylas.   May we discourse too
On honourable tearmes?
Thomas.   With any gentlewoman
That shall appeare at window: ye may rehearse too

        *24 wrong] *stet* Q   *25 will] *stet* Q   *29 please you] *stet* Q
        31 you] F 2; your Q   III.iii] *Scena Tertia.* Q

By your commission safely, some sweet parcels
Of poetry to a Chambermaid.
Hylas.   May we sing too?   10
For ther's my master-piece.
Thomas.   By no meanes, no boyes,
I am the man reserv'd for ayre, 'tis my part,
And if she be not rock, my voyce shall reach her:
Ye may record a little, or ye may whistle,
As time shall minister, but for maine singing,
Pray ye satisfie your selves: away, be carefull.
Hylas.   But hark ye one word *Tom*, we may be beaten.
Thomas.   That's as ye think good your selves: if you deserve it,
Why 'tis the easiest thing to compasse: beaten?
What bugbeares dwell in thy brains? who should beat thee?   20
Hylas.   She has men enough.
Thomas.   Art not thou man enough too?
Thou hast flesh enough about thee: if all that masse
Will not maintaine a little spirit, hang it,
And dry it too for dogs meat: get you gone;
I have things of moment in my minde: that doore,
Keep it as thou would'st keep thy wife from a Servingman.
No more I say: away *Sam.*
Sam.   At your will sir.
                    Exeunt Hylas *and* Sam.

Enter Launcelot *and* Fidler.

Launcelot.   I have him here, a rare rogue, good sweet master,
Doe something of some savour suddenly,
That we may eat, and live: I am almost starv'd,   30
No point manieur, no point devein, no Signieur,
Not by the vertue of my languages,
Nothing at my old masters to be hoped for,
O Signieur *du*, nothing to line my life with,
But cold Pyes with a cudgell, till you help us.
Thomas.   Nothing but famine frights thee: come hither Fidler,
What Ballads are you seen in best: be short sir.
Fidler.   Under your masterships correction, I can sing

The Duke of *Norfolke,* or the merry Ballad
Of *Diverus* and *Laʒarus,* the Rose of *England,*   40
In *Creet* when *Dedimus* first began,
Jonas his crying out against *Coventry*——
Thomas.   Excellent,
  Rare matters all.
Fidler.   *Mawdlin* the Merchants daughter,
  The Divell, and ye dainty Dames——
Thomas.   Rare still.
Fidler.   The landing of the Spaniards at *Bow,*
  With the bloudy battell at *Mile-end.*
Thomas.   All excellent:
  No tuning as ye love me; let thy Fidle
  Speake welch, or any thing that's out of all tune,
  The vilder still the better, like thy selfe,
  For I presume thy voyce will make no trees dance.   50
Fidler.   Nay truely, ye shall have it ev'n as homely.
Thomas.   Keep ye to that key: are they all abed trow?
Launcelot.   I heare no stirring any where, no light
  In any window, 'tis a night for the nonce Sir.
Thomas.   Come strike up then: and say the Merchants daughter,
  We'l beare the burthen: proceed to incision Fidler.

Song.

Enter Servant *above.*

Servant.   Who's there? what noyse is this? what rogue at these
      houres?
Thomas.   *O what is that to you my foole?*
            O what is that to you,
            Plucke in your face you bawling Asse,   60
            Or I will breake your brow.
                Hey down, down, adown.
  A new Ballad, a new, a new.

40 *Diverus*] *i.e. Dives*
41 *Dedimus*] *i.e. Daedalus; see Textual Note to lines 88–89*
*56.1 *Song.*] *see Textual Note*

Fidler.　　*The twelfth of Aprill, on May day,*
　　　　　My house and goods were burnt away, &c.
　　　　　　　　[*Enter*] Maid *above.*
Maid.　Why who is this?
Launcelot.　　*O damsell deere,*
　　　　　Open the doore, and it shall appeare,
　　　　　Open the doore.
Maid.　　*O gentle squire,*　　　　　　　　70
　I'le see thee hang first:
　　　　　　　Farewell my deere.
'Tis master *Thomas,* there he stands.

　　　　　　Enter Mary *above.*

Mary.　　　　　　　'Tis strange,
　That nothing can redeeme him: raile him hence,
　Or sing him out in's owne way, any thing
　To be deliver'd of him.
Maid.　　　　　Then have at him:
　　　　　My man Thomas *did me promise,*
　　　　　He would visite me this night.
Thomas. *I am here Love, tell me deere Love,*
　　　　　How I may obtaine thy sight.　　　80
Maid.　*Come up to my window love, come, come, come,*
　　　　Come to my window my deere,
　　　　The winde, nor the raine, shall trouble thee againe,
　　　　But thou shalt be lodged here.
Thomas.　And art thou strong enough?
Launcelot.　　　　　　Up, up, I warrant ye.
Mary.　What do'st thou meane to doe?
Maid.　　　　　　Good Mistresse peace,
　I'le warrant ye wee'l coole him: *Madge.*

　　　　　　[*Enter*] Madge *above.*

Madge.　　　　　　I am ready.

　　70 *Maid.*] C; *given to Launcelot* Q
　　71–72 I'le . . . first: | Farewell . . . deere.] this ed.; one line roman Q
　　81–84 Come . . . here.] see Textual Note

Thomas.   *The loue of Greece and it tickled him so,*
                  That he devised a way to goe.
Now sing the Duke of *Northumberland.*   90
Fidler.   *And climbing to promotion,*
                          He fell down suddenly.
          Madge with a divels viʒard roring, offers to kisse him,
                          and he fals down.
Maid.   Farewell sir.
Mary.   What hast thou done? thou hast broke his neck.
Maid.   Not hurt him,
He pitcht upon his legs like a Cat.
Thomas.   O woman:
Oh miserable woman, I am spoil'd,
My leg, my leg, my leg, oh both my legs.
Mary.   I told thee what thou hadst done, mischiefe go with
     thee.   [*Exeunt above.*]
Thomas.   O I am lam'd for ever: O my leg,
Broken in twenty places: O take heed,   100
Take heed of women, Fidler: oh a Surgeon,
A Surgeon, or I dye: oh my good people,
No charitable people, all despightfull,
Oh what a misery am I in: oh my leg.
Launcelot.   Be patient sir, be patient: let me binde it.

          Enter Samuel, *and* Hylas *with his head broken.*

Thomas.   Oh doe not touch it rogue.
Hylas.   My head, my head,
Oh my head's kil'd.
Sam.   You must be courting wenches
Through key-holes, Captain *Hylas*, come be comforted,
The skin is scarce broke.
Thomas.   O my leg.
Sam.   How doe ye sir?
Thomas.   Oh maim'd for ever with a fall, he's spoil'd too,   110
I see his braines.
Hylas.   Away with me for Gods sake,

A Surgeon.
Sam.   Here's a night indeed.
Hylas.   A Surgeon.
                    Exeunt all but [Thomas *and*] Fidler.

                    Enter Mary *and* servant *below.*

Mary.   Goe run for helpe.
Thomas.   Oh.
Mary.   Run all, and all too little,
  O cursed beast that hurt him, run, run, flye,
  He will be dead else.   [*Exit* servant.]
Thomas.   Oh.
Mary.   Good friend goe you too.
  Fidler.   Who payes me for my Musicke?
Mary.   Pox o'your Musicke,
  Ther's twelve pence for ye.
Fidler.   Ther's two groates againe forsooth,
  I never take above, and rest ye merry.   *Exit.*
Mary.   A grease pot guild your fidle strings: how do you,
  How is my deere?
Thomas.   Why well I thank ye sweet heart,   120
  Shall we walke in, for now ther's none to trouble us?
Mary [*aside*].   Are ye so crafty sir? I shall meet with ye.——
  I knew your tricke, and I was willing, my *Tom,*
  Mine owne *Tom,* now to satisfie thee: welcome, welcome,
  Welcome my best friend to me, all my deerest.
Thomas.   Now ye are my noble Mistresse: we loose time sweet.
Mary.   I thinke they are all gone.
Thomas.   All, ye did wisely.
Mary.   And you as craftily.
Thomas.   We are well met Mistresse.
Mary.   Come, let's goe in then lovingly: O my Skarfe *Tom.*
  I lost it thereabout, finde it, and weare it   130
  As your poore Mistresse favour.   *Exit.*
Thomas.   I am made now,
  I see no venture is in no hand: I have it,
  How now? the doore lock't, and she in before?

Am I so trim'd?

Mary [*above*].   One parting word sweet *Thomas*,
Though to save your credit, I discharg'd your Fidler,
I must not satisfie your folly too sir,
Ye'are subtle, but beleeve it Foxe, i'le finde ye,
The Surgeons will be here strait, rore againe boy,
And breake thy legs for shame, thou wilt be sport else,
Good night.   [*Exit.*] 140

Thomas.   She saies most true, I must not stay: she has bobd me,
Which if I live, I'le recompence, and shortly.
Now for a Ballad to bring me off againe.

 All yong men be warn'd by me, how you do goe a wooing.
 Seek not to climb, for feare ye fall, thereby comes your undoing,
             &c.
             Exit.

      Enter Valentine, Alice, *and* servant.   IV. i

Valentine.   He cannot goe and take no farewell of me,
 Can he be so unkinde? he's but retir'd
 Into the Garden or the Orchard: see sirs.
Alice.   He would not ride there certain, those were planted
 Onely for walkes I take it.
Valentine.   Ride? nay then,
 Had he a horse out?
Servant.   So the Groome delivers,
 Somewhat before the breake of day.
Valentine.   He's gone,
 My best friend's gone *Alice*: I have lost the noblest,
 The truest, and the most man I ere found yet.
Alice.   Indeed sir, he deserves all praise.
Valentine.   All sister,   10
 All, all, and all too little: O that honesty,
 That ermine honesty, unspotted ever,
 That perfect goodnesse.
Alice.   Sure he will returne sir,

  IV.i] *Actus Quartus, Scena Prima.* Q   6 a] F2; *om.* Q

He cannot be so harsh.

Valentine.　　　　　　　O never, never,
Never returne, thou know'st not where the cause lyes.

Alice.　He was the worthiest welcome.

Valentine.　　　　　　　He deserv'd it.

Alice.　Nor wanted, to our knowledge.

Valentine.　　　　　　　I will tell thee,
Within this houre, things that shall startle thee.
He never must returne.

Enter Michael.

Michael.　　　　　　　Good morrow Signieur.

Valentine.　Good morrow master *Michael.*

Michael.　　　　　　　My good neighbour,　20
Me thinks you are stirring early since your travell,
You have learn'd the rule of health sir, where's your mistres?
She keeps her warme I warrant ye, a bed yet?

Valentine.　I thinke she do's.

Alice.　　　　　　　'Tis not her houre of waking.

Michael.　Did you lye with her Lady?

Alice.　　　　　　　Not to night sir.
Nor any night this weeke else.

Michael.　　　　　　　When last saw ye her?

Alice.　Late yester night.

Michael.　　　　　　　Was she abed then?

Alice.　　　　　　　No sir,
I left her at her prayers: why doe ye aske me?

Michael.　I have been strangely haunted with a dreame
All this long night, and after many wakings,　　　30
The same dreame still; me thought I met yong *Cellide*
Just at Saint *Katherines* gate the Nunnery——

Valentine.　　　　　　　Ha?

Michael.　Her face slubber'd o're with teares, and troubles.
Me thought she cry'd unto the Lady Abbesse,
For charity receive me holy woman,
A Maid that has forgot the worlds affections,
Into thy virgin order: me thought she tooke her,

Put on a Stole, and sacred robe upon her,
And there I left her.
Valentine.   Dreame?
Michael.   Good Mistresse *Alice*
Doe me the favour (yet to satisfie me)   40
To step but up, and see.
Alice.   I know she's there sir,
And all this but a dreame.
Michael.   You know not my dreames,
They are unhappy ones, and often truths,
But this I hope, yet——
Alice.   I will satisfie ye.   *Exit.*
Michael.   Neighbour, how do's the gentleman?
Valentine.   I know not,
Dreame of a Nunnery?
Michael.   How found ye my words
About the nature of his sicknesse *Valentine*?
Valentine.   Did she not cry out, 'twas my folly too
That forc'd her to this Nunnery? did she not curse me?
For God sake speake: did you not dreame of me too,   50
How basely, poorely, tamely, like a foole,
Tir'd with his joyes——?
Michael [*aside*].   Alas poore gentleman.——
Ye promis'd me sir to beare all these crosses.
Valentine.   I beare 'em till I breake againe.
Michael.   But nobly,
Truely to weigh——
Valentine.   Good neighbour, no more of it,
Ye doe but fling flaxe on my fire: where is she?

Enter Alice.

Alice.   Not yonder sir, nor has not this night certaine
Bin in her bed.
Michael.   It must be truth she tels ye,
And now I'le shew ye why I came: this morning

45 Neighbour] L; Neighbours Q, F2
55 neighbour] L; neighbours Q, F2

482

A man of mine being employed about businesse,   60
Came early home, who at Saint *Katherines* Nunnery,
About day peep, told me he met your Mistresse,
And as I spoke it in a dreame, so troubled
And so received by the Abbesse, did he see her.
The wonder made me rise, and haste unto ye
To know the cause.
Valentine.   Farewell, I cannot speake it. *Exit* Valentine.
Alice.   For heaven sake leave him not.
Michael.   I will not Lady.
Alice.   Alas, he's much afflicted.
Michael.   We shall know shortly more, apply your own care
At home good *Alice*, and trust him to my counsell.   70
Nay, doe not weep, all shall be well, despaire not.

                                                Exeunt.

                Enter Sebastian, *and* a Servant.   [IV.] ii

Sebastian.   At *Valentines* house so merry?
Servant.   As a pie Sir.
Sebastian.   So gamesom dost thou say?
Servant.   I am sure I heard it.
Sebastian.   Ballads, and Fidles too?
Servant.   No, but one Fidle;
But twenty noyces.

                     Enter Launcelot.

Sebastian.   Did he do devises?
Servant.   The best devises sir: her's my fellow *Launcelet*
He can informe ye all: he was among 'em,
A mad thing too: I stood but in a corner.
Sebastian.   Come sir, what can you say? is there any hope yet
Your Master may returne?
Launcelot.   He went far else:
I will assure your worship on my credit   10
By the faith of a Travellor, and a Gentleman,

        IV.ii] *Scena Secunda.* Q   9 Your] F2; You Q

                         183

Your sonne is found againe, the sonne, the *Tom*.
Sebastian. Is he the old *Tom*?
Launcelot. The old *Tom*.
Sebastian. Goe forward.
Launcelot. Next, to consider how he is the old *Tom*.
Sebastian. Handle me that.
Launcelot. I would ye had seene it handled
Last night sir, as we handled it: *cap à pe*,
Footra for leers, and learings; O the noyse,
The noyse we made.
Sebastian. Good, good.
Launcelot. The windowes clattring
And all the Chambermaides, in such a whobub,
One with her smocke halfe off, another in hast   20
With a servingmans hose upon her head.
Sebastian. Good still.
Launcelot. A fellow rayling out of a loop hole there,
And his mouth stopt with durt.
Sebastian. Y'faith a fine Boy.
Launcelot. Here one of our heads broke.
Sebastian. Excellent good still.
Launcelot. The gentleman himselfe, yong Master *Thomas*,
Invirond with his furious Mermidons,
The fiery Fidler, and my selfe; now singing,
Now beating at the doore, there parlying,
Courting at that window, at the other scalling,
And all these severall noyses to two Trenchers,   30
Strung with a bottome of browne thred, which showd admirable.
Sebastian. There eate, and grow againe, I am pleas'd.
Launcelot. Nor here sir,
Gave we the frolicke over: though at length
We quit the Ladies Skonce on composition
But to the silent streetes we turn'd our furies:
A sleeping watchman here we stole the shooes from,
There made a noyse, at which he wakes, and followes:

*25, 91, 94, 110, 140, 149 Master] M. Q, F 2; Mr L–C
*26 Mermidons,] S; ~ ᴀ Q, F 2, L

The streetes are durty, takes a Queene-hithe cold,
Hard cheese, and that choakes him o' Munday next:
Windowes, and signes we sent to *Erebus*;   40
A crue of bawling curs we entertain'd last,
When having let the pigs loose in out parishes,
O the brave cry we made as high as Algate!
Downe comes a Constable, and the Sow his Sister
Most trayterously tramples upon Authority,
There a whole stand of rug gownes rowted mainly
And the Kings peace put to flight: a purblind pig here
Runs me his head into the Admiral's Lanthorne,
Out goes the light, and all turnes to confusion:
A Potter rises, to enquire this passion,   50
A Boare imbost takes sanctuary in his shop,
When twenty dogs rush after, we still cheering:
Down goes the pots, and pipkins, down the pudding pans,
The creame bols cry revenge here, there the candlesticks.

Sebastian   *If this be true, thou little tyny page,*
[*sings*].   *This tale that thou tell'st me,*
               Then on thy backe will I presently hang
               A handsom new Levery:
               But if this be false, thou little tyney page,
               As false it well may be,   60
               Then with a cudgell of foure foote long
               Ile beate thee from head to toe.

                    Enter Second Servant.

Will the boy come?
2. *Servant.*   He will sir.

                    Enter Thomas.

Sebastian.   Time tries all then.
Launcelot.   Here he comes now himselfe sir.
Sebastian.   To be short *Thomas*

46 mainly] D; manly Q, F2, L–W   47 to] F2; *om.* Q
48 Admiral's] S; Admirable Q, F2, L   *62.1 Second] D; *om.* Q, F2, L–W

185

Because I feele a scruple in my conscience
Concerning thy demeanour, and a maine one,
And therefore like a Father would be satisfi'd,
Get up to that window there, and presently
Like a most compleat Gentleman, come from *Tripoly*.
Thomas.   Good Lord sir, how are you misled: what fancies   70
(Fitter for idle boyes, and drunkards, let me speak't,
And with a little wonder I beseech you)
Choake up your noble judgement?
Sebastian.   You Rogue *Launcelet*,
You lying rascall.
Launcelot.   Will ye spoile all agen sir.
Why, what a devill do you meane?
Thomas.   Away knave——
Ye keepe a company of sawcy fellowes
Debosh'd, and daily drunkards, to deavoure ye,
Things, whose dull soules, tend to the Celler only,
Ye are ill advis'd sir, to commit your credit.
Sebastian.   Sirha, sirha.
Launcelot.   Let me never eate againe sir,   80
Nor feele the blessing of another blew-coate
If this yong Gentleman, sweet Master *Thomas*,
Be not as mad as heart can wish: your heart sir,——
Of yesternights discourse: speake fellow *Robin*,
And if thou speakest less then truth——
Thomas.   Tis strange these varlets——
Sebastian.   By these ten bones sir, if these eies, and eares
Can heare and see——
Thomas.   Extreame strange, should thus boldly
Bud in your sight, unto your sonne.
Launcelot.   O *deu guin*,
Can ye deny, ye beat a Constable
Last night?
Thomas.   I touch Authoritie ye rascall?   90
I violate the Law?
Launcelot.   Good Master *Thomas*.

66 thy] F 2; the Q   84 Of] If Q

486

Servant.   Did you not take two Wenches from the Watch too
And put 'em into pudding lane?
Launcelot.   We meane not
  Those civill things you did at Master *Valentines,*
  The Fidle, and the fa'las.
Thomas.   O strange impudence?
  I do beseech you sir give no such licence
  To knaves and drunkards, to abuse your sonne thus:
  Be wise in time, and turne 'em off: we live sir
  In a State govern'd civilly, and soberly,
  Where each mans actions should confirme the Law,   100
  Not cracke, and canzell it.
Sebastian.   *Lancelot du Lake*
  Get you upon adventers: cast your coate
  And make your exit.
Launcelot.   *Pur lamour de dieu——*
Sebastian.   *Pur* me no *purs*: but *pur* at that doore, out sirha,
  Ile beate ye purblind else, out ye eight languages.
Launcelot.   My bloud upon your head.   *Exit* Launcelot.
Thomas.   Purge me 'em all sir.
Sebastian.   And you too presently.
Thomas.   Even as you please sir.
Sebastian.   Bid my maid servants come: and bring my daughter,
  I will have one shall please me.   *Exeunt* Servants.
Thomas.   Tis most fit sir.
Sebastian.   Bring me the money there: here Master *Thomas,*   110

          Enter two Servants *with two bags.*

  I pray sit downe, ye are no more my sonne now,
  Good gentleman be cover'd.   [*Exeunt* Servants.]
Thomas.   At your pleasure.
Sebastian.   This money I do give ye, because of whilom
  You have bin thought my sonne, and by myselfe too,
  And some things done like me: ye are now another:
  There is two hundred pound, a civill some
  For a yong civill man: much land and Lordship

Will as I take it now, but prove temptation
To dread ye from your setled, and sweet carriage.
Thomas.   You say right sir.
Sebastian.   Nay I beseech ye cover.   120
Thomas.   At your dispose: and I beseech ye too sir,
 For the word civill, and more setled course
 It may be put to use, that on the interest
 Like a poore Gentleman——
Sebastian.   It shall, to my use,
 To mine againe: do you see sir: good fine gentleman,
 I give no brooding money for a Scrivener,
 Mine is for present trafficke, and so ile use it.
Thomas.   So much for that then.

Enter Dorothy, *and* foure Maids.

Sebastian.   For the maine cause Mounsieur
 I sent to treat with you about, behold it;
 Behold that peice of story worke, and view it.   130
 I want a right heire to inherit me,
 Not my estate alone, but my conditions,
 From which you are revolted, therefore dead,
 And I will breake my backe, but I will get one.
Thomas.   Will you choose there sir?
Sebastian.   There, among those Damsels,
 In mine owne tribe: I know their quallities
 Which cannot faile to please me: for their beauties
 A matter of a three farthings, makes all perfect,
 A little beere, and beeffe broth: they are sound too.
 Stand all a breast: now gentle Master *Thomas*   140
 Before I choose, you having liv'd long with me,
 And happely sometimes with some of these too,
 Which fault I never frown'd upon: pray shew me
 (For feare we confound our Genealogies)
 Which have you laid aboord? speake your mind freely,
 Have you had copulation with that Damsell?
Thomas.   I have.
Sebastian.   Stand you a side then: how with her sir?

488

Thomas.　How, is not seemely here to say.
Dorothy.　　　　　　　　　　Heer's fine sport.
Sebastian.　Retyre you too: speake forward Master *Thomas*.
Thomas.　I will: and to the purpose: even with all sir.　　　150
Sebastian.　With all? that's somewhat large.
Dorothy.　　　　　　　　　　And yet you like it.
　Was ever sinne so glorious?
Sebastian.　　　　　With all *Thomas*?
Thomas.　All surely sir.
Sebastian.　　　　　A signe thou art mine owne yet,
　In againe all: and to your severall functions.　　*Exeunt* Maides.
　What say you to yong *Luce*, my neighbours daughter,
　She was too yong I take it, when you travelled;
　Some twelve yeare old?
Thomas.　　　　　　Her will was fifteene sir.
Sebastian.　A pretty answere; to cut of long discourse,
　For I have many yet to aske ye of,
　Where I can choose, and nobly: hold up your finger　　　160
　When ye are right: what say ye to *Valeria*
　Whose husband lies a dying now? why two,
　And in that forme?
Thomas.　　　　　Her husband is recover'd.
Sebastian.　A witty morall: have at ye once more *Thomas*,
　The sisters of Saint *Albones*, all five; dat boy,
　Dat's mine owne boy.
Dorothy.　　　　　　Now out upon thee Monster.
Thomas.　Still hoping of your pardon.
Sebastian.　　　　　　　There needes none man:
　A straw on pardon: prethee need no pardon.
　Ile aske no more, nor thinke no more of marriage,
　For o' my conscience I shalbe thy Cuckold:　　　170
　Ther's some good yet left in him: beare your selfe well,
　You may recover me, ther's twenty pound sir,
　I see some sparkles which may flame againe,
　You may eat with me when you please, you know me.
　　　　　　　　　　　　　　　Exit Sebastian.

158 of] *i.e.* off *as in* F 2

Dorothy.   Why do you lye so damnably, so foolishly?

Thomas.   Do'st thou long to have thy head broke? hold thy
  peace
  And doe as I would have thee, or by this hand
  I'le kill thy Parrat, hang up thy small hound,
  And drinke away thy dowry to a penny.

Dorothy.   Was ever such a wilde Asse?

Thomas.   Prethee be quiet.   180

Dorothy.   And do'st thou think men will not beat thee
      monstrously
  For abusing their wives and children?

Thomas.   And do'st thou thinke
  Mens wives and children can be abus'd too much?

Dorothy.   I wonder at thee.

Thomas.   Nay, thou shalt adjure me
  Before I have done.

Dorothy.   How stand ye with your mistresse?

Thomas.   I shall stand neerer
  Ere I be twelve houres older: ther's my businesse,
  She is monstrous subtile *Doll*.

Dorothy.   The divell I thinke
  Cannot out subtle thee.

Thomas.   If he play faire play:
  Come, you must helpe me presently.

Dorothy.   I discard ye.   190

Thomas.   Thou shalt not sleep nor eate.

Dorothy.   I'le no hand with ye,
  No bawd to your abuses.

Thomas.   By this light *Doll*,
  Nothing but in the way of honesty.

Dorothy.   Thou never knew'st that road: I heare your vigils.

Thomas.   Sweet honey *Doll*, If I doe not marry her,
  Honestly marry her, if I meane not honourably——
  Come, thou shalt help me, take heed how you vex me,
  I'le help thee to a husband too, a fine gentleman,
  I know thou art mad, a tall yong man, a brown man,

178 hound] S; hand Q, F 2, L

490

I sweare he has his maidenhead, a rich man.   200
Dorothy.   You may come in to dinner, and I'le answere ye.
Thomas.   Nay I'le goe with thee *Doll*: four hundred a yeere
    wench.

Exeunt.

Enter Michael *and* Valentine.   [IV.] iii

Michael.   Good sir go back again, and take my counsell,
    Sores are not cur'd by sorrows, nor time broke from us
    Pul'd back again by sighes.
Valentine.   What should I doe friend?
Michael.   Doe that that may redeeme ye, goe back quickly,
    Sebastians daughter can prevaile much with her,
    The Abbesse is her Aunt too.
Valentine.   But my friend then
    Whose love and losse is equall ty'd?
Michael.   Content ye,
    That shall be my taske: if he be alive,
    Or where my travell and my care may reach him,
    I'le bringe him backe againe.
Valentine.   Say he come backe   10
    To piece his poor friends life out? and my mistresse
    Be vow'd for ever a recluse?
Michael.   So suddenly
    She cannot, haste ye therefore instantly away sir,
    To put that danger by: first as to a father,
    Then as a friend she was committed to ye,
    And all the care she now has: by which priviledge
    She cannot doe her selfe this violence,
    But you may breake it, and the law allowes ye.
Valentine.   O but I forc'd her to it.
Michael.   Leave disputing
    Against your selfe, if you will needs be miserable   20
    Spight of her goodnesse, and your friends perswasions,

IV.iii] *Scæna Tertia.* Q   14 danger] L; daughter Q, F 2
17 her selfe] S; her Q, F 2, L

Thinke on, and thrive thereafter.

Valentine.   I will home then,
And follow your advise, and good, good *Michael*——
Michael. No more, I know your soul's divided, *Valentine*,
Cure but that part at home with speedy marriage
Ere my returne, for then those thoughts that vext her,
While there ran any streame for loose affections,
Will be stopt up, and chaste ey'd honour guide her.
Away, and hope the best still: I'le worke for ye,
And pray too heartily, away, no more words.   30

Exeunt.

Enter Hylas *and* Sam.   [IV.] iv

Hylas. I care not for my broken head,
But that it should be his plot, and a wench too,
A lowzie, lazie wench prepar'd to doe it.
Sam. Thou hadst as good be quiet, for o' my conscience
He'l put another on thee else.
Hylas.   I am resolv'd
To call him to account, was it not manifest
He meant a mischiefe to me, and laughed at me,
When he lay roaring out, his leg was broken,
And no such matter: had he broke his necke,
Indeed 'twould ne'r ha' griev'd me: gallowes gall him.   10
Why should he choose out me?
Sam.   Thou art ever ready
To thrust thy selfe into these she occasions,
And he as full of knavery to accept it.
Hylas. Well, if I live, I'le have a new tricke for him.
Sam. That will not be amisse, but to fight with him
Is to no purpose: besides, he's truely valiant,
And a most deadly hand: thou never foughtst yet,
Nor o' my conscience hast no faith in fighting.
Hylas. No, no, I will not fight.
Sam.   Beside the quarrell,

IV.iv] *Scena Quarta.* Q

492

Which has a woman in't, to make it scurvy,
Who would lye stinking in a Surgeons hands
A moneth or two this weather; for beleeve it,
He never hurts under a quarters healing.
Hylas.   No upon better thought, I will not fight *Sam,*
But watch my time.
Sam.   To pay him with a project:
Watch him too, I would wish ye: prethee tell me,
Do'st thou affect these women still?
Hylas.   Yes faith *Sam,*
I love 'em ev'n as well as ev'r I did,
Nay, if my braines were beaten out, I must to 'em.
Sam.   Dost thou love any woman?
Hylas.   Any woman   30
Of what degree or calling.
Sam.   Of any age too?
Hylas.   Of any age, from fourscore to fourteen boy,
Of any fashion.
Sam.   And defect too?
Hylas.   Right.
For those I love to leade me to repentance:
A woman with no nose, after my surquedry,
Shewes like King *Philips* morall, *memento mort,*
And she that has a wooden leg, demonstrates
Like hypocrites, we halt before the gallowes:
An old one with one tooth, seemes to say to us
Sweet meats have sowre sawce: she that's full of aches,   40
Crum not your bread before you taste your porridge;
And many morals we may finde.
Sam.   'Tis well sir,
Ye make so worthy uses: but *quid igitur,*
What shall we now determine?
Hylas.   Let's consider,
An houre or two, how I may fit this fellow.
Sam.   Let's finde him first, he'l quickly give occasion.
But take heed to your selfe, and say I warn'd ye:

*38 hypocrites] C; *Hypocrites* Q

493

He has a plaguy pate.
Hylas.   That at my danger.

Exeunt.

Musick. Enter Saylors *singing; to them,*
Michael *and* Francis.

Saylor.   Aboard, aboard, the winde stands faire.
Michael.   These call for passengers, I'le stay, and see
  What men they take aboard.
Francis.   A boat, a boat, a boat.
Saylor.   Away then.
Francis.   Whether are ye bound friends?
Saylor.   Downe to the Straytes.
Michael.   Ha, 'tis not much unlike him.
Francis.   May I have passage for my money?
Saylor.   And welcome too.
Michael.   'Tis he, I know 'tis he now.
Francis.   Then merrily aboard: and noble friend
  Heauens goodnesse keep thee ever, and all vertue
  Dwell in thy bosome *Cellide*, my last teares   10
  I leave behinde me thus, a sacrifice,
  For I dare stay no longer to betray ye.
Michael.   Be not so quicke sir: Saylors I here charge ye
  By vertue of this warrant, as you will answer it,
  For both your ship and Merchant I know perfectly:
  Lay hold upon this fellow.
Francis.   Fellow?
Michael.   I sir.
Saylor.   No hand to sword sir, we shall master ye,
  Fetch out the manacles.
Francis.   I doe obey ye:
  But I beseech ye sir, informe me truely
  How I am guilty.

IV.v] *Scena Quinta.* Q
0.1 *Musick.*] L; *placed after preceding Exeunt.* Q, F2
0.1 *singing; to*] C; ~ ₐ ~ Q, F2

Michael.   Ye have rob'd a gentleman,   20
One that ye are bound to for your life and being:
Money and horse unjustly ye tooke from him,
And something of more note: but for y'are a gentleman——
Francis.   It shall be so, and here I'le end all miseries,
Since friendship is so cruell. I confesse it,
And which is more, hundred of these robberies:
This Ring I stole too from him: and this jewell,
The first and last of all my wealth: forgive me
My innocence and truth, for saying I stole 'em,
And may they prove of value but to recompence   30
The thousand part of his love, and bread I have eaten.
Pray see 'em render'd noble sir, and so
I yeeld me to your power.
Michael.   Guard him to'th water,
I charge you Saylors, there I will receive him,
And backe convey him to a Justice.
Saylor.   Come sir,
Look to your neck, you are like to sayle i'th ayre now.

                                        Exeunt.

Enter Thomas, Dorothy, *and* Maid.   [V. i]

Thomas.   Come quickly, quickly, quickly, paint me handsomly,
Take heed my nose be not in graine too,
Come *Doll, Doll*, disen me.
Dorothy.   If you should play now
Your divels parts againe——
Thomas.   Yea and nay *Dorothy.*
Dorothy.   If ye doe any thing, but that ye have sworne to,
Which onely is accesse——
Thomas.   As I am a gentleman:
Out with this hayre *Doll*, handsomely.
Dorothy.   You have your breeches?
Thomas.   I prethee away, thou know'st I am monstrous ticklish,
What, do'st thou think I love to blast my buttocks?

V.i] *Scena Sexta.* Q; *see Introduction*

491

Dorothy [*aside*].   I'le plague ye for this roguery: for I know well   10
  What ye intend sir.
Thomas.   On with my Muffler.
Dorothy.   Ye are a sweet Lady: come let's see you curtsie:
  What, broke i'th bum, hold up your head.
Thomas.   Plague on't,
  I shall bepisse my breeches if I cowre thus.
  Come, am I ready?
Maid.   At all points, as like sir
  As if you were my Mistris.
Dorothy.   Who goes with ye?
Thomas.   None but my fortune, and my selfe.   *Exit* Thomas.
Dorothy.   Blesse ye:
  Now run thou for thy life, and get before him,
  Take the by way, and tell my Cosin *Marie*
  In what shape he intends to come to cozen her;   20
  Ile follow at thy heeles my selfe: flie wench.
Maid.   Ile do it.   *Exit.*

                Enter Sebastian *and* Thomas.

Dorothy.   My Father has met him: this goes excellent,
  And ile away in time: looke to your skin *Thomas.*   *Exit.*
Sebastian.   What, are you growne so cornefed gooddy *Gillian.*
  You will not know your Father: what vaga'res
  Have you in hand, what out leapes, durty heeles,
  That at these houres of night ye must be gadding,
  And through the Orchard take your private passage;
  What, is the breeze in your breech, or has your brother   30
  Appointed you an houre of meditation
  How to demeane himselfe: get ye to bed, drab,
  Or ile so crab your shoulders: ye demure slut,
  Ye civill dish of sliced beefe, get ye in.
Thomas.   I wy' not, that I wy' not.
Sebastian.   Is't ev'n so Dame,
  Have at ye with a night spell then.
Thomas.   Pray hold sir.

    30 breeze] *i.e.* gadfly (*OED, sb*¹)   32 himselfe] *i.e.* oneself (yourself)

Sebastian. *Saint* George, *Saint* George, *our Ladies knight,*
   He walkes by day, so do's he by night,
    And when he had her found,
    He her beat, and her bound,   40
   Untill to him her troth she plight,
   She would not stir from him that night.
Thomas. Nay then have at ye with a counter-spell,
   From Elves, Hobs and Fayries,
   That trouble our Dayries,
   From Fire-drakes and fiends,
   And such as the divell sends,
   Defend us heaven.

     [*Knocks down* Sebastian *and*] *Exit.*

    Enter Launcelot.

Launcelot. Blesse my Master: looke up sir I beseech ye,
 Up with your eyes to heaven.
Sebastian.   Up with your nose sir, 50
 I doe not bleed, 'twas a sound knock she gave me,
 A plaguy mankinde girle, how my braines totters?
 Well, go thy waies, thou hast got one thousand pound more
 With this dog tricke.
 Mine owne true spirit in her too——
Launcelot.   In her? alas sir,
 Alas poore gentlewoman, she a hand so heavy
 To knocke ye like a Calfe down, or so brave a courage
 To beat her father? if you could beleeve sir——
Sebastian. Who wouldst thou make me beleeve it was, the
  divell?
Launcelot. One that spits fire as fast as he sometimes sir, 60
 And changes shapes as often: your sonne *Thomas:*
 Never wonder, if it be not he, straight hang me.
Sebastian. He? if it be so,
 I'le put thee in my Will, and ther's an end on't.
Launcelot. I saw his legs, h'as Boots on like a Player,
 Under his wenches cloaths: 'tis he, 'tis *Thomas*

In his own sisters cloaths, sir, and I canwast him.
Sebastian.   No more words then, we'l watch him: thou'lt
    not beleeve *Lance*,
How heartily glad I am.
Launcelot.   May ye be gladder,
  But not this way sir.
Sebastian.   No more words, but watch him.   70
                              Exeunt.

          Enter Mary, Dorothy, *and* Maid.   [V. ii]

Mary.   When comes he?
Dorothy.   Presently.
Mary.   Then get you up *Doll*,
  Away, I'le strait come to you: is all ready?
Maid.   All.
Mary.   Let the light stand far enough.
Maid.   'Tis placed so.
Mary.   Stay you to entertaine him to his chamber,
  But keep close wench, he flyes at all.
Maid.   I warrant ye.
Mary.   You need no more instruction?
Maid.   I am perfect.
        Exeunt [Mary *and* Dorothy, *hide* Maid].

        Enter Valentine *and* Thomas.

Thomas.   More stops yet? sure the fiend's my ghostly father:
  Old *Valentine*, what wind's in his poope?
Valentine.   Lady,
  You are met most happily: O gentle *Doll*,
  You must now doe me an especiall favour.   10
Thomas.   What is it Master *Valentine*? I am sorely troubled
  With a salt rheume falne i' my gums.
Valentine.   I'le tell ye,

      *67 canwast] *stet* Q
      V.ii] *Scena septima.* Q; *see Introduction*
      6.2 *Enter*] this ed.; *Scena Secunda. Enter* Q+

And let it move you equally: my blest Mistresse
Upon a slight occasion taking anger,
Tooke also (to undoe me) your Aunts Nunnery,
From whence by my perswasion to redeeme her,
Will be impossible: nor have I liberty
To come, and visite her: my good, good *Dorothy*,
You are most powerfull with her, and your Aunt too,
And have accesse at all houres liberally,　　　　　　　20
Speake now, or never for me.
Thomas.　　　　　　　　In a Nunnery?
That course must not be suffered Master *Valentine*,
Her mother never knew it: [*aside*] rare sport for me:
Sport upon sport——by th' breake of day I'le meet ye,
And feare not man, wee'l have her out I warrant ye,
I cannot stay now.
Valentine.　　　You will not breake?
Thomas.　　　　　　　　　By no meanes.
Good night.
Valentine.　Good night kinde Mistresse *Doll.*　　　　*Exit.*
Thomas.　　　　　　　　This thrives well,
Every one takes me for my sister, excellent:
This Nunnerys fal so pat too, to my figure,
Where there be handsome wenches, and they shall know it　　30
If once I creep in, ere they get me out againe:
Stay, her's the house and one of her Maids.
Maid.　　　　　　　　Who's there?
O Mistresse *Dorothy* you are a stranger.
Thomas [*aside*].　Still Mistresse *Dorothy*? this geere will cotton.
Maid.　Will you walke in forsooth?
Thomas.　　　　　　Where is your Mistresse?
Maid.　Not very well: she's gone to bed, I am glad
You are come so fit to comfort her.
Thomas.　　　　　　Yes, I'le comfort her.
Maid.　Pray make not much noise, for she is sure asleep,
You know your side, creep softly in, your company
Will warme her well.

*29 This Nunnerys fal] *stet* Q　　32 Maids.] Maids. | *Enter Maid.* | Q

Thomas.   I warrant thee I'le warme her.   40
Maid.   Your brother has been here, the strangest fellow.
Thomas.   A very rogue, a ranke rogue.
Maid.   I'le conduct ye
Even to her chamber door, and there commit ye.

                                                        Exeunt.

                    Enter Michael, Francis, *and* Officers.   [V. iii]

Michael.   Come sir, for this night I shall entertaine ye,
  And like a gentleman, how ere your fortune
  Hath cast ye on the worst part.
Francis.   How you please sir,
  I am resolv'd, nor can a joy or misery
  Much move me now.
Michael [aside].   I am angry with my selfe now
  For putting this forc'd way upon his patience,
  Yet any other course had been too slender:
  Yet what to thinke I know not, for most liberally
  He hath confess'd strange wrongs, which if they prove so—
  How ere the others long love may forget all;   10
  Yet 'twas most fit he should come back, and this way.——
  Drinke that: and now to my care leave your prisoner,
  I'le be his guard for this night.
Officers.   Good night to your worship.
                                                [*Exeunt.*]
Michael.   Good night my honest friends: Come sir, I hope
  There shall be no such cause of such a sadnesse
  As you put on.
Francis.   Faith sir, my rest is up,
  And what I now pull, shall no more afflict me
  Then if I plaid at span-counter, nor is my face
  The map of any thing I seeme to suffer,
  Lighter affections seldome dwell in me sir.   20
Michael [aside].   A constant gentleman: would I had taken
  A feaver when I took this harsh way to disturb him.——

            V.iii] *Scena Octava.* Q; *see Introduction*

Come walke with me sir, ere to morrow night
I doubt not but to see all this blown over.

Exeunt.

Enter Hylas.

V. iv

Hylas.   I have dog'd his sister, sure 'twas she,
And I hope she will come back again this night too:
Sam I have lost of purpose: now if I can
With all the art I have, as she comes backe,
But win a parley for my broken pate,
Off goes her maiden-head, and there's *vindicta.*
They stir about the house, I'le stand at distance.   *Exit.*

Enter Mary *and* Dorothy, *and then* Thomas *and* Maid   [V. v]
[*at the opposite door*].

Dorothy.   Is he come in?
Mary.   Speake softly,
He is, and there he goes.
Thomas.   Good night, good night wench.
A bed discovered with a black More in it.
Maid.   As softly as you can.   *Exit.*
Thomas.   I'le play the Mouse *Nan.*
How close the little thiefe lyes.
Mary.   How he itches?
Dorothy.   What would you give now to be there, and I
At home *Mull?*
Mary.   Peace for shame.
Thomas.   In what a figure
The little foole has pull'd it selfe together:
Anone you will lye streighter: ha, ther's rare circumstance
Belongs to such a treatise: doe ye tumble?
I'le tumble with ye straight wench: she sleeps soundly,   10
Full little thinkst thou of thy joy that's comming,

V.iv] *Actus Quintus. Scena Quarta.* Q; *see Introduction*
V.v] W; *no scene division* Q, F2, L–C

The sweet, sweet joy, full little of the kisses,
But those unthought of things come ever happiest.
How soft the rogue feeles? O ye little villaine,
Ye delicate coy thiefe, how I shall thrum ye?
Your *fy away, good servant, as ye are a gentleman*——
Mary.   Prethee leave laughing.
Thomas.   *Out upon ye* Thomas,
What do ye meane to do? ile call the house up.
O god, I am sure ye will not, shall not serve ye,
For up ye goe now, and ye were my Father.   20
Mary.   Your courage wilbe cold anon.
Thomas.   If I do hang for't,
Yet ile be quarterd here first.
Dorothy.   O feirce villaine.
Mary.   What would he do indeed *Doll*?
Dorothy.   You had best try him.
Thomas.   Ile kiss thee ere I come to bed: sweet *Mary*——
Mary.   Prethee leave laughing.
Dorothy.   O, for gentle *Nicholas*.
Thomas.   And view that stormy face, that has so thundered me;
A coldne's crept over't now, by your leave, candle,
And next doore by yours too, so, ah pretty, pretty,
Shall I now looke upon ye: by this light it moves me.
Mary.   Much good may it do you sir.
Thomas.   Holy saints, defend me.   30
The devill, devill, devill, devill, O the devill.
Mary, Dorothy.   Ha, ha, ha, ha, the devill O the devill.
Thomas.   I am abus'd most damnedly: most beastly,
Yet if it be a she devill: But the house is up,
And here's no staying longer in this Cassock.
Woman, I here disclaime thee; and in vengeance
Ile marry with that devill, but ile vex thee.
Mary.   By'r Lady, but you shall not sir, ile watch ye.
Thomas.   Plague o' your spanish leather hide; ile waken ye:
Devill, good night: good night good devill.

17 *Thomas.*] F2; *om.* Q
21 If I do hang for't] S; If it do hang for', Q   28 ah] D; a Q, F2, L–W

Moore.   Oh.   40
Thomas.   Rore againe, devill, rore againe.   *Exit* Thomas.
Moore.   O, O, sir.
Mary.   Open the doores before him: let him vanish.
  Now, let him come againe, ile use him kinder.
  How now Wench?
Moore.   Pray lye here your self next, Mistris,
  And entertaine your sweet heart.
Mary.   What said he to thee?
Moore.   I had a soft bed: and I slept out all,
  But his kind farewell: ye may bake me now
  For o' my conscience, he has made me venison.
Mary.   Alas poore *Kate*; ile give thee a new Petticoate.
Dorothy.   And I a Wastcoate, Wench.
Mary.   Draw in the bed Maides,   50
  And see it made againe; put fresh sheetes on too,
  For *Doll* and I: come Wench, lets laugh an houre now,
  To morrow earely, will wee see yong *Cellide*,
  They say she has taken Sanctuary: love, and hey
  Are thicke sowne, but come up so full of thistles.
Dorothy.   They must needs *Mall*: for 'tis a pricking age grown,
  Prethee to bed, for I am monstrous sleepy.
Mary.   A match, but art not thou thy brother?
Dorothy.   Would I were Wench,
  You should heare further.
Mary.   Come, no more of that *Doll.*
                                              Exeunt.

                    Enter Hylas, *and* Thomas.   [V.] vi

Hylas.   I heard the doores clap: now, and't be thy will,
        wench——
  By th' mas she comes: you are fairely met faire gentlewoman,
  I take it Mistris *Doll*, *Sebastians* daughter.
Thomas.   You take right sir: [*aside*] *Hylas*, are you feretting?

  54 hey] S; they Q, F2, L   V.vi] *Scena quinta.* Q
  2 fairely] C; surely Q, F2, L–S   2 met] F2; melt Q   4 You] S; I Q, F2, L

Ile fit you with a pennyworth presently.

Hylas.   How dare you walk so late sweet: so weak guarded?

Thomas.   Faith sir, I do no harme, nor none I looke for,
Yet I am glad, I have met so good a gentleman,
Against all chances: for though I never knew ye
Yet I have heard much good spoke of ye.

Hylas.   Harke ye,   10
What if a man should kisse ye?

Thomas.   That's no harme sir:
Pray God he scapes my beard, there lyes the mischiefe.

Hylas.   Her lips are monstrous rugged, but that surely
Is but the sharpnesse of the weather: harke ye once more,
And in your eare, sweet Mistresse, for ye are so,
And ever shall be from this houre: I have vow'd it.

Enter Sebastian *and* Launcelot.

Sebastian.   Why that's my daughter, rogue, do'st thou not see her
Kissing that fellow there, there in that corner?

Launcelot.   Kissing?

Sebastian.   Now, now, now they agree o'th match too.

Thomas.   Nay then ye love me not.

Hylas.   By this white hand *Doll.*   20

Thomas.   I must confesse, I have long desir'd your sight sir.

Launcelot.   Why ther's the Boots still sir.

Sebastian.   Hang Boots sir,
Why they'l weare breeches too.

Thomas.   Dishonest me?
Not for the world.

Sebastian.   Why now they kisse againe, there:
I knew 'twas she, and that her crafty stealing
Out the back way must needs have such a meaning.

Launcelot.   I am at my small wits end.

Thomas.   If ye meane honourably—

Launcelot.   Did she nev'r beat ye before sir?

Sebastian.   Why dost thou follow me?

6 sweet] F2; so sweet Q   12 beard] F2; heard Q

Thou rascall slave hast thou not twice abus'd me?
Hast thou not spoil'd the boy? by thine owne covenant,   30
Would'st thou not now be hang'd?

Launcelot.   I thinke I would sir,
But you are so impatient: do's not this shew sir,
(I do beseech ye speake, and speake with judgement,
And let the case be equally considered)
Far braver in your daughter? in a son now
'Tis nothing, of no marke: every man do's it,
But, to beget a daughter, a man maiden
That reaches at these high exploits, is admirable:
Nay she goes far beyond him: for when durst he,
But when he was drunke, doe any thing to speake of?   40
This is *Sebastian* truely.

Sebastian.   Thou sayest right *Lance*,
And ther's my hand once more.

Thomas.   Not without marriage.

Sebastian.   Didst thou heare that?

Launcelot.   I thinke she spoke of marriage.

Sebastian.   And he shall marry her, for it seems she likes him,
And their first boy shall be my heire.

Launcelot.   I marry,
Now ye goe right to worke.

Thomas.   Fye, fye sir,
Now I have promis'd ye this night to marry,
Would ye be so intemperate? are ye a gentleman?

Hylas.   I have no maw to marriage, yet this rascall
Tempts me extreamely: will ye marry presently?   50

Thomas.   Get you afore, and stay me at the Chappell,
Close by the Nunnery, there you shall finde a night Priest
Little sir *Hugh*, and he can say the Matrimony
Over without booke, for we must have no company
Nor light, for feare my father know, which must not yet be.
And then to morrow night——

Hylas.   Nothing to night sweet?

Thomas.   No, not a bit, I am sent of businesse
About my dowry, sweet, doe not you spoile all now,

'Tis of much haste. I can scarce stay the marriage,
Now if you love me, get you gone.
Hylas. You'l follow? 60
Thomas. Within this houre, my sweet chicke.
Hylas. Kisse.
Thomas. A rope kisse ye:
Come, come, I stand o' thornes.
Hylas. Me thinkes her mouth still
Is monstrous rough, but they have waies to mend it:
Farewell. [*Exit.*]
Thomas. Farewell: I'le fit ye with a wife, sir. [*Exit.*]
Sebastian. Come, follow close, I'le see the end she aymes at,
And if he be a handsome fellow *Launcelot*,
Fiat, 'tis done, and all my state is setled.

Exeunt.

Enter Abbesse, Cellide, *and Nuns.* [V.] vii

Abbesse. Come, to your Mattins Maids: these early houres,
My gentle daughter, will disturb a while
Your faire eyes, nurterd in ease.
Cellide. No vertuous mother,
Tis for my holy health, to purchase which
They shall forget the childe of ease, soft slumbers.
O my afflicted heart, how thou art tortur'd,
And Love, how like a tyrant, thou raign'st in me,
Commanding and forbidding at one instant:
Why came I hither that desire to have
Onely all liberty, to make me happy? 10
Why didst thou bring that yong man home, O *Valentine*,
That vertuous youth, why didst thou speake his goodnesse
In such a phrase, as if all tongues, all praises
Were made for him? O fond and ignorant,
Why didst thou foster my affection
Till it grew up, to know no other father,
And then betray it?

V.vii] *Scena Sexta.* Q

Abbesse.   Can ye sing?
Cellide.   Yes, Mother,
My sorrowes onely.
Abbesse.   Be gone, and to the Quire then.

Exeunt.
Musicke, singing.

Enter Michael *and* Servant, *and* Francis.   [V.] viii

Michael.   Ha'st thou inquir'd him out?
Servant.   He's not at home sir,
His sister thinks he's gone to th' Nunnery.
Michael.   Most likely: I'le away, an houre hence sirha,
Come you along with this yong gentleman,
Doe him all service, and faire office.
Servant.   Yes sir.

Exeunt.

Enter Hylas *and* Sam.   [V.] ix

Sam.   Where hast thou been man?
Hylas.   Is there nev'r a shop open?
I'le give thee a paire of gloves *Sam.*
Sam.   What's the matter?
Hylas.   What do'st thou thinke?
Sam.   Thou art not married?
Hylas.   By th' masse but I am, all to bemarried,
I am i'th order now *Sam.*
Sam.   To whom prethee?
I thought there was some such trick in't, you stole from me,
But who, for heaven sake?
Hylas.   Ev'n the sweetest woman,
The rarest woman *Samuel*, and the lustiest,
But wondrous honest, honest as the ice boy,
Not a bit before hand, for my life, sirha,

10

V.viii] *Scena septima.* Q   V.ix] *Scena Octava.* Q
4 bemarried] V; be married Q, F 2, L–S, W

And of a lusty kindred.
Sam.   But who *Hylas?*
Hylas.   The yong gentleman and I are like to be friends againe,
  The fates will have it so.
Sam.   Who, Monsieur *Thomas?*
Hylas.   All wrongs forgot.
Sam.   O now I smell ye *Hylas.*
  Do's he know of it?
Hylas.   No, ther's the tricke I owe him:
  'Tis done boy, we are fast, faith, my youth now
  Shall know I am aforehand, for his qualities.
Sam.   Is there no tricke in't?
Hylas.   None, but up and ride boy:
  I have made her no joynture neither, there I have paid him.
Sam.   She's a brave wench.
Hylas.   She shall be, as I'le use her,   20
  And if she anger me, all his abuses
  I'le clap upon her Cassocke.
Sam.   Take heed *Hylas.*
Hylas.   'Tis past that *Sam*, come, I must meet her presently,
  And now shalt see me, a most glorious husband.

                              Exeunt.

           Enter Dorothy, Mary, Valentine.   [V.] x

Dorothy.   In troth sir, you never spoke to me.
Valentine.   Can ye forget me?
  Did not you promise all your helpe and cunning
  In my behalfe, but for one houre to see her,
  Did you not sweare it? by this hand, no strictnesse
  Nor rule this house holds, shall by me, be broken.
Dorothy.   I saw ye not these two dayes.
Valentine.   Doe not wrong me,
  I met ye, by my life, just as you entred
  This gentle Ladies Lodge last night, thus suited
  About eleven a clocke.

             V.x] *Scena Nona.* Q

Dorothy.　　　　　　　　'Tis true I was there,
　But that I saw or spoke to you——
Mary [*to Dorothy*].　　　　　　I have found it,　　　　10
　Your brother *Thomas, Doll.*
Dorothy.　　　　　　　　Pray sir be satisfi'd,
　And wherein I can doe you good, command me.——
　What a mad foole is this?——stay here a while sir,
　Whilst we walke in, and make your peace.　*Exit* [*with* Mary].

　　　　　　　Enter Abbesse.

Valentine.　　　　　　　　　I thanke ye.　[*Exit.*]
　　　　　　　　　　　　　　　　Squeake within.
Abbesse.　Why, what's the matter there among these Maids?
　Now *benedicite*, have ye got the breeze there?
　Give me my holly sprinckle.

　　　　　　　Enter two Nuns.

1. Nun.　O Madam, ther's a strange thing like a gentlewoman,
　Like Mistresse *Dorothy*, I think the fiend
　Crept in to th' Nunnery we know not which way,　　　　20
　Playes revell rowt among us.
Abbesse.　Give me my holy water pot.
1. Nun.　　　　　　　　Here Madam.
Abbesse.　Spirit of earth or ayre, I do conjure thee,
　　　　　　　　　　　　　　Squeake within.
　Of water or of fire——
1. Nun.　　　　　　　Harke Madam, hark.
Abbesse.　　　*Be thou ghost that cannot rest:*
　　　　　　Or a shadow of the blest,
　　　　　　Be thou black, or white, or green,
　　　　　　Be thou heard, or to be seen——

　　　　　　　Enter Thomas *and* Cellide.

2. Nun.　It comes, it comes.
Cellide.　　　　　　What are ye? speake, speake gently,
　And next, what would ye with me?

　　　　17.1 *two* Nuns.] *2 Nun.* Q

　　　　　　　509

Thomas.   Any thing you'l let me.   30
Cellide.   You are no woman certaine.
Thomas.   Nor you no Nun, nor shall not be.
Cellide.   What make ye here?
Thomas.   I am a holy Fryer.
Abbesse.   Is this the Spirit?
Thomas.   Nothing but spirit Aunt.
Abbesse.   Now out upon thee.
Thomas.   Peace, or I'le conjure too Aunt.
Abbesse.   Why come you thus?
Thomas.   That's all one, her's my purpose:
   Out with this Nun, she is too handsome for ye,
   I'le tell thee (Aunt) and I speake it with teares to thee,
   If thou keptst her here, as yet I hope thou art wiser,
   Mark but the mischiefe followes.
Abbesse.   She is a Votresse.
Thomas.   Let her be what she will, she will undoe thee,   40
   Let her but one houre out, as I direct ye,
   Or have among your Nuns againe.
Abbesse.   You have no project
   But faire and honest?
Thomas.   As thine eyes, sweet *Abbesse.*
Abbesse.   I will be ruld then.
Thomas.   Thus then and perswade her——
   But do not iuggle with me, if ye do Aunt——
Abbesse.   I must be there my selfe.
Thomas.   Away and fit her.
Abbesse.   Come daughter, you must now be rull'd, or never.
Cellide.   I must obey your will.
Abbesse.   That's my good daughter.
                                        Exeunt.

                 Enter Dorothy, *and* Mary.   [V.] x

Mary.   What a coyle has this Fellow kept i'th' Nunnery,
   Sure he has run the *Abbesse* out of her wits.

       *38 keptst] stet Q   V.xi] Scena Decima. Q

Dorothy.   Out of the Nunnery I think, for we can neither see her
Nor the yong *Cellide*.
Mary.   Pray heavens he be not teasing.
Dorothy.   Nay you may thanke your selfe, 'twas your owne
structures.

Enter Hylas, *and* Sam.

Sam.   Why there's the gentlewoman.
Hylas.   Mas tis she indeed;
How smart the pretty theefe lookes? 'morrow Mistresse.
Dorothy.   Good morrow to you sir.
Sam.   How strange she beares it?
Hylas.   Maids must do so, at first.
Dorothy.   Would ye ought with us, gentlemen?
Hylas.   Yes marry would I   10
A little with your Ladiship.
Dorothy.   Your will sir.
Hylas.   *Doll*, I would have ye presently prepare your selfe
And those things you would have with you,
For my house is ready.
Dorothy.   How sir?
Hylas.   And this night not to faile, you must come to me,
My Friends will all be there too: For Trunks, and those things
And houshold stuffe, and clothes you would have carried
To morrow, or the next day, ile take order:
Onely, what money you have, bring away with ye,
And Jewels.
Dorothy.   Jewels sir?
Hylas.   I, for adornement.   20
There's a bed up, to play the game in, *Dorothy*,
And now come kisse me heartily.
Dorothy.   Who are you?
Hylas.   This Lady shalbe welcome too.
Mary.   To what sir?
Hylas.   Your neighbour can resolve ye.
Dorothy.   The man's foolish.
Sir, you looke soberly: who is this fellow,

And where's his businesse?
Sam.   By heaven, thou art abus'd still.
Hylas.   It may be so: Come, ye may speake now boldly,
  There's none but friends, Wench.
Dorothy.   Came ye out of Bedlam?
  Alas, tis ill sir, that ye suffer him
  To walke in th'open ayre thus: 'twill undoe him.   30
  A pretty hansome gentleman: great pitty.
Sam.   Let me not live more if thou be'st not cozend.
Hylas.   Are not you my Wife? did not I marry you last night
  At Saint *Michaels* Chappell?
Dorothy.   Did not I say he was mad?
Hylas.   Are not you Mistresse *Dorothy, Thomas* sister?
Mary.   There he speakes sence, but ile assure ye gentleman,
  I think no Wife of yours: at what houre was it?
Hylas.   S' pretious; you'll make me mad; did not the Priest
  Sir *Hugh* that you appointed, about twelve a clocke
  Tye our hands fast? did not you sweare you lov'd me?   40
  Did not I court ye, comming from this gentlewomans?
Mary.   Good sir, goe sleepe: for if I credit have
  She was in my armes, then, abed.
Sam.   I told ye.
Hylas.   Be not so confident.
Dorothy.   By th' mas, she must sir,
  For ile no husband here, before I know him:
  And so good morrow to ye: Come, let's goe seeke 'em.
                              [*Exit with* Mary.]
Sam.   I told ye what ye had done.
Hylas.   Is the devill stirring?
  Well, goe with me: for now I wilbe married.
                                          Exeunt.

                Enter Michael, Valentine, *and* Alice.   [V.] xi

Michael.   I have brought him backe againe.
Valentine.   You have don a friendship

          32 cozend] F2; cozens Q   V.xii] *Scena Undecima.* Q

Worthy the love you beare me.

Michael. Would he had so too.

Valentine. O he's a worthy yong man.

Michael. When al's tryde
I feare you'l change your faith: bring in the gentleman.

Enter Francis, *and servant*; *and* Abbesse, *and* Cellide, *severally.*

Valentine. My happy Mistresse too: now Fortune helpe me,
And all you starres, that governe chast desires
Shine faire, and lovely.

Abbesse. But one houre, deere Daughter,
To heare your Guardian, what he can deliver
In Loves defence, and his: and then your pleasure.

Cellide. Though much unwilling, you have made me yeeld,—— 10
More for his sake I see. how full of sorrow,
Sweet catching sorrow, he appeares? O love,
That thou but knew'st to heale, as well as hurt us.

Michael. Be ruld by me: I see her eye fast on him:
And what ye heard, beleeve, for tis so certaine
He neither dar'd, nor must oppose my evidence;
And be you wise, yong Lady, and beleeve too.
This man you love, Sir?

Valentine. As I love my soule, Sir.

Michael. This man you put into a free possession
Of what his wants could aske: or your selfe render? 20

Valentine. And shall do still.

Michael. Nothing was bard his libertie
But this faire Maide; that friendship first was broken,
And you, and she abus'd; next, (to my sorrow
So faire a forme should hide so darke intentions,)
He hath himselfe confes'd (my purpose being
Only to stop his Journey, by that pollicy
Of laying fellony to his charge, to fright the Saylors)
Divers abuses, done, thefts often practis'd,
Moneys, and Jewels too, and those no trifles.

Cellide. O where have I bestrew'd my faith: in neither: 30

*16 dar'd] *stet* Q   *30–31 O...bestrew'd...vertue] *stet* Q

513

Let's in for ever now, there is vertue.

Michael.   Nay do not wonder at it, he shall say it.
Are ye not guiltie thus?

Francis.   Yes: O my Fortune.

Michael.   To give a proofe I speake not enviously,
Looke here: do you know these Jewels?

Cellide.   In, good Mother.

     Enter Thomas, Dorothy, *and* Mary: *then* Sebastian
                and Launcelot.

Valentine.   These Jewels; I have knowne.

Dorothy.   You have made brave sport.

Thomas.   Ile make more, if I live Wench.
Nay doe not looke on me: I care not for ye.

Launcelot.   Do you see now plaine? that's Mistris *Dorothy*,
And that's his Mistris.

Sebastian.   Peace, let my joy worke easely.   40
Ha, boy: art there my boy: mine owne boy, *Tom* boy,
Home *Lance*, and strike a fresh peece of wine, the towne's ours.

Valentine.   Sure, I have knowne these Jewels.

Alice.   They are they, certaine.

Valentine.   Good heaven, that they were.

Alice.   Ile pawne my life on't,
And this is he; Come hither Mistris *Dorothy*,
And Mistris *Mary*: who do's that face looke like:
And view my brother well?

Dorothy.   In truth like him.

Mary.   Upon my troth exceeding like.

Michael.   Beshrew me,
But much: and maine resemblance, both of face
And lineaments of body: now heaven grant it.   50

Alice.   My brother's full of passion, I'le speake to him.
Now, as you are a gentleman, resolve me,
Where did you get these jewels?

Francis.   Now I'le tell ye,
Because blinde fortune yet may make me happy:
Of whom I had 'em, I have never heard yet,

But from my infancy, upon this arme
I ever wore 'em.
Alice.   'Tis *Francisco* brother,
  By heaven I ty'd 'em on: a little more sir,
  A little, little more, what parents have ye?
Francis.   None
  That I know yet, the more my stubborne fortune: 60
  But as I heard a Merchant say that bred me,
  Who, to my more affliction, di'de a poore man,
  When I reach'd eighteen yeers——
Alice.   What said that Merchant?
Francis.   He said, an infant, in the *Genoway* Galleyes,
  But from what place he never could direct me,
  I was taken in a sea-fight, and from a Marriner,
  Out of his manly pitty he redeem'd me.
  He told me of a Nurse that waited on me,
  But she, poore soule, he said was killed.
  A letter too, I had enclos'd within me,   70
  To one *Castructio* a Venetian Merchant,
  To bring me up: the man, when yeers allow'd me,
  And want of friends compell'd, I sought, but found him
  Long dead before, and all my hopes gone with him.
  The wars was my retreat then, and my travell
  In which I found this gentlemans free bounty,
  For which, heaven recompence him: now ye have all.
Valentine.   And all the worldly blisse that heaven can send me,
  And all my prayers and thanks.
Alice.   Down o' your knees, sir,
  For now you have found a father, and that father   80
  That will not venture ye againe in Gallyes.
Michael.   'Tis true, beleeve her sir, and we all joy with ye.
Valentine.   My best friend still: my deerest: now heaven blesse
      thee
  And make me worthy of this benefit.
  Now my best Mistresse——
Cellide.   Now sir, I come to ye.
Abbesse.   No, no, let's in wench.

77 recompence] S; recompenc'd Q, F 2, L

Cellide.   Not for the world, now, Mother,
  And thus sir, all my service I pay you,
  And all my love to him.
Valentine.   And may it prosper,
  Take her *Francisco*: now no more yong *Callidon*,
  And love her deerely, for thy father do's so.   90
Francis.   May all hate seek me else, and thus I seale it.
Valentine.   Nothing but mirth now, friends.

Enter Hylas *and* Sam.

Hylas.   Nay, I will finde him.
Sam.   What doe all these here?
Thomas.   You are a trusty husband,
  And a hot lover too.
Hylas.   Nay then, good morrow,
  Now I perceive the knavery.
Sam.   I still told ye.
Thomas.   Stay, or I'le make ye stay: come hither sister.
Valentine.   Why how now Mistresse *Thomas?*
Thomas.   Peace a little,——
  Thou would'st faine have a wife?
Hylas.   Not I, by no meanes.
Thomas.   Thou shalt have a wife, and a fruitful wife, for I finde
  Hylas,
  That I shall never be able to bring thee children.   100
Sebastian.   A notable brave boy, 'nown son agen.
Hylas.   I am very well sir.
Thomas.   Thou shalt be better *Hylas,*
  Thou hast seven hundred pound a yeer,
  And thou shalt make her three hundred joynture.
Hylas.   No.
Thomas.   Thou shalt boy, and shalt bestow
  Two hundred pound in clothes, look on her,
  A delicate lusty wench, she has fifteen hundred,
  And feasible: strike hands, or I'le strike first.
Dorothy.   You'l let me like?
Mary.   He's a good handsome fellow,

101 'nown son agen.] C; *known son agen.* Q

516

Play not the foole.
Thomas.   Strike, brother *Hylas*, quickly.   110
Hylas.   If you can love me, well.
Dorothy.   If you can please me.
Thomas.   Try that out soon, I say, my brother *Hylas*.
Sam.   Take her, and use her well, she's a brave gentlewoman.
Hylas.   You must allow me another Mistresse.
Dorothy.   Then you must allow me another servant.
Hylas.   Well, let's together then, a lustry kindred.
Sebastian.   I'le give thee five hundred pound more for that word.
Mary.   Now sir, for you and I to make the feast full.
Thomas.   No, not a bit, you are a vertuous Lady,
And love to live in contemplation.   120
Mary.   Come foole, I am friends now.
Thomas.   The foole shall not ride ye,
There lye my woman, now my man again,
And now for travell once more.
Sebastian.   I'le bar that first.
Mary.   And I next.
Thomas.   Hold your selfe contented: for I say I will travell,
And so long I will travell, till I finde a father
That I never knew, and a wife that I never look'd for,
And a state without expectation,
So rest you merry gentlemen.
Mary.   You shall not,
Upon my faith, I love you now extremely,   130
And now I'le kisse ye.
Thomas.   This will not doe it, Mistresse.
Mary.   Why when we are married, we'l doe more.
Sebastian.   Ther's all boy,
The keyes of all I have, come, let's be merry,
For now I see thou art right.
Thomas.   Shall we to Church straight?
Valentine.   Now presently, and there with nuptiall
The holy Priest shall make ye happy all.
Thomas.   Away then, faire afore.

                                        Exeunt.

FINIS.

TEXTUAL NOTES

I.i

22 young$_\Lambda$] The retention of Q's comma, though it is doubtless inten-
tionallyr hetorical, would create the tautology of 'youthful, | And young'.
117–119 power——...now,——] The construction of the passage, which
depends on the notion that Francis interrupts Valentine's speech and
Valentine briefly replies 'Ye wrong my tender love now,——' before
resuming his former sentence, was first recognized by Mason and has been
adopted by editors since W.

I.ii

8 *du gat awhee*] One need not quarrel with Colman's explanation, adopted
by all subsequent editors, that Q *du gata whee* represents a corruption of
Welsh *Duw cadw chwi*, 'God bless you', or 'God preserve you'. Yet the
phrase, in its setting among an unholy mixture of continental European
languages, sounds equally like mock-Dutch for 'you get away', re-empha-
sizing the preceding 'get you gone again'.

II.i

10–11 together: | Within these two daies deere——] Valentine, in what
would appear an echo of the opening of *MND*, embarks on a double
encomium of the impending wedding day, with a caesura at 'together:'.
To assume broken speech at 'deere——' implies that Cellide cannot bear
to hear him out, a psychological subtlety of characterization supported by
Alice's subsequent remark that no preparation has been made for the
wedding.

II.ii

3 your sweet] While Q's 'our sweet letter' has attraction in view of
Dorothy's having carried the letter, the bibliographical evidence of a space
in place of a piece of dropped type supports F 2's 'your' (from unobserved
variant state?).
30–32 Will...service] Dorothy and Thomas speak simultaneously. A
splitting of Q's hypermetrical line (29) reconstitutes lines 30 and 32 as
one continuous blank verse.
49 When your wants shall supply it.] S and all subsequent editors emend to
'When you want, shall supply it.' This does not markedly clarify the

construction, which for its meaning depends on the reference of 'it'. With 'it' = 'plate', Dorothy would appear to suggest to Thomas to help himself to what his father may deny him: 'There is plate in the parlour...when your circumstances of want/you in your straits, hardship (cf. *OED*, 'want', *sb²*, 3) shall supply (*OED*, 'supply', *v²* ≈ 'supplicate', *v* 2*b*) it'; or else, 'it' refers to the infant among the gypsies, whom Thomas 'in his straits/ hardship' may yet feel called upon to 'supply' = 'succour, relieve; support, maintain' (*OED*, 'supply', *v¹*, †1).

II.iii

135 a life] S's emendation 'as life', accepted by C, is rejected by subsequent editors who read 'a' life' and explain variously as 'at life' (W, following Tyrwhitt), or 'on my life, of my life' (D, following Todd, and Johnson's *Dictionary*).

II.iv

2 Phæses] F2 | spell 'faeces', and *OED* lists this passage as the first occurrence of 'faeces' = 'excrement'. But the uroscopy practised clearly establishes the earlier meaning of 'sediment; dregs' (*OED*, 1).

10 unflam'd] 'the pot's unflam'd yet': it is not quite clear from the context what observation, or matter, or what fulfilled or unfulfilled bodily functions the diagnosis is here being based upon. D and V, in emending to 'un-phlegm'd' (verbalizing a suggestion put forward by W), hold that uroscopy is still in question, and that 'the Second Doctor means that *phlegm* is not discharged into the vessel'. If so, Q's 'unflam'd' may equally constitute a reference to diagnosis by urinary colors (as discussed in Herbert Silvette, *The Doctor on the Stage* (Knoxville, 1967), p. 9). But we may do well to follow S and C in more acutely noting that the matter changes with the suggested remedies of clysters and a vomit, and the Second Physician's appreciation of the patient's stomach condition. Medically, a complete inertia of the bowels seems indicated, in which case the phrase would somewhat obscurely take on a meaning like 'the pot is unlined, or unfilled, yet'. Alternatively, the Second Physician may be reminding his colleagues of the condition of matter actually discharged (though mercifully inspected offstage). S/C's emendation 'enflam'd' would then be a possibility (cf. *OED*, 'inflamed', 3); and S's 'unclean'd', though arrived at by paleo-graphic rationalization, and unacceptable as an emendation, would euphe-mistically adumbrate the meaning. However, the uncertainty remaining as to the precise nature of the observation, combined with the possibility that, in stool examination as in uroscopy, color patterns were registered, suggests the retention of Q 'unflam'd'.

II.v

104–105 *Valentine.* What...treasure?] Q's original punctuation '...doe?' '...unsorrow'd?' '...treasure?' supports the critical decision to emend contrary to the copy-text and all previous editions and to consider the harshness of the lines as the tone of Valentine's self-reproach rather than that of contemptuous derision in Cellide.

III.i

101 aim'd] Q leaves a space (reproduced by F 2), indicating that copy was illegible. Of the two emendations proposed, this edition opts for 'aim'd' (V), accepting the explanation of K. Deighton (*The Old Dramatists* (London, 1896), p. 70) that the image is one of archery rather than of nature (as in C–D, 'born and shot together').

103 art of memory] Eliciting no satisfactory meaning, C, D and V have emended to 'act of memory', assuming no doubt that Cellide intimates in general terms the futility, for the younger partner, of a marriage with old age while it lasts, and after it has ended. Should however Q's 'art of memory' correctly carry its specific *OED* meaning, it becomes possible to read line 103 as a chiastically reversed and syntactically elliptical particularization of line 102, contrasting the fecund pastimes with a young husband (leaving behind a living name) with the fruitless doating over a game at cards with an old one.

293 for, say, the belly-ake] Modern pointing here simply brings out a possible seventeenth-century idiomatic usage (cf. *OED*, 'say', v^1, 10); 295 'therefore' consequently = 'therefor' (*OED*, 'therefore', I, 1a). There is no need to emend with D to 'for say the belly ache'.

297 *Hylas.*] Q runs on as *Sam*'s speech, changes to *Tom* at 299 (G 1, last line), and prefixes *Tom* again at 301 (G 1^v, line 2, after a probable change of compositor). This edition reduces Sam's part to the two half-lines at 295 and 302, and redistributes 296–301 by analogy to 281–283; after the belly-ake case, Hylas is allowed to present another teaser. Thomas, unable to restrain himself, helps to develop it, but Hylas takes the punch-line (301; see next note).

301 *Hylas.* Must...humour?] The line drives home a case consistently developed, though outrageous: from the hypochondria (the bowels), the melancholy vapours rise through a hernia in the diaphragm; swelling the kidneys below, they also cause the brains to become mouldy above (cf. *OED*, 'must', v^2). The sentence, therefore, is not elliptical, as all editions since F 2 – printing, apparently, from a copy of Q where frisket bite obliterated the '?' to further suggest auxiliary 'must' – have considered it.

365 split] In the immediate context of 'credit', which by itself easily suggests Q's 'spilt', 'split' is the *lectio difficilior*; since it carries the ship-

wreck imagery, it is accepted in accordance with all editions since F 2, even though the source is unauthoritative.

394 breeks]   Though all editions accept F 2 'break', and 'to break a person's head' is a common term of abuse in the language of the period, Q's form 'breeks' is not easily accounted for as a printing error, and may be a dialect variant. While lexically unrecorded, it is allowed to stand.

406 tipvaes]   The term is unrecorded, and its meaning somewhat obscure. As a measure to be danced at a huntsup, it may indeed, as Dyce suggests, be etymologically linked with 'tivy' (cf. *OED*, 'tivy' = 'tantivy').

III.ii

3 two fore-horses]   No editor has followed S in emending 'fore-horses' to 'Four Horses' (of a coach and four). But the intuition behind that emendation is valuable, since it helps to recognize that, by a reading of 'two' for 'to', the number of horses is still specified. This clarifies the construction of Sebastian's speech as an elliptically parallel set of two questions, one general and one particular: 'Should I leave my state to pins...and frownces? | [should I leave my] two fore-horses [and coach] to thee?'

4 behind'en]   Altered to 'behind 'em' (two words) in F 2; and so all subsequent editions. Q's original 'behind'en' (one word), however, though possibly influenced in respect of its apostrophe by the ubiquitous Fletcherian ''em', is acceptable as a survival of OE/ME 'behindan/behinden'.

24 wrong]   Since 'you have wrong' (*OED*, 'wrong', *sb*² 1†b; 8†a) is an idiomatic alternative for 'you are in the wrong', sense is also made of

25 will]   To Sebastian's 'You will realize (you shall know) you are wrong', Dorothy retorts bitterly, 'You will never do so. But I realize (I will know) my duty.'

29 please you]   All editions accept F 2's reversal to 'you please'. But in the word order of the first edition, the rhythmical pattern of the spoken line emphasizes the 'you: I' antithesis, the climax of Dorothy's emotional speech.

III.iii

56.1 *Song*.]   According to the implied direction in line 55, this should be *Maudline* (*Bishop Percy's Folio Manuscript*, ed. W. Hales and F. J. Furnivall (London, 1868), vol. III, pp. 374–84), or *The Merchant's Daughter of Bristol* (*Roxburghe Ballads*, ed. W. Chappell (London, 1869), vol. II pt I, pp. 86–95). On account of its length, however, the ballad as found in these and other sources could not possibly have been recited in full. But its opening plays with a sufficient number of motifs which, in a different constellation, are also those of *Monsieur Thomas*, to provide a fitting serenade for Thomas beneath Mary's window:

Behold: the touchstone of true loue,
   Maudlin, the Merchants daughter of Bristow towne,
whose ffirme affection nought cold moue!
   this ffauor beares the louely browne.
a gallant youth was dwelling by,
   which long time had borne this Lady great good will;
she loued him most ffaithffully,
   but all her ffreinds withstoode itt still.
the young man now perceiuing well
   he cold not gett nor winn the fauor of her ffreinds,
the fforce of sorrow to expell,
   to vew strange countryes hee intends;
& now to take his last ffarwell
   of his true loue & constant Maudlin,
with sweet musicke, that did excell,
   he playes vnder her windowe then:
'farwell,' quoth he, 'my owne true Loue!'
   'ffarwell,' quoth he, 'the cheeffest tresure of my Heart
Throughe ffortunes spite, that ffalse did proue,
   I am inforcet ffrom thee to parte
into the Land of Italye;
   there will I waite & weary out my dayes in woe.
seing my true loue is kept ffrom mee,
   I hold my liffe a mortall ffoe.
therfore, ffaire Bristow towne, now adew!
   for Padua shalbe my habitation now
although my loue doth Lodge in thee,
   to welcome whom alone my heart I vow.'
with trickling teares this did hee singe;
   with sighes & sobbs discendinge from his hart full sore,
he said, when hee his hands did wringe,
   'ffarwell, sweet loue, ffor euer-more!'
ffaire Maudline from a window hye
   beholding her true loue with Musicke where he stoode,
but not a word shee durst replye,
   ffearing her parents angry moode.

(Quoted from *Bishop Percy's Folio Manuscript*, vol. III, pp. 374–6)

70–72 *O...deere.*] No independent source for the song tags is known. C would seem correct in recognizing *O gentle squire* as the first line of the Maid's reply. Since none of it is in italics in Q, it cannot be shown just how it was divided between singing and speaking apart. But that it is meant to be so divided is suggested by the typically Fletcherian tag 'I'le see thee hang first.' This edition relines accordingly.

81–84 *Come up...here.*] With only slight modifications, the lines are repeatedly used in the Beaumont and Fletcher canon. See *Knight of the Burning Pestle* III.495–500; and *The Woman's Prize* I.iii, 45–7.

88–89 *The loue...goe.*] Two lines from the ballad which was quoted by distorted title in line 41. The textual differences between the three traceable manuscript versions are very marked. MS Tanner 306, fo. 306 (Oxford), apparently the earliest version extant (1563), reads:

> In create when dedalus begane
> His longe exile and state to waye
> thought [thoughe?] mynos wrathe had shut up then
> eche waye by land eche way by sea
> the Love of grece yet pricks him so
> that he devised a way to goe.

Rawl.poet.112, fo. 18 (Oxford), Harley 7578, fo. 103 (BL), and, deriving from it, MS Mus.d.184, fo. 19 (Oxford), all render the first line as 'In Crete when Dedalus first began' (Rawl.poet.112). But the penultimate line of the stanza suffers a surprising sea-change from 'The love of Greece it pricked him soo' (Rawl.) to 'the love of creett hyme pryeked so' (Harley) and 'the Lord of creatt hyme prycked so' (MS Mus.d.184).

IV.ii

25 Master] Here, and at lines 91, 94, 110, 140 and 149, the Quarto abbreviation is 'M.' It equally allows expansion to 'Monsieur'. At line 82, Launcelot addresses Thomas in an expanded form as 'Master *Thomas*'; at line 128, by contrast, Sebastian uses 'Mounsieur' sarcastically, and by itself. It might be tempting to distinguish between a form 'Master *Thomas*' as used by Launcelot, and 'Monsieur *Thomas*' as used by Sebastian. But the Q convention is apparently to apply 'M.' without distinction to Thomas and to Valentine (line 94); consequently, this edition expands to 'Master' uniformly throughout the scene.

26 Mermidons,] Depending on the absence or presence of punctuation, 'Mermidons' refers to either the Fidler and Launcelot, or Hylas and Sam.

62 1 Second] The opening s.d. has brought in 'Sebastian' *and* a servant.' Here, as Dyce observed, a second servant is required, unless the first one be made to go out in search of Thomas and to re-enter here. But there is no warrant in the text for such going and coming of the first servant, since at line 92 he continues to relate the events of the night before, and, with silent action, would be supporting Launcelot's report throughout. A second servant therefore heralds Thomas' entry and speaks three words only in line 63. The two servants go out together at line 109 and, according to the original Q direction, re-enter with the money bags two lines later. Since they are no longer required, this edition follows Dyce in removing them again immediately.

IV.iv

38 hypocrites] Q's *Hypocrites* wrongly (I take it) suggests *Hippocrates*.

67 canwast] The context suggests 'canvass' (*OED*, *v*, 4a, b), 'to scrutinize fully, to examine physically'; the -w- spelling, to be found in connotations of hawking ('canvas', *sb* 6; and 'canvas', *v†* 1), may suggest an overtone of 'catching out'.

V.ii

29 This Nunnerys fal] F2+ change number and tense to 'This Nunnery's faln'. But this is an unnecessary double sophistication if 'This' be read as plural 'These'.

V.ix

4 all to bemarried] A triple intensive construction, recognized as such by D and V, according to *OED*, 'To- *prefix²*', sense 3; and *OED* 'Be- *prefix*', senses 7, with 2 and 6.

V.x

38 keptst] The clearly conditional use validates Q 'keptst' – 'preterite of imagination', in O. Jespersen's term (*A Modern English Grammar on Historical Principles*, vol. IV (London, 1946), p. 117) – against F2's modernized 'keepst'.

V.xii

16 dar'd...must] 'Neither would he dare oppose...(nor must he do so).' 'Dar'd' signalizes a subjunctive construction, not an incongruence of tenses.

30–31 O...bestrew'd...vertue] 'Bestrew'd' appears acceptable – against all editions since L – if taken to carry a meaning of 'scattered' or 'squandered' (a semantic possibility within given lexical definitions; cf. *OED* 'bestrew'). In the subsequent line, 'Let's in now,...there is vertue', alternatives of punctuation affect the meaning. To read 'there is vertue' as 'In Valentine and Francis I see my illusions of virtue shattered' establishes an antithesis requiring a dash: 'now——there'. But if 'there' refers to the seclusion of the nunnery, the original Q punctuation is clearly satisfactory.

PRESS-VARIANTS IN Q

[NOTE: There are forty-one extant known copies of *Monsieur Thomas* (1639) and two of *Fathers own Son* (n.d., 1661/2?). Of these, twelve have been machine collated, another fifteen have been seen and checked for the press-variants revealed in the first twelve. The remaining sixteen copies have not been inspected.

Copies machine collated:
- (1) British Library, 644.b.28
- (2) British Library, Ashley 90
- (3) Bodleian Library, Malone Q1
- (4) Bodleian Library, Malone 203(1)
- (5) Bodleian Library, Malone 203(7)
- (6) Bodleian Library, *Fathers own Son*
- (7) Oxford, Worcester College Library
- (8) Oxford, Wadham College Library
- (9) Cambridge University Library
- (10) Edinburgh, National Library of Scotland
- (11) Glasgow University Library
- (12) Newcastle University Library

Copies seen:
- (13) Cambridge, Trinity College Library
- (14) Washington D.C., Folger Shakespeare Library, copy 1
- (15) do., copy 2
- (16) do., copy 3
- (17) San Marino, Henry E. Huntington Library 59777
- (18) do., 123833 (*Fathers own Son*)
- (19) Austin (Texas), University of Texas Library, Aitken–Swinburne copy
- (20) do., Ah F635 639m
- (21) do., Wh F635 639m
- (22) Philadelphia, University of Pennsylvania Library
- (23) Princeton University Library
- (24) do., Taylor Collection
- (25) New York, Pierpont Morgan Library
- (26) New Haven, Yale Elizabethan Club
- (27) Boston Public Library

Copies not inspected:
- (28) London, Victoria and Albert Museum, Dyce Collection
- (29) Cambridge, Emmanuel College Library
- (30) Cambridge, St John's College Library

(31) Chatsworth, Duke of Devonshire Library
(32) Carlisle Cathedral Library
(33) Washington D.C., Library of Congress
(34) Los Angeles, University of California Clark Library
(35) Fort Worth, Texas Christian Library
(36) Bloomington (Ind.), University of Indiana Library
(37) Urbana (Ill.), University of Illinois Library
(38) Chicago, University of Chicago Library
(39) Chicago, Newberry Library
(40) New York, Carl H. Pforzheimer Library
(41) Hartford (Conn.), Trinity College Watkinson Library
(42) Williamstown (Mass.), Chapin Library
(43) Cambridge (Mass.), Houghton Library]

SHEET B (*outer forme*)

Sig. B1   state a: head title *Thomas.*
        (3), (6), (11); *also* (15), (21).
        state b: head title *Thomas,*
        (1), (2), (4), (5), (7)–(10), (12); *also* (13), (14), (16)–(20), (22)–(27).

SHEET B (*inner forme*)

Sig. B2   state a: catchword I (present, though gradually dropping out)
        (1), (2), (4), (5) ,(8)–(10), (12); *also* (14), (16)–(19), (21), (24)–(27).
        state b: catchword (disappeared)
        (3), (6), (7), (11); *also* (13), (15), (20), (22), (23).

SHEET D (*outer forme*)

   Corrected: (1), (2), (5)–(7), (9), (10), (12); *also* (13)–(15),
                (17), (18), (20), (22), (23), (24), (27);
 Uncorrected: (3), (4), (8), (11); *also* (16), (19), (21), (25), (26).
Sig. D2ᵛ
  II.ii.18 perſwaſions] perſwaſion's
     27 tyes∧;] tyes;

SHEET E (*inner forme*)

      Corrected: (1)–(11); *also* (13)–(20), (22)–(27);
      Uncorrected: (12); *also* (21).
Sig. E3ᵛ
  II.v.58 aleagd] alleag'd

SHEET F (*inner forme*)

Sig. F2   state a: direction line F‖2   I h
(1), (7), (10); *also* (13), (18)–(20), (22)–(24).
state b: direction line F2   The
(2)–(6), (8), (9), (11), (12); *also* (14)–(17), (21), (25)–(27).

SHEET H (*inner forme*)

state a: (1), (5), (7),(9), (10); *also* (13), (20), (21), (23), (24);
state b: (2)–(4), (6), (8), (11), (12); *also* (14)–(19), (22), (25)–(27).
Sig. H4
   IV.i.52 his‸ joyes?] his joyes‸?

I.i

3 it. How] ~ , how Q; ~ : how F2
13 behaviour,] F2; ~ ∧ Q
18 (that...stil)] , ~ ... ~ , Q, F2
32 alter.] F2; ~ , Q
41 *Cellide*——] ~ . Q, F2
43 travell:] ~ ∧ Q; ~ , F2
58 onely——] F2; ~ ∧ Q
59 brother:] ~ , Q, F2
76 That, lay] ~ ∧ ~ Q; That ∧ lays F2

76 neck,] F2; ~ ∧ Q
76 travell:] ~ ∧ Q, F2
78 colts∧] F2; ~ ; Q
78 *Mary*] F2; Mary Q
84 visitation——] ~ . Q, F2
101 love;] ~ , Q, F2
110 returne——] F2; ~ . Q
117 power——] ~ . ∧ Q, F2
119 now,——] ~ , ∧ Q, F2
126 her:] ~ , Q, F2
136 *Valentine*] F2; Valentine Q
146 liking,] F2; ~ ∧ Q

I.ii

2 worship——] ~ : Q; ~ . F2
4 o'] O Q, F2
7 *Tom,*] F2; ~ : Q
7 *Thomas*:] ~ , Q, F2
10 punctually——] ~ . Q, F2
25 it, *Launcelot,*] F2; ~ ∧ ~ ∧ Q
31 neerest,] F2; ~ ∧ Q
35 *Thomas,*] F2; ~ ∧ Q
36 *Thomas*:] ~ , Q, F2
51 dog:——] ~ : ∧ Q; ~ . ∧ F2
53 conversion——] ~ , Q; ~ . F2
55 courses——] ~ . Q, F2
55.1 Dorothy] *Dorothea* Q, F2

56 sister:——] ~ ∧ ∧ Q, F2
57 picks,] F2; ~ ∧ Q
69 *Thomas.*] ~ , Q, F2
80 father's] F2; fathers Q
85 it. Deerest] ~ , deerest Q; ~ : dearest F2
89 minde——] ~ . Q, F2
96 faith] F2; fath Q
97 I'le——] F2; ~ . Q
101 mischeifes,] F2; ~ . Q
116 light——] ~ . Q, F2
123 ye?] F2; ~ . Q

I.iii

1 certaine,] F2; ~ ∧ Q
5 impression∧] F2; ~ ; Q
6 him;] ~ , Q, F2
15 him;] ~ , Q, F2
28 monstrous;] ~ ∧ Q, F2
28 shape,] F2; ~ ∧ Q
29 eyes,] F2; ~ ; Q
30 complexion——] ~ ∧ Q; ~. F2

32 making——] ~ . Q, F2
33 straiter,] F2; ~ . Q
44 follies——] ~ . Q, F2
55 s.d. Dorothy] *Dorothea* Q, F2
56 it:——] ~ : ∧ Q; ~ . F2
66 too.] F2; ~ : Q
70 heaven——] ~ . Q, F2
95 'pray.] F2; ~ : Q
101 friend,——] ~ , ∧ Q, F2

105 quartans] F2; quarterns Q
113 oh!] ~ : Q; ~ . F2
114 fingers.] F2; ~ , Q
122 *Indeed...ever.*] roman Q, F2

130 stile:] ~ . Q; ~ ? F2
131 *Deere Mistresse*] roman Q, F2
133 thinkes——] ~ . Q, F2

II.i

10 together:] ~ , Q, F2
11 deere——] ~ . Q, F2
13 preparation——] ~ . Q, F2
13 *s.d.* Francis] *Franck* Q, F2
18 is't] F2; i'st Q

20 feele:] ~ ₋ Q; ~ , F2
22 sir——] ~ , Q; ~ . F2
39 were).] ~)₋ Q; ~ .) F2
48 feele:] ~ , Q, F2
57 veyne——] ~ . Q, F2

II.ii

0.1 Dorothy] *Dorothea* Q, F2
12 debosh'd——] ~ ? Q, F2
17 Mistresse?] ~ ₋ Q; ~ . F2
18 perswasions] Q(u); perswasion's Q(c)
29–30 Till...ye. | Will...me

——] ~ ... ~ , will... ~ ₋ Q,
 F2 (*one line*)
30 me——] F2; ~' ₋ Q
31 Whut,] F2; ~ ₋ Q
32 any] ₋ ₋ny Q, F2

II.iii

1–2 Sirha...say: | Still...
 stiches:] ~ ... ~ ₋ still... ~ :
 Q, F2 (*one line*)
12 worship——] ~ . Q, F2
25 water.] F2; ~ , Q (*before omitted
 speech-prefix*)
33 rogue;] ~ , Q, F2
37 ever,——] ~ , ₋ Q; ~ . ₋ F2
42 agen:——] ~ : ₋ Q, F2
52 children:——] ~ : ₋ Q, F2
53 undone,] ~ : Q; ~ ; F2

53 me:] ~ , Q, F2
115 o'] F2, O Q
119 *Valentine,*₋] ~ , Q, F2
131 harke——] ~ . Q, F2
131 ——a] ₋ A Q, F2
134 *Alice*——] ~ . Q, F2
141 heaven——] ~ . Q, F2
142 so——] ~ . Q, F2
142 word——] ~ . Q, F2
144 visite,] F2; ~ ₋ Q
146 hir.] ~ ₋ Q; ~ ; F2

II.iv

7 low:] ~ , Q, F2

II.v

2 him;] ~ , Q, F2
25 think——] ~ . Q, F2
26 sir——] ~ . Q, F2
51 him——] ~ ₋ Q; ~ . F2
51 equall.] F2; ~ : Q

55 beauties] beautis Q; beautie F1
58 aleagd] Q(u); alleag'd Q(c)
66 pitty] pitiy Q; pity F2
98 (Yet...it,)] ₋ ~ ... ~ , Q, F2

III.i

352 man?] F2; ~ . Q
366 as——] F2; ~. Q
370 out-going——] ~ . Q, F2
378 *Tom,*] F2; ~ ∧ Q
383 ——How] ∧ ~ Q, F2
384 Juggler:] ~ ∧ Q; ~ ? F2
385.1 *Exeunt*∧] *Exit.* Q; *Ex.* F2

386 she?] F2; ~ . Q
396 then.] F2; ~ ∧ Q
403–404 Away...trusty,] *one line* Q,
F2
404 guid. Now] ~ ∧ now Q, F2
404 trusty,] F2; ~ ∧ Q

III.ii

1 againe.] ~ ∧ Q; ~ , F2
2 to∧] ~ , Q, F2
2 sticks,] F2; ~ ∧ Q
3 frownces?] F2; ~ , Q
10 pocket,] F2; ~ ∧ Q

11 it.] ~ ? Q, F2
19 late?] F2; ~ . Q
27 ²him,] F2, ~ ∧ Q
30 spoil'd,] F2; ~ ∧ Q
33 waits?] F2; ~ . Q

III.iii

3 boyes,] F2; ~ ∧ Q
27.1 *Exeunt*] F2; *Exit* Q
42 *Coventry*——] ~ , Q; ~ . F2
44 Dames——] ~ . Q, F2
52 key:] ~ , Q, F2
57 Who's...houres?] Who's...
rogue | At...houres? Q, F2
62 *Hey...adown.*] *as s.d. lined up
against line 61* Q, F2
64–65 *The...&c.*] *roman* Q, F2
67 69 *O...doore.*] *roman* Q, F2
69 *doore.*] ~ , Q, F2
70 *O...squire,*] *roman* Q, F2

70 *squire,*] ~ . Q, F2
71–72 I'le...first: | *Farewell...
deere.*] *one line roman* Q, F2
72 *deere.*] ~ , Q, F2
77 *promise,*] ~ . Q, F2
105.1 Samuel,] F2; ~ ∧ Q
112.1 *Exeunt*] *Exit* Q; *Ex.* F2
122 ye.——] ~ , ∧ Q, F2
123 willing,] ~ : Q, F2
124 thee:] ~ , Q, F2
142 shortly.] ~ , Q, F2
145 *full, thereby*∧] F2; ~ ∧ ~ , Q
145.1 *Exit*] *Exeunt* Q, F2

IV.i

5 Ride?] F2; ~ , Q
6 delivers,] ~ ∧ Q, F2
8 friend's] F2; friends Q
8 *Alice:*] ~ ? Q; ~ ; F2
32 Nunnery——] ~ . Q, F2
33 troubles.] ~ , Q, F2
42 dreame.] F2; ~ ? Q

44 yet——] ~ ∧ Q; ~ . F2
52 joyes——?] ~ ∧ ? Q, F2
52 gentleman.——] ~ . ∧ Q; ~ , ∧
F2
55 weigh——] ~ . Q, F2
64 her.] ~ ? Q; ~ , F2

IV.ii

1 Sir.] F 2; ~ : Q
2 gamesom] F 2; gameson Q
9 else:] ~ ∧ Q; ~ , F 2
17 noyse,] F 2; ~ ∧ Q
22 there,] F 2; ~ ∧ Q
25 himselfe,] F 2; ~ ∧ Q
26 Mermidons,] ~ ∧ Q, F 2
29 scalling,] ~ ∧ Q, F 2
32 sir,] F 2; ~ . Q
38 Queene-hith] queene-hith Q, F 2
50 passion,] F 2; ~ ∧ Q
51 shop,] F 2; ~ ∧ Q
52 cheering:] ~ ∧ Q; ~ , F 2
55–62 *If...toe.*] *roman* Q, F 2
55 *page,*] F 2; ~ ∧ Q
56 *me,*] F 2; ~ ∧ Q
58 *handsom*] F 2; handson Q
59 *page,*] ~ ∧ Q, F 2
60 *be,*] F 2; ~ ∧ Q
63 come?] F 2; ~ . Q
66 one,] F 2; ~ ∧ Q
71 speak't,] F 2; ~ ∧ Q
75 knave——] ~ , Q, F 2
83 sir,——] ~ , ∧ Q, F 2
84 *Robin,*] F 2; ~ ∧ Q
85 truth——] ~ . Q, F 2
85 varlets——] ~ . Q, F 2

87 see——] ~ . Q, F 2
88 *deu guin*] F 2; *roman* Q
88 *guin,*] ~ ∧ Q, F 2
90 night] F 2; ~ . Q
94 *Valentines,*] F 2; ~ ∧ Q
99 soberly,] F 2; ~ ∧ Q
103 *dieu*——] ~ ∧ Q; ~ . F 2
104 me no] *italic* Q, F 2
104 sirha,] F 2; ~ ∧ Q
108 daughter,] F 2; ~ ∧ Q
109 *Exeunt* Servants.] *Exit ser.* Q; *Exit servant.* F 2
115 another:] F 2; ~ ∧ Q
124 Gentleman——] ~ . Q, F 2
124 use,] F 2; ~ ∧ Q
130 it.] F 2; ~ ∧ Q
145 freely,] F 2; ~ ∧ Q
150 purpose:] ~ ; Q, F 2
151 all?] F 2; ~ ∧ Q
151 it.] F 2; ~ ∧ Q
152 *Thomas?*] F 2; ~ . Q
154.1 *Exeunt*] *Exit* Q; *Ex.* F 2
158 answere;] ~ , Q, F 2
160 nobly:] ~ , Q, F 2
165 *Albones*] F 2, *roman* Q
170 o'] F 2, O Q
189 play:] ~ , Q, F 2
196 honourably——] ~ , Q, F 2

IV.iii

2 us∧] ~ , Q, F 2
7 ty'd?] ~ | Q; ~ . F 2
8 taske:] ~ ∧ Q, F 2

14 by:] ~ ∧ Q; ~ ; F 2
23 *Michael*——] ~ . Q, F 2
28 her.] F 2; ~ ∧ Q

IV.iv

10 ha'] ha Q; have F2

41 porridge;] ~ , Q, F2

IV.v

0.1 *singing;*] ~ ∧ Q, F2
8 aboard:] ~ , Q, F2
23 note:] ~ , Q, F2

23 gentleman——] ~ . Q, F2
25 cruell.] ~ , Q, F2
27 jewell,] F2, ~ ∧ Q

V.i

1 handsomly,] F2; ~ ∧ Q
4 againe——] ~ . Q, F2
6 accesse——] ~ . Q, F2
9 What,] F2; ~ ∧ Q
13 What,] F2; ~ ∧ Q
13 on't,] F2; ~ ∧ Q
15 ready?] ~ . Q, F2
16 ye?] F2; ~ . Q
17 ye:] F2; ~ ∧ Q
20 her;] F2; ~ ∧ Q
21 wench.] F2; ~ ∧ Q
23 excellent,] F2; ~ ∧ Q
27 heeles,] F2; ~ ∧ Q
32 drab,] F2; ~ ∧ Q
33 slut,] F2; ~ ∧ Q
34 beefe,] F2; ~ ∧ Q

35 Dame,] ~ ∧ Q; ~ ? F2
37–42 *Saint* George...*night.*] ro-
    man Q, F2
37 *knight,*] F2; ~ ∧ Q
39 *found,*] F2; ~ ∧ Q.
44–47 *From...sends,*] From...
    Dayries, | From...sends, Q,
    F2
44–48 *From...heaven.*] roman Q,
    F2
54 tricke.] ~ , Q, F2
55 too——] ~ , Q; ~ . F2
55 her?] F2; ~ , Q
58 sir——] ~ . Q, F2
65 h'as] F2; has Q

V.ii

7 father:] ~ , Q, F2
8 *Valentine,*] ~ : Q; ~ ; F2

24 sport——] ~ , Q, F2

V.iii

9 so——] ~ , Q, F2
10 all;] ~ , Q, F2

11 way.——] ~ ʍ Q; ~ . ∧ F2
22 him.——] ~ , ∧ Q; ~ . ∧ F2

V.v

8 streighter: ha] ~ : | Ha Q, F2
9 tumble?] F2; ~ , Q
16–19 *fy...gentleman*——...*Out*
    ...*not,*] roman Q, F2

16 *gentleman*——] gentleman. Q,
    F2
17 Thomas,] F2; ~ ∧ Q
21 for't,] F2; for'[t]∧ Q

533

24 *Mary——*] ~ . Q, F 2
26 me;] ~ , Q, F 2
27 now,] ~ ; Q; ~ ? F 2
28 ²pretty,] F 2; ~ ∧ Q
35 Cassock.] F 2; ~ , Q
39, 48 o'] F 2; O Q
43 kinder.] F 2; ~ ∧ Q
44 Wench?] F 2; ~ . Q

44 your self∧ next,] F 2; ~ ~ , ~ ∧ Q
44 Mistris,] F 2; ~ ∧ Q
45 thee?] F 2; ~ . Q
52 *Doll*∧] F 2; ~ . Q
53 *Cellide,*] F 2; ~ ∧ Q
56 grown,] F 2; ~ ∧ Q

V.vi

1 wench——] ~ ∧ Q; ~ . F 2
4 feretting?] F 2; ~ ∧ Q
7 for,] F 2; ~ ∧ Q
10 Harke ye,] F 2; ~ ~ ∧ Q
11 sir:] ~ , Q; ~ ; F 2
23 me?] F 2; ~ ∧ Q
24 there:] ~ ∧ Q, F 2
27 honourably——] ~ . Q, F 2

45 marry,] F 2; ~ ∧ Q
53 *Hugh*] F 2; Hugh Q
55 be.] b[e∧] Q; ~ ; F 2
56 night——] ~ . Q, F 2
61 ye:] ~ , Q, F 2
63 it:] ~ , Q, F 2
64 Farewell:] ~ , Q, F 2

V.vii

1 houres,] ~ ∧ Q, F 2
2 while∧] F 2; ~ , Q

5 slumbers.] F 2; ~ , Q
18.2 *Musicke,*] ~ ∧ Q, F 2

V.ix

15 him:] ~ ∧ Q; ~ ; F 2

16 fast, ∧ faith] ~ ∧ 'faith Q, F 2

V.x

10 you——] ~ . Q, F 2
12 me.——] ~ , ∧ Q; ~ . ∧ F 2
13 this?——] ~ ? ∧ Q, F 2
24 fire——] ~ . Q, F 2

25–28 *Be...seen*——] ±F 2; Be
...blest, | Be...seen. Q
44 her——] ~ ∧ Q; ~ , F 2
45 Aunt——] ~ . Q, F 2

V.xi

1 Nunnery,] F 2; ~ ∧ Q
6 indeed;] F 2; ~ ∧ Q
19 what] F 2; What Q
20 Jewels.] F 2; ~ : Q

20 adornement.] ~ ∧ Q; ~ , F 2
24 foolish.] ~ ∧ Q; ~ , F 2
27 boldly,] F 2; ~ ∧ Q
44 sir,] ~ . Q; ~ ; F 2

V.xii

4.1 *servant*;] ~ , Q, F2

10 yeeld,——] ~ , ‸ Q, F2

11 sorrow,] ~ ‸ Q, F2

34 enviously,] F2; ~ ‸ Q

35 Jewels?] F2; ~ . Q

37 Wench.] ~ ‸ Q; ~ , F2

40 easely.] ~ ‸ Q; ~ , F2

41 *Tom*‸] ~ . Q; ~ , F2

42 peece‸] F2; ~ , Q

42 towne's] F2; townes Q

44 on't,] F2; ~ ‸ Q

54 happy:] ~ , Q, F2

60 yet,. . .fortune:] ~ :. . .~ , Q, F2

63 yeers——] ~ . Q, F2

65 me,] F2; ~ . Q

85 Mistresse——] ~ . Q, F2

97 little,——] ~ , ‸ Q, F2

101 boy,] ~ . Q, F2

102–103 Thou   shalt. . .yeer,]   *one line* Q, F2

103 seven] 7 Q, F2

104 three] 3 Q, F2

110 brother‸ *Hylas*,'] F2; ~ , ~ ‸ Q

129 not,] F2; ~ ‸ Q

135 nuptiall‸] F2; ~ . Q

HISTORICAL COLLATION

[The editions collated and their sigla are: F 2 (Second Folio, 1679), L (Langbaine, 1711), S (Seward, Sympson, Theobald, 1750), C (Colman, 1778), W (Weber, 1812), D (Dyce, 1843–6), V (Variorum, 1904–12).]

Dedication] *om.* L, S, C   Commendatory Verses] *om.* F 2, L–C

I.i

2 you] you are F 2, L–S
15 lyes] lie S–D
18 And...absence (...stil)] ~
    ...~...~ Q, F 2, L; (~ ...
    ~...~) S–V
59 allowes] allow C–D

76 lay] lays F 2, L–S
76 in] on C–V
90 *Hylas.*] *om.* Q, F 2, L
120 excepted] accepted Q, F 2, L
141 ere] e'er F 2+
151 unto] to F 2, L–S , D

I.ii

0.1 *old*] *om.* C, W, D
8 *du gat awhee*] *du gata whee* Q+
17–19 Is...ariv'd | To ask your
    (...sweetly) | Benediction] Is
    ...ask | (...sweetly) | Your
    Benediction S
20 furies] Juries S
31–32 To aske ye... | Your quo-
    tidian] To ask your... |
    Quotidian S
32 here he is] he's here S
38 much] much much Q

40 Ere] E'er L
51 howsoever] however F 2, L–S
64 *we*] we Q
72 Has] Have C, W
74 my] thy F 2, L–S
78 Ere] E'er F 2+
96 you] your Q
119–120 remember | You, you] re-
    member you, | You C, D;
    remember you, | You, you W;
    remember | You V
138 he] him F 2, L–S, D, V

I.iii

57 The] Thou W
76 He's] His Q

122 *law*] law Q–C; la W, D, V

II.i

11 two] too Q, F 2
12 Shall] Still C, W, D
15 all] *om.* V

25 harbingers] harbinger's Q, F 2,
    L

536

II.ii

3 your sweet] our sweet Q
16–17 with...Mistresse?] *variously indicated as quotation* S+

23 othes] others Q, F 2, L
49 your wants‿] you want, S+
57 better] betters S

II.iii

13 third] thirdly F 2, L–S
25 slept'st] sleep'st W
26 *Launcelot.*] om. Q
44 ¹ye] he Q, F 2, L–S
85 yea] ye Q
96 prentize] a ~ S; 'prentice W, D
105 that's] that Q

107 old] own F 2, L–S
110 Another] Anothers F 2
115 o'] O Q
118 dog] Dogs L, S
135 a] as S, C; a' W, D, V
144 visite] visit [Frank] D

II.iv

10 unflam'd] unclean'd S; enflam'd C; unphlegm'd D, V

II.v

25, 26 heaven] Heavens F 2, L–C
52 put me] put upon me W
55 beauties] beautis Q; beauties C, W, D
61 my selfe] I myself S

66 part] part's F 2, L–W, V; heart D
84 ere] e'r (e'er) F 2+
94 so] so so Q
104 Dye] *Cellide.* Dye Q+
106 *Cellide.*] om. Q+

III.i

0.1 a Pothecary] *an Apothecary* F 2, L+
2 those] these F 2, L, S
35 two] too Q
38 these] those C, W
52 O] Of Q
53 ye have] have ye F 2, L, S
54 not] no F 2, L, S
63 and] this S
65 to] too F 2, L–W, V; so D
88 friend] friends Q, F 2, L–W
90 you not] not you F 2, L, S
101 aim'd and shot] [*space*] and

shot Q, F 2, L; [*om.*] and shot up S; born and shot C–D
103 art] act C, D, V
120 imaculate] unaculate Q; the immaculate S–V
134 day] day's L, S
140 marke] make Q, F 2, L
144 to] so Q, F 2
153 With] *Cellide.* With Q, F 2, L
153 *Cellide.*] om. Q, F 2, L
173 Or] *Cellide.* Or Q
173 *Cellide.*] om. Q
179 Rigd] Ridg'd L+

180 mynes] minds F2, L
182 his] her Q, F2
215 patient] patent Q
227 no] an S
234 minister] mimister Q, F2, L, S
269 and] at S–V
279 feares] fevers D
293 belly-ake] belly ache (*noun+ verb*) D

297 *Hylas.*] *om.* Q, F2, L+
301 *Hylas.*] *Tom.* Q; *om.* F2, L+
353 curelesse] careless F2, L, S
365 split] spilt Q
371 Which] With Q, F2, L
394 breeks] break F2, L+
396 thee] the Q, F2, L, S
399 eyes] *om.* F2

III.ii

3 two] to Q, F2, L+
3 fore-horses] Four Horses S
4 a] an F2, L+
4 leather] leathern W
4 behind'en] behind 'em F2, L+
11 your] our W

14 shewes] shew D
24 wrong] wrong'd F2, L+
25 will] well F2, L+
26 ere] e'er L
29 please you] you please F2, L+
31 you] your Q

III.iii

2 her] the W
31 *No...Signieur,*] *No point man-ger, no point de vin, no, seigneur,* D
34 Signieur *du*] *Signieur Dieu* S, D

62 adown] *down* F2, L–S
70 *Maid.*] *given to* Launcelot Q, F2, L–S
71 hang] hang'd F2, L–S
132 is in no hand] nothing have S

IV.i

6 a] *om.* Q
9 ere] e're F2; e'er L, S, W–V

23 a bed] i'bed F2, L+
27 abed] 'bed F2

IV.ii

9 Your] You Q
32 Nor] Not L, S
46 mainly] manly Q, F2, L–W
47 to] *om.* Q
48 Admiral's] Admirable Q, F2, L
53 goes] goe F2, L–D
62 *head to toe*] Cap à pie S
62.1 Second] *om.* Q, F2, L–W, V
66 thy] the Q
84 Of] If Q+

87 Extreame] Extremely L
88 Bud] And D, V
88 *deu guin*] *Dieu guarde* S
104 *Sebastian.*] *om.* Q
108 servants] servant Q, F2, L
157 yeare] years F2, L–W
170 o'] O Q
178 hound] hand Q, F2, L
187 Ere] E're F2; E'er L, S

IV.iii

14 danger] daughter Q, F2
17 selfe] *om.* Q, F2, L

26 Ere] E're F2; E'er L

IV.iv

0.1 *Sam*] Samuel F2, L–S
10 ha'] have F2, L–W
19 Beside‚] Besides‚ F2, L–S, D;
    Besides C, W

38 hypocrites] *Hypocrites* Q, F2,
    L–S

IV.v

0.1 *Musick.*] *placed after preceding
    Exeunt.* Q, F2; *om.* C–V

0.1 *to them*] *om.* L, S, D
31 thousand] thousandth F2+

V.i

1 quickly, quickly, quickly] quick-
    ly, quickly F2, L–S, D, V
15 am I] I am F2, L–S
18 thou] *om.* F2, L–S
43 Nay] *om.* F2, L–S
48 *heaven*] *good heaven* F2, L–D

49 my] me F2, L–C, D
52 totters] totter L–D
65 h'as] has Q; he has W
67 canwast] can wast F2; can
    watch S, C; canvast W; can
    warrant D, V

V.ii

6.2 *Enter*] *Scena Secunda.* | *Enter*
    Q±
29 Nunnerys] Nunnery's F2, L+
29 fal] faln F2, L+

31 ere] e'er L, S
32 Maids.] Maids. | *Enter Maid.* |
    Q+

V.iv

V.iv] *Actus Quintus, Scena Prima.* F2, L+

V.v

V.v] *no scene division* Q, F2, L–C
11 thy] the D
17 *Thomas.*] *om.* Q
21 *Mary.*] *Ma.* Q; *Maid* F2, L
21 cold] cool'd F2+
21 If I do hang for't] If it do hang
    for' Q; If it do I'll hang for't
    F2, L

24 ere] e'er S
28 ah] a Q, F2, L–W
31 devill, devill, devill, devill,]
    devill, devill, devill, F2, L–S,
    D–V
54 Sanctuary] a ~ F2, L–S
54 hey] they Q, F2, L
58 Would] I would F2, L–S

V.vi

2 fairely] surely Q, F 2, L–S
2 met] melt Q
4 You] I Q, F 2, L–S
4 take] take it S

6 sweet] so sweet Q
12 beard] heard Q
27 end] ends F 2, L–S
58 not you] not F 2, L–S

V.vii

5 slumbers] slumber S, C

V.ix

4 all to bemarried] all to be married
Q, F 2, L–S, W; all to being
married C; all-to-be-married D;
all to-bemarried V

6 some such] so much W
7 heaven] Heavens F 2, L–W
24 now] thou S–W, V

V.x

17.1 *two* Nuns.] *2 Nun.* Q
38 keptst] keepst F 2, L+

39 a] but a W

V.xi

32 cozend] cozens Q

V.xii

16 dar'd] dare D, V
30 bestrew'd] bestow'd L+
31 vertue] no vertue S
42 towne's] townes Q
43 knowne] know F 2
62 a] *om.* S
76 this] that L, S

77 recompence] recompenc'd Q,
F 2, L
101 'nown son agen.] *known son
agen.* Q; *om.* F 2, L–S
103, 117 pound] pounds L, S, W
106 pound] pounds L, S, W, V

THE CHANCES

edited by

GEORGE WALTON WILLIAMS

TEXTUAL INTRODUCTION

The Chances (Greg, *Bibliography*, no. 646) was one in the list of plays by Beaumont and Fletcher entered to Humphrey Moseley in the Stationers' Register between 4 and 15 September 1646; it was first printed in the Folio of 1647. The present inquiry has found no occasion to question the common attribution that it is the unaided work of Fletcher.[1]

As he did often, Fletcher very likely turned to a Spanish source for the central fable of the play, Cervantes' *La Señora Cornelia*, first published in *Novelas Exemplares* in 1613, but perhaps more accessible to him in its French translation by Rosset and L'Audiguier in 1615.[2] Professor Bentley believes that the lines

> dost thou thinke
> The devill such an Asse as people make him?
> Such a poore coxcomb? such a penny foot post?
> Compel'd with crosse and pile to run of errands? (V.ii.9–12)

may echo Ben Jonson's *The Devil is an Ass*, performed at the Blackfriars in October or November 1616, and he therefore dates the composition of *The Chances* about 1617.[3] Though there are no records of performances of the play during Fletcher's lifetime, it is probable that a play that was to become most popular on the stage would have been so from the first. One allusive passage seems to point to a revival soon after Fletcher's death in 1626:

> The Duke of *Loraine* now
> Is seven thousand strong:...
> The Popes Buls are broke loose too, and 'tis suspected
> They shall be baited in *England*. (III.i.5–9)

These responses by the evasive Peter to the Land-lady, intentionally irrelevant (hence easily detached or substituted), can have had

---

[1] Cyrus Hoy, 'The Shares of Fletcher and his Collaborators in the Beaumont and Fletcher Canon (1)', *Studies in Bibliography*, VIII (1956), 132, 144–6.

[2] Gerald Eades Bentley, *The Jacobean and Caroline Stage* (Oxford, 1956), III, 318–23; E. K. Chambers, ed., *The Chances* (*The Variorum Edition*, London, 1912), IV, 437–8. [3] Bentley, III, 321–2; IV, 616.

meaning to a seventeenth-century audience only in reference to the mission in the spring of 1627 of Walter Montagu to the Duke of Lorraine in preparation for a war against France and to the publication in the same year of Henry Burton's *The Baiting of the Popes Bull*. The passage must have been inserted for a revival of the play for which probably also the Prologue was written (citing Fletcher's 'lovd memorie', line 12).[1] The first performance of record was on 30 December 1630, and there is a notice of another revival in 1638. After the Restoration the play was frequently staged as a great favorite, 'one of the most successful of Fletcher's comedies'.[2] Its popularity on stage encouraged alterations and revisions. The first was a 'droll', entitled *The Landlady*, in Kirkman's *Wits* of 1662 and 1672. George Villiers, second Duke of Buckingham, 'altered and very much improved' the play for the stage and published his version as *The Chances, A Comedy: As it is acted at the Theater Royal* (1682; subsequent editions 1692, 1711, 1735, 1755, 1776, 1791, 1817, 1826); David Garrick revised Buckingham's alteration and published the resulting version in 1773 (subsequent editions 1774, 1776, 1824, 1834, 1872), *The Chances. A Comedy. With Alterations*. His 'Advertisement' (pp. vii–viii) describes the history of the transmission of the stage version of the text:

The three first acts of *The Chances*, originally written by *Beaumont* and *Fletcher*, have been much approved of; but those authors, in this, as in many other of their plays, seeming to grow tir'd of their subject, have finished it with an unskilfulness and improbability which shew, at least, great haste, and negligence. The *Duke of Buckingham*, in his edition of this Comedy, gave a new turn and plan to the two last acts, and certainly added interest, and spirit, to the fable and dialogue; but the play, when it came out of his hands, was still more indecent than before. The familiar, and often irregular, versification of the original, is preserv'd in this edition; nor has the present editor chang'd into measure those parts, which the Duke thought proper to write in prose. Should this play be thought, in its present state, a more decent entertainment, it is all the merit that is claim'd from these necessary, tho' slight additions, and alterations.

In 1821, *Don John, or the Two Violettas, a musical drama* in three acts founded on *The Chances*, was played at the theater in Covent Garden.[3]

[1] Chambers, *loc. cit.*   [2] Bentley, III, 321.
[3] Alexander Dyce, ed., *Works of Beaumont and Fletcher* (London, 1844), VII, 217.

The Chances appears as the first play in Section 2 of the Folio, occupying signatures 3A1 through 3C3 (3C3^v is blank) (the quires are in fours, the normal pattern of the Folio.) The Section is presumably from the shop of Susan Islip.[1] As examination will show, the first quire was printed with a single skeleton, Quires B and C with two, the original skeleton alternating with a new one. The error in the running head on 3A2^v, '*The Change.*', demonstrates that the inner forme of the inner sheet was imposed first, since that error was corrected before the chase was used again. It would normally be expected, then, that the sequence of imposition would be from innermost to outermost forme, but Dr Gerritsen has plausibly argued on the basis of the alternation of skeletons that Quires B and C were imposed not in that sequence (2^v–3, 2–3^v, 1^v–4, 1–4^v) but in the sequence 2^v–3, 1^v–4, 2–3^v, 1–4^{v2}. This process of alternation, which obtains with some regularity throughout Susan Islip's Section, relates presumably to a policy of the shop to print both sheets of a quire before perfecting either. The pattern might suggest setting by formes, but the sequence of depletion and repletion of the initial letter for the character John in Quires B and C seems rather to suggest *seriatim* setting as the norm. It is clearly the intention of the compositor – and I agree with Dr Gerritsen that there is only one – to set the name of this character with an initial '*J*', '*John*'; the supply of that sort is, however, limited, and the compositor turns to the setting '*Iohn*'. (Words like '*Jewell*', '*Jaques*', '*Jeronimo*', he treats under a different scheme.) The repletion of the case occurs on a reasonably regular basis: after A3^v, after column A on B2, after column A on B3^v, after B4, after column A on C1, demonstrating that the compositor, though he set Quire A slowly (perhaps he was on other jobs), improved his rate of composition in Quire B and was probably moving so comfortably ahead of the press in that quire that he was able to set *seriatim*. On the basis of type shortage in Quire A, however, a fair argument can be made that the compositor is here setting by formes; such an argument receives some support from the fact that though in

---

[1] Johan Gerritsen, 'The Printing of the Beaumont and Fletcher Folio of 1647', *The Library*, Fifth Ser., III (March 1949), 235–48.

[2] *Ibid.* pp. 257–62.

signatures A 1 through A 3 there is a total of forty-six italic '*J*' sorts (all of which would be required for *seriatim* setting of Quire A), that kind of supply of this sort recurs nowhere in the signatures devoted to this play. Setting this quire by formes would require no more than twenty-two sorts for a forme, a figure which is more nearly in keeping with what seems to be the availability of this sort in the succeeding formes of the play.

There is little evidence on which to base a suggestion as to the nature of the copy for the Folio. Two stage-directions in F 1, deleted in F 2, would seem to derive from a prompt-book. Beside III.i.68–70 appears the direction '*Bottle of wine ready.*'; the wine is brought onstage at III.ii.26.1, ninety-two lines later. Beside IV.ii.13–14 appears the direction '*Bawd ready above.*'; the Bawd enters above at IV.iii.25, fifty lines later. It is not easy to see why these two activities should require special warnings; comparable items have no such advance notice. Entry directions are generally a line or two ahead of the first speech of the entrant, but this does not seem a mark of any consequence; entry directions are often squeezed into the right margin.

The play is entirely in verse, and it is notable that there are few errors in lineation. Two interesting errors of lineation occur at I.ii.50 and I.vi.1 where a single line of verse is divided and printed as two lines. Both of these errors occur at the bottom of column A (of A 1^v and of A 2), and it is tempting to speculate that they may derive from the compositor's need to use up an extra line of space in setting by formes. Since the same division of lines occurs on at least four other occasions in the play – but never at the foot of the column – this suggestion may not be particularly significant.

The Folio text is divided into acts and scenes, but, though the act division is acceptable, the scene division is in error in several places. In Acts II and III, the folio continues a scene which should properly be divided, and in Act I, it divides a scene which should properly be continued. At II.ii.50.1 there is a clear stage, and the succeeding dialogue indicates that the location of the scene has shifted from an outer or common room to a private chamber in the house; editors since Weber have begun a new scene (II.iii) with Constantia's entrance. At III.iv.107.1 there is a clear stage, and the succeeding dialogue indicates that the location of the scene has shifted from one part of the country to 'Another part of the country'; Dyce, Chambers and the present editor begin a new scene (III.v) with Francisco's entrance. (To the observation that the action here is continuous, the argument must be advanced that the dialogue and the stage movement depend upon a shift of location, though – it must be acknowledged – of no great distance.) At I.iii.31 s.d., though there is a clear stage, the succeeding dialogue gives no indication that the location has shifted, yet Dyce and Chambers move the play to 'Another street'. There is no necessity for a shift of location, one street serving as well as 'another' for these matters, and the Folio scene division, as Weber no doubt recognized when he omitted the scene break, divides a single line of verse in a manner that the dramatist surely did not intend. (It is perhaps worthy of comment that the three 'errors' in scene division all concern a clear stage followed by the entrance of a single character who soliloquizes.)

The play was evidently written to be performed with an interval between Acts III and IV (and thus presumably with intervals between the other acts as well), for the text requires the exit of four characters at the end of one scene and their immediate re-entry at the beginning of the succeeding scene. Such going and coming are meaningless unless an interval (of music?) intervenes. (This particular interval represents the movement of the characters from the country back to the city.)

The musical features of the play are not without interest. The play includes one recitation and four songs which are accompanied by a lute or by a consort. One of the songs, 'Song of John Dorry' (III.ii.28–34), though mentioned in dialogue and direction, is not printed in either Folio, probably because it was commonly known. Antonio requests this song as 'background music' for his operation; it is sung (and played?) by a group of musicians. Chambers quotes Weber's note that the song was 'an old three-man's song' in Cornwall in 1602 (p. 443). The text of the song, reprinted from Thomas Ravenscroft, *Deutromelia* (1609), p. 59, is given in the Textual Notes.

The first incantation, or recitation, by Vechio (V.iii.38–45), printed in F1 in italic type, has as its purpose the evoking of music, the '*soft winds*' which are to '*Raise these formes* [of the neighbor's children and Constantia]... *With a soft and happy sound*'. The incantation is successful; 'Soft Musick' (of the woodwinds?) immediately follows, and the shapes of the women pass by. Since its function was to produce instrumental music, the incantation was itself presumably unaccompanied. The printing in italic type then probably does not indicate that the incantation was sung as a song. The lines are, however, distinguished for some reason: perhaps they were intoned.

The second incantation by Vechio (V.iii.92–119) appears first in F2; it is a song, 'Come away, thou Lady gay', extant also in two manuscripts, one at the Bodleian and one at the Folger.[1] The texts have minor verbal differences (recorded in the Historical Collation). In neither of the MSS does the Land-lady, Gillian, respond as she does in F2 at lines 104 and 119; but in both she concludes the incantation with 'I come, I come' (as at line 96). Cutts believes that 'L'authenticité des "réponses" de l'édition de 1679 est très douteuse', and he regards the phrases 'Why when? Why when?' as the first response of the Land-lady.[2] Such an interpretation does not seem to yield a coherent dramatic reading of the song, nor do I detect any characteristic of the musical setting or of the MS versions that supports a theory of a second voice for those words. On the contrary, it would seem preferable to read the song in this fashion:

lines 92–95   in song Vechio calls the 'spirit' by name

96   in speech the Land-lady replies with the traditional termination of such conjurations; 'I come' is evidently her 'mumbling' (There is no music for this response.)

97–103   in song Vechio conjures the spirit by name a second time, using various beverages and requiring that she 'Appear and answer'; his impatience reveals itself in the repetition of his question, 'Why when?'

104   in speech the Land-lady replies (There is no music for this response.)

105–118   in song Vechio conjures the spirit a third time using various bodily ailments and requiring thrice (twice in Bodleian MS) that she 'Appeare'

119   in song the Land-lady replies

[1] John P. Cutts, *La musique de scène de la troupe de Shakespeare* (Paris, 1971), pp. 149–50.   [2] Cutts, *loc. cit.* But see V.iii.202.

The triple summons of the spirit necessitates a triple response. If the reconstruction is correct, the fact that the first two responses have no musical setting would explain why they would not appear in musical versions and hence might seem 'douteuses' or, indeed, spurious.

The two remaining songs (II.ii.18–28; IV.iii.14–21), printed first in F2, are both sung 'Within'. Such an undramatic technique may have its justification in the deception that Fletcher exploits here. The singer of the first song, 'Mercilesse love', is understood to be Constantia, solacing herself with music (in that assumption, this edition provides a speech-prefix for her); the singer of the second song, 'Welcome, sweet liberty', is understood to be Constantia also, but is in fact the Whore (the 'Second Constantia' as some editors term her). Since the two songs are sung out of the audience's sight, it is very likely that the same vocalist performed them both; and if he did, then the audience will agree with the Gentlemen that the voice is Constantia's, having already heard this singing voice and found it to have been Constantia's. The audience thus will share in the confusion that John and Fredrick suffer when they discover that the singer is the Whore – not Constantia, but someone else of the same name. (The Whore, who is, one may suppose, noted for her inconstancy, is given the same name as the faithful heroine in one of the 'chances' of the play in order to confuse John, Fredrick and the audience in the eavesdropping scene at III.v.8.)

The present text is based on the copy of the play in the 1647 Folio at the Huntington Library collated with fourteen other copies of various libraries. Four exemplars at the University of Illinois and eight at the University of Texas have been examined sporadically for variants.

The Historical Collation includes the two seventeenth-century folio editions, the eighteenth- and nineteenth-century collected editions, and the Variorum. The adaptations of the Duke of Buckingham and David Garrick are not included. The *Comments on the Plays of Beaumont and Fletcher* (London, 1798) by J. Monck Mason and the *Cursory Notes on Various Passages in the Text of Beaumont and Fletcher* (London, 1856) by John Mitford have been consulted also.

PERSONS REPRESENTED IN THE PLAY.

Duke of Ferrara.

Petruchio, *Governour of* Bolognia.

Don John,
Don Fredrick,� *two Spanish Gentlemen, and Comerades.*

Antonio, *an old Stout Gentleman, Kinsman to* Petruchio.

Three Gentlemen, friends to the Duke.

Two Gentlemen, friends to Petruchio.

Francisco, *A Musician,* Antonio's *Boy.*

Peter Vechio, *a Teacher of Latine and Musick, a reputed Wizard.*

Peter and⎫ *two Servants to Don* John *and* Fredrick.   10
Anthony,⎭

A Surgeon.

WOMEN.

Constantia, *Sister to* Petruchio, *and Mistriss to the Duke.*

Gentlewoman, Servant to Constantia.

Old Gentlewoman, Land-lady to Don John *and* Fredrick.

Constantia, *a Whore to old* Antonio.

Bawd.

[*Children, Servants, Musicians.*]

The Scene Bolognia.

Persons...Bolognia.] F 2; *om.* F 1

550

The Chances.

Enter two Serving-men, Peter *and* Anthony.

Peter. I would we were remov'd from this Town, *Anthony*,
That we might taste some quiet: for mine owne part,
I'me almost melted with continuall trotting
After enquiries, dreames, and revelations,
Of who knowes whom, or where? serve wenching soldiers,
That know no other Paradice but Plackets?
Ile serve a Priest in Lent first, and eate Bell-ropes.
Anthony. Thou art the froward'st foole——
Peter.   Why good tame *Anthony?*
Tell me but this: to what end came we hither?
Anthony. To wait upon our Masters.
Peter.   But how *Anthony?*   10
Answer me that; resolve me there good *Anthony?*
Anthony. To serve their uses.
Peter.   Shew your uses *Anthony.*
Anthony. To be imploy'd in any thing.
Peter.   No *Anthony,*
Not any thing I take it; nor that thing
We travell to discover, like new Islands;
A salt itch serve such uses; in things of moment,
Concerning things, I grant yee; not things errant,
Sweet Ladies things, and things to thank the Surgeon:
In no such things, sweet *Anthony:* put case——
Anthony.   Come, come,
All will be mended: this invisible woman   20
Of infinite report for shape and vertue,
That bred us all this trouble to no purpose,
They are determin'd now no more to thinke on,
But fall close to their studies.
Peter.   Was there ever

Men knowne to run mad with report before?
Or wander after that they know not where
To finde? or if found, how to enjoy? are mens braines
Made now a dayes of Malt, that their affections
Are never sober? but like drunken people
Founder at every new fame? I do believe too   30
That men in love are ever drunke, as drunken men
Are ever loving.
Anthony.   Prethee be thou sober,
And know, that they are none of those, not guilty
Of the least vanity of love, onely a doubt
Fame might too farre report, or rather flatter
The graces of this woman, made them curious
To finde the truth, which since they finde so boltted
And lock'd up from their searches, they are now setled
To give the wonder over.
Peter.   Would they were setled
To give me some new shooes too: for Ile be sworne   40
These are e'ne worne out to the reasonable soules
In their good worships businesse: and some sleep
Would not doe much amisse, unlesse they meane
To make a Bell-man on me: and what now
Meane they to study, *Anthony*, Morall Philosophy
After their mar-all women?
Anthony.   Mar a fooles head.
Peter. 'Twill mar two fools heads, and they take not heed,
Besides the Giblets to 'em.
Anthony.   Will you walke Sir,
And talke more out of hearing? your fooles head
May chance to finde a wooden night-cap else.   50
Peter. I never lay in any.

Enter Don John *and* Fredrick.

Anthony.   Then leave your lying,

26 wander] Langbaine; wonder F1–2
37 boltted] Chambers (Birch *conj.*); blotted F1, blocked F2
39 over] F2; ever F1

And your blinde Prophesying: here they come,
You had best tell them as much.
Peter.   I am no tell-tale.   *Exeunt.*
John.   I would we could have seen her though; for sure
She must be some rare creature, or report lyes,
All mens reports too.
Fredrick.   I could well wish I had seen her;
But since she is so conceal'd, so beyond venture
Kept and preserv'd from view, so like a Paradice,
Plac't where no knowledg can come near her, so guarded
As 't were impossible, though knowne, to reach her,   60
I have made up my beliefe.
John.   Hang me from this houre
If I more thinke upon her, or believe her,
But as she came a strong report unto me,
So the next Fame shall loose her.
Fredrick.   'Tis the best way:
But whither are you walking?
John.   My old round
After my meat, and then to bed.
Fredrick.   'Tis healthfull.
John.   Will not you stir?
Fredrick.   I have a little businesse.
John.   Upon my life this Lady still——
Fredrick.   Then you will loose it.
John.   Pray let's walke together.
Fredrick.   Now I cannot.
John.   I have something to impart.
Fredrick.   An houre hence   70
I will not misse to meet you.
John.   Where?
Fredrick.   Ith' high street;
For not to lye, I have a few Devotions
To doe first, then I am yours.
John.   Remember.
                              Exeunt [severally].

64 best] Chambers; next F 1–2

Enter Petruchio, Antonio, *and two Gentlemen.* [I.] ii

Antonio.   Cut his winde-pipe, I say.

1. Gentleman.   Fie *Antonio*.

Antonio.   Or knock his brains out first, and then forgive him.
  If you doe thrust, be sure it be to th' hilts,
  A Surgeon may see through him.

1. Gentleman.   You are too violent.

2. Gentleman.   Too open, undiscreet.

Petruchio.   Am I not ruin'd?
  The honour of my house crack'd? my bloud poyson'd?
  My credit, and my name?

2. Gentleman.   Be sure it be so,
  Before ye use this violence. Let not doubt,
  And a suspecting anger so much sway ye,
  Your wisedome may be question'd.

Antonio.   I say kill him,   10
  And then dispute the cause; cut off what may be,
  And what is, shall be safe.

2. Gentleman.   Hang up a true man,
  Because 'tis possible he may be theevish:
  Alas, is this good Justice?

Petruchio.   I know as certaine,
  As day must come againe; as cleare as truth,
  And open as beliefe can lay it to me,
  That I am basely wrong'd, wrong'd above recompence;
  Malitiously abus'd, blasted for ever
  In name and honour, lost to all remembrance,
  But what is smear'd, and shamefull; I must kill him,   20
  Necessitie compells me.

1. Gentleman.   But think better.

Petruchio.   There is no other cure left: yet witnesse with me
  All that is faire in man, all that is noble,
  I am not greedy of this life I seek for,
  Nor thirst to shed mans bloud; and would 'twere possible,
  I wish it with my soule, so much I tremble
  To offend the sacred Image of my Maker,

My sword could onely kill his crimes: no 'tis honour,
Honour, my noble friends, that idoll honour,
That all the world now worships, not *Petruchio*   30
Must doe this justice.
Antonio.   Let it once be done,
And 'tis no matter, whether you, or honour,
Or both be accessarie.
2. Gentleman.   Doe you weigh *Petruchio*
The value of the person, power, and greatnesse,
And what this sparke may kindle?
Petruchio.   To performe it,
So much I am ty'd to reputation,
And credit of my house, let it raise wild-fires,
That all this Dukedome smoak, and stormes that tosse me
Into the waves of everlasting ruine,
Yet I must through; if yee dare side me——
Antonio.   Dare?   40
Petruchio.   Ye're friends indeed; if not——
2. Gentleman.   Here's none flies from you,
Doe it in what designe ye please, wee'll back ye.
Petruchio.   But then be sure yee kill him.
2. Gentleman.   Is the cause
So mortall, nothing but his life——
Petruchio.   Beleeve me,
A lesse offence has been the desolation
Of a whole name.
1. Gentleman.   No other way to purge it?
Petruchio.   There is, but never to be hoped for.
2. Gentleman.   Thinke an houre more,
And if then ye finde no safer road to guide yee,
Wee'll set up our rests too.
Antonio.   Mine's up already,
And hang him for my part, goes lesse than life.   50
2. Gentleman.   If we see noble cause, 'tis like our swords
May be as free and forward as your words.
                                        Exeunt.

39 waves] F 2; stormes F 1   43 *Petruchio.*] Seward; 1. F 1–2

Enter Don John.   [I.] iii

John.   The civill order of this Towne *Bellonia*
Makes it belov'd, and honour'd of all travellers,
As a most safe retirement in all troubles;
Beside the wholsome seat, and noble temper
Of those mindes that inhabit it, safely wise,
And to all strangers vertuous: But I see
My admiration has drawne night upon me,
And longer to expect my friend may pull me
Into suspition of too late a stirrer,
Which all good Governments are jealous of.   10
Ile home, and thinke at liberty: yet certaine,
'Tis not so farre night as I thought; for see,
A faire house yet stands open, yet all about it
Are close, and no lights stirring: there may be foule play:
Ile venture to look in: if there be knaves,
I may doe a good office.
Woman (within).   Signieur?
John [aside].   What? how is this?
Woman (within).   Signieur *Fabritio*?
John [aside].   Ile goe nearer.
Woman (within).   *Fabritio*?
John [aside].   This is a womans tongue, here may be good done.
Woman (within).   Who's there? *Fabritio*?
John.   I.
Woman (within).   Where are ye?
John.   Here.
Woman (within).   O come, for heavens sake!
John [aside].   I must see what this meanes. 20

Enter Woman *with a childe.*

Woman.   I have stay'd this long houre for you, make no noise,
For things are in strange trouble: here, be secret,   [*Gives childe.*]
'Tis worth your care; begone now; more eyes watch us,
Then may be for our safeties.

John.   Harke ye?
Woman.   Peace: good night. [*Exit.*]
John.   She is gone, and I am loaden; fortune for me;
  It weighes well, and it feeles well; it may chance
  To be some pack of worth: by th' masse 'tis heavie;
  If it be Coyne or Jewels, 'tis worth welcome:
  Ile ne're refuse a fortune: I am confident
  'Tis of no common price: now to my lodging: 30
  If it hit right, Ile blesse this night.   *Exit.*

Enter Fredrick.

Fredrick.   'Tis strange,
  I cannot meet him; sure he has encountred
  Some light o' love or other, and there meanes
  To play at In and In for this night. Well *Don John,*
  If you doe spring a leak, or get an itch,
  Til ye claw off your curl'd pate, thank your night-walks:
  You must be still a bootehalling: one round more,
  Though it be late, Ile venture to discover ye,
  I doe not like your out-leaps.
                                              [*Exit.*]

Enter Duke, *and three Gentlemen.*   [I.] iv

Duke.   Welcome to Towne, are ye all fit?
1. Gentleman.   To point Sir.
Duke.   Where are the horses?
2. Gentleman.   Where they were appointed.
Duke.   Be private, and whatsoever fortune
  Offer it selfe, let's stand sure.
3. Gentleman.   Feare not us,
  'Ere ye shall be endangered, or deluded,
  Wee'll make a black night on't.
Duke.   No more, I know it;

34 In and In] (*a game of dice, popular at inns*)
37 bootehalling] *i.e.,* haling off booty

557

You know your Quarters?
1. Gentleman.   Will you goe alone sir?
Duke.   Ye shall not be farre from me, the least noise
  Shall bring ye to my rescue.
2. Gentleman.   We are counsell'd.

Exeunt.

Enter Don John [*with the childe*].   [I.] v

John.   Was ever man so paid for being curious?
  Ever so bob'd for searching out adventures,
  As I am? did the devill lead me? must I needs be peeping
  Into mens houses where I had no businesse,
  And make my selfe a mischiefe? 'Tis well carried;
  I must take other mens occasions on me,
  And be I know not whom: most finely handled:
  What have I got by this now? what's the purchase?
  A piece of evening Arras worke, a childe,
  Indeed an Infidell: this comes of peeping: 10
  A lumpe got out of lazinesse:——good white bread,
  Let's have no bawling with yee:——'sdeath, have I
  Knowne Wenches thus long, all the wayes of wenches,
  Their snares and subtilties? have I read over
  All their Schoole learnings, div'd into their quiddits,
  And am I now bum-fidled with a Bastard?
  Fetch'd over with a Carde of five, and in mine old dayes,
  After the dire massacre of a million
  Of Maiden-heads? caught the common way, ith' night too
  Under anothers name, to make the matter   20
  Carry more weight about it? well *Don John,*
  You will be wiser one day, when ye have purchas'd
  A beavy of these Butter prints together,
  With searching out conceal'd iniquities,
  Without commission: why, it would never grieve me,
  If I had got this Ginger-bread: never stirr'd me,
  So I had had a stroak for't: 't had been Justice
  Then to have kept it; but to raise a dayrie

558

For other mens adulteries, consume my selfe in caudles,
And scowring works, in Nurses, Bells and Babies,   30
Onely for charity, for meere I thank you,
A little troubles me: the least touch for it,
Had but my breeches got it, had contented me.
Whose e're it is, sure 't had a wealthy mother,
For 'tis well cloathed, and if I be not cozen'd,
Well lin'd within: to leave it here were barbarous,
And ten to one would kill it: a more sin
Then his that got it: well, I will dispose on't,
And keep it, as they keep deaths heads in rings,
To cry, *memento* to me; no more peeping.   40
Now all the danger is to qualifie
The good old gentlewoman, at whose house we live,
For she will fall upon me with a Catechisme
Of foure houres long: I must endure all;
For I will know this mother:——Come good wonder,
Let you and I be jogging: your starv'd trebble
Will waken the rude watch else:—— All that bee
Curious night-walkers, may they finde my fee.

                                                        Exit.

                Enter Fredrick.   [I.] vi

Fredrick. Sure hee's gone home: I have beaten all the purlewes,
But cannot bolt him: if he be a bobbing
'Tis not my care can cure him: To morrow morning
I shall have further knowledge from a Surgeons——
Where he lyes moord, to mend his leaks.

                Enter Constantia.

Constantia.   I'me ready,
And through a world of dangers am flown to yee.
Be full of haste and care, we are undone else:
Where are your people? which way must we travell?
For heaven sake stay not here sir.

29 caudles] Seward; candles F 1–2
33 contented] F 1(c), F 2; contended F 1(u)

Fredrick [*aside*].   What may this prove?
Constantia [*aside*].   Alas I am mistaken, lost, undone.   10
  For ever perish'd.—— Sir, for heaven sake tell me,
  Are ye a Gentleman?
Fredrick.   I am.
Constantia.   Of this place?
Fredrick.   No, borne in *Spain.*
Constantia.   As ever you lov'd honour,
  As ever your desires may gaine their ends,
  Doe a poore wretched woman but this benefit,
  For I am forc'd to trust yee.
Fredrick.   Y'ave charm'd me,
  Humanity and honour bids me helpe ye;
  And if I faile your trust——
Constantia.   The time's too dangerous
  To stay your protestations: I beleeve ye,
  Alas, I must believe ye: From this place,   20
  Good noble Sir, remove me instantly,
  And for a time, where nothing but your selfe,
  And honest conversation may come neare me,
  In some secure place settle me. What I am,
  And why thus boldly I commit my credit
  Into a strangers hand, the feares and dangers
  That force me to this wilde course, at more leisure
  I shall reveale unto you.
Fredrick.   Come, be hearty,
  He must strike through my life that takes ye from me.

                                        Exeunt.

                Enter Petruchio, Antonio *and two Gentlemen.*   [I.] vii

Petruchio.   He will sure come. Are yee well arm'd?
Antonio.   Never feare us.
  Here's that will make 'em dance without a Fiddle.
Petruchio.   We are to look for no weak foes, my friends,
  Nor unadvised ones.
Antonio.   Best gamsters make the best game,

We shall fight close and handsome then.

1. Gentleman.   *Antonio,*
 You are a thought too bloudy.

Antonio.   Why? all Physitians
 And penny Almanacks allow the opening
 Of veines this moneth: why doe ye talke of bloudy?
 What come we for, to fall to cuffes for apples?
 What, would ye make the Cause a Cudgell quarell? 10
 On what termes stands this man? is not his honour
 Open'd to his hand, and pickt out like an Oyster?
 His credit like a quart pot knockt together,
 Able to hold no liquor? cleare but this point.

Petruchio. Speak softly, gentle Couzen.

Antonio.   Ile speak truely;
 What should men doe ally'd to these disgraces?
 Lick o're his enemie, sit downe, and dance him?

2. Gentleman. You are as farre o'th' bow hand now.

Antonio.   And crie,
 That's my fine boy, thou wilt doe so no more, child.

Petruchio. Here are no such cold pitties.

Antonio.   By Saint *Jaques* 20
 They shall not finde me one: here's old tough *Andrew,*
 A speciall friend of mine, and he but hold,
 Ile strike 'em such a horne-pipe: knocks I come for,
 And the best bloud I light on; I profes it,
 Not to scarre Coster-mongers; If I loose mine owne,
 Mine audits cast, and fare-well five and fifty.

Petruchio. Let's talke no longer, place your selves with silence,
 As I directed yee; and when time calls us,
 As ye are friends, so shew your selves.

Antonio.   So be it.

               Exeunt.

   25 scarre] *i.e.,* scare (?) *26 cast] F2; lost F1

Enter Don John [*with the childe*] *and his* Land-lady. [I.] viii

Land-lady. Nay Son, if this be your regard——
John.   Good mother——
Land-lady.   Good me no goods; your Cozen, and your self
  Are welcome to me, whilst you beare your selves
  Like honest and true Gentlemen: Bring hither
  To my house, that have ever been reputed
  A gentlewoman of a decent, and faire carriage,
  And so behav'd my self——
John.   I know ye have.
Land-lady.   Bring hither, as I say, to make my name
  Stinke in my neighbours nostrills, your Devises,
  Your Brats, got out of *Alligant*, and broken oathes?   10
  Your Linsey Woolsey worke, your hasty puddings?
  I foster up your filch'd iniquities?
  Y'are deceiv'd in me, Sir, I am none
  Of those receivers.
John.   Have I not sworne unto you,
  'Tis none of mine, and shew'd you how I found it?
Land-lady.   Ye found an easie foole that let you get it,
  She had better have worne pasternes.
John.   Will yee heare me?
Land-lady.   Oathes? what doe you care for oathes to gaine your
        ends,
  When ye are high and pamper'd? What Saint know ye?
  Or what Religion, but your purpos'd lewdnesse,   20
  Is to be look'd for of ye? nay, I will tell ye,
  You will then sweare like accus'd Cut-purses,
  As far of truth too; and lye beyond all Faulconers:
  I'me sick to see this dealing.
John.   Heaven forbid Mother.
Land-lady.   Nay, I am very sick.
John.   Who waits there?
Anthony (within).   Sir.
John.   Bring down the bottle of Canary wine.
Land-lady.   Exceeding sick, heav'n helpe me.

John.   Haste ye sirrah.
  [*Aside*] I must ev'n make her drunk:——nay gentle mother.
Land-lady.   Now fie upon ye, was it for this purpose
  You fetch'd your evening walks for your digestions,   30
  For this pretended holinesse? no weather,
  Not before day could hold ye from the Matins.
  Were these your bo-peep prayers? ye'have praid well,
  And with a learned zeale: watcht well too; your Saint
  It seems was pleas'd as well:—— still sicker, sicker.

                 Enter Anthony *with a bottle of wine.*

John [*aside*].   There is no talking to her till I have drencht
         her.——
  Give me:—— here mother take a good round draught,
  'Twill purge spleen from your spirits: deeper mother.
Land-lady.   I, I, sonne; you imagine this will mend all.
John.   All y'faith Mother.
Land-lady.   I confesse the Wine   40
  Will doe his part.
John.   Ile pledge ye.
Land-lady.   But sonne *John*——
John.   I know your meaning mother, touch it once more;
  Alas you look not well, take a round draught;
  It warmes the bloud well, and restores the colour,
  And then wee'll talke at large.
Land-lady.   A civill gentleman?
  A stranger? one the Town holds a good regard of?
John [*aside*].   Nay I will silence thee.
Land-lady. One that should weigh his faire name? uh, a stich!
John.   There's nothing better for a stitch, good mother,
  Make no spare of it, as you love your health,   50
  Mince not the matter.
Land-lady.   As I said, a gentleman,
  Lodge in my house? now heav'ns my comfort, Signior!
John [*aside*].   I look'd for this.
Land-lady.   I did not thinke you would have us'd me thus;

                47 thee] F 2; there F 1

A woman of my credit: one, heaven knowes,
That lov'd you but too tenderly.
John.   Deare mother,
I ever found your kindnesse, and acknowledge it.
Land-lady.   No, no, I am a fool to counsell yee. Where's the
   infant?
Come, lets see your Workmanship.
John.   None of mine, Mother.
But there 'tis, and a lusty one.   [*Gives childe.*]
Land-lady.   Heaven blesse thee,   60
Thou hadst a hasty making; but the best is,
'Tis many a good mans fortune:——as I live
Your owne eyes Signior, and the nether lip
As like yee, as ye had spit it.
John.   I am glad on't.
Land-lady.   Blesse me, what things are these?
John.   I thought my labour
Was not all lost, 'tis gold, and these are jewels,
Both rich, and right I hope.
Land-lady.   Well, well sonne *John,*
I see ye are a wood-man, and can chuse
Your Deere, though it be i'th darke; all your discretion
Is not yet lost; this was well clapt aboard: 70
Here I am with you now; when as they say
Your pleasure comes with profit; when ye must needs do,
Doe where ye may be done to, 'tis a wisedome
Becomes a young man well: be sure of one thing,
Loose not your labour and your time together,
It seasons of a foole, sonne; time is pretious,
Worke wary whilst ye have it: since ye must traffick
Sometimes this slippery way, take sure hold Signior,
Trade with no broken Merchants, make your lading,
As you would make your rest, adventurously,   80
But with advantage ever.
John.   All this time mother,
The childe wants looking too, wants meat and Nurses.
Land-lady.   Now blessing o' thy care; it shall have all,

And instantly; Ile seek a Nurse my selfe, sonne;
'Tis a sweet childe:——ah my young *Spaniard*——
Take you no further care sir.
John.   Yes of these Jewels,
I must by your leave Mother: these are yours,
To make your care the stronger: for the rest
Ile finde a Master; the gold for bringing up on't,
I freely render to your charge.
Land-lady.   No more words,   90
Nor no more children, (good sonne) as you love me:
This may doe well.
John.   I shall observe your Morals.
But where's *Don Fredrick* (Mother)?
Land-lady.   Ten to one
About the like adventure: he told me,
He was to finde you out.   *Exit [with childe and Anthony].*
John.   Why should he stay thus?
There may be some ill chance in't: sleep I will not,
Before I have found him: now this woman's pleas'd,
Ile seek my friend out, and my care is eas'd.

                                                    Exit.

            Enter Duke *and Gentlemen.*   [I.] ix

1. Gentleman.   Beleeve sir, 'tis as possible to doe it,
As to remove the City; the maine faction,
Swarm through the streets like hornets, arm'd with angers
Able to ruine States: no safety left us,
Nor meanes to dye like men, if instantly
You draw not back againe.
Duke.   May he be drawne
And quarter'd too, that turnes now; were I surer
Of death then thou art of thy fears, and with death
More then those feares are too——
1. Gentleman.   Sir, I feare not.
Duke.   I would not crack my vow, start from my honour,   10
Because I may finde danger; wound my soule,

                    93 *Fredrick*] F2; *Ferdinand* F1

                            565

To keep my body safe.
1. Gentleman. I speak not sir,
Out of a basenesse to you.
Duke. No, nor doe not
Out of a basenesse leave me: what is danger,
More then the weaknesse of our apprehensions?
A poor cold part o'the bloud? who takes it hold of?
Cowards, and wicked livers: valiant mindes
Were made the Masters of it: and as hearty Seamen
In desperate stormes, stem with a little Rudder
The tumbling ruines of the Ocean,
So with their cause and swords do they do dangers.   20
Say we were sure to dye all in this venture,
As I am confident against it: is there any
Amongst us of so fat a sense, so pamper'd,
Would chuse luxuriously to lye a bed,
And purge away his spirit, send his soule out
In Sugar-sops, and Syrups? give me dying,
As dying ought to be, upon mine enemy,
Parting with man-kinde, by a man that's manly:
Let 'em be all the world, and bring along
Cain's envy with 'em, I will on.   30
2. Gentleman. You may sir,
But with what safety?
1. Gentleman. Since 'tis come to dying,
You shall perceive sir, here be those amongst us
Can dye as decently as other men,
And with as little ceremony: on brave sir.
Duke. That's spoken heartily.
1. Gentleman. And he that flinches
May he dye lowzie in a ditch.
Duke. No more dying,
There's no such danger in it: what's a clock?
3. Gentleman. Somewhat above your houre.
Duke. Away then quickly,
Make no noise, and no trouble will attend us.   40
Exeunt.

Enter Fredericke, *and* Peter, (*with a candle*).   [I.] x

Fredrick.   Give me the candle: so goe you out that way.
Peter.   What have we now to doe?
Fredrick.   And o' your life sirrah,
Let none come neare the doore without my knowledge,
No not my Landlady, nor my friend.
Peter.   'Tis done sir.
Fredrick.   Nor any serious businesse that concerns me.
Peter.   Is the winde there agen?
Fredrick.   . Be gone.
Peter.   I am sir.   *Exit.*
Fredrick.   Now enter without feare.

Enter Constantia *with a Jewell.*

                                                And noble Lady
That safety and civility yee wish'd for
Shall truely here attend you: no rude tongue
Nor rough behaviour knows this place, no wishes   10
Beyond the moderation of a man,
Dare enter here: your owne desires and Innocence,
Joyn'd to my vow'd obedience, shall protect you,
Were dangers more then doubts.
Constantia.   Ye are truely noble,
And worth a womans trust: let it become me,
(I doe beseech you sir) for all your kindnesse,
To render with my thanks, this worthlesse trifle;
I may be longer troublesome.   [*Offers a jewell.*]
Fredrick.   Faire offices
Are still their owne rewards: Heav'n blesse me Lady
From selling civill courtesies: may it please ye,   20
If ye will force a favour to oblige me,
Draw but that cloud aside, to satisfie me
For what good Angel I am engag'd.
Constantia.   It shall be.
For I am truely confident yee are honest:
The Piece is scarce worth looking on.   [*Draws her veil.*]

Fredrick.   Trust me
The abstract of all beauty, soule of sweetnesse——
[*Aside*] Defend me honest thoughts, I shall grow wilde else:
What eyes are there, rather what little heavens,
To stirre mens contemplations? what a Paradice
Runs through each part she has? good bloud be temperate: 30
I must look off: too excellent an object
Confounds the sense that sees it.——Noble Lady,
If there be any further service to cast on me,
Let it be worth my life, so much I honour ye,
Or the engagement of whole Families.
Constantia. Your service is too liberall, worthy sir,
Thus farre I shall entreat——
Fredrick.   Command me Lady.
You make your power too poore.
Constantia.   That presently
With all convenient haste, you would retire
Unto the street you found me in.
Fredrick.   'Tis done.   40
Constantia. There, if you finde a gentleman opprest
With force and violence, doe a mans office,
And draw your sword to rescue him.
Fredrick.   Hee's safe,
Be what he will, and let his foes be devills,
Arm'd with your pitty, I shall conjure 'em.
Retire, this key will guide ye: all things necessary
Are there before ye.
Constantia.   All my prayers goe with ye.
Fredrick. Ye clap on proof upon me:——   *Exit* [Constantia].
                              men say gold
Do's all, engages all, works through all dangers:
Now I say beauty can do more: The Kings Exchequer,   50
Nor all his wealthy *Indies*, could not draw me
Through halfe those miseries this peece of pleasure
Might make me leap into: we are all like sea-Cards,
All our endeavours and our motions,
(As they doe to the North) still point at beauty,

Still at the fairest: for a handsome woman,
(Setting my soule aside) it should goe hard,
But I would straine my body: yet to her,
Unlesse it be her owne free gratitude,
Hopes ye shall dye, and thou tongue rot within me,   60
E're I infringe my faith: now to my rescue.

Exit.

Enter Duke, *pursued by* Petruchio, Antonio, *and that Faction.*   II. i

Duke.   You will not all oppresse me?
Antonio.   Kill him ith' wanton eye: let me come to him.
Duke.   Then yee shall buy me dearely.
Petruchio.   Say you so sir?
Antonio.   I say cut his Wezand, spoile his peeping:——   ·
Have at your love-sick heart sir.

Enter Don John.

John.   Sure 'tis fighting.
My friend may be engag'd:——fie gentlemen,
This is unmanly oddes.
Antonio.   Ile stop your mouth sir.

Duke *fals down,* Don John *bestrides him.*

John.   Nay, then have at thee freely:
Ther's a plumb sir to satisfie your longing.
Petruchio.   Away: I hope I have sped him: here comes rescue.   10
We shall be endangered: where's *Antonio?*
Antonio.   I must have one thrust more sir.
John.   Come up to me. [*Wounds* Antonio.]
Antonio.   A mischiefe confound your fingers.
Petruchio.   How is't?
Antonio.   Well:
Ha's giv'n me my *quietus est,* I felt him
In my small guts, I'me sure, has feez'd me:
This comes of siding with ye.

*4 peeping] *i.e.,* piping, chirping

2. Gentleman.   Can you goe sir?
Antonio.   I should goe man, and my head were of,
   Never talke of going.
Petruchio.   Come, all shall be well then.
   I heare more rescue comming.

Enter the Dukes *Faction*.

Antonio.   Let's turne back then;
   My skull's uncloven yet, let me but kill.   20
Petruchio.   Away for heaven sake with him.
                    [*Exeunt* Petruchio, Antonio, *and that Faction*].
John.   How is't?
Duke.   Well sir,
   Onely a little stagger'd.
Men of the Dukes Faction.   Lets pursue 'em.
Duke.   No not a man, I charge ye:——thanks good coat,
   Thou hast sav'd me a shrewd welcome: 'twas put home too,
   With a good minde I'me sure on't.
John.   Are ye safe then?
Duke.   My thanks to you brave sir, whose timely valour,
   And manly courtesie came to my rescue.
John.   Ye'had foule play offer'd ye, and shame befall him
   That can passe by oppression.
Duke.   May I crave sir,
   But thus much honour more, to know your name?   30
   And him I am so bound to?
John.   For the Bond sir,
   'Tis every good mans tye: to know me further
   Will little profit ye; I am a stranger,
   My Countrey *Spaine*; my name *Don John*, a gentleman
   That lyes here for my study.
Duke.   I have heard sir,
   Much worthy mention of ye, yet I finde
   Fame short of what ye are.
John.   You are pleas'd sir,
   To expresse your courtesie: may I demand
   As freely what you are, and what mischance

570

Cast you into this danger?
Duke.   For this present   40
I must desire your pardon: you shall know me
Ere it be long sir, and a nobler thanks,
Then now my will can render.
John.   Your will's your owne sir.
Duke.   What is't you look for sir, have yee lost any thing?
John.   Onely my hat i'th scuffle; sure these fellowes
Were night-snaps.
Duke.   No, believe sir: pray ye use mine,
For 'twil be hard to finde your owne now.
John.   No sir.
Duke.   Indeed ye shall, I can command another:
I doe beseech ye honour me.   [*Gives his hat.*]
John.   I will sir,
And so Ile take my leave.
Duke.   Within these few dayes   50
I hope I shall be happy in your knowledge.
Till when I love your memory.
John.   I yours.
                    Exit Duke, *with his Faction.*
This is some noble fellow.

                    Enter Fredrick.

Fredrick.   'Tis his tongue sure.——
Don John?
John   Don *Fredrick?*
Fredrick.   Yo'are fairely met sir:
I thought ye had been a Bat-fowling: prethee tell me,
What Revelations hast thou had to night,
That home was never thought of?
John.   Revelations?
Ile tell thee *Fredrick*: but before I tell thee,
Settle thy understanding.
Fredrick.   'Tis prepar'd, sir.
John.   Why then mark what shall follow. This night *Fredrick*   60
This bawdy night——

Fredrick.   I thought no lesse.
John.   This blinde night,
What dost think I have got?
Fredrick.   The Pox it may be.
John.   Would 'twere no worse: ye talke of Revelations,
I have got a Revelation will reveale me,
An arrant Coxcombe while I live.
Fredrick.   What is't?
Thou has lost nothing?
John.   No, I have got I tell thee.
Fredrick.   What hast thou got?
John.   One of the Infantry, a childe.
Fredrick.   How?
John.   A chopping child, man.
Fredrick.   'Give ye joy, sir.
John.   A lump of lewdnesse *Fredrick*, that's the truth on't:
This Town's abominable.
Fredrick.   I still told ye *John*   70
Your whoring must come home; I counsell'd ye:
But where no grace is——
John.   'Tis none o'mine, man.
Fredrick.   Answer the Parish so.
John.   Cheated in troth,
Peeping into a house, by whom I know not,
Nor where to find the place agen: no *Fredricke*,
Had I but kist the ring fort; 'tis no poor one,
That's my best comfort, for't has brought about it
Enough to make it man.
Fredrick.   Where is't?
John.   At home.
Fredrick.   A saving voyage: But what will you say Signior,
To him that searching out your serious Worship,   80
Has met a stranger fortune?
John.   How, good *Frederick*?
A militant girle now to this boy would hit it?
Fredrick.   No, mine's a nobler venture: What do you think Sir
Of a distressed Lady, one whose beauty

Would oversell all *Italy?*
John.   Where is she——
Fredrick.   A woman of that rare behaviour,
  So qualified, as admiration
  Dwels round about her: of that perfect spirit——
John.   I, marry Sir.
Fredrick.   That admirable carriage,
  That sweetnes in discourse; young as the morning,   90
  Her blushes staining his.
John.   But where's this Creature?
  Shew me but that.
Fredrick.   That's all one, shee's forth comming,
  I have her sure Boy.
John.   Harke ye *Fredrick.*
  What truck betwixt my Infant?
Fredrick.   'Tis too light Sir,
  Stick to your charges good *Don John*, I am well.
John.   But is there such a wench?
Fredrick.   First tell me this,
  Did ye not lately as ye walk'd along,
  Discover people that were arm'd, and likely
  To doe offence?
John.   Yes mary, and they urg'd it
  As far as they had spirit.
Fredrick.   Pray goe forward.   100
John.   A Gentleman I found ingag'd amongst e'm,
  It seemes of noble breeding, I'm sure brave mettall,
  As I return'd to looke you; I set in to him;
  And without hurt (I thanke heaven) rescued him,
  And came my selfe off safe too.
Fredrick [*aside*].   My work's done then:——
  And now to satisfie you, there is a woman,
  Oh *John*, there is a woman——
John.   Oh, where is she?
Fredrick.   And one of no lesse worth then I assure ye;
  And which is more, falne under my protection.
John.   I am glad of that: forward sweet *Fredrick.*   110

Fredrick.   And which is more then that, by this nights wandring,
And which is most of all, she is at home too Sir.
John.   Come, lets be gone then.
Fredrick.   Yes, but 'tis most certaine,
You cannot see her, *John.*
John.   Why?
Fredrick.   She has sworne me
That none else shall come neare her: not my Mother
Till some few doubts are clear'd.
John.   Not look upon her?
What chamber is she in?
Fredrick.   In ours.
John.   Let's goe I say:
A womans oathes are wafers, breake with making,
They must for modestie a litle: we all know it.
Fredrick.   No, I'le assure you Sir.
John.   Not see her?   120
I smell an old dogtrick of yours, well *Fredrick,*
Ye talkt to me of whoring, let's have faire play,
Square dealing I would wish ye.
Fredrick.   When 'tis come,
Which I know never will be, to that issue,
Your spoone shall be as deep as mine Sir.
John.   Tell me,
And tell me true, is the cause honourable,
Or for your ease?
Fredrick.   By all our friendship, *John,*
'Tis honest, and of great end.
John.   I am answer'd:
But let me see her though: leave the doore open
As yee goe in.
Fredrick.   I dare not.
John.   Not wide open,   130
But just so, as a jealous husband
Would levell at his wanton wife through.
Fredrick.   That courtesie,
If ye desire no more, and keep it strictly,

I dare afford yee: come, 'tis now neare morning.

Exeunt.

Enter Peter and Anthony.

[II.] ii

Peter. Nay, the old woman's gone too.
Anthony.   Shee's a Catterwauling
  Among the gutters: But conceive me, *Peter,*
  Where our good Masters should be?
Peter.   Where they should be,
  I doe conceive, but where they are, good *Anthony*——
Anthony. I, there it goes: my Masters bo-peep with me,
  With his slye popping in and out agen,
  Argued a cause, a frippery cause.
Peter.   Beleeve me,
  They bear up with some carvell.
Anthony.   I doe believe thee,
  For thou hast such a Master for that chase,
  That till he spend his maine Mast——
Peter.   Pray remember   10
  Your courtesie good *Anthony*; and withall,
  How long 'tis since your Master sprung a leak,
  He had a sound one since he came.   *Lute sounds within.*
Anthony.   Harke.
Peter.   What?
Anthony. Doest not hear a Lute? Agen?
Peter.   Where is't?
Anthony. Above in my Masters chamber.
Peter.   There's no creature:
  He hath the key himself man.
Anthony.   This is his Lute:
  Let him have it.
Peter.   I grant you; but who strikes it?
Constantia within.   *Sing within a little.*
  Mercilesse Love, whom nature hath deny'd

8 carvell] *i.e.* caravel   17.1 *Constantia within.*] *om.* F 1-2
18-28 *Mercilesse...kill.*] F 2; *om.* F 1

The use of eyes, lest thou should'st take a pride
And glorie in thy murthers: why am I   20
That never yet transgress'd thy deity,
Never broke vow, from whose eyes never flew
Disdainfull dart, whose hard heart never slew,
Thus ill rewarded? thou art young and faire,
Thy Mother soft and gentle as the air,
Thy holy fire still burning, blown with praier.
Then everlasting Love restraine thy will
'Tis God-like to have power but not to kill.

Anthony.　　An admirable voice too, harke ye.
Peter.　　　　　　　　　　　　　*Anthony,*
　Art sure we are at home?
Anthony.　　　　　　　Without all doubt, *Peter.*   30
Peter.　　Then this must be the Devill.
Anthony.　　　　　　　Let it be.　　*Sing agen.*
　Good Devill sing againe: O dainty devill,
　Peter believe it, a most delicate devill,
　The sweetest Devill——

　　　Enter Fredrick *and* Don John [*wearing the* Duke's *hat*].

Fredrick.　　　　　　If ye could leave peeping——
John.　　I cannot by no meanes.
Fredrick.　　　　　　　Then come in softly,
　And as ye love your faith, presume no further
　Then yee have promised.
John.　　　　　　　*Basta.*
Fredrick.　　What make you up so early sir?
John.　　You sir in your contemplations?
Peter.　　O pray ye peace sir.
Fredrick.　　　　　　Why peace sir?   40
Peter.　　Doe you heare?
John.　　　　　　　'Tis your Lute.
Fredrick.　　　　　　　　Pray yee speak softly.
　[*Aside to John*]　She's playing on't.

24 *Thus ill rewarded?*] Seward; *those rewarders?* F 2
*34 *Enter . . . Don John.*] stet F 1–2　　　37 *Basta.*] F 2; *Basto.* F 1

Anthony.   The house is haunted sir,
For this we have heard this halfe yeare.
Fredrick.   Ye saw nothing?
Anthony.   Not I.
Peter.   Nor I Sir.
Fredrick.   Get us our breakfast then,
And make no words on't; wee'll undertake this spirit,
If it be one.   *Sing.*
Anthony.   This is no devill *Peter.*
Mum, there be Bats abroad.   *Exeunt Servants.*
Fredrick.   Stay, now she sings.
John.   An Angels voice Ile sweare.
Fredrick.   Why did'st thou shrug so?
Either allay this heat; or as I live
I will not trust ye.
John.   Passe: I warrant ye.   50
                                        Exeunt.

                Enter Constantia.   [II. iii]

Constantia.   To curse those starres, that men say governe us,
To raile at fortune, fall out with my Fate,
And taske the generall world, will helpe me nothing:
Alas, I am the same still, neither are they
Subject to helpes, or hurts: Our owne desires
Are our owne fates, our owne stars, all our fortunes,
Which as we sway 'em, so abuse, or blesse us.

        Enter Fredrick. Don John [*wearing the* Duke's *hat*] peeping
                [*at the doore*].

Fredrick.   Peace to your meditations.
John [*apart to Fredrick*].   Pox upon ye,
Stand out oth' light.
Constantia.   I crave your mercy sir,
My minde o're-charg'd with care made me unmannerly.   10

        3 taske] *i.e.* tax
        7.1 Fredrick. Don John] Dyce; *Fredrick, and Don John* F 1–2

                577

Fredrick.   Pray yee set that minde at rest, all shall be perfect.
John [*apart*].   I like the body rare; a handsome body,
  A wondrous handsome body: would she would turne:
  See, and that spightfull puppy be not got
  Between me and my light againe.
Fredrick.   Tis done,
  As all that you command shall bee: the gentleman
  Is safely off all danger.
John [*apart*].   *O de dios.*
Constantia.   How shall I thank ye sir? how satisfie?
Fredrick.   Speak softly, gentle Lady, all's rewarded.
  [*Aside*]   Now does he melt like Marmalad.
John [*apart*].   Nay, 'tis certaine,   20
  Thou art the sweetest woman I e're look'd on:
  I hope thou art not honest.
Fredrick.   None disturb'd yee?
Constantia.   Not any sir, nor any sound came neare me,
  I thank your care.
Fredrick.   'Tis well.
John [*apart*].   I would faine pray now,
  But the Devill and that flesh there o' the world,
  What are we made to suffer?
Fredrick [*aside*].   Hee'll enter;
  [*To John*]   Pull in your head and be hang'd.
John [*aside*].   Harke ye *Fredricke*,
  I have brought ye home your Pack-saddle.
Fredrick [*aside*].   Pox upon yee.
Constantia.   Nay let him enter: [*to John*] fie my Lord the Duke,
  Stand peeping at your friends?
Fredrick.   Ye are cozen'd Lady,   30
  Here is no Duke.
Constantia.   I know him full well Signior.
John [*aside*].   Hold thee there wench.
Fredrick [*aside*].   This mad-brain'd foole will spoile all.
Constantia.   I doe beseech your grace come in.
John [*aside*].   My Grace,
  There was a word of comfort.

Fredrick.   Shall he enter,
Who e're he be?
John [aside].   Well follow'd *Fredrick.*
Constantia.   With all my heart.
Fredrick.   Come in then.

Enter Don John.

John.   'Blesse yee Lady.
Fredrick.   Nay start not, though he be a stranger to ye,
Hee's of a Noble straine, my kinsman, Lady,
My Countrey-man, and fellow Traveller,
One bed containes us ever, one purse feeds us,   40
And one faith free between us; do not fear him,
Hee's truely honest.
John [aside].   That's a lye.
Fredrick.   And trusty
Beyond your wishes: valiant to defend,
And modest to converse with as your blushes.
John [aside].   Now may I hang my self; this commendation
Has broke the neck of all my hopes: for now
Must I cry, no forsooth, and I forsooth, and surely,
And truely as I live, and as I am honest.
Has done these things for 'nonce too; for hee knowes,
Like a most envious Rascall as he is,   50
I am not honest, nor desire to be,
Especially this way: h'as watch'd his time,
But I shall quit him.
Constantia.   Sir, I credit ye.
Fredrick.   Goe kisse her *John.*
John [aside].   Plague o' your commendations.
Constantia.   Sir, I shall now desire to be a trouble.
John.   Never to me, sweet Lady: Thus I seale
My faith, and all my service.
Constantia.   One word Signeur.
                              [*She talks with* Fredrick *apart.*]
John.   Now 'tis impossible I should be honest;
She kisses with a conjuration

Would make the devill dance: what points she at?   60
My leg I warrant, or my well knit body:
Sit fast *Don Fredrick*.
Fredrick.   'Twas given him by that gentleman
You took such care of; his owne being lost ith' scuffle.
Constantia.   With much joy may he weare it: [*to John*] 'tis a right
     one,
I can assure ye Gentleman, and right happy
May you be in all fights for that faire service.
Fredrick.   Why doe ye blush?
Constantia.   'T had almost cozen'd me,
For not to lye, when I saw that, I look'd for
Another Master of it: but 'tis well.   *Knock within*.
Fredrick.   Who's there?
          Stand ye a little close:——*Exit* Constantia.
          Come in Sir,   70

       Enter Anthony.

Now what's the newes with you?
Anthony.   There is a gentleman without,
Would speak with *Don John*.
John.   Who sir?
Anthony.   I do not know Sir, but he shews a man
Of no meane reckoning.
Fredrick.   Let him shew his name,
And then returne a little wiser.
Anthony.   Well Sir.   *Exit* Anthony.
Fredrick.   How doe you like her *John*?
John.   As well as you *Fredrick*,
For all I am honest: you shall finde it so too.
Fredrick.   Art thou not honest?
John.   Art thou not an Asse?
And modest as her blushes? What block-head
Would e're have popt out such a dry Apologie,   80

71 gentleman] F2; gentlemen F1
78 thou not an] Dyce; thou an F1–2
79 What] F2; What a F1

For his deare friend? and to a Gentlewoman,
A woman of her youth, and delicacy,
They are arguments to draw them to abhorre us.
An honest morall man; 'tis for a Constable:
A handsome man, a wholsome man, a tough man,
A liberall man, a likely man, a man
Made up like *Hercules*, unslak'd with service;
The same to night, to morrow night, the next night,
And so to perpetuitie of pleasures:
These had been things to hearken too, things catching: 90
But you have such a spiced consideration,
Such qualmes upon your worships conscience,
Such chil-blaines in your bloud, that all things pinch ye,
Which nature, and the liberall world makes custome,
And nothing but faire honour, O sweet honour:
Hang up your Eunuch honour: That I was trusty,
And valiant, were things well put in; but modest!
A modest gentleman! ô wit where wast thou?
Fredrick.   I am sorrie *John.*
John.   My Ladies gentlewoman
Would laugh me to a Schoole-boy, make me blush   100
With playing with my Codpeece point: fie on thee,
A man of thy discretion?
Fredrick.   It shall be mended:
And henceforth yee shall have your due.
John.   I look fort:

Enter Anthony.

How now, who is't?
Anthony.   A gentleman of this towne
And calls himselfe *Petruchio.*
John.   Ile attend him.   [*Exit* Anthony.]

Enter Constantia.

Constantia.   How did he call himselfe?
Fredrick.   *Petruchio,*
Doe's it concerne you ought?

Constantia.   O gentlemen,
The houre of my destruction is come on me,
I am discover'd, lost, left to my ruine:
As ever ye had pitty——   [*Kneels.*]
John.   Doe not feare,   110
Let the great devill come, he shall come through me:
Lost here, and we about ye?
Fredrick.   Fall before us?
Constantia.   O my unfortunate estate, all angers
Compar'd to his, to his——
Fredrick.   Let his, and all mens,
Whilst we have power and life:—— stand up for heaven sake.
                                        [*She rises.*]
Constantia.   I have offended heaven too; yet heaven knows——
John.   We are all evill:
Yet heaven forbid we should have our deserts.
What is a?
Constantia.   Too too neare to my offence sir;
O he will cut me peece-meale.
Fredrick.   'Tis no Treason?   120
John.   Let it be what it will: if a cut here,
Ile find him cut-worke.
Fredrick.   He must buy you deare,
With more than common lives.
John.   Feare not, nor weep not:
By heaven Ile fire the Towne before yee perish;
And then, the more the merrier, wee'll jog with yee.
Fredrick.   Come in, and dry your eyes.
John.   Pray no more weeping:
Spoile a sweet face for nothing? my returne
Shall end all this I warrant you.
Constantia.   Heaven grant it.
                                        Exeunt.

128 you] F1(c), F2; yoe F1(u)

582

Enter Petruchio *with a Letter.*

Petruchio. This man should be of speciall rank: for these commends
Carry no common way, no slight worth with 'em:

Enter Don John.

A shall be he.
John. 'Save yee sir: I am sorrie
My businesse was so unmannerly, to make ye
Wait thus long here.
Petruchio. Occasions must be serv'd sir:
But is your name *Don John*?
John. It is Sir.
Petruchio. Then,
First, for your owne brave sake I must embrace yee:
Next, from the credit of your noble friend
Hernando de Alvara, make yee mine: 10
Who layes his charge upon me in this Letter
To look yee out, and for the goodnesse in yee,
Whilst your occasions make yee resident
In this place, to supply yee, love and honour yee;
Which had I knowne sooner——
John. Noble sir,
You'll make my thanks too poore: I weare a sword, sir,
And have a service to be still dispos'd of,
As you shall please command it.
Petruchio. Gentle sir,
That manly courtesie is half my businesse:
And to be short, to make ye know I honour ye,   20
And in all points believe your worth like Oracle,
And how above my friends, which are not few,
And those not slack, I estimate your vertues,
Make your selfe understand: This day *Petruchio*,
A man that may command the strength of this place,
Hazzard the boldest spirits, hath made choice
Onely of you, and in a noble office.
John. Forward, I am free to entertaine it.
Petruchio. Thus then:

I doe beseech ye mark me.

John. I shall doe it.

Petruchio. *Ferrara's* Duke, would I might call him worthie,
But that he has raz'd out from his family, 30
As he has mine with Infamie, This man,
Rather this powerfull Monster, we being left
But two of all our house, to stock our memories,
My Sister, and my selfe; with arts, and witch-crafts,
Vowes, and such oathes heaven has no mercy for,
Drew to dishonour this weak maid: by stealthes,
And secret passages I knew not of,
Oft he obtain'd his wishes, oft abus'd her:
I am asham'd to say the rest: This purchas'd,
And his hot bloud allay'd, as friends forsake us 40
At a miles end upon our way, he left her,
And all our name to ruine.

John. This was foule Play,
And ought to be rewarded so.

Petruchio. I hope so;
He scap'd me yester-night: which if he dare
Againe adventure for, heaven pardon him,
I shall with all my heart.

John. For me, brave Signior,
What doe yee intend?

Petruchio. Onely, faire sir, this trust,
Which from the commendations of this Letter,
I dare presume well placed, nobly to beare him
By word of mouth a single challenge from me, 50
That man to man, if he have honour in him,
We may decide all difference.

John. Faire, and noble,
And I will doe it home: When shall I visite ye?

Petruchio. Please you this after-noon, I will ride with yee;
For at a Castle six mile hence, we are sure
To finde him.

John. Ile be ready.

Petruchio. To attend ye,

My man shall wait: with all my love.
John.   My service shall not faile yee.   *Exit* Petruchio.

Enter Fredrick.

Fredrick.   How now?
John.   All's well: who dost thou think this wench is?
  Ghesse, and thou canst?
Fredrick.   I cannot.
John.   Be it knowne then,   60
  To all men by these presents, this is she,
  She, she, and only she, our curious coxcombs
  Were errant two moneths after.
Fredrick.   Who, *Constantia?*
  Thou talk'st of Cocks and Bulls.
John.   I talke of wenches,
  Of Cocks and Hens *Don Fredrick*; this is the Pullet
  We two went proud after.
Fredrick.   It cannot be.
John.   It shall be;
  Sister to *Don Petruchio*: I know all man.
Fredrick.   Now I beleeve.
John.   Goe to, there has been stirring,
  Fumbling with Linnen *Fredrick*.
Fredrick.   'Tis impossible,
  You know her fame was pure as fire.
John.   That pure fire   70
  Has melted out her maiden-head: she is crackt:
  We have all that hope of our side, boy.
Fredrick.   Thou tell'st me,
  To my imagination, things incredible:
  I see no loose thought in her.
John.   That's all one,
  She is loose ith' hilts by heaven: but the world
  Must know a faire way, upon vow of marriage.
Fredrick. There may be such a slip.
John.   And will be *Fredrick*,

Whil'st the old game's afoot: I feare the boy too
Will prove hers I took up.
Fredrick.   Good circumstance
May cure all this yet.
John.   There thou hitst it, *Fredrick*:   80
Come, let's walke in and comfort her: her being here
Is nothing yet suspected: anon Ile tell thee
Wherefore her brother came, who by this light
Is a brave noble fellow, and what honour
H'as done to me a stranger: there be Irons
Heating for some, will hisse into their heart blouds,
'Ere all be ended; so much for this time.
Fredrick.   Well sir.
                          Exeunt.

             Enter Land-lady *and* Peter.   III. i

Land-lady.   Come ye doe know.
Peter.   I do not by this hand Mistris.
But I suspect.
Land-lady.   What?
Peter.   That if egges continue
At this price, women wil ne're be sav'd
By their good works.
Land-lady.   I will know.
Peter.   Yee shall, any thing
Lyes in my power: The Duke of *Loraine* now
Is seven thousand strong: I heard it of a fish-wife,
A woman of fine knowledge.
Land-lady.   Sirrah, sirrah.
Peter.   The Popes Buls are broke loose too, and 'tis suspected
They shall be baited in *England*.
Land-lady.   Very well sir.
Peter.   No, 'tis not so well neither.
Land-lady.   But I say to yee,   10
Who is it keeps your Master company?

78 afoot] Langbaine; a foot F1–2
78–79 boy too...hers] Weber; boy too...hers too F1; boy...hers too F2

Peter.   I say to you, *Don John.*
Land-lady.   I say what woman?
Peter.   I say so too.
Land-lady.   I say againe, I will know.
Peter.   I say 'tis fit yee should.
Land-lady.   And I tell thee
   He has a woman here.
Peter.   And I tell thee
   'Tis then the better for him.
Land-lady.   You are no Bawd now?
Peter.   Would I were able to be call'd unto it:
   A worshipfull vocation for my elders;
   For as I understand it is a place
   Fitting my betters farr.
Land-lady.   Was ever Gentlewoman   20
   So frumpt off with a foole? well sawcy sirrah,
   I will know who it is, and for what purpose;
   I pay the rent, and I will know how my house
   Comes by these Inflamations: if this geere hold,
   Best hang a signe-post up, to tell the Signiors,
   Here ye may have lewdnesse at Liverie.
Peter.   'Twould be a great ease to your age.

                    Enter Fredrick.

Fredrick.   How now?
   Why what's the mater Land-lady?
Land-lady.   What's the matter?
   Ye use me decently among ye gentlemen.
Fredrick.   Who has abus'd her, you sir?
Land-lady.   'Ods my witnesse   30
   I will not be thus treated, that I will not.
Peter.   I gave her no ill language.
Land-lady.   Thou lyest lewdly,
   Thou tookst me up at every word I spoke,
   As I had been a Mawkin, a flurt Gillian;
   And thou thinkst, because thou canst write and read,
   Our noses must be under thee.

Fredrick.   Dare you sirrah?
Peter.   Let but the truth be known Sir, I beseech ye,
  She raves of wenches, and I know not what sir.
Land-lady. Go to, thou know'st too well, thou wicked varlet,
  Thou instrument of evill.
Peter.   As I live Sir,   40
  She is ever thus till dinner.
Fredrick.   Get ye in,
  Ile answer you anon sir.
Peter [*aside*].   By this hand
  Ile break your possit pan.
Land-lady [*aside*].   Then by this hood
  Ile lock the meat up.   *Exit* [Peter].
Fredrick.   Now your grief, what is't?
  For I can ghesse——
Land-lady.   Ye may with shame enough,
  If theer were shame amongst yee; nothing thought on,
  But how yee may abuse my house: not satisfi'd
  With bringing home your Bastards to undoe me,
  But you must drill your whores here too; my patience
  (Because I beare, and beare, and carry all,   50
  And as they say am willing to groan under)
  Must be your make-sport now.
Fredrick.   No more of these words,
  Nor no more murmurings Lady: for you know
  That I know something. I did suspect your anger,
  But turne it presently and handsomely,
  And beare your selfe discreetly to this woman,
  For such a one there is indeed——
Land-lady.   'Tis well sonne.
Fredrick.   Leaving your devils Matins, and your melanchollies,
  Or we shall leave our lodgings.
Land-lady.   You have much need
  To use these vagrant wayes, and to much profit: 60
  Ye had that might content
  (At home within your selves too) right good gentlemen,
  Wholsome, and yee said handsome: But you gallants,

Beast that I was to beleeve ye——
Fredrick.   Leave your suspicion:
For as I live there's no such thing.
Land-lady.   Mine honour;
And 'twere not for mine honour——
Fredrick.   Come, your honour,
Your house, and you too, if you dare beleeve me,
Are well enough: sleek up your self, leave crying,
For I must have yee entertain this Lady
With all civility, she well deserves it,   70
Together with all secresie: I dare trust yee,
For I have found yee faithfull: when you know her
You will find your owne fault; no more words, but doe it.
Land-lady. You know you may command me,

Enter Don John.

John.   Worshipfull Lady,
How does thy Velvet scabbard? by this hand
Thou look'st most amiably: now could I willingly
And 'twere not for abusing thy *Geneva* print there,
Venture my body with thee.
Land-lady.   You'll leave this roperie,
When you come to my yeares.
John.   By this light
Thou art not above fifteen yet, a meere girle,   80
Thou hast not half thy teeth: come
Fredrick.   Prethee *John*
Let her alone, she has been vex'd already:
Shee'll grow starke mad, man.
John.   I would see her mad,
An old mad woman——
Fredrick.   Prethee be patient.
John. Is like a Millers Mare, troubled with tooth-ache.
Shee'll make the rarest faces.
Fredrick.   Goe, and doe it,
And doe not mind this fellow.

64 Beast] F2; Boast F1

Land-lady.   Well *Don John.*
There will be times agen; when O good Mother,
What's good for a carnosity in the Bladder?
O the green water, mother.
John.   Doting take yee,   90
Doe ye remember that?
Fredrick.   She has payd ye now sir.
Land-lady.   Clarry, sweet mother, Clarry.
Fredrick.   Are ye satisfied?
Land-lady.   Ile never whore againe; never give Petticoats
And Wastcoats at five pound a peece; good Mother,
Quickly Mother: now mock on Son.
John.   A devill grinde your old chaps.
Fredrick.   By this hand wench
Ile give thee a new hood for this.   *Exit* Land-lady.
Has she met with your Lordship?
John.   Touch-wood rake her.
Shee's a rare ghostly mother.

Enter Anthony.

Anthony.   Below attends yee
The Gentlemans man sir that was with yee.
John.   Well Sir; [*Exit* Anthony.]   100
My time is come then: yet if my project hold,
You shall not stay behinde: Ile rather trust
A Cat with sweet milk *Fredrick.*

Enter Constantia.

                    By her face
I feele her feares are working.
Constantia.   Is there no way,
I doe beseech yee think yet, to divert
This certaine danger?
Fredrick.   'Tis impossible:
Their honours are engag'd.

92 Clarry] (*a sweet wine, thought to have curative power*)
98 *John.*] F2; *om.* F1

Constantia.   Then there must be murther,
Which, Gentlemen, I shall no sooner heare of,
Then make one in't: you may, if you please sir,
Make all goe lesse yet.
John.   Lady wer't mine owne cause,   110
I could dispence: but loaden with my friends trust,
I must go on; though generall massacres
As much I feare——
Constantia.   Doe ye heare sir; for heavens pittie
Let me request one love of you.
Fredrick.   Yes any thing.
Constantia.   This gentleman I find too resolute,
Too hot, and fiery for the cause: as ever
You did a vertuous deed, for honours sake
Go with him, and allay him: your fair temper
And noble disposition, like wish'd showres,
May quench those eating fires, that would spoile all else.   120
I see in him destruction.
Fredrick.   I will doe it;
And 'tis a wise consideration,
To me, a bounteous favour:——harke ye *John*,
I will goe with yee.
John.   No.
Fredrick.   Indeed I will,
Ye goe upon a hazzard: no denyall;
For as I live, Ile goe.
John.   Then make ye ready
For I am straight a horse-back.
Fredrick.   My sword on,
I am as ready as you:——what my best labour,
With all the Art I have can work upon 'em,
Be sure of, and expect faire end: the old gentlewoman   130
Shall wait upon you; she is both grave and private,
And yee may trust her in all points.
Constantia.   Ye are noble.
Fredrick.   And so I kisse your hand.

133 *Fredrick.*] Seward; *om.* F 1–2

John.   That seale for me too,
And I hope happy issue Lady.
Constantia.   All heavens care upon yee, and my prayers.
John.   So, now my mind's at rest.
Fredrick.   Away, 'tis late *John.*
                                    Exeunt [*severally*].

            Enter Antonio, a Surgeon, *and two Gentlemen.*   [III.] ii

1. Gentleman.   Come sir, be hearty: all the worst is past.
Antonio.   Give me some Wine.
Surgeon.   'Tis death Sir.
Antonio.   'Tis a horse sir.
'Sbloud, to be drest to the tune of Ale onely,
Nothing but sawces to my sores.
2. Gentleman.   Fie *Antonio,*
You must be govern'd.
Antonio.   Has given me a dam'd Glister,
Only of sand and snow water, gentlemen,
Has almost scour'd my guts out.
Surgeon.   I have giv'n you that sir
Is fittest for your state.
Antonio.   And here he feeds me
With rotten ends of rooks, and drown'd chickens,
Stewd Pericraniums, and Pia-maters;   10
And when I goe to bed, by heaven 'tis true gentlemen,
He rolls me up in Lints, with Labels at 'em,
That I am just the man ith' Almanack,
In head and face, is *Aries* place.
Surgeon.   Wilt please ye
To let your friends see ye open'd?
Antonio.   Will it please you sir
To let me have a wench: I feele my body
Open enough for that yet?
Surgeon.   How, a wench?
Antonio.   Why look yee gentlemen; thus I am us'd still,
I can get nothing that I want.

1. Gentleman.   Leave these things,
And let him open ye.
Antonio.   Doe'ye heare Surgeon?   20
Send for the Musick, let me have some pleasure
To entertaine my friends, beside your Sallads,
Your green salves, and your searches; and some wine too,
That I may onely smell to it: or by this light
Ile dye upon thy hand, and spoyle thy custome.
1. Gentleman.   Let him have Musick.
Surgeon.   'Tis ith' house, and ready,

Enter Servant with wine [and Musicians].

If he will aske no more: but wine——   *Musick.*
2. Gentleman.   He shall not drink it.
Surgeon.   Will these things please yee?
Antonio.   Yes, and let 'em sing
John Dorrie.
2. Gentleman.   'Tis too long.
Antonio.   Ile have *John Dorrie,*
For to that warlike tune I will be open'd.   30
Give me some drinke:——have yee stopt the leakes well
          Surgeon?
All will runne out else.
Surgeon.   Feare not.
Antonio.   Sit downe Gentlemen:
And now advance your plaisters.
                              Song of John Dorry.
Give 'em ten shillings friends: *[Exeunt Musicians.]*
                    how doe ye finde me?
What Symptomes doe you see now?
Surgeon.   None Sir, dangerous:
But if you will be rul'd——
Antonio.   What time?
Surgeon.   I can cure ye
In forty dayes, so you will not transgresse me.
Antonio.   I have a dog shall lick me whole in twenty:

*26.1 Servant] Rowl. F 1–2   *29 John Dorrie] see Textual Note*

In how long canst thou kill me?

Surgeon. Presently.

Antonio. Doe it; there's more delight in't.

1. Gentleman. You must have patience. 40

Antonio. Man, I must have busines; this foolish fellow
Hinders himselfe: I have a dozen Rascalls
To hurt within these five dayes: good man-mender,
Stop me up with Parsley, like stuft Beefe,
And let me walke abroad——

Surgeon. Ye shall walke shortly.

Antonio. For I must finde *Petruchio.*

2. Gentleman. Time enough.

1. Gentleman. Come lead him in, and let him sleep: within
these three dayes
Wee'll beg yee leave to play.

2. Gentleman. And then how things fall,
Wee'll certainly informe yee.

Antonio. But Surgion promise me
I shall drinke Wine then too.

Surgeon. A little temper'd. 50

Antonio. Nay, Ile no tempering Surgion.

Surgeon. Well, as't please ye,
So ye exceed not.

Antonio. Farewell: and if ye finde
The Mad slave, that thus slasht me, commend me to him,
And bid him keep his skin close.

1. Gentleman. Take your rest sir.

Exeunt.

Enter Constantia, *and* Land-lady. [III.] iii

Constantia. I have told yee all I can, and more then yet
Those Gentlemen know of me; ever trusting
Your Councell and concealement: for to me
You seem a worthy woman; one of those
Are seldome found in our sex, wise and vertuous,
Direct me I beseech ye.

Land-lady.   Ye say well Lady,
And hold yee to that poynt; for in these businesses
A womans councell that conceives the matter,
(Doe ye marke me, that conceives the matter Lady)
Is worth ten mens engagements: She knows something,   10
And out of that can worke like wax: when men
Are giddy-headed, either out of wine,
Or a more drunkennesse, vaine ostentation,
Discovering all, there is no more keep in 'em,
Then hold upon an Eeles taile: nay 'tis held fashion
To defame now all they can.
Constantia.   I, but these gentlemen——
Land-lady.   Doe not you trust to that: these gentlemen
Are as all Gentlemen of the same Barrell:
I, and the selfe same pickle too. Be it granted,
They have us'd yee with respect and faire behaviour,   20
Yet since ye came: doe you know what must follow?
They are Spaniards, Lady, Gennets of high mettle,
Things that will thrash the devill, or his dam,
Let 'em appeare but cloven——
Constantia.   Now heaven blesse me.
Land-lady.   Mad Colts will court the wind: I know 'em Lady
To the least haire they have; and I tell you,
Old as I am, let but the pinte pot blesse 'em,
They'll offer to my yeares ——
Constantia.   How?
Land-lady.   Such rude gambolls——
Constantia.   To you?
Land-lady.   I, and so handle me, that oft I am forc'd
To fight of all foure for my safety: there's the yonger,   30
Don John, the arrantst *Jack* in all this City:
The other, time has blasted, yet he will stoop,
If not ore-flowne, and freely on the quarry;
Has been a Dragon in his dayes. But *Tarmont,*
Don Jenkin is the Devill himselfe, the Dog-dayes,

----

*14 keep in 'em] *stet* F1-2   30 of all foure] *i.e.,* on all fours
34 But] F2; Bur F1   34 *Tarmont*] *i.e., Termagant*(?); an oath

The most incomprehensible whore-master,
Twenty a night is nothing: Beggers, Broom-women,
And those so miserable, they look like famine,
Are all sweet Ladies in his drink.
Constantia. He's a handsome Gentleman.
Pitty he should be master of such follies. 40
Land-lady. Hee's ne're without a noise of Sirrenges
In's pocket, those proclaim him; birding pills;
Waters to coole his conscience, in small Viols;
With thousand such sufficient emblemes: the truth is,
Whose chastity he chops upon, he cares not.
He flies at all; Bastards upon my conscience,
He has now in making multitudes; The last night
He brought home one; I pitty her that bore it,
But we are all weake vessels, some rich woman
(For wife I dare not call her) was the mother, 50
For it was hung with Jewels; the bearing cloath
No lesse then Crimson Velvet.
Constantia. How?
Land-lady. 'Tis true Lady.
Constantia. Was it a Boy too?
Land-lady. A brave Boy; deliberation
And judgement shewd in's getting, as I'le say for him,
He's as well paced for that sport——
Constantia. May I see it?
For there is a neighbour of mine, a Gentlewoman,
Has had a late mischance, which willingly
I would know further of; now if you please
To be so curteous to me——
Land-lady. Ye shall see it:
But what do ye thinke of these men now ye know 'em, 60
And of the cause I told ye of? Be wise,
Ye may repent too late else; I but tell ye
For your owne good, and as you will find it Lady.
Constantia. I am advis'd.
Land-lady. No more words then; do that,

*50 wife] wise F1–2

And instantly, I told ye of, be ready:——
Don John, I'le fit ye for your frumps.
Constantia.   I shall be:
But shall I see this Child?
Land-lady.   Within this halfe houre,
Let's in, and there thinke better; she that's wise,
Leapes at occasion first; the rest pay for it.

                                        Exeunt.

                Enter Petruchio, Don John, *and* Fredrick.   [III.] iv

John.   Sir, he is worth your knowledg; and a Gentleman
If I that so much love him, may commend him,
Of free and vertuous parts; and one, if foule play
Should fall upon us, for which feare I brought him,
Will not flie backe for phillips.
Petruchio.   Ye much honour me,
And once more I pronounce ye both mine.
Fredrick.   Stay,
What Troope is that below i'th valley there?
John. Hawking I take it.
Petruchio.   They are so;
'Tis the Duke, 'tis even he Gentlemen:——
Sirrah, draw backe the Horses till we call ye.——   10
I know him by his company.
Fredrick.   I thinke too
He bends up this way.
Petruchio.   So he does.
John.   Stand you still
Within that Covert till I call: you *Fredrick*,
By no meanes be not seen, unlesse they offer
To bring on odds upon us; he comes forward,
Here will I waite him fairely: to your Cabins.
Petruchio.   I need no more instruct ye?
John.   Feare me not,
I'le give it him, and boldly.   *Exeunt* Petruchio *and* Fredrick.

              5 phillips] *i.e.*, fillips
                        597

Enter Duke *and his faction.*

Duke.   Feed the Hawkes up,
  Wee'l flie no more to day:——O my blest fortune,
  Have I so fairely met the man!
John.   Ye have Sir,   20
  And him you know by this.   [*Points to his hat.*]
Duke.   Sir all the honour,
  And love——
John.   I do beseech your Grace stay there,
  (For I know you too now): that love and honour
  I come not to receive; nor can you give it,
  Till ye appeare faire to the world; I must beseech ye
  Dismisse your traine a little.
Duke.   Walke aside,
  And out of hearing I command ye:——   [*Exeunt his faction.*]
                                        Now Sir.
John.   Last time we met, I was a friend.
Duke.   And Nobly
  You did a friends office: let your businesse
  Be what it may, you must be still——
John.   Your pardon,   30
  Never a friend to him, cannot be friend
  To his own honour.
Duke.   In what have I transgress'd it?
  Ye make a bold breach at the first Sir.
John.   Bolder
  You made that breach that let in infamy
  And ruine, to surprize a noble stocke.
Duke. Be plaine Sir.
John.   I will, and short; ye have wrong'd a Gentleman
  Little behind your selfe, beyond all justice,
  Beyond the mediation of all friends.
Duke.   The man, and manner of wrong?
John.   Petruchio,   40
  The wrong, ye have whord his Sister.

39 the] Sympson; *om.* F 1–2

598

Duke.   What's his will in't?
John.   His will is to oppose you like a Gentleman,
  And single, to decide all.
Duke.   Now stay you Sir,
  And heare me with the like beliefe: this Gentleman
  His Sister that you named, 'tis true I have long loved,
  Nor was that love lascivious, as he makes it;
  As true, I have enjoy'd her: no lesse truth
  I have a child by her: But that she, or he,
  Or any of that family are tainted,
  Suffer disgrace, or ruine, by my pleasures,   50
  I weare a Sword to satisfie the world no,
  And him in this cause when he please; for know Sir,
  She is my wife, contracted before Heaven,
  (Witnesse I owe more tye to, then her Brother)
  Nor will I flye from that name, which long since
  Had had the Churches approbation,
  But for his jealous danger.
John.   Sir, your pardon,
  And all that was my anger, now my service.
Duke.   Faire sir, I knew I should convert ye; had we
  But that rough man here now too——
John.   And ye shall Sir: 60
  Whoa, hoa, hoo.
Duke.   I hope ye have laid no Ambush?
John.   Only friends.

                    Enter Petruchio.

Duke.   My noble Brother welcome:
  Come put your Anger off, we'l have no fighting,
  Unlesse you will maintaine I am unworthy
  To beare that name.
Petruchio.   Do you speake this hartely?
Duke.   Upon my soule, and truly; the first Priest
  Shall put you out of these doubts.
Petruchio.   Now I love ye;

            66 *Duke.* Upon] F 2; *Duke* upon F 1

                        599

And I beseech you pardon my suspitions,
You are now more then a Brother, a brave friend too.
John. The good man's over-joy'd.

Enter Fredrick.

Fredrick.   How now, how goes it?   70
John. Why, the man 'has his mare agen, and all's well *Fredrick*,
  The Duke professes freely hee's her husband.
Fredrick. 'Tis a good hearing.
John [*aside*].   Yes for modest Gentlemen.——
  I must present ye:——may it please your Grace
  To number this brave Gentleman, my friend
  And noble kinsman, amongst those your servants.
Duke. O my brave friend! you showre your bounties on me.
  Amongst my best thoughts Signior, in which number
  You being worthily dispos'd already,
  May place your friend to honour me.
Fredrick.   My love sir,   80
  And where your Grace dares trust me, all my service.
Petruchio. Why? this is wondrous happy: But now Brother,
  Now comes the bitter to our sweet: *Constantia*——
Duke. Why, what of her?
Petruchio.   Nor what, nor where, do I know:
  Wing'd with her feares last night, beyond my knowledge,
  She quit my house, but whether——
Fredrick.   Let not that——
Duke. No more good Sir, I have heard too much.
Petruchio.   Nay sinke not,
  She cannot be so lost.
John.   Nor shall not Gentlemen;
  Be free agen, the Ladie's found; that smile Sir,
  Shewes ye distrust your Servant.
Duke.   I do beseech ye.   90
John. Ye shall beleeve me: by my soule she is safe.
Duke. Heaven knows, I would beleeve Sir.
Fredrick.   Ye may safely.

*86 whether] *i.e.,* whither(?)

600

John.   And under noble usage: this faire Gentleman
  Met her in all her doubts last night, and to his guard
  (Her feares being strong upon her) she gave her person,
  Who waited on her, to our lodging; where all respect,
  Civill and honest service now attend her.
Petruchio.   Ye may beleeve now.
Duke.   Yes, I do, and strongly:
  Well my good friends, or rather my good Angels,
  For ye have both preserved me; when these vertues   100
  Dye in your friends remembrance——
John.   Good your grace
  Lose no more time in complement, 'tis too pretious,
  I know it by my selfe, there can be no hell
  To his that hangs upon his hopes; especially
  In way of lustly pleasures.
Petruchio.   He has hit it.
Fredrick.   To horse againe then, for this night I'le crowne
  With all the joyes ye wish for.
Petruchio.   Happy Gentlemen.
                                              Exeunt.

                    Enter Francisco.   [III. v]

Francisco.   This is the maddest mischiefe: never foole
  Was so fubd off, as I am; made ridiculous,
  And to my selfe, mine owne Asse: trust a woman,
  I'le trust the Devill first; for he dare be
  Better then's word sometime: what faith have I broke?
  In what observance failed? Let me consider,
  For this is monstrous usage.

                Enter Don John, *and* Fredrick.

Fredrick.   Let them talke,
  Wee'll ride on faire and softly.
Francisco.   Well *Constantia*——
Fredrick [*apart*].   *Constantia,* what's this fellow? stay by all means.
Francisco.   Ye have spun your selfe a faire thred now.

Fredrick [*apart*].   Stand still *John*. 10
Francisco.   What cause had you to fly? what feare possest ye?
  Were you not safely lodg'd from all suspition?
  Us'd with all gentle meanes? did any know
  How ye came thether, or what your sin was?
Fredrick [*apart*].   *John*.
  I smell some juggling *John*.
John [*apart*].   Yes, *Fredrick*,
  I feare it will be found so.
Francisco.   So strangely,
  Without the counsell of your friends; so desperatly
  To put all dangers on ye?
Fredrick [*apart*].   'Tis she.
Francisco.   So deceitfully
  After a strangers lure?
John [*apart*].   Did ye marke that *Fredrick*?
Francisco.   To make ye appeare more monster; and the Law   20
  More cruell to reward ye? to leave all,
  All that should be your safeguard, to seeke evils?
  Was this your wisedome? this your promise? well
  He that incited ye——
Fredrick [*apart*].   Marke that too.
John [*apart*].   Yes Sir.
Francisco.   'Had better have plough'd farther off; now Lady,
  What will your last friend, he that should preserve ye,
  And hold your credit up, the brave *Antonio*,
  Thinke of this slip? he'll to *Petruchio*,
  And call for open justice.
John [*apart*].   'Tis she *Fredrick*.
Fredrick [*apart*].   But what that he is *John*——
Francisco.   I do not doubt yet 30
  To bolt ye out, for I know certainly
  Ye are about the Towne still: ha, no more words.   *Exit*.
Fredrick.   Well.
John.   Very well.
Fredrick.   Discreetly.
John.   Finely carried.

Fredrick.　You have no more of these tricks?
John.　　　　　　　　　　　　Ten to one Sir,
　I shall meet with 'em if ye have.
Fredrick.　　　　　　　　Is this honest?
John.　Was it in you a friends part to deale double?
　I am no asse *Don Fredrick.*
Fredrick.　　　　　　　And *Don John*,
　It shall appeare I am no foole; disgrace me
　To make yourselfe a lecher? 'tis boyish, 'tis base.
John.　'Tis false, and most unmanly to upbraid me,　　　40
　Nor will I be your bolster Sir.
Fredrick.　Thou wanton boy, thou hadst better have been Eunuch,
　Thou common womans curtesie, then thus
　Lascivious, basely to have bent mine honour.
　A friend? I'le make a horse my friend first!
John.　　　　　　　　　　　Holla, holla,
　Ye kicke to fast sir: what strange braines have you got,
　That dare crow out thus bravely? I better been a Eunuch?
　I privy to this dog tricke? cleare your selfe,
　For I know where the wind sits, and most nobly,
　Or as I have a life——　　　*A noyse within like horses.*
Fredrick.　　　　　No more: they'r horses.　　　　50
　Nor shew no discontent: to morrow comes;
　Let's quietly away: if she be at home,
　Our jealousies are put off.
John.　　　　　　The fellow
　We have lost him in our spleenes, like fooles.

Enter Duke, Petruchio.

Duke.　　　　　　　　　Come Gentlemen,
　Now set on roundly: suppose ye have all mistresses,
　And mend your pace according.
Petruchio.　　　　　Then have at ye.
　　　　　　　　　　　　　　　Exeunt.

Enter Duke, Petruchio, Fredrick, *and* John. IV.i

Petruchio. Now to *Bollonia,* my most honoured brother,
I dare pronounce ye a hearty, and safe welcome,
Our loves shall now way-lay ye; welcome Gentlemen.
John. The same to you brave Sir;——*Don Fredrick*
Will ye step in, and give the Lady notice
Who comes to honour her?
Petruchio. Bid her be suddain,
We come to see no curious wench: a night-gowne
Will serve the turne: here's one that knowes her neerer.
Fredrick. I'le tell her what ye say Sir. *Exit* Fredrick.
Duke. My deare brother,
Ye are a merry Gentleman.
Petruchio. Now will the sport be 10
To observe her alterations; how like wildfire
She'll leap into your bosome; then seeing me,
Her conscience, and her feares creeping upon her
Dead as a fowle at souse, she'll sinke.
Duke. Faire brother,
I must entreat you——
Petruchio. I conceive your mind Sir,
I will not chide her: yet ten duckets Duke,
She falls upon her knees, ten more she dare not——
Duke. I must not have her frighted.
Petruchio. Well you shall not:
But like a summers evening against heate,
Marke how I'le guild her cheekes?

Enter Fredrick *and* Peter.

John. How now.
Duke. Ye may Sir. 20
Fredrick. Not to abuse your patience, noble friends,
Nor hold ye off with tedious circumstance,
For you must know——

17 her] F2; he F1   20 *Duke.*] Seward; *Fred.* F1–2
21 *Fredrick.*] Seward; *om.* F1–2

604

Petruchio.   What?
Duke.   Where is she?
Fredrick.   Gone Sir.
Duke.   How?
Petruchio.   What did you say Sir?
Fredrick.   Gone, by heaven, removed,
  The woman of the house too.
John.   Well *Don Fredrick.*
Fredrick.   *Don John,* it is not well, but——
Petruchio.   Gone?
Fredrick.   This fellow
  Can testifie I lye not.
Peter.   Some foure houres after
  My Master was departed with this Gentleman,
  My fellow and my selfe, being sent of businesse,
  (As we must thinke, of purpose)——
Petruchio.   Hang these circumstances,   30
  They appeare like owles, to ill ends.
John [*aside*].   Now could I eate
  The devil in his own broath, I am so tortur'd.——
  Gone?
Petruchio.   Gone?
Fredrick.   Directly gone, fled, shifted:
  What would you have me say?
Duke.   Well Gentlemen,
  Wrong not my good opinion.
Fredrick.   For your Dukedome
  I will not be a knave Sir.
John.   He that is
  A rot run in his bloud.
Petruchio.   But harke ye Gentlemen,
  Are ye sure ye had her here, did ye not dreame this?
John.   Have you your nose Sir?
Petruchio.   Yes Sir.
John.   Then we had her.
Petruchio.   Since you are so short, beleeve your having her   40
  Shall suffer more construction.

John.   Let it suffer,
  But if I be not cleere of all dishonour,
  Or practice that may taint my reputation,
  And ignorant of where this woman is,
  Make me your Cities monster.
Duke.   I beleeve ye.
John [aside].   I could lye with a witch now, to be reveng'd
  Upon that Rascall did this.
Fredrick.   Only thus much
  I would desire your Grace, for my minde gives me
  Before night yet she is yours: stop all opinion,
  And let no anger out, till full cause call it,   50
  Then every mans owne work's to justifie him,
  And this day let us give to search: my man here
  Tels me, by chance he saw out of a window
  (Which place he has taken note of) such a face
  As our old Landladies, he beleeves the same too,
  And by her hood assures it: Let's first thether,
  For she being found, all's ended.
Duke.   Come, for heavens sake;
  And Fortune, and thou beest not ever turning,
  If there be one firme step in all thy reelings,
  Now settle it, and save my hopes: away friends.   60

                                             Exeunt.

                Enter Antonio *and his Servant.*   [IV.] ii

Antonio.   With all my jewels?
Servant.   All Sir.
Antonio.   And that money
  I left i'th' trunke?
Servant.   The Trunke broke, and that gone too.
Antonio. *Franscisco* of the plot?
Servant.   Gone with the wench too.
Antonio.   The mighty poxe go with 'em: belike they thought
  I was no man of this world, and those trifles
  Would but disturbe my conscience.

Servant.   Sure they thought Sir,
  You would not live to persecute 'em.
Antonio.   Whore and Fidler,
  Why, what a consort have they made? Hen and bacon?
  Well my sweet Mistris, well good Madame martaile?
  You that have hung about my neck, and lick't me,   10
  I'le try how handsomely your Ladyship
  Can hang upon a Gallowes, there's your Master-piece;——
  But harke ye Sirrah, no imagination
  Of where they should be?
Servant.   None Sir, yet we have search'd
  All places we suspected; I beleeve Sir,
  They have taken towards the Ports.
Antonio.   Get me a conjurer,
  One that can raise a water devill, I'le port 'em;
  Play at duck and drake with my money? take heed Fidler;
  I'le dance ye by this hand; your Fidle-sticke
  I'le grease of a new fashion, for presuming   20
  To medle with my degamboys:——get me a Conjurer,
  Enquire me out a man that lets out devils:——
  None but my C. Cliffe serve your turne?
Servant.   I know not——
Antonio.   In every street, Tom foole; any bleare-eyd people
  With red heads, and flat noses can performe it;
  Thou shalt know 'em by their half gowns and no breeches:——
  Mount my mare Fidler? ha boy? up at first dash?
  Sit sure, I'le clap a nettle, and a smart one,
  Shall make your filly firck: I will fine Fidler,
  I'le put you to your plundge boy:——Sirrah meet me   30
  Some two houres hence at home; In the meane time
  Find out a conjurer and know his price,
  How he will let his devils by the day out,
  I'le have 'em, and they be above ground.   *Exit* Antonio.
Servant.   Now blesse me,
  What a mad man is this? I must do something
  To please his humour: such a man I'le aske for,

29 fine] F2; find F1

And tell him where he is: but to come neare him,
Or have any thing to do with his *don* devills,
I thanke my feare, I dare not, nor I will not.

> *Exit.*

> *Enter* Duke, Petruchio, Fredrick, John, Peter,   [IV.] iii
> [*and at another doore a*] *Servant with bottles.*

Fredrick.   Whether wilt thou lead us?
Peter.   'Tis hard by sir.
  And ten to one this wine goes thether.   [*Exit Servant.*]
Duke.   Forward.
Petruchio.   Are they growne so merry?
Duke.   'Tis most likely
  She has heard of this good fortune, and determines
  To wash her sorrowes off.
Peter.   'Tis so; that house sir
  Is it: out of that window certainly
  I saw my old Mistrisses face.   [*Laughing within.*]
Petruchio.   They are merry indeed,   *Musicke.*
  Harke I here Musicke too.
Duke.   Excellent Musick.
John [*aside*].   Would I were ev'n among 'em and alone now,
  A pallat for the purpose in a corner,   10
  And good rich wine within me; what gay sport
  Could I make in an houre now?   *Song.*
Fredrick.   Harke a voice too;
  Let's not stir yet by any meanes.

> *Sing within.*

> *Welcome sweet liberty, and care farewell,*
>   *I am mine own,*
> *She is twice damn'd, that lives in Hell,*
>   *When Heaven is shown.*
> *Budding beauty, blooming years*
> *Were made for pleasure, farewell feares,*

1 *Peter.*] F1(c) (*Pet.*); *Petr.* F1(u), F2
13.1 *Sing within.*] om. F1–2   14–21 *Welcome...hand.*] om. F1

For now I am my selfe, mine own command,   20
My fortune alwayes in my hand.

John. Was this her own voyce?

Duke.   Yes sure.

Frederick   'Tis a rare one.

Duke. The Song confirmes her here too: for if ye marke it,
It spake of liberty, and free enjoying
The happy end of pleasure.

Enter Bawd (*above*).

Peter.   Looke ye there sir,
Do ye know that head?

Fredrick.   'Tis my good Landlady,
I find feare has done all this.

John.   Shee I sweare,
And now do I know by the hanging of her hood,
She is parcell drunke: shall we go in?   [*Exit* Bawd.]

Duke.   Not yet Sir.

Petruchio. No, let 'em take their pleasure.

Duke.   When it is highest,   30
Wee'll step in, and amaze 'em: *Musicke.*

                    peace more Musicke.

John [*aside*].   This Musick murders me; what bloud have I now?

Enter Francisco.

Fredrick.   I should know that face.

John.   By this light 'tis he *Fredrick*,
That bred our first suspitions, the same fellow.

Fredrick.   He that we overtooke, and overhoard too
Discoursing of *Constantia.*

John.   Still the same;
Now he slips in.   *Exit* [Francisco].

Duke.   What's that?

Fredrick.   She must be here Sir:
This is the very fellow, I told your Grace
We found upon the way; and what his talke was.

                25 *Peter.*] Seward; *Petr.* F 1–2   30 *Petruchio.*] F 2; *Pet.* F 1

Enter [above] Francisco.

Petruchio.   Why, sure I know this fellow; yes, 'tis he,   40
Francisco, Antonio's Boy, a rare Musitian,
He taught my Sister on the Lute, and is ever
(She loves his voice so well) about her: certaine,
Without all doubt she is here: it must be so.
John.   Here? that's no question: what should our hen o'th game
    else
Do here without her? if she be not here
(I am so confident) let your Grace beleeve,
We two are arrant Rascalls, and have abus'd ye.
Fredrick.   I say so too.

[Enter Bawd *above.]*

John.   Why there's the hood againe now,
The card that guides us; I know the fabricke of it.   50
And know the old tree of that saddle yet, 'twas made of;
A hunting hood, observe it.   *[Exit* Bawd *with* Francisco.]
Duke.   Who shall enter?
Petruchio.   I'le make one.
John.   I, another.
Duke.   But so carry it,
That all her joyes flow not together.
John.   If we told her,
Your Grace would none of her?
Duke.   By no meanes Signior,
'Twould turne her wild, starke frantick.
John.   Or assur'd her——
Duke.   Nothing of that sterne nature. This ye may sir:
That the conditions of our feare yet stand
On nyce and dangerous knittings: or that a little
I seeme to doubt the child.
John.   Would I could draw her   60
To hate your Grace with these things.

*50 card] Seward; guard F1–2
57 that sterne nature.] F2 (stern); that? starve nature? F1

Petruchio.   Come let's enter.——
[*Aside*]   And now he sees me not, I'le search her soundly.
                                        Exeunt Petruchio *and* John.
Duke.   Now lucke of all sides.   *Musick.*
Fredrick.   Doubt it not: more Musicke:
  Sure she has heard some comfort.
Duke.   Yes, stand still sir.
Fredrick.   This is the maddest song.
Duke.   Applyed for certaine
  To some strange mellancholly she is loden with.
                                        Claping of a doore.
Fredrick.   Now all the sport begins——harke?
Duke.   They are amongst 'em,
  The feares now, and the shakings?   *Trampling above.*
Fredrick.   Our old Lady
  (Harke how they run) is even now at this instant   *Cease Musick.*
  Ready to loose her head peice by *Don John*,   70
  Or creeping through a Cat hole.
Petruchio (*within*).   Bring 'em downe,
  And you sir, follow me.
Duke.   Hee's angry with 'em,
  I must not suffer this.
John (*within*).   Bowle downe the Bawd there
  Old *Erra mater*: you Lady leachery
  For the good will I beare to'th game, most tenderly
  Shall be lead out, and lash'd.

      Enter Petruchio, John, Whore, *and* Bawd, *with* Francisco.

Duke.   Is this *Constantia?*
  Why Gentlemen? what do you meane? is this she?
Whore.   I am *Constantia* sir.
Duke.   A Whore ye are sir.
Whore.   'Tis very true: I am a Whore indeed sir.
Petruchio.   She will not lye yet, though she steale.
Whore.   A plaine whore,   80
  If you please to imploy me.
Duke.   And an impudent——

Whore. Plaine dealing now is impudence.
　One, if you will sir, can shew ye as much sport
　In one halfe houre, and with as much variety,
　As a far wiser woman can in halfe a yeare:
　For there my way lies.
Duke. Is she not drunk too?
Whore. A little guilded o're sir,
　Old sack, old sacke boyes.
Petruchio. This is valiant.
John. A brave bold queane.
Duke. Is this your certainty?
　Do ye know the man ye wrong thus, Gentlemen? 90
　Is this the woman meant?
Fredrick. No.
Duke. That your Landlady?
John. I know not what to say.
Duke. Am I a person
　To be your sport Gentlemen?
John. I do beleeve now certaine
　I am a knave; but how, or when——
Duke. What are you?
Petruchio. Bawd to this peece of pye meat.
Bawd. A poore Gentlewoman
　That lyes in Towne, about Law businesse,
　And't like your worships.
Petruchio. You shall have Law, beleeve it.
Bawd. I'le shew your mastership my case.
Petruchio. By no meanes,
　I had rather see a Custard.
Bawd. My dead husband
　Left it even thus sir.
John. Blesse mine eyes from blasting, 100
　I was never so frighted with a case.
Bawd. And so sir——
Petruchio. Enough, put up good velvet head.
Duke. What are you two now,

88 valiant] Chambers (Bullen *conj.*); saliant F1; *saliant* F2

By your owne free confessions?
Fredrick.   What you shall thinke us;
  Though to my selfe I am certaine, and my life
  Shall make that good and perfect, or fall with it.
John.   We are sure of nothing (*Fredrick*) that's the truth on't:
  I do not think my nam's *Don John*, nor dare not
  Beleeve any thing that concernes me, but my debts,
  Nor those in way of payment:——things are so carried,
  What to entreat your Grace, or how to tell ye   110
  We are, or we are not, is past my cunning,
  But I would faine imagine we are honest,
  And o' my conscience, I should fight in't——
Duke.   Thus then,
  For we may be all abus'd.
Petruchio.   'Tis possible,
  For how should this concerne them?
Duke.   Here let's part——
  Untill to morrow this time: we to our way,
  To make this doubt out, and you to your way;
  Pawning our honours then to meet againe,
  When if she be not found——
Fredrick.   We stand engaged
  To answer any worthy way we are cald to.   120
Duke.   We aske no more.
Whore.   Ye have done with us then?
Petruchio.   No Dame.
Duke.   But is her name *Constantia*?
Petruchio.   Yes a moveable
  Belonging to a friend of mine:——come out Fidler,
  What say you to this Lady? be not fearfull.
Francisco.   Saving the reverence of my Masters pleasure,
  I say she is a whore, and that she has robb'd him,
  Hoping his hurts would kill him.
Whore.   Who provok't me?
  Nay sirrah squeak, Ile see your treble strings
  Ty'd up too; If I hang, Ile spoyle your piping,
  Your sweet face shall not save yee.

Petruchio. Thou dam'd impudence, 130
And thou dry'd devill; where's the Officer?

Enter Officer.

Peter. Hee's here sir.
Petruchio. Lodge these safe, till I send for 'em;
Let none come to 'em, nor no noise be heard
Of where they are, or why: away.
    [*Exit Officer with* Bawd, Francisco, *and* Whore.]
John [*aside*]. By this hand.
A handsome whore: Now will I be arrested,
And brought home to this officers: a stout whore,
I love such stirring ware: pox o' this businesse,
A man must hunt out morsells for another,
And starve himself: a quick-ey'd whore, that's wild-fire,
And makes the bloud dance through the veines like billowes. 140
I will reprive this whore.
Duke. Well, good luck with ye.
Fredrick. As much attend your Grace.
Petruchio. To morrow certaine——
John. If we out-live this night sir.
    [*Exeunt* Duke *and* Petruchio.]
Fredrick. Come *Don John*,
We have something now to doe.
John. I am sure I would have.
Fredrick. If she be not found, we must fight.
John. I am glad on't,
I have not fought a great while.
Fredrick. If we dye——
John. Ther's so much money sav'd in lecherie.

          Exeunt.

Enter Duke, Petruchio *below, and* Vechio *above*. V. i

Duke. It should be here abouts.
Petruchio. Your grace is right,

138 hunt] F 2; haunt F 1

614

This is the house I know it.

Vechio [*apart*].   Grace?

Duke.   'Tis further
By the description we received.

Petruchio.   Good my Lord the Duke,
Believe me, for I know it certainly,
This is the very house.

Vechio [*apart*].   My Lord the Duke?   [*Exit* Vechio.]

Duke. Pray heaven this man prove right now.

Petruchio. Beleeve it, hee's a most sufficient Scholler,
And can doe rare tricks this way; for a figure,
Or raising an appearance, whole Christendome
Has not a better; I have heard strange wonders of him.   10

Duke. But can he shew us where she is?

Petruchio.   Most certaine,
And for what cause too she departed.

Duke.   Knock then,
For I am great with expectation,
Till this man satisfie me: I feare the Spaniards,
Yet they appeare brave fellows: can he tell us?

Petruchio. With a wet finger, whether they be false.

Duke. Away then.

Petruchio.   Who's within here?

Enter Vechio.

Vechio.   Your Grace may enter.

Duke. How can he know me?

Petruchio.   He knowes all.

Vechio.   And you sir.

Exeunt.

Enter Don John, *and* Fredrick.   [V.] ii

John. What do you call his name?

Fredrick.   Why, *Peter Vechio.*

John. They say he can raise devills, can he make 'em
Tell truth too, when he has rais'd 'em? for beleeve it,

These devils are the lyingst Rascalls.

Fredrick.   He can compell 'em.

John.   With what? can he
Tye squibs in their tailes, and fire the truth out?
Or make 'em eate a bawling Puritan,
Whose sanctified zeale shall rumble like an Earthquake?

Fredrick.   With Spels man.

John.   I with spoones as soone; dost thou thinke
The devill such an Asse as people make him?   10
Such a poore coxcomb? such a penny foot post?
Compel'd with crosse and pile to run of errands?
With *Asteroth*, and *Behemoth*, and *Belfagor?*
Why should he shake at sounds, that lives in a smiths forge?
Or if he do——

Fredrick.   Without all doubt he do's *John.*

John.   Why should not Bilbo raise him, or a paire of bullyons,
They go as big as any? or an unshod Car,
When he goes tumble, tumble o're the stones,
Like *Anacreons* drunken verses, make him tremble?
These make as fell a noyse; me thinkes the collick   20
Well handled, and fed with small beere——

Fredrick.   'Tis the vertue——

John.   The vertue? nay, and goodnesse fetch him up once,
'Has lost a friend of me; the wise old Gentleman
Knowes when, and how; I'le lay this hand to two pence,
Let all the Conjurers in Christendome,
With all their spells, and vertues call upon him,
And I but thinke upon a wench, and follow it,
He shall be sooner mine then theirs; where's vertue?

Fredrick. Thou art the most sufficient, (I'le say for thee)
Not to beleeve a thing——

John.   O sir, slow credit   30
Is the best child of knowledge; I'le go with ye,
And if he can do any thing, I'le thinke
As you would have me.

19 him] Weber (Mason *conj.*); us F 1; *om.* F 2

Fredrick.   Let's enquire along,
 For certaine we are not far off.
John.   Nor much nearer.

                                                        Exeunt.

           Enter Duke, Petruchio, *and* Vechio.   [V.] iii

Vechio.   You lost her yesternight.
Petruchio.   How thinke you sir?
Duke.   Is your name *Vechio*?
Vechio.   Yes sir.
Duke.   And you can shew me
 These things you promise.
Vechio.   Your graces word bound to me,
 No hand of Law shall seize me.
Duke.   As I live sir ——
Petruchio.   And as I live, that can do something too sir.
Vechio.   I take your promises: stay here a little,
 Till I prepare some Ceremonies, and I'le satisfie ye.
 The Ladies name's *Constantia*?
Petruchio.   Yes.
Vechio.   I come straight.   *Exit* Vechio.
Duke.   Sure hee's a learned man.
Petruchio.   The most now living;
 Did your grace marke when we told all these circumstances,   10
 How ever and anon he bolted from us
 To use his studies helpe?
Duke.   Now I thinke rather
 To talke with some familiar.
Petruchio.   Not unlikely,
 For sure he has 'em subject.
Duke.   How could he else
 Tell when she went, and who went with her?
Petruchio.   True.
Duke.   Or hit upon mine honour: or assure me
 The Lady lov'd me dearely?
Petruchio.   'Twas so.

                   33 along] F2; a long F1

Enter Vechio *in his habiliments.*

Vechio.   Now,
I do beseech your Grace sit downe, and you sir;
Nay pray sit close like brothers.
Petruchio.   A rare fellow.
Vechio.   And what ye see, stir not at, nor use a word,   20
Untill I aske ye; for what shall appeare
Is but weake apparition and thin ayre
Not to be held, nor spoken too.
Duke.   We are counselled——

                                   Knocking within.

Vechio.   What noise is that without there?
Fredrick (within).   We must speake with him.
Servant (within).   Hee's busie Gentlemen.
John (within).   That's all one, friend,
We must, and will speake with him.
Duke.   Let 'em in sir,
We know their tongues and businesse, 'tis our owne;
And in this very cause that we now come for,
They also come to be instructed.
Vechio.   Let 'em in then:

            Enter Fredrick, *and* John.

Sit down, I know your meaning.
Fredrick.   The Duke before us?   30
Now we shall sure know something.
Vechio.   Not a question,
But make your eyes your tongues——
John.   This is a strange jugler,
Neither indent before hand for his payment,
Nor know the breadth of the businesse; sure his devell
Comes out of Lapland where they sell men winds,
For dead drinke, and old doublets.
Fredrick.   Peace, he conjures.

            29.1 and John.] *Iohn, and Servant.* F 1–2
            35 where] F 2; were F 1

                        618

John.   Let him, he cannot raise my devill.
Fredrick.   Prethee peace.
Vechio.   *Appeare, appeare,*
           And you soft winds so cleare,
           That dance upon the leaves, and make them sing   40
           Gentle love-layes to the Spring,
           Gilding all the vales below
           With your verdure as ye blow,
           Raise these formes from under ground
           With a soft and happy sound.
                                    Soft Musick.

John.   This is an honest Conjurer, and a pretty Poet;
I like his words well, there's no bumbast in 'em,
But do you thinke now, he can cudgell up the devill,
With this short staffe of Verses?
Fredrick.   Peace the spirits— —

                   Two Shapes of women passe by.

John.   Nay, and they be no worse——
Vechio.   Do ye know these faces?   50
Duke.   No.
Vechio.   Sit still upon your lives then: and marke what follows:
Away, away.   [*Exeunt the two Shapes.*]
John.   These devils do not paint sure?
Have they no sweeter shapes in hell?
Fredrick.   Harke now *John.*

                   Constantia *passes by.*

John.   I marry, this moves something like, this devill
Carries some metall in her gate.
Vechio.   I find ye,
You would see her face unvail'd?
Duke.   Yes.
Vechio.   Be uncovered.
Duke.   O heaven!
Vechio.   Peace.
Petruchio.   See how she blushes.
John.   *Fredrick,*

This devill for my money; this is she Boy,
Why dost thou shake? I burne.
Vechio.   Sit still, and silent.
Duke.   She lookes back at me; now she smiles sir.
Vechio.   Silence.   60
Duke.   I must rise, or I burst.   *Exit* Constantia.
Vechio.   Ye see what followes——
Duke.   O gentle sir this shape agen.
Vechio.   I cannot,
'Tis all dissolv'd againe: this was the figure?
Duke.   The very same sir.
Petruchio.   No hope once more to see it?
Vechio.   You might have kept it longer, had ye spar'd it,
Now 'tis impossible.
Duke.   No meanes to find it?
Vechio.   Yes that there is: sit still a while, there's wine
To thaw the wonder from your hearts: drinke well sir.
                            Exit Vechio.

John.   This Conjurer is a right good fellow too,
A lad of mettle; two such devils more   70
Would make me a Conjurer: what wine is it?
Fredrick.   Hollock.
John.   The devil's in it then, looke how it dances?
Well, if I be——
Petruchio.   We are all before ye,
That's your best comfort sir.
John.   Byth'mas brave wine;
Nay, and the Devils live in this hell, I dare venture
Within these two months yet to be delivered
Of a large legion of 'em.

                    Enter Vechio.

Duke.   Here 'a comes,
Silence of all sides Gentlemen.
Vechio.   Good your grace,
Observe a stricter temper, and you too gallants,
You'l be deluded all else. This merry devill   80

620

That next appeares, for such a one you'l find it,
Must be cal'd up by a strange incantation,
A Song, and I must sing it: pray beare with me,
And pardon my rude pipe; for yet ere parting
Twenty to one I please ye.

Duke.   We are arm'd Sir.

Petruchio.   Nor shall you see us more transgresse.

Fredrick.   What think'st thou
   Now *John?*

John.   Why, now do I thinke *Fredrick,*
   (And if I thinke amisse heaven pardon me,)
   This honest Conjurer, with some foure or five
   Of his good fellow devils, and my selfe,   90
   Shall be yet drunke ere midnight.

Fredrick.   Peace, he conjures.   *Song.*

Vechio.   *Come away, thou Lady gay,*
            Hoist; how she stumbles?
            Hark how she mumbles.
                  Dame Gillian.

Answer [within].   *I come, I come.*

Vechio.   *By old Claret I enlarge thee,*
            By Canary thus I charge thee,
            By Britain *Mathewglin, and Peeter,*
            Appeare and answer me in meeter.   100
                  Why when?
                  Why Gill?
                  Why when?

Answer [within].   *You'll tarry till I am ready.*

Vechio.   *Once again I conjure thee,*
            By the pose in thy nose,
            And the gout in thy toes;
            By thine old dry'd skin,
            And the mummie within;
            By thy little, little ruff,   110
            And thy hood that's made of stuff;

---

*92–119 Come...here.] F2; om. F1   92, 97, 105 Vechio.] Colman; om. F1–2
99 Britain...Peeter] (two wines)   106 pose] i.e., catarrh

By thy bottle at thy breech,
And thine old salt itch;
By the stakes, and the stones,
That have worn out thy bones.
      Appeare.
      Appeare.
      Appeare.
Answer [within]. *Oh I am here.*
John.   Why, this is the Song *Fredrick*: twenty pound now   120
To see but our *Dame Gillian.*

        Enter Land-lady *and the Child.*

Fredrick.   Peace it appeares.
John.   I cannot peace: devils in French hoods *Fredrick*?
Sathans old Siringes?
Duke.   What's this?
Vechio.   Peace.
John.   She, Boy.
Fredrick.   What dost thou meane?
John.   She, Boy, I say.
Fredrick.   Ha?
John.   She, boy.
The very child too *Fredrick.*
Fredrick.   She laughes on us
Aloud *John*, has the devill these affections?
I do beleeve 'tis she indeed.
Vechio.   Stand still.
John.   I will not;
Who calls *Jeronimo* from his naked bed?
Sweet Lady, was it you? If thou beest the devill,
First, having crost my selfe, to keep out wildfire,   130
Then said some special prayers to defend me
Against thy most unhallowed hood: have at thee.
Land-lady.   Hold sir, I am no devill.
John.   That's all one.
Land-lady.   I am your very Landlady.

         121 Dame] Don F 1–2

622

John.   I defie thee:
  Thus as St. *Dunstan* blew the devils nose
  With a paire of tongs, even so right worshipfull——
Land-lady.   Sweet son, I am old *Gillian.*
Duke.   This is no spirit.
John.   Art thou old *Gillian*, flesh and bone?
Land-lady.   I am Son.
Vechio.   Sit still sir, now I'le shew you all.   *Exit* Vechio.
John.   Where's thy bottle?
Land-lady.   Here, I beseech ye son——
John.   For I know the devill   140
  Cannot assume that shape.
Fredrick.   'Tis she *John*, certaine——
John.   A hogs poxe o' your mouldy chaps, what make you
  Tumbling and juggling here?
Land-lady.   I am quit now Signior,
  For all the prankes you plaid, and railings at me,
  For to tell true, out of a trick I put
  Upon your high behaviours, which was a lye,
  But then it serv'd my turne, I drew the Lady
  Unto my kinsmans here, only to torture
  Your *Don*-ships for a day or two; and secure her
  Out of all thoughts of danger: here she comes now.   150

                Enter Vechio, *and* Constantia.

Duke.   May I yet speake?
Vechio.   Yes, and embrace her too,
  For one that loves you deerer ——
Duke.   O my sweetest.
Petruchio.   Blush not, I will not chide ye.
Constantia.   To add more
  Unto the joy I know, I bring ye, see sir,
  The happy fruit of all our vowes.
Duke.   Heavens blessing
  Be round about thee ever.
John.   Pray blesse me to,
  For if your grace be well instructed this way

You'l find the keeping halfe the getting.
Duke. How sir?
John. I'le tell ye that anon.
Constantia. 'Tis true, this Gentleman
　Has done a charity worthy your favour, 160
　And let him have it deare sir.
Duke. My best Lady
　He has, and ever shall have:——so must you sir,
　To whom I am equall bound, as to my being.
Fredrick. Your Graces humble servants.
Duke. Why kneele you sir?
Vechio. For pardon for my boldnesse: yet 'twas harmlesse
　And all the art I have sir; those your grace saw
　Which you thought spirits, were my neighbours children
　Whom I instruct in Grammer, here, and Musick;
　Their shapes, the peoples fond opinions,
　Beleeving I can conjure, and oft repairing 170
　To know of things stolne from 'em, I keepe about me,
　And alwaies have in readinesse; by conjecture
　Out of their owne confessions, I oft tell 'em
　Things, that by chance have fallen out so: which way
　(Having the persons here, I knew you sought for)
　I wrought upon your grace: my end is mirth,
　And pleasing, if I can, all parties.
Duke. I beleeve it,
　For you have pleas'd me truly: so well pleas'd me,
　That when I shall forget it—— [*Knocking within.*]
Petruchio. Here's old *Antonio*,
　I spide him at a window, comming mainely 180
　I know about his whore, and the man you light on,
　As you discovered unto me: good your Grace,
　Let's stand by all, 'twill be a mirth above all,
　To observe his pelting fury.
Vechio. About a wench sir?

　　162 He] F2; She F1
　　181 whore, and the] Chambers (Mason *conj.*); whore, the F1–2
　　181 light] *i.e.*, lit

Petruchio.   A young whore that has rob'd him.
Vechio.   But do you know sir,
  Where she is?
Petruchio.   Yes, and will make that perfect——
Vechio.   I am instructed well then.
John.   If he come
  To have a devill shew'd him, by all meanes
  Let me be he, I can rore rarely.
Petruchio.   Be so,
  But take heed to his anger.
Vechio.   Slip in quickly,   190
  There you shall find suites of all sorts: when I call,
  Be ready and come forward.——   *Exeunt all but* Vechio.
                            Who's there? come in.

                    Enter Antonio.

Antonio.   Are you the Conjurer?
Vechio.   Sir I can do a little
  That way, if you please to imploy me.
Antonio.   Presently
  Shew me a devill that can tell——
Vechio.   Where your wench is.
Antonio.   You are i' th' right; as also where the Fidler
  That was consenting to her.
Vechio.   Sit ye there sir,
  Ye shall know presently: can ye pray heartily?
Antonio.   Why, is your devill so furious?
Vechio.   I must shew ye
  A forme, may chance affright ye.
Antonio.   He must fart fire then: 200
  Take you no care for me.
Vechio.   Ascend *Asteroth*,
  Why, when? appeare I say——

                    Enter Don John *like a Spirit.*

  192 Who's there? come in.] Dyce; Who's there come in? F1; Who's there comes
in? F2

                            625

                Now question him.

Antonio.   Where is my whore *Don* devill?

John.   Gone to *China,*

  To be the great *Chams* Mistris.

Antonio.   That's a lye devill:

  Where are my jewels?

John.   Pawn'd for Peticoates.

Antonio.   That may be; where's the Fidler?

John.   Condemn'd to th' Gallowes,

  For robbing of a Mill.

Antonio.   The lyingst devill

  That e're I dealt withall, and the unlikeliest:

  What was that Rascall hurt me?

John.   I.

Antonio.   How?

John.   I.

Antonio.   Who was he?

John.   I.

Antonio.   Do ye here conjurer,   210

  Dare you venture your devill?

Vechio.   Yes.

Antonio.   Then I'le venture my dagger;

  Have at your devils pate: do ye mew?

              Enter all.

Vechio.   Hold.

Petruchio.   Hold there,

  I do command ye hold.

Antonio.   Is this the devill?

  Why Conjurer——

Petruchio.   'Has been a devill to you sir.

  But now you shall forget all: your whores safe,

  And all your Jewels: your Boy too.

John.   Now the devill indeed

  Lay his ten claws upon thee, for my pate

  Finds what it is to be a fend.

Antonio.   All safe?

Petruchio. Pray ye know this person: all's right now.

Antonio.   Your grace
May now command me then: but where's my whore?   220

Petruchio. Ready to goe to whiping.

Antonio.   My whore whipt?

Petruchio. Yes, your whore without doubt Sir.

Antonio.   Whipt? pray Gentlemen——

Duke. Why, would you have her once more rob ye? the young
  boy
You may forgive, he was intic'd.

John.   The Whore sir,
Would rather carry pitty: a hansome Whore.

Antonio. A Gentleman, I warrant thee.

Petruchio.   Let's in all,
And if we see contrition in your whore sir,
Much may be done.

Duke.   Now my deare faire, to you,
And the full consummation of my Vow.

              [*Exeunt.*]

FINIS.

Prologue.

Aptnesse for mirth to all, this instant night
Thalia hath prepar'd for your delight,
Her choice and curious Viands, in each part,
Season'd with rarities of wit, and Art;
Nor feare I to be tax'd for a vaine boast,
My promise will finde credit with the most,
When they know Ingenuous Fletcher *made it, hee*
Being in himselfe a perfect Comedie.
And some sit here, I doubt not, dare averre,
Living he made that house a Theater   10
Which he pleas'd to frequent; and thus much we
Could not but pay to his lovd memorie.
For our selves we doe entreat that you would not
Expect strange turnes, and windings in the Plot,
Objects of State, and now and then a Rhime,
To gall particular persons, with the time;
Or that his towring Muse hath made her flight
Nearer your apprehension then your sight:
But if that sweet expression, quick conceit,
Familiar language, fashion'd to the weight   20
Of such as speake it, have the power to raise
Your grace to us, with Trophies to his praise:
We may professe, presuming on his skill,
If his Chances *please not you, our fortune's ill.*

4 *and*] F 2 (1653); *as* F 1
12 *lovd*] Dyce; *loud* F 1–2
19 *expression*] Dyce (1653); *expressions* F 1–2

Epilogue.

We have not held you long, nor doe I see
One brow in this selected company
Assuring a dislike; our paines were eas'd,
Could we be confident that all rise pleas'd:
But such ambition soares too high: If wee
Have satisfi'd the best, and they agree
In a faire censure, We have our reward;
And in them arm'd, desire no surer guard.

TEXTUAL NOTES

I.vii

26 cast]   The original 'lost' retains the metaphor of loss in the preceding
line, but 'cast' (see for other *a:o* errors, I.i.26, II.ii.37) is the normal idiom
for the final balancing of accounts and regularly serves as a euphemism for
death. Perhaps the appearance of 'Coster-' assisted in the compositor's
confusion.

II.i

4 peeping]   That is, 'piping', or chirping. For the same use see IV.iii.129,
'Ile spoyle your piping', and V.iii.84, 'pardon my rude pipe'.

II.ii

34 *Enter*...Don John.]   Dyce adds to this direction '*who remains at the
door, peeping*'. This is indeed the situation at II.iii.7.1, but there is no occasion here for Don John to 'peep' into a room already occupied by two
servants, evidently one of the common rooms of the lodging house. The
next scene (II.iii) is laid in the private chamber in which Constantia has
locked herself, and it is into this room that Don John peeps – 'as a jealous
husband | Would levell at his wanton wife' (II.i.131–132), through a
partially opened door. The conversation between the two friends at
II.ii.34–37 refers to their earlier discussion on this topic (II.i.129–134) and
not to the situation at the moment. It does not therefore describe actions
and gestures appropriate to this point, as Dyce evidently thought it did.
It may, furthermore, be considered poor stagecraft to use the clumsy device
of peeping through a door (the same door on stage probably) on two
occasions only twenty-five lines apart.

III.ii

26.1 *Servant*]   The 1647 Folio reads '*Rowl.*' at this point. Editors have
reasonably supposed that the abbreviation represents the name of an actor,
Fleay suggesting William Rowley and Dyce and Chambers—Rowland.
W. C. Powell has proposed Rowland Dowle, a minor actor for the King's
Men in the 1630s ('A Note on the Stage History of...*The Chances*',
MLN, LVI (February, 1941), 122–7); Bentley concurs: 'It was probably for
the revival of 1638 that his name was inserted in the stage direction of
The Chances' (*The Jacobean and Caroline Stage* (Oxford, 1956), II, 425–6).
29 *John Dorrie*]   The text of the song is reprinted from Thomas Ravenscroft,
Deutromelia (1609), p. 59:

As it fell on a holy day,
  and upon an holy tide a,
Iohn Dory bought him an ambling Nag,
  to *Paris* for to ride a.

And when *Iohn Dory* to Paris was come,
  a little before the gate a
Iohn Dory was fitted, the porter was witted,
  to let him in thereat a:

The first man that *Iohn Dory* did meet,
  was good King *Iohn* of France a;
Iohn Dory could well of his courtesie,
  but fell downe in a trance a.

A pardon, a pardon my Liege & my king,
  for my merie men and for me a;
And all the Churles in merie England,
  Ile bring them all bound to thee a.

And *Nicholl* was then a Cornish [man,]
  a little beside Bohyde a;
And he mande forth a good blacke Barke,
  with fiftie good oares on a side a.

Run up, my boy, unto the maine top,
  and looke what thou canst spie a.
Who, ho; who, ho; a goodly ship I do see,
  I trow it be *Iohn Dory*.

They hoist their Sailes both top and top,
  the meisseine and all was tride a;
And every man stood to his lot,
  whatever should betide a.

The roring Cannons then were plide,
  and dub a dub went the drumme a:
The braying Trumpets lowde they cride,
  to courage both all and oome a

The grapling hooks were brought at length,
  the browne bill and the sword a:
Iohn Dory at length, for all his strength,
  was clapt fast under board a.

III.iii

14 keep in 'em]   Perhaps the reading should be 'keep 'em in'?
50 wife]   The Folio 'wise' sets up a contrast with the adjective 'rich' – not
  a particularly significant contrast; the emendation 'wife' sets up a contrast

with the noun 'woman'. The Land-lady declines to dignify the mother of the child with the title 'wife' whom she has already termed 'an easie foole' (I.viii.16). The emendation supposes the common misreading of 'f' and long 's'.

III.iv

86 whether——] Modernizing editors read 'whither——' with F2, and such is surely the sense of IV.iii.1 where the same spelling occurs: 'Whether wilt thou lead us?'; but the interruption in the speech in F1 precludes final certainty in the matter here.

IV.iii

50 card] The F1 reading 'guard' is an interesting example of compositorial anticipation and conflation: MS 'the card that guides' becomes 'the guard that guides'.

V.iii

29.1 *Enter* Fredrick, *and* John.] The 1647 Folio adds a Servant to this direction; all editors follow. The Servant has spoken to Frederick and John 'within' (line 25), and he is mentioned in the direction that in the Folio follows the direction for '*Knocking within*' (line 23.1); but he has no speeches in the rest of the scene, and this edition deletes him from the entry, supposing his presence there to be the result of contamination. Since there is no exit direction for him, there is no reason to suppose that even a brief appearance (to show the gentlemen in) is intended.

92–119 *Come...here.*] In F2 the word 'Answer' and the response are printed, like the song, in italic type. To indicate that the word was a prefix, Langbaine distinguished 'Answer' in Roman, followed by all editors, and Dyce emended to '*Gillian*' (*i.e.*, *Land-lady*). The short monometric lines and the three lines of 'Answer' appear in F2 at the right-hand margin. F2 understood line 99 to list three wines and hence placed a comma after 'Britain'; but 'Britain' is an adjective distinguishing this domestic wine from the imported wines. See also Textual Introduction.

121 *Dame Gillian*] The reading '*Don Gillian*' of F1 and all subsequent editions seems to have provoked no critical discussion, yet 'Don' is surely a curious title to give to a woman. I have ventured to emend to 'Dame', the title the character receives in line 95 in the Song (from F2); 'Don' is not a difficult misreading of 'Dame' (*a:o*; *m:n*).

PRESS-VARIANTS IN F1 (1647)

[Copies collated: Bodl (Bodleian Library B.1.8.Art.), Camb¹ (Cambridge University Library Aston a.Sel.19), Camb² (Cambridge University Library SSS.10.8); CSmH (Henry E. Huntington Library 112111), DFo¹ (Folger Shakespeare Library copy 1), DFo² (Folger Shakespeare Library copy 2),† NCD (Duke University), NCU (University of North Carolina, Chapel Hill), NN¹ (New York Public Library, Berg Collection/Beaumont Copy¹), NN² (New York Public Library, Berg Collection/Beaumont Copy²), NN³ (New York Public Library, Berg Collection/Beaumont Copy³), NN⁴ (New York Public Library, *KC/1647/Beaumont (Astor Copy)), NN⁵ (New York Public Library, Arents Collection 232, Acc. 3583), ViU¹ (University of Virginia 217972), ViU² (University of Virginia 570973).]

QUIRE 3A (*inner sheet, outer forme*)

Corrected: the rest
Uncorrected: Bodl, Camb¹, Camb², CSmH, NCU, NN¹,²,³,⁵, ViU²

Sig. 3A2
I.v.33 contented] contended

QUIRE 3A (*inner sheet, inner forme*)

Corrected: the rest
Uncorrected: Bodl, Camb¹, Camb², NN⁵

Sig. 3A2ᵛ
I.viii.0.1 *Land-lady*] *Landlady*
I.viii.19 pamper'd?] pamper'd:
Sig. 3A3
I.ix.15 our] onr

QUIRE 3B (*outer sheet, outer forme*)

Corrected: the rest
Uncorrected: Camb¹, Camb², CSmH, NCU, NN¹

Sig. 3B1
II.iii.119 Too too] Too, too
II.iii.128 you] yoe
II.iv.7 your] yonr
Sig. 3B4ᵛ
IV.iii.1 *Pet.*] *Petr.*

† This copy is no longer at the Folger Library; present location unknown.

EMENDATIONS OF ACCIDENTALS

Dramatis Personae

2, 5, 7, 13 Petruchio] Petruccio F 2;
  om. F 1
4, 10.1, 15 Fredrick] Frederick F 2;
  om. F 1
9 Vechio] Vecchio F 2; *om.* F 1

11 Anthony] Anthonie F 2; *om.* F 1
13, 14, 16 Constantia] Constancia
  F 2; *om.* F 1
15 *Land-lady*] *Landlady* F 2; *om.* F 1

I.i

I.i] *Actus primus. Scæna prima.* F 1–2
  1 *Anthony,*] F 2; (~) F 1
  6 Plackets?] ~ : F 1–2
 17 things,] ~ ∧ F 1–2
 17 yee;] ~ , F 1–2

19 *Anthony:*] ~ , F 1–2
19–20 Come,... woman] *one line of
  verse* F 1–2
59 her,] ~ ; F 1–2
60 knowne,] F 2; ~ ∧ F 1

I.ii

In this scene, after line 1, *prefixes for
the Gentlemen are simple numerals
in* F 1; *are numerals and* 'Gent.'
in F 2.
I.ii] Scæn. 2. F 1–2
  2 him.] ~ ∧ F 1; ~ , F 2
 25 possible,] F 2; ~ ∧ F 1

40 me——] ~ . F 1–2
41 indeed;] ~ , F 1–2
41 not——] ~ . F 1–2
44 life——] ~ ? F 1–2
50 And...life.] F 1–2 *line*: And...
  part, | Goes...life.

I.iii

I.iii] Scæne. 3. F 1–2
 16 office. | *Woman (within).*] office.
  (*Woman within.* | *Within.* F 1–2
 17 (*twice*), 19 (*twice*), 20 *Woman
  (within).*] *Within.* F 1–2

19 Who's there? *Fabritio?*] F 1–2
  line: Who's there? | *Fabritio?*
31 *Enter*] Scæne 4. *Enter* F 1–2

I.iv

In this scene, prefixes for the Gentlemen *are simple numerals in* F 1; *are

numerals and* 'Gent.' *in* F 2
I.iv] Scæne 5. F 1–2

I.v

I.v] Scæne 6. F1–2
11 lazinesse:——] ~ ; ‸ F1–2
11 bread,] ~‸ F1–2
12 yee:——] ~ : ‸ F1–2

30 Nurses,] ~ ‸ F1–2
34 't had] F2; t'had F1
45 mother:——] ~ : ‸ F1–2
47 else:——] ~ : ‸ F1–2

I.vi

I.vi] Scæn. 7. F1–2
1 Sure...purlewes,] F1–2 *line*:
Sure...home: | I...purlewes,
11 perish'd.——] ~ . ‸ F1–2

18 trust‸——] ~ . —— F1–2
24 settle] sentle F2; sertle F1
26 dangers ‸] ~ , F1–2
29.1 *Exeunt*.] F2; *Exi* F1

I.vii

I.vii] Scæne 8. F1–2
16 disgraces?] ~ , F1–2
18 2. *Gentleman*.] F2; 2. F1

18 crie,] ~ ; F1–2
19 more,] ~ ‸ F1–2

I.viii

I.viii] Scæne. 9. F1–2
1 regard——] ~ . F1–2
1 mother——] ~ . F1–2
7 self——] F2; ~ ? F1
9 nostrills,] ~ ? F1–2
25 Anthony (*within*). Sir.] *Ant*. Sir.
within. F1–2
27 sirrah.] ~ , F1–2
28 drunk:——] ~ ; ‸ F1–2
35 well:——] ~ : ‸ F1–2
36 her.——] ~ . ‸ F1–2
37 me:——] ~ : ‸ F1–2

41 *John*——] ~ . F1–2
42 mother,] ~ ; F1–2
42 more;] ~ , F1–2
43 well,] ~ ; F1–2
43 draught;] ~ , F1–2
62 fortune:——] ~ : ‸ F1–2
69 darke;] ~ , F1–2
76 sonne;] ~ , F1–2
85 childe:——] ~ : ‸ F1–2
85 *Spaniard*——] ~ , F1–2
91 me:] ~ , F1–2
93 (Mother)?] ( )‸ F1; ‸~‸ ? F2

I.ix

In this scene, after line 1, *prefixes for
the* Gentlemen *are simple numerals
in* F1; *are numerals and* 'Gent.' *in*
F2
I.ix] Scæne. 10. F1–2
3 through] throgh F1; though F2

9 too——] ~ . F1–2
18 it:] F2; ~ , F1
20 Ocean,] ~ : F1–2
31 *Cain's*] F2; *Cain's* F1
38 There's...clock?] F1–2 *line*:
There's...it: | What's a clock?

I.x

I.x] Scæne 11. F1–2
  0.1 *candle*).] ~ .) F1–2
  7 feare.] ~ .—— F1–2
  7 *Enter...Jewell.] after line* 6
    F1–2

26 sweetnesse——] ~ , F1–2
32 it.——] ~ . $_\wedge$ F1–2
37 entreat——] ~ . F1–2
48 me:——] ~ : $_\wedge$ F1–2
48 *Exit.] after line* 47 F1–2

II.i

II.i] *Actus Secundus. Scæna prima.*
  F1–2
  4 Wezand,] ~ $_\wedge$ F1–2
  4 peeping:——] ~ : $_\wedge$ F1; ~ ; $_\wedge$
    F2
  6 engag'd:——] ~ : $_\wedge$ F1–2
  7.1 *Duke...him.] in margin beside*
    lines 7–9 F1–2
  19 *Enter...Faction.] after* then. *in*
    line 18 F1–2
  22 *Men of the Dukes Faction.] Fac-*
    tion Du. F1–2
  23 ye:——] ~ : $_\wedge$ F1–2
  52.1] *Exit...Faction.] Exit Duke,*
    & c. (after memory). F1–2

53 *Enter* Fredrick.] *location as* F2;
  after yours. *in line* 52 F1
53 sure.——] ~ . $_\wedge$ F1–2
58 *Fredrick:*] ~ . F1; ~ , F2
61 night——] ~ . F1; ~ , F2
73 in troth] introth F1–2
73 troth,] ~ . F1; ~ : F2
89 I,] I $_\wedge$ F1–2
103 you;] ~ , F1–2
105 then:——] ~ : $_\wedge$ F1–2
116–117 Not look...she in?] *one*
  line in F1–2
134.1 *Exeunt.] Ex.* F1; *Exit.* F2

II.ii

II.ii] Scæne 2. F1–2
  14 Dost...Agen?] F1–2 *line:* Dost
    ...Lute? | Agen? |
  15–17 Above...it?] F1–2 *line:*
    Above...chamber. | There's
    ...man. | This...it. | I grant
    ...it?
  17.1 *Sing...little.] after* have it *in*
    line 17 F1–2
  18–28 *Mercilesse...kill.] after* man.
    in line 16 F2; *om.* F1
  18 *Mercilesse] Merciless* F2; *om.* F1
  20 *why] Why* F2; *om.* F1
  22–24 Never...faire,] F2 *lines:*

Never broke...never | *Flew...*
dart | *Whose...never,* | *Slew...*
rewarders? | *Thou...fair,* ; *om.*
F1
23 *dart,] ~ $_\wedge$ F2; om.* F1
23 *never $_\wedge$] ~ ,* F2; *om.* F1
23 *slew,] ~ $_\wedge$* F2; *om.* F1
24 *thou...faire] Thou...fair* F2;
  om. F1
27 *restraine] restrain* F2; *om.* F1
34 peeping——] ~ . F1–2
39 contemplations?] ~ . F1–2
43 nothing?] F2; ~ ; F1
46 *Sing.] after* Peter. F1–2

II.iii

II.iii] *om.* F 1–2
  19 rewarded.] ∼ , F 1–2
  25 there∧] ∼ , F 1–2
  30 friends?] ∼ . F 1–2
  42 trusty∧] ∼ : F 1–2
  58 honest:] ∼ , F 1–2
  70 close:——] ∼ : ∧ F 1–2
  70 *Exit* Constantia.] F 2 (*after* Sir.);
    om. F 1
  70.1 *Enter* Anthony.] *after* there?
    in line 70 F 1–2
  87 service;] ∼ : F 1–2
  89 pleasures:] ∼ ; F 1–2

  93 Such∧] Such- F 1–2
  95 honour:] ∼ , F 1–2
  103–104 I look...is't?] *one line* F 1–
    2
  103.1 *Enter* Anthony.] *after* due. *in*
    line 103 F 1–2
  105.1 *Enter* Constantia.] *after* Petru-
    chio. in line 105 F 1–2
  106 himselfe? F 2; ∼ . F 1
  115 life:——] ∼ : ∧ F 1; ∼ ∧ ——
    F 2
  124 perish;] ∼ , F 1–2

II.iv

II.iv] Scæne 3. F 1–2
  1–2 This...'em:] F 1–2 *line*: This
    man...rank: | For...way, |
    No...'em:
  2.1 *Enter*...John.] *after* he. *in line*
    3 F 1–2
  23 understand:] ∼ , F 1 2

  36 maid:] ∼ , F 1–2
  58 *Exit* Petruchio.] *after* love *in*
    line 57 F 1–2
  65 *Frederick*] F 2; *Frerdick* F 1
  75–76 She...marriage.] F 1–2 *line*:
    She is...know | A faire...
    marriage.

III.i

III.i] *Actus Tertius. Scæna prima.*
  F 1–2
  0.1 *Enter*] F 2; *Eter* F 1
  1 Come] F 2; CCome F 1
  27 *Enter* Fredrick.] *after line* 26
    F 1–2
  44 *Exit.*] *after* pan. *in line* 43 F 1–2
  57 indeed——] ∼ . ∧ F 1–2
  66 honour——] ∼ . F 1–2
  67 me,] ∼ ∧ F 1–2
  69 Lady] F 2; Lady *Bowle of wine*
    ready. F 1 (*beside lines* 68–70)
  74 Don] F 2; ∼ . F 1
  83 mad, man] F 2; ∼ ∧ F 1
  84 woman——] F 2; ∼ ∧ F 1

  97 *Exit* Land-lady.] *after* chaps. *in*
    line 96 F 1–2
  99 *Enter* Anthony.] *after* her. *in line*
    98 F 1–2
  103 *Fredrick.* By] ∼ ; by F 1–2
  103 *Enter* Constantia.] *in right mar-*
    gin beside lines 102–103 F 1; *after*
    line 102 F 2
  116 cause:] ∼ , F 1; ∼ ; F 2
  123 favour:——] ∼ : ∧ F 1; ∼ , ∧
    F 2
  128 you:——] ∼ : ∧ F 1; ∼ ; ∧ F 2
  132 noble.] ∼ : F 1; ∼ ; F 2
  136 So...rest.] F 1–2 *line*: So, |
    Now...rest.

III.ii

III.ii] Scæne 2. F 1–2
20 Doe'ye] De'ye F 1; D'ye F 2
23 searches;] ~ , F 1; ~ , F 2
26.1 *Enter...wine.*] *after* Musick.
  in line 26 F 1–2

31 drinke:——] ~ , , F 1–2
31–32 Surgeon?...else.] ~ , ...
  ~ ? F 1–2
42 man-] F 2; ~ , F 1
45 abroad——] ~ . F 1–2

III.iii

III.iii] Scæn. 3. F 1–2
14 all,] ~ : F 1; ~ ; F 2
24 cloven——] ~ . F 1–2

42 pills;] ~ , F 1–2
59 me——] ~ . F 1–2
65 ready:——] ~ : , F 1; ~ ; , F 2

III.iv

III.iv] Scæne 4. F 1–2
0.1 John,] F 2; ~ . F 1
6–9 And...Gentlemen:——] F 1–
  2 *line*: And...mine. | Stay...
  Troope | Is...there? | Hawking
  ...ir. | They...Gentlemen,
8 it.] F 2; ir. F 1
9 Gentlemen:——] ~ , , F 1–2
10 ye.——] ~ , , F 1–2
19 day:——] ~ : , F 1; ~ , , F 2
23 now):] ~) , F 1–2
27 ye:——] ~ : , F 1–2
33 Bolder,] ~ , F 1–2

37 I...Gentleman] F 1–2 *line*: I
  will...short; | Ye...Gentleman
49 tainted,] F 2; ~ , F 1
60 Sir:] ~ , F 1; ~ , F 2
62 *Enter* Petruchio.] *after* Ambush?
  in line 61 F 1–2
73 Gentlemen.——] ~ . , F 1–2
74 ye:——] ~ : , F 1–2
77 me.] ~ , F 1–2
83 *Constantia*——] ~ . F 1–2
84 know:] ~ ? F 1–2
90 distrust] F 2; distruct F 1

III.v

III.v] *om.* F 1–2
7 *Enter...Frederick.*] *in margin
  beside lines* 6–7 F 1; *after line* 6
  F 2
8 *Constantia*——] ~ , F 1; ~ .
  F 2
14 was?] ~ . F 1–2
15–16 Yes...found so.] *one line*
  F 1–2

30 *John*——] ~ . F 1; ~ ? F 2
38–39 It...base.] F 1–2 *line*: It...
  foole; | Disgrace...lecher? |
  'Tis....base.
50 *A...horses.*] *after* horses. F 1–2
54 *Enter...Petruchio.*] *after* fellow
  in line 53 F 1–2

IV.i

IV.i] *Actus Quartus. Scæna prima.*
  F 1–2
  4 Sir;——] ~ ; ∧ F 1–2
  20 *Enter*. . .Peter.] *after line* 18
  F 1–2
  23 know∧——] F 2; ~ , —— F 1
  24 heaven,] ~ ∧ F 1–2

30 thinke, of purpose)] thinke) of
  purpose F 1–2
32 tortur'd.——] ~ . ∧ F 1–2
33–34 Directly. . .me say?] *one line*
  F 1–2
38 this?] F 2; ~ . F 1
57 sake;] ~ , F 1–2

IV.ii

IV.ii] Scæne 2. F 1–2
  12 Master-piece;——] ~ ; ∧ F 1–2
  13 imagination] F 2; imagination
  Bawd ready above. F 1
  17 'em;——] ~ ; ∧ F 1–2
  19 hand;] ~ , F 1–2

21 degamboys:——] ~ : ∧ F 1–2
22 devils:——] ~ : ∧ F 1–2
24 foole;] ~ , F 1–2
26 breeches:——] ~ : ∧ F 1–2
30 boy:——] ~ : ∧ F 1–2
38 *don*] don F 1–2

IV.iii

IV.iii] Scæne 3. F 1–2
  3 merry?] F 2; ~ . F 1
  14–21 *Welcome*. . .*hand.*] *after* now.
  in line 12 F 2; *om.* F 1
  14, 19 *farewell*] *farewel* F 2; *om.* F 1
  19 *feares*] *fears* F 2; *om.* F 1
  20 *selfe*] *self* F 2; *om.* F 1
  25 *Enter*. . .*above).*] *after line* 22
  F 1–2
  31 *Musicke.*] *after* highest, *in line* 30
  F 1–2
  32.1 *Enter* Francisco.] *Enter Fran.*
  and Exit. F 1–2
  37 *Exit.*] *after line* 33 F 1–2
  51 of;] ~ , F 2; ~ ∧ F 1
  57 This. . .sir:] this. . .sir. F 1;
  this. . .sir, F 2
  61 enter.——] ~ , ∧ F 1; ~ . ∧ F 2

62.1 *Exeunt*] *Exit.* F 1; *Ex.* F 2
  (*after line* 61 F 1–2)
66.1 *Claping*. . .*doore.*] *after line* 65
  F 1; *om.* F 2
71 *Petruchio* (*within*).] *Petr. and*
  Iohn within. in right margin F 1–2
73 *John* (*within*).] F 2; *Iohn within.*
  in right margin F 1
83 One,] F 2; ~ ∧ F 1
103 us;] ~ , F 1–2
106 *Fredrick*] *Fred.* F 1–2
109 payment:——] ~ : ∧ F 1–2
119 found ∧ ——] ~ . ∧ F 1–2
123 mine:——] ~ : ∧ F 1–2
124 Lady?. . .fearfull.] F 2; ~ ;. . .
  ~ ? F 1
131.1 *Enter Officer.*] *after* sir. *in line*
  132 F 1–2

V.i

V.i] *Actus Quintus. Scæna prima.*
  F 1–2

6 prove] F 2; Prove F 1
14 Spaniards] *Spaniards* F 1–2

V.ii

V.ii] Scæne. 2. F1–2
  2 They...'em] F1–2 *line*: They
  ...devills, | Can...'em

9 man.] F2; ∼ ? F1
9 soone;] ∼ , F1–2
14 forge?] F2; forg? F1

V.iii

V.iii] Scæne 3. F1–2
17 *Enter . . . habiliments.*] *after*
  dearely? F1–2
23.1 *Knocking within.*] *after* too. *in*
  line 23 F1–2
23.1 *Knocking within.*] *Knocking*
  within. John, Fredrick, and a Ser-
  vant within. F1–2
24, 25 (*within*)] *Within.* F1; *within*
  F2
25 one,] ∼ ∧ F1–2
27 owne;] ∼ , F1–2
29.1 *Enter*...John.] *after* meaning.
  in line 30 F1–2
30 us?] F2; ∼ , F1
?2 eyes ∧] F2; ∼ , F1
45.1 *Soft Musick.*] Soft Musick. F1–2
  (*on line* 45)
51 follows:] ∼ ; F1–2
63 figure?] F2; ∼ . F1
91 *Song.*] *after* midnight. F1–2
  (*centered in* F2)
92–119 *Come*....*here.*] *after* midnight. *in line* 91 F2; *om.* F1
96, 104, 119 Answer.] *Answer.* F2
  (*not as speech-prefix*); *om.* F1

99 Britain∧] ∼ , F2; *om.* F1
100 *Appeare*] *Appear* F2; *om.* F1
106–115 *pose...bones.*] *initial capitals*
  for all nouns F2; *om.* F1
108 *dry'd*] *dryed* F2; *om.* F1
116, 117, 118 *Appeare*] *Appear* F2;
  om. F1
137 *Gillian*] F2; *Gillion* F1
160 Has] F2; 'Has F1
162 have:——] ∼ : ∧ F1–2
164 servants. ∧] ∼ ∧ —— F1–2
192 Be ready] F2; Bready F1
192 forward.——] ∼ . ∧ F1–2
192 there?...in.] ∼ ∧ ... ∼ ? F1
194–195 Presently...tell——] *one*
  line in F1–2
201 *Asteroth*] *Asterth* F1–2
202 when?] ∼ , F1–2
202 *Enter...Spirit.*] *after line* 201
  F1–2
222 Gentlemen——] ∼ . F1–2
226 Gentleman,] ∼ ∧ F1–2
229.2 FINIS.] *om.* F1–2 (*after* Epilogue *in* F1

Epilogue

3 *dislike*;] ∼ , F1–2

HISTORICAL COLLATION

[This collation against the present text includes the two seventeenth-century Folio texts (F1, 1647, F2, 1679) and the editions of Langbaine (L, 1711), Theobald, Seward and Sympson (S, 1750), Colman (C, 1778), Weber (W, 1812), Dyce (D, 1843) and Chambers (Variorum) (V, 1912). The collation also includes the edition of Beaumont's *Poems* (1653) for the Prologue and Epilogue, and Bodleian MS Don c. 57, 119 (129)(B) and Folger MS 452, 4, f. 56 (Fo) for the song at V.iii.92–119. Omission of a siglum indicates that the text concerned agrees with the reading of the lemma.]

I.i

6 know] knows F2
16 moment,] ~ ₐ F2, L, S
26 wander] wonder F1–2
26 that] *om.* F2
28 a dayes] adays F2; a-dayes L

37 boltted] blotted F1; blocked
F2+ (V)
39 over] ever F1
44 on] of C, W
64 best] next F1+ (−V)

I.ii

39 waves] stormes F1
41 Ye're] Y'are F2, L, S; Ye are W
43 *Petruchio.*] *1.* F1, F2, L; *Ant.* C,
W, D

43 *2. Gentleman.*] *1. Gent.* S
46 *1. Gentleman.*] *2. Gent.* F2, L, S,
C, W
48 And] *om.* S

I.iii

4 Beside] Besides C, W
14 lights] light C

21, 24 *Woman.*] *Within.* F1–2, L, S

I.iv

3 private] private all S, C, W

I.v

15 learnings] Learning S
22 ye have] ye've S; you've C; you
have W, D

29 caudles] candles F1–2, L, C
33 contented] contended F1(u)

I.vi

16 Y'ave] You've L, S; You have   17 bids] bid C, W
    C, W, D

I.vii

25 scarre] scare F 2 +   26 cast] lost F 1

I.viii

6 a] *om.* V
12 I] I, F 2
13 Y'are] You're L; You are S, C,
    W, D
33 ye'have] you've L, S, C; you
    have W, D; ye have V

47 thee] there F 1
57 acknowledge] knowledge F 2, L
64 ye had] y'had S, C; you had D
76 It] Is S
93 *Fredrick*] *Ferdinand* F 1

I.ix

3 through] throgh F 1; though F 2

I.x

14 Ye are] Ye're S, C; You are W,
    D

24 yee are] ye're S; you're C; you
    are W, D

II.i

4 peeping] piping F 2, L, S, C, W
14 Ha's] H'has C; He has W; H'as
    D; 'Has V
15 has] h'as S; h'has C; he has W,
    D; 'has V
28 Ye'had] Y'ad L, S, C; You had
    W, D

38 You are] You're C
44 yee] you F 2 + (−V)
54 Ye'are] Ye're F 2, L; Y'are S, V;
    You're C, D; You are W
55 ye had] you'd C; you had W, D
95 charges] charge S, C

II.ii

5 Masters bo-peep] Master bo-
    peeps L; Masters bo-peeps S;
    master's bo-peeps C, W;
    master's bo-peep D, V
10 spend] spends C, W
17.1 *Constantia within.*] *om.* F 1 +

18–28 *Mercilesse...kill.*] *om.* F 1
23 *never*] *none e'er* S, C; *om.* F 1
24 *Thus ill rewarded*] *those rewarders*
    F 2, L; *om.* F 1
37 *Basta*] *Basto* F 1

II.iii

3 taske] tax F2, L, S, V
7.1 Fredrick. Don John] *Fredrick, and Don John* F1+ (−D)
25 o' the world] O the World! S
30 Ye are] You're C; You are W, D
41 faith] faith's S
49 Has] H'has C; He has W; H'as D; 'Has V

52 h'as] H'has C; He has W; 'has V
71 gentleman] gentlemen F1
78 thou not an] not thou an C; thou an F1–2, L, S, W
79 What] What a F1, V; Why, what S
111 come through] go through L, S
119, 121 a] he F2–D; 'a V
128 you] yoe F1(u)

II.iv

3 A] He F2–D; 'A V
30 he has] h'has S, C
78 afoot] a foot F1–2
78–79 boy too...hers] boy...hers

too F2, L, S, C; boy too...hers too F1
85 H'as] H'has C; He has W; 'Has V

III.i

57 a] an L, S, C, W
64 Beast] Boast F1
78 roperie] Roguery F2, L, S, C
91 She has] Sh'has C
94 a peece] apiece F2, L, S, C; a-piece W, D

98 *John.*] *om.* F1
98 rake] take F2, L, S, C, D
132 Ye are] You're S, C; You are W, D
133 *Fredrick.*] *om.* F1–2, L

III.ii

3 'Sbloud] *om.* F2, L, S
5 Has] H'as F2, L, S, D; H'has C; He has W; 'Has V
14 In] My S, C, W
14 ye] you, sir, W
15 ye] you F2, L, S, C, W, D
20 Doe'ye] De'ye F1; D'ye F2, L, S, V; Do you C, W, D
22 beside] besides F2, L, S, C, W

23 searches] Searcloths S
26.1 *Servant*] *Rowl.* F1–2; Rowland L, S, C, W, D, V
36 ye] you F2, L, S, C, W, D
37 so] if F2, L, S
44 up] *om.* S
44 with] with some F2, L, S, W, D, V

III.iii

15 upon] up W
21 Yet] Ere F2, L, S, C
34 Has] H'as L, S, D; H'has C; He has W; 'Has V
34 But] Bur F1

42 birding] Purging S
47 He has] He 'as S; H'has C
50 wife] wise F1+
62, 66 ye] you F2, L, S, C, W, D

643

III.iv

29 did] did me S
37, 41, 61 ye have] ye've S; You've
C; You have W, D
39 the] *om.* F 1–2, L
45 'tis true I have] true, I've S
57 danger] Anger S, C
63 we'l have no] we'l no F 2, L; we
will no S

66 *Duke.* Upon] *Duke* upon F 1 (*as
dialogue*)
70 How now, how] How, how,
how F 2, L, S
102 complement] Compliment L, S,
C, W, D, V
106 crowne] crowne ye S

III.v

2 fubd] fob'd F 2, L, S, C
10 Ye have] Ye've S; You've C;
You have W, D
25 'Had] Had C, W, D

47 a] an F 2+
50 they'r] Their S, C; They are
W; they're D, V

IV.i

2 ye a] y'a S, C; you a W, D
11 like] like a F 2, L, S
17 her] he F 1
20–21 *Duke.* Ye...*Fredrick.* Not

...] *Fred.* Ye...Not... F 1–2,
L, C, W
51 work's] works L, S, C
54 note] notice F 2, L, S

IV.ii

29 fine] find F 1

IV.iii

1 *Peter.*] *Petr.* F 1(u), F 2; *Pet.* F 1
(c), S
3 most] most most F 2
9 among] amongst C
14–21 *Welcome...hand.*] *om.* F 1
25 *Peter.*] *Petr.* F 1–2, L; *Pet.* S
30 *Petruchio.*] *Pet.* F 1
50 card] guard F 1–2, L

57 that sterne nature.] that ? starve
nature? F 1
88 valiant] saliant F 1, W, D;
saliant F 2, L, S, C
113 should] would L, S
121 Ye have] Y'have S; Ye've C
138 hunt] haunt F 1

V.ii

3 he has] h'has C
9 thou] *om.* S
10 as] as the S
19 make him tremble] make us
tremble F 1, C; *om.* F 2, L, S

23 'Has] H'as F 2, L, S, D; H'has
C; He has W
33 along] a long F 1

V.iii

29.1 *and* John.] *Iohn, and Servant.*
    F1+
35 where] were F1
41 *love-layes*] *Love-lay* L (*final* s
    scarcely visible in F2)
64 *Petruchio.*] *om.* F2, L, S, C
71 Hollock] Hock S, C, W
77 'a] he F2, L, S, C, W, D
92–119 *Come...here.*] *om.* F1
92, 97, 105 Vechio.] *om.* F1–2, L, S
92 *Come away*] Comc away, come
    away B, Fo
93 *Hoist*] Harke Fo
95 *Dame* Gillian] Dame Gillian,
    Dame Gillian B, Fo
96 Answer...*come.*] *om.* B; Why
    when? Why when? Fo
97 *thee*] *om.* B
98 *thus I*] I thus Fo
99 Britain *Mathewglin*] Brettainy
    'metheglin B; brittaine, water,
    glim Fo
101 *Why when?*] Why when? Why
    when? B; *om.* Fo
102 *Why*] What B (w^t); *om.* Fo
103 *Why when?*] *om.* Fo
104 Answer...*ready.*] *om.* B, Fo
105 *Once...Nbod*] *om.* Fo
106 *pose*] poxe Fo
108 *thine*] thy B, Fo
108 *dry'd*] dry B, Fo

109 *mummie*] mumble Fo
111 *thy*] the B
111 *that's made of*] that now is B
112 *thy bottle*] the bottle B, Fo
113 *thine*] thy B, Fo
114, 115 *By...bones.*] *om.* Fo
117, 118 *Appeare.*] *om.* Fo
119 Answer...*here.*] I come B
    (*thrice*); I come Fo (*twice*)
121 *Dame*] *Don* F1+
142 make] makes F2, L, S, C
145 true] truth W
159 ye] you F2, L, S, C, W, D
162 He] She F1
164 servants] servant F2, L, S, C, W,
    D
181 whore, and the] whore, the F1–2,
    L, S, C, W, D
181 light] lit C, W
182 unto] to S
188 shew'd] shewn C, W
192 Who's there? come in.] Who's
    there come in? F1; Who's there
    comes in F2, L, S, C, W
210, 213 ye] you F2, L, S, C, W, D
210 here] hear F2+
212 do ye] do you F2, L, S, W, D;
    D'you C
214 'Has] He has F2, L, S, W;
    H'has C; H'as D
218 All] All's W

Prologue

4 and] as F1
12 lovd] loud F1–2, L, S, C, W,
    1653

9 *expression*] *expressions* F1–2, L,
    S, C, W, V